SHAKESPEARE
MAN AND ARTIST

SHAKESPEARE
MAN AND ARTIST

By

EDGAR I. FRIPP

Late William Noble Fellow, University of Liverpool. A Life Trustee of Shakespeare's Birthplace. Author of *Master Richard Quyny, Bailiff of Stratford-upon-Avon; Shakespeare's Stratford; Shakespeare's Haunts near Stratford; Shakespeare Studies*, &c. Editor of *Minutes and Accounts of the Corporation of Stratford-upon-Avon and other Records*, 1553–1620

VOLUME II

LONDON
OXFORD UNIVERSITY PRESS
NEW YORK TORONTO

Oxford University Press, Amen House, London E.C.4

GLASGOW NEW YORK TORONTO MELBOURNE WELLINGTON
BOMBAY CALCUTTA MADRAS KARACHI LAHORE DACCA
CAPE TOWN SALISBURY NAIROBI IBADAN ACCRA
KUALA LUMPUR HONG KONG

First published 1938
Second impression 1964

REPRINTED LITHOGRAPHICALLY IN GREAT BRITAIN
AT THE UNIVERSITY PRESS, OXFORD
BY VIVIAN RIDLER
PRINTER TO THE UNIVERSITY

'What king has he not taught state, as Talma taught Napoleon?
What maiden has not found him finer than her delicacy?
What lover has he not outloved?
What sage has he not outseen?
What gentleman has he not instructed in the rudeness of his behaviour?'

(*Emerson on Shakespeare, one Sunday morning in the avenue to Stratford Church on the way to worship.*[1])

[1] JAMES WALTER, *Shakespeare's True Life*, p. 256.

CONTENTS

VOLUME II

LIST OF ILLUSTRATIONS

VOLUME II

§ 78. SHAKESPEARE AND HIS GARDEN

SHAKESPEARE's love of his garden and practical acquaintance with gardening appear in his earlier as in his later work. He must have been his own gardener for years in Henley Street, and have employed one or more gardeners at *New Place*. In his poems and plays written before 1597 he speaks of mint and parsley, fennel, onions, leeks, garlic; of apples, pears, plums—

> The mellow plum doth fall, the green sticks fast,
> Or, being early pluck'd, is sour to taste,[1]

damsons, cherries, quinces, figs, 'dangling apricocks' (grown as a standard, not against the wall), grapes, strawberries, dewberries, mulberries, medlars, walnuts, chestnuts, hazelnuts and their 'kernels'; of carnations, lilies, roses, 'nodding violets', marigolds, 'pale primroses', oxlips, columbine, woodbine and its 'honey-suckle' flowers, eglantine or sweet-brier, pansies ('love-in-idleness'), myrtle, marjoram, rosemary, and rue. To these he adds in subsequent writings, cabbage and carrot, potato, eringo, lettuce, hyssop, thyme, savory, radish, gourd ('gross watery pumpion'), turnip; gooseberry and peach; daffodils 'that come before the swallow dares'; lavender, orchids or 'long purples', 'crown-imperials', and, noticeable, the box-tree. In an early play (*Rich. II*, III. iv. 29–64) he reveals his knowledge of pruning—

> We at time of year
> Do wound the bark, the skin of our fruit-trees,
> Lest, being over-proud in sap and blood,
> With too much riches, it confound itself;

and in a late play (*The Winter's Tale*, IV. iv. 85–103) he shows his familiarity with grafting:

> We marry
> A gentler scion to the wildest stock,
> And make conceive a bark of baser kind
> By bud of nobler race: this is an Art
> Which does mend Nature.[2]

He understood the virtue of 'digging and dunging', like the

[1] *Ven. & Ad.* 527 f.

[2] This advocacy of grafting on a lower stock by the aristocratic father who disapproves of his son's alliance with a peasant maiden is fine dramatic irony.

dresser of the vineyard in the parable.[1] He speaks of 'lean, sterile, and bare land manured, husbanded and tilled with excellent endeavour';[2] and of

> Covering discretion with a coat of folly,
> As gardeners do with ordure hide those roots
> That shall first spring and be most delicate.[3]

He was feelingly aware of the mischievous effects of weeds ('unwholesome', 'choking weeds'), caterpillars, blight ('eating canker', 'envious worm'), frost ('untimely, biting, killing, sap checked with frost'), cold wind and storms ('unruly blasts', 'the tyrannous breathing of the North').

His favourite fruit is the Apple, which he names at least thirty times, and of which he mentions half a dozen kinds—the crab, the pippin, the bitter-sweeting, the pome-water, the apple-john, the leather-coat. And his best-loved flower is the Rose. He refers to it, including his allegorical and emblematical allusions, more than a hundred times, and specifies eight sorts—the white rose, the red rose, the variegated—

> A third nor red nor white had stolen of both,[4]

the musk, the damask, the rose of Provençe, the canker or dog-rose, and the sweet-brier. On its beauty he has lavished his praise. Of nothing has he written more exquisitely: e.g.

> She looks as clear
> As morning roses newly washed with dew.[5]
> So sweet a kiss the golden sun gives not
> To those fresh morning drops upon the rose.[6]
> The rose
> (On) the fair forehead of an innocent love.[7]
> O rose of May,
> Dear maid, kind sister, sweet Ophelia![8]
> Sweet rose, fair flower, untimely pluck'd, soon faded,
> Pluck'd in the bud, and faded in the spring![9]
> A Silver Basin
> Full of rose-water and bestrew'd with flowers.[10]

and twenty more passages as beautiful.[11]

[1] Luke xiii. 8. [2] *2 Hen. IV*, IV. iii. 129 f. [3] *Hen. V*, II. iv. 38–40.
[4] Sonnet xcix. [5] *Tam. Sh.* II. i. 173 f.
[6] *Love's L. L.* IV. iii. 26 f. [7] *Haml.* III. iv. 42 f. [8] *Ib.* IV. v. 157 f.
[9] *Pass. Pil.* x. 1 f. (notice the green plum, 5 f., and the legal touches in 8, 12).
[10] *Tam. Sh.* Induct. i. 55 f.
[11] Ellacombe has collected them in his charming book, *The Plant-Lore and Garden Craft of Shakespeare*, 243–55.

The 'great garden' at *New Place*, no doubt, was typically Elizabethan, consisting of the kitchen-garden, the flower-garden, and the orchard. The flower-garden would be formally, not to say mathematically, laid out, such 'a curious-knotted garden' as we hear of in *Love's Labour's Lost* (I. i. 249 f.), with ingeniously designed beds and paths, trellises and an arbour, the whole surrounded by a brick wall or a high hedge carefully cultivated and cut into shapes often fantastic. In the orchard would be grass, 'kept finely shorn',[1] and probably a 'thick pleached alley', like Antonio's in *Much Ado about Nothing* (I. ii. 9 f.), wherein the Prince and Count Claudio walked and were overheard by a servant of the house in secret conversation. In such an alley, between and under the thickly interlacing boughs of two rows of trees—thorn, sweet-brier, privet, or whatnot—the Poet would find welcome retreat with his book or writing.[2]

1597

§ 79. *THE FIRST PART OF KING HENRY THE FOURTH*

ANOTHER work of the autumn of 1597 and further evidence of a new lease of splendid literary life was the first part of a great English-History trilogy, in continuation of *Richard the Second* and preparation for *Henry the Sixth*. Civil War again is the political theme. The prophecy of the Bishop of Carlisle in *Richard the Second*—

> The blood of English shall manure the ground . . .
> Disorder, horror, fear and mutiny
> Shall here inhabit, and this land be called
> The field of Golgotha and dead men's skulls—[3]

begins to be fulfilled. Civil strife, as a retribution for usurpation, is in the background of the laughable scenes in Cheapside and on Gadshill, and comes to the forefront of the stage. Prince Henry

[1] Bacon, *Essays* (xlvi: 'Of Gardens').

[2] Cf. Milton, *Il Penseroso*,

> retired leisure,
> That in trim gardens takes his pleasure.

[3] IV. i. 136, 142–4.

succeeds King Richard, and is consciously contrasted with him, the 'dissolute' young soldier, more dissolute in repute than fact, who rises where the indulgent poet monarch fell. 'Can no man tell me', cries Bolingbroke, near the close of *Richard the Second*,

> of my unthrifty son?
> If any plague hang over us, 'tis he.
> I would to God, my lords, he might be found:
> Inquire at London, 'mongst the taverns there,
> For there, they say,[1] he daily doth frequent,
> With unrestrained loose companions . . .
> Which he, young wanton and effeminate boy
> Takes on the point of honour to support
> So dissolute a crew.[2]

Half-way through *The First Part of Henry the Fourth* Prince Henry is warned of 'the skipping king', who

> Ambled up and down,
> With shallow jesters and rash bavin wits.[3]

His father tells him,

> For all the world
> As thou art to this hour was Richard then.[4]

Of a nobler blood than Richard, 'inclined to mirth'[5], 'gracious' (that saving merit in an Elizabethan), with

> a tear for pity and a hand
> Open as day for melting charity,[6]

Hal is beset by a more attractive circle of reprobates. Bushy, Bagot and Green are mean and beggarly scoundrels in comparison with Falstaff and his satellites, who are rich beyond the dreams of avarice in their humorous rascality.

After Shylock, Falstaff—or, to give him his baptismal name (for which Shakespeare was not responsible),[7] Sir John Oldcastle.

[1] See again l. 6, 'Even such, *they say*', &c., and Percy's *report* of his rival's bravado in 16–19. See also Warwick's defence of the Prince in *2 Hen. IV*, IV. iv. 67–78 (a welcome speech, put into the mouth of a Warwickshire magnate!).

[2] V. iii. 1, 3–7, 10–12.

[3] III. ii. 60 f.

[4] 93 f.

[5] *2 Hen. IV*, IV. iv. 38.

[6] 31 f.

[7] He took the name from the old play of *The famous Victories of Henry the Fifth*. Evidence of his adoption of it is in I. ii. 47 ('my Old lad of the Castle'). He substituted for it the Sir John Falstaff (*not* Fastolf) of *1 Henry VI*, who 'played the coward' (I. i. 131), 'the treacherous Falstaff' (I. iv. 35), 'cowardly knight' (III. ii. 104). This is tradition, not history, which Shakespeare accepted, and an indication of his estimate of his own creature's exploits at Gad's Hill and Shrewsbury.

The difference is extraordinary. Shylock is medieval, he is foreign, he steps out of romance and rumour. Shakespeare may have seen the famous Lopez, the Earl of Leicester's and the Queen's Jewish physician, who was executed on a charge of treason in 1594; but he never entered, never saw a Synagogue. Falstaff is late Elizabethan, and from London. He carries with him the atmosphere of the Boar's Head and King's Tavern; and his followers, Bardolf, Nym, Pistol, Mistress Quickly, are redolent of these fusty and familiar head-quarters. To bring them into the country and give them an airing is to reveal their cockney habitat.

Shakespeare had more than recovered his equanimity when he created this amazing company. He could sit in his garden and laugh. Pen in hand he chuckled at the troop of jolly oddities imagination bodied forth within his brain. He astonished himself with the exuberance of his invective and repartee. The nonsense of it was immense. Tragedy, however, blended inextricably with the humour.

1597–8

§ 80. *LOVE'S LABOUR'S LOST* REVISED

A BY-PRODUCT of this autumn was a revision, probably at the request of the Queen,[1] of *Love's Labour's Lost*. By happy accident[2] considerable fragments of the play in its earlier form have been preserved, and we are able to compare Shakespeare's workmanship in the comedy of 1593 with that of 1597. He 'corrects and augments' in his revision, changing 'Duke Ferdinand' to 'King' and 'Princess' to 'Queen', adding the 'dialogue' of the Owl and the Cuckoo at the end,[3] and more than touching

[1] We are expressly informed that the play was 'presented before her Highness this last Christmas' 1597, or possibly but improbably (after the death of Burleigh) 1598. She had, without doubt, seen it previously.

[2] The printers failed to note marks of deletion in the Quarto and mixed up old and new stage-directions and speech-headings in the Folio. See Dover Wilson, in 'The New Shakespeare' edition.

[3] v. ii. 894–942. This second pageant and its songs (among the Poet's best) unduly lengthen a very long scene, and are apologized for: 'But, most esteemed Greatness, will you hear the dialogue that the two learned men have compiled?' 'Call them forth quickly; we will do so.'

up the speeches of Berowne. Here is Berowne's apology of 1593 for the Love of the Eyes:

> And where that you have vowed to study, lords,
> In that each of you have foresworn his book,
> Can you still dream, and pore, and thereon look?
> For when would you, my lord, or you, or you,
> Have found the ground of Study's excellence
> Without the beauty of a Woman's face?
> From Women's Eyes this doctrine I derive;
> They are the ground, the books, the Académes,
> From whence doth spring the true Promethean fire.
> Why, universal plodding prisons up
> The nimble spirits in the arteries,
> As motion and long-during action tires
> The sinewy vigour of the traveller.
> Now, for not looking on a Woman's face,
> You have in that forsworn the use of Eyes,
> And Study too, the causer of your vow;
> For where is any author in the world
> Teaches such beauty as a Woman's Eye?
> Learning is but an adjunct to ourself,
> And where we are our Learning likewise is;
> Then, when ourselves we see in Ladies' Eyes,
> Do we not likewise see our Learning there?[1]

This is early work, in thought and verse, after the manner of the Sonnets. Here is the same re-written four years later, the new matter being printed in italics:

> O, *we* have *made a* vow to study, lords,
> *And* in that *vow we* have forsworn *our* book*s*.
> For when would you, my *liege*, or you, or you,
> *In leaden contemplation* have found *out*
> *Such fiery numbers as the prompting Eyes*
> *Of* beauty's *tutors have enriched you with?*
> *Other slow arts entirely keep the brain;*
> *And therefore finding barren practisers,*
> *Scarce show a harvest of their heavy toil;*
> *But Love, first learned in a* Lady's Eyes;
> *Lives not alone immuréd in the brain;*
> *But, with the motion of all elements,*
> *Courses as swift as thought in every power,*
> *And gives to every power a double power,*
> *Above their functions and their offices.*
> *It adds a precious seeing to the eye,*

[1] IV. iii. 296–317.

A lover's eyes will gaze an eagle blind;
A lover's ear will hear the lowest sound
When the suspicious head of the eft is stopped:
Love's feeling is more soft and sensible
Than are the tender horns of cockled snails;
Love's tongue proves dainty Bacchus gross in taste;
For valour, is not Love a Hercules,
Still climbing trees in the Hesperides?
Subtle as Sphinx; as sweet and musical
As bright Apollo's lute, strung with his hair;
And when Love speaks, the voice of all the gods
Make Heaven drowsy with the harmony.
Never durst poet touch a pen to write
Until his ink were temper'd with Love's sighs;
O then his lines would ravish savage ears,
And plant in tyrants mild humility.
From Woman's Eyes this doctrine I derive,
They sparkle still the *right* Promethean fire,
They are the books, *the arts*, the Académes,
That show, contain, and nourish all the world—
Else none at all in aught proves excellent.[1]

Nearly all is new and better, more graceful and musical. Yet in thought and verse it is in the 'early' style, a specimen of pretty sentiment in dainty 'pentameters', *evidence of the Poet's willingness to revert to his youthful manner when occasion demands it.* Few of the lines but have five stresses, few if any run on, none has a weak ending or a pause but at the close. This is as it should be for such superficial reflection.

In a later scene (v. ii) six jingling lines (827–32) of question and answer by Berowne and Rosaline in 1593 become a serious dialogue of thirty-three lines (847–79) in 1598:

1593

BEROWNE. And whát to mé, my lóve? and whát to mé?
ROSALINE. You múst be púrgéd tóo, your síns are rácked,
You áre attaínt with fáults and pérjurý:
Therefóre if yóu my fávour méan to gét,
A twélvemonth shåll you spénd, and néver rést,
But séek the wéary béds of péople sick.

1598

BEROWNE. Stúdies my lády? místress, lóok on mé;
Behóld the window of my héart, mine Eýe,

[1] 318–54.

What húmble súit atténds thy ánswer thére:
Impóse some sérvice ón me for thy lóve.

ROSALINE. Óft have I héard of yóu, my Lórd Berówne,
Befóre I sáw you; | and the wórld's lárge tóngue
Procláims you for a mán replète with móckś,
Fúll of compárisons and woúnding flóuts,
Which yóu on áll estátes will éxecute
That líe withín the mércy of your wít.
To wéed this wórmwood from your fruítful braín
And thérewithál to wín me, if you pléase,
Withóut the whích I ám not to be wón,
You shåll this twélvemonth térm from dáy to dáy
Vísit the spéechless síck, | and stíll convérse
With groáning wrétches; | and your tásk shall bé
With áll the fíerce endéavour of your wít
To enfórce the paíned ímpotent to smíle.

BEROWNE. To móve wíld láughter in the thróat of déath?
It cánnot bé; | it ís impóssible:
Mirth cannot móve a sóul in ágony.

ROSALINE. Why, thát's the wáy to chóke a gíbing spírit,
Whose ínfluence is begót of that lóose gráce
Which shállow láughing héarers gíve to fóols:
A jést's próspérity líes in the éar,
Of hím that héars it, néver in the tóngue
Of hím that mákes it: | thén, if síckly éars,
Déaf'd with the clámours of their ówn déar gróans,
Will héar your ídle scórns, | contínue thén,
And Í will háve you, and that fáult withál;
But íf they wíll not, | thrów awáy that spírit,
And Í shall fínd you émpty of that faúlt,
Ríght jóyful of your réformátion.

The expanded version is not early work, nor after the manner of it. Berowne begins with his prattle about his 'heart' and 'eye', and is pulled up sharply. What follows is serious thought, in lines one-half of which contain pairs of balanced stresses, and one-fourth have a pause in the middle.

It adds to the interest of Berowne's revised speeches that the Poet himself may have taken the part.[1] One of the minor features of the lengthened scene v. ii is a revision (at least) of Costard's reproof of 'Alisander', with allusion to Harington's unsavoury Court jest: 'You will be scraped out of the painted cloth for this; your Lion, that holds his poll-ax sitting on a close-stool, will be given to Ajax.'[2]

[1] p. 362.

[2] 578–81. See pp. 362, 423.

The persistence of *Love's Labour's Lost*, at first sight so slight a thing and limited to select audiences, is noteworthy. Huguenot France, which had excited enthusiasm in England, was crushed or exiled, and the France now in power did not commend itself to the English mind. For four years Shakespeare held up to ridicule her levity in speech and love, and divorce of culture from action. Michael Lord of Montaigne was a poor exchange for honest Hubert Languet.

1598

§ 81. THE EARL OF SOUTHAMPTON

SHAKESPEARE after his first sojourn in *New Place* arrived in London richly provided for the Christmas season 1597–8. He had learnt of the relaxation of the Council's stern order of 28 July,[1] and of the reopening of the theatres. He heard of the decision by the Queen's Justices on 15 November that a party, *after judgement in the Courts*, could not be 'relieved in Equity'—a legal matter of interest to him as an old lawyer, hardly as a dramatist, and the occasion of Falstaff's grumble in *The First Part of Henry the Fourth*, 'An the Prince and Poins be not two arrant cowards there's no Equity stirring'.[2] On 24 November the bill of complaint of himself, and his father and mother, against John Lambert was heard in Chancery. It was doomed to failure, and the ancestral estate of Asbies to perpetual alienation.[3] But the plays were a triumphant success. Shakespeare and his company performed at Whitehall, on the morrow of Christmas, New Year's Day, Twelfth Day, and Shrove Sunday (26 February 1598).[4] They performed also at the *Curtain*,[5] and in noblemen's houses. Falstaff took Londoners by storm, and Shylock probably was only less popular. *The First Part of Henry the Fourth* was entered at Stationers' Hall on 25 February,[6] and printed

[1] p. 458.

[2] II. ii. 106 f.

[3] Witnesses were appointed on 5 July 1598 (Richard Lane, John Combe, Thomas Underhill, and Francis Woodward, gentlemen) and again on 27 June 1599, but they do not seem to have been examined (Halliwell-Phillipps, *Outlines*, ii. 14–17, 204 f.).

[4] Chambers, IV. iii. 165.

[5] The *Theatre* was probably closed, see p. 457.

[6] 'A booke intituled The historye of Henry the iiij^th with his battaile at Shrewsburye against Henry Hottspurre of the Northe, with the conceipted mirthe of Sir John Falstoff.'

before the summer, when Falstaffian aphorisms were freely quoted. Before 25 February Shakespeare had changed the name 'Oldcastle' to 'Falstaff', but the public would not have it. For years the first name, so immediate was the attachment between him and the audience, stuck to the rollicking knight. Poor John Lyly was overwhelmed by his rival's ascendancy. His 'hopes' and 'wits' were 'shipwrecked'. He petitioned the Queen:

Vouchsafe some plank or rafter to waffe me into a country where in my sad and settled devotion I may in a thatched cottage write prayers instead of plays—prayers for your long and prosperous life.[1]

The Merchant of Venice was registered on 22 July, but held over pending a licence from the Lord Chamberlain Hunsdon, the players' patron.[2] *Love's Labour's Lost* was published this year, 'as it was presented before her Highness this last Christmas: newly corrected and augmented'.[3]

This year, while his friends enjoyed Falstaff, the Earl of Southampton was under a cloud. We get glimpses of him and his troubles in contemporary correspondence. Rowland White writes to Sir Robert Sidney (Philip's brother) on 14 January 1598:

I hear my Lord of Southampton goes with Master Secretary [Cecil] to France, and so onwards on his travels; which course of his doth exceedingly grieve his mistress [Elizabeth Vernon], that passes her time in weeping and lamenting.[4]

On 19 January:

I heard of some unkindness between the Earl of Southampton and his Mistress [the Queen], occasioned, by some report of Master Ambrose Willoughby. The Earl called him to account; the matter was made known to the Earl of Essex and my Lord Chamberlain, who had them under examination. I see the Earl of Southampton is full of discontentments.

On 21 January:

The quarrel was this, that [the Earl], with Sir Walter Raleigh and Master Parker, being at primero in the presence-chamber, the Queen was gone to bed, and [Master Willoughby] being there as squire of the body, required them to give over.

On 28 January:

My Lord of Southampton is now at Court [Whitehall], who for a while, by her Majesty's command, did absent himself from it.

[1] Feuillerat, *Lyly*, p. 557.
[2] Arber, iii. 122.
[3] *Ib.*
[4] Collins, *Sidney Papers*, ii. 81.

On 1 February:

My Lord of Southampton is much troubled at her Majesty's strangest use of him. Somebody hath played unfriendly parts with him. Master Secretary hath procured him licence to travel. His fair mistress doth wash her fairest face with too many tears. I pray God his going away bring her to no such infirmity as is, as it were, hereditary to her name.

On 2 February:

It is secretly said that my Lord of Southampton shall be married to his fair mistress.

She was with child at the moment of the Earl's contemplated departure for the Continent. A licence was granted to him on 6 February to travel beyond seas for two years, with ten servants, six horses, and £200. On the 10th he set out with Master Cecil and Lord Brooke. Rowland White continues on 12 February: 'My lord of Southampton is gone, and hath left behind him a very desolate gentlewoman, that hath almost wept out her fairest eyes.'[1]

Old Burghley was approaching his end. He wrote to his son, Southampton's companion in France, on 1 March: 'The bearer will report my great weakness. God bless you on earth and me in Heaven, the place of my present pilgrimage.'[2]

He rallied, and on 27 April the Privy Council met for his convenience at his house in the Strand. The Court was at Whitehall until 2 May, when it moved to Greenwich. Cecil was on his way home. He landed at Portsmouth on 29 April, and wrote to the Earl of Essex to procure him a coach at Staines:

I have written to no creature living, not even to my most dear Father, of whom I will steal a sight on my way to the Court.[3]

We learn from John Chamberlain, in a letter to Dudley Carleton:

Master Secretary returned the first of this month May, somewhat crazed with his posting journey. The report of his father's dangerous estate gave him wings; but for ought I can learn the old man's case is not so desperate but he may hold out another year. Matters in Ireland are worse. They cannot decide on a Deputy—Raleigh, Sidney, and Blount have refused.[4]

[1] Collins, *Sidney Papers*, ii. 90.

[2] *S.P. Dom. Eliz.* cclxvi. This letter was received at Angier on 21 March.

[3] *S.P. Dom. Eliz.* cclxvi.

[4] *Letters* (Camden Society), pp. 6–7.

On 20 May, Chamberlain wrote to Carleton, 'Sir William Harvey is said to have married the Countess of Southampton.'

This was the Earl's mother, who had lost her second husband, Sir Thomas Heneage, in October 1595. She was forty-six years of age and had nine years to live.

In May or June John Harington wrote from Bath:

I have been to visit my Lord Treasurer, and found him and another cripple together, my cousin of Exton. It grieved me to see so much discretion, wisdom and learning in peril of death. My Lord doth seem dead on one side, and my cousin on the other (though both in their health were ever on one side!). It gave me some comfort to hear their religious discourse, and how each did despise his own malady and hold death in derision, because both did not despair of life eternal. The Treasurer smiles to see me look gravely at their serious talk. Her Highness doth much lament her good servant's malady.[1]

Harington, if he loved a joke, was no buffoon.

Southampton was in Paris on 11 July, when Sir Charles Danvers wrote to Cecil that he had delivered his commendations to the Earl.[2] On 4 August Burghley died at his house in the Strand. His funeral took place on the 29th at Westminster, and afterwards at Stamford. Southampton seized the opportunity, when London was crowded with five hundred lordly mourners, to come over in secret and marry his betrothed. Chamberlain writes in his tattling fashion on 30 August:

I came up from Oxfordshire to see the funeral . . . Mistress Vernon is from the Court and lies in Essex House. Some say she hath taken a *venue* under the girdle and swells upon it; yet she complains not of foul play but says the Earl will justify it. *And it is bruited underhand that he was lately here four days in great secret of purpose to marry her and effected it accordingly.*[3]

The secret was out on Sunday, 3 September, when Cecil wrote from Greenwich Palace to Southampton in France:

Her Majesty knows that you came over very lately and returned very contemptuously; that you have also married one of her maids of honour without her privity; for which, with other circumstances informed against you, I find her grievously offended. And she commands me to charge you expressly (all excuses set apart) to repair hither to London and advertise your arrival, without coming to the Court until her pleasure be known.[4]

[1] *Nugae Antiquae*, i. 236 f. [2] *S.P. Dom. Eliz.* cclxvii.

[3] *S.P. Dom. Eliz.* cclxvii. The conjecture of the editors of *The New Shakespeare*, that the Poet revised *A Midsummer Night's Dream* for performance at this hasty and secret wedding, is indefensible (x. 100). [4] *S.P. Dom. Eliz.* cclxvii.

This was followed up by a letter to the English Agent in Paris, Sir Thomas Edmondes:

> You know the nature of his [lordship's] offence and what it is like to prove, which makes me wish that [he] should take heed [not] to make it worse with any contempt, a matter that cannot danger his fortune further than the cloud of her Majesty's favour, who punisheth the form rather than the substance.[1]

On 9 September, before he received Cecil's communication, Southampton wrote from Paris to the Earl of Essex:

> I have by your messenger sent a letter to Master Secretary wherein I have discovered unto him my marriage with your lordship's cousin, withal desiring him to find the means of acquainting her Majesty therewith in such sort as may least offend.

Apparently the Countess was committed to prison:

> Yesterday the Queen was informed of the new Lady of Southampton and her adventures; whereat her patience was so much moved that she came not to the Chapel. She threatens them all to the Tower . . . I now [7 September] understand the Queen has commanded to be provided for the new Countess the sweetest and best appointed lodging in the Fleet. Her lord is by command to return upon his allegiance with all speed. These are but the beginnings of evils. Well may he hope for that merry day ἐν θάνατῳ which I think he did not find ἐν θαλαμῳ.[2]

The young Earl declined to face the royal thunder. He would let it roll by, and he was justified by consequences. Early in November his wife had a daughter.[3] Then, or immediately after, he was with her; and on the 11th he was sent to the Fleet. But Fortune favoured him. There was rebellion in Ireland, and the Queen could not afford to keep her gallant officers in prison. 'I hear', wrote Chamberlain on the 22nd, '[the Earl] is already upon his delivery. Messengers come daily out of Ireland, like Job's servants laden with ill-tidings.' Essex was to go as Deputy in the spring, and he wanted his new kinsman. They were closer than ever friends, and playing together 'hard' at 'the tables' in the presence-chamber before Christmas.

1 The date is the 19th, French, our 9th.

2 An anonymous writer at Court: *S.P. Dom. Eliz.* cclxviii.

3 'The new Countess of Southampton is brought a bed of a daughter, and to mend her portion the Earl her father hath lately lost 1800 crowns at tennis in Paris' (Chamberlain to Dudley Carleton, 8 Nov.).

1598

§ 82. *PALLADIS TAMIA*

THIS autumn (entered Stationers' Hall 7 September 1598) appeared *Palladis Tamia* by Francis Meres, containing a valuable 'Comparative Dis-Course of Our English Poets'.[1] Meres was a minister and schoolmaster, M.A. of Cambridge, incorporated at Oxford on 10 July 1593.[2] He was a well informed and enthusiastic admirer of contemporary English literature, art, and music. Puritan in his condemnation of Rabelais and Machiavelli (as 'hurtful to age' as 'Amadis de Gaul to youth') and old medieval romances (he censures most of those in Master Cox's library), he is liberal in his appreciation of Elizabethan writers. He is severe on Peele, Greene, and Marlowe for their personal vices,[3] but praises highly Sidney, Spenser, Daniel, Drayton, and Shakespeare. Some of his *dicta* are memorable:

Sir Philip Sidney writ his immortal poem, *The Countess of Pembroke's Arcadia* in prose, and yet our rarest *poet* . . . I say of Spenser's *Faerie Queene*, I know not what more excellent or exquisite poem may be written . . . Spenser's Eliza, the Faerie Queene, hath the advantage of all the Queens in the world, to be eternised by so divine a poet . . . Daniel hath divinely sonnetted the matchless beauty of Delia; . . . every one passionateth when he readeth the afflicted death of Rosamond . . . Drayton is termed golden-mouthed for the purity and preciousness of his style and phrase . . . He is penning in English verse a poem called *Polyolbion* . . . Among scholars, soldiers, poets and all sorts of people he is held for a man of virtuous disposition, honest conversation, and well-governed carriage, which is almost miraculous among good wits in these declining and corrupt times, when [and here he quotes Falstaff] there is nothing but roguery in villainous man.[4]

Remarkable is his defence of Nashe:

As Actaeon was worried of his own hounds, so is Tom Nash of his *Isle of Dogs*;[5] but be not disconsolate, gallant young Juvenal! Linus the son of Apollo died the same death. Yet God forbid that so brave a wit should so basely perish! Thine are but paper dogs . . . comfort thyself, sweet Tom!

[1] Arber, iii. 125.

[2] *Register*, II. i. 353.

[3] 'As Anacreon died by the pot, so George Peele by the pox'—a statement probably more alliterative than true. 'Robert Greene died by a surfeit of pickled herrings and Rhenish wine: as witnesseth Thomas Nash who was at the fatal banquet.'

[4] *1 Hen. IV*, II. iv. 138.

[5] pp. 457–8.

Of Shakespeare, who was less within his ken than Drayton or Nashe, he says:

> As the soul of Euphorbus was thought to live in Pythagoras,[1] so the sweet witty soul of Ovid lives in mellifluous and honey-tongued Shakespeare: witness his *Venus and Adonis*, his *Lucrece*, his sugared Sonnets among his private friends, *etcetera*.
>
> As Plautus and Seneca are accounted the best for comedy and tragedy among the Latins, so Shakespeare among the English is the most excellent in both kinds for the stage: for comedy witness his *Gentlemen of Verona*, his *Errors*, his *Love's Labour's Lost*, his *Love's Labour's Won*, his *Midsummer Night's Dream*, and his *Merchant of Venice*: for tragedy, his *Richard II*, *Richard III*, *Henry IV*, *King John*, *Titus Andronicus*, and his *Romeo and Juliet*.
>
> As Epius Stolo said that the Muses would speak with Plautus's tongue if they would speak Latin,[2] so I say that the Muses would speak with Shakespeare's fine-filed phrase if they would speak English.

If under *etcetera* we include Sonnets and *A Lover's Complaint*, and by *Love's Labour's Won* understand *The Taming of the Shrew*,[3] we have here a complete list of the Poet's works to date, with the exception of *Henry VI*, which was only partly his. Evidently the genius of Marlowe in *Henry VI* was more distinctive and memorable than the crude talent of the first author in *Titus Andronicus*. Meres's acquaintance, whatever it was, with the Sonnets, among the Poet's 'private friends' (wherein, by the by, he notes nothing to censure) connects him with the Shakespeare-Southampton lawyer circle. He was resident in London in Botolph Lane, Eastcheap, in 1597, when he published a sermon, *God's Arithmetic*; and still in London when he dedicated in May 1598 *Granado's Devotion*, 'exactly teaching how a man may truly dedicate and devote himself unto God', to William Sammes of the Middle Temple, and *Sinners' Guide*, 'a work containing the whole regiment of Christian life', to Sir Thomas Egerton. In London also he wrote the dedication, on 19 October 1598, of *Palladis Tamia* to 'the right worshipful and virtuous gentleman, Master Thomas Eliot of the Middle Temple, esquire'.[4] From 1602 until his death in 1647 he was rector of Wing in Rutland. Shakespeare did not lack admirers among the 'grave' and 'godly'.

[1] Ovid, *Metamorphoses*, xv. 160–4.

[2] *Bacchides*, iv. 9–13.

[3] There is no sound reason for identifying this with *All's Well that Ends Well*: see pp. 600–8.

[4] F. S. Ferguson in *Times Literary Supplement*, 7 June 1928.

Another quotation from Falstaff, in September, is in a letter of the 20th from Tobie Matthew to Dudley Carleton in Ostend:

Sir Francis Vere is coming towards the Low Countries, and Sir Alexander Ratcliffe and Sir Robert Drury with him. *Honour pricks them on*, and the world thinks that *honour will quickly prick them off again.*[1]

Two days later Ben Jonson killed his fellow actor and late fellow prisoner in the Marshalsea,[2] Gabriel Spenser, in a duel in Hoxton Fields. For a brief period Spenser had joined Shakespeare's company from Pembroke's Men,[3] and then he passed to the Admiral's Men. He was buried at St. Leonard's, Shoreditch, from his house in Hog Lane, on Sunday 24 September.[4] Henslowe wrote on 26th from the Bankside to Edward Alleyn at Ringmere in Sussex, where he was the guest, with his wife, of Master Arthur Langworth:

Now to let you understand news, I will tell you some, but it is for me hard and heavy. Since you were with me, I have lost one of my company, which hurteth me greatly, that is, Gabriel. For he is slain in Hogsdon Fields by the hands of Benjamin Jonson, bricklayer. Therefore I would fain have a little of your counsel, if I could.[5]

Jonson was indicted (as a 'yeoman') at Newgate. He confessed to slaying Spenser with a rapier, which penetrated his right side six inches and killed him instantly; asked for the Book, read his 'neck-verse' (*Misere mei Deus secundum magnam misericordiam tuam et secundum multitudinem miserationum tuarum dele iniquitatem meam*, Psalm li. 1), proving thereby he was a scholar (*clericus*); was branded on the left thumb with T (for Tyburn), and set free *juxta formam statutis*, i.e. of 18 Elizabeth.[6]

If duellists, however, received mercy, less criminal offenders had a rough time this autumn. 'The Lord Chief Justice', wrote Chamberlain on 20 October to Carleton, 'hath played *rex* of late among whores and bawds, and persecutes poor pretty wenches out of all pity and mercy.' This did not escape the notice of the lawyer-poet, ever ready to support a Lord Chief Justice, who was now Sir John Popham. Scenes I. ii and II. i in *The Second Part of Henry the Fourth*, and the dragging in of Mistress Quickly

[1] *S.P. Dom. Eliz.* cclxvii. Cf. *1 Hen. IV*, v. i. 130 f.
[2] p. 458.
[3] He took the part of Messenger in *3 Hen. VI* (I. ii): see p. 712.
[4] *Register*.
[5] *Henslowe Papers*, 47 f.
[6] Jeaffreson, *Middlesex County Records*, i. xxxviii; iv. 350.

and Doll Tearsheet by the Beadles in the same play (v. iv), would not be uncomplimentary to Popham.

One more event of interest to Shakespeare must be noted. On Wednesday, 1 November, Richard Field and a brother stationer represented their Company at the Lord Mayor's Feast. Shakespeare and Richard Quyney were both in London at this date, and may have witnessed the Procession.

1597–9

§ 83. PUBLICATION OF SHAKESPEARE'S PLAYS

EVIDENCE of Shakespeare's popularity is the demand for his plays in print. In 1597 were published *Romeo and Juliet*, *Richard the Second* (entered S.H. 29 August), and *Richard the Third* (S.H. 20 October); in 1598, *The First Part of Henry the Fourth* (S.H. 25 February), *Richard the Second* (a second edition), *Richard the Third* (a second edition), and *Love's Labour's Lost.* These were 'stolen and surreptitious' ventures, 'piracies' of the publishers, of varied worth but all valuable to the student. *Romeo and Juliet* is a hasty and very imperfect production, but it throws light on a subsequent edition of 1599. In *Love's Labour's Lost* we have noted the embodiment of new and discarded passages. The printer, 'W. W.' of London, does very much as Field did with the poems. He saves his type and line-space by abbreviation of the author's spelling, use of contractions, and revision of provincialisms (London pronunciation being almost invariably curter than that of the country); yet he leaves enough of the original for us to recognize the features familiar to us in Warwickshire script and unmistakable in the published *Venus and Adonis* and *Lucrece*. Similar results appear from the other quartos. Their printers are rival craftsmen, who take individual lines, but are at one in the economy of their paper and type, regard for the appearance of the page, and drastic shortening of the Poet's redundant, provincial orthography. Fortunately, they have their own ideas of convenient and sufficient spelling, follow more or less faithfully that particular spelling, and by no means agree in their individual selection; so that they take over from the manuscript original forms, which may be put together fruitfully for the reconstruction of the Poet's text. The quartos of *Richard the Second*, 1597 and 1598, are particularly interesting and useful. They are from the same printer and publisher, but the second is not a reprint of the first. The type has been distributed and set up again, largely but not entirely from the old manuscript. Where the editions differ they supplement each other not unfrequently with original spellings.

Collation of these early printed texts, with one another and with later texts, gives us much, approximately, as it left Shakespeare's hand, rich and strong and individual, in comparison with the tame correctness and monotony of modern standardized, impersonal letterpress. It is delightful to reconstruct and read, not to say hear, a bit of comedy-nonsense of the Sonnet type, like the following:

KING (disguised as a 'Muscovite', and accompanied by 'Muscovites', and 'Black Moores' as musicians; to Rosaline, who is disguised as the Princess, with ladies):

Vouchsafe to shewe the Sonneshine of your face
That wee like savages maye worshippe it.
R. My face is but a Moone, and clouded too.
K. Blessed are cloudes to doe as such cloudes doo.
Vouchsafe, bright Moone, and these thy starres, to shyne,
Those cloudes remoovde, uppon oure waterie eyne.
R. O vaine peticioner, begge a greater matter—
Thou nowe requestst but Mooneshine in the watter.
K. Then, in oure measure vouchsafe but one chaunge;
Thou bidst mee begge, this begginge is not straunge.
R. Playe, musique, then! naye, you must doe it soone.
Not yet, no daunce; thus chaunge I like the Moone.
K. Will youe not daunce? howe came you thus estraungde?
R. You tooke the Moone at fulle, but nowe shee's chaungde.
K. Yet stille shee is the Moone, and I the Man.

Rosaline's reply is lost, rhyming with 'Man'. The King continues:

The musique playes; vouchsafe some motion to it.
R. Our eares vouchsafe it.
K. But your legges should do it.
R. Since youe are straungers, and come heere by chaunce,
Weel not bee nice: take handes; wee will not daunce.
K. Whie take you handes then?
R. Onlie to parte frendes
Curtsie, sweete hartes;—and soe the measure endes
K. More measure of this measure, bee not nyce.
R. Wee can affoorde noe more at such a pryce.

The broad vowel-music, set off by the doubled consonants (nn, pp, rr, gg, tt, dd, ll), is very different from the present thin, Cockney 'change', 'strange', 'dance', 'chance', 'sun', 'afford'.

Still more, the Stratford songs want the Stratford man's spelling—e.g.

When ysicles hange by the walle,
And Dick the shepheard blowes his nayle,
And Tom beares logges into the halle,
And milke comes frozen home in payle:
When bloud is nippte, and waies bee fowle,
Then nightlie singes the staringe Owle:
  Tu-whit, tu-who: a merrie noatte,
  Whyle greasie Joane dooth keele the potte.

In *Richard the Third* Richmond's exhortation to his army gains from the author's orthography:

The wretched, bloudie and usurpinge Boare,
That spoylde your Sommer fieldes and fructfulle vines,
Swilles your warm bloud like washe, and makes his trough
In your imbowellde boosomes: This fowle Swyne
Is nowe een in the Center of this Ile,
Neere to the towne of Leycester, as wee learne:
From Tomwoorth thither is but one dayes marche.
In Goddes name, cheerelie on, couragious freendes,
To reape the harvest of perpetualle Peace
By this one bloudie tryall of sharpe Warre.

Shakespeare gives Falstaff 'bowelles' (with two *l*s and an *e*), and a good deal besides in *1 Henry IV*. The physical endowment of this old scoundrel in this one play is remarkable. He is 'a fatte oulde man' (I doubt not with two *t*s), 'a tunne of man', 'fillde-uppe with guttes and midriffe' (two *l*s, two *p*s, two *t*s, two *f*s), 'a stuffte cloake-bagge of guttes' (two *f*s, two *g*s, and again two *t*s), 'an oylie rascall', 'a whooresonne obscene, greasie tallowe catch', 'a boultinge-hutch of beastlinesse', 'a trunke of humours', 'a swolne parcell of dropsies', a 'roasted Manningtree Oxe, with the puddinge in his bellie', a 'hudge hille of flesh' (we suspect with the *d* in 'huge'), 'a bedde-presser' (with two *d*s), 'a horse-back breaker'; but a 'clay-braynde guttes', a 'knottie-pated foole', a 'sweete creature of bumbast', his 'skinne (two *n*s) hanges about him', 'a sanguine cowarde', his eyes 'redde' (two *d*s and an *e*) with 'sack', a 'white-bearded Sathan' (with an *h* in 'Satan'), as his 'hayres doe witnesse'.

There is very much in *1 Henry IV* where modern spelling breaks down, is feeble, without character. It is the drama in which Shakespeare discovered and displayed his immense, unparalleled wealth of expression. No printer could or can do justice to it with purposes or notions of his own, or canons of convention to follow.

1598

§ 84. *THE SECOND PART OF KING HENRY THE FOURTH* AND *KING HENRY THE FIFTH*

SHAKESPEARE, we may believe, spent the autumn of 1598 on *The Second Part of King Henry the Fourth*, and its sequel, *King Henry the Fifth*. Anxious about the fate of Asbies, annoyed with the ground-landlord of the *Theatre* and determined to have a playhouse under his control, disgusted by the abuses of the recruiting for Ireland, grave at the death of the great Lord Treasurer, eager for intelligence of the Court, in high spirits nevertheless, in the flush of strength and success, he bent, as he himself tells us—

> with rough and all-unable pen
> Our bending author[1]—

to the portrayal of his young Soldier King.

Serious political division immediately followed Burghley's departure. Southampton's independence, not to say defiance, had more behind it than his marriage. He was restless under the Cecil yoke, and devoted to the cause of his kinsman. Essex was Earl Marshal, and leader of all malcontents, Puritan and Romanist. He was loud for the succession of King James, had the secret support of the Scottish king, was an extraordinary favourite with the people. And there is little doubt that Shakespeare, at this time, with many of the best minds in England, had considerable faith in him. Some who knew him better shook their heads. Half a year later, when the Poet was sanguine about the Earl's prospects in Ireland, a discerning critic observed:

> He goeth not forth to serve the Queen's realm, but to humour his own revenge . . . If he performs in the field what he hath promised in the Council, all will be well; but . . . If my Lord Treasurer had lived longer matters would

[1] *Hen. V*, Epilogue, 1 f.

go on surer. *He was our great Pilot, on whom all cast their eyes and sought their safety.* The Queen's Highness doth often speak of him in tears, and turn aside when he is discoursed of, nay, even forbiddeth any mention to be made of his name in the Council.[1]

In this psychological context, of national bereavement and challenge, Shakespeare drew his splendid picture of Youth and Age—of romantic Youth and tragic Age, Youth beset by the failures and sins of elders, their forebodings:

> The blood weeps from my heart when I do shape
> In forms imaginary the unguided days
> And rotten times that you shall look upon;[2]

their evil examples, mean ambitions, senile sensualities; but confronting all this decrepitude, encountering it with magnificent good nature, humour, and vitality, and overcoming it.

As the drama unfolds, the laughter at the *Boar's Head* and in Shallow's garden becomes as 'the crackling of thorns under a pot'. Harry turns from it. He has played the fool, but not deeply; he has been a prig, but superficially. So the Poet shows us at the outset.[3] 'Most subject is the fattest soil to weeds',[4] 'best men are moulded out of faults'[5]: this is his philosophy, and his Prince exemplifies it. The young king coming from his coronation rebukes the old voluptuary fiercely because of the voluptuous in himself:

> I know thee not, old man: fall to thy prayers.[6]

[1] Robert Markham to John Harington (March 1599).

[2] *2 Hen. IV*, IV. iv. 58–60. Cf. III. iii. 45 ff., IV. v. 66–76.

[3] *1 Hen. IV*, I. ii. 218–41 ('I know you all', &c.). Shakespeare builds the character, as already said, on Holinshed: 'Persons . . . by slanderous report sought not only to spot his good name but to sow discord betwixt him and his father . . . privily charg[ing] him with riot and other uncivil demeanor unseemly for a prince. Indeed he was youthfully given, grown to audacity, and had chosen him companions agreeable to his age; with whom he spent the time in such recreations, exercises and delights as he fancied. But yet it should seem he had a care to avoid doing of wrong and to tedder his affections within the tract of virtue' (*Chronicles*, iii. 539). Cf. also iii. 543: As 'king . . . he determined to put on him the shape of a new man. For whereas aforetime he had made himself a companion unto misruly mates of dissolute order and life, he now banished them all from his presence (but not unrewarded or else unpreferred), inhibiting them upon a great pain not once to approach, lodge or sojourn within ten miles of his Court or presence.' And iii. 583, a glowing tribute to his kingship. Shakespeare does not depart from this conception. The only licentious speech he puts in Harry's mouth is *1 Hen. IV*, II. iv. 396–9, and it is bravado.

[4] *2 Hen. IV*. IV. iv. 54.

[5] *Meas. for M.* V. i. 444.

[6] *2 Hen. IV*. V. v. 51.

He rises strongly into the simple, God-fearing, practical young ruler. Nothing 'bookish', pedantic, introspective, or agnostic impedes him. He asks,

> May I with right and conscience make this claim?[1]

And satisfied by his advisers he prosecutes it, 'weighing time to the utmost grain'.[2] At Agincourt he is the Christian Knight—

> O God of battles! steel my soldiers' hearts—[3]

and the battle is the Christian's warfare with evil, more worthy of a morality than a history-play,

> O God, thy arm was here;
> And not to us but to thy arm alone
> Ascribe we all![4]

But the Morality feature cannot disguise a genuine contempt for France, for her 'gallants' in high places and 'superfluous lackeys'. There is national antipathy, as in *King Henry the Sixth*, but more. The ridicule in *Love's Labour's Lost* has become scorn in the parade of high-sounding titles by Pistol's prisoner:

> Je pense que vous êtes gentilhomme de bonne qualité. . . . O Seigneur Dieu! . . . Je suis gentilhomme de bonne maison: gardez ma vie, et je vous donnerai deux cents écus. . . . Sur mes genoux je vous donne mille remercîmens; et je m'estime heureux que je suis tombé entre les mains d'un chevalier, je pense, le plus brave, vaillant, et très distingué seigneur.[5]

The French princess, whatever her charm, is a poor little heroine for Shakespeare. He might have given his young King a worthier helpmate, but of that stock he will not. He betrays his want of respect by a gross jest.[6]

Satire is keener for the Poet's knowledge and marvellous portrayal of abuses in England. He is on ground altogether familiar. He brings Falstaff and his tattered wide-legged levies by the road he knows so well through St. Albans ('Albones') and Daventry ('Daintry') into Warwickshire.[7] Recruiting was a scandal. The Privy Council complained of 'corruption' in 'commissaries for the musters' (18 November 1597),[8] and in 'captains' who for 'private and unhonest gain' 'dismissed' soldiers and

[1] *Hen. V*, I. ii. 96.
[2] II. iv. 137 f.
[3] IV. i. 306.
[4] IV. viii. 111 ff.
[5] IV. iv.
[6] III. iv. 54–63.
[7] *I Hen. IV*, IV. ii. 50 f., 56.
[8] *Acts*, XXVIII. 128.

'entertained' others (12 July 1598).[1] They issued instructions to commissaries to demand of captains the muster-rolls, and compare them with the men, and observe whether there had been changes since their delivery, and to have special care that 'victuallers, horse-boys, hirelings or vagrant *pas volents* did not offer to pass musters in the bands' (6 August).[2] A body of recruits revolted at Towcester on their way from London to Chester (an occasion of letters from the Council on 4 and 5 October).[3] Two hundred men were raised in Gloucestershire, one hundred and fifty in Warwickshire, and one hundred and fifty in Worcestershire during the summer and autumn (the commission was issued from Greenwich on 18 June)[4] and 'coat-and-conduct money' was provided.[5] Shakespeare takes us to the heart of all this, as no historian can, with satirical comment, in the vivid scenes before Justice Shallow's house.[6] Shallow, when a youth, studied at Clement's Inn and picked up sufficient law to make him a disreputable country magnate. He is a commissary for musters. He is not all ass. He can make a bargain, is alert about prices,[7] sows even 'the headland',[8] deducts the price of a sack from William's wages,[9] bids Davy 'cast' the blacksmith's bill ere he pay it.[10] He welcomes Falstaff with an eye to business: 'a friend in Court is better than a penny in purse'.[11] 'God' in his mouth is on the lips of a fool,[12] but he has a solemn dread of Death:

And is old Double dead?[13]

He is shocked by Falstaff's barefaced 'dismissing' of his best recruits, Mouldy and Bullcalf. Bardolf has received £4 from them, of which he gives £3 to Falstaff.[14] Bardolf is no match for his master, but he more than holds his own among the country men. He is greeted as a gentleman from Court, he inspires in Davy the desire to see London, he impresses Shallow by his use

[1] *Acts*, xxviii. 571.
[2] *Ib.* xxix. 17, 19 f.
[3] *Ib.* 214 f., 217 f.
[4] *Ib.* xxviii. 524.
[5] Three score and eight pounds six shillings and eight pence were voted by the Council on 16 April 1599 to be delivered to Robert Somerville for coat-and-conduct of 150 men levied in the County of Warwick at two several times for Her Majesty's service of Ireland (xxix. 728).
[6] *2 Hen. IV*, III. ii, V. i and iii.
[7] III. ii. 42 f., 54–7.
[8] V. i. 15–17.
[9] 24–9.
[10] 19–21.
[11] 33 f.
[12] III. ii. 312 f.
[13] III. ii. 58.
[14] III. ii. 239, 247 f., 264.

of the word 'accommodated' ('it comes of *accommodo*'),[1] he is 'sweet sir' and 'most sweet sir' to Davy (notwithstanding his 'marvellous foul linen')[2] when Davy is a little drunk. There was virtue in sack to make Bardolf sweet. It is hot summer weather. Falstaff sweats, he would have Simon Shadow 'to sit under'.[3] We are on the Cotswolds—whence came that interesting youth (whose name suggests the black pigs of the district), Will Squele. We hear of Woncot, and Barston, and The Hill. Tamworth[4] and Hinckley are on the horizon. The fairs in these towns (on 27 July and 15 August) are just past. Falstaff is acquainted with Tewkesbury mustard.[5] He has learnt of an order by the Privy Council on 27 August to restrain Gloucestershire glass-blowers, who had erected 'houses and furnaces' to the detriment of Sir Jerome Bowes and his lucrative monopoly in the making of 'drinking-glasses'.[6] To lend the fat knight money Quickly must pawn her plate and her tapestry.[7] 'Glasses, glasses', he replies, 'is the only drinking'.[8]

His comment on the tapestry should be noted:

> For thy walls, a pretty slight drollery, or the story of the Prodigal, or the German Hunting, in water-work is worth a thousand of these bed-hangings and these fly-bitten tapestries.[9]

The Parable of the Prodigal Son is in poor company. Falstaff knows it well. 'You would think', he says, at the head of his recruits, 'that I had a hundred and fifty tattered Prodigals lately come from swine-keeping, from eating draff and husks.'[10] He knows another parable even better. He calls his soldiers, 'slaves as ragged as Lazarus in the painted-cloth where the Glutton's dogs licked his sores'.[11] The Glutton is Dives, Nashe introduced him under the head of Gluttony in his representation of the Seven Deadly Sins, 'a fat churl', 'with a belly as big as the Round Church in Cambridge'.[12] Falstaff is half afraid that he may be that Glutton, and meet with his fate. He remembers his hot

[1] *2 Hen. IV*, III. ii. 78. [2] V. i. 38. [3] III. ii. 133.

[4] 'Stamford' of the Folio is too far afield. The Quarto has 'Samforth', which is, surely, as Gray suggests (*A Chapter in the Early Life of Shakespeare*, 76 f.), a corruption of 'Tamworth'.

[5] *2 Hen. IV*, II. iv. 262.

[6] *Acts*, xxix. 101 f.

[7] *2 Hen. IV*, II. i. 152.

[8] II. i. 155.

[9] *Ib.* 155–9.

[10] *1 Hen. IV*, IV. ii. 36–9.

[11] 27–9.

[12] McKerrow, i. 199 f.

tongue in Hell. He says to Bardolf, in mingled jest and terror, 'I never see thy face but I think upon Hell-fire, and Dives that lived in purple, for there he is, in his robes, burning, burning, burning.'[1] 'Let him be damned', he says of his tailor (because he will not accept Nym and Bardolf for sureties), 'like the Glutton! pray God his tongue be hotter.'[2]

Falstaff (Oldcastle) was brought up on the Bible.[3] No character in Shakespeare knows it better. That, it may be said, does not speak well for the Bible; in Shakespeare's eyes it does not speak well for Falstaff. He sins against the light, and he knows it. Hence it is that this incomparably comic figure is tragic. We see him on his death-bed in Mistress Quickly's bit of matchless prose.[4] He is the victim of the pot and the pox, disillusion, and a broken heart. He dies where he has lived and reigned, in the Tavern. So sociable in life, he is solitary in death. Quickly and the boy are with him; no friend, no minister is present. The spiritual consolation he receives is from the hostess, who mixes up Arthur and Abram. She knows Malory better than the Bible. The scraps of Scripture are from the dying man's lips—'Abraham's bosom', 'the soul in Hell', 'the Whore of Babylon', the 'green fields' of the twenty-third psalm,

> He shall feed me in a green pasture, and lead me forth beside the waters of comfort.[5]

There is grim irony in the close:

> 'How now, Sir John!' quoth I: 'what, man! be o' good cheer.' So a' cried out, 'God, God, God!' three or four times. Now I, to comfort him, bid him a' should not think of God; I hoped there was no need to trouble himself with any such thoughts yet. *So a' bade me lay more clothes on his feet.*[6]

It was all the comfort she could give. No scene in Shakespeare is more profoundly religious.

[1] *1 Hen. IV*, III. iii. 35. [2] *2 Hen. IV*, I. ii. 33 f.

[3] Oldcastle was a Lollard leader, and subject of a mocking ballad:

> It is unkindly for a Knight
> That should a Kinges Castle keep,
> To babble the Bible day and night
> In resting time when he should sleep.

[4] *Hen. V*, II. iii.

[5] Prayer Book. 'A' babbled of green fields': Theobald's emendation, which is undoubtedly correct. 'Bibble-babble' was a scornful phrase for Lollards and Puritans wont to quote Scripture: see Foxe, *Actes and Monuments*, viii. 340.

[6] *Hen. V*, II. iii. 18–23.

Facts and clues as to the distribution of the parts are instructive. Rossill (Russell) played Bardolf,[1] Sinkler (1st Keeper in *3 Henry VI* and 1st Player in *The Taming of the Shrew*)[2] the Beadle.[3] Sinkler was evidently a tall thin fellow—'nut-hook', 'thin man in a censer', 'famish'd correctioner', 'starved bloodhound', 'Goodman Death' and 'Goodman Bones', 'atomy' (anatomy), 'thin thing'. 'Lean Poluphagus', Ben Jonson calls him, insatiable cormorant. The reader sees his gaunt figure. Burbage was slim and active, if he impersonated Hal—'a fine thief of two-and-twenty or thereabout' in *1 Henry IV*, in comparison with Falstaff a 'starveling, elf-skin, dried neat's tongue, bull's-pizzle, stock-fish, tailor's yard, sheath, bowcase', a 'vile standing-tuck' in Falstaff's exuberant mockery;[4] in *2 Henry IV* a young, beardless, well-trained athlete, able to digest anything,[5] without trace of corpulency. Pope, presumably, took the part of Falstaff, and Kemp that of Shallow.[6] Falstaff's description of the 'starved Justice', in youth as in old age, is a brilliant sketch, in burlesque, of the famous comedian, in and without his get-up. We wonder whether Kemp altogether appreciated it. Laughter at his expense (and there certainly must have been that) may have been an occasion of coolness.

> I do remember him [says the unwieldy caricaturist] like a man made after supper of a cheese-paring: when a was naked he was for all the world like a forked radish, with a head fantastically carved upon it with a knife . . . And now is this Vice's dagger become a squire . . . If I were sawed into quantities, I should make four dozen of such bearded hermits' staves as Master Shallow.[7]

Shakespeare, unfortunately, has not left us such a portrait of himself, burlesque or other, in any of his kingly parts—of which 'Henry IV' would be the chief—or other roles assigned or assignable to him. Old Adam's appearance is undefined. The Ghost in *Hamlet* is almost hidden under armour—a 'fair and warlike

[1] *1 Hen. IV* (Q. 1598), I. ii. 181, II. iv. 193–9.

[2] pp. 291, 401.

[3] V. 4 (Q. 1600), 'Enter Sinclo, and three or four Officers.'

[4] III. iii. 210–12, II. iv. 274–8.

[5] I. ii. 22–30, 165 f., II. iv. 265–77 ('eat conger and fennel').

[6] *The Return from Parnassus*, IV. iv. 56–8, *Kemp* (to *Studioso*), 'Methinks you should belong to my tuition, and your face methinks would be good for . . . a foolish Justice of Peace: mark me (*grimaces*).'

[7] *2 Hen. IV*, III. ii. 331–5, 343 f.; V. i. 69–72.

form', with 'slow and stately' walk, showing a 'pale' and 'frowning' face, and 'sable silver'd beard' through his beaver.[1] These outward features would suit 'Henry IV'.

1597–8

§ 85. SHAKESPEARE AND RICHARD QUYNEY

ABRAHAM STURLEY was a chamberlain of the borough when Stratford was desolated by the fires of 1594 and 1595. His house was burnt down, and he had the expense of a son at Oxford—his eldest son, Henry, who matriculated from Exeter College on 7 January 1595. With pious resignation and courage he met his responsibilities. Sir Thomas Lucy was his friend, who paid no less than five official visits to the town (one with Lady Lucy) in 1595. His bailiwick followed in 1596. He was sworn 1 October with Master Barber of the *Bear* as his deputy. Plague broke out in November, which lasted until April. Vicar Bramhall, whose sermons had not saved the town from 'profanation of the Sabbath' and 'God's judgment by Fire',[2] died,[3] and was succeeded by Richard Byfield in January. That month Sir Edward Greville, the lord of the manor, received the congratulations of the Corporation on his knighthood. Richard Quyney entertained him, in the Bailiff's stead, in his house in High Street, the Chamberlain sending a gift of wine and sugar at the command of the Bailiff by the hand of the Serjeant. These are courtesies and formalities not to be lost sight of. Sturley's house in Wood Street was not yet available for hospitalities.

In the Hilary Term 1597 (23 January–13 February) Sturley and his clerk made a six days' expedition to London to prosecute William Underhill for non-payment of tithe—two or three months before Shakespeare's purchase from this gentleman of *New Place*. In March[4] the plague reached its height. There were three interments on the 6th, three on the 7th, five on the 10th, three on the 17th, three on the 20th. Sudden improvement took

[1] *Hamlet*, I. i. 47, 62; ii. 200–2, 230–3, 242.
[2] Lewis Baily, *The Practice of Piety*, p. 226.
[3] He was not buried in Stratford.
[4] And the end of February: there were four funerals on the 27th, five on the 28th.

place after 2 April, whereon four persons were buried. The Serjeant William Rogers, the old Beadle Meekins, the old Flemish weaver Thomas Deege, were among those who died. Eight old folk were buried out of the Almshouse, and apparently the School was attacked next door. Two ten-year-old boys, sons of leading parishioners, were buried within three days of each other, Fulke, son of Master Richard Woodward, on Thursday 17 March, and Thomas Sturley, the son of the Bailiff, on Sunday following.[1] From what we know of their fathers we may conclude that the boys were pupils at the *Schola Grammaticalis* of Master Aspinall, and probably schoolfellows of Shakespeare's son, Hamnet. Abraham Sturley's troubles were not ended. One of the four victims buried on 2 April was his clerk, Thomas Edkins. This young man ('servus Magistri Sturley', 'his man') was not a native of Stratford. He may have been the Thomas Edkins of Aston Cantlow who was born before April 1580, son of Thomas Edkins yeoman, Shakespeare's cousin.[2] If so, the Poet was not the only one in his connexion who had professionally to do with law.

On 6 May the Bailiff's second son, Richard Sturley, matriculated at Oxford from Balliol. And this day William Parsons' son, John, matriculated from the same college, and Nicholas Byfield, son of the new vicar, matriculated from Henry Sturley's college, Exeter. Their names thus appear in the register:[3]

1597, 6 May. Balliol, Parson (Parsons), John, Warwickshire, plebis filius, 15.
" " Balliol, Sturley, Richard, Worcestershire, plebis filius, 16.
" " Exeter, Byfeild, Nicholas, Warwickshire, plebis[4] filius 17.

We will note that in Shakespeare's town, in this difficult time, neighbours in Wood Street, who had suffered severe loss by fire, managed to keep sons at the University, Parsons one, Sturley two.

On the termination of his bailiwick in the autumn, Sturley was requested by the Corporation to join Richard Quyney in London on behalf of their petition for financial relief and enlargement of their charter. The relations between Sturley and

[1] *Register*, p. 58. [2] *Dugd. Soc.* v. 58. [3] ii. 2. 219.

[4] *plebis* may be a slip for *clerici*; or Nicholas may have been a nephew of the Vicar.

Quyney were at this time most cordial. Four letters and the fragment of a fifth, from the former in Stratford to the latter in London, testify to their friendship. The fragment is the worn epistle at the top of a bundle of papers endorsed by Quyney, 'These letters and writings concern our Town Business, and my warrant to follow some suits for them.' In Sturley's handwriting we decipher the characteristic close of an affectionate communication: '*Salutem in Christo.* I have no more time . . . God Almighty bless you and us . . . this messenger can tell you more.'[1]

Sturley and Quyney were absent from 'hall' on 16 December, probably being in London. Sturley was home again on the 31st; but Quyney spent Christmas in the metropolis and was there when Sturley, after visits to Cambridge and Bedford on behalf of the Fire fund, wrote to him from Stratford on 18 January (1598) in Latin. The letter must be given in full as typical of Stratford culture in both the writer and the recipient:[2]

Quam possum brevissime, sed quam amantissime nec possum litteris exprimere neque mente concipere quidem. Multifarias tuas ante et post Nativitatem epistolas accepi, etiam Magistro Wendaio datas et Westone eius clerico Cantabrigiae vidi et magna voluptate animi perlegi ad Sessiones Pacis. Sed quomodo ad te rescriberem propter itinerationis tuae incertitudinem facile conjectare non potui. Per quas ad nos proxime dedisti et Magistro Wendaio scripsisti opinor te Londinum perventum esse et illic et hiis meis obvium dare, et de rebus omnibus iis quantum memoriae dabitur recordari sic habete. Tui tuaeque omnes bene valent. Res tuae domesticae patris cura, conjugis industria, ancillarum labore, benedicente Domino, succedunt pene ad votum. Leonardus Bennett mutuo dedit 50ta libras, stipulatore Johanne Sadlero tantum, Magister Thomas Barber nec ego ullas. Magister Ballivus, Aldermannus et consociatio nostra omnis valet. Robertus Bedill deest; et cognatus Badger dissociatus (uti accepi) ad Camerariorum computationem, agente me ipso Bedfordiae et Cantabrigiae. Quibus locis quid a me actum est, cum domum veneris (si interim non illic) accipies. Cantabrigiae dies solum datus est, Bedfordiae partim ad manus venerunt partim in expectatione pendent. Quae in illis comitatibus V^{li} expectationibus V^{li} optionibus nostris responderunt. Eorum omnium laudes Magistro nostro Burgoino debentur meritissime secundum Deum. Jam tuo peregrinationis socio me commendatum habe: cuius uxor ac familia valetudine fruuntur desiderata rebus aliquanto arctioribus et pressioribus. Utcunque bene sit vobis in negotiis vestris valde, immo pervalde, desiderati estis. Quare omni iam excusatione cessante domum celeriter advolate. Johannes Rogerus promisit se omni rationi promptum et alacrem sed nihil ad huc praestitum est. Cognatus dominus Combe vasa argentea et aureata pro

[1] *Misc. Doc.* ii. 17.

[2] Saunders MS., ff. 132 a–133 a. Malone, *Life of Shakespeare*, ii. 561.

vado tenet ex suasione et deliberatione Danielis Baker, quo cum etiam valde succensebat tua gratia, sed illius concitationis et iracundiae illum poenituisse puto, sed quidem ignoro an in gratiam rediit adhuc. Sed ne verbum unum addam amplius. Sed incolumem te servet Deus omnipotens ut te sospitem mittat ad nos omni festinatione festinantius. Quia iam ad me Soror ut litteras ad te exarem suo nomine. Illius igitur et nostri reliqua habebis vernaculo sermone; haec enim hebetiora. Stretfordiae Januarij 18 vespere datas 1597.

Tuus utcunque suus Abraham Strellij,

Si otium dabitur siste lites inter Magistrum Clopton et me, ac etiam inter Dominum Burtonum. Metuo non sine multo timore a Magistra Warda.

Those of us who may not read Latin so easily as Shakespeare's mercer friend, may, like *Soror*, that mercer's good wife, appreciate a rendering in the 'mother tongue':

As briefly as I can, but with what affection I can neither express in writing nor indeed conceive in mind. Thy various letters before and after Christmas I have received; and those to Master Wenday and his clerk, Weston, I saw at Cambridge and read with great pleasure at the Sessions of Peace. But how to reply to thee I could not easily hit upon a way, because of the uncertainty of thy movements. From thy last letter to me, and that thou wrotest to Master Wenday, I gather thou hast arrived in London and there also wilt meet with this of mine. And of all those matters, so far as my memory can record them, take the following account. All thine, male and female, are very well. Thy home affairs by thy father's care, thy wife's industry, the labour of the maids, the Lord granting His blessing, are as flourishing almost as thou couldst wish. Leonard Bennet has lent £50 on the sole security of John Sadler. Master Thomas Barber nor I pledged anything. Master Bailiff,[1] the Alderman,[2] and all our company are well. Robert Bedill is dead; and Cousin Badger, as I heard, was amoved from the Council at the Chamberlains' Account, while I was away at Bedford and Cambridge. What I did in these places thou shalt hear when thou comest home, if not in the meantime where thou art. At Cambridge only the day has been named, at Bedford part has come to hand, part is still in expectation. In those counties they have responded to our expectations £5, and to our hopes £5. The praises of them all are deservedly due to our Master Burgoine, under God. Commend me now to the companion of thy pilgrimage, whose wife and family are in the enjoyment of good health: a desideratum where circumstances are somewhat narrow and pinched. That it may be as well as possible with you in your business, is greatly, yea very greatly, desired for you. Wherefore now all excuse failing fly home with speed! John Rogers promised that he would be prompt and quick in all reason, but nothing is forthcoming so far. Your cousin, Sir Combe, holds the silver and gold plate in pledge, on the advice and persuasion of Daniel Baker; with whom indeed he was very angry on thine account; but I think he has repented of

[1] John Gibbs, p. 578.

[2] Thomas Rogers, p. 497.

his rage and passion, though I am not aware that he has as yet taken him back into favour. But let me not add one word more. But God Almighty keep thee all unharmed that He may send thee to us sound more swiftly than all swiftness. Why, even now Sister cometh to me to indite thee a letter in her name. Her news and what is left of mine thou shalt have in the mother tongue, for they are somewhat tedious.

Given at Stratford, January 18, in the evening, 1597.

Thine howsoever his
Abraham Strellij.

If leisure be given thee, stay the proceedings between Master Clopton and me; also between Sir Burton and myself. I am afraid, not without much anxiety, of action on the part of Mistress Ward.

Robert Biddle was the shoemaker in Sheep Street. He was buried on 28 December.[1] Master Burgoyne was High Sheriff of Warwickshire in Sturley's bailiwick, and was welcomed by him to Stratford. To him was dedicated in 1598 *A Godly Form of Household Government by R.C.* The unfortunate George Badger suffered, not only from both the fires and his Catholic opinions, but from the suspicion and abuse of fellow councillors, who charged him with buying up timber and corn, and, by pretence of poverty, avoiding payment of subsidy and service in the Corporation. He was fined £5 in July 1597 for absences and £10 in September for refusal to be Bailiff. Later it was resolved 'by the voices of nineteen of the Aldermen and Burgesses present, being the greater number, that he was of sufficient ability to take the office upon him' and therefore should pay the £10. Richard Quyney voted against the resolution. In January 1598 it was voted that Badger should no longer be one of the Aldermen 'for that he will not be ordered by the statutes of the House'.

'Sir Combe' in Sturley's letter is sarcastic. It refers evidently to John Combe the money-lender. He seems to have visited his wrath on Daniel Baker for failure on the part of his kindred—the Sturley, Baker, Quyney connexion—to meet an obligation, and, on Baker's persuasion, to have accepted their gold and silver plate, like a pawn-broker, in lieu of present payment. Sturley, who read his Bible in the Vulgate, hints that Lord Combe was as merciless to his townsfolk as the Lord was merciful to his People in the Exodus: *Et petierunt ab Aegyptiis vasa argentea et aurea. Dominus autem dedit gratiam populo coram Aegyptiis ut commodarent*

[1] '1597 Dec. 28 Robert Byddell' (*Register*, p. 60).

eis et spoliaverunt Aegyptios (Exod. xii. 35 f.). We conclude that *Dominus Combe spoliavit Stratfordienses.*

Sturley wrote again on 24 January 1598 a long and interesting letter in English.[1] It contains a reference to Shakespeare, and implies that Quyney was in touch with Shakespeare in London.

> This is one special remembrance from your father's motion: It seemeth by him that our countryman, Master Shakespeare, is willing to disburse some money upon some odd yard-land or other at Shottery or near about us. He thinketh it a very fit pattern to move him to deal in the matter of our Tithes. By the instructions you can give him thereof, and by the friends he can make therefor, we think it a fair mark for him to shoot at, and not unpossible to hit. It obtained would advance him indeed, and would do us much good. *Hoc movere et quantum in te est permovere ne necligas, hoc enim et sibi et nobis maximi erit momenti. Hic labor, hoc opus esset eximie et gloriae et laudis sibi.*[2]

Shakespeare, apparently, had written to his wife that he was willing to buy her old home at Shottery, her step-mother having recently died. Old Quyney has heard of this, and suggests a more attractive investment, in keeping with a coat of arms. He was aware of the Poet's desire to stand well in the neighbourhood. He knew also, as did everybody else, his honesty, and the credit he would be as a regular payer, unlike his predecessor at *New Place*, of the Tithe Rent. Neither 'disbursement' came off at the time; but in 1605 Shakespeare made a big purchase of the Tithes, and in 1610, probably with his assistance, Bartholomew Hathaway bought the Shottery farm.

Sturley gives a lively account of local discontent caused by the high price of corn and the widespread poverty:

> You shall understand, brother, that our neighbours are grown, with the wants they feel through the dearness of corn, malcontent. They have assembled together in a great number, and travelled to Sir Thomas Lucy on Friday last to complain of our maltsters, on Sunday to Sir Fulke Greville and Sir John Conway: I should have said on Wednesday to Sir Edward Greville first. There is a meeting here expected tomorrow. The Lord knoweth to what end it will sort. Thomas West returning from the two knights of the Woodland [Sir Fulke Greville of Beauchamp's Court and Sir John Conway

[1] *Misc. Doc.* i. 135.

[2] 'Do not neglect to move in this and, as much as in you lies, move deeply, for it will be both to himself and us of the greatest importance. This is the labour, this is the work that would be exceedingly to his honour and praise.' *Hic labor hoc opus est* was proverbial (see Gosson, *Apology of the School of Abuse*, Arber, p. 70), derived from Virgil, *Aeneid*, vi. 126–9.

'THE NOATE OF CORNE & MALTE', 1598

of Arrow, both in the 'Woodland', as the forest country on the right bank of the Avon was called] came home so full that he said to Master Baily [Gibbs] that night, *he hoped within a week to lead some of them in a halter*, meaning the maltsters; and *I hope*, saith John Grannams, *if God send my Lord of Essex down shortly, to see them hanged on gibbets at their own doors*. To this end I write this chiefly that there might by Sir Edward Greville some means be made to the Knights of the Parliament for an ease and discharge of such taxes and subsidies wherewith our town is like to be charged; and, I assure you, I am in great fear and doubt by no means able to pay . . . I am left in the greatest need of £30 that possibly may be: in truth, brother, to you be it spoken and to none else, for want thereof know scarce which way to turn me. *Det Deus misericordiae Dominus exitum secundum bene placitum suum.*[1]

An inquiry was held at Stratford on 4 February, and it was reported that Parsons had 8 quarters of malt, Sturley 5 of his own, 12½ belonging to Sir Thomas Lucy, 11½ to other clients; Wheeler 5, William Smith of Henley Street 2, Richard Tyler 15, Alexander Aspinall 11, William Shakespeare at *New Place* 10, the Vicar Byfield 6 of his own and 4 of his sister's, Daniel Baker 3 of his own and 2½ of Master Tovey's, the assistant minister, Richard Quyney 14 of his own and 7 of Master Rafe Huband's, Henry Walker 6, and Thomas Rogers 7 of his own and 5 of Master Rafe Huband's.

Quyney was home at last on 8 February. Next day Parliament was dissolved, after voting three subsidies for the defence of the realm of 4*s*. in the £ on land, 2*s*. 8*d*. in the £ on goods, and six-fifteenths on personalty. From these taxes Stratford men, including Shakespeare, sought exemption. On 27 September Quyney was appointed to 'ride to London about the suit to Sir John Fortescue for discharging of the Tax and Subsidy'. Fortescue was Chancellor of the Exchequer. Quyney's sojourn in London on this business led to a correspondence which is in part preserved, and throws light on Shakespeare's friends and acquaintance and on himself.

A letter[2] to Quyney in Latin from his little son, Richard, written probably at school on his eleventh birthday, early in October (the boy was baptized on 8 October 1587), is evidence of Stratford culture. Something of Cicero, something of Aspinall, is in the phrasing and sentiment.

[1] 'God, the Lord of Mercy, give an issue according to His good pleasure' (*Misc. Doc.* i. 135).

[2] Malone, ii. 564.

Patri suo amantissimo Magistro Richardo Quinye

Richardus Quinye filius Salutem Plurimam Dicit.

Ego omni officio ac potius pietate erga te (mi pater) tibi gratias ago iis omnibus beneficiis quae in me contulisti; te etiam oro et obsecro ut provideres fratri meo et mihi duos chartaceos libellos quibus maxime caremus hoc presenti tempore; si enim eos haberemus, plurimus profecto iis usus esset nobis; et praeterea gratias tibi ago quia a teneris, ut aiunt, unguiculis[1] *educasti me in sacrae doctrinae studiis usque ad hunc diem: Absit etiam verbulis meis vana adulationis suspicio, neque enim quenquam ex meis amicis cariorem aut amantiorem mei te esse judico, et vehementer obsecro ut maneat semper egregius iste amor tuus sicut semper antehac, et quanquam ego non possum remunerare tua beneficia, omnem tamen ab intimis meis praecordiis tibi, exoptabo salutem. Vale.*

Filiolus tuus tibi obedientissimus
Richardus Quinye.

We may render as follows:

To his most loving father, Master Richard Quinye,

Richard Quinye the son bids very good health.

With all respect, nay, rather with filial affection, towards thee, my father, I give thee thanks for all those kindnesses which thou hast bestowed upon me; also I pray and beseech thee that thou wouldst provide for my brother and me two paper books, which we very much want at this present time; for if we had them we should truly find great use for them; and moreover, I give thee thanks that 'from tender soft nails', as they say, unto this day thou hast instructed me in the studies of Sacred Learning. Far be from my poor words even the vain suspicion of flattery, for I deem not any one of my friends to be dearer or more loving of me than thou art, and earnestly I pray that that surpassing love of thine may always remain as always hitherto; and although I am not able to repay your kindnesses, nevertheless I shall wish you from my heart of heart all prosperity. Farewell.

Thy little son, most obedient unto thee,
Richard Quinye.

The 'brother', also in want of a copy-book, was probably Thomas (baptized 26 February 1589), the future husband of Shakespeare's daughter, Judith, who was an excellent penman.

Sturley wrote on 16 October:

I thank you for your remembrance of me . . . Did not Jonathan take care for his David? . . . Our Christian love should be more if it might be . . . Your and our brother, William Wheate, hath procured me an hundred to come in about the 22 of November. I stand in some present need the while.[2]

Again on 22 October 1598:

Your letter of 6 of October came unto me the 21 late at night. We are very

[1] Cicero, *Epistolae ad Familiares*, i. 6. 2.

[2] Saunders MS. f. 134.

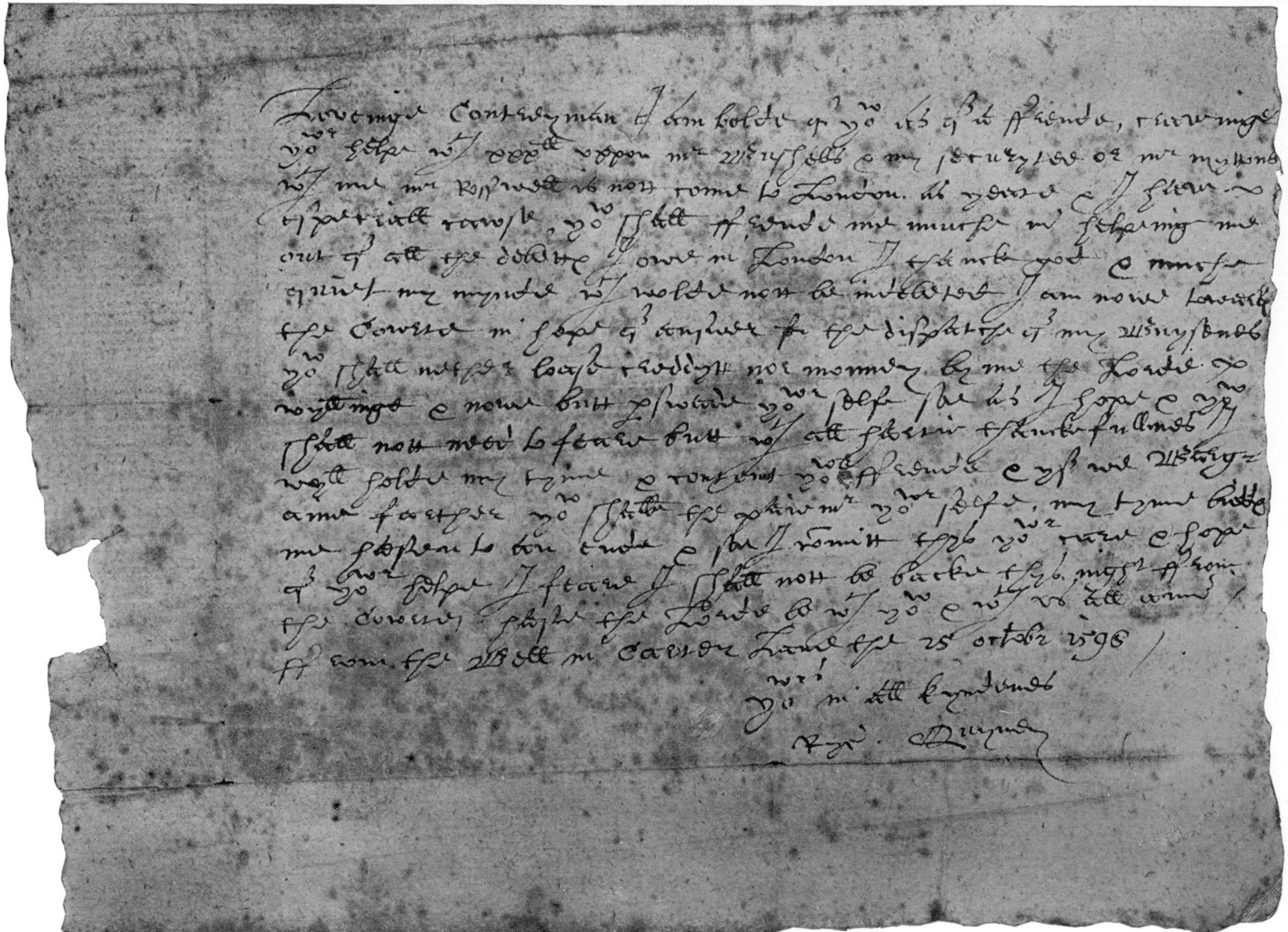

Loveinge Contreyman, I am bolde of yowe as of a ffrende, craveinge
yowe helpe with xxxll vppon Mr Bushells & my securytee or Mr Myttons
with me. Mr Rosswell is nott come to London as yeate & I have
especiall cawse. Yowe shall ffrende me muche in helpeinge me
out of all the debettes I owe in London, I thancke god, & muche
quiet my mynde which wolde nott be indebeted. I am nowe towardes
the Cowrte in hope of answer for the dispatche of my Buysenes.
Yowe shall neither loase creddytt nor monney by me, the Lorde
wyllinge, & nowe butt perswade yowe selfe soe as I hope & yowe
shall nott need to feare butt with all hartie thanckefullenes I
wyll holde my tyme & content yowe ffrende, & yf we Bargaine
farther yowe shalbe the paiemaster yowe self. My tyme biddes
me hasten to an ende & soe I committ thys yowe care & hope
of yowe helpe. I feare I shall nott be backe thys night ffrom
the Cowrte. Haste. The Lorde be with yowe & with vs all Amen.
ffrom the Bell in Carter Lane the 25 October 1598.

Yowes in all kyndenes

Ryc. Quyney

LETTER OF RICHARD QUYNEY TO SHAKESPEARE, 1598

glad of your good hope. Be valiant. If the Lord bless you with success it will pay itself.[1]

Three days later, having received Sturley's letter of the 16th and his pressing request for more help, Quyney wrote to Shakespeare for a loan of £30:

Loveinge Contreyman I am bolde of yo^{w} as of a ffrende, craveinge yo^{wr} helpe w^{t}h xxx^{li} vppon m^{r} Bushells & my securytee or m^{r} myttons[2] w^{t}h me m^{r} Rosswell[3] is nott come to London as yeate & I have especiall cawse, yo^{w} shall ffrende me muche in helpeinge me out of all the debettes I owe in London I thancke god & muche quiet my mynde w^{c}h wolde nott be indebeted I am nowe towardes the Cowrte in hope of answer for the dispatche of my Buysenes yo^{w} shall nether loase creddytt nor monney by me the Lorde wyllinge & nowe butt perswade yo^{wr}selfe soe as I hope & yo^{w} shall nott need to feare butt w^{t}h all hartie thanckefullenes I wyll holde my tyme & content yo^{wr} ffrende & yf we Bargaine farther yo^{w} shalbe the paie m^{r} yo^{wr}selfe, my tyme biddes me hasten to an ende & soe I committ thys [to] yo^{wr} care & hope of yo^{wr} helpe I feare I shall nott be backe thys night ffrom the Cowrte. haste the Lorde be w^{t}h yo^{w} & w^{t}h vs all amen / ffrom the Bell in Carter Lane the 25 october 1598 /.

yo^{wrs} in all kyndenes
Ryc. Quyney

To my Loveinge good ffrend
& contreymann m^{r} w^{m}
Shackespere dlr thees /

This letter,[4] here given in its original spelling, deserves, in passing, careful consideration. It is a typical example of an educated Stratford man's script, who has been in touch a good deal with London and to some extent with the Court, and has dropped something of his provincialism and redundancy of spelling. Interesting to Shakespeareans are the forms he retains, and the remarkable uniformity of his spelling.[5] The orthography, however, is that of a man of business, not of a dramatic poet.

[1] Saunders MS. f. 96 a–96 b.

[2] Richard Mytton, official receiver in Warwickshire of the Coat and Conduct Money for the recruits for Ireland.

[3] Peter Rosswell, servant to Sir Edward Greville.

[4] In the Birthplace Museum.

[5] Written in haste and consisting of 214 words (of which 25 have been abbreviated and 1 omitted), the epistle includes 38 which occur more than once and as many as 21 which occur thrice or oftener. Among these repeated words variation of spelling is practically negligible—*ffrende* once out of 4 dropping the silent *e*, and *countreyman* once having the old-fashioned double *n* (*-mann*). In spite of his haste Quyney adds the silent *e* to 24 words, and he strengthens *k* with *c* in *thancke*, *thanckefullnes*, and *Shackespere*. *Uppon*, *yeate*, *mynde*, *loase*, *tyme* (twice), *wyll* (twice), *bidde*, *hartie*, are good Stratford.

Quyney, evidently, was about to take boat to Richmond, where the Court was sitting, and where the Privy Council met three times that day. He directs his letter without address, intending to dispatch it by a messenger well acquainted with his whereabouts. On his way, however, to the River, he seems to have met the Poet, and received from him a favourable answer to his request. In the evening, on his return from Richmond, he wrote to Sturley that Shakespeare would provide them money. The letter, undelivered and not destroyed, has come down to us, the sole relic of the Poet's correspondence.

The Poet's readiness to find money was known to Adrian Quyney early in November (if not before), when he wrote to his son: 'If you bargain with William Shakespeare, or receive money there, bring your money home.'[1]

He wanted it put into wares that would sell speedily at a profit, such as 'knit-stockings', of which there was 'great buying at Evesham'. Sturley wrote to Richard Quyney on 4 November 1598:

> Your letter of 25 of October came to my hands the last of the same at night *per* Greenway, which imported . . . that our countryman, Master William Shakespeare would procure us money, Which I will like of as I shall hear when and where and how, and, I pray, let not go that occasion if it may sort to any indifferent conditions.[2]

On 27 October Quyney obtained at Richmond the royal 'consideration' of the Stratford petition, which was referred by Doctor Caesar to the Exchequer.[3] Here probably he had a friend in Sir Thomas Fanshawe, father of Mistress Timothy Lucy. In November or December he secured the Chancellor's approval:

> In mine opinion it is very reasonable and conscionable for Her Majesty to grant in relief of the Town, twice afflicted and almost wasted by fire.[4]

His business was now again at the Court, which sat at Whitehall. On 17 December he learnt from Doctor Herbert her Majesty's 'clemency' that a 'book should be drawn for the discharge of the subsidy and tax'.[5] For this Quyney proceeded to the Solicitor-General. He spent Christmas in London, his second in succession, a Christmas of thrilling interest to Shakespeare.

The Poet 'as a friend' found £30 (some £360 at least in our post-War money) for Quyney, though engaged in an expensive

[1] *Misc. Doc.* i. 131.
[2] i. 136.
[3] v. 17.
[4] *Misc. Doc.* v. 17.
[5] *Ib.*

and hazardous undertaking with the Burbages. The lack of an address on Quyney's letter of 25 October may not be unconnected with Shakespeare's change of his lodging. He had removed from St. Helen's, Bishopsgate, where the collectors of the Subsidy reported his levy of 13*s.* 4*d.* as unpaid on 1 October. The debt was defrayed the following year in the Clink on Bankside, and there is little doubt that he resided near the scene of operations during the erection of the *Globe*.[1]

1598–9

§ 86. THE BUILDING OF THE *GLOBE*

SHAKESPEARE'S company performed before the Queen at Whitehall on 26 December 1598 and 1 January 1599, and at Richmond on Shrove Tuesday, 20 February.[2] Negotiations with the ground-landlord of the *Theatre* had failed, and he claimed the building. On 28 December 1598, two days after their performance at Whitehall, Shakespeare's company, under the direction of a builder named Peter Street, bodily removed the structure to Bankside. Armed with daggers, swords, bills, and axes, these 'riotous persons, to the number of twelve', pulled down the timber-work and, resisting interference from the landlord's servants (he himself was in the country), conveyed it across the Thames to a site in the parish of St. Saviour's,[3] apparently on the north side of Maiden Lane.[4] Of this site, which was the property of Sir Thomas Brend, Cuthbert and Richard Burbage, in conjunction with 'William Shakespeare, John Heminge, Augustine Phillips, Thomas Pope and William Kemp', had a lease for thirty-one years from Christmas last past at a rent of £14 10*s.* 0*d.* per annum.[5] On New Year's day they performed, as stated, at Whitehall, notwithstanding this act of temerity, which brought Peter Street for the moment to the Marshalsea. In the second

[1] *Lay Subsidy Roll* 146/369 (Hunter, *New Illustrations*, 76 ff.). *Pipe Roll* 40, 41 Eliz.

[2] Chambers, iv. 111, 166.

[3] Bill of Complaint, Allen *v.* Burbage, 44 Eliz.

[4] 'Maiden Lane, a long straggling place with ditches on each side, the passages to the houses being over little bridges, with little garden-plots before them, especially on the north side, which is best both for houses and inhabitants' (Stow, *Survey of London*).

[5] 21 Feb. 1599.

raid on 20 January 1598/9 they carried off what material was left.[1] Shakespeare was more than a ringleader. On 16 May, when the new playhouse had been open a few weeks, it was described in the post-mortem inquisition on Sir Thomas Brend as *una domus de novo edificata in occupacione Willelmi Shakespeare et aliorum*[2]—'a building of late erected in the occupation of William Shakespeare and others'. And so long as he had to do with it, though he owned but one of the ten shares, the *Globe* was Shakespeare's and others'. He provided his share of the money, and of the acting: he provided also the play, and he meant to have it after his own heart.

Quyney was in London (with a brief visit to Stratford) until the end of February. In a letter to a gentleman in authority, probably in the Exchequer, he pleaded for the conclusion of his suit:

> Most humbly beseecheth your Worship the poor suitor for Stratford-upon-Avon, whose purse is weakened with long lying in London and heart much grieved he can not effect to the expectation of his neighbours this poor suit with more speed and less charge, and whose entreaty is now to your Worship, as to one whose power is sufficient and will, by common report, of no less value, by your merciful and good inclination to do well to and for distressed people: that you would be well pleased accordingly to hasten the end of this suit.
>
> The certificate from our Justices with our petition do speak more than your poor suppliant can write, and if the Lord give leave I distrust not your Worship's good help herein, neither the Lord's providence to stay His leisure and your fit time. I will to my power thankfully requite your travail, and with my poor prayer to God never forget to call to Him to recompence you besides. And many hundreds with me shall you bind to pray for your increase of health with much worldly dignity in this life, and eternal glory in the life to come.[3]

1599

§ 87. THE EARL OF ESSEX

THE darling of the moment was the Earl of Essex—

> The expectancy and rose of the fair state,
> The glass of fashion and the mould of form,
> The observed of all observers.[4]

To employ him the Queen sent him to Ireland, on the advice

[1] *Coram Rege Roll 1362*, 42 Eliz., rot. 587.
[2] Chambers, ii. 415.
[3] *Wheler Papers*, i. 54.
[4] *Haml.* III. i. 160–2.

HONI SOIT QUI MAL Y PENSE
The most noble ROBERT
Earle of Essex and Eue, Earle
Marshall of England, Vicount He-
reford and Bourgcher, Lord Ferres
of Chartley, L. Bourgcher and
Louayn, and her Maiesties
lieutenant, and Gouernour generall
of the Kingdome of Irland. 1601.
HIC TVVS ILLE COMES GENEROSA ESSEXIA NOSTRIS
QVEM QVAM GAVDEMVS REBVS ADESSE DVCEM.

ROBERT DEVEREUX, EARL OF ESSEX

(British Museum)

of his enemies, who were glad to get rid of him. He was made Lord Deputy on 14 January. John Chamberlain wrote to Carleton on the 17th:

On Twelfth Day the Queen danced with the Earl of Essex, very richly and freshly attired . . . Essex's journey to Ireland is postponed till March . . . Spenser, our principal poet, coming lately out of Ireland died at Westminster on Saturday last.[1]

Edmund Spenser had been recommended by the Privy Council on 30 September as Sheriff of the County of Cork, 'a gentleman well known for his good and commendable parts, endowed with good knowledge in learning and not unskilful or without experience in the service of the wars'.[2] In October his castle of Kilcolman, the old home of the Desmonds, was plundered and burnt by insurgents. He escaped to England and died, as Chamberlain informs us, on 13 January. He was buried in the Abbey, near the tomb of Chaucer, at the expense of the Earl of Essex. Poets bare the pall (*poetis funus ducentibus*) and threw memorial verses, with their pens, into his grave—among them, without doubt, Shakespeare.

Essex was not likely to succeed where Spenser, and almost every Englishman, had failed. Sir George Carew was appointed his treasurer on 1 March, an able colleague. The Earl was confident. He wrote to John Harington:

I shall provide you to a command of horsemen in consort of the Earl of Southampton . . . I have beaten Knowles and Mountjoy in the Council; and, by God, I will beat Tyrone in the field.

On 27 March 'about two o'clock in the afternoon', says Stowe, the Earl

took horse in Seething Lane; and from thence, being accompanied with divers noblemen and many others, himself being very plainly attired, rode through Gracechurch Street, Cornhill, Cheapside, and other high streets; in all which places and in the fields, the people pressed exceedingly to behold him, especially in the high ways, for more than four miles' space, crying and saying, *God bless your lordship! God preserve your honour!* &c., and some followed him until the evening only to behold him.[3]

Shortly afterwards, about the time of Shakespeare's thirty-fifth birthday—

Nel mezzo del cammin di nostra vita—

[1] *Letters* (Camden Soc.), p. 41.
[2] *Acts*, xxix. 204 f.
[3] Howes, 1631, p. 788.

the *Globe* was opened, to an audience, probably, such as had never assembled in a London theatre, and with a pageantry which must have crowded its stage to the utmost. The building was circular, with galleries, and open to the sky save that a thatched roof covered the top gallery and extended, for the protection of the actors, over the stage. This last projected half-way into the pit, and had the twofold advantage of giving the player command of his audience and enabling the spectator to see and hear the performer. Every stress and intonation, every facial expression, would tell.[1] Careful and elaborate costume helped the illusion, and the story was not held up by scenery. The effect was statuesque rather than pictorial.

Henry the Fifth was the piece presented. Already it was talked of. A gentleman who had witnessed it at Christmas, L. Lytton, wrote to Dudley Carleton on 15 January, with the scene of the Dauphin bragging of his horse (III. vii) in his mind,

> I have sent you my hobby, who will brag with the proudest jennet in the French Court, and if he would not be too busy with his breath, he were a beast for the King.[2]

Shakespeare added or enlarged the Chorus, with apology before the first act for his limited platform, and with compliment before the fifth to the Earl of Essex. Chorus says,

> pardon, gentles all,
> The flat unraised spirits that have dared
> On this unworthy scaffold to bring forth
> So great an object: can this cockpit hold
> The vasty fields of France? or may we cram
> Within this wooden O the very casques
> That did affright the air at Agincourt? . . .
> On your imaginary forces work, . . .
> Suppose within the girdle of these walls
> Are now confined two mighty monarchies . . .
> Piece out our imperfections with your thoughts.

And again,

> Behold
> In the quick forge and working-house of thought
> How London doth pour out her citizens!
> As, by a lower but loving likelihood,

[1] See p. 831. 'You will think you see so many lines drawn from the circumference of so many ears while the actor is the centre.'

[2] *S.P. Dom. Eliz.* cclxx.

Were now the General of our gracious Empress
As in good time he may, from Ireland coming
Bringing rebellion broached on his sword,
How many would the peaceful City quit
To welcome him!

Portions of the Chorus, as that before Act IV, reach the very summit of epic narration. We not only 'sit and see' but *hear*:[1]

Steed threatens steed in high and boastful neighs,
Piercing the night's dull ear; and from the tents
The armourers accomplishing the knights,
With busy hammers closing rivets up,
Give dreadful note of preparation:
The country cocks do crow, the clocks do toll
And the third hour of drowsy morning name.

Disappointment at Falstaff's brief appearance (and it *is* an appearance in Mistress Quickly's report of his death) was in part requited by the bustling advent of Fluellen. This delightful Briton sprang into being probably in rivalry with 'a Welshman' about whom Michael Drayton, in collaboration with Thomas Dekker and Henry Chettle, was busy in a play for the Admiral's Men in March 1598.[2] He obliterated their creation, who has left not even his name behind. Fluellen's humours, his courage in the wars, his infliction of righteous chastisement on Pistol ('Goodman Puff of Barson'),[3] and glorification of the leek, must have given unqualified satisfaction to the Tudor Queen's Welsh colony in London. For the absence of a heroine, and the shortcomings of her countrymen, the French Princess makes amends.

[1] Cf.

Hear the shrill whistle which doth order give
To sounds confused (Prol., Act III. 9 f.).

[2] 'Lent unto Drayton and Chettle the 13 of March 1598' (159⅞), 'in part payment of a book wherein is a part of a Welshman written, which they have promised to deliver by the 20th day next following, I say lent ready money, 40*s*.'

'Lent unto the Company to pay Drayton and Dickers and Chettle their full payment for the booke called *The Famous Wars of Henry the First and the Prince of Wales*, the sum of £4 5*s*. 0*d*.'

'Lent at that time unto the Company for to spend at the reading of that book at The Sun in New Fish Street, 5*s*.' (*Henslowe's Diary*, p. 85). This three-author effort was no doubt to rival *Henry the Fourth*. Drayton made vain attempts to emulate Shakespeare. With three others (Munday, Wilson, and Hathaway) he wrote *Sir John Oldcastle* in 1599, another obvious rival to *Henry the Fourth*.

[3] *2 Hen. IV*, v. iii. 94 (Barston or, more probably, Barcheston (pronounced Barson) in Warwickshire).

She may owe something to Master Field's wife, Jaquenetta, or to Mary Montjoy of Silver Street, daughter of the Poet's Huguenot *perruquier.*[1] In one of their households Shakespeare probably found the French Geneva Bible which he quotes in *Henry the Fifth*, III. vii. 68 f.: 'Le chien est retourné a son propre vomissement, et la truie lavée au bourbier' (2 Peter ii. 22).

Essex had not reached Dublin before trouble began. He dismissed his marshal, Sir Charles Blount, an abler man than himself and his rival for the deputyship. Blount was in love with his sister, Penelope, Lady Rich, Sidney's 'Stella'. On his arrival Essex made Southampton General of his Horse. On 15 April 1599 Southampton reprimanded Lord Grey, and had the support of his chief. Grey appealed to the Privy Council. Rumours were abroad in London in June that Essex and the Queen 'had each threatened the other's head', and 'all kindness was forgotten between them'.[2] Unable to 'beat Tyrone in the field' Essex treated with him, to her Majesty's indignation. In September he deserted his post, journeyed with indecent haste to Nonsuch, and throwing himself at her feet in her bedchamber, begged forgiveness. The mud, it was remarked, was on his face.[3]

This contemptible home-coming was a shock to his supporters. In six months he had forfeited every claim to statesmanship. It was one of the disillusions of the Poet's life. He had mistaken his man, else he could not have prophesied his return 'in good time', bringing 'rebellion broached on his sword'. A scrap of humour alone brightens up, for lovers of Shakespeare, this sorry adventure of his patron's friend. Writing from Chartley on 8 July to her husband in Ireland, the Countess of Southampton informs him of the desire of her hostess, Lady Rich, to take her to London to reside with her, in his absence, at Essex House. To an affectionate letter she adds an amusing piece of gossip:

> All the news I can send you that I think will make you merry is that I read in a letter from London that Sir John Falstaff is by his mistress, Dame Pintpot, made father of a goodly miller's thumb, a boy that is all head and very little body. But this is a secret.[4]

'Peace, good Pintpot' is Falstaff's rebuke of Hostess Quickly in

[1] pp. 574–5, 629, 760. [2] George Fenner to a correspondent in Venice.
[3] Rowland White to Sidney, 29 Sept. 1599.
[4] *Hist. MSS. Com.* iii. 145.

1 Henry IV, II. iv. 438. The 'miller's thumb' is a fish with a small body and a big head; Falstaff's head was small in comparison with his belly. Who were this corpulent gentleman and his lady we have no means of knowing. The story is evidence of Shakespeare's vogue at Court.[1]

Early in June 1599 there was a public burning of satirical and other writings condemned by Whitgift and the Bishop of London. Among them was Marlowe's youthful translation, which had been printed without authority, of Ovid's Elegies.[2] Shakespeare was aware of this proceeding, and he does not fail, as we shall see, to refer to it.[3] Before leaving the metropolis for his summer sojourn he obtained, on 27 June, on behalf of his father and mother, a further commission to examine witnesses in the suit for the recovery of Asbies.[4] About the same time he applied to the Heralds' College for the right to impale his father's coat of arms with that of his mother's family, the Ardens.[5] He had probably left home by 5 September, when his wife's stepmother, Widow Hathaway (or Widow Gardner, as she seems to have been called), was buried in Stratford.[6] He took with him, as the work of this summer, his fine tragedy, *Julius Caesar*, and the outline at least of his brilliant comedy, *Much Ado about Nothing*. The former was on the boards at the *Globe* by 21 September.

1599

§ 88. *JULIUS CAESAR*

AFTER King Harry, Brutus. It is a striking and, surely, intentional contrast. After the young English ruler, straightforward, practical, untroubled by a doubt, rich in humour, tempted but triumphantly successful, we have the Roman patriot, philosophic, complex, perplexed and perplexing to himself, incorruptible but without a grain of humour, a noble and tragic failure. Compared with Brutus, Harry intellectually is a school-

[1] The insinuation (Lee, p. 665) that 'Sir John Falstaff' was Shakespeare, is not a credit to the intelligence or character of those who make it.

[2] Arber, iii. 677 f.

[3] p. 539.

[4] Halliwell-Phillipps, *Outlines*, ii. 204 f.

[5] p. 520.

[6] 'Sep. 5 Jone Gardner de Shottrey' (*Register*, p. 63). I owe to Sir E. K. Chambers the identification of this Jone with Widow Hathaway.

boy. He has not reached the level of thinking where abstract truth or doubt begins. But he is human, abroad in the night in devotion to his army, in touch with John Bates, Alexander Court, Michael Williams, and the rest, sensitive to their rough criticism, not regarding them from the height of a lofty pity or generous rationalism. We cannot imagine him saying,

> Since Cassius first did whet me against Caesar,
> I have not slept;[1]

nor can we conceive of his yielding to the theoretical but fallacious arguments which plunge Brutus into crime and his country into civil war.

Brutus comes of a righteous stock, and is true to it. In vain Cassius appeals to his self-interest. He believes in reason and liberty. Caesar says of Cassius,

> He thinks too much: such men are dangerous;
> He reads much.[2]

Here the despot speaks. Brutus as a democrat welcomes thought and books. He is introduced thinking, he reads far into the night. He would be judicious and just:

> What you would work me to, I have some aim:
> How I have thought of this and of these times,
> I shall recount hereafter . . . What you have said
> I will consider; what you have to say
> I will with patience hear, and find a time
> Both meet to hear and answer such high things.[3]

Thought and verse are bridled. It takes a month for this logical assassin to make up his mind. He would be persuaded that the course is right. And persuaded, he would persuade the citizens. He asks them to 'open their ears', addresses them in prose, would show them the wherefore of Caesar's killing. He insists on Antony being heard, against the advice of Cassius. He has faith in the impartiality of the people, as they have faith in his integrity:

> He sits high in all the people's hearts.[4]

For this influence with the masses, the conspirators want him; when he joins, others join; and he immediately takes the lead, overriding frequently the better judgement of Cassius. Nor is

[1] II. i. 61 f.
[2] I. ii. 195, 201.
[3] I. ii. 163–5, 167–70.
[4] I. iii. 157.

he a cold ethical person, who has his way by an impressive manner. Far from it. Beneath the restrained demeanour is a volcano of feeling. Brutus also loves the individual—his wife, his friend Caesar, his page-boy. He can say,

> In all my life
> I found no man but he was true to me.[1]

But he has a passion for freedom. He hates tyranny with all his being. He murders his friend in blind devotion to liberty. 'Brutus', says Plutarch, 'for his virtue and valiantness was well-beloved of the people, esteemed of noble men and hated of no man, not so much of his enemies; he was a marvellous lowly and gentle person.' But he adds, and here Shakespeare breaks away from his authority, 'He would never be in any rage.' Shakespeare's Brutus is frequently, and in every critical moment, 'in a rage'. He is a man of ideas, who is invariably carried away by passion. His reason for killing Caesar, that to crown him 'might change his nature', though he has never known (we must note the irony here) '*when his affections swayed more than his reason*',[2] is no reason at all, and would be dismissed by him were he not the victim of sleeplessness, confused by superstitious omens, and played upon and inflamed in his frenzy-spot by Cassius. In the quarrel-scene he upbraids his fellow general with a vehemence out of all proportion to the offence—which was never committed:

> he was but a fool
> That brought my answer back.[3]

'Choleric' Cassius can laugh at the intruder poet, but the 'philosophic' Brutus beats him savagely.[4] How shall we account for this collapse of the Stoic and Platonist? Grief for Portia's death, a gnawing sense of wrong to Caesar, a consciousness of liberty departing rather than secured, an impatient distrust of the superhuman course of things.[5] At Philippi reason and religion vanish in intoxicated sentiment. 'If we lose,' asks Cassius, 'what are you then determined to do?' Brutus calm replies,

> Even by the rule of that philosophy
> By which I did blame Cato for the death
> Which he did give himself. I know not how,
> But I do find it cowardly and vile
> For fear of what might fall so to prevent

[1] v. v. 34 f. [2] II. i. 19–21. [3] IV. iii. 83 f. [4] 129–38. [5] 144–282

The time of life: arming myself with patience
To stay the Providence of some High Powers
That govern us below.[1]

Had he followed this philosophy he would not have slain Caesar, nor himself. Cassius says,

Then, if we lose this battle,
You are contented to be led in triumph
Through the streets of Rome?

Brutus, in sudden fury, cries,

No, Cassius, no: think not, thou noble Roman,
That ever Brutus will go bound to Rome;
He bears too great a mind.[2]

Feeling (and verse) is let go, and ethics thrown to the winds. Brutus cares more about the reputation of Brutus as the apostle of liberty than for Providence and the Will of the High Powers. A little humour, a touch of Falstaff in him, would have saved him from this unspeakable folly.

Here are problems, of liberty and authority, friendship and patriotism, which were *vexatae questiones* in the last years of Elizabeth. Into them Shakespeare brings the critique of his Stratford Protestantism. Caesar, like Elizabeth, is the instrument of Heaven to guide the Empire and maintain peace—to save the country from that 'domestic fury' which in 1598–1603 was the nightmare of English statesmen. Caesar is no perfect character—Shakespeare gives him weaknesses for which there is no precedent in Plutarch; yet always he is the indispensable head, who got

the start of the majestic world
And bears the palm alone.[3]

To lift up hands against him is to strike at Olympus and threaten Fate. He is not, as he imagines, a god—he is mortal, deaf,[4] timid; but behind him are the Immortal Powers, which are altogether too strong for Brutus and his virtues, and, like an avenging Deity, pursue the noble rebel until it is a relief to him to run upon his sword and die:

Caesar, now be still:
I killed not thee with half so good a will.[5]

[1] v. i. 101–8. [2] 109–13. [3] I. ii. 130 f.
[4] I. ii. 212 f.: always I am Caesar.
Come on my right hand, for this ear is deaf.
[5] v. v. 50 f.

A foreign visitor, Thomas Platter of Basle, witnessed *Julius Caesar* at the *Globe* shortly before Michaelmas. He says in his *Reisebeschreibung*,

> On the twenty-first of September, I, with my companions, after dinner, somewhere about two o'clock, was rowed across the River to see, in the straw-thatched House there, the tragedy of the first Emperor, *Julius Caesar*, acted extremely well by scarcely more than fifteen players.[1]

There was little in *Julius Caesar* for Kemp and his groundlings; but a 'jig' followed, in which no doubt he was the leading spirit, 'according to custom, very elegant indeed, by two dressed as men and two as women, in wonderful combination'. A jig was a facetious dialogue in rhyme, accompanied with dancing, such as the 'French brawl' satirically described by Moth in *Love's Labour's Lost*:

> to jig off a tune at the tongue's end, canary to it with your feet, humour it with turning up your eye-lids, sigh a note and sing a note, sometime through the throat as if you swallowed love with singing love, sometime through the nose as if you snuffed up love by smelling love; with your hat pent-house-like o'er the shop of your eyes, with your arms crossed on your thin-belly doublet, like a rabbit on a spit; or your hands in your pocket, like a man after the old painting; and keep not too long in one tune, but a snip and away.[2]

Kemp excelled in such performances. One was entered at Stationers' Hall on 21 October 1595 as 'A ballad, called Kemp's New Jig, betwixt a Soldier and a Miser and Sym the Clown'.

1599

§ 89. 'OUR BENDING AUTHOR'

DANTER's quarto of *Romeo and Juliet*, 1597, was a hastily concocted version of the new and popular tragedy. The 'platt' (or paper of stage-directions, usually pasted on cardboard and hung up in the dressing-room of the theatre for the guidance

[1] Chambers, ii. 364. In *1 Oldcastle*, v. i. 42 (Nov. 1599) may be a reminiscence of Shakespeare's tragedy:

> To have the King at Council and there murder him,
> As Caesar was, among his dearest friends.

For the size of Shakespeare's company see p. 567.

[2] III. i. 11–22.

of the actors), parts obtained from certain of the players (some of them copied from the Poet's manuscript), and reports, short-hand or other, of other parts have been woven together by some versifier, with links of his own composition, and supplied to the reading public, with the motto *Aut Nunquam aut Nunc* ('Now or Never'). To this first edition, imperfect as it is, we owe the preservation of many true readings and otherwise lost passages.

It was followed in 1599 by an admirable quarto 'printed by Thomas Creede for Cuthbert Burby', entitled '*The Most Excellent and lamentable Tragedie, of Romeo and Iuliet. Newly corrected, augmented, and amended: As it hath bene sundry times publiquely acted, by the right Honourable the Lord Chamberlaine his Seruants*'. Obviously it was intended to supersede Danter's edition. It bore the motto *Viressit Vulnere Veritas*[1] ('Truth gathers strength from a wound'), as if the publisher voiced a consciousness of injury done to Shakespeare's work by Danter's premature publication.

This second edition of *Romeo and Juliet* is probably the most valuable issue in print of any work by Shakespeare in his lifetime. It has been typed with care and fidelity (whatever its errors) from a much revised manuscript, probably the dramatist's own original copy. It did not enjoy, indeed, as did *Venus and Adonis* and *Lucrece*, his oversight and correction in the press,[2] but on this very account it sometimes takes us nearer than these poems to the 'bending author' at his writing-table.

Both Danter and Creede, of course, have an eye to economy. Danter reduced the size of his type before the end of the second act. Both saved space by printing the Nurse's long speech in I. iii as prose, and Creede further produced Mercutio's speech on Queen Mab in prose. Creede adopted a small type throughout, yet ran the verse over the line some fifteen times, and employed abbreviations half a hundred times. And obviously he made short work of the Poet's superfluous letters.[3] Nevertheless when he has done his worst (and it is not a bad worst) his *Romeo and Juliet* is a treasure-house of Shakespeare orthography.

We recognize, both in Danter and Creede, the broad-vowelled

[1] A variant of that of Gellius—*Virescit vulnere virtus*.

[2] p. 379.

[3] He prints, e.g., *wil, so, we, me, here*, &c., and *dog, dug, kis, he, she, shal, sink, run, od, pin, cat, sun, upon*; also *bewtie* and *bewtious*.

auncient and *chaunge*, &c., *graundsire* and *herauld*, &c., *affoord*, &c., *bloud* and *floud*, *roong* and *swoong*, *umpeere*, *woonder*, &c., the initial *im-* and *in-*, the terminal *-ie*, the adjectival *-ious*, the rolled *r*, the initial *y* (e.g. *ytch*) and interior *y* (e.g. *joynt*), the fortifying *c* (e.g. *hereticque*, *banckrout*), Saxon survivals (*yeolow*, *eugh*, *deawe*) and French (*sodaine*, *marchandize*, *vertue*, *maister*), the preterite *-de* (for *-ed*), and the familiar *hearbe*, *theame*, *sommer*, *sute*, *tane*, *ore*, *inough*, *Eccho*, *wrack*, not to mention the variants for eye-rime, *kisse* and *kis*, *spight* and *spite*, *anie* and *any*, &c.

Apparently Shakespeare wrote swiftly, and not always very legibly; yet so tidily that, in spite of erasures and corrections, he left few 'blots on his papers'. Not only his *f* and *s* (long), *h* and *s* (long), *c* and *t*, pairs of letters easily confused, but his vowels, especially *a*, *e*, and *o*, were sometimes indistinguishable. *Flapmouthd* was read *slapmouthd*, *passing* as *puffing*, *switch* as *swits*, *iaunte* as *iaunce*, *humor* as *honor*, *honor* as *houre*, *hollow* as *hallow*, *iocond* as *iocand*, *agat* as *agot*, *loind* as *liand*, *pronaunce* as *pronaunt*, and, more interesting, *Atomie* as *ottamie*, the capital *A* being deciphered *ot* and the *o* as *a*. Remarkable is the misreading twice of *Eugh* (possibly *Yeugh*) as *yong*.

More personal than the spelling is the revision, of which fascinating examples are forthcoming. A case of simple erasure is the following. Shakespeare wrote in 1596 (as we learn from Danter), approximately:

> The date is out of such prolixitie;
> Weele have noe Cupid hudwinckte with a Scarfe,
> Bearinge a Tartars paynted bowe of lathe,
> Scaringe the Ladies like a Crowekeeper;
> Nor noe withoutbooke Prologue faintlie spoke
> After the Prompter, for our enteraunce;
> But let them measure us by what they wille,
> Weele measure them a measure, and bee gonne.

Later, as we learn from Creede, he omitted lines 5 and 6, showing good taste. Prologue and Prompter after Cupid are too much of the players' profession, and 'shop'.

An instance of re-writing occurs at the end of II. ii and beginning of iii. Shakespeare had finished the scene with Romeo's couplet:

> Sleep dwell vpon thine eyes, peace in thy breast
> Would I were sleepe and peace so sweet to rest!

And he began the next with the Friar's soliloquy:

> The grey-eyed morne smiles on the frowning night,
> Checkring the Easterne clowdes with streakes of light;
> And darknesse fleckted like a drunkard reeles,
> From forth daies pathway, made by Tytans wheeles.

Then he pauses, returns to Romeo, and gives him a further couplet, linking the scene with the next:

> Hence will I to my ghostly Friers close celle
> His helpe to craue, and my deare hap to tell.

Then, beginning again the Friar's speech, he improves it:

> The grey-eyed morne smiles on the frowning night,
> Checkring the Easterne clowdes with streaks of light,
> And fleckeld darknesse like a drunkard reeles
> From forth daies pathe and Tytans fierie wheeles.

He does not put his quill through the superseded lines, but marks them by an omission-sign in the margin. This revision was prior to Danter's quarto of 1597, which has the added couplet, 'Now wille I', &c. Creede, not observing the marginal sign, prints the whole.

Another example of unobservant (but for us illuminating) printing is in Romeo's last speech. Creede gives us, save that he misreads 'pallace' as 'pallat' and 'tombest' as 'tumblest':

> Ah deare Iuliet
> Why art thou yet so faire? I will beleeue,
> Shall I beleeue, that vnsubstantiall death is amorous,
> And that the leane abhorred monster keepes
> Thee here in darke to be his parramour?
> For feare of that, I still will staie with thee,
> And neuer from this pallace of dym night
> Depart againe, come lye thou in my arme.
> Heer's to thy health, where ere thou tombest in.
> O true Appothecarie!
> Thy drugs are quicke. Thus with a kisse I die.
> Depart againe, here, here, will I remaine,
> With wormes that are thy Chamber-maides: O here
> Will I set vp my everlasting rest:
> And shake the yoke of inauspicious starres
> From this world wearied flesh, eyes looke your last:
> Armes take your last embrace: And lips, O you
> The doores of breath, seale with a righteous kisse
> A datelesse bargaine to ingrossing death:
> Come bitter conduct, come vnsavoury guide,
> Thou desperate Pilot, now at once run on

The dashing Rocks, thy seasick weary barke:
Heeres to my Loue. O true Appothecary:
Thy drugs are quicke. Thus with a kisse I die.

Danter gives us little help here; but it is not difficult to see what has happened. Shakespeare wrote, 'I will beleeve' (l. 2); then correcting, turned the sentence into a question, 'Shall I beleeve'. He wrote on until 'Thus with a kisse I die' (l. 11); but dissatisfied returned to 'Depart againe' (l. 8) and re-wrote, expanding, seized with new imagery, converting ll. 8 f. into 12–22.[1] This revision again, as we know from Danter,[2] was at the time of composition, 1596, probably at Stratford.

That the manuscript, however, was a theatre document appears from the stage directions, and the mention, by interpolation or otherwise, of two of the actors. Directions, if they do not instruct like Danter's 'platt', include stage properties, such as 'swords and bucklers' for the servants of the rival houses, 'clubs or partysons' for the citizens, Capulet's 'gowne', masks and torches for Romeo and his party, napkins for Potpan's grumbling fellows, music for the dancing, the Friar's 'basket', the 'cords' (rope-ladder) for the Nurse, 'spits and logs and baskets' for Capulet's serving-men, the Friar's 'lanthorne, crowe and spade'. There is interesting reference to 'Romeo and Juliet aloft'—Danter's 'Romeo and Juliet at the window', from which he (without) and then she (within) 'goeth downe'. A great play and good players did not suffer from a simple projecting platform with a two-storied tiring-house in the rear.

The two players whose names have found their way into the manuscript are Will Kemp and Martin Slaughter. Kemp took the droll part of Peter, as we learn from *Enter Will Kemp* in IV. v. 101 instead of *Enter Peter*, and from the concocted scene IV. iv in Danter, where Capulet says to his servant carrying logs, 'Go, go, choose dryer: Will will tell thee where thou shalt fetch them.' Kemp was wont to thrust himself into the play. He took also the part of Balthazar, as we conclude from *Enter Romeo and Peter*, instead of *Enter Romeo and Balthazar*, at V. iii. 22. But at V. iii. 199 the Watchman says,

Here is a Friar, and Slaughter, Romeo's man.

[1] *Romeo und Julia*, Tycho Mommsen, pp. 33–5.
[2] His text here is a garbled report of the expanded passage.

'Romeo's man' is the description, again and again, of Balthazar, and Slaughter has been inserted from the margin. The correction 'slaughter'd Romeo's man' is unjustified—Romeo was not slaughter'd, he drank poison. Slaughter left the Admiral's Men in 1597, as Henslow records in his diary: 'marten slather went for [the] the company of my lord admeralles men the 18 of July 1597'.[1] Evidently he joined Shakespeare's company (the Lord Chamberlain's men), and superseded Kemp as Balthazar—a solemn role the comedian might not be sorry to relinquish.

1599–1600

§ 90. *MUCH ADO ABOUT NOTHING*

SHAKESPEARE's company played three times before the Queen at Christmas, on 26 December 1599, 6 January and 3 February 1600.[2] One of their pieces was *Much Ado about Nothing*. That the Poet found time for this brilliant new comedy is astonishing. It bears the marks of pressure. Two-thirds of it are prose, and the verse is not comparable with that of *Henry the Fifth* and *Julius Caesar*. Save the songs, there is little outstanding poetry.[3] The Friar's speeches, the best in verse, are cramped and sometimes unmusical—

> Marry, this well-carried shall on her behalf
> Change slander to *remorse*, that is some good:
> *But* not for that dream I on this strange *course*,
> *But* on this travail look for greater birth.
> She, dying, as it must be so maintain'd,
> Upon the instant that she was *accused*,
> Shall be lamented, pitied and *excused*
> Of every hearer.[4]

[1] Greg, p. 54. [2] Chambers, iv. 112, 166.

[3] In his enthusiasm for the Quarto, Prof. Dover Wilson is hardly just to the Folio, which is invaluable, if for nothing else, for its correction of the disastrous repetition of 'Heavily, heavily' in the dirge, v. iii. 21. Rightly and beautifully the Folio gives that 'solemn hymn' with a triumphant ending:

> Midnight, assist our moan,
> Help us to sigh and groan
> Heavily, heavily!
> Graves, yawn and yield your dead,
> Till Death be uttered
> Heavenly, Heavenly!

Graves shall yield their ghosts until Death is out-ered (outdone and defeated) at the Last Day in Heavenly victory.

[4] IV. i. 212–19.

Few parts are more difficult to learn, for the reason that the author was hurried, working in snatched moments amid rehearsals and interruptions. The Quarto of the play published in 1600 confirms bibliographically what is apparent to the critical reader. It was printed from a manuscript which, if not the Poet's own, was a copy for the prompter and full of corrections. It tells us that a character was at first introduced and then dropped, namely 'Innogen', wife of Leonato. Whatever speeches were given to her, in I. i and II. i, were afterwards deleted. Speeches by other characters were also deleted. Names of actors were given for speakers, whereby we learn that Kemp played Dogberry and Richard Cowley[1] Verges, and that Kemp was known among his fellows as 'Andrew', i.e. Merry Andrew.[2]

Much Ado, we may believe, was written in a quarter of the time occupied by *Love's Labour's Lost*, with which it should be compared as a Court-play and a satire on the Court. The characters are Court ladies and gentlemen and their subordinates. The former are brilliant talkers and busy contrivers, but disastrous 'doers'; the latter muddle along in delicious and mischievous incompetence. On every side, to employ a key-note phrase in *Hamlet*,[3] there is seeking 'by indirections to find directions out'. The Prince and Count Claudio are overheard by a servant of Leonato in an orchard, and again by Borachio behind the arras. Benedick learns the truth about himself and Beatrice hidden in the arbour, Beatrice the truth about herself and Benedick concealed in 'the pleached bower'. The Prince and Claudio

[1] p. 567.

[2] Dover Wilson (*Much Ado*, 'The New Shakespeare', pp. 89–107), keen to scent revision and *substrata*, detects, as he thinks, an early version of *Much Ado*, also by Shakespeare, embodied in the Quarto. He has identified a number of loose ends, but the 'old play' is another matter. The verse which he denominates 'early' (I. i. 292–330, II. i. 179–89, III. i, IV. i. 24–256, V. i. 1–109, 269–312, V. iii) is not great, but it is not juvenile—it contains too few conceits, too many run-on lines, too many double endings, too frequent pauses within the line. And it is good enough, for Claudio and Hero and their secondary interest in the play; it is not good enough for Benedick and Beatrice, who for lack of time on the Poet's part laugh and tease and love in brilliant *prose*. Shakespeare in 1599–1600 was capable of somewhat indifferent verse in *Much Ado* and of touches of inspired poetry in *A Midsummer Night's Dream*.

[3] II. i. 66. Cf. *Rich. III*, IV. iv. 225, 'Thy head all indirectly gave direction'; and *K. John*, III. i. 275, 'Though indirect, yet indirection thereby grows direct.'

are duped into the belief that they witness Hero's unfaithfulness. The leading instrument in this deception, in his turn, is overheard and taken by the watchmen in wait under a penthouse. Talk and intrigue have banished common sense, sometimes with criminal consequence. On the very morning of the wedding Dogberry and Verges (they leave a bitter taste in the mouth) wait on Leonato with evidence of the plot in their possession, but longer-winded than usual, in a matter of urgency, they fail to get to the point before he is summoned to the church. Still, what 'wisdoms could not discover, these shallow fools', with help of the Sexton, 'bring to light'.[1] The two personages who *do* most in the play are those who *say* least. They are Don John the Bastard, who hatches the plot, and old Francis Seacole the sexton, who kills it. The villain is from Spain, the ghost of Don John of Austria, bastard brother of King Philip the Second, who died, with the reputation of a conspirator, in 1578 when Shakespeare was at school. The sexton is from Stratford, a familiar figure under another name, father and son, George and John Pinder, sacristan and parish clerk, who wore a gown, led the responses at church, had to do with registers, and could read and write, and deserved the 'stool and cushion' on which to record the 'examination'.[2]

Queen Elizabeth would appreciate Beatrice—her wit and her fire. Like Portia and, as we shall see, Rosalind, Beatrice is born in love and trouble. She leaps to life in passionate sympathy with Hero. She *knows* that she is wronged—any question of it is insult. Her burning words are like rapier-thrusts after her gay sparkle of nonsense:

Kill Claudio! . . . you kill me to deny it . . . There is no love in you. Let me go! . . . in faith, I will go! O that I were a man! What, bear her in hand until they come to take hands, and then, with public accusation, uncovered slander, unmitigated rancour! O God, that I were a man! I would eat his

[1] v. i. 239 f.

[2] 'Town Clerk' in the stage direction in the Quarto is a curious blunder (IV. ii). It could not possibly stand for 'parish clerk' in Stratford or elsewhere, the difference in status was so great.

The 'Constables' with gowns in the same stage direction are Dogberry and Verges, the 'Master Constables' or 'Head-boroughs', annually elected Town officers responsible for the watch in their ward. With them, as a witness, is 'the constable of the watch' or chief watchman and bearer of the lantern, chosen by

heart in the market-place... But manhood is melted into courtesies, valour into compliment, and men are only turned into tongue.[1]

Beatrice has Tudor blood in her. She is cousin to the gallant, high-tempered old Lady who, notwithstanding her age and infirmities, still held, as the Earl of Essex discovered to his cost, the reigns of government.

Kemp, then, impersonated Dogberry. None could do it better, or worse. We suspect that he took liberties with the part and grievously offended Shakespeare. In Lent 1600, which began on 6 February, the *Globe* was closed in obedience to the authorities.[2] Kemp made his famous dance to Norwich. Leaving the Lord Mayor's house on 11 February he arrived at Master Mayor's gates in Norwich on 8 March.[3] He did not participate in a performance by Shakespeare's company on 6 March, when the Lord Chamberlain entertained the Flemish ambassador Verreiken at his house in the Blackfriars. 'There, in the afternoon,' says White in a letter to Sidney, 'his players acted Sir John Oldcastle to his great contentment.'[4] This was probably *Henry the Fourth, Part One*, or *Part Two*, which bore the additional titles (as entered in the Stationers' Register in 1598 and 1600),[5] 'the Conceited Mirth of Sir John Falstaff' and 'the Humours of Sir John Falstaff'.

Proceedings in regard to the Wilmcote property in Michaelmas term 1599 resulted in the failure of the suit, or in compromise whereby John Lambert retained possession.[6] Certainly his mother's farm did not appear in the Poet's estate. Nor did the Lamberts hold it long. In the Will of John's son, John ('Old Sly's' grandson), dated 24 March 1654, there is no mention of it.[7] More successful was Shakespeare's application for impalement of his father's coat of arms with that of his mother's family, though for a reason of peculiar interest he did not avail himself

them out of the rest, a salaried servant of the Corporation, George Seacole—not to be confused (as by Dover Wilson, *Much Ado*, p. 97) with the Sexton (who may be his brother), Francis Seacole. See III. iii. 10–25 and III. v. 62–4.

[1] IV. i. 291–323.

[2] The *Rose* was closed for the Lenten interval: Henslowe, *Diary* (Greg), 118 ('Lent unto the Company the 6 of February 1599 for to buy a drum when to go into the country, xj^{s}. vj^{d}').

[3] *Nine Days' Wonder*, Camd. Soc. 3, 17.

[4] *Sydney Papers*, ii. 175.

[5] Arber, iii. 105, 170.

[6] pp. 31, 157. Halliwell-Phillipps, *Outlines*, ii. 205.

[7] P. C. C. Aylett 442: one of the testator's granddaughters, Mary (it is interesting to note), had married a Gibbes.

of the grant. Garter and Clarenceux (William Dethick and William Camden) duly considered the request, and on a date between 17 November 1599 and 25 March 1600[1] acceded to it, in the following terms:

We have assigned, granted, and confirmed, and by these presents exemplified, unto the said John Shakespeare and to his posterity, that shield and coat of arms (heretofore assigned to him),[2] and we have likewise upon one other escutcheon impaled the same with the ancient arms of the said Arden of Wellingcote,[3] signifying thereby that it may and shall be lawful for the said John Shakespeare, gentleman, to bear and use the same, single or impaled, during his natural life, and for his children, issue, and posterity to bear, use, and quarter, and show forth the same.

Shakespeare's Coat of Arms from the Grant of 1596.

Shakespeare's Arms impaled (with revision) 1599.

A sketch of the impalement is given in the margin of the draft with, however, a significant revision. The shield contained at first the Shakespeare spear and the *ermine fess checky* of the Park Hall Ardens; but for the latter has been substituted the *three cross-crosslets fitchée* of John Shakespeare's old Protestant kinsman, Simon Arden, then still living and resident at Longcroft, Yoxall, in Staffordshire.[4] The Ardens of Park Hall had been in disgrace since Edward Arden's treason with John Somerville and execution in 1583; and the old Puritan John Shakespeare, we may believe, preferred to be connected with the house of Simon. The

[1] 'in the xlii year, 1599.'

[2] In 1576 (see pp. 74–6), but this draft says incorrectly, 'whilst he was Bailiff', i.e. 1568–9.

[3] Wilmcote.

[4] pp. 29, 46. There is no need with Lee (pp. 283–5), who follows a writer in *The Herald and Genealogist*, i. 510 ff., to go to the Cheshire Ardens for the coat of cross-crosslets and assume the dishonesty of both the Shakespeares and the heralds. See French, *Shakespeareana Genealogica*, pp. 416–30.

Poet, however, probably for his mother's sake, was not so satisfied with the substitution; at any rate, so far as we know, he never used the impalement.[1]

Kemp returned to London but not to the *Globe*. He had 'danced himself', as he tells us, 'out of the World'.[2] Liberties in

Master Kemp and his taborer, Thomas Sly.

I have seen
Him caper upright, like a wild Morisco,
Shaking the bloody darts, as he his bells,
Full often, like a shag-hair'd craftie Kerne.
2 Henry VI, III. i. 364–7.

the role of Dogberry probably brought matters to a head. He was an honest fellow, as we may read in his *Nine Days' Wonder*, unrivalled as a low comedian but incapable of suppressing impromptu jest. After twelve years he and Shakespeare parted. He sold his interest in the *Globe* and prepared for a 'dance' on the Continent. In his *Wonder* (an account of his 'morris to Norwich', entered at Stationers' Hall 22 April 1600) he said, addressing

1 The 'single' escutcheon is on his memorial in the church at Stratford.

2 Epistle to Mistress Fitton in *Nine Days' Wonder*. The 'World' is Ben Jonson's name for the *Globe*: see p. 782. There is, no doubt, an allusion to Kemp's departure as Chief Fool from the *Globe* in *The Return from Parnassus*, IV. v. 30:

STUDIOSO. God save you, Master Kemp; welcome, Master Kemp, from dancing the morris over the Alps.

KEMP. Well, you merry knaves, you may come to the honour of it one day. Is it not better, to make a fool of the World, as I have done, than to be fooled of the World, as you scholars are?

ballad-makers who had made free with his name and doings, 'I am shortly, God willing, to set forward as merrily as I may, whither I myself know not. Wherefore employ not your little wits in certifying the world that I am gone to Rome, Jerusalem, Venice, or any other place at your idle appoint.'

1599–1600

§91. ROBERT ARMIN

KEMP was succeeded in Shakespeare's company by Robert Armin. Tarleton's 'adopted son', without leaving literature or, altogether, his craft of goldsmith,[1] had joined Lord Chandos's players, among whom he went by the name of Pinck and gained the reputation of a clown free of 'flattery and fiction' (otherwise falsehood). William Lord Chandos lived at Sudeley Castle in Gloucestershire, and his players were well known in Shakespeare's country. They visited Coventry in 1587, 1592, 1593, 1595, 1597, 1599; Stratford at least once (in 1583, before Armin joined them), and Evesham and Pershore at least once (after Armin had joined them). Of this last tour Armin himself gives interesting particulars, in a story of a local clown, who called himself after him, 'Grumball'. This was an Evesham man, Jack Miller, one of many, no doubt, with histrionic aspirations and abilities in the neighbourhood. He was a simple fellow, and 'much made of in every place'. He would 'imitate plays', Armin tells us, 'in gentlemen's houses, doing all himself—King, clown, gentleman and all: having spoke for one, he would suddenly go in, and again return for the other'. His stammering 'made mighty mirth', and 'to conclude, he was a right innocent, without any villany at all', some thirty years old, he thought. Evidently Jack fell in love with 'Grumball', would embrace him, and vowed he would follow him 'all the world over'. When, however, the players set out for Pershore, 'the gentleman that kept the Hart, an inn in the town whose back-side looked to the way that led to the river-side to Partiar' (a local pronunciation of Pershore), 'locked up Jack in a chamber next the Avon', where he could 'see the players pass by'. Not to be daunted, he crept through the window and cried, 'I come to thee, Grumball!'

[1] p. 729.

There was a great frost and the river was 'frozen over thinly'. 'Very dangerously the fellow made his way down' from the window, and without more ado, to the horror of Armin and his fellows, crossed the cracking ice, 'which, by the Long Bridge, as I guess, was some forty yards over'. 'My heart', he says, 'ached to see it, and my ears heard the ice crack all the way.' They rated him for his folly. He entreated Armin 'to whip him but with rosemary' (rosemary is for remembrance). 'In jest', and something more, they 'breeched him till the blood came.' He took it laughing, 'for it was his manner ever to weep in kindness and laugh in extremes'.

Armin joined Shakespeare's company, no doubt at Shakespeare's invitation, at the *Curtain* in 1599, when he described himself as 'Clounico de Curtanio Snuffe', in a collection of tales, including the above story of Jack Miller, *Fool Upon Fool, or Six Sorts of Sots*, published in 1600. Proceeding to the *Globe* in 1600, he changed his name to 'Clounico del Mondo Snuffe' in a second edition of the book which appeared in 1605. His first part with Shakespeare, presumably, was that which we know he filled, and which Kemp had just laid down, namely Dogberry[1]; and that he gave the Poet pleasure we conclude from the fact that he remained in the company until his death, with a reputation for 'honest, harmless mirth'. He was the man for a higher type of Clown than Kemp's kindly droll, a little fellow, like Kemp, but more intellectual, spiritual, critical—or, in representation, degenerate. He filled, we do not doubt, such roles as Touchstone, Feste, Lavache, Fool in *King Lear*, and kindred parts like Hugh Evans and Trinculo.

1599–1601

§ 92. THE *ROSE* AND THE *FORTUNE*

THE removal of Shakespeare and his fellows from the *Curtain* in Shoreditch to the *Globe* had brought them into close proximity and keener rivalry with the Admiral's Men at the *Rose*. The two companies, hitherto parted by the river and city,

[1] 'Pardon, I pray you, the boldness of a beggar, who hath been *writ down an ass* in his time, and pleads under *forma pauperis* in it still *notwithstanding his Constableship and office*' ('The Italian Tailor and his Boy', 1609).

now performed within a few yards of one another on the Bankside. The Chamberlain's had the advantage of their new theatre, as well as their vastly superior wit and drama. The *Rose* was twelve years old, in 'decay', and its site was 'noisome' in winter.[1] Henslowe, moreover, was unwilling to spend on it in view of the expiration of the lease in 1605, and his determination to build elsewhere. In the meantime he did his best. The venture of the Admiral's men in 1598, *The Famous Wars of Henry the First and the Prince of Wales wherein is a part of a Welshman*, the joint effort by Drayton, Dekker, and Chettle,[2] must have been a futile competitor with Shakespeare's great trilogy. Undaunted, however, they brought out in the autumn of 1599 an acknowledged rival to the Falstaff cycle, *The True and Honorable History of the Life of Sir John Oldcastle, the good Lord Cobham*. It was the work of Drayton with Anthony Munday, Robert Wilson, and one Richard Hathaway (whom only conjecture connects with the family of Shakespeare's wife). An entry in Henslowe's accounts of 16 October is for £10 to these authors in payment for 'the first part' and 'in earnest of the second'.[3] A further entry is of 'a gift' to them of 10*s*.—'at the playing of *Sir John Oldcastle* the first time' early in November (1–8).[4] It was evidently a success—'gifts' by Henslowe are uncommon—and on account of its challenge to Shakespeare:

> It is no pamper'd glutton we present,
> Nor aged counsellor to youthful sin,
> But one whose virtue shone above the rest,
> A valiant martyr and a virtuous peer.

It was poor stuff, paying Shakespeare the doubtful compliment of feeble imitation in every scene.

Next year Henslowe with Alleyn's assistance built the *Fortune*, 'situate near Golding Lane in the parish of St. Giles without Cripplegate': a square playhouse, otherwise, save in one or two particulars, after 'the fashion of the late erected house on the Bank called *The Globe*'.[5] It was a timber and lath edifice, on a foundation of piles and brick, of three stories of 12, 11, and 9 feet. Without, it was 80 by 80 feet; within, 55 by 55. The stage, 43 feet wide, extended to the middle of the 'yard' or pit, and was

[1] *Henslowe Papers*, p. 49. [2] p. 505. [3] *Diary*, p. 113.
[4] *Ib.* [5] *Papers*, pp. 4–7.

covered with a roof of tile—as were the top gallery and staircases. The contractor was Peter Street, the builder of the *Globe*, and his price was £440, exclusive of painting and decoration.[1]

Alleyn had left the stage in 1597,[2] but now returned to take part in the undertakings of his old company at the *Fortune*—fortified by the express wish of the Queen that he should resume his services as a player.[3] In the summer of 1601 they were busy on an elaborate and ambitious production, then and in the autumn, of *Cardinal Wolsey*, in two parts, of which the first, called *The Rising of Cardinal Wolsey*, was brought out after the second. Payments by Henslowe were to the authors—Chettle, Munday, Drayton, and Wentworth Smith—of £12; for coats 50*s*., a doctor's velvet gown 30*s*., a splendid Cardinal's robe of 'two pile velvet of carnadine' at 20*s*. a yard, satins at 12*s*., taffeties at 12*s*. 6*d*., tinsel and tiffeny and lining and other things £3 10*s*. 0*d*., altogether £24 10*s*. 0*d*.; tailors' bills £8 4*s*. 0*d*. and 7*s*., divers things 30*s*., and tiffeny 14*d*.[4] *Cardinal Wolsey*, with its appropriate lavishness of dress, did not escape, we may believe, the notice of Shakespeare at the *Fortune*; nor did the production of a play at the *Rose* in the spring of 1599 entitled *Troilus and Cressida*. He handled both these themes when his art, and not mere rivalry, demanded.

1600

§ 93. PUBLICATION OF *A MIDSUMMER NIGHT'S DREAM*

Six plays by Shakespeare were published or entered at the Stationers' Hall for the first time in 1600, among them the old and popular comedy *A Midsummer Night's Dream*, and a new one, fresh from the author's hand and not yet staged, probably

[1] *Papers*, p. 4.

[2] *Diary*, p. 81.

[3] *Papers*, p. 51 ('Whereas her Majesty, having been well pleased with the services of Edward Allen whereof of late he hath made discontinuance, hath sundry times signified her pleasure that he should revive the same again'). Alleyn could do more than 'strut and bellow'.

[4] *Diary*, p. 146 f. Cf. *Papers*, p. 53 (an inventory of Alleyn's theatrical apparel includes 'Harry the viii gown, black velvet gown with white fur, a Cardinal's gown', &c.).

unfinished, *As You Like It.*[1] The *Dream* had undergone revision more than once since its first appearance in 1594–5. It was beloved of the Poet and his public, and served as no other play heretofore for a wedding-feast. Hence its enrichment from time to time until its registration on 8 October 1600 and publication soon afterwards with the sub-title, 'As it hath beene sundry times publickely acted, by the Right honourable, the Lord Chamberlaine his seruants. Written by William Shakespeare. Imprinted at London, for Thomas Fisher, and are to be soulde at his shoppe, at the Signe of the White Hart, in Fleetestreete, 1600.' It is a good quarto, evidently from Shakespeare's own manuscript, with his country grammar and spelling—'as' for 'like', 'perfit' for 'perfect', 'thorough' for 'through', 'sprite' for 'spirit', 'pelting' for 'petty', 'swound' for 'swoon', 'murther' for 'murder', 'till' for 'to', 'aby', for 'abide', 'vilde' for 'vile', 'hanged' for 'hung'. If the play was performed, as it probably was, at 'the great marriage' in June 1600 of Lord Henry Herbert and Lady Anne Russell,[2] it was touched up for the last time, and finely, then. The Queen came from Greenwich on 16 June to be present at the ceremony and festivities in the Blackfriars, and was carried in her chair from the waterside through the City, as we see her in the familiar painting by Gheeraerts (or one of his school), with her lords and ladies.[3] After supper, her maids of honour played a mask, among them Mistress Mary Fitton, a fair young lady of two-and-twenty with light brown hair and grey eyes, a bold young person and a good dancer. She 'went to the Queen and wooed her to dance. Her Majesty asked What she was? *Affection*, she said. *Affection?* said the Queen; *Affection is false*. Yet her Majesty rose and danced.' Next day the Queen returned to Greenwich, where 'the solemnities continued till Wednesday',[4] the 18th.

Shakespeare would not repeat his *Dream* at Greenwich without amendment; and the Quarto shows some very striking recent additions to the part, which doubtless the Poet impersonated, of Theseus.[5] They occur at the beginning of the

[1] I have not a particle of belief in Prof. Dover Wilson's 1593 edition of *As You Like It* (*The New Shakespeare*). His argument seems to me fantastically ingenious.

[2] Rowland White to Sir Robert Sidney (*Sydney Papers*, ii. 195, 197, 201, 203).

[3] Reproduced in *Shakespeare's England*, frontispiece, vol. i.

[4] Chamberlain to Carleton, 79, 83.

[5] p. 397.

fifth Act, and have been interpolated in the old 1594–5 draft. Here is the first and chief, in italics, with its context:

Enter THESEUS, HIPPOLYTA, *and* PHILOSTRATE.

HIP. Tis strange, my Theseus, that these louers speake of.
THE. More straunge then true. I never may beleeue
These antique fables, nor these Fairy toyes.
Louers, and mad men haue such seething braines,
Such shaping phantasies, that apprehend
More then coole reason euer comprehends.
The lunatick, the louer, and the Poet
Are of imagination all compact.
One sees more diuels, then vast hell can holde:
That is the mad man. The louer, all as frantick,
Sees Helens beauty in a brow of Ægypt.
The Poets eye, in a fine frenzy rolling,
Doth glance from heauen to earth, from earth to heauen.
And as imagination bodies forth
The formes of things vnknowne, the Poets penne
Turnes them to shapes, and giues to ayery nothing
A locall habitation and a name.
Such trickes hath strong imagination,
That if it would but apprehend some ioy,
It comprehends some bringer of that ioy.
Or in the night, imagining some feare,
How easie is a bush suppos'd a Beare?

The new matter has evidently been written between the lines and in the margin of old manuscript.[1] There was nothing about the poet in the original—Shakespeare has brought him in as an afterthought, magnificently. The last four lines he deleted or intended to omit—the 'bush and bear' is feeble after what he has added, and the 'apprehend' 'comprehends' he has re-written above (5 f.).

Another addition and its context are as follows:

THES. What are they, that doe play it?
PHIL. Hard handed men, that worke in Athens here,
Which neuer labour'd in their minds till now:
And now haue toyled their vnbreathed memories,
With this same Play, against your nuptiall.
THES. And wee will heare it.
PHIL. No, my noble Lord,
It is not for you. I haue heard it ouer,
And it is nothing, nothing in the world;

[1] Dover Wilson, *The New Shakespeare*, 80–5.

Vnlesse you can finde sport in their entents,
Extreamely stretcht, and cond with cruell paine,
To do you seruice.

THES. I will heare that play;
For neuer any thing can be amisse,
When simplenesse and duety tender it.
Goe, bring them in, and take your places, Ladies.[1]

The 'gracious words' here deliberately inserted draw us greatly to the Poet.[2]

To the latest revision also, we must believe, belongs that purple patch, already referred to and in part quoted,[3] Oberon's speech,

My gentle Puck, come hither. Thou remembrest—

and the rest, seventeen lines of superb poetry, beyond the capacity of even Shakespeare in 1594.

1600

§ 94. DEATH OF SHAKESPEARE'S PRESUMED GODFATHER

THIS summer, prolific in work bearing the mark of Stratford, saw the death of Shakespeare's old neighbour and probable godfather, William Smythe the haberdasher of Henley Street. His picturesque house and the *Angel* next door may have suffered in the fire of 1594. If so, they had been restored by 1599, being reported in the survey of April that year as on the street 'tiled', the latter as with 'a barn on the Gild-Pits side amiss'; the only grievance resulting from the restoration, if there was one, being a soreness on Arthur Cawdrey's part about a 'hovel' on his neighbour's premises.

Shakespeare's godfather, if William Smythe were he, died well off. Apart from his leases, which he had distributed among his five sons, and marriage-portions to his four daughters, he left goods and chattels to the value of £164, which, with the exception of £10 to his son, Roger, £3 to the poor of Stratford, and parting gifts to his children and young unconfirmed godsons, he bequeathed to his widow and son, William. His house was (and

[1] v. i. 71–84. [2] Dover Wilson, 85. [3] pp. 393–7.

WOOD STREET (EAST END), STRATFORD-UPON-AVON

The house connecting Wood Street with Henley Street may be that of Lawrence Holmes, the cardmaker. The house visible in Henley Street, on the right, is that of William Smythe, haberdasher

is) of two stories, as was (but no longer is) the *Angel*. Its frontage was (and is) 40 feet 3 inches. It contained a shop, a hall, a parlour, a little parlour, a maids' chamber, a men's chamber, a chamber over the shop, chambers over the hall and little parlour, an upper chamber where he lay, a kitchen and 'spence', or buttery. We may follow the appraisers (John Gibbs of Rother Market,[1] Francis Ainge—an able young man of five-and-twenty, a baker in Back Bridge Street, next door to the *Angel*—and others) from room to room and note the simple, admirable contents: the oak furniture and wainscoting, painted cloths and cushions, four-post bedsteads and bedding, coffers, 'a great chest', 'a carpet for the table', two dozen of table napkins, ten hand-towels, and brass and pewter we should like to keep in our drawing-rooms. The stock of the shop does not appear in the inventory, having been made over, no doubt, to the son, William; and items given show that the father's business was as much with husbandry as with haberdashery: wheat and malt £10, wood and timber £13 (a goodly supply, probably for building purposes after the fires of 1594 and 1595), eight oxen £26, two wains and a tumbrel for oxen, with bows for oxen, tows and yokes and harness, and a plough and harrows £4, nine kine and a bull £19, two heifers £3, a sow and six stores 26*s.* 8*d.*, a bald mare 20*s.*, corn in the common fields of Stratford £20, and at Rushbrooke £10.

William Smythe made his will on 16 April 1600 and died in June, being buried on the 27th. His goods were valued[2] on the 30th, a week before the death at Charlecote of Sir Thomas Lucy.

§ 95. DEATH OF SIR THOMAS LUCY

SIR THOMAS LUCY survived his loved wife four and a half years. He wrote on her monument that she was

> a true and faithful servant of her good God, never detected of any crime or vice, in Religion most sound, in love to her husband most faithful and true, in friendship most constant, to what in trust was committed to her most secret, in wisdom excelling, in governing of her house and bringing up of youth in the fear of God most rare and singular, a great maintainer of hospitality, greatly esteemed of her betters, misliked of none unless of the envious.

[1] p. 578.

[2] *Misc. Doc.* vii. 61.

Her 'betters' were the Dudleys; the 'envious' probably included her son-in-law, Sir Edward Aston of Tixhall in Staffordshire, who called her 'vixen'.

Lucy maintained his close and friendly relations with Stratford. We have noticed his visits to the town after the fires of 1594 and 1595, during the chamberlainship of his man, Master Sturley. He was welcomed to Stratford by Sturley on the latter's election to the bailiwick in November 1596, nine months after the death of Lady Lucy. In the dearth of corn of 1598, and discontent with maltsters, he was more than sympathetic, receiving a deputation from the town, and entertaining Sturley and Master Robert Sheldon of Warwick, at Charlecote, and in his turn being entertained at Master John Smythe's tavern in Stratford at a banquet. The Privy Council more than continued their confidence in him, putting him on commissions for the campaign in Ireland until within a few weeks of his death. On 3 February 1600, in a letter rebuking Sir Thomas Leigh and Sir Edward Greville of Milcote (lord of the manor of Stratford) for their remissness, they praise Lucy for his 'care and endeavour for the accomplishment and good effecting' of the service required, and quote a letter from him complaining of their absence from Warwickshire and their duties. They also thank him, and the high sheriff (Thomas Holt) and Richard Verney, personally:

> We perceive the care and speedy course you took according to the direction given by Her Majesty. We have good cause to note your diligence and endeavour. Your labour and travail hath been the greater . . . by reason of the absence and indisposition of the rest.

He died 7 July, and was buried beside his wife in Charlecote Church on 7 August, William Camden attending as Clarenceux and superintending the ceremonies. The rector of Hampton Lucy, Richard Hill, preached the sermon—an Oxford man, 'honest and towardly' in the judgement of the Puritan censor of 1586, and kinsman, by the marriage of his sister to Robert Fulwood of Aston Cantlow in 1596, to old Alderman Shakespeare. 'Chief mourner' was the son and heir, Sir Thomas Lucy, and 'assistant' was the deceased's brother, Master Timothy Lucy. The new master of Charlecote was not of the quality of the old, nor was the exchange exceptional. A sense of 'good old' times, and of 'good' men in them, is a feature of *As You Like It*.

SIR THOMAS LUCY

from his effigy in Charlecote Church

1600

§ 96. *AS YOU LIKE IT*

By 4 August (the moment of the completion of the *Fortune*) *As You Like It* was sufficiently ready for registration, to prevent piracy, with *Henry the Fifth* and *Much Ado about Nothing*, at Stationers' Hall.[1] These were re-entered the same month for publication, but *As You Like It* was held over. Shakespeare had readers as well as spectators. His name spelt money for publishers, and prompt-copy might get into print. Evidence of his status as an *author* is the entry of *Much Ado* and *2 Henry IV* as 'written by Master Shakespeare'. This is the first appearance of his name in the Stationers' Register, and it has the noticeable prefix 'Master'.

As You Like It is pure Stratford—its woodland solitude, hermit-cell,[2] deer, huntsmen, foresters, shepherds, yokels, young squire and old retainer, girl-friends of rank and the honoured father of one of them, hardship and fellowship, songs, cheeriness, common sense, religion. It is radiant with health and happiness. There is nothing dismal in Arden, nothing decadent and *blasé* save the stranger. Monsieur Jaques alone is out of his element. Always 'Monsieur' and French, he is the occasion of discord. His name, pronounced Jakes and Jakës, was the common epithet for a Frenchman and for a privy,[3] and was in evidence on account of Sir John[4] Harington's *Metamorphosis of A-jax*.[5] From 'Mounsir What-ye-call't', as Touchstone euphemistically addresses him,[6] emanates an unsavoury odour in the sweet air. He is an old voluptuary somewhat Falstaffian in appearance

[1] Arber, iii. 170.

[2] Oliver meets with a 'religious' (v. iv. 165 f.). Cf. Drayton in his description of Arden,

> Whereas the hermit leads a sweet retired life
> From villages replete with ragg'd and sweating clowns,
> And from the loathsome airs of smoky citied towns.
> (*Polyolbion*, xiii. 164–6.)

[3] 'Jaques Scabb'd-hams', Nashe calls the Frenchman, and associates him with a close-stool (*Pierce Pennilesse*, McKerrow, i. 169, 177).

[4] As he now was: he was knighted by Essex in Ireland; p. 503.

[5] Harington was still in disgrace at Court in March 1599: see Markham's letter to him of this date.

[6] III. iii. 73.

(if Pope impersonated him),[1] with 'a tormenting laughter' and 'goggle eye' (if we accept Ben Jonson's description of Pope),[2] and nothing of Falstaff's good fellowship. On the contrary, he is out of sympathy with young and old, and a censor of the world. He says,

Give me leave
To speak my mind, and I will through and through
Cleanse the foul body of the infected world.

The Duke, for once in anger, replies

Most mischievous foul sin in chiding sin:
For thou thyself hast been a libertine,
As sensual as the brutish sting itself.[3]

Shakespeare dismisses him, or rather lets him dismiss himself. The Duke, who has tolerated him long, is willing that he should remain—'Stay, Jaques, stay.' He answers, 'To see no pastime I.' He's 'for other than dancing measures'—being a superior person.[4] He serves as a foil to the good folk about him—Amiens, the Duke, Orlando, Touchstone, Rosalind, and the whole happy company at the close. Always he is the discordant note. His last hit is a nasty one. He says of the lovers, four pairs of them, 'There is sure another Flood toward, and these *couples* are coming to the Ark.'[5] The 'unclean beasts' went in 'by couples', the 'clean by sevens' (Genesis vii. 2, Geneva Version).

Jaques is 'compact of jars: if he grow musical we shall have discord in the spheres'.[6] He parodies the thrush. Amiens sings,

Under the greenwood tree
Who loves to lie with me,
And turn his merry note
Unto the sweet bird's throat—
Come hither, come hither, come hither.[7]

(Shakespeare's thrush, more accurately than Browning's, sings each song *thrice* over.[8]) Jaques, like a crow, mocks the song with

Ducdame, ducdame, ducdame—[9]

[1] Baldwin, *The Organization and Personnel of the Shakespearean Company*, p. 409.
[2] See below, p. 567.
[3] II. vii. 58–60. [4] V. iv. 200. [5] 35 f.
[6] II. vii. 5 f. He holds up the music at the close—'Sir, by your patience' (V. iv. 186).
[7] II. v. 1–5, 44. Cf. the Angel in *The Faerie Queene*: 'Come hither, come hither, O come hastily!' (II. viii. 3). [8] *Home-Thoughts from Abroad.*
[9] II. v. 56. *Ducdame* is surely a misprint for *Duedamé*.

THE SEVEN AGES OF MAN
Mosaic Pavement in the Cathedral, Siena
Inscription: 'Tempore D. Savini MCCCCLXXVI'

otherwise

God-dammé, God-dammé, God-dammé.[1]

He burlesques the venerable device of the Seven Ages of Man.[2] It was one of the sacred 'Sevens' of the Medieval Church—others being the Seven Sacraments, the Seven Deadly Sins, the Seven Cardinal Virtues, the Seven Acts of Mercy, the Seven Sciences. It is hardly less familiar than these in the art and literature of the fourteenth and fifteenth centuries. *Infantia* was Babyhood (or as Eliot-Cooper gives it, 1578, 'Babyship'), the period of learning to speak, from birth to the age of seven. *Pueritia* was Childhood, the period of learning to read and write, from the age of seven to twelve or fourteen. *Adolescentia* was Youth or 'Young Age' ('Stripling Age', Wilson calls it[3]), the period of learning a craft or profession, from twelve or fourteen to twenty-one or twenty-five years. *Juventus* was Early Manhood, the period of taking out one's freedom and acquiring the mastery, from twenty-one or twenty-five to thirty-five years.[4] *Virilitas* was Full Manhood, the period of mastership, from thirty-five to fifty. *Senectus* was Old Age, the period of declining strength, from fifty to seventy. *Decrepitas* was Extreme Old Age, the period of 'labour and sorrow' 'at the pit's brink', from threescore and ten to fourscore and upward. In the famous mosaic on the floor of Siena Cathedral, a work of 1476, so far as one can read the stones worn by the knees and feet of centuries of worshippers, *Infantia* is represented by a child playing with his hobby-horse and picking flowers in a garden; *Pueritia* by a pretty schoolboy, in the same garden; *Adolescentia* by a scholar in hat and cloak, also in this garden; *Juventus* by a young man with a falcon on his fist; *Virilitas* by a learned doctor in his robes, carrying a book of the law; *Senectus* by an elderly gentleman, with a staff in his right

[1] Cf. *Comedy of Errors*, IV. iii. 53 f. (Folio): 'God dam me.'

[2] In the form of a drama of seven scenes. The idea of the World as a stage is as old as Petronius (*Totus mundus agit histrionem*) and appears in Withal's *Short Dictionary in Latin and English*, in use in schools when Shakespeare was a youth:

This life is a certain interlude or play;
The world is a stage full of chance every way;
Every man is a player, &c.

[3] *The Arte of Rhetorique*, 1560 (Mair, p. 12).

[4] The ages are variously conceived, but Psalm xc. 10 ('The days of our age are threescore years and ten') is the shaping thought. At thirty-five, Youth is ended, and the second half of life begins.

hand and a rosary in his left: all three again in the garden, which is the Garden of the World, among flowers and trees; and *Decrepitas* by a very old man, who leans heavily on two staves, and looks with bowed head into his tomb, within the House of God: *the largest and central picture of the series, with a Cross behind it.*

After this happy and dignified representation of Life, Jaques's delineation is a clever travesty. It is a gibe at the old conception. Like Montaigne Jaques is clever, but, unlike the Seigneur, he is cynical.[1] The smartness and vividness of his description, wherein we are made to *hear* as well as see[2] the successive types,[3] give point to the cynicism. The infant is all mouth, crying, sucking, and throwing up his milk; the boy blubbers, soiling his new-washed face as he crawls to school; the lover is a young fool penning a sonnet; the soldier curses under his bristling moustache, eager for a quarrel and a duel, ready to throw away his life for a 'bubble'; the justice, well fed on bribes[4] and round-bellied, discourses sententiously; the thrifty dotard, with his thin legs and a pair of spectacles on his running nose, leans on a stick and carries a handkerchief in his pouch at his side; and the old nonentity at the end has lost his memory, is toothless and blind, and no longer able (the last as the first mark of man) *to taste.*[5]

This may be a voice from Paris or even London in 1600, not from Stratford. Hooker complains of 'trencher-mates' in 'the miserable times whereinto we are fallen', who have 'a new method' of 'turning things that are serious into mockery, an art of contradiction by way of scorn, a learning graced with a wanton superfluity of wit'.[6] Shakespeare is of Hooker's opinion.

[1] See further, Fripp, *Shakespeare Studies*, 151–68.

[2] How Shakespeare *saw* his characters while he heard them speak, and even when they were inaudible, we may observe in such a passage as *Wint. T.* IV. iv. 134–61 ('this robe of mine . . . what you do . . . are doing . . . the true blood peeps through your youth . . . *he tells her something that makes her blood look out*').

[3] The child, the boy, the lover, the soldier, the justice, the pantaloon, the dying senile, all utter a characteristic *sound*—mewling, whining, sighing, swearing, speechifying, wheezing, expiring.

[4] Corrupt country magistrates were known as 'capon justices'. Hales, *Notes and Essays on Shakespeare*, p. 220.

[5] The modern actor very rarely understands the part of Jaques. He pronounces the speech of the Seven Ages as a piece of profound philosophy, and not as a sneer. It ruins not only the scene but the play.

[6] *Ecclesiastical Polity*, v. ii. 2.

His children, boys, lovers, soldiers, justices, grey-beards, and tottering veterans are, with rare exceptions, of an honourable mould. We think of little Mamilius and Marcius, of young Lucius and Arthur, of Romeo and Florizel, Henry and Hotspur, the Lord Chief Justice and Vincentio, Bellarius and Leonato, Kent and Lear, among many representatives. They are as noble as Monsieur's caricatures are mean. Orlando's entrance with Adam on his back at the moment of the final pronouncement,

> *Sans* teeth, *sans* eyes, *sans* taste, *sans* everything,[1]

is the Poet's dramatic answer to the scoffer. In Old Adam, as in *Decrepitas*, 'though the outward perish, the inward man is renewed day by day':[2]

> He that doth the ravens feed,
> Yea, providently caters for the sparrow,
> Be comfort to my age! Here is the gold;
> All this I give you. Let me be your servant:
> Though I look old, yet I am strong and lusty;
> For in my youth I never did apply
> Hot and rebellious liquors in my blood,
> Nor did not with unbashful forehead woo
> The means of weakness and debility;
> Therefore my age is as a lusty winter,
> Frosty, but kindly; let me go with you.[3]

It is significant that Shakespeare himself took the part of this 'venerable' and lovable character.[4]

Orlando (taken by Burbage: with 'chestnut' hair and 'little beard', an athlete) lacks Prince Henry's humour, and has escaped his follies; but he is of the same manly type, an athletic, unsophisticated young Englishman. He recalls Bassanio in his

[1] An echo, probably, of Montaigne (Florio, ii. 12): 'Sans tongues, sans eyes and sans ears.'

[2] 2 Corinthians iv. 16.

[3] II. iii. 43–53.

[4] Oldys has preserved a tradition, traced to one Master Thomas Jones of Turbich (or Tarbick, Tardebigg) in Worcestershire, wrong no doubt in its association with a *brother* of the Poet, but certainly reliable as a recollection of the Poet's performance, that taking part 'in one of his own comedies, wherein being to personate a *decrepit* old man, he wore a long beard, and appeared so weak and drooping and unable to walk that he was forced to be supported and carried by another person to a table, at which he was seated among some company who were eating, and one of them sung a song'. I have italicized the absolutely correct term 'decrepit'.

simplicity and strength,[1] and in his good fortune to be loved by one of Shakespeare's perfect heroines.

English girlhood in Portia and Beatrice has opened her heart to the Poet and he is worthy of the confidence. She is too good for leisure and idleness. She is 'sad' under it, craves occupation and adventure. Portia wants something to do, and some one to love. She is a new being in Bassanio's presence, as he is in hers. They have outgrown Arcadian romance. If the attraction of 'a lady richly left', 'fair', 'of wondrous virtues', with 'speechless messages in her eyes', drew him to Belmont, he turns from 'gaudy gold' to win her hand—

> thou, thou meagre lead,
> *Which rather threatenest than doth promise aught,*
> Thy plainness moves me more than eloquence;
> And here choose I: joy be the consequence![2]

And she is the clinging girl, with all her intellect and state,

> unschool'd, unpractis'd,
> Happy in this, she is not yet so old
> But she may learn.[3]

Beatrice is of the same strain, clever, open-eyed, clinging:

> Benedick, love on: I will requite thee,
> Taming my wild heart to thy loving hand.[4]

After Portia and Beatrice, Rosalind. Her sadness, which is not *taedium vitae* but sorrow for a banished father,[5] is alleviated by the friendship of Celia—a gleam, as her name suggests, of the Heavenly Grace—but transformed into animation, wit, glee, a babbling stream of banter, by her love for Orlando. '*Did you call, sir?*' Here is his triumph, and she triumphs the same instant. He cannot speak for love. He is happy to be teased, stands blissfully by while she does what she will with him, a beautiful young creature, proud of and playing with his masculine strength. At the sight of blood, however, his blood, she swoons.[6]

[1] I do not recognize (with 'Q', *All's W.* xxvi f.) any resemblance in Bassanio to the 'selfish, contemptuous, callous, lustful young Bertram'. Such a Bassanio would not love Portia, nor any Shakespeare heroine, but would prefer, like Bertram, a 'mistress'.

[2] *Mer. of Ven.* III. ii. 101–6.

[3] 161–3.

[4] *Much Ado*, III. i. 111 f. Again the image from Falconry: see p. 388.

[5] We must note Rosalind's love for her father (and correct the senseless reading in I. iii. 11, 'child's father' to 'father's child', as in *Mer. of Ven.* II. iii. 17).

[6] *As You L. It*, IV. iii. 157.

Only one who knew the height and depth of pure sweet love could say of it, as Shakespeare says in *As You Like It*,

> It is to be all made of fantasy,
> All made of passion, and all made of wishes;
> All adoration, duty and observance,
> All humbleness, all patience and impatience,
> All purity, all trial, all obedience.[1]

This is love that lasts, that can take and keep 'that great vow' which, as Brutus says to Portia, 'did incorporate and make us one'[2]—'from this day forward, for better for worse, for richer for poorer, in sickness and in health, to love and to cherish till death us depart'.[3]

The play is simply and broadly religious. Not dogma and the Creeds, but the Sermon on the Mount[4] and the Parables,[5] breathe through it. The disciple of Hooker, more liberal even than his master, speaks. As dear to him as *A Midsummer Night's Dream*, and as spontaneous an utterance of himself, it is as rich in the jewels of spiritual expression for things most after his heart—'Innocent as Grace',[6] 'Sermons in stones[7] and good in everything' (let no one say that he sneered at preaching, though he found the 'homily' of the parish 'pulpiter' not unfrequently 'tedious'),[8] 'Gentle Virtues sanctified and holy',[9] 'the Way to Heaven by deeds of hospitality',[10] in 'better days' where 'Bells have knoll'd to Church', 'Holy Bell' and 'drops that Sacred Pity hath engendered',[11] a Kiss 'as full of sanctity as the touch of Holy Bread',[12] 'Holy is my love and I in poverty of Grace',[13] Love 'all made of Faith and Service',[14] 'a wedlock-Hymn',[15] and

> Then is there mirth in Heaven
> When earthly things made even
> Atone together.[16]

[1] v. ii. 100–4 (the Folio has 'observance' in both 102 and 104 by printer's error).

[2] *Jul. Caes.* II. i. 272 f.

[3] Here, I think, we may part with that disreputable fiction of the 'Dark Lady'.

[4] Henry Morley, *English Writers*, x. 422–9. See II. iii. 43 f. (Sparrow, Ravens).

[5] Prodigal Son, I. i. 38–47, 56, III. i. 5 f.; Lost Sheep, III. i. 5 f., v. iv. 114–16.

[6] I. iii. 56.

[7] II. i. 17.

[8] III. ii. 163.

[9] II. iii. 12 f.

[10] II. iv. 81 f.

[11] II. vii. 113–23.

[12] III. iv. 14 f.

[13] III. v. 99 f.

[14] v. ii. 95.

[15] v. iv. 143.

[16] *Ib.* 114–16. Cf. 'Joy shall be in Heaven', Luke xv. 7; 'Joy in the presence of the Angels', *ib.* 10.

1600

§ 97. SHAKESPEARE'S TRIBUTE TO MARLOWE

TWICE in *As You Like It* Shakespeare pays honour to the memory of Marlowe. There were various reasons why he should do so. Nobody had come upon the scene comparable with his old master and rival. He had welcomed Ben Jonson, recommended his *Every Man in his Humour* and taken part in it, and also recognized, undoubtedly, the lower-*genre* order of his genius. Nor did successive claimants to poetic and dramatic fame, worthy craftsmen as they were—Chapman, Drayton, Daniel—approach within measurable distance of the inspired author of *Doctor Faustus* and *Hero and Leander*. Yet Chapman had undertaken to continue and conclude the unfinished 'Musaean story', and with his addition *Hero and Leander* was printed in 1598. Shakespeare must have groaned as he turned from the original to the supplement, from passion, colour, melody to hammered-out rhetoric.[1] Then Marlowe's reputation had suffered at the hands of preachers, who moralized over his atheism and wicked death.

'As Jodelle, a French tragical poet', wrote Meres, 'being an Epicure and an Atheist, made a pitiful end, so our tragical poet, Marlowe, for his Epicurism and Atheism, had a tragical death: you may read of this Marlowe more at large in *The Theatre of God's Judgments* in the 25th chapter entreating of Epicures and Atheists. As the poet Lycophron was shot to death by a certain rival of his, so Christopher Marlow was stabbed to death by a bawdy serving-man, a rival of his in his lewd love.'

Thomas Beard's *Theatre of God's Judgments* was published in

[1] Marlowe's poem, left a fragment in 1593, consists of 818 lines in couplets; Chapman's continuation is almost twice as long (1,558 lines), and was written after the Expedition to Cadiz in 1596 (Sestyad iii. 204–6), and apparently after the production of *The Merchant of Venice* (in 1597), to which there seems to be an allusion in Sest. vi. 266 f.:

> To filthy usuring rocks that would have blood
> Though they could get of him no other good.

The address in Sest. iii. 183–98 to the Muse, bidding her visit the Spirit of Marlowe, and convey to him the Continuator's pledge of consecration to his task, does not warrant the conclusion that Marlowe entrusted the task to him. Marlowe's 'late desires' that Chapman should 'surrender to light' (publish) his 'soul's dark offspring' have reference to a work written before Marlowe's death, probably his *Shadow of Night*.

1597. So speedily had the 'Blatant Beast' interpreted Marlowe's unhappy supper-party as Epicurism, his Arianism as Atheism, and his quarrel with Master Fryser about the reckoning as a brawl with 'a bawdy serving-man' about a harlot.[1] Again, as we have seen, Marlowe's translation in verse, a crude schoolboy effort, of Ovid's Elegies, recently published surreptitiously, was publicly burned by command of Whitgift and Bancroft, on 4 June 1599.

Hence the pointed allusion by Touchstone to the occasion of Marlowe's death, and to his 'verse' and 'good wit' as the victims of stupidity:

> When a man's verses cannot be understood, nor a man's good wit seconded with the forward child, Understanding, it strikes a man more dead than a great reckoning in a little room.[2] Truly, I would the gods had made thee poetical.[3]

With affection for the traduced poet, Shakespeare must have put his famous line[4] into the mouth of the shepherdess, with praise of him dead,

> Dead Shepherd, now I find thy saw of might—
> 'Who ever loved that loved not at first sight?'[5]

[1] See p. 340.

[2] A reference both to Marlowe's death in the parlour at Deptford and to a fine line of his in *The Jew of Malta* (I. i. 37): 'Infinite riches in a little room'. See p. 341.

[3] III. iii. 12–16. See letters from O. W. F. Lodge in *Times Literary Supplement*, 14 May, 4 June 1925, 6 Jan. 1927.

[4] *Hero and Leander*, i. 176.

[5] III. v. 82 f. Cf. IV. i. 100–6. I have no belief in a 1593 version (*New Shakespeare* editors) of *As You Like It*. The work is mature, in sentiment and form, in every part of it. The 'verse-fossils' are fiction. It would be strange if the Poet, after ten years of verse, did not drop occasionally into verse-rhythm in his prose. What we should expect we find. The inconsistencies are very few, and due, when not to copyist, printer, or stage exigencies, to the Poet's wonted and enforced haste. The marvel is that there are not many more discrepancies. Shakespeare did not change his mind, but, owing to circumstances, he could not always have it. The reading 'taller' or 'smaller' in I. ii. 284 would depend on the respective heights of the boy actors at his disposal, with corresponding changes or omissions at I. iii. 117 and IV. iii. 88. And may not Orlando address Diana in the early morning sky (III. ii. 2–4)? She is invoked at all times in *Pericles*, and by Helena in the day (*All's W.* II. iii. 80). Shakespeare, too, was more likely to praise Marlowe in 1599–1600 after defamation, than in 1593 after his rival's indisputably disreputable end. The sensation of his death, among players and their public, would still be fresh after six or seven years, and probably revived by the publication of *Hero and Leander*. For Oliver Martext see pp. 224 ff. The 'Marprelate' controversy was still in evidence in 1595, in Job Throgmorton's *Defence* against Sutcliffe and Sutcliffe's *Answer*. Nor was it forgotten in 1600.

1601

§ 98. REVOLT OF THE EARL OF ESSEX

SHAKESPEARE and his fellows played before the Queen at Whitehall on 26 December 1600, 6 January 1601, and, to their immense relief, on 24 February following.[1] Between the second and third of these dates occurred events which caused them deepest anxiety. On 7 February, young bloods in the faction of the Earl of Essex, after dinner at Gunter's over against Temple Gate, crossed the water to witness a performance, at their own request, of Shakespeare's *Richard the Second* at the *Globe*. They had asked for this play because of the scene (omitted in the quartos of 1597 and 1598) of the Deposition of the King. Essex in 1597 was charged, half in jest, by Sir Robert Cecil, with advocating the deposition of Queen Elizabeth and playing the part of 'Bolingbroke'. Raleigh was not a little relieved when Essex, on the suggestion of it, laughed at it as a bad joke. 'He was wonderful merry', wrote Raleigh to Cecil on 6 July,[2] 'at your conceit; I hope it shall never alter, as the true way to all our good, quiet and advancement, and most of all for Her sake whose affairs shall thereby find better progression.' The Queen, too, was sensitive on the subject—whence the omission of the passage (IV. i. 154–318) from the quartos. When the keeper of the records at the Tower, William Lambarde, was showing her Majesty the rolls on 4 August 1601, she startled him by saying, at the mention of King Richard II, 'I am Richard II, know you not that?' 'Such a wicked imagination', he replied, 'was indeed attempted by a most unkind gentleman, the most adorned creature that ever your Majesty made.' Presently she added, 'That tragedy was played forty times in open streets and houses.'[3] Shakespeare's drama condemns deposition. Nobody, with anything of the artist in him, could interpret it as supporting usurpation. For this reason, probably, the Chamberlain's men, though they thought it (in Augustine Phillips's words) 'so old, and so long out of use, that they should have small or no company', consented to perform it when offered 'forty shillings more than

[1] Chambers, iv. 113, 166.

[2] Edwards, *Life of Raleigh*, ii. 169 f.

[3] *Brit. Mus. Addit. MS.* 15664, f. 226.

their ordinary to do so'.[1] But the young gentlemen, full of the Earl's designs and, no doubt, wine, paid their money and witnessed the play; and next morning, which was Sunday 8 February, they joined in the fatuous attempt, while the Lord Mayor and his Brethren were at a sermon in St. Paul's, to seize the City and intimidate the Court. Their ostensible object was to declare King James of Scotland heir to the English throne, change the personnel of the Privy Council, and remodel the Church on Presbyterian lines, with a certain toleration for Catholics—an admirable programme, but not to be effected by a *coup d'état.* Essex and his 150 followers quickly found themselves in prison, from which they were not released with their heads or without ruinous penalties. Essex and Southampton were tried and convicted on 19 February. The former was executed on 25 February, which was Ash Wednesday. Shakespeare and his fellows, out of danger, played before the Queen the previous evening, Shrove Tuesday. We are not told what play they performed, but none would have fitted the moment better than *Julius Caesar.* It might almost have been written for it. Sir Gelly Merrick, Sir Charles Danvers, and Sir Christopher Blount were beheaded in March. In May the Earl of Rutland was fined £30,000, the Earl of Bedford £20,000, Lord Sandys £10,000, Lord Monteagle £8,000, Lord Cromwell £6,000, Robert Catesby of Lapworth, of whom we shall hear again, 4,000 marks, Francis Tresham 3,000 marks, Sir Charles Percy and Sir Joceline Percy £500 each, and Francis Manners £500, Edward Bushell 100 marks, Christopher Wright and John Wright £40 apiece. Of these offenders Merrick, Monteagle, Blount, Charles Percy, and Bushell, with Captain Thomas Lee (who on 12 February tried to coerce the Queen in the presence-chamber and on 17th was beheaded at Tyburn) and others, had witnessed *Richard the Second* at the *Globe.*[2] The fate of the Earl of Southampton was for some time in the balance. He wrote from the Tower immediately on the failure of the rising to his wife, Elizabeth Vernon:

Sweetheart, I doubt not but you shall hear, ere my letter come to you,

[1] Deposition, 18 Feb. See pp. 412–15.

[2] *State Trials*, i. 1445; *Acts of the Privy Council*, xxxi. 147 ff.; Halliwell-Phillipps, *Outlines*, ii. 359–61.

of the misfortune of your friends. Be not too apprehensive of it, for God's Will must be done, and what is allotted to us by destiny cannot be avoided. Believe that in this time there is nothing that can so much comfort me as to think that you are well and take patiently what has happened; and contrariwise I shall live in torment if I find you vexed in my cause. Doubt not but that I shall do well; and bless yourself with the assurance that I shall ever remain your affectionate Husband.

To my Bess.[1]

Sympathy with him was widespread. Cecil wrote on 26 February, 'I grieve for the young Earl of Southampton, who was drawn in merely for love of Essex . . . It will be hard to save him, yet I despair not, he being penitent and the Queen merciful.' And on 21 March, 'I hope the Earl shall be spared.' He was spared, but remained in the Tower until King James set him free.

1601

§ 99. SIR EDWARD GREVILLE

TROUBLE with Sir Edward Greville brought Richard Quyney and other friends of Shakespeare to London at the time of the Essex outbreak. Greville was a high-handed person, whether against wealthy Catholic recusants[2] or unfortunate Puritan neighbours. He claimed the bestowal of the office of collector of the toll-corn, then the toll-corn itself, at Stratford. On the death of that steadfast friend of the Corporation, Sir Thomas Lucy, he seized the town commons. Lucy died on 7 July 1600. Early in 1601 Greville enclosed the Bankcroft. The Corporation had hitherto resisted him passively, if firmly; to the seizure of the Bankcroft they responded with violence. On 21 January the Bailiff and others, including Richard Quyney, John Sadler, Daniel Baker, and Shakespeare's friend, Henry Walker, armed with mattocks and spades, broke into the Croft, levelled the

[1] Stopes, *Southampton*, p. 196. We should not expect such a letter from the 'Friend' of Shakespeare's Sonnets as conceived by our sentimentalists. The writer in 1592–3 was the youth to whom Shakespeare addressed Sonnet lxx ('And thou presentst a pure unstained prime', &c.). He is now twenty-seven, with a passion for national affairs, not feeble sensualities. See p. 420.

[2] 'Felton has a new large commission for finding all recusants' lands and goods; and with him are now Sir Edward Greville, and Sir Henry Bromley. And this course is prosecuted with all violence.' (Fenner to correspondent at Venice, 30 June 1599. *S.P. Dom. Eliz.*)

hedges and mounds, drove in 'horses, oxen, kine, swine and hoggerels', and 'then and there', in the language of Sir Edward, 'did depasture, tread down and consume to the value of forty shillings; and forty willows did lop, and the wood thereof (six loads to the value of six pounds) took and carried away, and other enormities in the other enclosures, to the damage of £40'.[1] Next day they carried off the toll-corn, taking, however, no toll of Sir Edward's corn in the market, his man having dared any one put his hand into the sacks 'on the risk of leaving it behind him'.[2] Arrested for 'riot', these leaders rode to London to the Marshalsea, where they were immediately liberated on bail.

The Hilary term lasted from 23 January to 12 February. Quyney consulted Thomas Greene, Shakespeare's cousin at the Middle Temple, now solicitor to the Stratford Corporation, and perhaps already resident at *New Place*.[3] 'Three days together' they waited on the Attorney-General, Sir Edward Coke, but 'could not have him at leisure by the reason of these troubles'[4]—that is the Essex Rising. Quyney had returned to Stratford by 27 February,[5] with first-hand news of what had happened, and answers more or less reassuring to anxious inquiries about Shakespeare.

In Trinity term (12 June–1 July) Quyney was again in London on behalf of the Corporation. He took with him a statement (which we have in his handwriting)[6] of their case drawn up by the Steward, John Jeffreys, in consultation with Adrian Quyney, John Shakespeare, Thomas Barber, and a fourth oldest inhabitant and officer, Simon Biddle (the old cutler in High Street, who had charge of the armour in the memorable year of the Northern Rebellion, 1569).[7] The Poet's father was over seventy years of age, and had but a few weeks to live. We read with pleasure the document which testifies to his continued interest in the borough and national affairs. Lord Burghley is cited in evidence of the Council's right to elect the toll-gatherer. His letter to them, recommending a servant of his own for the post, was 'extant', and 'of the Lord Treasurer's wisdom and

1 *Misc. Doc.* ix. 20.
2 *Ib.* v. 20.
3 p. 168.
4 *Misc. Doc.* v. 148.
5 He kept the minutes that day of a meeting of the Corporation (*Council Book B.* 79).
6 *Misc. Doc.* v. 20.
7 Dugdale Soc. iii. 36.

knowledge let them judge who knew him'. The Bailiff, Henry Wilson, wrote to Quyney in London on 17 June:

I pray you, remember that, if you perceive that we shall have a trial at the next Assizes, to get the Court moved that Master Under Sheriff have not the return of our jury; neither the High Sheriff, for upon that occasion lately happened myself and some other of our company were with him, but *find no hope of favour at his hands but rather have cause to fear his displeasure.*

The High Sheriff was Sir Thomas Lucy the Second. Here was a change at Charlecote. The old knight would have turned in his grave had he known that his neighbours in Stratford, within a year of his death, found 'no hope of favour' at the hands of his successor, but rather had 'cause to fear his displeasure'.

The cordial relations of half a century were broken. Charlecote was linked with that hated citadel of tyranny, Milcote, and the *luce* of the old coat had suddenly become a *louse*.

Quyney enclosed this disturbing letter in a note of his own to Thomas Greene at the Middle Temple:

By this letter you may perceive Master Bailiff's mind: whereunto I subject [submit].[1] My want of good health letteth[2] my coming to you at this time; I pray you, be at home after supper, and in meantime, I beseech you, think of our motion[3] by this occasion, and by Sir Edward Greville's words, of which you are not ignorant, *Sir, What I urge dare not go against me;* then, *My Lord Anderson*[4] *was his uncle.* Now the last accident, to move Master High Sheriff[5] by the Under Sheriff's means, I leave to Master Sadler's relation.[6] I pray your care, though in regard of your conscionable[7] feeling I need [to make] no such entreaty. I leave it to you and us all in the Lord.[8]

Quyney was at home in July. On the 22nd Greene wrote to him ('to my very loving and good friend'):

After the writing of my last letters, namely on Monday [20th] at night at Master Harborne's,[8] what was done, they showed me a Jury returned by Sir Thomas Lucy: Master Harborne saying that they would go to trial . . . I have herein sent you the copy of the Jury . . .

Had not your Assizes fallen out in our Reading,[9] with great desire I would

[1] So Shakespeare in *As You L. It*, II. iii. 36 f.: 'I rather will subject me to the malice of a bloody brother.'

[2] Hindereth.

[3] Legal action.

[4] Sir Edmund Anderson, Lord Chief Justice of the Common Pleas.

[5] Master Robert Burdett.

[6] John Sadler, Quyney's companion in London.

[7] Conscientious. So Shakespeare in *Oth.* II. i. 241 ff.: 'a knave, no further conscionable than in putting on the mere form of civil and humane seeming'.

[8] *Misc. Doc.* i. 122.

[9] p. 242.

have left all other business apart and been glad to have bestowed my best endeavour for the rectifying of things, but seeing things stand as they do I most heartily crave pardon.[1]

To prevent, if possible, further proceedings, Quyney and Sturley rode to Worcester and interviewed the new bishop, Gervase Babington. The result was a letter from his lordship to Sir Edward suggesting arbitration. Greville replied from Milcote on 27 July expressing his willingness.[2] Thereupon the Bishop visited Stratford, and was entertained at supper at the house of Master Smythe, vintner, who was Head Alderman.[3] The Corporation, and Sir Edward, presumably, were present. The suit in consequence was stayed.

But the supper and drinking by no means concluded the matter. Master Smythe suddenly and violently took the side of the lord of the manor. On 12 August it was unanimously resolved by the Council that for his 'abuses', his 'obstinate and wilful hindering of execution of process out of the Court of Record, his detaining of the Serjeant's mace, and keeping of the keys where the Company could not come by the Book of Orders for the perusing of certain leases', he should be 'dismissed' from his office of High Alderman and 'expelled' from the Council.[4] Ill health partly explains this exhibition of fierce eccentricity in the Smythe blood, of which we have seen something in his father, William Smythe of Henley Street, Shakespeare's godfather, recently deceased.

Quyney's labours were not lightened by these performances, which probably encouraged Greville in the belief that he had a backing in the Council. On Quyney's election to the bailiwick in September, Sir Edward's consent, as nine years previously, was withheld.[5] The battle was renewed, on old and fresh ground. Quyney wrote to Greene with instruction to consult Sir Edward Coke. Greene replied on 23 September:

'Sir, I salute you in the Almighty. I have been yesterday with Master Attorney, who answered that he was not of counsel with Sir Edward [Greville] and would, with all his heart, be of your counsel . . . According

[1] *Misc. Doc.* i. 120.

[2] 'I received your lordship's letter this xxvijth of July, being newly returned out of Dorsetshire.'

[3] *Chamberlains' Account*, 8 Jan. 1602.

[4] *Council Book B.* 82.

[5] *Council Book B.* 83. See p. 311.

to the small leisure he then had, he looked upon your book; and for the first proviso, the Toll, he resolved as your other lawyers have done; for your Justices of Peace', the Bailiff and Head Alderman, 'he saith they may only deal with matters which tend to the breach of the peace; and so referred me over until this morning, to come to him to his chamber again . . . But this morning here, being very foul, he is not (our horn having blown to dinner half an hour since)[1] yet come to his chamber. So after dinner, God willing, I will wait upon him, and by the next convenient messenger certify you fully . . .

'Your assured loving friend *per posse suo* . . .'[2]

On 26 September (we will note in passing) the *Inquisitio post mortem* on Sir Thomas Lucy was held at Warwick. On the jury were John Greene of the *Crown* (kinsman of Thomas Greene and Shakespeare) and Thomas Haward (Harvard) of Tardebigg (kinsman of Shakespeare's old schoolmaster, Simon Hunt).[3]

Quyney was sworn on 2 October, Sir Edward and the want of a mace notwithstanding; on which day 'Master Thomas Rogers and Henry Walker, being sent unto John Smythe vintner for the Serjeant's mace, brought answer from him that they *should not have it,* and that he *would spend twenty times more than the mace was worth before he left it.*'[4]

On the 24th Greene sent to Quyney Coke's opinion:

Here have you resolved under Master Attorney's hand two questions: the one an assurance that the office of Baily may be exercised as it is taken upon you (Sir Edward's consent not being had to the swearing of you) without damage to you or to your Charter; the other being a good mean to enforce men chosen to take the office upon them. These I thought at your request most material and needful to be procured under his hand.

For the Toll and other questions, he agreeth fully with the rest of your counsel; and therefore, methinks, you should rest settled in your minds and purposes for those things.

He hath now had a third fee.

Master Wilkinson[5] and myself think good you be here by Allhallowntide at the furthest.[6]

That was but a week off, and Quyney could not get away. He wanted money for the journey and law expenses. A fund was

[1] By ancient custom a porter blew a horn in the different Courts half an hour before dinner. He still does it—in the evening, however, instead of midday. The dinner was an important function, the students being known as 'diners'.

[2] *Misc. Doc.* i. 119.

[3] p. 530.

[4] *Council Book B.* 84.

[5] The attorney in London to the Stratford Corporation.

[6] *Misc. Doc.* xii. 60.

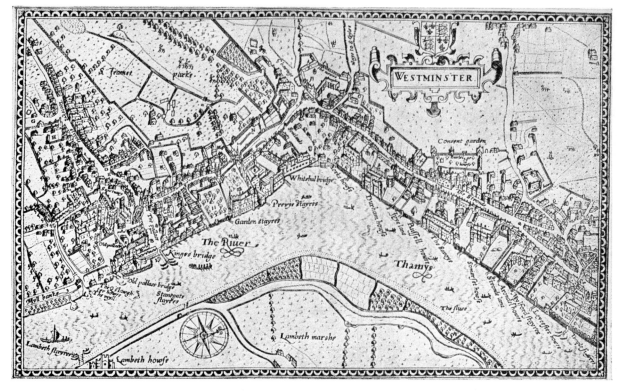

NORDEN'S MAP OF WESTMINSTER, 1593

raised, Thomas Rogers and Shakespeare's friend, Henry Walker, lending £2 apiece, Barber, Aspinall, Francis Smythe, Daniel Baker, Valentine Taunt £1, John Wilmore, William Walford, and John Gibbs 10*s.*, and the Chamberlain, John Smith, ironmonger, out of his own pocket £4 7*s.* 0*d.* On Thursday 5 November Quyney and Henry Wilson the late Bailiff 'set forwards' for Oxford, walking their horses up the Edge Hill to the Rising Sun, and thence descending to Banbury, twenty miles from Stratford, where they dined. Proceeding, they reached the University City and spent the night. That day and night they laid out 6*s.* 8*d.* On Friday they rode to High Wycombe, dinner and horsemeat there costing 2*s.* 1*d.*, and on to Uxbridge where their charges were 5*s.* On Saturday they arrived in London, putting up, no doubt, at Quyney's old haunt, the *Bell* in Carter Lane, kept by Mistress Griffin, where they dined and had a fire in their chamber and afterwards supped. On Sunday they breakfasted on bread and beer, which cost them 2*d.*, received a visit at dinner from Master Jeffreys (the Stratford steward), paid 12*d.* for the carriage to London of a copy of the Town Charter, and supped together in the evening. Monday was a busy day. At breakfast they entertained Master Greene their solicitor, on something more substantial than beer and bread, paying 15*d.* for their repast. His fees for various services they defrayed, amounting to 50*s.* Quyney dined with their proctor, upon whom he bestowed 'extra ordinary 12*d.*' He paid fees to their attorney, Master Wilkinson, 20*s.*, and their counsel, Master Dyot, 10*s.*, and Master Morgan 20*s.* In the evening he supped with friends, bestowing upon them a quart of sack. Tuesday was quieter. On Wednesday morning 'brother Bannister' called and was regaled, otherwise our friend Nicholas Barnhurst of Stratford.[1] Master Greene came again, and was refreshed, 8*d.* On Thursday Quyney took boat to Westminster, and paid 13*d.* for renewing the writ against Master Smythe, vintner, for the recovery of the mace, and 8*d.* for a draft of the Corporation's answer to Greville. He and Wilson supped together at night, and after supper drank ale and *aqua vitae* with friends in their chamber. On Friday 13 November, after dinner, they started on their return journey, paying 9*s.* 9*d.* for horsemeat and to the ostlers, 5*s.* 6*d.* for faggots

[1] pp. 48, 162, 192–3, 306, 308, 794.

in their chamber, and to the chamberlain and servants. The roads were hard with frost, and they bestowed 9*d*. on shoeing and frost-nailing their horses. They spent the night at Aylesbury. Next day they dined and baited at Banbury, and reached Master Jeffrey's house at Walton. On Sunday, after giving 14*d*. 'amongst his people', they rode home to Stratford. The charter followed them, packed in a trunk 'with some things of Master Greene's', trunk and carriage costing 4*s*. 6*d*.[1]

The writ against Master Smythe was unnecessary. He had made his will on 5 November, and been buried, probably as an alderman within the church, on Sunday the 8th.[2] So departed the obstinate townsman and recusant, with a taste for gay clothes, whom we have taken to be John Shakespeare's godson. How entirely he had gone over to the enemy we learn from his direction—

I desire the right worshipful Sir Edward Greville, my brother Francis Smythe,[3] and my loving friend, Peter Roswell, to be overseers.[4]

The mace was recovered (first the shaft, then the head) and the Serjeants were able to execute precepts. The Bailiff attended meetings on 2, 18, and 30 December and kept the minutes. Among tasks for the new year he noted—

What were best to do to Sir Edward Greville; the suits of our Town; how the money last borrowed may be repaid; what leases be expired; a view of our houses be taken; inmates, that the headboroughs take notice of them; the poor, that a time be appointed to the collectors; to draw all our townsmen into companies; a sale be made of trees; order to be taken for our tipplers; wood and coal money, how it is bestowed; perfect all our accounts.[5]

A pleasant break in all this labour is suggested by an invitation on Christmas Eve from Sir Fulke Greville, to the Bailiff and his Brethren, to make merry with him at Beauchamp's Court.[6]

Sir [wrote his secretary, Edward Worthington, to Quyney], myself being hindered by many occasions from coming to you this day, I must entreat you to accept of these few lines as a message from my Master, showing his desire to see you, and some other his good friends with you, sometime this Christmas. I hope it shall not need for me in particular to solicit every man in this kind or otherwise by any other messenger than by your self and your good means, whose aid I do earnestly pray herein; as also to understand by

[1] *Chamberlains' Account*, 8 Jan. 1602; *Misc. Doc.* v. 148.
[2] *Register*, p. 66.
[3] Of the Corner House.
[4] *P.C.C. 54 Bolein.*
[5] *Misc. Doc.* i. 142.
[6] Near Alcester.

this bearer the day you purpose of coming, because I would willingly take such course as no day ought to be passed idly without some good company. You may do well to bring the good company that accompanied you to Warwick, that they may see for whom they travailed, and my Master understand who hath so well deserved his love and to acknowledge the same. And thus with my kind remembrance and love to yourself, I rest your assured loving friend.[1]

Evidently the Stratford men had rendered their old Recorder good service, and the relationship between them (notwithstanding the Chamberlain William Wyatt's grumble of 12 January 1599 that Sir Fulke did 'nothing' for his fee of forty shillings) was very cordial. It was the more welcome to Quyney and his friends in view of the changed attitude of Charlecote.

1601

§ 100. *HAMLET* AND *THE MERRY WIVES OF WINDSOR*

IN these days Shakespeare wrote *Hamlet*, and, apparently, while engaged on this great drama, produced for the pleasure of the failing Queen *The Merry Wives of Windsor*. The folly of Essex and his beheadal left the forces of 'progression' demoralized, and the Court for the rest of the Queen's reign in deepest depression.

The story of the Danish prince, who feigned madness in revenging his father's death on an uncle who had murdered him, seized his throne, and married his queen, was known in England when Shakespeare was a boy.[2] It was dramatized about the time Shakespeare began his career as a player by a second-rate writer, Thomas Kyd, who added to the story the character of Horatio, the visitation of the Ghost, the play-scene, and the introspective, wavering workings of the hero's mind. The play is lost, but we know it was the tragedy of a youthful prince who fumed passionately and impotently in a difficult and bloody situation.[3] Shakespeare knew it, possibly had acted in it,[4] and he made it the

[1] *Misc. Doc.* i. 118.

[2] In a French work, Belleforest's *Histoires Tragiques*, vol. v (1570).

[3] Boas, *Thomas Kyd*, xlv–xlviii.

[4] It was performed on 10 June 1594 at Newington Butts theatre, apparently by the Chamberlain's men, when they and Alleyn's company played for a couple of weeks there. (p. 371.)

basis of his matchless study of decadence of culture, disillusion, and paralysis. His treatment of the 'bookish' leader we have seen in successive portraits of Navarre, Henry the Sixth, Richard the Second, and Brutus. In Hamlet it is fullest and most finished. He is the overgrown student, who would return to Wittenberg and its academic seclusion, to books, foils, and plays, when his presence is called for, and sternly demanded, on the field of public affairs. With almost every conceivable spur to action, he can only reflect and comment, as in a note-book, on the scene and task before him. He sees clearly, is conscious of every feature, every detail, but is unable, as Lady Macbeth would say (that little incarnation of *volition*), to 'screw his courage to the sticking-place'.[1] His thought has been trained at the expense of his will. And it results not merely in 'smoky ineffectuality'[2] but in deeper difficulty. Seven times we see Hamlet in monologue—that is, *thinking*. The fine language and feeling of all this brainwork must not conceal its worse than futility. Instead of furthering his purpose, it defeats it. His feigned madness, and deception of Ophelia (in order to deceive others), and his *chef d'œuvre*, the Play, are his undoing. They betray him. So also the schemes of his enemies recoil invariably on the contrivers' heads—the 'windlasses and essays of bias' (II. i. 65) of Corambus[3] (Polonius), Guildenstern, and Rosencrantz bring all three to their death, while the elaborate piece of treachery by Laertes and the King, with poisoned cup and foil, carries them both off, together with the Queen. Unpremeditated action, on the other hand, does Hamlet yeoman service. His effective doings are on the impulse. He follows the Ghost, he reads the dispatches and leaps to the deck of the pirate, he lays aside the drink and exchanges the foils, without thinking, and 'praised be rashness for it'.[4]

A worse malady, however, than artifice or 'bookishness' remains. Hamlet has noble qualities—fine moral sensitiveness, generosity, hatred of hypocrisy. He almost worships his father, is devoted to his friend, loves Ophelia for her simplicity and sweetness. He has a pure,[5] reverent nature—'this goodly frame

[1] *Macb.* I. vii. 60. [2] Carlyle, *Historical Sketches*, p. 56.

[3] 'Corambis' in Q[1], more correctly 'Corambus' in the German Version, *Der bestrafte Brudermord*; 'Polonius' in Q[2] and Folio. The name 'Corambus' turns up in *All's W.* IV. iii. 185. [4] V. ii. 6–10.

[5] We must distinguish, as in the case of Shakespeare himself, between his

the earth, this majestical roof fretted with golden fire';[1] and 'What a piece of work is man! how noble in reason... in apprehension how like a God!'[2] He speaks of 'sweet Religion',[3] sees 'Providence in the fall of a sparrow',[4] the hand of God 'shaping our ends, rough-hew them as we may'.[5] And because he has a noble nature, disillusion is the more cruel—his father's murder, his mother's 'incestuous' marriage (for so it was regarded) with the murderer (a despicable creature, 'a king of shreds and patches'), the state of Denmark under such a ruler (drunken, and on the verge of revolution), and Ophelia's petty lying. His culture fails him, his manly strength, his popularity, and, chiefly, his *good cheer*.

He confesses to a 'bestial oblivion',[6] a morbid apathy which asks, 'Is there any good in all our labour under the sun?' It is Albrecht Dürer's 'Melancolia', the disease which threatened through all the Renaissance, the gloom not of occupation unworthy the faculty, nor of opportunity too limited for the power (*ars longa vita brevis*), nor of evil greater than the forces of good, but of *good not worth the while*. Hamlet says in a vital moment, 'Thou would'st not think how ill all's here about my heart; *but it is no matter*.'[7] And again, 'Since no man has aught of what he leaves, what is't to leave betimes? *Let be!*'[8] Here is the root cause of his forgetfulness, procrastination, secretiveness, moodiness, brooding on suicide and death, and those wild outbursts more worthy of a lunatic than a sane man.

The malady was as out of place in Arden as the cynicism of Jaques. Shakespeare studied it in the quiet of *New Place*, in consultation, perhaps, with his neighbour and future son-in-law, Doctor John Hall. It is as much a 'case', and the subject of a medical 'observation', as the peculiar mental breakdown of

transparent honesty, in matters of sex as in everything else, and his occasional licence of speech (in III. ii. 119–29, for example). The theory that he had seduced Ophelia is worthy only of our sentimentalists. His love and reverence for her are very real (III. i. 89 f.; v. i. 292–4). His outburst, 'Get thee to a nunnery!', is for the benefit of Polonius, whose hiding he has detected behind the arras ('Ha, ha! are you honest?').

[1] II. ii. 310–13. 'The frame of that heavenly arch erected over our heads' (Hooker, *Eccles. Polity*, i. 155).

[2] *Ib.* 315–19.

[3] III. iv. 47.

[4] v. ii. 231.

[5] 10 f.

[6] IV. iv. 40.

[7] v. ii. 222 f.

[8] *Ib.* 234 f.

Ophelia, wherein also the Poet may have had the advantage of conference with his *medicus peritissimus*.

Stratford Calvinism was as strenuous and optimistic as Hamlet's philosophy was fatalistic. Sturley writes in a dark hour to his friend (1598):

Brother Quyney, judge what I say. If the matter be compassed with difficulties and impossibilities now, which before seemed open, easy, possible and plain, know that the Lord of lords hath met with you.[1] He seeth sufficient matter of your unworthiness both in you and us; but if all this be worse reported and taken than indeed it is, and your possibilities do stand as before, let this be a spur to stir you up more courageously, a *caveat* to add, if it may be, more circumspection and diligence. Ply Sir Edward night and day, weary him, howsoever he may seem to be weary of your importunity[2] yet stick to him, that in the night he may dream of you and waking may bethink him how he may be rid of you:[3] which should be no way but by endeavouring to help and farther you.[4]

Stratford yeomen, mercers, glovers, wooldrivers, weavers had no inclination, even when their houses were burned out and the lord of the manor threatened their commons and liberties, to bewail the weariness and unprofitableness of 'the uses of the world',[5] nor leisure in their idlest moments to speculate 'how the dust of Alexander may stop a bunghole'.[6]

Queen and Court were sick with melancholy. Outwardly, on occasion, she would make a show of vigour and even sprightliness, but to her intimates she was a despondent, broken old woman. Sir John Harington, writing to Sir Hugh Portman from Kelston on 9 October, gives a pitiable picture of her condition in the spring:

For six weeks I left my oxen and sheep and ventured to Court [apparently at Whitehall, before she went to Greenwich in May]. I feared her Majesty more than Tyrone, and wished I had never received my Lord of Essex's honour of knighthood [in Ireland].[7] She is quite disfavoured and unattired, and these troubles waste her much. She disregardeth every costly cover, and taketh little but manchet and succory pottage. Every new message from the City doth disturb her, and she frowns on all the ladies. I had a sharp message from her, brought by my Lord Buckhurst [Lord Burghley's successor as Lord Treasurer, the last of her old Councillors] namely thus:

[1] As the Lord met with Balaam and made him speak other than Balak wished (Numbers xxiii).

[2] Luke xi. 8.

[3] *Ib.* xviii. 4–7.

[4] 14 Nov. 1598: *Misc. Doc.* i. 144.

[5] *Haml.* I. ii. 133 f.

[6] *Ib.* v. i. 224 ff.

[7] In 1599: p. 503.

Go, tell that witty fellow, my godson, to get home; it is no season now to fool it here. I liked this as little as she doth my knighthood, so took to my boots and returned to the plough in bad weather. I must not say much even by this trusty and sure messenger, but the many evil plots and designs have overcome all her Highness's sweet temper. She walks much in her Privy Chamber, and stamps with her feet at ill-news, and thrusts her rusty sword at times into the arras in great rage.[1] My Lord Buckhurst is much with her, and few else since the City business.[2] But the dangers are over, and yet she always keeps a sword by her table. Her Highness hath worn but one change of raiment for many days.[3]

From Greenwich she removed to Windsor, arriving on 8 August. She was here until the 28th,[4] and it was probably during this her last sojourn in the Castle that Shakespeare, for her pleasure and at her request, at very short notice produced *The Merry Wives of Windsor.*[5] She had laughed at Falstaff, and she wanted more of him—Falstaff in love. Obediently Shakespeare brought him out of his grave, and rejuvenated him to be the sport of her Majesty's neighbours of Windsor. In a fortnight, we are told,[6] he wrote this rollicking farce. It is a 'prodigious' achievement, as Gildon remarks, 'when all is so well contrived and carried on without the least confusion'.[7] A few loose threads and errors of time are the only signs of haste.[8] Theme, character,

[1] Cf. *Haml.* III. iv. 22–6.

[2] The Essex Rebellion.

[3] *Nugae Antiquae*, i. 317.

[4] Chambers, iv. 114.

[5] A pirated edition of the *Merry Wives* was published in 1602 (entered at S.H. 18 Jan. 1602), bearing on the title-page the valuable statement, 'As it hath been divers times acted by the Right Honourable my Lord Chamberlain's Servants, both *before Her Majesty* and elsewhere'.

[6] Dennis, Epistle to *The Comical Gallant*, 1702.

[7] *Remarks on the Plays of Shakespeare*, 1710.

[8] *The New Shakespeare*, xiii f., xvi–xviii. There is no evidence here for a previous *Merry Wives*. Nor is there in a supposed substitution of 'Falstaff' for 'Oldcastle'. Conceivably there is an echo of the first name of the hero in the Host's allusion in IV. v. 6 to 'his chamber, his house, his *castle*'; but 'bully-rook' the Host distributes freely, to Page and Ford and Shallow, as well as Falstaff, with other 'bully' compounds, such as 'bully-Hercules' (to Falstaff, I. iii. 6), 'bully-Hector' (to Falstaff, I. iii. 10), 'bully-Doctor' (to Caius, II. iii. 18), 'bully-stale' (to Caius, II. iii. 30), 'bully-Knight' (to Falstaff, IV. v. 17). On the other hand, 'Falstaff' occurs in the text of the play nearly thirty times, five times in verse (I. iii. 92, 106; IV. iv. 42, 75; IV. vi. 16); and in no instance (if we accept the emendation of the line IV. vi. 16 in the light of the Quarto, and read 'Without the show of both: wherein fat Falstaff') could 'Oldcastle' be substituted without destruction of the verse, or injury to the rhythm or alliteration of the prose. For the alliteration, '*f*at Fals*taff*', cf. Fals*taff* *v*arlet *v*ile' I. iii. 106, '*f*igh*t*, John Fals*t*aff' II. i. 19, 'Fa*l*staff *l*oves your wi*f*e' 139, 're*v*enged on Falsta*ff*' II. ii. 326, '*f*ind Falsta*ff*' III. ii. 47, 'posi*t*i*v*e as the

dialogue (which is nearly all in prose) are *con amore* and child's play after *Hamlet* and *Julius Caesar*. Working swiftly, and with masterly ease, the Poet blends homely folk with fantastic personages, the most ridiculous being 'the fat knight', allowed as a 'gentleman' and 'made an ass of', an 'unwholesome humidity' and 'gross watery pumpion' taught 'to know turtles from jays'.[1] He is thrown into the Thames with dirty linen, cudgelled in the garb of the old woman of Brentford, tormented by fairies, ridden with a Welsh goat. Much is from Windsor,[2] more from Stratford. The Poet draws on his school-life, his father's shop, his youthful sports, his neighbours and their hospitalities, his law, his Ovid, his Bible and Metrical Psalms. Flashes of satire give point to the humour. Parson Evans fails to recognize Scripture;[3] Master Slender in future will be 'drunk with those that have the fear of God';[4] Rugby is 'an honest, willing, kind fellow but given to prayer, and something peevish that way: nobody but has his fault';[5] 'Mistress Page', so Quickly reports, is 'one that will not miss morning or evening prayer', and bade her say 'that her husband is seldom from home but she hopes there will come a time';[6] 'as I am a gentleman', says Falstaff to 'Master Brooke', 'you shall, if you will, enjoy Ford's wife';[7] and again, 'what I have suffered to bring this woman to evil for your good'.[8] There's much talk of 'honesty' by dishonest rogues, especially by 'that foolish carrion', Quickly.[9] One of the few passages in verse is in honour of the Queen, the ancient Castle, and the Order of the Garter:

> Search Windsor Castle, elves, within and out:
> Strew Good-luck, ouphes, on every sacred room,

earth is *f*irm tha*t* Fal*staff* is there' 49 f., 'Falsta*ff*'s a kna*ve*' v. v. 114. 'Oldcastle' here, and amid the easy flow of the sentences, would be gravel to the teeth. 'Sir John Falstaff' figures prominently on the title-page of the Quarto 1602, and in the entry in the Stationers' Register, 18 Jan. 1602.

1 III. iii. 42–4.

2 There were Fords and Pages at Datchet, as we know from the church registers.

3 I. i. 150–3. Cf. Luke viii. 8.

4 I. i. 188–90.

5 I. iv. 10–15. Why Prof. Dover Wilson selects Slender for puritanism (*New Shakespeare*, 106) and not Rugby or Mistress Page, I do not see. Slender's kinship with Shallow, who was a Papist, his getting drunk, his books of Sonnets and Riddles, his fencing and bear-baiting and coursing, hardly suggest a strict or a Biblical upbringing.

6 II. ii. 101–6.

7 263–5.

8 III. v. 96–8.

9 I. iv. 10, 75–89, 148, 160, 177.

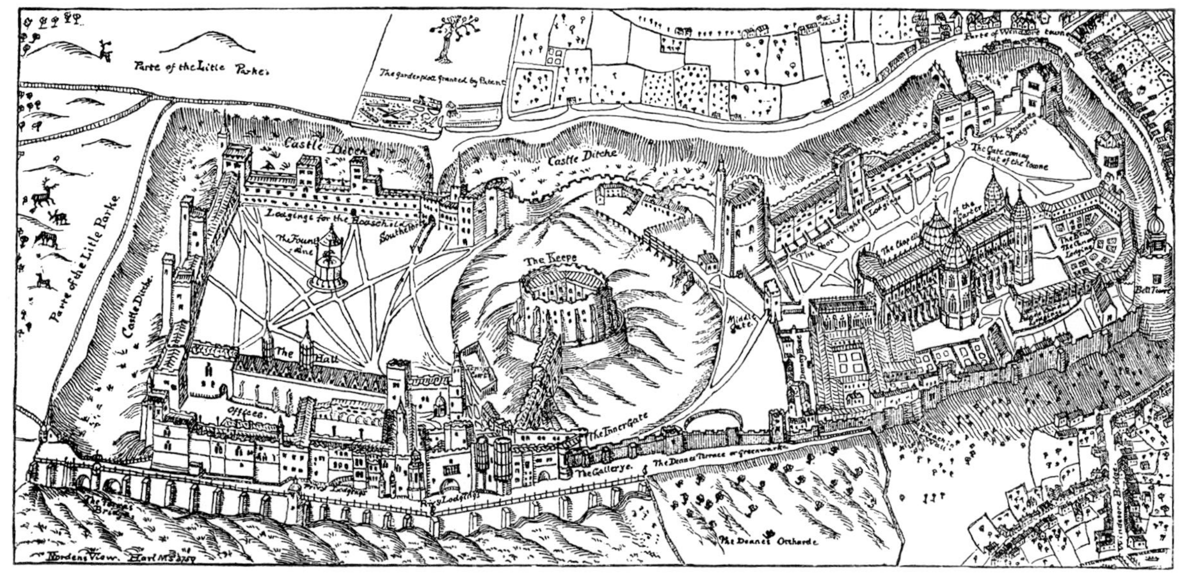

NORDEN'S PLAN OF WINDSOR CASTLE, 1607

Harleian MS. 3759

That it may stand till the perpetual Doom,
In state as wholesome as in State 'tis fit:
Worthy the Owner and the owner It.[1]
The several chairs of Order look you scour
With juice of balm and every precious flower:
Each fair instalment, coat, and several crest
With loyal blazon evermore be blest!
And nightly, meadow-fairies, look you sing,
Like to the Garter's compass, in a ring:
The expressure that it bears, green let it be,
More fertile-fresh than all the field to see;
And *Honi Soit Qui Mal Y Pensé* write
In emerald tufts, flowers purple, blue, and white;
Like sapphire, pearl, and rich embroidery,
Buckled below fair Knighthood's bending knee:
Fairies, use flowers for their charactery.[2]

A welcome and charming feature of the story, a thread of golden silk in the linen and sack-cloth, is the romance of 'sweet Anne Page' and her lover, Master Fenton.

After this interlude Shakespeare, apparently, returned to Stratford and *Hamlet*, to find his father dying or dead. The old gentleman was held in just esteem.[3] He lived to see the election of Richard Quyney to his second bailiwick on 2 September, and six days later he was buried in the parish church:[4]

1601 Septem. 8 M[agiste]r Johannes Shakespeare.

The Ghost in *Hamlet*, so nobly impressive, the part which Shakespeare took himself, without doubt owes something to his bereavement. Touches of tenderness recall those in *Romeo and Juliet* after the death of Hamnet:

GHOST. If thou didst ever thy dear father love—
HAMLET. O God! . . .[5]
GHOST. Adieu, adieu! Hamlet, remember me.
HAMLET. . . . Remember thee!
Ay, thou poor ghost, while memory holds a seat
In this distracted globe . . .[6]
My father, in his habit as he lived![7]

[1] Note the absence of flattery.

[2] v. v. 60–77. Charactery is writing.

[3] See above, p. 450.

[4] Shakespeare had not yet purchased the tithes which gave him the right of burial in the chancel, but his father, as an old Alderman, was entitled to interment within the church.

[5] I. v. 23 f.

[6] *Ib.* 91, 95–7.

[7] III. iv. 135.

After his father's death the Poet, as heir to the Birthplace (subject to his mother's dower), let the East house to one Lewis Hiccocks of Welcombe, who converted it in 1603 into an inn, with the sign of the Maiden Head. The rest of the house he let to his sister, Joan Hart, at the nominal rent of 12*d*. Presumably he took his aged mother to live with him at *New Place*.

A lesser but a real loss in the year 1601 was the death, in April, of the Poet's and his wife's old friend, Thomas Whittington. He had been the Hathaways' shepherd for many years, probably since Anne was a child.[1] He lived in their home at Shottery and, apparently, never married. Anne's father, Richard Hathaway, took care of his savings, which amounted in 1581 to £4 6*s*. 8*d*. He remained with the family after her marriage with Shakespeare in 1582, first with her step-mother, Widow Joan Hathaway, then with her step-brothers, John and William Hathaway, until his death. When he made his will on 25 March 1601 he was worth £50 1*s*. 11*d*.[2] Of this £6, less 'a quarter of a year's board', was in the keeping of his employers. Forty shillings more he had entrusted to Mistress Shakespeare as a bequest to the poor:

> I give unto the poor people of Stratford Forty Shillings that is in the hand of Anne Shakespeare, wife unto Master William Shakespeare, and is due debt unto me, being paid to mine executor by the said William Shakespeare or his assigns, according to the true meaning of this my will.[3]

On Sunday 19 April his body was borne across the fields from Shottery to Stratford churchyard and there laid to rest—as we read in the register:

> Thomas Whitingtoune, shepard.[4]

We think of Corin, Celia's shepherd 'in the purlieus of the Forest'—

> Sir, I am a true labourer: I earn that I eat, get that I wear, owe no man hate, envy no man's happiness, glad of other men's good, content with my harm, and the greatest of my pride is to see my ewes graze and my lambs suck.[5]

[1] Dugdale Soc. v, p. 90.

[2] His Will and the Inventory of his 'Goods and Chattels' are at Birmingham.

[3] There is no foundation for the statement by Lee (*Life*, p. 280) that the Poet's wife, in poverty during 'the poet's absence', borrowed this 40*s*. from Whittington and kept it unpaid until his death, when his executor was directed to 'recover it'. Such 'due debts' from a master to his servant are common in the wills and inventories, and represent savings or investments.

[4] *Register*, p. 65.

[5] *As You L. It*, III. ii. 78–82.

1601

§ 101. *THE PHOENIX AND THE TURTLE*

ANOTHER bereavement of this time, the death together of a young married couple, probably in the circle of the Poet's Court friendship, inspired his lovely elegy, *The Phoenix and the Turtle.* Subscribed by the author, 'William Shake-speare', the poem was included in a collection published under the title, *Loves Martyr: or Rosalins Complaint. Allegorically shadowing the truth of Loue, in the constant Fate of the Phoenix and Turtle. A Poeme enterlaced with much varietie and raritie; now first translated out of the venerable Italian Torquato Caeliano, by Robert Chester. With the true legend of famous King Arthur, the last of the nine Worthies, being the first Essay of a new Brytish Poet: collected out of diuerse Authenticall Records. To these are added some new compositions, of seuerall moderne Writers whose names are subscribed to their seuerall workes, vpon the first subiect: viz. the Phoenix and Turtle. Mar:—Mutare dominum non potest liber notus. London Imprinted for E. B. 1601.* The 'new compositions' have their separate title-page, from which we gather that the subjects of Shakespeare's elegy were of the family or kindred of Sir John Salisbury: '*Hereafter follow diverse Poeticall Essaies on the former Subiect; viz: the Turtle and Phoenix. Done by the best and chiefest of our moderne writers, with their names subscribed to their particular works: neuer before extant. And (now first) consecrated by them all generally, to the love and merite of the true-noble knight, Sir John Salisburie. Dignum laude virum Musa vetat mori. Anchora Spei. MDCI.*' Contributions are from John Marston, George Chapman, and Ben Jonson.

Of the Phoenix, and other wondrous creatures, Elizabethan poets read in such a work as *De Proprietatibus Rerum* by an English Franciscan, Bartholomew, translated among others by Berthelet.

The Phoenix is a bird [they were told], and there is but one of that kind in all the wide world. Therefore lewd men wonder thereof, and among the Arabs, there this bird is bred, he is called singular, alone . . . he maketh a nest of right sweet-smelling sticks, that are full dry, and in summer when the western wind blows, the sticks and the nest are set on fire with burning heat of the sun. Then this bird cometh wilfully into the nest, and is there burnt to ashes . . . Within three days a little worm is gendered of the ashes, and waxeth little and little, and taketh feathers and is shapen to a bird.

Other information was that 'the Culvour is messager of peace, ensample of simpleness, clean and kind, plenteous in children, follower of meekness, friend of company, forgetter of wrongs'. 'The Eagle hath principality among fowls; but when the prey is not sufficient, as a king she giveth it among the others.' 'The Swan singeth sweetly, and is the most merriest bird in divinations.' 'The Crow is a bird of long life.' Shakespeare's Culvour, or Turtle-dove, married the Phoenix, but was not 'plenteous in children'. The Pair died before they were old enough to cohabit. To the funeral the sacred Gallus summoned the mourners—all chaste birds; but he banned the Screech-owl, Ovid's ill-boding *bubo*, and birds of prey save the Eagle. Priest shall be the Swan; and the venerable Crow, which, like Pliny's raven, does not conceive by kind, but by billing at the mouth, shall walk in the procession. Around the Tree of the burning nest, songsters unite in an anthem; and Reason as chorus pronounces the 'threnos'.

The poem has suffered less than usual at the hand of the printer.[1] A change or two gives us, for example, the spelling and dainty music of what one conceives to have been the original in lines 28–32:

Harts remote, yet not asonder;
Distaunce, and noe space was seene
Twixt the Turtle and his Queene,
But in them it were a wonder.

Two or three slight restorations are sufficient in the Threnos:

Beautie, Trueth and Raritie,
Grace in alle Simplicitie,
Heere encloasde in Cynders lie.

Death is nowe the Phoenix nest,
And the Turtles loyall brest
To Eternitie doth rest.

Leavinge noe Posteritie,
Twas not their Infirmitie,
It was married Chastitie.

[1] Shakespeare forms are numerous, such as *herauld, shrike, augour, troupe, obsequie, devine, starre, tragique.*

Trueth maie seeme, but cannot bee;
Beautie bragge, but tis not shee:
Trueth and Beautie buried bee.

To this Urne lette those repaire
That are eyther trewe or faire;
For these dead Birdes sighe a Praire.

1601–2

§ 102. *TWELFTH NIGHT*

WITH a third play Shakespeare was ready for the Christmas festivities of 1601–2. This was *Twelfth Night*, written to cheer the Queen and delight the lawyers of the Middle Temple. It is the last of his merry comedies and in many ways the greatest, an astounding mixture of romance, drollery, and satire. Love's young dream is told in loveliest verse, and interspersed in prose are the speeches of those inspired Philistines, Sir Toby Belch, Sir Andrew Aguecheek, and Malvolio. The young Duke Orsino and the youthful Countess Olivia alike suffer the pangs of unrequited love, but attain, by ways they wot not of, to the blissful state of 'holy' matrimony. They are children of inconsistent fancies. For seven years Olivia will hide herself, as in a cloister, mourning for a brother—

will veiléd walk
And water once a day her chamber round
With eye-offending brine;[1]

but in a day or two she is hopelessly in love with a pretty, well-born youth, her persistent suitor's messenger:

Even so quickly may one catch the plague;
Methinks I feel this youth's perfections
With an invisible and subtle stealth
To creep in at mine eyes.
Fate, show thy force: ourselves we do not owe;
What is decreed must be, *and be this so*.[2]

Orsino is made up of fitful longings, for music, for his garden, for loneliness, for company, for Feste. His 'mind is a very opal', reflecting the passing impression. In the same scene he says,

Our fancies are more giddy and unfirm,
More longing-wavering, sooner lost and worn,
Than women's are;

[1] I. i. 28–30. [2] I. v. 314–17, 329 f.

and

> There is no woman's sides
> Can bide the beating of so strong a passion
> As love doth give my heart; no woman's heart
> So big to hold so much; they lack retention.[1]

In the end Olivia marries not Cesario but Sebastian, and Orsino not Olivia but Viola. The latter is fortunate in such a wife, as the former in such a husband. Storm-tossed and thrown upon stern realities, Viola and her brother will be the pillars of their respective households.

Sir Toby Belch suffers from indigestion. It is a lesser malady than Falstaff's, but sufficiently disagreeable. By birth, like Falstaff, a gentleman, Sir Toby when sober has the carriage of a gentleman. He has also, as Falstaff has not, the courage of a gentleman: he stands up to Sebastian—Falstaff's one exploit is to beat Pistol downstairs. He sponges, like Falstaff, on his friends—on his rich young niece and the foolish Sir Andrew. And, like Falstaff, he drinks too much; but whereas Falstaff is never intoxicated, Belch is drunk nightly. He is not a hypocrite, and, like Falstaff, he has humour. Because she has wit, and the key of the wine-cellar, he marries Maria.

Sir Toby gains by such a foil as Sir Andrew Aguecheek. This is the Prince of Ninnies. Shakespeare had probably made a hit with Master Slender in *The Merry Wives*. Sir Andrew is Master Slender glorified, a perfect piece of nonsense created out of nothing, absolutely the most ludicrous figure on the Shakespeare stage. His inanities take us to the summit of foolery—'I have it in my nose too', 'I was adored once too', 'That's me, I warrant you', 'I knew it was I, for many do call me fool'.[2]

It is hard to believe that any one should see in the mouth of such an absolute ass Shakespeare's opinion on anything: yet we are gravely informed that his abuse of the Puritans is the Poet's own.[3] 'Sometimes', says Maria of Malvolio, 'he is a kind of Puritan.' Sir Andrew exclaims, 'O if I thought that I would beat him like a dog!' 'What!' says Sir Toby, 'for being a Puritan? thy exquisite reason, dear knight?' 'I have no exquisite reason for it', answers the imbecile, 'but I have reason good enough.'[4] This is

[1] II. iv. 34–6 and 96–9.
[2] II. iii. 177, 197, II. v. 87, 89 f.
[3] Lee (*Life*, p. 465).
[4] II. iii. 151–8.

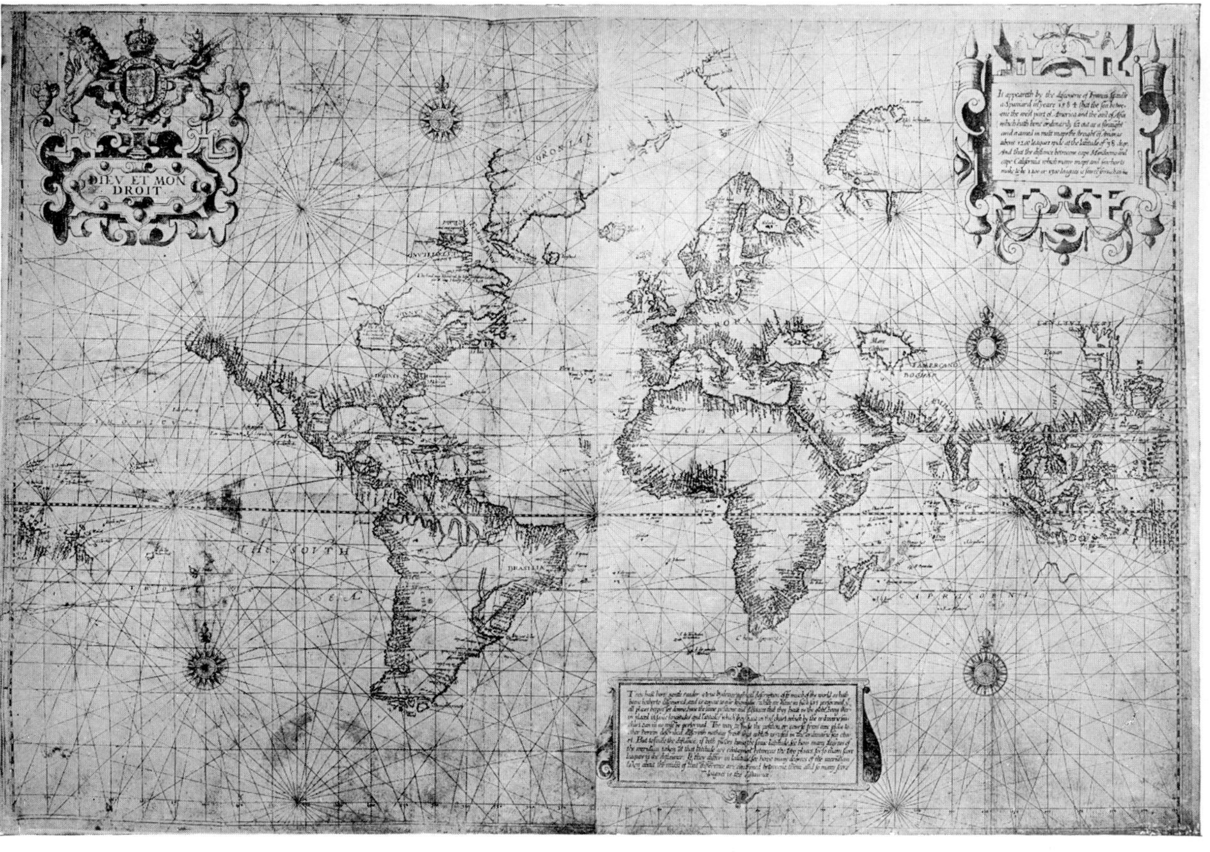

MAP OF THE WORLD, 1600

'He does smile his face into more lines than are in the new map with the augmentation of the Indies' (*Twelfth Night*, III. ii. 84–6) the artist's way of showing his audience that such disparagement of earnest men is the mark of an idiot.[1] He must have felt pretty sick at times of titled persons who abused the tenets of his father.

Shakespeare, indeed, goes out of his way to emphasize the fact that his objection to Malvolio is not on the ground of his religion. 'The devil a Puritan that he is', says Maria, 'or anything constantly but a time-pleaser, an affectioned ass, that cons state without book and utters it by great swarths: the best persuaded of himself, so crammed as he thinks, with excellencies that it is his grounds of faith that all that look on him love him, and on that vice in him will my revenge find notable cause to work.'[2] 'Sick of self-love', so Olivia describes him,[3] and without a grain of humour[4] (the essence of which is that sense of proportion which enables a man to laugh at himself), he steps right into the net which Maria spreads for him, and becomes 'the most notorious geck and gull that e'er invention played on'.[5] He cannot stand praise any better than blame. Olivia, who values his services as steward highly, says, 'Let some of my people have a special care of him: I would not have him miscarry for the half of my dowry.'[6] This commendation, which he overhears, completes his downfall. Substitute 'God' (doubtless the original reading) for 'Jove' of the Folio, and his vanity is blasphemous: 'God and my stars be praised! . . . God, I thank thee! . . . It is God's doing, and God make me thankful! God, not I, is the doer of this, and He is to be thanked.'[7]

The Poet dislikes him, as he dislikes Jaques, and allows him, as he allows Jaques, to take himself off.

Maria is noteworthy. She is a little person with a *will*:[8] the first of three women in Shakespeare famous for these characteristics of body and mind.[9] She achieves her end, which is the hand of Sir Toby, with 'quantity of dirty lands'.[10] He was worth

[1] Sir Andrew and his 'Anglicanism' were hardly a credit to his party. He speaks of 'devil incardinate', confuses Jezebel and Judas, and writes, 'God have mercy upon one of our souls! He may have mercy upon mine but my hope is better' (v. i. 185, II. v. 46, III. iv. 183–5).

[2] II. iii. 159–62.

[3] I. v. 97.

[4] 89–106.

[5] v. i. 351 f.

[6] III. iv. 68, 70.

[7] II. v. 187 f., 194; III. iv. 83, 91 f.

[8] 'Your giant' (I. v. 218), 'wren' (III. ii. 70).

[9] pp. 550, 651, 718.

[10] II. iv. 85.

catching. She will put up with his drunkenness if she may enjoy the proud title of 'Lady Belch'.[1]

Shakespeare's company played before the Queen on 26 and 27 December 1601, 1 January and 14 February 1602.[2] *The Merry Wives of Windsor* was entered at Stationers' Hall on 18 January,[3] probably after performance on one of the earlier dates at Whitehall. *Twelfth Night* was given at the Middle Temple on 2 February, and most likely on 14 February (St. Valentine's) before her Majesty. John Manningham, a student of the Middle Temple, describes the performance there in his diary thus:

> Febr. 1601. 2. At our feast wee had a play called Twelue night or what you will. much like the commedy of errores, or Menechmi in Plautus,[4] but most like and neere to that in Italian called Inganni. A good practise in it to make the steward beleeue his Lady widdowe[5] was in Loue with him by counterfayting a lettre, as from his Lady in generall termes, telling him what shee liked best in him, and prescribing his gesture in smiling his apparraile &c. And then when he came to practise making him beleeue they tooke him to be heady.[6]

The Templars had two annual feasts, at All Saints' and Candlemas. Their 'readers' held them, were the hosts, and bore the cost. These were two experienced members, elected annually, responsible for the education of the 'scholars'. At this time they were Master Henry Hall and Master Augustine Nicholls. Among the 'scholars' was Shakespeare's kinsman, Thomas Greene, whose inability to attend the Warwick assizes on account of the 'reading' at the Middle Temple we have noted.[7] His pleasure and pride in Shakespeare's achievement at Candlemas may be imagined. Legal terms and wit would be appreciated—Sir Toby's 'Judgment and Reason' as 'grand-jurymen since before Noah was a sailor',[8] 'Scout me for him like a bum-baily',[9] 'Very competent injury',[10] 'Except before excepted';[11] Viola's 'Bar-ful strife',[12] and 'Action in durance at Malvolio's suit';[13] Feste's 'Misprision in the highest degree',[14] 'Names' and 'words

[1] Henry Morley, *English Writers*, x. 354.
[2] Chambers, iv. 114, 167.
[3] Arber, ii.
[4] p. 406.
[5] Olivia was in mourning for her brother, not a husband.
[6] *Harl. MS.* 5353, f. 12*b*.
[7] p. 544.
[8] III. ii. 16–18.
[9] III. iv. 193 f.
[10] III. iv. 270.
[11] I. iii. 7.
[12] I. iv. 41.
[13] V. i. 282 f.
[14] I. v. 61.

MIDDLE TEMPLE HALL, LONDON

very rascals since bonds disgraced them',[1] 'Good report after fourteen years' purchase',[2] and his ludicrous 'Impeticos thy gratillity' (mixing-up *impeticote* and *impetico*, otherwise *exactio in jure*: gratuities not unfrequently being exactions illegal);[3] Olivia's 'Schedules' of her 'beauty', 'inventoried, as item . . . item',[4] 'Unjust extent against thy peace',[5] and 'thou shalt be both the plaintiff and the judge in thine own cause';[6] Antonio's 'If I be lapsed in this place I shall pay dear';[7] Fabian's 'Keep you from the blow of the law' and 'o' the windy side of the law';[8] and Sir Andrew's outburst, 'I'll have an action of battery against him, if there be any law in Illyria; though I struck him first, yet it's no matter.'[9] Such professional allusions, however, are not more frequent than usual. There are as many in *The Merry Wives*, and very many more in *Hamlet*.

1602–3

§ 103. 'THROWING ABOUT OF BRAINS'

THE title *Twelfth Night* was suggested by 'la Notte di Beffana' ('the Night of Epiphany') in the play referred to by Manningham, *Gli Ingannati*, and that it has no particular significance is indicated by the sub-title, *What You Will*. There was no performance at Court on Twelfth Night (5 January 1602), but the Children of the Royal Chapel played on Twelfth Day at night (6 January).[10] These clever choir-boys were popular and rivals of the Chamberlain's men, as we learn from *Hamlet*:

ROSENCRANTZ. There is, sir, an eyrie of Children, little eyases, that cry out on the top of the question[11] and are most tyrannically clapped for it: these are now the fashion, and so berattle the common stages—so they call them—that many wearing rapiers are afraid of goose-quills, and dare scarce come thither.

HAMLET. What, are they Children? who maintains 'em? how are they escoted?[12] Will they pursue the quality[13] no longer than they can sing? will they not say afterwards, if they should grow themselves to common players

[1] III. i. 20–5.
[2] IV. i. 24 f.
[3] II. iii. 27.
[4] I. v. 263–8.
[5] IV. i. 57 f.
[6] V. i. 362 f.
[7] III. iii. 36 f.
[8] III. iv. 168 f., 181.
[9] IV. i. 36–9.
[10] Chambers, iv. 114.
[11] Semi-legal term = controversy, debate, dialogue.
[12] *es-scot-ed* (scot, shot, tax) = paid, maintained.
[13] profession.

—as it is most like, if their means are no better,—their writers do them wrong to make them exclaim against their own succession?

ROSENCRANTZ. Faith, there has been much to do on both sides, and the nation holds it no sin to tarre them to controversy: there was for a while no money bid for argument unless the poet and the player went to cuffs in the question.[1]

HAMLET. Is't possible?

GUILDENSTERN. O, there has been much throwing about of brains.

HAMLET. Do the boys carry it away?

ROSENCRANTZ. Ay, that they do, my lord; Hercules and his load too.[2]

'Instructions' to a young gentleman about town at this time are to the effect that

he must acquaint himself with gallants of the Inns of Court, and those that spend most; his lodging must be about the Strand, remote from the handicraft scent[3] of the City; his eating in some famous tavern, as the Horn, the Mitre or the Mermaid; and after dinner he must venture in a pair of oars to the Bankside, where he must sit out the breaking up[4] of a comedy or the first cut of a tragedy; or rather, if his humours so serve him, call in at the Blackfriars, where he should see a nest of boys able to ravish a man.

The phrase 'nest of boys' suggests that the writer (in 1604)[5] had heard Shakespeare's complaint at the *Globe* ('aery of children' did not appear in print until 1623), while 'ravish' is striking testimony to the quality of the boys' performances.

The Choir-boys of Paul's played in their singing-school by the Cathedral, those of the Chapel Royal in the Blackfriars theatre, before private and select audiences 'not choked with the stench of garlic'.[6] They rivalled the 'common' or public players, and they rivalled each other, the former engaging the talent of Marston and Dekker, the latter that of Ben Jonson. They excelled in singing and saucy satire. What formidable competitors they might be to the professional actors we know from the enthusiastic account by a member of the Duke of Stettin-Pomerania's suite of a boy's singing at the Blackfriars on Saturday 18 September 1602, '*cum voce tremula*, to the accompaniment of a bass-viol, so delightful that unless the nuns of Milan excelled him we heard not his equal on our travels';[7] and from Ben Jonson's

[1] Semi-legal term = controversy, debate, dialogue.

[2] II. ii. 354–79.

[3] The City was looked down upon by the courtiers and lawyers as the domain of tradespeople.

[4] carving.

[5] Author of *Father Hubbard's Tales* (quoted in Cunningham's *Handbook of London*, and by Hales, *Notes and Essays*, p. 238).

[6] *Jack Drum's Entertainment*, 1600.

[7] Chambers, ii. 46 f.

tribute to the boy player, Salathiel Pavey, for three years 'the stage's jewel': who

> did act (what now we mourn)
> Old men so duly
> As sooth the Parcae[1] thought him one,
> He played so truly:

and decreed his death aged 'scarce thirteen'.[2]

The *Globe*, with its sign of Hercules bearing the World on his shoulders, and motto from Petronius, *Totus Mundus Agit Histrionem*,[3] suffered from these 'little eyases' with their unbroken voices[4] and amusing personalities. Audiences were attracted by the polemics of their poets, who sometimes lost their tempers. Battles of 'goose-quills' occasionally led to encounters of rapiers. Ben Jonson, who was quarrelsome and jealous for his merits, came to blows with Marston, and would have drawn Shakespeare if he could into the stage controversy.

There is probably an allusion to Shakespeare in *Histriomastix*, an old academic play revised by Marston for Paul's boys in 1599. Two of the hundred and odd characters are Troilus and Cressida, who enter for the following brief dialogue, not unjustly described by the lordly onlooker as 'lame stuff indeed', and lamer for us in a corrupt text:

> TROILUS. Come Cressida, my cresset light,
> Thy face doth shine both day and night.
> Behold, behold thy garter blue
> . . . .[5]
> Thy Knight his valiant elbow weare,[6]
> That when he *shakes* his furious *speare*
> The foe in shivering fearful sort
> May lay him down in death to snort.
> CRESSIDA. O Knight, with valour in thy face,
> Here take my screen,[7] wear it for grace,
> Within thy helmet put the same
> Therewith to make thine enemies lame.[8]

[1] The Fates. [2] *Epigrams*, cxx.

[3] *Totus Mundus Exerceat Histrioniam* (Fragments 10).

[4] 'I shall see some squeaking Cleopatra boy my greatness' (*Ant. & Cleop.* v. ii. 219 f.).

[5] A line has dropped out, the last word rhyming with 'blue'.

[6] misprinted 'wears'.

[7] veil, mantling for the helmet.

[8] II. 269–79.

Why Shakespeare should be burlesqued in the person of Troilus does not appear; but the allusion may be to his grant of coat-armour, which was an object of Jonson's satire in *Every Man out of his Humour* (III. i) in 1599–1600 at the *Globe*:

CARLO BUFFONE. But ha' you arms? ha' you arms?

SOGLIARDO. I' faith, I thank God, I can write myself 'Gentleman' now; here's my patent, it cost me thirty pound, by this breath.

PUNTARVOLO. A very fair coat, well charged and full of armory.

SOGLIARDO. 'Gyrony of eight pieces, azure and gules; between three plates, a chevron; engrailed checquy; or, vert, and ermins, on a chief argent, between two ann'lets sable, a boar's head, proper.'

PUNTARVOLO. Let the word be, *Not Without Mustard.*

The patent is nonsense, but there is no mistaking the pungent reference in the 'word', or motto, to *Non Sanz Droict.*[1]

Jonson laughed at *Histriomastix* in this play, and returned to the attack in *Cynthia's Revels* (1600) at the Blackfriars, including Dekker in his ridicule. Marston replied at Paul's in *What You Will* (1600), Dekker at the *Globe* in *Satiromastix* (1601). The last brought Jonson into collision with his late comrades on the Bankside. In his *Poetaster* (1601) at the Blackfriars he attacked Marston and Dekker and the Chamberlain's men.[2] He introduces a Chamberlain's man, 'Histrio' (Augustine Phillips, manager of the company), as the means of satirical talk about his fellowship of 'common players' on 'the other side of Tiber' (Thames), who present not 'Humours', 'Revells', and 'Satires', like the plays at Blackfriars,[3] but 'ribald' pieces which 'the sinners in the suburbs applaud daily'—'sinners' being a hit at the *Globe* in its proximity to the Stews on Bankside.[4] 'Histrio', it is complained, 'stalks by', not at all like 'a player'. Augustine Phillips could, and doubtless did, hold up his head as a 'gentleman'.[5] 'Captain Tucca', a 'man of war', will take him down: 'You are proud, you rascal? . . . you grow rich, do you? and purchase, you two-penny tearmouth . . . Come, we must have you turn fiddler again, slave, get a base viol at your back, and march in a tawny coat, with one sleeve, to Goose Fair'—an allusion, in Jonsonian fashion, to the actor's skill as a musician,

[1] pp. 449, 519–20.
[2] III. i.
[3] i.e. 'Every Man in his *Humour*', 'Every Man out of his *Humour*', 'Cynthia's *Revels*' and 'Poetaster, a comical *Satire*'.
[4] pp. 501–4.
[5] p. 295.

and his beloved instrument, bequeathed in his will to his old apprentice, Samuel Gilburne.[1] Of the 'twenty-five' said to comprise the fellowship (Tucca suggests 'six and thirty': evidently Shakespeare's company had the reputation for size as well as quality),[2] five are rudely caricatured, as 'the lean Poluphagus' (Great-eater), with a 'belly like Barathrum' (*barathrum macelli* of Horace,[3] the bottomless pit of the market), probably that 'famished correctioner, Goodman Bones', Sinkler;[4] 'the villanous out-of-time fiddler, Aenobarbus' (Redbeard), presumably Cowley,[5] 'musician' and player of five small parts in *Four Plays in One* in 1592, performer of 'Verges', and probably of 'Slender' (with 'a little whey face' and 'little yellow beard, a Cain-coloured beard') and 'Aguecheek' ('a thin-faced knave', with hair 'like flax on a distaff'); 'Aesop, your politician', whose 'mouth' is to be 'ram'd up with cloves', no doubt Heminge, 'stuttering Heminges',[6] grocer as well as player, and 'politician' for the company in dealings with the Court;[7] 'Frisker, my zany, a good skipping swaggerer'—little, lively, Robin Armin; and 'your fat fool, my Mango', with 'his over-familiar playing face', 'saucy, glavering grace, and goggle eye', who 'roars out barren jests, with a tormenting laughter between drunk and dry', and a habit of borrowing a sword or military scarf—an interesting sketch, however extravagant and offensive ('mango' is 'pander'), of the able performer of 'Falstaff', 'Jaques', and 'Belch', namely Thomas Pope. There is bare allusion to Burbage as 'Seven Shares-and-a-Half', as if he were proprietor of the *Globe*, though as chief owner he possessed but three and a half. Shakespeare comes in for marked attention:

TUCCA. Dost thou not know that Pantolabus there?
HISTRIO. No, I assure you, Captain.
TUCCA. Go, and be acquainted with him then; he is a gentleman, parcel-poet, you slave; his father was a man of worship, I tell thee. Go, he pens high, lofty, in a new stalking strain, bigger than half the rhymers in the

[1] pp. 210–11.

[2] As a matter of fact the number was 'scarcely more than fifteen', to the surprise of Thomas Platter on 21 Sept. 1599: see p. 511.

[3] *Epistles*, i. 15, 31.

[4] p. 490.

[5] Baldwin, 233 n., 399.

[6] pp. 206, 294, 633, 879.

[7] He was payee of his company for performances at Court, with Bryan in 1596, with Pope in 1597, 1598, and 1599, with Richard Cowley in 1601, and by himself in 1600, 1602, and subsequent years.

Town again; he was born to fill thy mouth, Minotauros, he was; he will teach theee to tear and rand. Rascal, to him, cherish his Muse, go; thou hast forty-forty shillings, I mean, stinkard; give him in earnest, do, he shall write for thee, slave! If he pen for thee once, thou shalt not need to travel with thy pumps full of gravel any more, after a blind jade and a hamper, and stalk upon boards and barrel-heads to an old crack'd trumpet.[1]

From this fantastic and envious compliment we learn that *Johannes Factotum*[2] has advanced into favour in high places and is acquiring wealth (a *Pantolabus Scurra*[3] or all-grasping, fine-gentleman buffoon in the suite of the mighty), stands head and shoulders above contemporary poets, and as a dramatist (his acting is not alluded to) is of such value to his company that they need not travel to get a living.

How the Chamberlain's men had been hit by the popularity of the boy players we learn from Histrio's confession, 'This winter has made us all poorer than so many starved snakes: nobody comes at us, not a gentleman.'

Shakespeare, moreover, had a rival in Kemp. The latter had returned from his 'dance' on the Continent, the worse for 'many mistakes' and 'misfortunes', in the summer of 1601 and joined the Worcester's men. On 2 September he was in London, when his free speech on Sir Anthony Shirley, whom he had met in Rome, was noted in his diary by one Richard Smith of Abingdon.[4] He and his fellows performed at Court on Sunday 3 January 1602,[5] two days after Shakespeare's company. There must have been comment on the parting of these old colleagues. Shakespeare states his case in *Hamlet*:

Let not your clowns speak more than is set down. There be of them, I can tell you, that will laugh themselves to set on some quantity of barren spectators to laugh with them, albeit there is some necessary point in the play then to be observed. O 'tis vile, and shows a pitiful ambition in the fool that useth it. And then, you have some again that keep one suit of jests as a man is known by one suit of apparel, and gentlemen quote his jests down in their tables before they come to the play, as thus—*Cannot you stay till I eat my porridge?* and *You owe me a quarter's wages*; and *My coat wants a cullisen*,[6] and

[1] For players on tour see pp. 321, 458. [2] p. 310.

[3] Horace, *Sat.* I. viii. 11, II. i. 22.

[4] '1601 Sep. 2. Kemp, mimus quidam, qui peregrinationem quandam in Germaniam et Italiam instituerat, post multos errores, et infortunia sua reversus: multa refert de Anthonio Sherley, equite aurato, quem Romae (Legatum Persicum agentem) convenerat' (*Sloane MS.* 414, f. 56).

[5] Chambers, iv. 114. [6] scutcheon.

Your beer is sour; and blabbering with his lips and thus keeping in his cinque pace of jests, when, God knows, the warm[1] clown cannot make a jest unless by chance, as the blind man catcheth the hare, Masters, tell him of it.[2]

That Kemp perpetrated such inanities, for 'lungs tickle o' the sere', is confirmed by the occurrence of that about 'coat' and 'cullisen' in Ben Jonson's *Every Man out of his Humour*, where Sogliardo, a bumpkin clown, is guilty of the speech, which Carlo Buffone plays with, 'My humour is not for boys; I'll keep men, and I'll give coats, but I lack a cullisen' (I. i). Kemp probably took the part of Sogliardo, 'a kinsman to Justice Silence' and therefore to (his late part) 'Justice Shallow'.

Kemp's extemporalities and liberties were proverbial. The testimony of Nashe in 1592 has already been quoted.[3] Later, in Day, Rowley, and Wilkins's play of the *Brothers Shirley*, Kemp is made to say, 'I am somewhat hard of study, but if they will invent any extemporal merriment, I'll put out the small sack of my wit I have left in venture with them.' This was in 1607. A generation later, in Brome's *Antipodes* (*c.* 1640), Letoy corrects Byplay for interpolations and omissions, and for addressing the audience. 'That is a way has been allowed', pleads Byplay, 'on elder stages to more mirth and laughter.' 'Yes', replies Letoy, 'in the days of Tarleton and Kemp, before the stage was purged of barbarism.' Shakespeare was right in thinking such intrusion barbaric and prohibiting it at the *Globe*.

We know, then, why Armin now played 'Dogberry',[4] and clowns of a caustic wit, 'Touchstone' and 'Feste', figure in recent plays instead of the old Kemp droll.[5] Kemp was in poor circumstances and near the close of his career. Henslowe advanced him 5*s.* on 22 August 1602 to make him 'a pair of giant's hose'—a comic garb for the little man; then 30*s.* on 3 September to buy him 'a suit'; and again 8*s.* 8*d.* on 4 September for the 'making' of this suit and another for his 'boy'.[6] He was introduced this

[1] at his ease, at his best.

[2] III. ii. 26–43 Quarto[1]. The passage was revised and greatly reduced in subsequent editions.

[3] p. 422.

[4] 'Pardon, I pray you, the boldness of a beggar who hath been *writ down an ass* in his time, and pleads under forma pauperis in it still, notwithstanding his *Constableship* and *Office*' (Armin to Lord Haddington in *The Italian Tailor and his Boy*, 1609).

[5] Baldwin, 244 f., 394 f.

[6] Henslowe, *Diary*, i. 179 f.

autumn into the Cambridge play, *The Return from Parnassus*, with Burbage. A speech put into his mouth is interesting evidence that the battles of the Children and their Poets were taken up keenly beyond London:

> Few of the University-men play well; they smell too much of that writer Ovid, and talk too much of Proserpina and Jupiter. Why, here's our fellow Shakespeare puts them all down, aye, and Ben Jonson too. O that Ben Jonson is a pestilent fellow; he brought up Horace giving the poets a pill; but our fellow Shakespeare hath given him a purge that made him bewray his credit.

In *Poetaster* Jonson brought on the stage Augustus Caesar and the Augustan poets, and himself in the guise of Horace. Shakespeare's 'purge' was probably his *Troilus and Cressida*.[1]

On 10 March 1603 Kemp borrowed 20*s*. of Henslowe for his 'necessary uses'.[2] Eight months later he was buried at St. Saviour's, Southwark. It was plague-time, and the register records barely,

> '1603 November 2nd William Kemp, a man.'

An 'epitaph' was composed by Richard Braithwaite:

> Welcome from Norwich, Kemp! all joy to see
> Thy safe return morriscoed lustily!
> But out, alas! how soon is thy morris done!
> When pipe and tabor, all thy friends, be gone,
> And leave thee now, to dance the second part
> With feeble Nature, not with nimble Art:
> When all thy triumphs, fraught with strains of mirth,
> Shall be caged up within a chest of earth—
> Shall be? they are: thou hast danced thee out of breath,
> And now must make thy parting dance with Death.[3]

§104. SHAKESPEARE, PLAYER AND MANAGER

THAT Shakespeare was an actor as well as a dramatist, and the producer of his plays as well as a performer, becomes increasingly obvious as his work proceeds. From the beginning he employs the language and devices of his craft, and shows both sensitiveness to the presence and behaviour of the actor and

[1] pp. 579–84.
[2] Henslowe, *Diary*, i. 163.
[3] *Remains after Death* (Collier, *Memoirs*, 119).

consciousness of his audience. His use of such terms as *theatre*, *stage*, *act*, *scene*, *part*, *cue*, *enter*, and *exit*, in their technical and figurative sense, is common. He introduces 'the play within the play' in at least four dramas, and the mask with its machinery in as many more. In *Hamlet* the inset play is preceded by a dumb show. In all this there is a stage sense and dexterity. More apparent is the 'producer' in the structure of a masterpiece like *Romeo and Juliet*. From the servants of the rival houses the quarrel spreads to their chiefs, and prepares us for the hero and the heroine, their meeting, their love at first sight, protestation, and marriage—in less than a dozen scenes, with help twice of Chorus. As swiftly and inevitably follows the rest—Mercutio's killing, then Tybalt's, and Romeo's flight after his one night with Juliet, the Friar's friendly aid and its frustration, Juliet's trance and burial, Romeo's suicide in her tomb, her awaking and suicide, the terrified grief of the hostile families and their reconciliation—in thirteen scenes more, without a hitch, without a pause. The whole is an amazing piece of stagecraft—

> the two hours' traffic of our stage.[1]

Shakespeare does not forget his characters—though occasionally he may dispose of one unceremoniously when he gets in his way (like the harmless Antigonus in *The Winter's Tale*, who is conveniently devoured by a bear).[2] He sees them and hears them, is critically observant of their look and gesture and speech. This we know from Hamlet's searching advice, or rather instruction, to the players. It is a voice from the stage to those on it, a voice of authority at the *Globe*:

> Speak the speech *as I pronounced it to you*, trippingly on the tongue ... Use all gently ... acquire a temperance that may give it smoothness ... Be not too tame neither, suit the action to the word, the word to the action, o'erstep not the modesty of Nature. The purpose of playing, both at the first and now, was and is, to hold as 'twere the mirror up to Nature: to show Virtue her own feature, Scorn her own image, and the very age and body of the Time his form and pressure. This overdone or come tardy off, though it make the unskilful laugh, cannot but make the judicious grieve, the censure of the which one must in your allowance o'erweigh a whole theatre of others.[3]

[1] Act I, Chorus.
[2] III. iii. 58, 102–4, 108 f.
[3] *Haml.* III. ii. 1–32.

Shakespeare gesture appears frequently. 'Can'st thou quake,' asks Richard,

and change thy colour,
Murder thy breath in middle of a word,
And then again begin and stop again,
As if thou wert distraught and mad with terror?

Buckingham replies,

I can counterfeit the deep tragedian,
Speak and look back and pry on every side,
Tremble and start at wagging of a straw,
Intending deep suspicion.[1]

Hubert says,

Young Arthur's death is common in their mouths:
And when they talk of him they shake their heads,
And whisper one another in the ear;
And he that speaks doth gripe the hearer's wrist,
Whilst he that hears makes fearful action,
With wrinkled brows, with nods, with rolling eyes.[2]

The *Globe* men did not stand like ciphers. Nor did they 'tear a passion to tatters'. Portia says to Brutus,

You suddenly arose, and walked about
Musing and sighing with your arms across;
And when I asked you what the matter was,
You stared upon me with ungentle looks:
I urged you further; then you scratch'd your head,
And, too, impatiently stamp'd with your foot:
Yet I insisted, yet you answered not,
But with an angry wafture of your hand,
Gave sign for me to leave you.[3]

Macduff pulls his hat over his brows.[4] Coriolanus holds Volumnia 'by the hand silent'.[5]

Equally aware is the Poet of his audience—its varied elements, censure ('serpent's tongue'),[6] and approbation. He knows the 'groundlings' capable *for the most part* of nothing but 'dumb-shows and noise',[7] the city apprentices that 'thunder' at the play-house and 'fight for bitten apples',[8] the Christopher Slys who

[1] *Rich. III*, III. v. 1–8.
[2] *K. John*, IV. ii. 187–92.
[3] *Jul. Caes.* II. i. 239–47.
[4] *Macb.* IV. iii. 208.
[5] *Cor.* V. iii. 183.
[6] *Mid. N. D.* V. i. 440.
[7] *Haml.* III. ii. 12–14.
[8] *Hen. VIII*, V. iv. 63 f.

enjoy 'a Christmas gambold or a tumbling trick',[1] and 'simpering' young men more interested in the ladies in the galleries than in the play.[2] At one time he felt bitterly the 'laugh' of the 'unskilful' and the 'grief' of the 'judicious' at the drama in which he participated.[3] But it was not for long. To the end Jonson grumbled and growled at the public. Shakespeare very manifestly gained their attention and regard, and at the *Globe*, as at the Court, their enthusiastic admiration. Only a dramatist confident of his audience, in close touch with them, could appeal to them as he does in *Henry V*:

Pardon, gentles all,
The flat unraised spirits that have dar'd
On this unworthy scaffold to bring forth
So great an object . . .
On your imaginary forces work . . .
Piece out our imperfections with your thoughts . . .
Work, work your thoughts. . . . Be kind,
And eke out our performance with your mind.[4]

The people are his, as he is theirs, for such address to be possible. Hence, as we are told,

Let but Falstaff come,
Hal, Poins, the rest, you scarce shall have a room,
All is so pestered; let but Beatrice
And Benedick be seen, lo, in a trice
The cockpit, galleries, boxes, all are full.[5]

Whatever the limitations of the Elizabethan and Jacobean playgoer (and it is chiefly from the unsuccessful playwright that we hear of them), he had sufficient of the artist in him, whether in the pit or box, for the Supreme Artist to work his magic there—

O, how the audients
Were ravished, with what wonder they went hence![6]

[1] *Tam. Shrew*, Ind. ii. 140.

[2] *As You L. It*, Epilogue.

[3] Sonnet CX.

[4] Act I, Chorus 8–11, 18, 23, Act III, Chorus 25, 35.

[5] Digges (prefixed to Shakespeare's *Poems*, 1640).

[6] *Ib.* Orazio Busino, a Venetian in London, unable to understand a word of English, when taken to a tragedy in one of the theatres in December 1617, was impressed by the magnificent dress of the actors and their gestures, and by the presence of nobles and their ladies, listening *con tanto silenzio e modestia* (J. S. Smart, *Shakespeare Truth and Tradition*, p. 155 f.).

1602–4

§ 105. SHAKESPEARE AND THE MONTJOYS

FOR quiet, we may believe, Shakespeare in 1602 'or thereabouts'[1] removed his lodging from the Bankside to the house of his Huguenot wigmaker, Christopher Montjoy, at the corner of Silver Street and Monkwell Street in Cripplegate. Hither, beneath the wall of the north-west corner of the City, near Barber-Surgeons' Hall (where he might see the portrait of Doctor Butts of *Henry VIII*)[2] and its garden in Monkwell Street, surrounded by Gothic churches—St. Olave's, St. Mary's Steyning, St. Alban's, St. Mary's Aldermanbury, St. Alphege's[3]—he could escape from the calls and casual fellowship of the *Globe*.[4] In a few minutes he could walk to the river—down Wood Street, past the sign of the Splayed Eagle (where Richard Field now lived with his second wife, Jane), past the Counter (as hateful to Falstaff as 'the reek of a lime-kiln'),[5] across Cheapside, down Bread Street, past the house of the scrivener, John Milton, and the *Mermaid* tavern—and take boat to the Bankside. Dressed for his part, and bewigged under the hand of Monsieur or his apprentice, Stephen Bellott, he needed but a cloak for the journey from his lodging to the stage.

Montjoy had a second apprentice, his younger brother, Noel Montjoy. He had a wife also, and a daughter, his only child, Mary. There was a servant, Joan, who evidently waited on Shakespeare. She says that 'Master Shakespeare lay in the house',

[1] The Poet said on 11 May 1612 he had known Montjoy and his apprentice Bellott 'for the space of ten years or thereabouts'.

[2] v. ii.

[3] See the maps of Aggas (*c.* 1560) and Leak (1666, after the Fire).

[4] Silver Street had a reputation for wealth and comfort. Stow says (*A Survey of London*, 1603), 'In Wood Street is Silver Street (I think of silver-smiths dwelling there), in which be divers fair houses; and on the north side thereof is Monkswell Street so called of a well at the north end thereof.' Ben Jonson has (*The Staple of News*, iii), '*Censure.* A notable tough rascal this old Penny boy! right city-bred. *Mirth.* In Silver Street, the region of money, a good seat for an usurer.' It was known for its wig-makers. In Jonson's *The Silent Woman* (iv. 1) *Otter* says of his wife, 'All her teeth were made in the Blackfriars, both her eye-brows in the Strand, and her hair in Silver Street.'

[5] 'I fear', says Mistress Ford, 'you love Mistress Page.' Falstaff replies, 'Thou mightst as well say I love to walk by the Counter-gate, which is as hateful to me as the reek of a lime-kiln.' This is one of the bits of London which Falstaff brings with him to Windsor (*Merry W.* III. iii. 82 f.).

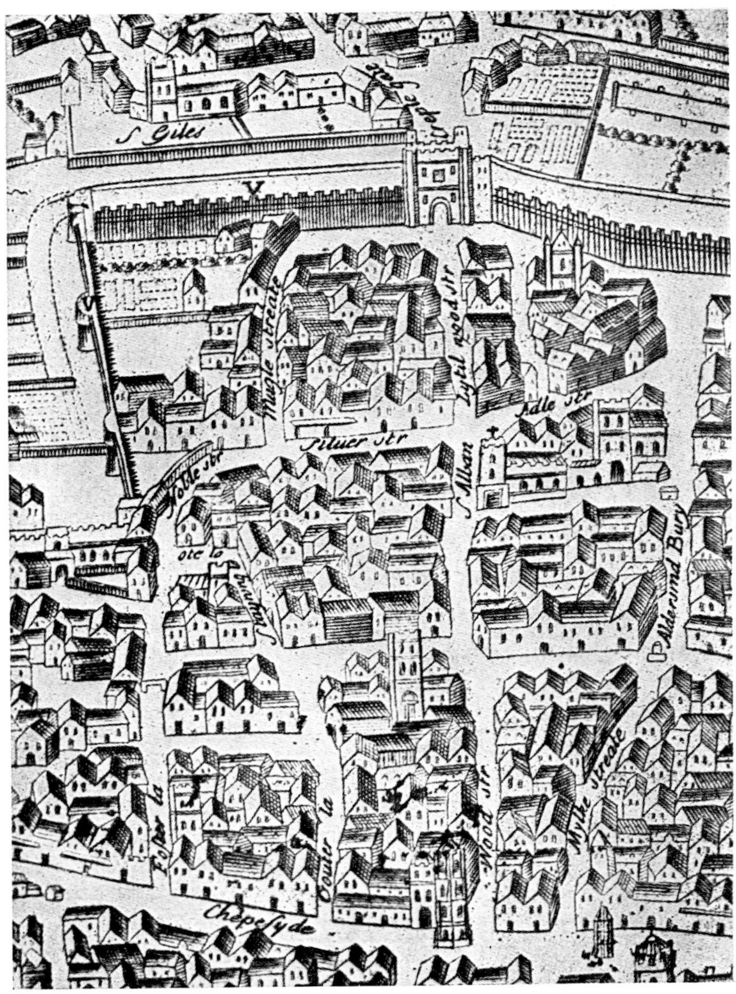

WHERE SHAKESPEARE LODGED WITH THE MONTJOYS

From Aggas's map, c. 1560

The house, at the corner of Silver Street and Monkswell ('Mugle') Street, though conventionally drawn (with gable, a pair of windows, and a door), marks the spot, and the pentice may be a genuine feature

that her master moved him to use his influence with Stephen Bellott to bring him to a marriage with Mary, and that Stephen was regarded as 'a very good servant' by Monsieur, who bore him 'great goodwill and affection'. Stephen was in love with his master's daughter, as she with him, but he needed encouragement to aspire to her hand. At Madame's entreaty, Shakespeare says, he 'did move and persuade him thereunto'. All went well, and 'they were made sure by Master Shakespeare', that is betrothed, 'by giving their consent, and agreed to marry,[1] giving each other's hand to the hand of the other',[2] being thus 'handfast'. The marriage ceremony followed on 19 November 1604, in St. Olave's Church in Silver Street.[3]

1602

§ 106. DEATH OF RICHARD QUYNEY

IN 1602, in consequence of the 'fashion' for the 'eyrie of Children' and their 'writers', Shakespeare and his fellows 'travelled'. It was their first tour, so far as we know, since 1597. Not that they journeyed, in Ben Jonson's scornful language, with their 'pumps full of gravel, after a blind jade and a hamper', and 'stalked upon boards and barrel-heads to an old cracked trumpet'.[4] They took *Hamlet* to the Universities,[5] where it was certain of an enthusiastic reception. What other towns they visited besides Oxford and Cambridge we have no information. In the absence of notices in the Corporation records we are justified in the belief that their tour was confined to colleges and private mansions. Shakespeare was not in Stratford on 1 May when his brother, Gilbert, acted on his behalf in the purchase from William Combe of Warwick (and the Middle Temple) and John Combe of Old Stratford, of 'four yard-land within the parish, fields or town of Old Stratford, containing by estimation one hundred and seven acres, with the common of pasture for

[1] These words are scored through as irrelevant.

[2] See the depositions in Bellott *v.* Montjoy of 11 May, 19 and 23 June 1612. Court of Requests, published by their discoverer, Dr. Charles William Wallace, in *Harper*, March 1910, and *University Studies*, Nebraska.

[3] p. 629.

[4] *The Poetaster*, iii. 1.

[5] See the title of the pirated quarto of *Hamlet*, p. 592.

sheep, horse, kine, or other cattle in the fields of Old Stratford to the said four yard-land belonging', in the several tenures of Thomas Hiccocks and Lewis Hiccocks, for the sum of three hundred and twenty pounds.[1]

In the indenture of his purchase the Poet is 'William Shakespeare of Stratford-upon-Avon, gentleman'. That is the title he aspired to from the beginning, and enjoyed to the end. He was never 'of London'. When he bought a house in the Blackfriars in 1613 he was still 'William Shakespeare of Stratford-upon-Avon in the County of Warwick, gentleman'.[2]

On 10 May 1602 the Heralds, William Dethick and William Camden, replied to exceptions which had been taken to the grant of coat-armour to twenty-three 'gentlemen', including Master John Shakespeare and the Poet's fellow player, Richard Cowley. They pointed out that John Shakespeare's patent did not usurp the coat, as alleged, of Lord Manley, because the *spear* on the bend made 'a patible difference'. Cowley's arms were also confirmed.[3]

This month died Shakespeare's friend at Stratford, Richard Quyney, the Bailiff. We have noted Quyney's memoranda of work for 1602.[4] On 8 January the borough council voted to him the toll-corn claimed by Sir Edward Greville 'towards his great charges that he is and shall be at'.[5] He presided as usual at the 'hall' on 3 February.[6] In March his godson (as we have assumed), Richard Badger, son of his sorely-tried Catholic kinsman, Master George Badger of Sheep Street and Henley Street, entered the service of a London stationer (one of Richard Field's craft and fellowship), Peter Short, to whom the youth bound himself apprentice on 12 April.[7] Peter Short interests us as the printer in 1594 of *The Taming of a Shrew*, in 1595 of *The True Tragedie*, in 1598 of the second edition of *Lucrece* and the first edition of *King Henry the Fourth, Part One*. One of Quyney's burdens was the presence in the town of soldiers wounded, physically and morally, in the Irish wars. Among them was a ruffian, not unworthy of Shakespeare's Pistol, a swaggering

[1] Halliwell-Phillipps, *Outlines*, ii. 17–19.
[2] *Ib*. 31–4.
[3] *Heralds' College MS*. *Off*. *Arm*. W–Z, 276.
[4] pp. 546–8.
[5] *Council Book B*. 88.
[6] *Ib*. 89.
[7] Arber, ii. 261 ('John' is a slip for 'George').

drinking bully, who afterwards committed murder, one Lewis Gilbert. On 13 April the council renewed a petition to the magistrates of the shire, of the previous year, respecting their relief from such undesirable characters. We learn from this petition that there were still seven hundred poor in the parish in receipt of assistance.[1]

Another of Quyney's troubles was Sir Edward Greville's bailiff, Robin Whitney of Milcote. Like his master, Whitney was a thorn in the side of the Corporation. For Sir Edward's sake Quyney showed him courtesy until he proved intolerable. He forbade him his house, and advised honest folk to have nothing to do with him. Whitney wrote to him:

I must not come to expostulate matters with you, for that I am informed that *you have the good abarring against me*. It will *make me so much the better husband to forbear your house*. I know *you do it altogether for my good*. I would willingly know from where all the malice doth proceed: I am sure not from either of our natures. If I might have a protection from yourself I would willingly speak with you; if it may not be granted I will rest contented.

Milcote, this Thursday at night. Your friend as before, if he be used accordingly. I pray you, let me receive an answer from you as soon as you may conveniently. Give these with speed.[2]

The Thursday of this urgent letter was probably 29 April. The May Fair was approaching, and Quyney was determined to have the tolls. The Fair began on Monday and lasted until Tuesday evening—3 and 4 May. Quyney, we know, kept the toll-book of the horses that changed hands. Here is an item out of it:

John Cale of Dossington *in Comitatu Gloucestrense* hath sold to Richard Maydes of Snitterfield *in Comitatu Warwicense* a grey mare trotting whole-eared, price 45*s*. Toll 2*d*.[3]

Sir Edward Greville's men, who came to intercept the toll-corn, seem to have contented themselves with getting drunk and making a brawl. They gathered at the house of one who may have been a friend of their master, but in their drink they quarrelled and drew their daggers on him. This apparently was on Monday night. What then took place shall be told in the words of the chronicler:

The Bailiff being late abroad to see the town in order, and coming by in

[1] *Misc. Doc.* vii. 95.
[2] *Ib.* i. 123.
[3] *Ib.* vii. 30.

that hurly-burly,[1] came into the house and commanded the peace to be kept; but could not prevail, and in his endeavour to still the brawl, had his head grievously broken by one of his men: whom neither himself punished nor would suffer to be punished.[2]

In the fray, then, by one of his own officers, accidentally, Richard Quyney was grievously, and as it proved fatally, struck on the head. It being an accident, however careless, he would not have the man punished. He lived nearly four weeks, and was buried on 31 May,[3] Trinity Monday, doubtless within the Church. Never before had a bailiff died in office. The Corporation met in force after attending the funeral, and elected Master John Gibbs bailiff for the rest of the year. Old Adrian Quyney was present, for the first time for seven months. Abraham Sturley kept the minutes.[4]

The Greville ringleaders escaped in the 'hurly-burly' but were taken by County magistrates, Master Verney and Master William Combe, in the neighbourhood. So we conclude from an item in the Chamberlains' Account, presented and passed 7 January 1603, for 'two quarts of sack and two quarts of Rhenish', given to these gentlemen by Master Gibbs, 'when the rogues were taken at Clifford Barn'.

The news of Quyney's death would reach Thomas Greene in London not later than 8 June when the Chamberlain, Francis Smith the younger, paid him there a fee for work for the Corporation.[5] Shakespeare, if not in Stratford, might hear it about the same time. On 26 July *Hamlet* was entered, in anticipation of piracy, at Stationers' Hall under the title *The Revenge of Hamlett, Prince of Denmarke, as yt was latelie Acted by the Lord Chamberleyne his servantes.*[6] On 28 September Shakespeare's purchase from Walter Getley (Gatcliff) of a cottage in Chapel Lane, Stratford, was reported, in his absence, at the View of Frankpledge at Rowington.[7] This cottage, with a garden, was on the opposite side of the lane to *New Place*, below the 'mudwall' of the Gild Orchard. On Sunday 3 October Shakespeare may have

[1] *Macb.* I. i. 3.

[2] Shakespeare's Birthplace, *Wheler MS.* 1, f. 59.

[3] *Register*, p. 67.

[4] *Council Book B.* 89.

[5] Chamb. Accts.: 'Item delivered unto Master Greene at London the 8 day of June, x^{s}.'

[6] Arber, ii.

[7] Halliwell-Phillipps, *Outlines*, ii. 19.

been in London, as sponsor at the christening of his friend John Heminge's son, William, in St. Mary's Aldermanbury, a few yards from his lodging in Silver Street. In the Michaelmas term a second fine was levied in connexion with his purchase of *New Place*.[1] Whatever momentary check he and his company experienced at the *Globe*, his prosperity shows no decline. Tucca might say to Histrio, in spite of a bad winter, 'You grow rich, and purchase.'[2]

1602–3

§ 107. *TROILUS AND CRESSIDA*

WE approach now the last theatrical season of the Queen's reign. Shakespeare brought thither no new gay comedy as had been his wont for years past. His fountain of merriment had run dry, and in the same measure it never flowed again. He had passed another stage of his career. Early-manhood comedy had succeeded youthful poetry and sonnetry, and gone its way; and again mental suffering, but public, not private, marked the transition. The Poet was sick of the rivalries and personalities, not merely theatrical and academic but political and social, which embittered the present and darkened the future. The great Queen was dying, and the era, of such paramount significance, of which she was the embodiment was dying with her, amid the din of quarrels and jealous expectations and literary fopperies, not to be drowned by laughter. Again Shakespeare, as in *King John*, is revolutionary and denunciatory, not of the old 'Commodity', but the petty ambition and recrimination rampant since the death of the Lord Treasurer Burghley. He will not utter sweet words, saying 'peace, peace', when there is no peace.

Of late he had been thinking sarcastically on the lauded theme of the Trojan War, and on the story popularized by Chaucer of Troilus and Cressida. That was not his mood when he drew the realistic picture of Priam's 'Troy' in *Lucrece*, though he did not spare Helen ('the strumpet that began this stir') and laughed at

[1] *Ib.* ii. 105. [2] p. 566.

'grave Nestor's beard wagging up and down';[1] nor when he put in Lorenzo's mouth in *The Merchant of Venice* the lines,

> Troilus methinks mounted the Troyan walls,
> And sighed his soul toward the Grecian tents
> Where Cressid lay that night (v. i. 4–6).

But from Pistol's lips we hear of 'the lazar kite of Cressid's Kind' (*Henry V*, II. i. 80); Benedick in *Much Ado about Nothing* (v. ii. 31) and Rosalind in *As You Like It* (IV. i. 97) poke fun at Troilus as a lover, and the former calls him 'the first employer of pandars'; Pistol in *The Merry Wives* declines to play the part of Sir Pandarus,[2] as the Clown in *Twelfth Night* would willingly play it in the sense of adding a mate to Viola's gratuity.[3] In all this, perhaps, we may recognize caricature of the *Troilus and Cressida* at the *Rose* Theatre in 1599.[4] In his own drama of this title the Poet expresses almost fierce derision. The editors of the Folio of 1623 were puzzled by the drama—they placed it first after *Romeo and Juliet* as a tragedy of love, then between the Tragedies and the Histories. Their perplexity is not surprising. *Troilus and Cressida* stands alone among Shakespeare's plays as a piece of scornful irony. That cannot be called a comedy which ends with the murder of the best character in it; nor a history which from beginning to end is fiction; nor a tragedy which is throughout satirical. It holds up to mockery, in the spirit of Swift or Hogarth rather than of Cervantes, the unreal ideals of the prevailing Medievo-Renaissance chivalry. Hence its association with the battles of the theatres.[5] Without personalities it carries the war into the heart of the classical camp.[6]

The 'small Latin' of Ben Jonson's dictum was misleading in his day, as we have seen,[7] and is false in ours. But the 'less Greek' is not exaggeration. We look in vain in Shakespeare's writings for proof that he read Greek, or cared for Greek learning. His acquaintance with the Homeric heroes was through Ovid[8] and Chapman's translation of the *Iliad*.[9] There is no good evidence that he knew the Greek drama. Aristotle's 'dramatic unities' he

[1] 1471, 1406. [2] I. iii. 83. [3] III. i. 58–62.
[4] p. 523. [5] pp. 581–4.
[6] 'Masticke jaws', I. iii. 73, is surely a misprint for 'mastiffe jaws', and not a feeble play on *Histriomastix*! The allusion to Shakespeare in *Histriomastix* (see p. 565) is very slender evidence that *Troilus and Cressida* was in existence in 1599.
[7] pp. 114–16. [8] p. 102. [9] 'Seven Books', 1598 (Bks. I, II, VII–XI).

more than disregards.[1] *The Tempest* is the one play in which he observes the unities of time and place, and there conformity ends. In *Timon of Athens* he shows no trace of Milton's enthusiasm for the 'mother of arts and eloquence'. His Greek men and women are wordy, weak, and treacherous. So unsympathetic, indeed, is his attitude towards Greek models that we must seek a ground for it in his age and in himself.

Briefly, his English temper resented the tendency to subordinate Teutonic and Christian ideals to the Classical and Pagan. In his love of liberty, his contempt for 'rules' about Truth and Beauty, his disdain of mere neatness, smoothness, and symmetry, his grim humour, his honest uncouthness and coarseness in scorn of vicious elegancies, and his deep unobtrusive reverence, he is a Goth among the Classicists. A child of the Renaissance, he is never its slave. While he borrows of the good things which are poured in on him from Greece and Rome, he preserves his independence of genius and race.

The heroes of the Trojan War are roughly handled in *Troilus and Cressida*. They are 'fools on both sides',[2] engaged in a verbose and vainglorious contest for a harlot.[3] When Paris asks Diomedes who best deserves Helen, himself or Menelaus, he gets a blunt reply:

> He merits well to have her that doth seek her
> Not making any scruple of her soilure,
> With such a Hell of pain and world of charge[4] . . .
> For every false drop in her bawdy veins
> A Grecian's life hath sunk, for every scruple
> Of her contaminated carrion-weight
> A Trojan hath been slain.[5]

She is a 'starved subject',[6] the source of 'hollow factions'.[7]

[1] He refers to Aristotle's *Ethics* or *Works* (read either for 'checks') in *Tam. Sh.* I. i. 32. Another allusion to Aristotle is in *Tro. & Cres.* II. ii. 166.

[2] I. i. 93.

[3] She is always such in Elizabethan literature. See *Euphues* (Arber, pp. 91, 97, 119, 180, 185, 196, 202, 208, 279), Marlowe (in *Doctor Faustus* she is the instrument of Satan, in *Edward II* 'the Greekish strumpet' II. v. 15), Nashe (McKerrow, i. 217, iii. 184), &c. See Chamberlain to Carleton 13 June 1600: 'Mistress Fowler is a very Helen and the cause of all the evil, carrying the right picture of a courtesan in her countenance.'

[4] IV. i. 55–7.

[5] 69–72.

[6] I. i. 96.

[7] I. iii. 80.

The Greek camp is a nest of rivalry and intrigue. The chiefs parade their weaknesses. Agamemnon is a sententious, pompous person, living on his reputation: 'an honest fellow enough, and one that loves quails' (less innocent than those after whom the Israelites 'fell a-lusting').[1] Nestor is a dotard, who says ditto to Agamemnon. Achilles is a braggart. He lounges in his tent laughing at the incompetence of his brother generals. Drawn at last to avenge the death of Patroclus, he plays the coward and the traitor. Ajax apes Achilles, and proves an ass in his vanity. Ulysses is a wiseacre, full of maxims and wiles. Deferential to Agamemnon, he flatters Nestor and plays off Ajax against Achilles.[2] Diomedes is 'a false-hearted rogue', guilty of sin with Cressida for which he condemns Helen. And up and down the Greek camp creeps the foul-mouthed Thersites (Shakespeare's 'Blatant Beast'), uttering shamelessly the thoughts and whispers of the rest with mocking comment. The Trojans are little better. Priam is an adulterer, Paris an effeminate seducer, Troilus a greenhorn, Aeneas a boaster, Calchas a deserter. Hector alone is noble. He contrasts with all the men of the play, as his wife, Andromache, with the women. He is faithful in love, wise in counsel, a brave and generous soldier. He argues with his brothers:

> The reasons you allege do more conduce
> To the hot passion of distempered blood
> Than to make up a free determination
> 'Twixt right and wrong; for pleasure and revenge
> Have ears more deaf than adders[3] to the voice
> Of any true decision . . .[4]
> What nearer debt in all humanity
> Than wife is to the husband? . . .
> If Helen, then, be wife to Sparta's King,
> As it is known she is, these moral laws
> Of nature and of nations speak aloud
> To have her back returned; thus to persist
> In doing wrong extenuates not wrong
> But makes it much more heavy.[5]

[1] v. i. 56 f. 'Quail', like 'partridge', was a cant term for a harlot, derived from Numbers xi. 32, Psalm lxxviii. 29, note (Geneva).

[2] Shakespeare is sterner than Gosson, who complains of Maximus Tyrius that he 'taketh upon him to defend the discipline of these Doctors [the Poets] under the name of Homer, wresting the rashness of Ajax to valour, the cowardice of Ulysses to policy, the dotage of Nestor to grave counsel' (*The School of Abuse*, Arber, p. 21).

[3] Psalm lviii. 3.

[4] II. ii. 168–73, 175 f.

[5] *Ib.* 183–8.

Hector spares both Ajax and Achilles, the one as a kinsman, the other as unfit by 'rest and negligence' to fight.[1] And for his chivalry he is treacherously slain by Achilles, who ties his body to his horse's tail and drags it in false triumph over the field.[2]

With the same sarcasm Shakespeare handles the medieval tale of Troilus and Cressida. Troilus is barely mentioned, and Cressida[3] is unnamed, by Homer. They appear, not yet connected, in *Historia de Excidio Trojae* ascribed to Dares. A trouvère of the twelfth century, Benoît de Saint-Maure, made them lovers. Boccaccio developed the story, and added Pandarus. Chaucer gave the whole life and beauty, changing Pandarus from a gay young knight into a fourteenth-century Falstaff. The Elizabethans satirized the tale.[4] Shakespeare is merciless. Troilus in his hands is a typical victim of the high-flown sentiment burlesqued in *Don Quixote* at this very time.[5] He is blindly devoted to his 'Trojan drab',[6] to his 'brother-lackey', Pandarus (a brainless animal, not to be mentioned in the same breath with Falstaff or Belch),[7] and to a war of 'Honour'.[8] He is guilty of the 'mad idolatry' which makes 'the service greater than the god'.[9] Disillusion is the fruit of his infatuation. For relief he does 'mad and fantastic execution',[10] changing one form of recklessness for another. Not Troilus, but Hector, is the 'prince of chivalry',[11] who loves Andromache though he uses no hysterical language about her and can chide her,[12] and is true to the law of arms, mingling mercy with blows, and dying for his magnanimity.

Shakespeare and his fellows played at Whitehall on 26 December 1602 and at Richmond on 2 February 1603.[13] That they performed *Troilus and Cressida* before the Queen is highly improbable; but that they included it in their Christmas repertoire in or near London seems evident from its entry on 7 February in the Stationers' register: 'The Book of Troilus and Cressida, *as it is acted by my Lord Chamberlain's men.*' It would suit an audience of

[1] IV. v. 118–48, V. vi. 13–19. [2] V. viii. 1.

[3] Unless her name is a corruption of that of Chryseis (*Il.* I. iii).

[4] p. 525.

[5] Published 1605 (First Part: *El Ingenioso Hidalgo Don Quixote de la Mancha*).

[6] V. i. 104.

[7] V. x. 33. Like Shallow he ekes out his lack of matter with vain repetition, i.e. 'fair', III. i. 46–50, 'sweet Queen', 51–160.

[8] II. ii. 26, 47, 68, 124, 199 f. [9] II. ii. 6 f. [10] V. v. 38.

[11] I. ii. 249. [12] I. ii. 6. [13] Chambers, iv. 115 f., 167.

politicians, lawyers, scholars, or others on some special occasion. It was speedily forgotten, to be discovered years afterwards and published as 'a new play never staled with the stage'.

On 19 March 1603 the Queen was dying. Stage-plays in London were forbidden in view of her decease. On the 24th at Richmond she passed away.

Inscription on the coffin of Queen Elizabeth.

1603

§ 108. ACCESSION OF KING JAMES

ELIZABETH died at two in the morning.

'And forthwith', says Edmund Howes, gentleman, continuator of Stow's *Chronicle*, 'the princes, peers of the land and privy councillors of estate, in their wisdoms' foresight, for the preservation and continuance of our long enjoyed peace and tranquillity, (being a matter which all nations held impossible to perform, by reason of so many laws made, not only against competitors and pretenders but against all future right of succession), the lords aforesaid (knowing above all things delays to be most dangerous) within six hours after, made proclamation at the Court gates, signifying and assuring the people her Majesty was dead, and that the right of succession was wholly in James the King of Scots, now justly intitulated unto the

KING JAMES, 1574. *By* TADDEO ZUCCHERO

By permission of the National Portrait Gallery

BEATI PACIFICI
Crounes haue their compasse, length of dayes their date,
Triumphes their tombes, felicitie her fate:
Of more then earth, can earth make none partaker,
But knowledge makes the KING most like his maker.
Simon Passæus sculp: Lond.
Ioh: Bill excudit.

JAMES I

By SIMON DE PASSE

crown of England; and about eleven of the clock at the west side of the High Cross in Cheapside, where were assembled the most part of the English princes, peers, divers principal prelates, and an extraordinary and unexpected number of gallant knights and brave gentlemen of note well mounted, besides the huge number of common persons: all which with great reverence gave attention unto the proclamation, being most distinctly and audibly read by Master Secretary Cecil, and at the end thereof, with one consent cried aloud, *God save King James!* being not a little glad to see their long-feared danger so clearly prevented. After that, the lords sent three heralds and a trumpeter to proclaim the same within the Tower; at the hearing whereof, as well prisoners as others rejoiced, namely[1] the Earl of Southampton, in whom all signs of great gladness appeared. I should have told you before that at the first Sir Robert Carey, unknown to the lords, rid post unto his Majesty with wondrous expedition, and by the way sent certain knowledge of all things to Warwick, unto his brother, Sir John Carey, who presently proclaimed the King's right.'[2]

Sir George Carew of Clopton heard of the Queen's death on his journey from Ireland, at Nantwich in Cheshire, and of the King's proclamation by the mouth of Sir Henry Danvers, in or near Coventry: whence he wrote on 27 March to Sir Robert Cecil that the proclamation

hath much eased my heart, that was before in anxiety, fearing many distempers in the State, whereof as far as I can judge, there is now no appearance but all men are exceedingly satisfied, and praise God, who of His goodness hath so miraculously provided for us, contrary to the opinions of the wisest, who for many years past trembled to think of her Majesty's decease, as if instantly upon it the kingdom would have to be torn in sunder.[3]

The sense of relief was astonishing. Thomas Egerton, Lord Ellesmere, wrote from London on 13 April to Lord Henry Howard,

I condoled with you in the sickness and decease of our late gracious Queen, and will ever rejoice with you in the greatest and most blessed happiness that ever any people enjoyed, in that it hath pleased God to place in the royal throne over us *sine caede et sanguine*[4] our liege-lord and sovereign the King's Majesty, and that so speedily, so peaceably, with such general acclamation and applause as precedent times cannot exemplify and in all future ages will be admirable. I have read of *Halcyonis dies*[5] and *laetus introitus*[6] and *Sol occubuit, nox nulla secuta*:[7] we see and feel the effects of that which they feigned and imagined. We had *heaviness in the night but joy in the morning*.[8] It is the

[1] Especially.
[2] *Annales*, p. 816.
[3] *Cecil Papers*, 99, 54.
[4] 'Without slaughter and blood.'
[5] *Halcyonei* or *Halcyonides dies*, Halcyon days, of unwonted calm.
[6] 'Happy entrance' on an office.
[7] 'The Sun set, no Night followed.'
[8] Psalm xxx. 5 (Prayer Book).

great work of God: to Him only is due the glory and praise for it, and we are all bounden to yield to Him our continual prayers, praise and thanks. When I took pen in hand I meant only to scribble a few commendatory lines unto you, but I am now transported I wot not whither.[1]

In a similar strain wrote John Davies—

> Now wisest men with mirth do seem stark mad
> And cannot choose, their hearts are all so glad.[2]

Political satisfaction, however, far exceeded personal appreciation of King James. The symbol and instrument of outward peace, he was nevertheless most unattractive to Englishmen. Elizabeth had more than disliked him, lamented to her Council his 'childishness, folly, and cowardice'.[3] The prospect of his succession, which was a political necessity (anything was better than civil war), deepened if it did not occasion her melancholy. *Jacobus Rex Pacificus* was a canny fool, and all but himself were speedily aware of it. Courtiers said openly, *Rex fuit Elizabeth nunc est Regina Jacobus*.[4] His queen and elder son, Henry, made no disguise of their disdain.

Happily for Shakespeare His Majesty had a taste, of a kind, for the drama, nor was it a misfortune for him and his fellows that they had been, however remotely, connected with the Essex rising. The Earl of Southampton was released from the Tower on 10 April, while the King was yet on his journey to London. A malignant outbreak of plague, the first since 1594, diverted the royal procession from the City to Whitehall, and thence to Greenwich, whither it arrived on 13 May. Four days later at Greenwich the King granted a licence to Shakespeare's company as his 'Servants'. The letters patent issued on the 19th *pro Laurentio Fletcher et Willielmo Shakespeare et aliis* permitted them to use and exercise their faculty as 'well for the recreation of our loving subjects, as for our solace and pleasure when we shall think good to see them', both 'within their now usual house called *The Globe*', when 'the infection of the plague shall decrease', and 'within any town-halls or moot-halls or other convenient places in any city, university, town or borough whatsoever, Willing and Commanding all Justices, Mayors,

[1] *Egerton Papers*, p. 361 f.

[2] *Microcosmos*, 1603.

[3] Burghley to Walsingham, 10 March 1588/9.

[4] Fane, 'Commonplace Book', p. 2.

HENRY WRIOTHESLEY, THIRD EARL OF SOUTHAMPTON

A MEMBER OF GRAY'S INN

Shakespeare's Patron

Copyright of the Duke of Devonshire

Sheriffs, Constables, Headboroughs and other our officers not only to permit them, but to aid and assist them'. The members of the company, henceforth 'the King's Men', with this remarkable privilege and commendation, are thus named: 'Lawrence Fletcher, William Shakespeare, Richard Burbage, Augustine Phillips, John Hemings, Henry Condell, William Sly, Robert Armin, Richard Cowley, and the rest of their associates.'[1] Fletcher leads for the moment in virtue of his having performed before the King in Edinburgh,[2] but the real leader, of course, was Shakespeare. The patent conferred the right to wear on all ceremonial occasions the royal livery of red doublet, hose, and cloak with the royal arms on the sleeve. The plague increased, the Coronation was postponed, and 'the King's Men', with permission to perform practically wherever they wished or right to compensation for not performing, went on tour—to Ipswich (30 May),[3] Cambridge, Coventry, Shrewsbury, Bath, and Oxford. At Coventry, Shakespeare would turn aside for Stratford. At Cambridge and Oxford he and his fellows played *Hamlet*.

The King was crowned on 25 July at Westminster; but he avoided the plague-stricken City, deferring his State-entry until 'the angry hand of God had worked the will of His all-commanding power' and 'the infection ceased'. With his queen and children, he 'progressed in the country, and dealt honours as freely to our nation as their hearts could wish, as creating knights of gentlemen, lords of knights, and earls of lords'.[4]

The burials at St. Saviour's, Southwark, were 25 from 1 to 11 July, then 158 from 12 to 31 July. In August the number rose to 620, in September to 735. In October it fell to 292. By 21 October Shakespeare's company had ventured into the neighbourhood in hope of reopening the *Globe*. Edward Alleyn received at Bexhill the following letter of this date from his wife on the Bankside:

My entire and well-beloved sweet-heart, still it joys me and long, I pray God, may I joy to hear of your health and welfare, as you of ours. Almighty

[1] Halliwell-Phillipps, *Outlines*, ii. 82 f.

[2] In 1599 (Lee, p. 83) and 1601 (J. T. Murray, i. 104, n. 3).

[3] J. T. Murray, i. 183; but 1601–2 is a slip for 1602–3, it being in the highest degree improbable that any company would take, or any corporation allow, the title of 'the King's Players' in England in 1602. See further, p. 618.

[4] Gilbert Dugdale, Arber's *Garner*, v. 648.

God be thanked, my own self (your self), and my mother, and whole house, are in good health, and about us the Sickness doth cease, and is likely more and more, by God's help, to cease. *All the companies be come home*, and are well, for aught we know; but that Browne of the Boar's Head is dead, and died very poor: he went not into the country at all. And all of your own company are well, at their own houses. My father is at the Court: but where the Court is, I know not. I am of your own mind that it is needless to meet my father at Basing,[1] the incertainty being as it is; and I commend your discretion . . . For your coming home, I am not to advise you, neither will I: Use your own discretion. Yet I long and am very desirous to see you; and my poor and simple opinion is, if it shall please you, you may safely come home. Here is none now sick near us. Yet let it not be as I will, but at your own best liking. I am glad to hear you take delight in hawking; and though you have worn your apparel to rags, the best is you know where to have better, and as welcome to me shall you be with your rags as if you were in cloth of gold or velvet; try and see!

She concludes this charming epistle with greetings: 'Nick and James be well, and commend them. *So doth Master Cooke and his wife, in the kindest sort.*'[2]

Master Cooke was probably Shakespeare's fellow, whom we saw as a boy, 'Saunder', in the female parts of Videna and Progne in 1592.[3] He had recently married, and was living in Hill's Rents in Southwark. Their child, Francis, was baptized in St. Saviour's in 1605.[4] That a junior member of Shakespeare's company, like Cooke, should be 'Master' is significant of their status.

But the plague, though less on the Bankside than in many parishes,[5] was not gone. There were 7 interments at St. Saviour's on 1 November, 2 on the 2nd, including, as we have seen, William Kemp; 7 on the 3rd, 4 on the 4th, 6 on the 5th, 3 on the 6th, 2 on the 7th and 8th, then 7 on the 9th before the normal 2 on the 10th and 1 on the 11th and 12th.[6] Kemp, whose dwelling was in Langley's New Rents, Southwark,[7] as recently as 1602, had returned home too soon. In December on the 19th, Mary Kemp, probably his wife, followed him to the grave.[8]

[1] The Court was at Basing, the residence of the Marquis of Winchester, 17–23 Aug., and thither apparently there was some expectation of its return *en route* from Wilton to Hampton Court.

[2] *Henslowe Papers*, 59 f., 61. [3] p. 293. [4] Chambers, ii. 311 f.

[5] Cripplegate, for instance, where 2,531 persons were buried in July–Dec.

[6] Burial Register. [7] Chambers, ii. 327.

[8] This seems the natural inference from the entry (the name is uncommon in the register): '1603 December 19 Marye Kempe a woman.' A child, Cicely Kempe, was buried 13 Feb. 1604/5, probably their daughter.

Shakespeare in November, with members of his company, was at Mortlake, where Augustine Phillips, perhaps to avoid the recurring pestilence, had lately bought a country house. A victim of the plague may have been their old 'fellow', Thomas Pope. He had left the company shortly before 19 May—his name does not appear in the list of the King's Men of this date. As a clown,[1] like Kemp, he may have caused Shakespeare tribulation. The fact that he left nothing, though he was well-off, to his brother players, save Robert Gough and John Edmunds who were his apprentices, possibly suggests estrangement. Unlike Kemp, he retained his share in the *Globe*; but at the time of his death he had secured at least a provisional lease of the *Rose*, as successor to Henslowe, at a rent increased from £7 to £20. He may have contemplated a theatrical venture of his own.[2] He made his will on 22 July 1603, when he declared himself 'in good and perfect health'—the plague had just begun. But he died not long afterwards, in flight apparently from Southwark, where, in St. Saviour's, he was not interred, in spite of a handsome legacy of £20 for burial there and a monument. His will was proved 13 February 1603/4.[3] To Gough and Edmunds he bequeathed his 'wearing apparel and arms'—which would include his theatrical outfit. Edmunds married his legatee, probably his niece, Mary Clarke *alias* Wood, and inherited in her right half his interest in the *Curtain* and *Globe*. Shortly after his death objection was raised to his having taken the coat-armour of Sir Thomas Pope (founder in 1558 of Trinity College, Oxford). 'Pope the player', complained Rouge Dragon pursuivant, William Smith, to Dethick and Camden, 'would have no other

[1] 'Pope the clown' (Samuel Rowlands, *Letting of Humour's Blood*).

[2] 'Memorandum—that the 25 of June 1603 I talked with Master Pope, at the scrivener's shop where he lies, concerning the taking of the lease anew of the *Little Rose*: and he showed me a writing betwixt the parish and himself, which was, to pay twenty pound a year rent and to bestow a hundred marks upon building. Which I said I would rather pull down the playhouse than I would do so; and he bade me do [it], and said he gave me leave, and would bear me out, for it was in him to do it.' Henslowe's *Diary* (Greg, 178). The scrivener was evidently Pope's 'loving friend', Basil Nicholl, to whom he bequeathed £5, and whom he appointed an executor. Pope was owner of the house, wherein he lodged with his tenant, Nicholl. Rather than pay the new rent and spend one hundred marks on rebuilding the *Rose* (which stood on the garden of the house known as *Little Rose*), Henslowe would pull down the old playhouse and carry off the materials.

[3] Collier, *Memoirs*, 125–8; Chambers, ii. 334 f.

arms but the arms of Sir Thomas Pope, Chancellor of the Augmentations.' He complained likewise that 'Phillips the player had graven in a gold ring the arms of Sir William Phillip, Lord Bardolph, with the said Lord Bardolph's coat quartered, which I showed to Master York at a small graver's shop in Foster Lane'.[1] 'Master York' was Ralph Brooke, York Herald, another critic of his superior officers in the Heralds' College. It was Brooke who excepted in 1602 to the arms granted to the players, Shakespeare and Richard Cowley.

Ballad-writers published verse on the Queen's death and King James's 'Entrance', but the chief poets refrained judiciously. It was a dangerous theme, as Drayton discovered. He says:

> It was my hap before all other men
> To suffer shipwreck by my forward pen
> When King James entered:[2] at which joyful time
> I taught his title to this Isle in rhyme,
> And to my part did all the Muses win
> With high-pitch't pæans to applaud him in;
> When cowardice had tied up every tongue,
> And all stood silent, yet for him I sung.[3]

Shakespeare was no 'coward', but he would wait for a less controversial moment to do honour to Elizabeth. He 'stood silent' when called upon personally in the following terms:

> You Poets all, brave Shakespeare, Jonson, Greene,
> Bestow your time to write for England's Queen;[4]

and again when his old acquaintance, Henry Chettle, fat and rather foolish, appealed to him thus:

> Nor doth the silver-tonguéd Melicert
> Drop from his honeyed muse one sable tear
> To mourn her death that gracéd his desert
> And to his lays open'd her royal ear.
> Shepherd, remember our Elizabeth
> And sing her 'Rape', done by that Tarquin, Death.[5]

'Brave Shakespeare' is worth noting in view of Drayton's charge.

[1] Lee, *Life*, 285 f. [2] *To the Majesty of King James; a Gratulatory Poem.*

[3] *To Master George Sandys*, 19–26.

[4] *A Mournful Ditty entitled Elizabeth's Loss, together with A Welcome for King James.* Greene was ten years dead; whence a sarcastic reference in John Cooke's *Epigrams* (S.H. 22 May 1604) to him who 'craves

For help of spirits in their sleeping graves'.

[5] *Englandes Mourning Garment; Worne here by plaine Shepheardes; in memorie of their*

More welcome is the praise of Shakespeare, and his fellow Burbage, in this year 1603, by John Davies of Hereford in *Microcosmos*.[1] Davies, a writing-master in the University of Oxford (who taught penmanship in aristocratic families, and later had Prince Henry for a pupil)[2] and no mean poet, congratulated the Earl of Southampton on his liberation from the Tower—

> Welcome to shore, unhappy-happy lord,
> From the deep seas of danger and distress.[3]

He may have known the Earl—as well as Shakespeare and Burbage, whom he admired as actors, at the Court or the *Globe*, still more as respectively a poet and a painter, and most of all as gentlemen of parts fit for higher fortune. He wrote, setting the initials R. B. and W. S. against the third line:

> Players, I love ye and your quality
> As ye are men that pass time not abused;
> And some I love for painting, poesy,
> And say fell Fortune cannot be excused
> That hath for better uses you refused—
> *Wit, courage, good shape, good parts, and all good*
> (As long as all these *goods* are no worse used);
> And though the stage doth stain pure gentle blood,
> Yet generous ye are in mind and mood—

generous being the proud title in the records, *generosus*. From Spenser in 1591[4] to John Davies in 1603, and to the end of the Poet's life,[5] the testimony is the same. He was at home in any circle, of shepherds, burghers, lawyers, poets, nobles, princes, a striking, honourable, and lovable presence.

sacred Mistresse, Elizabeth, Queene of Vertue while shee liued, and Theame of Sorrow being dead. To which is added the true manner of her Emperiall Funerall. After which foloweth the Shepheards Spring-Song, for entertainement of King Iames our most potent Soueraigne. Dedicated to all that loued the deceased Queene, and honor the liuing King. Non Verbis sed Virtute. There is further reference to Shakespeare as Melicert: 'O, saith Thenot, in some of those wrongs resolve us, and think it no unfitting thing, for thou that hast heard the songs of that warlike poet, Philisides, good Melœbee, and smooth tongued Melicert, tell us what thou hast observed in their saws, seen in thine own experience and heard of undoubted truths touching those accidents, for that they add, I doubt not, to the glory of our Eliza.' Philisides, of course, was Sidney. The Queen's funeral took place on 28 April in Westminster Abbey.

[1] *Chertsey Worthies Library*, Grosart, i.

[2] He wrote, before his death in 1618, *The Writing School master or the Anatomy of Fair Writing, wherein is exactly expressed each several character*, of which the sixteenth edition was published in 1636.

[3] p. 586. [4] p. 279. [5] For Davies, see further, p. 729.

Until November there was no prospect of the *Globe* being reopened, and Shakespeare devoted himself to work for the entertainment of his royal patron. He wrote, apparently, two new plays, *All's Well that Ends Well* and *Measure for Measure*, and re-wrote *Hamlet*.

1603–4

§ 109. *HAMLET* REVISED

THE entry of *Hamlet*, already in a revised state, at Stationers' Hall on 26 July 1602, did not save it, in its first form, from piracy. A garbled version (of great interest to scholars) found its way into print in 1603 under the title, *The Tragicall Historie of Hamlet, Prince of Denmarke, by William Shake-speare. As it hath beene diuerse times acted by his Highnesse Seruants in the Cittie of London: as also in the two Vniuersities of Cambridge and Oxford, and else-where.* It was printed 'at London for N. L and John Trundell'. This called forth an authorized revised edition in 1604, by the printer to whom it had been entered in 1602, James Roberts. It bore the title, *The Tragicall Historie of Hamlet, Prince of Denmarke, By William Shakespeare. Newly imprinted and enlarged to almost as much againe as it was, according to the true and perfect coppie.*[1] As the pirated quarto of 1603 gives us, very imperfectly, the *Hamlet* of 1601, so the quarto of 1604 gives us the speedy and drastic revision of 1602 and later.

As Shakespeare first portrayed him, Hamlet was a youth of about twenty years of age—in his 'primy nature',[2] of 'young blood',[3] 'a noble youth',[4] his 'chin scarce fledged' (as Falstaff would say), 'the expectancy and rose of the fair state, the glass of fashion and the mould of form':[5] shocked at his mother's sin, and wishing that the 'too much grieved and sallied[6] flesh' of man (his own included) might 'melt to nothing' and Creation return to 'Chaos'. In the revision the Poet changed him into a man of thirty,[7] with a full beard,[8] robust, inclining through much study

[1] Arber, ii. [2] I. iii. 7. [3] I. v. 16.
[4] *Ib.* 38. [5] III. i. 160 f.
[6] Cf. 'unsallied lily' (*Love's L.L.* v. ii. 352), 'sullied night' (Sonnet xv).
[7] In the first Quarto, Yorick, who played with Hamlet when a boy, has been dead 'this dozen year' (v. i. 62), in the second Quarto 'twenty-three years' (v. i. 190).
[8] Q1 has, 'Who plucks me by the beard?'; Q2, 'Who calls me villain? plucks off my beard and blows it in my face?' (II. ii. 599 f.).

to fatness, 'too too solid flesh',[1] in spite of 'continual practice' in fencing,[2] and walking 'for hours together' book in hand in the lobby.[3] The intention is obvious. The youthful hero ('young Hamlet' in years) was pardonably unequal to the problem before him; the mature shall have no excuse on the ground of age. 'Young Hamlet' as distinguished from his father, Old Hamlet, is a powerful Northman, outwardly a great rough fellow, gentle underneath, tender and true—a Hercules to look at,[4] exhibiting from time to time a giant strength;[5] but in mind sensitive and hesitant, incapable of exerting the force he possesses in the direction demanded. Pathetic beyond words is the contrast of his massiveness and ineffectiveness with the smart, commonplace success of the 'delicate and tender' Fortinbras. It is the tragedy of England's capacity going to waste, the national strength and lustihood for reformation, freedom, statesmanship, achievement by land and sea, expending itself on rhetoric, speculation, pedantry, fatalism, and gloom. Sir Walter Raleigh, after witnessing *Hamlet*, might have embraced the author, with tears and curses.

But Raleigh may not have seen the play in its revised form until after Shakespeare's death. On Sunday 8 May 1603 at

[1] 'This too too solid flesh' (I. ii. 129), 'the King shall drink to Hamlet's better breath' (v. ii. 282), 'he's fat and scant of breath' (v. ii. 298), 'Come, let me wipe thy face' (v. ii. 305).

[2] v. ii. 221.

[3] II. ii. 160 f.

[4] I. ii. 152 f., v. i. 314.

[5] This is the Hamlet who, as Bradley finely says, 'scarcely once speaks to the King without an insult, or to Polonius without a gibe; who storms at Ophelia and speaks daggers to his mother; who, hearing a cry behind the arras, whips out his sword in an instant and runs the eavesdropper through; who sends his "school-fellows" to their death and never troubles his head about them more; who is the first man to board a pirate ship, and who fights with Laertes in the grave; the Hamlet of the catastrophe, an omnipotent fate, before whom all the court stands helpless, who, as the truth breaks upon him, rushes on the King, drives his foil right through his body, then seizes the poisoned cup and forces it violently between the wretched man's lips, and in the throes of death has force and fire enough to wrest the cup from Horatio's hand (By Heaven, I'll have it!) lest he should drink and die' (*Shakespearean Tragedy*, p. 102). It cannot be said that Shakespeare has always successfully combined the earlier and later conceptions: see p. 550. Burbage played the part doubtless in both forms. His elegist speaks of his 'Young Hamlet', a description preserved in the revision (I. i. 170, v. i. 160) to distinguish the hero from his father. 'Oft have I seen him', he says, 'leap into the grave', and play 'so lively' that spectators, amazed, 'thought he died indeed.'

Theobalds, where he welcomed King James, he was informed of the royal pleasure that the office he held under the late Queen, of Captain of the Guard, should be filled by Sir Thomas Erskine: 'whereunto in very humble manner he did submit himself.'[1] The Countess of Dorset was at Theobalds at the same time, wife of the old Lord Buckhurst; and she wrote, 'We all saw a great change between the fashion of the Court as it was now and of that in the Queen's day. We were all lousy by sitting in Sir Thomas Erskine's chambers.' Raleigh despised King James, preferred Arabella Stuart for his sovereign, and in July was imprisoned in the Tower, to remain there until 30 January 1616.[2]

The extension of Hamlet's age upset the 'balance of nature', in himself and others. His letter to Ophelia, and fantastic behaviour in her chamber, for example, are too juvenile for a man of thirty. His mother is now fifty instead of forty, less her husband's 'Mouse' and object of his 'reechy kisses', and more open to her son's reproaches.[3] The lines:

> You cannot call it love, for at your age
> The hey-day in the blood is tame, it's humble
> And waits upon the judgement,

appear for the first time in the Quarto 1604 (III. iv. 74–6). Shakespeare developed, we may believe, her motherly side, both towards Hamlet and Ophelia. Her account of Ophelia's drowning, and farewell in the churchyard—

> Sweets to the sweet: Farewell!
> I hoped thou shouldst have been my Hamlet's wife;
> I thought thy bride-bed to have deck'd, sweet maid,
> And not t'have strew'd thy grave (V. i. 266–9)

befit one whose heart has outgrown physical attractions.

Horatio is more vitally affected. From a youth of Hamlet's age, his fellow-student at Wittenberg, who, twelve years since,[4] a 'liegeman of the Dane' but not a native of Denmark, had un-

[1] *Acts of the Privy Council*, xxxii. 498.

[2] Edwards, i. 373, 562 f.

[3] There is no ground for believing, whatever Hamlet's suspicion (III. iv. 28–30) that the Queen was privy to her husband's murder, or married the murderer knowing him to be such. Her sin was twofold—in committing adultery before marriage, and then in marrying the 'beast', her late husband's *brother*, being thereby guilty of *Incest* (I. ii. 139–57, V. 42–57, 82–8; III. iii. 90; V. ii. 336).

[4] V. i. 190, Q1: 'here's a skull hath been here this dozen year, aye, ever since our last King Hamlet slew Fortinbras.'

forgettable sight of Old Hamlet in armour, with his beaver up, showing black hair touched with grey,[1] he becomes Hamlet's senior—that boyhood glimpse of royalty receding thirty years, to the year of Hamlet's birth. The welcome, therefore, from Wittenberg and contemplated return thither, and Horatio's strangeness at the Court, ill suit the new conception of long and mature friendship, and touching dependence of the gifted and romantic hero on his relatively stolid and even commonplace comrade. Shakespeare knew the value and power of such a friendship. Was he thinking of his own 'acquaintance and coetanean',[2] Richard Quyney, when he added in 1602–4 the lines:

> Since my dear soul was mistress of her choice
> And could of men distinguish, her election
> Hath seal'd thee for herself; for thou hast been
> As one in suffering all that suffers nothing,
> A man that Fortune's buffets and rewards
> Hast ta'en with equal thanks; and blest are those
> Whose blood and judgement are so well commingled
> That they are not a pipe for Fortune's finger
> To sound what stop she please. Give me that man
> That is not passion's slave and I will wear him
> In my heart's core, ay, in my heart of heart,
> As I do thee.[3]

1603

§ 110. FLORIO'S *MONTAIGNE*

ANOTHER feature is the addition of passages which prove Shakespeare's knowledge of Florio's *Montaigne*—the *Essays of Michel Lord of Montaigne, translated by John Florio*, entered at Stationers' Hall in 1595 and again in 1600, and published in 1603.[4] An advance, or manuscript, copy was in his library in 1601, and he was probably acquainted with the book in 1599, when he drew the portrait of that French courtier and *philosophe*, Monsieur Jaques. Not that Montaigne was a cynic (he was too mild for that), but like Jaques he was melancholy, sensual, self-

[1] I. i. 14, 60–2, ii. 160–75, 187, 211 f., 240–2.

[2] Fripp, *Master Richard Quyny*, pp. 196–9.

[3] III. ii. 68 ff. These lines are not in the Quarto of 1603.

[4] Edited by Henry Morley, 1886.

absorbed and solitary, full of 'many matters', eager for things 'to be heard and learn'd'. A speech by Shallow in *The Merry Wives*, II. i. 232–4—'You stand on distance, your passes, stoccadoes, and I know not what: 'tis the heart, Master Page, 'tis here, 'tis here'—was probably inspired by a passage in *The Essays* in Bk. i, c. 30: 'It is a prank of skill and knowledge to be cunning in the art of fencing, and which may happen unto a base and worthless man: the reputation and worth of a man consisteth in his heart and will.' Montaigne may be the 'strange fellow' quoted by Ulysses in *Troilus and Cressida*, as author of the saying III. iii. 96–102:

> That man how dearly ever parted,
> How much in having, or without or in,
> Cannot make boast to have that which he hath,
> Nor feels not what he owes, but by reflection;
> As when his virtues shining upon others
> Heat them and they retort that heat again
> To the first giver.

More than once Shakespeare employs the thought—as in *Measure for Measure*:

> Spirits are not finely touch'd
> But to fine issues,[1]

which in various forms (less finely) is expressed by Montaigne.[2]

Michel Seigneur de Montaigne died in 1592, aged 59, lamenting the *ancien régime*[3] and the corruption of life by the civil wars in France. He had more belief in the 'cannibals' of the New World than in his own generation of countrymen.[4] A Catholic liberal with a fair estate, he hated, so far as he hated anything, the Reformation and its disturbances—the translation of the Bible into the vulgar tongue and the metrical psalms, and, notwithstanding his academic plea for equality,[5] 'the uncontroll'd

[1] I. i. 36. [2] J. M. Robertson, *Montaigne and Shakespeare*, pp. 95–107.

[3] See p. 598. 'It is a wonder to think on the strange tales I have heard my father report of the chastity of his time . . . His demeanour and carriage was ever mild, meek, gentle, and very modest, and, above all, grave and stately . . . He was wont to say that in a whole province there was scarce any woman of quality that had an ill name. He would often report strange familiarities, namely of his own, with very honest women, without any suspicion at all . . . When he was married he was yet a pure virgin, yet had he long time followed the wars beyond the Mountains . . . and he was well stricken in years when he took a wife . . . being full three-and-thirty years old' (Morley, p. 171).

[4] *Ib.* 92–9. [5] *Ib.* 128–33.

liberty' in their use;[1] the 'sway' in 'ecclesiastical laws' by 'children and women' (such as Edward VI and Queen Elizabeth);[2] the cruelty and barbarism of religious controversy, the decline of friendship, reason, moderation, discipline, until 'the very imagination of virtue is far to seek and seems to be no other thing than a College supposition and a gibberish word'.[3] Not a little in this small, lusty Frenchman, with the big moustache, in the English dress of Florio, would appeal to Shakespeare—his Latinity from a child and love of Ovid's *Metamorphoses*,[4] his study of law and experience of civic government, his reverence for Plutarch, his wealth and shrewdness of observation, his reasonableness and tolerance, his humour, his originality, his good temper, his contempt for duelling, for the affectations of courtesy and dress in men ('apish breeches' and 'dangling locks')[5] and cosmetics and scent ('to smell sweet is to stink')[6] in women, his frankness even to the exposure of his nakedness, his appreciation of the drama, his devotion to his horse (like Shakespeare he composed on horseback)[7] and liking for his cat. But much would rouse the Englishman's antagonism, not to say indignation. The *Essays* indeed was a book to read and enjoy, indispensable to the dramatist,[8] the book of the day and for a long time after, on everybody's lips, a unique contribution to letters, the first of its kind;[9] and Shakespeare wrote his name in it, with care, the best of his signatures.[10] But it was a book to quarrel with, if not to grapple with, to the impressionable Poet both a stimulus to his thought and a challenge to righteousness. The dark background of

[1] Morley, pp. 157–9. [2] *Ib.* 160. [3] *Ib.* 105.

[4] *Ib.* 78 f. His love of Ovid's *Metamorphoses* as a boy recalls Shakespeare's (p. 102): 'The first taste or feeling I had of books was of the pleasure I took in reading the fables of Ovid's *Metamorphoses*; for, being but seven or eight years old, I would steal and sequester myself from all other delights only to read them' (79).

[5] *Ib.* 134. [6] *Ib.* 156.

[7] *Ib.* 446: 'On horseback, at the table, in my bed, but most on horseback where my amplest meditations and farthest reaching conceits are.' Cf. above, p. 389.

[8] To Ben Jonson as to Shakespeare. Their copies with their autographs are in the British Museum.

[9] Bacon followed Montaigne as a writer of 'Essays', otherwise Assays or attempts at analysis.

[10] It is very like the first signature to the Will, but even better written, with characteristic variations which preclude forgery. See Tannenbaum's convincing reply to those who have doubted the autograph, in his *Problems in Shakespeare's Penmanship*.

Hamlet, of *Troilus and Cressida*, of *All's Well that Ends Well*, of *Measure for Measure*, bears witness among other shadows to that of the fashionable and gifted *roué*, with his complacent conscience, light-hearted vice, remoteness from duty, incapacity for stern action, servitude to self, and lack of high seriousness.

Confessedly Montaigne was an old lecher, a connoisseur in sexual indulgence. There can be few pieces of elegant writing more salacious than his chapter with the euphemistic title, 'Upon some Verses of Virgil'.[1] Poor Virgil! because he too warmly paints the charms of 'marital Venus',[2] is made the text of a nauseating apology for unlawful intercourse. 'Wedlock' to our *Chevalier* is an unromantic relationship, conventional and cold, an affair of 'means' and 'alliance', necessary for the family and posterity, the 'pleasure' whereof is 'moderate, staid and mixed with severity', and its 'appetite drowsy and sluggish'.[3] 'Love' is for illicit intimacy, 'a vigilant, lively, and blithe agitation', 'wholesome and fit to rouse a dull spirit, to keep him awake and in strength': 'I have no other passion', he declares, 'that keeps me in breath'; it would 'restore me the vigilancy, sobriety, grace, and care of my person, assure my countenance against the wrinkled frowns of age, reduce me to serious, sound, and wise studies whereby I might procure more love and purchase more estimation, purge my mind from despair of itself and of its use, divert me from thousands of irksome tedious thoughts', to which he is subject as a gentleman 'without occupation' or definitely employed 'leisure', 'uphold the drooping chin and lengthen the shrunken sinews'. If 'the marital Venus', therefore, does not 'solicit and tickle him' into vitality, the harlot-goddess does, 'alluring, all naked, quick and panting'—when she is to be had! For 'the commerce needs relation and mutual correspondency', is 'a sport' to give as well as 'receive the sweet contentment and sense-moving earnestness', and is thus a 'generous' solace. He fancies (this is his brutal substitute for 'pudency so rosy')[4] some 'tender, irresolute and ignorant girl, *which yet trembleth for fear of the rod* and will blush' at the deed, 'whose love-sparkling eyes' call forth 'the vigorous exercise of an officious and active night'. Such is Seigneur's chivalry, his reverence for womanhood. We

[1] iii. 5. Morley, pp. 427–57.
[2] *Aeneid*, viii. 387–406.
[3] Cf. Shakespeare's Brutus and Portia, p. 509.
[4] *Cymb.* II. v. ii.

can understand the fierce puritan cry, of which we shall hear more than an echo in *Measure for Measure* and *King Lear*, against the fornicator, 'Pluck out his eyes!'[1]

To return, however, to *Hamlet*. The hero, alien in every other respect, owes to Montaigne something of his meditative, analytic, bookish, and sceptical ineffectiveness. Shakespeare had read in *The Essays*, Bk. i, c. 40: 'That the taste of goods or evils doth greatly depend on the opinion we have of them . . . If that which we call evil and torment, be neither torment nor evil, but that our fancy only gives it that quality, it is in us to change it';[2] and he wrote, 'There is nothing either good or bad but thinking makes it so.'[3] He read in Bk. iii, c. 8: 'My consultation doth somewhat roughly hew the matter, . . . the main and chief point of the work I am wont to resign to Heaven';[4] and he wrote,

> There's a divinity that shapes our ends,
> Rough-hew them how we will.[5]

Again he read, in Bk. iii, c. 12: 'Death . . . if it be a consummation of one's being, it is also an amendment and entrance into a long and quiet night. We find nothing so sweet in life as a quiet rest and gentle sleep and without dreams';[6] and he wrote,

> To die: to sleep;
> No more; and by a sleep to say we end
> The heartache and the thousand natural shocks
> That flesh is heir to, 'tis a consummation
> Devoutly to be wished. To die, to sleep;
> To sleep: perchance to dream?[7]

Hamlet's phrase, 'discourse of reason' (I. ii. 150), is probably from this work, where it occurs at least four times.[8] Bacon may have had it thence in his *Advancement of Learning* (1605).[9] Shakespeare employs it in *Troilus and Cressida*, II. ii. 116, and the variant 'reason and discourse' in *Measure for Measure*.[10] The Duke's aphorisms in this drama about Death, brushed aside in an instant by Claudio when he sees a hope of Life, are of the kind in which Montaigne indulges.[11]

[1] For this terrible expression see Wilson's *Arte of Rhetorique* (Mair, p. 28). Cf. *Meas. for M.* IV. iii. 124; *K. Lear*, III. vii. 5, 57.

[2] Morley, p. 116 f.

[3] *Haml.* II. ii. 255–7.

[4] Morley, p. 476.

[5] *Haml.* V. ii. 10 f.

[6] Morley, p. 540.

[7] *Haml.* III. i. 60–5.

[8] Robertson, pp. 46–8.

[9] I. iv. 2.

[10] i. ii. 190.

[11] Morley, pp. 26–35, 310–13, and elsewhere.

1603

§ 111. *ALL'S WELL THAT ENDS WELL*

RHYMED passages in *All's Well that Ends Well*, which at first sight may recall the Poet's early verse, on examination do not bear the marks of his immature workmanship. Their thought is ripe—indeed the rhyming is reserved for sententious, epigrammatic speech, as in Helena's lines at the close of I. i, the Countess of Rousillon's in I. iii. 134–41, the King's and Helena's dialogue in II. i. 133–213, Helena's verse (in contrast with Lafeu's prose) in II. iii. 80–110, the King's admonition of Bertram in this scene, 132–51, and his parting reflections and directions in V. iii. 60–70, 325–40. In the Poet's blank-verse of 1603 these speeches would not have quite their distinctive character and emphasis.[1] Nor is their rhyme-verse youthful. Run-on lines are common, and the pause falls frequently within the line. By every canon of metrical development, I. i. 231–4, 239–42 (note the extra syllables in the closing couplet), II. i. 141–7, 172–7, 204–13, II. iii. 109–11, 134–51 (note the penultimate stress and mid-line pause in these last passages—'táke you', 'sérvice', 'hónour', 'títle', 'foregóers', 'tróphy', 'dówer'), and V. iii. 60–2, 69 f. are mature verse.[2]

Nor has the story to which these passages contribute the least resemblance to the conventional plots of Shakespeare's early Comedy. Those are in harmony with Elizabethan gaiety and propriety. The theme of *All's Well* is 'improper' and oppressive. To identify this drama with *Love's Labour's Won*, mentioned by Meres in 1598, is to overlook its bold disregard of decorum and unmistakable reflection of Court indelicacy. The late Queen and her ladies were far from squeamish, but by no stretch of imagination can we conceive of her approval of Helena's behaviour, or allowance of the play in her royal festivities. Nor can we concede such an indiscretion on the part of the Poet. On the other hand, *All's Well*, and the drama, which probably followed it, *Measure for Measure*, are peculiarly after the taste of King

[1] Even later we find such rhyme, e.g. *K. Lear*, III. vi. 109–20; *Oth.* I. iii. 202–19; *Macb.* V. iv. 16–20; *Cor.* II. iii. 120–31.

[2] Not, therefore, 'boulders from the old strata embedded in the later deposits'.

James. His Majesty delighted in such casuistical questions as are therein handled. 'The King's table', says John Hacket, 'was a trial of wits. The reading of some books before him was very frequent while he was at his repast; otherwise he collected knowledge by variety of questions . . . *He was ever in chase after some disputable doubts*, which he would wind and turn about with the most stabbing objections that ever I heard.'[1] At Oxford, in 1605, he concluded the students' disputations with a determination of his own on such subjects as whether pastors are obliged to visit the plague-stricken, whether a judge shall give sentence according to the evidence or the truth known privately to himself, whether gold can be made by art,[2] whether imagination can produce real effects, whether an enemy detained in port by adverse winds may be put to death, whether just and unjust are such by law only or by nature. A canny intelligence of this debating-club order would appreciate the problems, whatever the indecorums, of Helena and Diana, Claudio and Juliet, Isabella and Mariana of the Moated Grange.

Scriptural sanction would weigh with His Majesty, as with the Poet, whose genius transformed both the story and the heroine out of Paynter's *Palace of Pleasure*.[3] Her stratagem recalls Laban's trick with Leah on Jacob,[4] and Tamar's device with Judah[5]—whose ring, like Bertram's, is an important piece of evidence. Court gossip added piquancy to the play. Edward Earl of Oxford, who married Lord Burghley's daughter Anne in 1571 and was father on 2 July 1575 of Elizabeth Vere (whom the young Earl of Southampton declined to marry, Shakespeare's Sonnets I–XXVI notwithstanding, in 1590), owed his parentage of this young lady, so it was said, to his wife's resort to Helena's deceit. Young Francis Osborne calls it 'virtuous'.[6] The King's ladies and gentlemen, as we shall see, were little disturbed by improprieties. His own punctilios were theological.

Boccaccio's tale of Giletta as retold by Paynter, easy and graceful but colourless, without passion or humour, Shakespeare quickens into life, and the life of 1603, adding to the personages

[1] *Life of Archbishop Williams*, i. 38.

[2] By alchemists with their grand elixir. See *All's W*. v. iii. 101 f.: Plutus, the god of alchemy and wealth, 'knows the tinct and multiplying medicine'.

[3] 1575.

[4] Genesis xxix. 21–8.

[5] Genesis xxxviii. 12–18, 24–6.

[6] *Memoires*.

of the story creations of his own, also vividly contemporary. Outstanding figures—Helena (Giletta) and Bertram, the King and the Countess—he portrays with care, lesser characters with sufficient breadth, heightening worth and purity by plentiful splashes of dirt. He takes us, as Paynter (and Boccaccio) cannot do, into France, where feudal distinction, and the divorce of Old and New, were infinitely more marked than in England. The *ancien régime* of Montaigne *père* and Hubert Languet, religious (Catholic or Huguenot), virtuous, dignified, admonitory, clashed with the new order of Montaigne *fils*, sceptical and licentious, and was plunged in melancholy. King and Countess and, on its lighter side, Lafeu, represent the Old. They live in the past, on its faith, its wisdom, and its friendship, and despise the New, in Bertram, Parolles, and the Clown. The King says to Bertram:

It much repairs me
To talk of your good father. In his youth
He had the wit which I can well observe
To-day in our young lords; but they may jest
Till their own scorn return to them unnoted,
Ere they can hide their levity in honour;
So like a Courtier: contempt nor bitterness
Were in his pride or sharpness . . . Such a man
Might be a copy to these younger times;
Which, followed well, would demonstrate them now
But goers backward (I. ii. 30–7, 45–8).

Bertram's father, the old Count of Rousillon, was of the same mind:

'Let me not live',
Thus his good melancholy oft began,
On the catastrophe and heel of pastime,
When it was out: 'Let me not live', quoth he,
'After my flame lacks oil, to be the snuff
Of younger spirits, whose apprehensive senses
All but new things disdain; whose judgements are
Mere fathers of their garments; whose constancies
Expire before their fashions' (55–63).

Venerable fatherhood is a feature, even more than of *Hamlet*, of *All's Well*, and owes something, we must believe, to the Poet's recent bereavement. 'Six months' since, Helena had lost an honoured parent, 'whose skill was almost as great as his honesty'.

Old Lafeu, friend of the King and the Countess, is impatient of 'boy' Lords, stern with Lavache, contemptuous of Parolles, and indignant with 'philosophical persons' who 'make modern[1] and familiar things supernatural and causeless',[2] whence 'we make trifles of Terrors, ensconcing ourselves into seeming knowledge when we should submit ourselves to an Unknown Fear' (II. iii. 1–6).

Gravity and impertinence clash. If, as is probable, Shakespeare himself took the role of the King (one of those 'kingly parts' he would not delegate to an inferior actor), he would pronounce (as no one else could) the speech above and others as quietly wise:

Good alone
Is good without a name . . . Honours thrive
When rather from our acts we them derive
Than our foregoers: the mere word's a slave,
Deboshed on every tomb, on every grave
A lying trophy, and as oft is dumb
Where dust and damned oblivion is the tomb
Of honoured bones indeed (II. iii. 132–6, 142–8).
Oft our displeasures, to ourselves unjust,[3]
Destroy our friends and after weep their dust:
Our own love waking cries[4] to see what's done,
While shameful hate sleeps out the afternoon (V. iii. 60–6).

The Countess, too, has moral sagacity—as in her commendation of Helena (I. i. 43–67), her benediction on her son (70–7: as brief and sound as that of Polonius on Laertes is but a string of maxims), her meditation on her own youthful love. Others have had ethical experience, 'The web of our life', says 1st Lord, 'is of a mingled yarn, good and ill together: our virtues would be proud, if our faults whipped them not, and our crimes would despair, if they were not cherished by our virtues' (IV. iii. 82–7). Jostling and colliding with this wisdom, in pathetic contrast, the irreverent and 'greasy' satire (which is not without point) of Lavache, and the empty, unsavoury chatter of Parolles, demonstrate their feebleness, and fitness for the stable[5] and the privy.[6]

[1] commonplace. [2] miraculous, and not to be scientifically explained.

[3] Our offences to others, discreditable to ourselves. [4] weeps.

[5] IV. v. 61–5. Lavache, with all his coarseness, is sanity and honour compared with Montaigne. The latter's 'elegance' is lower than Falstaff's grossness. Sir John says, borrowing an expression from deer-craft (Turberville, *Venerie*, p. 205): 'Send me a cool rut-time, Jove, or who can blame me to piss my tallow?' *Merry W.* v. v. 16; Seigneur, like a 'gentleman', speaks of 'emptying' his 'seminary vessels' (Morley, p. 446). [6] V. ii. 10–18.

In such a France 'little Helena' is born, and plays her valiant part. She belongs to the Old Order, while she faces and triumphs in the New. She inherits 'her dispositions' and 'her honesty' from her father, a skilful but poor physician, Gerard de Narbon, resident attendant on the Count de Rousillon—Bertram's father, husband of the Countess, to whom in widowhood, Helena in her orphanhood, becomes a young waiting 'gentlewoman' (plain 'Helen' in the wealthy household).[1]

She is hopelessly in love with her young 'Master':

> There is no living, none,
> If Bertram be away.
> In his bright radiance and collateral light
> Must I be comforted, not in his sphere . . .
> 'Twas pretty (though a plague)
> To see him every hour, to sit and draw
> His archèd brows, his hawking eye, his curls
> In our heart's table . . .
> But now he's gone, and my idolatrous fancy
> Must sanctify his relics (I. i. 95–100, 103–6, 108 f.).

She is a Huguenot, apparently, with some knowledge of astronomy.

After Hamlet—Helena; after the big Dane, big in thought and stature, with a paralysed will, ineffective and incapable, in spite of every call to action and means of success, the gloomy victim of 'Fatism'—the little Frenchwoman, hardly more than a child, simple, tearful as a child, pure in her infatuation for the youth she loves, great of will, winning through, against every obstacle, to her desired end, carried along and piloted by *Grace*.

Wisdom in the play, confronted by folly and vice, is not merely ethical. King, Countess, Lafeu, Lords, Diana, above all, Helena, are religious. The King says to Bertram:

> As thou lovest her
> Thy love is to me *religious* (II. iii. 189 f.).

He can say nothing higher. The Countess blesses her son—

> What Heaven more will,
> That thee may furnish and my prayers pluck down,
> Fall on thy head (I. i. 77–9).

[1] I. iii. 70, 73, 101.

and blesses Helena's adventure—

> I'll stay at home,
> And pray God's blessing into thy attempt (I. iii. 259 f.).

(*Into*, we will notice, not merely *on*.) She will not listen to abuse of either papist or puritan (54–61). Lafeu bows before the 'Unknown Fear',[1] is a reader of the tract, *A Showing of a Heavenly Effect in an Earthly Actor*,[2] quotes his Bible, more than once aptly.[3] Diana reproves Bertram,

> What is not holy, that we swear not by,
> But take the Highest to witness: then, pray you, tell me
> If I should swear by God's great attributes
> I loved you dearly, would you believe my oaths
> When I did love you ill? This has no holding,
> To swear by Him whom I protest to love
> That I will work against Him (IV. ii. 23–9).

And when Bertram, not knowing all he says, declares:

> A heaven on earth I have won by wooing thee!

she replies, in words that go to the heart of the play:

> For which live long to thank both Heaven and me (66 f.).

Very much to the point is the remark and rejoinder of the Lords: '*2nd Lord.* Now God lay[4] our *rebellion*! as we are *ourselves*, what things are we! *1st Lord.* Merely our own traitors' (IV. iii. 23–5). '*Natural rebellion*', the Countess calls it,

> done in the blaze of youth,
> When oil and fire, too strong for reason's force,
> O'erbears it and burns on (V. iii. 6–9).

It is the rebellion of the '*natural* man' which 'perceiveth not the things of the Spirit', 'the law in my members *rebelling* against the law of my mind', from which 'by Grace ye are saved, and that not of *yourselves*: it is the Gift of God'. We cannot mistake the Poet's thought. Bertram, without grace, is a *traitor* to himself; Helena, with grace, is *more* than herself, and brings him to *himself*. Truly, if whimsically, she is called 'The Herb of Grace' in

[1] II. iii. 6.

[2] 27 f.

[3] I. i. 64 f. (Ecclesiasticus xxxviii. 16–18), II. v. 51–3 (Matthew v. 44).

[4] 1 Cor. ii. 14, Rom. vii. 23 (Geneva), Eph. ii. 8. 'God delay' of the Folio is a misreading of Shakespeare's manuscript: 'Godde lay'.

the nosegay[1]—Rue, 'herb-of-grace o' Sundays':[2] for, as we learn from the *Schola Salerni*,

Ruta facit castum, dat lumen, et ingerit astum.[3]

Bertram is a royal ward, under twenty-one, say eighteen, 'young Bertram', 'proud scornful boy', 'rash unbridled boy', 'foolish, lascivious, young boy'; but brave, more sinned against than sinning by companionship of an officer, a good deal older than himself, with a reputation for courage, travel, and 'the tongues'. Helena sees partly through Parolles, knows him to be a liar, thinks him 'a great-way fool, and solely a coward'; but loves him, she says, for Bertram's sake, and suffers him, more or less unheeding, to discourse, after Court fashion, on the well-worn theme of Virginity (familiar to Elizabethans since 1560 in Wilson's *Arte of Rhetorique*),[4] with innuendoes she is too pre-occupied to recognize, but sufficiently 'greasy' to reveal his character to the adult audience.[5]

Parolles and Lavache, as their names indicate ('Words', and 'The Cow' with suggestion of the byre), are descendants of the Morality Drama on which Shakespeare was brought up, but living personages nevertheless. Parolles is of the kindred of Jaques, and, like Jaques, always and emphatically *Monsieur*, unworthy, that is, to be an Englishman. He is a well-groomed, bearded, red-faced 'cockscomb', in red and saffron uniform with scarves, 'a snipt-taffeta fellow', a 'red-tailed humble-bee', fierce-looking like Pistol, without 'honesty' (in the sense of chastity or any sense) and without religion. He embraces convenient doctrine (in this case Lafeu's),[6] will 'take the Sacrament how and which way you will',[7] has 'a smack' of the Bible (as of languages), and mixes up Balaam and Bajazeth (a stage-hero from

[1] IV. v. 18.

[2] *Haml.* IV. v. 181 f.

[3] Ellacombe, *Plant-lore and Garden Craft of Shakespeare*, p. 261 ('Rue makes chaste, gives light, imparts craft'). See Alleyn's allusion to 'herb of grace' and 'Grace of God' above, p. 347.

[4] Mair, 39–63. The 'Epistle by Erasmus', made use of by Shakespeare in his Sonnets i–xxvi: see p. 267, n. 5.

[5] I. i. 121–79 is, apparently, an expansion in prose of a much shorter dialogue in verse, written by Shakespeare, subsequent to Gunpowder Plot ('underminers and blowers up'), for the clever actor (whoever he was) who played the popular part of Parolles.

[6] II. iii. 1–45.

[7] IV. iii. 156 f.

1 Tamburlaine).[1] Lavache knows his Bible, and sins, like Falstaff, against the light. From his abuse of papist and puritan we might conclude that, like Sir Andrew Aguecheek, he was a prelatist.[2] Whitgift and Bancroft would not be proud of their champion. The Countess endures him for her late husband's sake, who enjoyed his satirical wit and bequeathed to him his place: a favour which the knave took to be 'a patent of his sauciness'.[3] It is no small humiliation for 'Monsieur Parolles', the comrade of a Count, to be brought to beg a mean favour of 'Monsieur Lavache'.[4] They are a foil to each other, as well as to the heroine.

Helena is a beautiful girl of, say, seventeen, universally admired by the men, devoted to her haughty boy-idol, a Griselda in humility, with a touch of Deborah in her courage and energy, 'assured of God's favour and aid'.[5] She says:

> Our remedies oft in ourselves do lie
> Which we ascribe to Heaven: the fated Sky
> Gives us free scope, only doth backward pull
> Our slow designs when we ourselves are dull (I. i. 231–4).

She is no fatalist. She believes that God helps those who obey His call and vision:

> *What Power is it which mounts my love so high?*
> *That makes me see? and cannot feed mine eye?* (235 f.)

[1] The conjectural reading of the Cambridge Editors, 'Bajazet's mate' (Zabina, the 'termagant', wife of Bajazet in *1 Tamburlaine*) for 'Bajazet's mule' is not a happy one. Parolles, beginning to eat his words (that is, himself), says, 'I find my tongue is too foolhardy; my heart hath the fear of Mars' (not of God) 'before it and of his creatures, not daring the reports of my tongue . . . Tongue, I must put you into a butter-woman's mouth, and buy myself another of Bajazet's mule' —otherwise Balaam's ass, which saved her rider from death by the sword with a few timely words (Numbers xxii. 28–31). With such a tongue (certainly not with a termagant's), there would be some hope for him. His recognition of this, too late, and through fear, is the only sign of grace in him.

[2] His foolery in I. iii is crammed with Biblical language and allusions (the damned rich and the beggar, Lk. xvi; better to marry than to burn, 1 Cor. vii. 9; the unbelieving husband sanctified by the wife, vii. 14; a woman of the world, i.e. married, vii. 34; children an inheritance of the Lord, Ps. cxxvii. 3; thou 'shalt be blessed, it shall be well with thee', Ps. cxxviii. 2; (the world, the flesh, and the devil) 'flesh and blood', 1 Cor. xv. 50 and margin Geneva; one in ten, Lk. xvii. 17). So again in iv. 5 (Nebuchadnezzar eating grass, Dan. iv. 32, Geneva (Bishops' Bible has Nabuchodonosor); the Prince of devils, Matt. xii. 24; Prince of Darkness, Eph. vi. 11 f.; everlasting fire for the Devil, Matt. xxv. 41; Prince of this world, John xii. 31; the strait and wide gate, the broad and narrow way, Matt. vii. 13 f.).

[3] IV. v. 67–70.

[4] V. ii. 1 (read here 'Monsieur', not 'Master').

[5] Judges iv. 14 and margin (Geneva).

Purity itself in her passion, she asks for sympathy of the Countess:

if yourself,
Whose aged honour cites a virtuous youth,
Did ever in so true a flame of liking,
Wish chastely and love dearly, that your Dian
Was both herself and Love:[1] O, then, give pity
To her whose state is such that cannot choose
But lend and give where she is sure to lose (I. iii. 215–21).

But she will not lose. Affection, in which Diana is as strong as Venus, *with Grace* will take her first to Paris, where she cures the King and is rewarded with Bertram as a husband; then, on his refusal to cohabit with her (save on conditions, on the face of it impossible), as a pilgrim, lamenting her unworthiness, to Saint Jaques le Grand (located by the Poet in Italy), in order to leave him free to return from the War and its dangers, and on the way thither, incidentally to Florence; where by accident that is providential, she discovers him, and the means to hand, providential if unconventional, to share his bed. Let us follow her.

Of her father's prescription she says:

There is Something in it
More than my father's skill (I. iii. 248 f.).

As the gift of God, by the hand of a maid, she exhorts the King to try it:

He that of greatest works is Finisher,
Oft does them by the weakest minister:[2]
So Holy Writ in babes hath judgement shown,
When judges have been babes; great floods have flown
From simple sources; and great seas have dried,
When miracles have by the greatest been denied (II. i. 139–44).

[1] The sentence is rather involved but the meaning is clear: 'If yourself . . . did ever wish chastely and love dearly, in so true a flame of liking that your Dian was both herself and Love . . .' Malone's conjecture (adopted by the Cambridge Editors), 'Love chastely and wish dearly', is not only unnecessary but injurious to the passage, greatly lowering Helena's expression of admiration for the Countess.

[2] 'Finisher and minister' links two great words of the Bible ('Author and *Finisher* of our Faith', Heb. xii. 2; 'His *ministers* a flaming fire', Ps. civ. 4; 'the child did *minister* unto the Lord', 1 Sam. ii. 11) and is perfect vowel-rhyme, better than hundreds of examples in lovely passages of the Poet's work (e.g. *Mid. N. D.* IV. i. 92–7).

To refuse it—

Inspirèd merit so by breath is barred.
It is not so with Him that all things knows
As 'tis with us that square our guess by shows;
But most it is presumption in us when
The help of Heaven we count the act of men (151–5).

Moved, he asks:

Within what space
Hopest thou my cure? (162 f.)

She replies, her young voice rising in prophetic fervour:

The Greatest Grace lending grace,
Ere twice the horses of the Sun shall bring
Their fiery torcher his diurnal ring—
Ere twice in murk and occidental damp
Moist Hesperus hath quenched his sleepy lamp—
Or four-and-twenty times the pilot's glass
Hath told the thievish minutes how they pass—
What is infirm from your sound parts shall fly,
Health shall live free, and sickness freely die! (163–71)

Grace in him persuades him to try:

Methinks in thee some Blessed Spirit doth speak (178).

She smacks of Something Greater than herself. He is cured, and she ascribes the fact to God. 'Heaven hath through me', she says, 'restored the King'; and with a touch of gaiety unwonted in her (she is a solemn little thing), she cries:

Now Dian, from thy altar do I fly,
And to Imperial Love! (II. iii. 80 f.)

But her joy is turned to grief by Bertram's petulant repudiation:

A poor physician's daughter my wife! Disdain
Rather corrupt me ever! (122 f.)

Says the King (and Shakespeare, true democrat):

Strange is it, that our bloods,
Of colour, weight, and heat, poured all together,
Would quite confound distinction, yet stand off
In differences so mighty (125–8).

She gives way to despair:

That you are well restored, my lord, I am glad:
Let the rest go (154 f.).

The King, however, insists. Exercising his right as guardian, he bestows his ward upon her. In his presence they are betrothed and married.

There is no trace of boldness here, or in the sequel. St. Jaques (wherever it might be) is her genuine destination, not Florence, as we learn from her sonnet-letter to the Countess (now her 'Mother'), so different in its urgency and sincerity from the sonnet-vapourings of *Love's Labour's Lost*. She writes:

Write, write, that from the bloody course of war
My dearest master, your dear son, may hie:
Bless him at home in peace; whilst I, from far,
His name with zealous fervour sanctify (III. iv. 8–11).

And straightway the Countess, catching the spirit and wording of the poem, commands,

Write, write, Rinaldo,
To this unworthy husband . . .
Dispatch the most convenient messenger (29 f., 34).

Providential circumstance ('Fortune', as Paynter translates), nothing that Helena has foreseen and prepared, gives her the opportunity (as it proved, 'God so disposed the matter', Paynter says) of fulfilling the conditions of her husband's love. She seizes it, without a qualm of conscience, dismissing the thought of censure, whether of 'superfluous Folly' or 'Virtue's steely bones bleak in the cold air'.[1] Neither 'false adulterate eyes', as the Poet had written of himself a decade before, nor pharisaic 'spies',

Which in their wills count bad what I think good,[2]

shall deter her:

to-night
Let us assay our plot; which if it speed,

(and here the language is that of the old attorney's clerk, with experience of cases of casuistry at the Inns of Court, rather than of his girl-pilgrim),

Is 'wicked' meaning in a 'lawful' deed,
And 'lawful' meaning in a 'wicked'[3] act,
Where both not 'sin', and yet a 'sinful' fact:
But let's about it! (III. vii. 43–8)

The conundrum and its conclusion would probably interest King James as much as the play itself.

[1] I. i. 14–16. [2] Sonnet cxxi. See p. 330.
[3] Read thus for the repeated, wrongly, 'lawful'.

'Heaven aiding' Helena succeeds; and her accomplice, Diana, as 'Heaven hath fated', obtains a dowry. Diana is delightful, with humour that Helena lacks. Pure and maidenly, and too clever for her amorous gallant, she secures for Helena her marriage-right and the conditional token:

> I see that men may cope us in such a stour[1]
> That we'll forsake ourselves. *Give me that ring* (IV. ii. 38 f.).

Heart and soul she enters into the fatiguing enterprise, and arrives at length in Paris, to puzzle and play with the recovered King, to the amusement of the audience, while she brings the mystery to light. The whole theatre must have roared when she turns upon the dignified and astounded old gentleman, Lafeu, with the saucy retort (to his, 'This woman is an easy glove . . . off and on at pleasure'):

> By Jove, if ever I knew man, 'twas *you*! (V. iii. 288)

Helena's appearance solves the 'riddle', without narration of her 'plot',[2] and brings Bertram, the first sign of grace in him, to his knees:

> O, pardon! . . .
> If she, my liege, can make me know this clearly,
> I'll love her dearly ever, ever dearly (309, 316 f.).[3]

Hall-marks of Shakespeare's authorship are throughout—the Bible, *Metamorphoses*, Law, Sport, Stage-consciousness (as in Helena's changes of countenance and gesture in I. iii. 142, 146–8, 155–8, 175–85, 195–7). To these must be added his new interest in medicine, due, we may believe, to friendship with Doctor Hall. The French physician, his 'prescriptions' and 'notes' (such as Doctor Hall kept record of and left in his case-book); the

[1] So I would restore the corrupt reading 'make rope's in such a scarre'. *Stour* is a frequent word in Spenser, meaning stir, storm, tumult, passion, frenzy, love-fit. Una suffers from a woeful stour; Duessa from a heavy stour; and Colin Clout declares,

> And eke tenne thousand sithes I blesse the stoure
> Wherein I saw so fayre a sight as shee.

For *cope* see *As You L. It*, II. i. 67, 'I love to cope him in these sullen fits'; and *Oth.* IV. i. 87, 'He is again to cope your wife'.

[2] In Paynter, 'to the great admiration of the Count, and of all those that were in presence', she 'rehearsed unto them in order all that which had been done and the whole discourse thereof'.

[3] The removal of a printer's comma after the first 'dearly' saves the line from unscholarly parody.

King's 'fistula' and its semi-miraculous healing; the 'congregated College', otherwise the Royal College of Physicians, and 'authentic fellows'; the fathers of the ancient and modern schools of medicine, Galen and Paracelsus; 'empirics' or quacks, and 'artists', 'medicines' and 'practisers'; 'leave-off', 'anatomize', and 'application', may well have been topics, or terms, of conversation at New Place or the Croft between the Poet and his future son-in-law.

If Shakespeare took the part of the King he fittingly pronounced the Epilogue. To Burbage we may assign Bertram, to Heminge the peppery Lafeu (who laments his loss of teeth),[1] to Armin the Clown, to Cowley the 'Cockscomb'; 'E' and 'G' (Eccleston and Gough or Gilburne) played the Brother Lords.[2]

1603

§ 112. *MEASURE FOR MEASURE*

IF *All's Well that Ends Well* has its improprieties and lawlessness, what shall we say of *Measure for Measure*? With open and judicious eyes, and undismayed, the Poet would have us look on the darkest evils. Hiding nothing, he would show us the difference between convention and morality, fanaticism and statesmanship, hypocrisy and righteousness.

The heroine, unlike Helena, is a young austere figure in a licentious world, from which she will escape to the cloister. Vienna (London) and its 'suburbs' (Shoreditch and Bankside in particular) reek with corruption. Brothels and jails show forth their inmates—Lucio, a dissolute 'fantastic'; Froth, 'a foolish gentleman' and patron of the stews; Mistress Overdone, a bawd, and her servant, Pompey; Barnardine, a drunken prisoner; Abhorson, the executioner; and Elbow, 'a simple constable', elected eight years together for want of a more competent representative of his ward. The Duke, who is King James, partly as he is (ingenious and indirect, shrinking from contact with the populace), partly as he thinks himself to be (the wise orator and overseer, with knowledge of men and affairs, keeping watch on his

[1] II. iii. 65 f.

[2] As we learn from the Folio, II. i; III. vi; IV. i. and iii.

officials from the background), will endeavour a drastic purification. Stern laws which he has neglected shall be put into operation by means of an energetic deputy of 'precise' principles —one Angelo, with a reputation worthy of his name, and of the gold coin, honoured throughout Europe. Not that he has complete faith in the policy or the man, but he will give both a fair trial and take note of what happens in the disguise of a Friar.

Angelo, like Malvolio, is without spiritual perspective. He is unable to distinguish bird-bolts from cannon-bullets. Instantly, in the same moment, he issues a proclamation for the plucking down of the Stews and arrests a comparatively innocent young couple, Claudio and Juliet. They have committed the offence, still widely regarded as venial, of cohabiting between contract and marriage. Puritan opinion was strong against the practice. Robert Cleaver, while acknowledging that in Deuteronomy xxii. 23 f.,[1] 'God calleth the betrothed a *wife*', urged parents not to delay the wedding, and parties affianced to abstain from intercourse until after that ceremony. Stern laws were proposed on the lines of Old Testament legislation, and at Stratford, as elsewhere, clergy and churchwardens brought no light pressure to bear on erring couples.[2]

On 27 July 1622, Michael Palmer and Jane his wife were presented at Stratford by the churchwardens as having acknowledged with penitence 'their incontinency before marriage and their offence in being married without banns or licence', and

[1] 'If a maid be betrothed unto an *husband* and a man find her in the town and lie with her, then shall ye bring them both out unto the gates of the same city and shall stone them with stones to death: the maid because she cried not, being in the city, and the man, because he hath humbled his neighbour's *wife*.'

[2] In July 1621 the vicar of Feckenham (between Alcester and Droitwich), John Trueman, wrote to the vicar of Stratford, Thomas Wilson, thus: 'So it is, that there is a man of your flock, one William Ball, servant to Master Henry Smith, who has contracted himself to one of my parish, Anne Delves, servant to the right worshipful Sir Francis Edgeock, before sufficient witness; and now understanding that the same Ball hath a purpose to contract himself to another woman, one Mary Watson, contrary to all truth, may it please you to consider the premisses and truly to examine the business, that no proceedings may be, before the truth may appear from the said Anne Delves; for they be man and wife before God and the world, although matrimony be not solemnized: which he, the said William Ball, did intend to perfect before St. James' day next [25 July], and, upon the same words, delivered to the same Anne Delves a token: as shall appear by sufficient witness.'

'promised from henceforth they will live as Christians ought to do'. Their child, Thomas, had been baptized on 28 April, and being the offspring of contracted parents, was not marked 'notus', 'spurius', or 'bastard'.[1]

Claudio thinks little of his 'trespass' with Juliet:

She is fast my wife,
Save that we do the denunciation lack
Of outward order.[2]

They had unwarrantably postponed their marriage because her dowry was in the possession of friends not yet favourable to the match. Angelo, by an obsolete law, sends them to prison and to their *death*. Juliet, because she is with child, has respite, but Claudio will be executed immediately.

He is brother to Isabella, to whom he sends to plead for him with Angelo. His messenger, with dramatic irony, is Lucio. Under the new administration, Claudio is in prison awaiting his death, Lucio the seducer and perjurer goes free. Lucio finds Isabella at the door of the convent. *Roué* and noble maiden face each other. He is courteous, reverential—her presence makes him so:

I hold you as a thing enskied and sainted.[3]

He is not then altogether evil. His boldness encourages her:

Our doubts are traitors,
And make us lose the good we oft might win
By fearing to attempt.[4]

She puts off her restraint, warms to her work, speaks passionately, splendidly to Angelo:

Alas, alas!
Why, all the souls that were were forfeit once;
And He that might the vantage best have took
Found out the remedy. How would you be
If He, which is the top of judgement, should
But judge you as you are?[5] . . . Merciful God,
Thou rather with Thy sharp and sulphurous bolt
Split'st the unwedgable and gnarled oak
Than the soft myrtle; but man, proud man,
Dress'd in a little brief authority,
Most ignorant of what he's most assured—

[1] *Register*, p. 101.
[2] *Meas. for M.* I. ii. 151–3.
[3] I. iv. 34.
[4] 77–9.
[5] II. ii. 72–7.

His glassy essence[1]—like an angry ape
Plays such fantastic tricks before high Heaven
As make the angels weep.[2] . . . Go to your bosom;
Knock there, and ask your heart what it doth know
That's like my brother's fault: if it confess
A natural guiltiness such as is his,
Let it not sound a thought upon your tongue
Against my brother's life.[3]

The beautiful Puritan girl, with glowing cheeks, affects him as neither expected:

Can it be
That modesty may more betray our sense
Than woman's lightness? . . .
O cunning Enemy, that, to catch a saint,
With saints dost bait thy hook![4]

Angelo was 'saintly' because never tempted; tempted, he topples over. Isabella with difficulty understands his base proposal. With swift intelligence she turns it to her brother's account. She demands his pardon on the penalty of exposure. But in vain, for who will believe her? Accusation of Angelo will rebound upon herself as calumny. Then,

brother die:
More than our brother is our chastity.[5]

She will to Claudio, to comfort him and be comforted.

The Duke is before her. He pours into Claudio's ear the consolations of philosophy, from many sources, including Montaigne—

Reason thus with life:
If I do lose thee, I do lose a thing
That none but fools would keep; a breath thou art
Servile to all the skyey influences,
That doth this habitation, where thou keep'st,
Hourly afflict: merely, thou art Death's fool,[6]

and so on, three dozen lines of platitude to his young blood. It is brushed aside the moment he has a chance of life. And with it, so

[1] 'A man that beholdeth his natural face in a glass . . . and forgetteth immediately what manner of one he was.' Marg. 'men know not themselves' (James i. 23 f.).

[2] II. ii. 114–22.

[3] 136–41.

[4] 168–70, 180 f.

[5] II. iv. 184 f.

[6] III. i. 6–11. Cf. *Rich. II*, I iii. 275–93.

feeble is philosophy without religion, goes all sense of his sister's shame:

CLAUDIO. Death is a fearful thing.
ISABELLA. And shamed life a hateful.
CLAUDIO. Ay; but to die, and go we know not where;
To lie in cold obstruction and to rot;
This sensible warm motion to become
A kneaded clod . . .
The weariest and most loathed worldly life
That age, ache, penury, and imprisonment
Can lay on nature is a paradise
To what we fear of death.
ISABELLA. Alas, alas!
CLAUDIO. Sweet sister, let me live . . .
ISABELLA. O faithless coward! O dishonest wretch!
Wilt thou be made a man out of my vice?
Die, perish![1]

She clears again the filthy air, and lets in the light of Heaven—of cleanness, perspective, sanity. Her denunciation of life that is lower than animal existence, with loss of that which is life indeed, is one of the great things in Shakespeare. She is an unanswerable reply to Montaigne.

Angelo proves guilty of the offence for which he condemned Claudio, and, in spirit, of a far greater crime. So deep is his descent from the pinnacle of virtue that he both breaks faith with Isabella and hastens the hour of her brother's execution. She is committed to ward as crazy, and Mariana's evidence fails. Angelo triumphs; but in the moment of triumph the Duke reveals himself. Angelo stands condemned, stript and bare in his sins. The only grace he can ask is immediate sentence and 'sequent death'.

He deserves to die, as Claudio, at the price of his sister's shame, does not deserve to live. But his desire to die, in retribution of his wickedness, proves Angelo's worthiness to live; as the thankfulness of Parolles in *All's Well*, disgraced and despised for his lies and treachery, to be yet *alive*, proves that he is not worth the killing—

Captain I'll be no more;
But I will eat and drink and sleep . . .
Safest in shame; being fool'd by foolery thrive;
There's place and means for every man *alive*.[2]

[1] III. i. 116–21, 129–33, 137 f., 144.
[2] IV. iii. 367 f., 374 f. So also 147, 154, 182, 270–4 ('My life, sir, in any case . . .

Shakespeare had been reading, not only Montaigne, but a book, regarded in his day (which his father and schoolmaster had taught him in the despised 'vulgar tongue'), containing much about 'life after the Spirit' and 'after the flesh', 'life' which is 'more than meat' and is not 'by bread alone', and these searching exhortations:

'Walk in the Spirit; ye shall not fulfil the lusts of the flesh . . . Brethren, if a man be suddenly taken in any offence, through the malice of the flesh and the devil, ye which are spiritual restore such one with the spirit of meekness, *considering thyself lest thou also be tempted. For they commonly are most severe Judges which forget their own infirmities.* Bear ye one another's burden and so fulfil the law of Christ. For if any man seem to himself that he is somewhat when he is nothing, he deceiveth himself in his own imagination.'[1]

Measure for Measure is indeed in London. Its thickly splashed mud is that of the metropolis—moral filth and falsehood, rats and 'plague' and 'angry apes'. But Stratford sets it off—the 'unfolding star' that 'calls up the shepherd', 'the unwedgeable and gnarled oak' (a veritable bit of Arden), fishing, falconry, and archery, lapwings, 'breaks', and scarecrows, the killing of the fowl for the season; blossoming-time, gardens with their violets, roses, medlars and the soft myrtle, the milkmaid in love, the carman whipping his jade, horsemanship; the rating of the house 'by the bay', and much law fresh from the Court of Record, including the life-like holding of the Court in the palace of Angelo.

Markworthy is Isabella's marriage. Whatever tradition the Poet may have inherited of a Dame Isabella Shakespeare, prioress of Wroxall, who died in or shortly before 1504,[2] and whatever respect he may have expressed in *A Midsummer Night's Dream* for the conventual life—

Thrice-blessed they that master so their blood
To undergo such maiden pilgrimage,[3]

he bestows the heroine of *Measure for Measure* on the Duke, as helpmate to whom in his struggle with the corruption of the city

let me live, sir, in a dungeon, i' the stocks, or anywhere, so I may live'), 344 f. There was example for it: 'O that it would please her good Grace to give me life, yea the life of a dog, if I might but live and kiss her feet! . . . O my good lord, remember how sweet life is and how bitter the contrary!' (John Dudley from the Tower to the Earl of Arundel on the eve of his execution, 21 August 1553).

[1] Galatians v. 16, 24, vi. 1–3, Geneva Version, 1587, and marginalia.

[2] Fripp, *Shakespeare's Haunts*, p. 66.

[3] I. i. 74 f.

she will be of greater service than in retreat, however 'enskied and sainted', in the cloister. Social problems are not solved by celibacy, nor sexual evils atoned by prayers of 'saints' and 'hermits' and 'wrongèd souls', whatever efficacy may have been attributed to these in early plays.[1]

1603–4

§ 113. THE NEW PATRON

KING JAMES did not wait until Christmas for a taste of his Players' quality. He was at Wilton, to avoid the plague in London, from October to December, hunting with his courtiers in the noble park of the Countess of Pembroke—'Sidney's Sister' of the *Arcadia* and its sports and pleasures, mother now of Shakespeare's admirers, the young Earl of Pembroke, William Herbert, and his brother, Philip. The Countess and her sons were probably as eager to show Shakespeare's genius to the King as the latter was to witness it. The Poet and his fellows were at Mortlake (where, as we have noted, Augustine Phillips resided) in anticipation of the reopening of the *Globe*, when they received the royal summons to perform at Wilton. They rode down, and on Friday 2 December played before His Majesty. The piece, whatever it was, gave great satisfaction, for they were paid next day the handsome sum of £30.[2] The old Queen had rewarded Shakespeare with thrifty recompense and rare mental appreciation, the new King stuttered fulsome praise and filled his pocket. Eight times the following Christmas and Shrovetide Shakespeare and his company played at Hampton Court—on 26, 27, 28, 30 December, 1 January (twice), 2 and 19 February; and they received in payment £53 on 18 January, £30 on 8 February ('for maintenance and relief, being prohibited to present any plays publicly in or near London by reason of great

[1] *Tit. Andr.* III. ii. 41; *Rich. III*, v. iii. 241. For contempt of the hermit, however, in early dramas, see *1 Hen. VI*, II. v. 117; *Love's L. L.* IV. iii. 242; *2 Hen. IV*, v. i. 71 f.

[2] Chambers, iv. 168: ('John Hemings, one of his Majesty's Players, . . . for the pains and expenses of himself and the rest of the Company in coming from Mortlake in the County of Surrey unto the Court aforesaid and there presenting before His Majesty one play.' £30. 3 December 1603).

MARY SIDNEY, COUNTESS OF PEMBROKE, 12 MARCH 161$\frac{4}{5}$

By permission of the National Portrait Gallery

peril that might grow through the extraordinary concourse and assembly of people, to a new increase of the plague'), and £20 on 29 February.[1] One of the plays on New Year's Day was *Robin Goodfellow*, no doubt *A Midsummer Night's Dream*.[2] Theseus as huntsman would delight the King, and Oberon's benediction would be as suitable for Hampton Court as for Greenwich Palace.

In the meantime at Hampton Court, on 14, 16, 18 January, the King met the Prelatical and Puritan leaders in the English Church, and after conference with them, in which he made no secret of his break with 'Scotch Presbytery' and hatred of the same, as agreeable with 'Majesty' as the Devil with God, and pronounced his aphorism, 'No Bishop, no King!', he left Whitgift and Bancroft charmed beyond the limits of expectation, and their opponents correspondingly disappointed. 'Undoubtedly', said Whitgift, 'your Majesty speaks by the special assistance of God's Spirit'. 'I protest', cried Bancroft, on his knees, 'my heart melteth for joy that Almighty God, of His singular mercy, hath given us such a King as since Christ's time hath not been'. Whitgift died on 29 February, and Bancroft succeeded him as Archbishop of Canterbury. Cartwright had died on 27 December, at Warwick, and been buried in St. Mary's Church, his friend, John Dodd, preaching the funeral sermon..

By March the plague had sufficiently abated to permit the royal entry into London and the assembling of Parliament.[3] On 15 March Shakespeare and eight of his fellows as 'Grooms of the Chamber' rode or walked in their red liveries in the procession from the Tower to Westminster.[4] Pageants were presented on the route, and at Temple Bar a young actor (who may or may not have been of the King's Men) won by his oration deserving commendations. Alleyn, who had led the Admiral's Men into the service of young Prince Henry, made a 'gratulatory speech' to the King, in the person of 'Genius', with 'excellent action' and in 'a well tuned audible voyce'.[5] On 9 April the Privy Council granted the reopening of the theatres of the three companies, the

[1] Chambers, iv. 168. [2] *Ib.*, p. 118.

[3] Parliament met on the 19th.

[4] New Shak. Soc. Pub. 1877–9, app. ii. Law, *Shakespeare as a Groom of the Chamber*, p. 8. The list is that of 1603 (p. 587) but Shakespeare leads.

[5] Gilbert Dugdale (Arber, *Garner*, v. 650).

King's, the Prince's, and the Queen's, namely 'The *Globe* situate in Maiden Lane on the Bankside, the *Fortune* in Golding Lane, and the *Curtain* in Holywell'.[1]

Shakespeare, then, was busy in London when, on Sunday 18 March, his wife, as we may believe, attended as godmother the christening at Stratford of Thomas Greene's first child, Anne.[2] The Greenes, as we have seen,[3] were probably living with her at *New Place*. As Town Clerk Greene attended meetings of the Stratford Corporation on 30 March and 14 April, and kept the minutes.[4] For the Easter Term (25 April–21 May) he would be in London. In the absence of Greene and Shakespeare from Stratford, Philip Rogers the apothecary ran up a considerable account for the purchase of malt at *New Place*. Mistress Shakespeare's good nature seems to have been imposed on. Rogers bought malt of her on 27 March and 10 April, 3 May, 16 May, and 30 May, when the sum owing was forty shillings all but two pence.[5] Greene was at home on 1 June, when he kept the minutes of the Council-meeting and no doubt, with the Corporation, attended the Perrott Sermon in the Chapel after it.[6] Rogers got no more malt; but on 25 June, when apparently Shakespeare, after a visit to Oxford between 7 May and 16 June, was at home, he had the audacity, instead of paying anything, to borrow two shillings. He may have been Doctor Hall's apothecary, and Susanna Shakespeare, therefore, perhaps befriended him.

From 6 June to 2 August the Chapel-roof was under repair, Julines Shaw providing some timber for the leads.[7] On 16 July a seminary priest, Master John Sugar, captured at Rowington by that indefatigable puritan magistrate, Robert Burgoyne of Wroxall, was executed at Warwick, his body being cut down before he was dead, disembowelled, decapitated and quartered—the quarters being set as a warning on the Town gates.[8] Hatred

[1] Chambers, iv. 336.
[2] *Register*, p. 69.
[3] p. 543.
[4] *Council Book B.* 113 f.
[5] Halliwell-Phillipps, *Outlines*, ii. 77. The six purchases are all stated to have been from William Shakespeare; but if one and all were from Mistress Shakespeare it is probable that the borrowing from him and subsequent payment of 6*s*. to him would be in the terms given. For the recovery of the residue, Shakespeare instructed his attorney.
[6] *Council Book B.* 115.
[7] *Chamberlains' Account*, 11 Jan. 1605.
[8] Ryland, *Records of Rowington*, 174 ff.

of the Catholics was inflamed rather than quenched by James's pacific policy towards Spain. The Spanish ambassador was shortly expected in London for the ratification of a treaty of peace. He arrived on 10 August, Fernandez de Velasco, Constable of Castile, and was entertained at Somerset House; where, as Grooms of the Chamber, the King's players, to the number of twelve—including Heminge and Phillips and, of course, Shakespeare—were appointed to wait upon him. They were in attendance from the 9th to the 27th, and received for their services £21 12*s*. 0*d*. As they were not called upon to play, and it was their fate to witness such sports as bear-baiting and bull-baiting, rope-dancing, tumbling, and feats of agility on horseback, we may wonder what the Poet thought of this intolerable waste of his time whilst engaged on *Othello*.

1604

§ 114. *OTHELLO*

THIS, it seems, was the masterly work which occupied him amid scenes homely and trivial, and politically tragic, in the summer and autumn of 1604. It marks an astonishing development after *All's Well that Ends Well* and *Measure for Measure*. Those dramas, comedies only in name, part Tragedy from Tragedy—the *Tragedy of Thought* in *Julius Caesar* and *Hamlet*,[1] from the *Tragedy of Passion* in *Othello* and its successors, *Macbeth*, *King Lear*, *Antony and Cleopatra*, *Timon*, and *Coriolanus*. There was everything to make the Poet grave. Worse than decrepitude was maturity that is senile—talkative, dictatorial, idle, indulgent, spendthrift. At a glance Shakespeare saw the character of King James, and might have groaned:

> O nation miserable,
> When shalt thou see thy wholesome days again?[2]

His ablest minister, Sir James Melville, had told James when King of Scotland, that his subjects

'marvelled with stupefied minds to see his affairs so unluckily handled, complaining that his country was never in greater disorder, the Kirk never worse

[1] They are this, though in both Feeling predominates.

[2] *Macb.* IV. iii. 103, 105.

contented, its dissatisfaction influencing the whole Kingdom, his house at so evil a point, the nobility so divided, the barons never in greater poverty, the commons never more oppressed, never more taxations raised, mostly applied to the utility of private persons, never more parliaments holden, never more laws broken, his proclamations no ways obeyed'.[1]

Scotland in those days was far afield, but Elizabeth knew what was in store. It was probably the chief cause of her melancholy. Her successor's incapacity was only a lesser evil than a civil war. He imprisoned Raleigh and promoted Bacon, made peace with Spaniards and war on his Puritan subjects—who included, as Osborne, himself no Puritan, tells us, not only 'brainsick fools' but 'all the conscientious men of the nation'[2]—gabbled theology, and made favourites of the godless, and by reiteration of his 'divine right' did his best to undermine the doctrine among Protestant Englishmen. His neglect of business, his prodigal expense, his mean pleasures, the feuds of Scots and English, the feasting, drunkenness, and adultery of the Court, quickly rendered the whole environment of royalty contemptible.

For such a patron and his entourage Shakespeare provided strong meat. He has done with sexual 'grease', dismisses sensualist and lecher in words of unparalleled contempt from a woman:

> They are all but stomachs, and we all but food;
> They eat us, hungerly; and when they are full,
> They belch us.[3]

He draws now a 'demi-devil',[4] a villain calculated to shock the most reckless into sobriety. Iago is the most terrible human that has yet appeared in drama, not a Marlowean grotesque but a living iniquity. He is without that quality which the Elizabethan Christian called *Grace*.[5] He does not possess it, he does not believe in it, his psychology expressly excludes it. Man is made, not, as the good old Friar says in *Romeo and Juliet*,[6] of 'Grace' and 'rude Will', but of 'Reason', 'Will', and 'Sensuality', the last

[1] *Memoirs*, p. 185.

[2] *Historical Memoires.*

[3] *Oth.* III. iv. 104–6.

[4] V. ii. 299 f.: 'demand that demi-devil why he hath thus ensnared my soul and body?' Cf. 'fear him which is able to destroy both my soul and body in Hell' (Matthew x. 28).

[5] II. i. 86. In mockery Iago calls upon Grace and Heaven in III. iii. 373.

[6] II. iii. 28.

including what Hooker distinguishes as Appetite and Affection.[1] 'Virtue!' cries Iago (the 'virtue' of the Gospel,[2] which 'went out of Him', the influence and efficacy of the Divine Spirit), 'a fig!', and then follows the baldest statement of libertarianism, horrible to Protestant theologians:

''Tis in *ourselves* that we are thus or thus. Our bodies are our gardens, to the which our Wills are gardeners . . . If the balance of our lives had not one scale of Reason to poise another of Sensuality, the blood and baseness of our natures would conduct us to most preposterous conclusions; but we have Reason to cool our raging motions, our carnal stings, our unbitted lusts; whereof I take this that you call *love* to be a sect or scion . . . a lust of the blood and *a permission of the Will.*'[3]

Iago is no sensualist. He is the incarnation of what he terms *Will.* As Midas changes everything he touches into gold, and Hamlet into thought, so Iago turns it to determination. A Venetian, he hates Othello the Moor and Cassio the Florentine; as his superior officers, he envies them; but his malice is the excuse rather than the cause of his torture of them, in the execution of which he is immoderately industrious. That it is difficult and perilous and exciting, rather than it is cruel, is the chief attraction. After the tumult in the guardroom he exclaims,

By the mass, 'tis morning;
Pleasure and action make the hours seem short.[4]

And when Othello falls in a trance at his feet, he says:

Work on,
My medicine, work! Thus credulous fools are caught.[5]

These are supreme moments, not of hatred but of intellectual and volitional triumph.

His coldness, self-control, and lack of moral sense assist him. His *simplicity* disarms suspicion. Othello, Cassio, Desdemona, Roderigo, even his ill-used wife, Emilia, believe in him. On all sides he is the 'honest Iago'.[6] How shall we account for this but

[1] *Ecclesiastical Polity*, i. 167. Cf. Philippians iv. 7, Geneva margin: 'He divideth the mind into the heart—that is, into that part which is the seat of the *will* and *affections*, and into the higher part, whereby we *understand* and *reason* of matters.'

[2] Mark v. 30 ('Jesus being touched with true faith, although it be but weak, doth heal us by his virtue').

[3] I. iii. 322–40.

[4] II. iii. 384 f.

[5] IV. i. 45 f.

[6] I. iii. 295; II. iii. 6, 177, 341; V. i. 31, ii. 72, 154.

on the assumption that *he believes in himself*? His conscience does not trouble him. Circumstances, moreover, are greatly in his favour. Time, place, accident seem to conspire on his behalf. What momentous issues depend on Desdemona's loss of her handkerchief, and her little, wretched white lie prompted by love of her husband! Like the detention of the Friar's messenger in *Romeo and Juliet* and the old man's stumbling among the graves, they are out of all proportion to their consequences. So, too, is Cassio's cup of wine. Satan might be at the back of these incidents. Most of all, Iago is aided and abetted by the temperament of those on whom he works. Roderigo is a simpleton, Cassio a gallant, Desdemona a child. The last drops her unlucky words as she does her handkerchief. They were unpardonable were they not so artless. How a girl born and bred in Venice can be so innocent is a miracle. She is above caution and tact, and we rejoice that she is: we would not have her on a lower plane; but it means her husband's ruin and her death. And of Othello, what can we say but with Emilia, noble as he is,

> O gull, O dolt, as ignorant as dirt?[1]

After Hamlet, Othello—the hero who cannot think, great in impulse and instinct, but 'when he thinks thinks wrong'.[2] He is a mixture of the simple and profound, a handsome swarthy Arab in the prime of life, 'declining into the vale of years yet not much',[3] ten years older than Iago, if ten years younger in knowledge of the world; a brave and trained soldier, more at home in the camp than the city, devoted to Venice, where with the zeal of a convert, and the singleness of his primitive nature, he has embraced the Christian religion.

Othello is not easily jealous. He believes implicitly in Desdemona, as in Iago; and his faith in her is only disturbed by his faith in him. He has no shadow of doubt of either until the play is half over. Nor is his wrath easily excited. He maintains a dignified serenity when Brabantio and his party come upon him in the night with drawn swords and insulting cries. But when suspicion is aroused, he is

> Perplexed in the extreme;[4]

[1] v. ii. 163 f.

[2] Raleigh, *Shakespeare*, 141 f.

[3] III. iii. 265 f. Past the half of threescore years and ten; say 38.

[4] v. ii. 345.

and his rage is terrible, dominating his reason:

My blood begins my safer guides to rule
And passion, having my best judgment collied,
Assays to lead the way.[1]

He might learn of Iago to control his passion. Iago knows it, and insidiously injects the poison, until it burns in his veins like a fever:

OTHELLO. I would have him nine years a-killing. A fine woman! a fair woman! a sweet woman!

IAGO. Nay, you must forget that.

OTHELLO. Ay, let her rot, and perish, and be damned to-night, for she shall not live . . . O, the world hath not a sweeter creature, . . . so delicate with her needle, . . . an admirable musician . . . of so high and plenteous wit and invention . . . of so gentle a condition!

IAGO. Ay, too gentle.

OTHELLO. Nay, that's certain: *but yet the pity of it, Iago! O Iago, the pity of it, Iago!*[2]

Here is the Christian, with his love of whatsoever things are true and beautiful, and sense of loss irreparable. We hear the lamentation of his noble riven heart in the words,

Othello's occupation's gone![3]

the wail of which is continued in the *o*-s of the lines that follow (so preposterous in their *reasoning*, enough to make Iago grin):

Villain, be sure thou prove my love a whore;
Be sure of it; give me the ocular proof;
Or, by the worth of mine eternal soul,
Thou had'st been better have been born a dog,[4]
Than answer my waked wrath.[5]

The worth of mine eternal soul. Iago knows that Othello's baptism and the sacraments are sacred to him, as his love for Desdemona—

Were't to renounce his Baptism,
All Seals and Symbols of redeemed sin.[6]

[1] II. iii. 205–7.

[2] IV. i. 188–207. Note the repetition, in the last line of the name of his friend.

[3] III. iii. 357.

[4] It troubles Iago lightly that he is no 'better than a dog', even of the eastern, scavenger, outcast kind Othello has in mind.

[5] III. iii. 359–63.

[6] II. iii. 349 f.

The Moor and his wife are pious.[1] They meet in Cyprus after the storm as in 'the haven where they would be':

> If after every tempest come such calms,
> May the winds blow till they have wakened death,
> And let the labouring bark climb hills of seas
> Olympus high, and duck again as low
> As Hell's from Heaven![2]

His Christian spirit mingles and struggles with his jealousy:

> If thou dost slander her and torture me,
> *Never pray more*; abandon all remorse;
> On horror's head horrors accumulate;
> Do deeds to make Heaven weep, all earth amazed;
> For nothing can'st thou to damnation add
> Greater than that.[3]

Verbiage to Iago, who never prayed in his life, nor felt a twinge of remorse, or any sense of righteous horror, nor cares a straw for Heaven's tears or his own 'damnation', these words reveal the depth of Othello's faith. Passionately Christian is his denunciation of Desdemona. It is his agonizing duty to tell her what she is:

> this hand of yours requires
> A sequester from liberty, fasting and prayer.[4]

With his sense of cruel personal wrong blends that of her offence against God. Image after image comes into his mind from the Bible—the Sermon on the Mount,[5] Job,[6] Proverbs,[7] the

[1] Both are accustomed to pray. She follows the injunction, 'But when thou prayest, enter into thy closet, and when thou hast shut thy door, pray unto thy Father which is in secret' (Matthew vi. 6). Othello has observed her:

> A closet lock-and-key of villanous secrets:
> And yet she'll kneel and pray, I have seen her do 't (IV. ii. 22 f.).

Othello cries to the brawling officers, 'For *Christian* shame, put by this *barbarous* brawl!' (II. iii. 172). He is infinitely more Christian than the degenerate, conventional believers among whom he is thrown.

[2] 'He commandeth and raiseth the stormy wind, and it lifteth up the waves thereof. They mount up to the heaven, and descend to the deep. He turneth the storm to calm, so that the waves thereof are still. When they are quieted they are glad, and He bringeth them unto the haven where they would be' (Psalm cvii. 23 ff.).

[3] III. iii. 368–73.

[4] III. iv. 39 f.

[5] IV. ii. 22 f. (prayer in secret).

[6] *Ib.* 47–52 (Heaven's trial by affliction, sores, poverty, captivity, patience).

[7] *Ib.* 59–62 (Proverbs v. 15: 'Drink the water of thy cistern'; 18, 'let thy fountain be blessed, and rejoice in the wife of thy youth').

Decalogue,[1] John,[2] Thessalonians,[3] Matthew xvi.[4] And the murder scene is less painful because the personal motive has vanished, and all is for Righteousness:

It is the Cause, it is the Cause, my soul:
Let me not name it to you, *you chaste Stars.*[5]
                                        I must weep,
But they are cruel tears; this sorrow's Heavenly,
It strikes where it doth love.[6]
Have you prayed to-night, Desdemona? . . .
If you bethink yourself of any crime
Unreconciled as yet to God and Grace,
Solicit for it straight . . .
I would not kill thy unprepared spirit:
No, God forfend, I would not kill thy soul.[7]

He stifles her. And 'Chaos is come again'[8]—

Methinks it should be now a huge Eclipse
Of sun and moon, and that the affrighted Globe
Should yawn at alteration.[9]

He is ready for the end of the world. At this moment, too late, he learns the awful truth. Emilia's outburst, which redeems her from all evil, scatters at last the cloud of hideous misunderstanding. Chaos now is insufficient. He deserves Hell:

                    When we shall meet at 'Compt,[10]
This look of thine will hurl my soul from Heaven,
And fiends will snatch at it.[11]

[1] IV. ii. 70, 72, 76, &c. (Exodus xx. 14: 'Thou shalt not commit adultery').

[2] *Ib.* 78 ('The bawdy wind that kisses all.' Cf. John iii. 8: 'The wind bloweth where it listeth, with free and wandering blasts.' Geneva with margin. So elsewhere in Shakespeare—'idle wind', 'strumpet wind', 'chartered libertine').

[3] *Ib.* 83 ('vessel'. Cf. 1 Thessalonians iv. 3 f.: 'Every one should possess his vessel in holiness').

[4] *Ib.* 91 ff. ('You have the office opposite to St. Peter and keep the gate of Hell. I pray you, turn the key.' Cf. Matthew xvi. 18 f.: 'Thou art Peter, and upon this rock I will build my church, and the gates of Hell shall not overcome it. And I will give unto thee the keys of the Kingdom of Heaven').

[5] V. ii. 1 f.

[6] 20–2. Cf. Proverbs iii. 12: 'The Lord correcteth him whom He loveth.'

[7] 25–32.

[8] III. iii. 92.

[9] V. ii. 98 ff. Cf. Ovid, *Metam.* i and Revelation vi. 12: 'A great earthquake, and the sun was black . . . and the moon like blood, and the stars fell into the earth.'

[10] Account, the Last Judgement.

[11] 273–5.

He calls for it. The torments from which Claudio shrank he welcomes:

> Whip me, ye devils,
> From the possession of this heavenly sight!
> Blow me about in winds! roast me in sulphur!
> Wash me in steep-down gulfs of liquid fire!
> O Desdemona! Desdemona! dead!
> Oh! Oh! Oh![1]

He has kissed and slain the most pure and innocent. He is another Judas, and like Judas he will take his cursed life:

> Speak of me as I am . . .
> Of one not easily jealous, but being wrought
> Perplex'd in the extreme; of one whose hand,
> Like the base Judean,[2] threw a pearl away
> Richer than all his tribe;[3] of one whose subdued eyes,
> Albeit unused to the melting mood,
> Drop tears as fast as the Arabian trees
> Their medicinal gum. Set you down this;
> And say besides, that in Aleppo once
> Where a malignant and a turban'd Turk
> Beat a Venetian and traduced the state,
> I took by the throat the circumcised dog,
> And smote him, thus. [*He stabs himself.*][4]

With Christian fervour, he kills himself as an *infidel*. Bending over his wife, and kissing her again as one worthy of Christ, he likens himself again to the archtraitor—

> I kissed there ere I killed thee: no way but this,
> Killing myself to die upon a kiss.[5]

Shakespeare and his company played *Othello*, Burbage taking the part of the Moor, on Hallowmas Day, in the great banqueting-house at Whitehall,[6] which was made ready for the occasion at a cost of 78*s*. 8*d*.[7] Three days later, Sunday 4 November, they gave *The Merry Wives of Windsor*,[6] in the same place. The

[1] v. ii. 277–82.

[2] Editors who read 'Indian' for 'Judean', and would admit in this great speech a paltry allusion to an Indian chief who scattered gems upon the sea, are best unnamed and forgotten.

[3] The pearl thrown away was Desdemona, richer than all the tribe of Othello; as Christ was the pearl of great price cast away by Judas, richer than all the tribe of Judas, to which Jesus belonged.

[4] v. ii. 342–56.

[5] *Ib.* 358 f. Cf. Matthew xxvi. 49, xxvii. 5.

[6] Chambers, iv. 171.

[7] Halliwell-Phillipps, *Outlines*, ii. 165.

building, Holinshed tells us, was 'in the manner and form of a long square, three hundred, thirty and two foot in measure about', the sides having 'ten heights of degrees for people to stand upon'.[1] It was too large. Justice could not be done to Shakespeare's lines in an auditory where the actor had to strain his voice to be heard. The 'great chamber', therefore, was prepared, at a charge of 39*s.* 4*d.*,[2] for the Christmas performances.

1604–5

§ 115. PUBLIC AND PERSONAL

ON 19 November Shakespeare probably attended the marriage in St. Olave's in Silver Street of Stephen Bellot and Mary Montjoy, the young people in whose welfare he had interested himself as a resident in her father's house.[3] In December he and his fellows attracted large audiences at the *Globe* with a play on the King's escape in Scotland (on 5 August 1600) from what is known as the 'Gowrie Conspiracy'. Great mystery attached to this affair, about which the King romanced extravagantly. The players did shrewdly in giving a dramatic version of it, presumably favourable to his Majesty, on the stage; but there was risk all the same of displeasure. John Chamberlain wrote from London to Sir Ralph Winwood on 18 December,

> *The Tragedy of Gowrie*, with all actions and actors, hath been twice represented by the King's Players, with exceeding concourse of all sorts of people; but whether the matter or manner be not well handled, or that it be thought unfit that princes should be played on the stage in their life-time, I hear that some great councillors are much displeased with it, and so it is thought it shall be forbidden.[4]

Whatever objection, if any, was taken, the King's Players were much in evidence at the Court at Christmas. They performed *Measure for Measure* on 26 December, *The Comedy of Errors* on the 28th, *Henry the Fifth* on 7 January, and Jonson's *Every Man out of His Humour* on the 8th.[5] They also played *Love's Labour's Lots* before the Queen at the house of the Earl of Southampton, or of

[1] *Chronicles*, iii. 1315.

[2] Halliwell-Phillipps, *Outlines*, ii. 165.

[3] 'November 19. Stephen Plott and Mary Montjoye' (Register).

[4] Winwood, ii. 41.

[5] Chambers, iv. 171 f.

Robert Cecil (now Viscount Cranborne). Sir Walter Cope writes to Cecil early in the new year:

I have sent and been all this morning hunting for players, jugglers, and such kind of creatures, but find them hard to find; wherefore leaving notes for them to seek me, Burbage is come, and says there is no new play that the Queen hath not seen, but they have revived an old one called *Love's Labour's Lost*: which for wit and mirth, he says, will please her exceedingly; and this is appointed to be played tomorrow night at my Lord of Southampton's: unless you send a writ to remove the *corpus cum causa* to your house in Strand. Burbage is my messenger, ready attending your pleasure.[1]

The extension of the Christmas festivities beyond 6 January was an indulgence of the new reign, and is thus commented on by Dudley Carleton in a letter to Chamberlain of 15 January:

It seems we shall have Christmas all the year, and therefore I shall never be out of matter. The last night's revels were kept at my Lord of Cranborne's, where the Queen, with the Duke of Holst, and a great part of the Court were feasted; and the like two nights before at my Lord of Southampton's. The Temples have both of them done somewhat since Twelfthtide, but nothing memorable save that it was observed on Friday last at night (11 January) the greatest part of the female audience was the sisterhood of Blackfriars.[2]

If the 'last night' was Monday 14 January, the night of revelling at the Earl of Southampton's would be Saturday the 12th; and we shall not be far wrong in dating Cope's letter the 11 January.[3]

Shakespeare and his fellows were again to the front at Shrovetide. They played Jonson's *Every Man in His Humour* on 2 February (Candlemas); had a piece ready on Sunday the 3rd, which for some reason was 'discharged': performed *The Merchant of Venice* on Shrove Sunday the 10th, a play called *The Spanish Maze* on the 11th, and *The Merchant of Venice*, a second time by the King's command, on Shrove Tuesday the 12th.[4]

They received in payment £60 on 21 January, £40 on 24

[1] *Hist. MSS.* iii. 148.

[2] *S.P. Dom. Jac. I.* xii. 13.

[3] There is a curious notice of the performance of *Love's Labour's Lost* in the Audit Office Account (Chambers, iv. 172): 'Between New Year's Day and Twelfth Day a play of Loves Labours Lost.' As no payment was made by the Treasurer of the Chamber for this performance we may wonder why the entry was made. It was evidently an afterthought, and hence a slip in the date. The latter was between New Year's Day and the conclusion of Christmas, correctly 6 Jan., but at the Court this year at least a week later.

[4] Chambers, iv. 171 f.

February, and £10 more on 28 April for the play not presented on 3 February.[1]

Master Greene spent Christmas in Stratford, where he attended Council Meetings on 14 December 1604 and 11 January 1605,[2] and no doubt accompanied the brethren to Charlecote on 28 December and to Snitterfield on 2 January when they were entertained respectively by Sir Thomas Lucy the Second and Master Bartholomew Hales. He would return to London for the Hilary term (23 January to 12 February), and apparently he was not in Stratford again until May. His deputy kept the minutes at Council meetings on 5 and 24 April.[3] At the latter meeting it was

agreed, that whereas heretofore the Bailiff and Burgesses have been suitors to Sir Julius Caesar for the renewing of the Charter, Master Greene shall have all the notes of the proceedings and acquaint Sir Julius Caesar with the same, and deal with him in such sort as he shall think fit for the effecting thereof: which notes are now delivered to Francis Collins to be delivered to Master Greene: which notes are six in number and in paper.

It was now Easter term (17 April to 13 May), and into Greene's capable hands were delivered the papers aforesaid by Shakespeare's solicitor in Stratford, Francis Collins. At the end of term Greene rode home, attended a Council meeting on 24 May,[4] heard the Perrott sermon in the Chapel the same day (preached by Master Knowles of Alveston in place of the vicar, Master Byfield, who had just left Stratford), and joined in the 'drinking' or 'banquet', which followed the sermon, at Master Wyatt's house.[5] His sojourn was a brief one, for he had to be in London for Trinity term (31 May to 19 June).

In the meantime players and playwriters were in trouble for their free comment on public affairs. Within three months of the King's state-entry into London he was ridiculed on the stage, and his queen joined in the laughter at his expense. 'For pity's sake', wrote the French ambassador, de Beaumont, who did not love the queen, on 14 June 1604, 'consider what must be the state and condition of a Prince whom the preachers openly attack in the pulpit, whom the comedians of the metropolis bring

[1] Chambers, iv. 171 f.

[2] *Council Book B*, 120 f.

[3] *Ib.* 122 f.

[4] *Ib.* 124.

[5] *Chamberlain's Account*, 13 Jan. 1606.

upon the stage, and whose wife attends these representations in order to enjoy the laugh against her husband.'[1] Queen Anne's countenance encouraged these liberties which grew to a head the following year. 'They do not forbear', Calvert wrote to Winwood on 28 March 1605, 'to present upon the stage the whole course of this present time, not sparing the King, state or religion, in so great absurdity and with such liberty that any would be afraid to hear them.'[2] The Children at the Blackfriars, in a play called *Eastward Ho!* by Ben Jonson, Chapman, and Marston, satirized the greed of hungry Scots for lucrative offices in England, and the King's creation of titles as a means of raising money. A boy actor mimicked the royal brogue, 'I ken the man weel: he is one of my thirty-pound knights'. The authorities at last took action. Jonson and Chapman were sent to prison, where they were in danger of losing their ears,[3] and Marston, the chief offender, fled, to find his way to Newgate later.[4] Shakespeare, whatever his opinion of King or Court, did not indulge in personalities.

His quiet in Silver Street cannot have been unaffected by differences between Montjoy and his son-in-law, which resulted in the latter's departure with his wife, in or near April 1605, into the parish of St. Sepulchre's, to lodge with Shakespeare's acquaintance, the writer, George Wilkins.[5] That month Robert Harvard of Southwark married Katherine Rogers at Stratford.[6] Their home was in the parish of St. Saviour's, not far from the *Globe*, and here their famous son, John Harvard, was born in November 1607.[7] In May, Shakespeare lost his friend and fellow, Augustine Phillips. He died at Mortlake after making his will on the 4th of that month, which was proved by his widow on the 13th.[8]

I commend my soul [he declared] into the hands of Almighty God, my Maker and Saviour and Redeemer, in whom and by the merits of the

[1] Von Raumer, *History of the Sixteenth and Seventeenth Centuries*, ii. 206.

[2] Winwood, ii. 54.

[3] Chambers, i. 326, ii. 51, iii. 254.

[4] In June 1608. *Ib.* iii. 428.

[5] Wallace, *Nebraska University Studies*, x. 289.

[6] 'Apriell 8 Robertus Harwood to Katharina Rogers' (*Register*, p. 21).

[7] He was baptized in St. Saviour's: 'Nov. 29 John Harvye, s. of Robert a Butcher.'

[8] Collier, *Memoirs of Actors*, p. 24.

Second Person, Jesus Christ, I trust and believe assuredly to be saved, and to have clear remission and forgiveness of my sins; and I commit my body to be buried in the chancel of the parish-church.

He was 'gentleman' and well-off, left £5 to the poor of Mortlake, 20*s.* to the preacher of his funeral sermon (which assuredly Shakespeare heard), and bequests to his widow and children, brothers and sisters (or their children), and comrades at the *Globe*. These last are thus enumerated:

to my fellow, William Shakespeare, a thirty shilling piece in gold; to my fellow, Henry Condell, one other thirty shilling piece in gold; to my servant, Christopher Beeston, thirty shillings in gold; to my fellow, Lawrence Fletcher, twenty shillings in gold; to my fellow Robert Armin, twenty shillings in gold; to my fellow, Richard Cowley, twenty shillings in gold; to my fellow, Alexander Cooke, twenty shillings in gold; to my fellow, Nicholas Tooley, twenty shillings in gold.

Three others of his 'company' are executors—John Heminge, Richard Burbage, and William Sly: to whom he bequeaths a bowl of silver, of the value of £5, apiece.[1] His 'apprentices', as we have seen, were not forgotten.[2]

The prosperity and, it should be noticed, the 'frugality' of the King's Players are the subject of satirical comment in the whimsical 'biography' of Gamaliel Ratsey, a highwayman executed at Bedford on 26 March. 'The very best' of players, says the hero, 'have sometimes been content to go home at night with fifteen pence apiece; others, whom Fortune hath favoured, by penny sparing and long practice of playing are grown so wealthy that they have expected to be knighted, or at least to be conjunct in authority and to sit with men of great worship on the bench of justice.' And addressing 'the chiefest' of a company whom he meets on tour in the country, he says, with obvious reference to Burbage, 'Thou hast a good presence, methinks thou darkenest thy merit by playing in the country; get thee to London, for if one man were dead they will have much need of such a one as thou art; I durst venture all the money in my purse on thy head to play Hamlet with him for a wager.' He continues, with an equally obvious allusion to Shakespeare, 'There thou shalt learn to be *frugal*, and when thou feelest thy purse well-lined, buy thee some *Place* or lordship in the country, that growing weary of playing thy money may there bring thee to

[1] Collier, *Memoirs of Actors*, pp. 85–8.

[2] Vol. i, pp. 210–11.

dignity and reputation.' The highwayman concludes by making the player kneel down and receive the title 'Sir Simon Two Shares-and-a-Half'. Burbage had two-and-a-half shares in the *Globe*.

As a result of his thrift and industry, Shakespeare was able to purchase, on 24 July, a moiety of the lease of the Stratford Tithes, of late the property of Sir John Huband of Ipsley, for the large sum of £440, of which only £20 was unpaid on 31 January 1606.[1] The conveyance exists, signed by the vendor, Sir John's brother and heir, Rafe Huband, in the presence of William Huband, Anthony Nash (Shakespeare's friend at Welcombe), and Francis Collins, his lawyer. The same day, 24 July 1605, his sister Joan Hart's son, Thomas, was baptized in the parish church of Stratford.

1605

§ 116. DEATH OF SIR THOMAS LUCY THE SECOND

SIR THOMAS LUCY made his peace, as we have seen, with the Stratford Corporation. For his father's sake they would take a good deal at his hands. He suffered from ill health, and on his return home, after search for health, in November 1604, they gave him a welcome, sending him a present of fish and cake. On his part he entertained them at Charlecote on 28 December, when the bailiff, Master John Smith, ironmonger, nephew of the late John Watson, Bishop of Winchester, bestowed on the 'usher of the hall', the 'yeoman of the pantry', the 'butler', and the 'cook' half a crown apiece, and on the 'porter' two shillings. Lucy died the following summer, on 16 July, and was buried on 20 August at Charlecote. His decease was noted in October with that of other 'Parliament-men of mark'; and his will was proved in November, when the country was alarmed over Gunpowder Plot. He was twice married, had many children, cared for riding and reading, but lacked the force of his father. His bequest to his son and heir, Thomas, interests us chiefly because of that father mentioned in it:

'To my son and heir, Thomas, the gilt bason and ewer graven which was my

[1] As we learn from an item in Rafe Huband's Inventory of this date: 'There was Owinge by Mr. Shakespre xx li.' (E. A. B. Barnard, *New Links with Shakespeare*, p. 61.)

MONUMENT TO SIR THOMAS LUCY (1551–1605) IN CHARLECOTE CHURCH

From Shakespeare's Warwickshire Contemporaries *by Charlotte C. Stopes, by permission of the Shakespeare Head Press*

father's, with the two gilded engraven livery pots, and a nest of gilded bowls with a cover, and a gilded salt, together with a dozen of gilded spoons; to whom I also give all my household stuff at Sutton'—his mother's home near Tenbury—'and my best horse and furniture at his choice, both to be chosen by him. And all my French and Italian books.'

This third Thomas, born in 1586 and educated at Magdalen College, Oxford, and Lincoln's Inn, was already a knight and a lover of horses. He proved a mild namesake of his grandfather, more keen on chasing the deer than a papist, with long locks instead of a round head, a gentleman of leisure and learning rather than a statesman.

1605

§ 117. *THE ADVANCEMENT OF LEARNING*

BACON's interest in Shakespeare we have noted.[1] What evidence is there of Shakespeare's interest in Bacon? The latter published in 1597 the first edition of his *Essays*, a little work of ten short disquisitions on 'studies', 'discourse', 'ceremonies and respects', 'followers and friends', 'suitors', 'expense', 'health', 'honour and reputation', 'faction', and 'negociations'. They show the thinker, scholar, and lawyer—keen, cautious, politic, timid, delicate, cold. If Shakespeare read this little book, as he probably did, he must have recognized its merits and felt its limitations. 'There is little friendship in the world,' says the author, 'and least of all between equals.'[2] Shakespeare's drama is full of friendship, and much of it is between equals. We think of Romeo, Mercutio, and Benvolio, Antonio and Bassanio, Hamlet and Horatio, Benedick and Claudio, and a score of others, and of girl and woman friends still more numerous.

In 1605 Bacon brought out his important volume, with a dedication to King James, '*Of the Proficience and Advancement of Learning*'. Shakespeare was acquainted with this work, probably in an earlier form. When writing *Troilus and Cressida*, probably therefore prior to February 1603,[3] in manuscript, he read the following:

Therefore we see the iron in particular sympathy moveth to the load-

[1] pp. 424–7. [2] *Essay*, iv.

[3] It is possible that the passages adduced were part of a revision of the play prior to its publication in 1609.

stone, but yet if it exceed a certain quantity it moveth to the earth, which is the region and country of massy bodies; so may we see that water and massy bodies move to the centre of the earth, but rather than to suffer a divulsion in the continuance of Nature they will move upwards from the centre of the earth (II. xx. 7).

And he wrote—

As iron is adamant, as earth to the centre (III. ii. 186);

and—

as the very centre of the earth,
Drawing all things to it.

It is unnecessary to assume, as some have done, that either Bacon or Shakespeare anticipated Newton.

Again the Poet read:

Is not the opinion of Aristotle worthy to be regarded wherein he saith, That young men are no fit auditors of moral philosophy, because they are not settled from the boiling heat of their affections, nor attempered with time and experience (II. xxii. 13).

And he put into the mouth of Hector these lines:

Paris and Troilus, you have both said well;
And on the cause and question now in hand—

(the subject of Helena)—

Have glozed, but superficially; not much
Unlike young men whom Aristotle thought
Unfit to hear moral philosophy.
The reasons you allege do more conduce
To the hot passion of distempered blood
Than to make up a free determination
Twixt right and wrong (II. ii. 163–71).

Such parallels, however, are far to seek.

On the other hand, if Bacon was sufficiently interested in 1596 in Shakespeare's *Richard the Second* to secure a copy of the drama for his collection of manuscript pieces,[1] we may not unreasonably look for some reflection of Shakespeare's work in *The Advancement of Learning*.

Bacon had become 'Sir Francis' on King James's accession, and high promotion awaited him if he could win the royal confidence. In his excuse it must be said that his amazing address to the King in the *Advancement* was penned at the outset of his

[1] pp. 424–7.

FRANCIS BACON, VISCOUNT ST. ALBANS

By permission of the National Portrait Gallery

disastrous reign, and with the justifiable eagerness of a man of genius who had not received the recognition he expected and deserved at the hands of the late Queen. Much as Elizabeth appreciated the pretty and clever youth, she did not love the man; nor was this due merely or chiefly to his opposition in Parliament or the jealousy of his kinsmen, the Cecils. She liked, as already said, manly men about her, who had the courage, on occasion and with due respect, to stand up against her, spirited and athletic, and if handsome all the better. Bacon was not handsome nor athletic nor courageous. He was soft in physique, luxurious in his tastes, unenthusiastic save for knowledge, and incapable of fellowship with Raleigh or Essex. He was led, moreover, by a cringing prudence, as different as can be from the shrewd and courteous wisdom of old Burghley. He thus delivers himself to the King:

> I have been touched, yea, and possessed with an extreme wonder at those your virtues and faculties which the philosophers call intellectual, and largeness of your capacity, the faithfulness of your memory, the swiftness of your apprehension, the penetration of your judgment, and the facility and order of your elocution . . . Your Majesty's manner of speech is indeed Prince-like, flowing as from a fountain, and yet streaming and branching itself into Nature's order, full of facility and felicity, imitating none and inimitable by any . . . There hath not been since Christ's time any king or temporal monarch which hath been so learned in all literature and erudition, divine and human.

This by way of preface. Coming to his object he says:

> to have the true testimonial concerning the dignity of learning to be better heard, I think good to deliver it from the discredits and disgraces which it hath received . . . And as for the disgraces which learning receiveth from politics, they be of this nature: that learning doth soften men's minds and makes them more *unapt for the honour and exercise of arms*, that it doth *mar and pervert men's dispositions for matter of government* and policy in making them *too curious and irresolute* by variety of reading, or too peremptory or positive by strictness of rules and axioms, . . . or at least that it doth *divert men's travails from action and business* and bringeth them to *a love of leisure and privateness*.

Shakespeare must have smiled as he read this. Who was the most recent offender but himself? Where is there a better understanding or criticism of his repeated portrayal of the 'bookish' prince? So much, indeed, of this is applicable to Hamlet that if King James had been in the least conscious of his failings, he might have thought the dramatist rather personal. But, continues Bacon, 'it is almost without instance that ever any government was disastrous that was in the hands of learned governors'. Twenty years later Englishmen had reason to form a different opinion. King James and Bacon proved a feeble exchange for Queen Elizabeth and Burleigh. The best minds sighed for the old days. Than under Elizabeth, Bacon confesses, 'this part of the Island never had forty years of better times'. He adds, 'not through the calmness of the season, but through the wisdom of her regiment'. Unfortunately by 'wisdom' he means *learning*— 'language, science, divinity, humanity' or classical knowledge: which, as Shakespeare has shown us, are another matter. King James, Bacon, Hamlet were learned; but in 'regiment', otherwise statesmanship, they were not wise.

1605

§ 118. GUNPOWDER PLOT

POLITICAL wisdom might have prevented the Gunpowder Plot. King James was too busy with 'divinity' and pleasure, and too ignorant of *men*, to understand toleration for Catholics and Puritans. In July and August 1605 he was on progress. He came to Hanwell, Sir Anthony Cope's, on 20 August—on which day Sir Thomas Lucy the Second was buried at Charlecote. Proceeding through Wroxton, Sir William Pope's, and Woodstock, he arrived in Oxford on the 27th. It was his first formal visit to the University City, and he was accompanied by the Queen and Prince Henry. The royal party were greeted with a pageant of the 'Three Sibyls' (*Tres Sibyllae*) devised by Doctor Matthew Gwynne, Regius Professor of Physic. He had read in Holinshed's *Historie of Scotlande*[1] how 'three women in strange and ferly apparel resembling creatures of an elder world' met Macbeth and Banquo on their journey to Forres, and welcoming the first with the successive titles, Thane of Glamis, Thane of Cawdor, and 'Macbeth that hereafter shalt be King', promised his companion 'greater benefits', for 'he shall reign, but with an unlucky end, neither leave any issue behind him; contrarily

[1] ii. 170.

thou shalt not reign, but of thee those shall be born which shall govern the kingdom by long order of continual descent'. Three students of St. John's, clad in the becoming garb of Sibyls, singing in turn charming incantations, pronounced themselves those sisters who predicted the succession to Banquo's issue. They had come again, to foretell to His Majesty a long and happy reign, a lineage of many kings, and a never-failing heir to the British crown.

Shakespeare, as a groom of the chamber, may have been present and witnessed the pageant, or he may have heard of it on a subsequent visit to Oxford with his company on 9 October.[1] The seeing or hearing of it certainly sent him to Holinshed, where he found material for *Macbeth*. Interpreting the 'Sibyls' or 'Weird Sisters' of the story as 'witches' and 'handmaids of Hecate', and fastening on the idea of 'illusion', in its profound Biblical sense, he worked with his usual haste on the drama and was in the fever of composition, we may think, when 'Hell and its instruments' were suddenly confronted and baffled by the discovery of the Gunpowder Plot.

Warwickshire was a meeting-ground of the conspirators. Robert Catesby was the son and heir of the late Sir William Catesby of Bushwood, near Lapworth; John Wright was his tenant at Lapworth; John Grant was the son of Thomas Grant of Northbrooke, Snitterfield; Robert Winter lived at Huddington in Worcestershire. To be in their neighbourhood, young Sir Everard Digby of Gothurst, Buckinghamshire, rented Coughton Court, near Alcester, and Ambrose Rookwood of Coldham Hall, Suffolk, hired Clopton House about Michaelmas 1605. To provide funds for the enterprise Catesby sold Bushwood to Sir Edward Greville. On Monday 4 November at night Guy Fawkes was arrested in the vaults of Thomas Percy's tenement adjoining the Parliament House at Westminster, and the conspirators, gathered in London for the opening of Parliament next day, fled into the country—to Dunchurch, Warwick, Northbrooke, Alcester, and thence to Huddington, where they arrived about 2 o'clock in the afternoon of Wednesday the 6th. Before daybreak of Thursday they were off again for Wales. They reached Holbeach House on the Staffordshire border at

[1] J. T. Murray, *Engl. Dramatic Companies*, ii. 379.

10 o'clock at night. They got no farther. In the early hours of Friday, Catesby, Rookwood, and Grant were severely burned by an explosion of gunpowder which they were drying at the fire. They were unable to proceed, and their companions fled or resolved to face the worst. In the meantime Warwick, Stratford, and Alcester had been aroused. Hue and cry pursued the fugitives. Winter was struck by a blacksmith in Warwick, and sixteen of the party were captured.[1] Marmaduke Ward (of Newby in Yorkshire) was seized in Alcester riding through the town an hour after the main body of the conspirators.[2] The Bailiff of Stratford, William Wyatt, on Wednesday the 6th bought up gunpowder in the town, armed the constables with calivers, put the gaol in readiness, and raided Clopton House, where he attached Master Thomas Pearse, and seized a large quantity of Romanist relics.[3] Others at Clopton followed the main troop to Alcester and there, seeing the town disturbed, turned aside to Bidford, where they were taken.[4] Thomas Tempest of Bridgetown, Stratford, a retainer of Lord and Lady Carew, the owners of Clopton, wrote to him on the 8th at the Savoy—

May it please your honours to be certified of the news which is lately happened in Warwickshire. As upon Monday night last, being the fourth of this month,[5] the Castle stable at Warwick was broken, eight or nine great horse for service, worth some threescore pound or a hundred mark a horse, carried away by one Master Winter of Huddington and one Master Grant of Northbrooke your neighbour hereby with divers other gentlemen yet unknown. Master Rookwood, the gentleman at Clopton, is greatly suspected, for that he hath not been there this ten or twelve days, but it is certainly known that a brother of his is in the action. It is reported that these gentlemen be now at Winter's house, whither old Sir Fulke Greville hath raised the country for their apprehension. I fear me greatly that Master Rookwood is one, for he had some five or six great horse besides his road-geldings; now they be all gone, not one left there, nor never a man about the house but his wife, one Mistress Momson, Mistress Key, and servant-maids, and a little boy his page. Here is a cloakbag stayed by the Bailiff of Stratford, which came from Northbrooke to be delivered to one George Badger there.[6] It is full of copes, vestments, crosses, crucifixes, chalices and other massing

[1] *Discourse of the Powder Treason* by the King.

[2] *Gunpowder Plot Books*, i. 47.

[3] *Misc. Doc.* x. 4.

[4] *Gunpowder Plot Books.*

[5] It was the night of Tuesday the fifth: *State Papers Dom. Jas. I.*

[6] For George Badger see pp. 50, 156, 192, 873.

CLOPTON HOUSE

Water-colour drawing by ROBERT BELL WHELER, *1801*

relics.[1] The party that brought them is sent to the Gaol. I have seized all the goods in Clopton to the use of my lord—it is not much, the most of their furniture is hired and borrowed, some of one and some of another. I would gladly know your honours' pleasure therein.

Thus desiring Almighty God to keep your honours in all safety, I end. This eight of November, Bridgetown, *anno* 1605. Your obedient servant, Thomas Tempest.

The Sheriff[2] was at Clopton with a great company as upon Wednesday last to search the house, and seemed to make seizure of the goods. He comforted the gentlewoman, and so went away.[3]

That day, Friday, the fugitives were overtaken about 11 o'clock at Holbeach. Intrepid Thomas Winter, younger brother of Robert, shall tell what happened:

As I walked into the court I was shot in the shoulder [with an arrow from a cross-bow.] The next shot was the elder Wright [John] striken dead, after him the younger Wright [Christopher] and fourthly, Ambrose Rookwood. Then said Master Catesby to me, standing before the door they were to enter, *Stand by me, Tom, and we will die together. Sir*, quoth I, *I have lost the use of my right arm, and I fear that will cause me to be taken.* So as we stood close together, Master Catesby, Master Percy and myself, they two were shot, as far as I could guess, with one bullet; and then the company entered upon me, hurt me in the belly with a pike, and gave me other wounds until one came behind and caught hold of both my arms.[4]

Visitors at Clopton, with Rookwood and his wife, from time to time had been Catesby, Grant, Winter, Wright, one Master Bott, Master Robert Key and Mistress Key of Drayton in Northamptonshire, Mistress Momson, Sir Edward Bushell, and the three taken at Bidford—Master Thomas Rookwood and his servant and one Master Townsend.[5]

Less innocent than these young desperadoes was Henry Garnet *alias* Farmer, the head of the Jesuits in England. He was at the rendezvous in Warwickshire on 6 November. With the priest, Hugh Hall, whom we have met before as the chaplain of the Ardens at Park Hall, he found refuge at Hindlip with Thomas Habington. Here they were traced and, after an eight days' search, discovered, in a secret place in a chimney, on 27 January,

[1] For a full list of the 'relics' taken at Clopton see the Inquisition of 26 Feb. 1606 (Document at the Birthplace, *Cat.* 9; also *Misc. Doc.* x. 4). It includes a silver bell, an altar of stone, paper pictures, five Latin books, beads of amber and bone, and a pax.

[2] Sir Richard Verney.

[3] *S.P. Dom. Jas. I*, xvi. 34.

[4] Confession, 23 November.

[5] *Gunpowder Plot Books*, i. 12.

so distressed that they could not have held out a day longer but must have 'squealed or perished'.[1] Ambrose Rookwood and Thomas Winter were hanged with Guy Fawkes in Old Palace Yard, Westminster, on 31 January.

The King paid a special tribute to 'old Sir Fulke Greville' for his stout and honest services, and praised the Warwickshire folk who would not so much as give the fugitives a cup of drink but with execrations detested them.[2]

The 'Priest's Chamber' is still a feature of Clopton, a small bedroom at the top of the ancient part of the house, whence escape would be possible under or over the roof. Its mural paintings have been for the most part obliterated or over-written with texts of a pronounced Protestant character (dwelling on 'the Word', on giving 'ear to instruction', otherwise sermons, and on the 'wickedness of the heart') from the Authorized Version of 1611. But more ancient inscriptions can be detected, the outline of a Heart which now contains texts may be the 'Sacred Heart', symbol of the 'Hart' which 'desireth the water-brooks' (*ita desiderat anima mea ad te, Deus*), and visible is the monogram IC of a symbolical representation of the ΙΧΘΥΣ, or Sacred Fish, with a line and hook from the Hand in Heaven. Ancient also is an admonitory stanza (evidence that the chamber was a bedroom and not a chapel):

> Whether you Rise Yearlye/
> or goe to bed late/
> Remember Crist Jesus※
> that Died ffor your sake/[3]

1595–1605

§ 119. THE SCHOOLMASTER AT STRATFORD

ENERGETIC in this crisis was the schoolmaster, Alexander Aspinall. We saw him married, and settled in 1594 in the Chapel Quad, a few yards from *New Place*. With his wife (Widow Shaw, Julines Shaw's mother) and step-daughter Anne Shaw (aged sixteen) and a maid (or a pupil, possibly a son by a

[1] The proclamation for Garnet's apprehension was made on 15 January. The account of his capture is in *Harl. MS.* 38B.

[2] *Discourse of the Powder Treason.*

[3] Fripp, *Shakespeare's Haunts*, 132–4.

first wife, aged thirteen), Aspinall was returned in the Corn Inquiry of December 1595 as 'in house four persons'. 'Besides his office' as Schoolmaster, we learn, 'he hath the trades of buying and selling of wool and yarn, and making of malt, and hath 32 quarters of malt'. He had been forbidden on 4 November to make more malt under a penalty of £100: such was the poverty of the town and dearth of corn after the second Fire. On 14 February 1595 it was resolved 'by the Bailiff and the greater number of the Company that there shall be no School kept in the Chapel from this time following'. There is a curious allusion to the practice, and possibly to Aspinall, in *Twelfth Night* (III. ii. 77–81):

MARIA. He's in yellow stockings.
SIR TOBY. And cross-gartered?
MARIA. Most villanously, like a pedant that keeps a school in the church.

Such a case was probably peculiar in Shakespeare's experience, and a double incongruity. Like the Lady Olivia's pompous steward, the dignified Stratford schoolmaster may have worn the homely yellow worsted of Warwickshire yeomen, and he may have found the youthful cross-gartering an extra comfort in the unheated Chapel in winter.

Next year, on 18 August, 1596, he was elected a Burgess of the Council. It was an unusual appointment, and justified by his undoubted abilities and subsequent services to the Corporation. On 22 September his step-daughter married Henry Smythe, son of Shakespeare's godfather (as we have assumed), William Smythe of Henley Street. Like his brothers (Francis, William, and Roger) Henry Smythe was a mercer and prosperous. To him and his young wife, Aspinall let the house adjoining his own —the old Priests' House.

On 31 May 1602, the day of Richard Quyney's memorable funeral, Aspinall was elected an Alderman in his stead. This was an undoubted mark of trust, and no small gratification, we may believe, to his vanity. His efficiency and self-importance as Chamberlain in the years of 1603–6 remind us of Malvolio. His colleague, James Elliotts, played a passive part. Their 'Accompts', presented 11 January 1605 and 13 January 1606, were made by the great man with exemplary fullness and formality, and not a little intrusion of the first person plural: as,

On St. Thomas day last (21 Dec. 1604) we went to the Charity House—usually known as the Almshouse—to see the rents paid; and we found that some had paid, some came and paid when we were present, and some sent their rent afterwards.

Again,

We took one of the Almsfolks with us and went to them in Tinkers' Lane; but none of them was at home, save Fitter, which said he had not his money ready then. For these sums we are not countable.

It was not for Master Aspinall to be running after Charity folk.

Certain items are admonitory—John Smith pays rent for 'ground that *he is to build on*'; Master Woodward's executors pay 'for the use of Master Perrott's money *which they kept so long in their hands*'; Master Badger promises 'to signify by writing the cause *why he payeth not 5s.; we were willing at all times to go and distrain for* Master Badger's 5s.' It was more congenial to him to distrain on Master Badger, Catholic, and more than suspect for complicity in the Gunpowder Plot, than to collect the rents of Charity tenants, who might not be at home. He enjoyed an encounter—as with William Trout, an objectionable tenant in the High Street. He himself sat up in the house to evict him.

Items in his Accompt of 13 January 1606 prove the activity of himself and the Bailiff, and other neighbours of Shakespeare, in encountering the danger of Gunpowder Plot. He was more occupied in the Armoury, we may believe, than in the Schoolroom in those thrilling days, 6–9 November 1605. We read:

'Paid the vjth of November to Richard Dawes for two pounds of gunpowder, ij^{s} iiij^{d}; to Mistress Quyney the same day for two pounds of gunpowder, ij^{s} iiij^{d}; also to her for a pound of match, vj^{d}; the same day for scouring of one musket, four calivers, four flasks, and one bandoleer, to Henry Broom xvj^{d}; to Bircher for scouring of one musket, iij calivers, and for a stick and iron for one of them, xxij^{d}; to Henry Smythe for two pounds of shot, vj^{d}.'

Dawes, or Dawkes, was a plumber in Sheep Street, married to the late vintner, John Smythe's daughter, Anne, and father of a first child, William, baptized four days earlier, on 2 November. Mistress Quyney was Richard Quyney's widow in High Street. Broom was a cutler, as was William Bircher,[1] Henry Smythe was Aspinall's kinsman above.

[1] Bircher had a daughter born in March 1606 (at least, baptized on the 5th),

Under date 7 November is the item, 'to Mistress Quyney for wine that was brewed for Master Hales, when he came to survey the armour, xxiij^{d}'. Mistress Quyney had now the tavern (No. 36) next her mercer's shop in High Street. She supplied the wine, taken in hot water with sugar, on the visit of Master Hales from Snitterfield. On the 9th are payments to Bircher 'for making a new spring at the end of the seer[1] in Rafe Smythe's piece and mending the tumbler,[2] viij^{d}; for making a new scourer in Lewes Rogers' piece and making it clean, vj^{d}'; 'for mending the pan of William Merrell's piece, iiij^{d}'; 'for mending William Shaw's piece, having a new seer made for it, vj^{d}' (Rafe Smythe, Lewes Rogers, William Merrell, and William Shaw, Julines' younger brother, being trained recruits); '*the same day at night, when it was said that Sir Fulke Greville's house was besieged, at Mistress Quyney's for wine, by the appointment of Master Bailiff's and other*, ij^{s}'. This gathering at the tavern was something like an all-night sitting, a pound of candles being requisitioned, as we learn from the item, 'paid the xth of November for a pound of candles which John Heminges had fetched the night before, iiij^{d} ob'.

The anxiety had not passed on the 13th, when 8½ lb. of bullets were purchased of Dawkes for 18*d*.; nor on the 21st, when Bircher was paid the large sum of 6*s*. 8*d*. for altering two 'head pieces', and Henry Smythe no less than 10*s*. 6*d*. for gunpowder. Bircher was kept busy making or mending weapons. On 2 December Aspinall paid him 10*s*. for three swords and three daggers, and on the 5th 20*s*. for swords and daggers. Aspinall, as Chamberlain, superintended the hanging-up of the swords and daggers on the 10th, in the Armoury adjoining his Schoolroom, paying 1*d*. for nails to hang them on; and on Saturday before Christmas, 21 December 1605, he paid his old friend and neighbour, the curate, Sir William Gilbert *alias* Higges, 2*d*. for

who on 1 Nov. 1614, when eight years old, was apprenticed to a shoemaker, Richard Holmes, and his wife Susanna, for eight years, to learn 'weaving bone-lace and housewifery'.

[1] Sear, a portion of a gun-lock which engages with the notches of the tumbler in order to keep the hammer at full or half-cock, and which is released (at full cock) by pressure upon the trigger. *O.E.D.*

[2] In a gun-lock, a pivoted plate through which the mainspring acts on the hammer, and in the notches of which the sear engages. *O.E.D.*

sallet-oil for the lubrication of the same. Thus they could eat their Christmas dinner in peace, whilst they talked of the Pope, Guy Fawkes, and the Devil.

1605–6

§ 120. *MACBETH*

ON the news of the plot and its failure reaching Count Frederick Palatine, he wrote to Prince Henry expressing his thankfulness that he had been delivered by God from 'Hell and its instruments', and assuring him of his desire to 'second him in maintaining and defending the Truth against the assaults of the Father of Lies'.[1]

King James was only a profounder believer than his people in witchcraft as the work of the Devil.[2] From Bacon[3] downwards the superstition was universal. Protestant theologians, with the exception of Reginald Scot,[4] were unanimous.

'God warneth us', said Tyndale, 'to beware of witchcraft, sorcery and all crafts of the Devil. Thou wilt haply say, *They tell a man the truth.* What then? God wills that we care not to know what shall come, but only to keep His commandments and commit all chances unto Him.'[5]

Calfhill wrote:

'So hath the Devil his conjurors, his witches, his figure-flingers and his sorcerers, *with the spirit of illusion* to work strange effects.'[6]

Bullinger:

'Satan eggeth enchanters against us, whereunto belong deceitful jugglings and witchcraft; devils are the instruments of God's wrath; for Paul saith, the coming of anti-christ is after the working of Satan in all signs and wonders of lying';[7]

[1] 10 Dec. 1605 (Birch, *Life of Prince Henry*, p. 65).

[2] 'His Majesty did much press for my opinion touching the power of Satan in matter of witchcraft, and asked me, with much gravity, if I did truly understand why the Devil did work more with ancient women than others. I said we were taught hereof in Scripture, where it is told that "*the Devil walketh in dry places*" (Harington to Sir William Paulet, January 1604). An Act of Parliament came into force on 29 Sept. 1604, which enjoined that any one invoking or consulting with evil spirits and practising witchcraft should be put to death. (Cf. Exodus xxii. 18: 'Thou shalt not suffer a witch to live.')

[3] *Advancement of Learning*, II. i. 4.

[4] *Discouerie of Witchcraft*, 1584.

[5] *Prologue to Exodus*, 1530 (*Parker Soc.* i. 413).

[6] *Answer to Martial*, 1565 (*Parker Soc.* 14).

[7] *Decades* (*Parker Soc.* iv. 9).

Sandys, Bishop of Worcester:

'They which gave greatest credit to idolatrous spirits of divination were but *deluded; none had fairer promises of prosperous events than they whose ends were most unfortunate*';[1]

Gifford:

'The witch is an instrument under a colour' whereby Satan 'leadeth men into the depth of sin, that they may be drowned in the deeper condemnation';[2] and, '*Woe be to them that call good evil and evil good.* Doth not the apostle say, *God will send them strong delusion to believe lies?* And mark well, I pray you, the power of devils is in the hearts of men—as to *harden the heart*, blind the eyes of the mind, and inflame them unto wrath, malice, envy and *cruel murders*, to puff them up in pride, arrogancy and *vainglory*. Satan pursueth the innocent with suspicion that men may be *guilty of innocent blood. He telleth the truth sometimes to the end he may be credited when he doth lie. For let no man be so simple as to think that he will ever tell truth but for some wicked purpose.*'[3]

Here is good commentary on *Macbeth*.[4] Still better is the passage from St. Paul, which underlies these Puritan exhortations, in the vigorous English of the Geneva Version:

'And then shall that wicked man'—otherwise Antichrist—'be revealed, whose coming is by the effectual working of Satan, with all power and signs and lying wonders, and in all deceivableness of unrighteousness, among them that perish, because they received not the love of the truth that they might be saved. *And therefore God shall send them strong delusion that they should believe lies.*'[5]

Macbeth is a magnificent morality on this text. The Witches betray at once their Satanic origin, 'Fair is foul and foul is fair'.[6] Hovering in the air, the words are caught up by the victim, 'So foul and fair a day I have not seen'. He is greeted with the 'All-Hail' of Judas,[7] and a promise which is immediately fulfilled.

[1] *Parker Soc.* 373. [2] *Discourse*, 1587, xi. [3] *Dialogue*, 1593.

[4] Better than some modern editions of the play. A little knowledge of contemporary theology would have saved us much nonsense about the Witches and Hecate.

[5] 2 Thessalonians ii. 8–11.

[6] Isaiah v. 20: 'Woe be unto them that call evil good and good evil.' See the quotation from Gifford above, and *Love's Labour's Lost*, below (note 7).

[7] Mark xiv. 45: Judas went to Jesus and said 'Hail, Master! and kissed him'. The salutation is from Holinshed, who may or may not have seen its identity with that of Judas. Shakespeare certainly recognized it. He has 'Judas kissed his Master and cried All-hail!' (*3 Hen. VI*, v. vii. 33 f.); 'Did they not sometime cry All-hail to me? So Judas did to Christ' (*Rich. II*, IV. i. 169 f.); 'Fair in All-hail is foul' (*Love's L. L.* v. ii. 340). So Bacon of Essex, that he gave 'an All-hail and a kiss to the City' (Spedding, ii. 230, 282).

'What!' cries Banquo, 'can the Devil speak true?' The 'Father of Lies' is not to be trusted:

> oftentimes, to win us to our harm,
> The instruments of darkness tell us truths,
> Win us with honest trifles, to betray 's
> In deepest consequence.[1]

Equivocation is the theme of the grinning porter-scene which follows the murder.[2] Crime leads to crime—Banquo's death is the result of Duncan's. Still Hecate is unsatisfied. She wants *evil for its own sake*:

> All you have done
> Hath been but for a wayward son,
> Spiteful and wrathful; who, as others do,
> Loves for his own ends, not for you.[3]

The witches must provide a thicker Hell-broth and redouble their charms, while she will raise spirits

> *As by the strength of their illusion*
> *Shall draw him on to his confusion:*[4]

that awful fate against which the Christian prays in the concluding line of *Te Deum*,

> Let me never be *confounded*.

The Head, Macbeth's own, 'Knows his thought' and bids him beware Macduff; the Bloody Child, 'more potent than the first', is Macduff, ript from his mother's womb; and the Child Crowned with a Tree is Malcolm in his attack on Dunsinane. His recognition of the first misleads him in the belief that he understands the second and third, by which he is betrayed.[5]

As the Welsh were prominent in Elizabeth's reign and figure largely in the plays which Shakespeare wrote for her pleasure—the Welsh Captain in *Richard the Second*, Glendower and Lady Mortimer in *Henry the Fourth*, Fluellen in *Henry the Fifth*, Sir

[1] *Macb.* I. iii. 123–6.
[2] See further, p. 653.
[3] III. v. 10–13.
[4] *Ib.* 28 f.
[5] IV. i. 69, 76, 92–4. There are critics who dislike this allegory; but to disapprove of it does not disprove Shakespeare's authorship. We can forgive Coleridge his objection to the porter-scene, for genius has its aberrations; but 'competent scholars' who deny to Shakespeare the panting Serjeant's speech (they might as well condemn the agitated verse of Horatio's speech to the Ghost), large passages in the Witches' scenes, and the part of Hecate, are best left to oblivion. Nor has the play been shortened. A line more would have injured it.

Hugh Evans in *The Merry Wives*—so Macbeth and Lady Macbeth are the poet's nobler offering to the genius of King James's Scotland. Macbeth is the semi-savage Highlander, on his fog-enveloped, spirit-haunted heath, a fierce, powerful, pitiless clansman, with a deep vein of religion in him and nothing of the Saxon's animality, highly strung, imaginative, the victim of supernatural terrors. He is 'Bellona's bridegroom lapped in proof'[1]—has saved his country from rebel and invader, is sensitive to nothing so keenly as the charge of cowardice—as his wife knows, when she throws at him the taunt, 'Art thou afeard?'[2] Yet, to be king, he commits a dastardly crime. Duncan is old, gentle, has conferred signal favour on Macbeth, is his kinsman and his *guest*. A 'deep damnation' is his 'taking-off'.[3] The two elements of Conscience, the sinfulness of the deed and the fear of its consequence—vibrate together and shake the 'peerless' warrior to pieces. He says,

> If it were *done* when 'tis *done*, then 'twere well
> It were *done* quickly—[4]

uttering three times the terrible word that tolls through the play, 'I have *done* the deed' (II. ii. 15), 'what's *done* is *done*' (III. ii. 12), and 'What's *done* cannot be *undone*' (V. i. 75)—and he slays the grooms,

> One cried *God bless us!* and *Amen* the other,
> As they had *seen* me with these hangman's hands.

But he adds,

> I could not say *Amen* . . .
> I had most need of blessing, and *Amen*
> Stuck in my throat.[5]

He takes horrible precautions—his casual inquiries of Banquo, his friend, with murderous intent in every word, are worthy of the Celt at his lowest—wrecker, moonlighter, *sansculotte*.[6] But his cunning overleaps itself. His intellect, awake and on the stretch, cannot relax, cannot rest. He suffers from ghastly dreams and hallucinations, sees daggers in the day-time. From *within*, far more than from without, comes retribution:

> All is but toys, Renown and Grace is dead;[7]

[1] I. ii. 54.
[2] I. vii. 39.
[3] *Ib.* 20.
[4] *Ib.* 1–2.
[5] II. ii. 26–33.
[6] III. i. 19, 24, 36.
[7] II. iii. 99.

and

> Good things of Day begin to droop and drowse.[1]

He has known innocent happiness, a poet's joy in Nature and the surroundings of his castle—has looked upon the sun as the 'tender eye of pity' on the world, ridden home in the evening free to observe the flight of the bat, the hum of the cockchafer as it beat against his face, the cawing of the rooks in the wood, and rejoiced to be in his hall again as the night descended with its 'black agents' outside.[2] All this has left him. In the last act he is a worn-out man, shouting for his armour, despatching his servants hither and thither, countermanding his orders, mad with a tortured brain.[3] Poet to the last, crowding image upon image as only a Celt can, he utters in matchless verse his despair:

> To-morrow, and to-morrow, and to-morrow,
> Creeps in this petty pace from day to day,
> To the last syllable of recorded time;
> And all our yesterdays have lighted fools
> The way to dusty death. Out, out, brief Candle![4]
> Life's but a walking shadow,[5] a poor player
> That struts and frets his hour upon the stage,
> And then is heard no more: it is a tale[6]
> Told by an idiot, full of sound and fury,
> Signifying nothing.[7]

Almost as painful is our sense of 'the pity of it' in the case of Lady Macbeth. She is no demon of cruelty. She is a Celt, and says more than she means. She says,

> I have given suck, and know
> How tender 'tis to love the babe that milks me:
> I would, while it was smiling in my face,
> Have pluck'd my nipple from his boneless gums,
> And dash'd the brains out, had I so sworn as you
> Have done to this.[8]

But *would* she? She tells of Duncan,

> Had he not resembled
> My father as he slept, I had done it.[9]

And when Macbeth recalls the scene of Duncan in his bed,

> His silver skin laced with his golden blood—[10]

she swoons.

[1] III. ii. 52. [2] *Ib.* 40–53. [3] V. iii. [4] Job xviii. 6.
[5] Psalm xxxix. 6. [6] Psalm xc. 9. [7] V. v. 19–28.
[8] I. vii. 54–9. [9] II. ii. 13 f. [10] II. iii. 118.

She is a little woman with a will.[1] She loves her husband, as she had loved her father and her child. Nothing shall stand, if she can remove it, between Macbeth and the object of his great ambition:

> Glamis thou art, and Cawdor, and shalt be
> What thou art promised.[2]

There is no thought of herself, no desire whatever to be Queen—and here Shakespeare departs from Holinshed.[3] Her husband, because he has set his heart upon it, shall be King. Whole-heartedly she unites herself with him in the moment of his crime. Her welcome to him as he staggers from the chamber is, *My husband!*[4]

But there is *effort* in it all. She takes wine.[5] She, too, cannot sleep. Physical dejection, and the fact that she is losing hold on Macbeth, that she cannot control his 'sorry fancies', and no longer shares his full confidence, breaks her down. She says, before the feast,

> Gentle, my lord, sleek o'er your rugged looks;
> Be bright and jovial among your guests to-night.

He replies,

> So shall I, love; *and so, I pray, be you.*[6]

After the feast she sinks exhausted. She lets her husband ramble on, unable to attend to his questions. She speaks as from a distance. From afar she begins to see the man she has loved going over the precipice.[7]

Unconsciously she does the thing she fears Macbeth will do—namely, disclose the crime. Awake, she can suppress her thoughts; but at night, when for a moment her will is at rest, they rise up in insurrection against her. She has a maid to lie with her, and burns a lamp by her bed—in vain. Her thought possesses

[1] She speaks of 'this little hand' (v. i. 57), and lacks physique—has lost her child, faints, takes stimulant; and, as Bradley points out (*Short Studies*, p. 126), her husband admires her 'undaunted mettle'.

[2] I. v. 16 f.

[3] 'She was very ambitious, burning in unquenchable desire to bear the name of a Queen' (*Chronicle of Scotland*, p. 24). The well-known portrait by Sargent (in the National Gallery) of Miss Terry as Lady Macbeth lifting the crown to her head gives us Holinshed, not Shakespeare.

[4] II. ii. 14. For the significance of the word see *Ant. & Cleop.* v. ii. 290.

[5] II. ii. 1.

[6] III. ii. 27–9.

[7] III. iv. 122–9.

her, she acts it, she goes through the whole horrible business of the murder in her dream. Every sense is quickened, as in triumph after repression. She hears the clock strike, urges her husband to the deed, sees Duncan in his blood, washes her hands of the stains, *smells the odour of the blood*, hears the knocking at the gate, leads Macbeth trembling back to bed. *And her Conscience at last is liberated.* Macbeth had said,

> What hands are here? ha! they pluck out mine eyes!
> Will all great Neptune's ocean wash this blood
> Clean from my hand? No; this my hand will rather
> The multitudinous seas incarnadine,
> Making the green one red—[1]

giving utterance to that *infinite* quality which attaches to wickedness. She replied, but she could not have meant it—she would suppress her real sentiments at that moment—

> A little water clears us of this deed:
> How easy is it then![2]

In her sleep the truth will out:

> All the perfumes of Arabia will not sweeten this little hand. Oh, oh, oh![3]

For this searching diagnosis of mental torture—a broken heart, an accusing conscience, insomnia and sleep-walking—the poet may have owed something to conversations with Doctor John Hall. Was his future son-in-law (a devout Puritan) the 'good' Doctor in the play?

Macbeth was probably one of the ten pieces produced by Shakespeare's company at Whitehall from Christmas Day 1605 to 24 March 1606 when Heminge was paid £100 for their performances. Henry Garnet was tried at the Guild Hall in London on 28 March, and found guilty of complicity in Gunpowder Plot. The King himself was present in secret, like Duke Vincentio in *Measure for Measure* in the 'Vienna' prison.[4] There had been much talk of a Jesuit book, *The Defence of Equivocation* (a plea that the persecuted were justified in telling lies), by one 'Farmer', who was strongly suspected to be Garnet. Hence the

[1] II. ii. 59–63. Imagine, if we can, the Poet's exquisite pleasure in writing
> The multitudinous seas incarnadine,
> Making the green *One Red*—

supreme lines, worthy of their sublime thought.

[2] *Ib.* 67 f. [3] V. i. 56–8. [4] II. iii, III. i, ii, IV. i, ii, iii, V. i.

Porter's grim jest, 'Here's a farmer, that hanged himself'. On 13 February, on his examination at Whitehall, Garnet declared that he only corrected the book, which he did not want printed. On the 23rd he was overheard, in conversation with his fellow-prisoner Hugh Hall, to utter incriminating evidence, which at his trial he first denied and then, confronted with Hall, confessed.[1]

'And being now asked how he could salve this lewd perjury, he answered that so long as he thought they had no proof, he was not bound to accuse himself; but when he saw they had proof, he stood not long in it; and then he fell into a large discourse of defending equivocations, with many weak and frivolous distinctions.'[2]

Whence the Porter's further merriment, added to the text after this date, 'Here's an Equivocator, *that could swear in both the scales against either scale*; who committed treason enough for God's sake, yet could not equivocate to Heaven.' Garnet was executed on 3 May at the west gate of St. Paul's. *Macbeth* is referred to in a play entitled *The Puritan or The Widow of Watling Street*, performed by the Children of Paul's on 15 July.[3]

1606

§ 121. *KING LEAR*

DELIVERED from the Gunpowder Plot, Parliament voted generous supplies to the King, and passed a bill to restrain the name of God in stage-plays.[4] Money was forthcoming for needy Scots (against whom feeling was growing fierce in June)[5] and for wasteful hospitalities. There was money, too, for Shakespeare, and restriction henceforth, with damaging effect, on his employment of the Divine Name. Three times he played before King Christian of Denmark during his visit to his sister, Queen Anne—twice at Greenwich, where His Majesty stayed on 18–24 and 28–31 July and 8–9 August, once at Hampton Court, on

[1] *S.P. Dom. Jac. I.*
[2] Chamberlain to Winwood, 5 April.
[3] Fleay, *Chronicle of the English Drama*, ii. 93. Sir Godfrey Plus says (alluding to Banquo's ghost): 'We'll have the ghost in the white sheet set at the upper end of the table.' The reference in III. vi. 289 to Tuesday 15 July gives us the year 1606.
[4] *3 Jac. I* (between 21 Jan. and 24 March 1606).
[5] Dr. Lionel Sharpe to the Privy Council 25 June.

7 August.[1] The 'swinish phrase' which 'soiled the addition', as Hamlet tells us,[2] of the Danish Court, was, on this occasion, applicable to the English. Sir John Harington, who was no Puritan, wrote from London of the 'rich doings'.

'I came here', he said, 'a day or two before the Danish King, and until this hour I have been well nigh overwhelmed with carousals and sports of all kinds. The sports began each day in such manner and such sort as well nigh persuaded me of Mahomet's paradise. I think the Dane hath strangely wrought on our good English nobles, for those whom I never could get to taste good liquor, now follow the fashion, and wallow in beastly delights. The ladies abandon their sobriety, and are seen to roll about in intoxication.'

One evening ladies performing in the masques were the worse for drink. 'The Queen of Sheba' fell at the throne-steps with a tray full of 'wine, cream, jelly, beverage, cakes and spices' into the lap of King Christian, bestowing her presents on his garments. He rose up to dance with the unfortunate dame, but fell and was carried helpless to 'an inner chamber, and laid on a bed of state'. 'Faith, Hope, and Charity' also disgraced themselves—Hope forgot her part and 'withdrew', and Faith 'staggered' after, leaving Charity to apologize, who found her sisters 'sick and spewing in the lower hall'.

'I have much marvelled', he continues, 'at these strange pageantries, and they do bring to my remembrance what passed of this sort in our Queen's days, of which I was some time an humble presenter. I ne'er did see such lack of good order, discretion and sobriety. The Gunpowder fright is got out of all our heads, and we are going on as if the Devil was contriving every man should blow up himself by riot, excess, and devastation of time and temperance. The great ladies do go well masked, it be the only show of their modesty.'[3]

Weldon in his fierce way speaks, a little later, of 'a foul State and Court, wherein pride, revenge, and luxury (lechery) abounded'.[4]

The plague increased dangerously in London,[5] the theatres were closed, and Shakespeare's company went on tour. We trace them at Saffron Walden, Leicester, Oxford, Marlborough, Dover, and Maidstone.[6] Shakespeare probably left his fellows in August, when they played at Leicester, and rejoined them

[1] Chambers, iv. 121. [2] *Haml.* I. iv. 19 f.

[3] To Master Secretary Barlow, *Nugae Antiquae*, i. 348 ff.

[4] *The Court of King James*, p. 113.

[5] Chambers, iv. 350. [6] J. Tucker Murray, i. 183 f.

before their visit to Dover, about 4 October, working in the interval on *King Lear*. Edgar's speech on the summit of Dover Cliff is from recent, personal observation:[1]

Stand still. How fearful
And dizzy 'tis to cast one's eyes so low!
The crows and choughs that wing the midway air
Show scarce so gross as beetles. Half-way down
Hangs one that gathers samphire, dreadful trade!
Methinks he seems no bigger than his head.
The fishermen that walk upon the beach
Appear like mice; and yond tall anchoring bark
Diminished to her cock, her cock a buoy
Almost too small for sight. The murmuring surge,
That on the unnumbered idle pebbles chafes,[2]
Cannot be heard so high. I'll look no more,
Lest my brain turn, and the deficient sight
Topple down headlong.[3]

Never was a great work of art less in touch with its immediate context, or more completely an expression of the artist, than *King Lear*. We look around in vain for anything that bears the least resemblance to it in contemporary drama, or for any one outside the circle of his 'fellows' and 'grave', 'judicious' friends, who would entirely understand it. King James and the majority of his courtiers could only regard with astonishment its annihilation of commonplace morality and theology; and of disciples like Burbage, and admirers like John Stephens,[4] we can only say, Happy were they to share the Master's thought and representation! Yet only with knowledge of his time and experience of his art can we hope to get at the secret of this incomparable tragedy, the noblest spiritual utterance since *La Divina Commedia*.[5]

The story of Lear is older than Dante. It is told in *Historia*

[1] Shakespeare had been in Dover twice before—in Feb. 1588 and Sept. 1597: pp. 216, 458.

[2] The beach at Dover impressed Shakespeare—its unnumbered pebbles, the grinding noise of the retiring waters which it seems to devour, and the murmur of the waves upon it heard from above. See *Cor.* v. iii. 58 f.: 'let the pebbles on the hungry beach fillip the stars'; and *Cymb.* I. vi. 35 f.: 'the fiery orbs above and the stones upon the unnumbered beach.' Both stars and pebbles are beyond number, in their magnificence and insignificance.

[3] IV. vi. 11–24. Notice how the Poet *hears*, as well as sees, his surroundings (the murmuring surge chafes the pebbles). Cf. pp. 124–33.

[4] See pp 817, 831.

[5] I do not forget the sculpture on Giotto's Tower in Florence.

Britonum by Geoffrey of Monmouth, who lived in the reign of Stephen. Thence it passed into Layamon's *Brut* and the *Gesta Romanorum*. In Elizabeth's reign it was told in Holinshed's *Chronicle*, *The Mirror for Magistrates*, Spenser's *Faerie Queene*, and in a play, *King Leir and his Three Daughters*, acted in 1594 and published in 1605. In all these forms it has a happy ending. Notwithstanding painful features, it is 'comedy' in the sense that 'poetic justice' is done to the injured. Lear regains his kingdom and Cordelia succeeds him on the throne.

Such a termination has small interest for Shakespeare. He has outgrown (at the age of two-and-forty) utilitarian ethics. The recovery of the crown cannot make good the wrong inflicted. They are incommensurable. In Shakespeare's hands Lear's folly and his daughters' cruelty result in irreparable disaster to themselves, and irretrievable misery to the innocent. 'Sweet are the uses of adversity', such as hardship in the Forest; but what of torments which 'cut to the brain'?[1] The fruit of the tragedy is *Chastening*. The proud, reckless old King passes through a savage school of discipline to knowledge of himself—to lowliness, justice, tenderness; and out of Cordelia's sacrifice come the influences that punish and bless. It is worth while to *go through* all that Lear endures, to arrive at last at his sweet moments of sanity, and to suffer all Cordelia's woes, to rise into her perfectness. To *be*, not to *have*, is the sum of all.

The original setting of the story is pagan. In Geoffrey, Holinshed, and *The Mirror for Magistrates*, Lear is a heathen. In the play of 1594 the scene is transferred to Christian times. The author introduces Scripture and moralizes. He hints at the death of their mother as a cause of the unfilial behaviour of Goneril and Regan. Lear laments her decease. Though in a moment of 'doting frenzy', egged on by her sisters, he disinherits Cordelia, he is a gentle, pious old man, who wants to exchange his throne for the cloister; and Cordelia is a Puritan maiden, whose demure and precise ways excite the envy of the sisters, and blunt speech the wrath of her father. Something of Cordelia is taken over by Shakespeare; and doubtless he would have preserved the

[1] IV. vi. 197. The Arcadian company of *As You L. It* (II. i. 12) are schoolboys and schoolgirls in suffering compared with Lear, Gloucester, Cordelia, Kent, and Edgar.

Christian background, as in *Macbeth*, were it not for the Act, forbidding the use of 'God', 'Jesus Christ', and 'Holy Ghost'. Without the name 'God' he was deprived of the greatest word in the language. In *Macbeth* he was able to say 'God bless us!' and 'Amen', 'the Lord's anointed temple', 'In the great hand of God I stand', 'with Him above to ratify the work', 'God, God, forgive us all!', 'God's soldier he, his hurts before'; in *Lear* he is reduced to the feeble substitutes: 'Gods', 'Powers', 'Wills', 'Heaven' and 'Heavens', 'Apollo', 'Jupiter', 'Goddess', 'Fortune', 'Juno', 'Justicers', 'Summoners', 'Stars', 'Fairies', anything he can lay hold of, with adjectives to express Christian sentiment—'dear', 'blest', 'high-judging', 'kind', 'mighty', 'opposeless', 'dearest', 'ever-gentle'. The play suffers from this restriction, especially in the greatest passages. 'By Jupiter' and 'By Juno' in II. iv. 21 f. are almost ludicrous. We should expect 'By God!' and 'By the Lord!'

For the underplot of Gloucester and his sons we must go to Sidney's *Arcadia*. There we read of a 'Paphalgonian King', whose bastard by 'poisonous hypocrisy' led him to hate the legitimate brother. 'Drunk in his affection for that unlawful and unnatural son', the king suffered himself to be governed by him and, ere he was aware, thrown out and sent blinded into the wilderness. The other son sheltered him, beneath a rock whence he would have cast himself and ended his misery.[1]

Out of this slender material Shakespeare creates the lesser but excessively painful tragedy of the adulterous Gloucester and his unlawful, demon-like offspring, Edmund, the ill-treatment and fidelity of his legitimate son, Edgar, his loss of his eyes and expulsion into the tempest, his wandering to Dover and projected suicide from the cliff, his deliverance, as he believes, by miraculous powers, his submission to God, his patience and happy death. Gloucester, too, *attains*.

The two stories, one of a father and his daughters, the other of a father and his sons, both of heart-rending family dissension, are skilfully blended, and made to supplement and enforce each other. Lear and Gloucester are bad fathers, who meet with unmerited cruelty and undeserved devotion from their children, and undergo that 'chastening' which is not 'joyous but grievous',

[1] Bk. ii. 10.

'but afterward bringeth the quiet fruit of righteousness unto them which are thereby exercised'.[1]

The play opens with significant dialogue. In the background is the dark and sinister figure of the Bastard. He is always 'Bastard' in the old editions, in the Quarto and Folio (save here and there by printer's error), though modern editors weakly prefer the less offensive 'Edmund'. Once before, in 1596, Shakespeare introduced the dominating figure of a bastard, in manly contrast with conventional and hypocritical goodness. His Bastard of 1606 is a different creature, as baser than his birth as the other was nobler, an expression of the Poet's wrath against godless licentiousness. Shakespeare does not write now—

> Some sins do bear their privilege on earth,
> And so doth yours: your fault was not your folly.[2]

He writes instead,

> The Gods are just, and of our pleasant vices
> Make instruments to scourge us.[3]

Gloucester is not forward to introduce his illegitimate son. Kent has to ask, 'Is not this your son, my lord?' Gloucester replies, putting a bold face on the matter, 'His breeding hath been at my charge: I have so often blushed to acknowledge him that now I am brazed to it.' Gloucester had been married more than a twelvemonth and was the father of a son when he committed adultery.[4] He speaks lightly of his sin—'there was good sport at his making'. He will speak in a different key later. Edmund, we learn, has been 'out nine years *and away he shall again*'. Bastard sons are inconvenient encumbrances. Gloucester has had small opportunity of knowing Edmund. He knows his son Edgar even less.[5] He has little reason to be loved by either, and that both condemn him when he is least to be condemned cannot surprise us.[6] Edgar had grounds for 'sullenness'.[7]

[1] Hebrews xii. 11 f.

[2] *K. John*, I. i. 261 f.

[3] *K. Lear*, v. iii. 170 f. ('scourge' is the reading of the Quarto).

[4] *Ib.* I. i. 19 f. Shakespeare is careful to represent Edmund as the younger: cf. I. ii. 5.

[5] *Ib.* I. i. 20 f., 'no dearer', which does not mean much. If Gloucester had really 'tenderly and entirely' loved Edgar, as he professes, he would not have accepted Edmund's lying tale about him and the forged letter in i. 2.

[6] v. iii. 170–4.

[7] The first edition of the play, 1608, has the sub-title: 'With the unfortunate

Lear here enters with his train. He proceeds to do what is expressly forbidden in the Bible, and was regarded in Shakespeare's time as the mark of weakness and dereliction of duty:

'Hear me, O ye great men of the people . . . Give not thy son and wife, thy brother and friend, power over thee while thou livest; and give not away thy substance to another, lest it repent thee and thou entreat for the same again. As long as thou livest and hast breath, give not thyself over to any person. For better it is that thy children should pray unto thee than that thou shouldest look up to the hands of thy children. At the time when thou shalt end thy days and finish thy life, distribute thine inheritance.'[1]

In Geoffrey, Holinshed, and *The Mirror for Magistrates*, Lear is dispossessed by his sons-in-law; in *The Faerie Queene* he resigns his crown to 'lead a private life'; in the old play he lays it down that he may 'think upon the welfare of his soul'. Shakespeare's treatment resembles that in *Gorboduc* by Sackville and Norton, where they paraphrase the passage in *Ecclesiasticus*.[2] Lear, like Gorboduc, is determined

To shake all cares and business from our age,
Conferring them on younger strengths, while we
Unburthened crawl towards death.[3]

Crawling towards death means hunting with the hounds. The old King's next entrance is to the sound of the horn. Already he begins to see his mistake—'I have perceived a most faint neglect'.[4] His Fool rubs it in—'I'ld keep my cockscombs

life of Edgar, son and heir to the Earl of Gloucester, and his sullen and assumed humour of Tom of Bedlam.' See especially his judgement on his father in v. iii. 170–3.

[1] I. i. 34 ff. Ecclesiasticus xxxiii. 17–22.

[2] Act I, scene i:

When fathers cease to know that they should rule,
The children cease to know they should obey.
So while the Gods prolong your royal life
Prolong your reign . . .
Arm not unskilfulness with princely power:
But you that long have wisely ruled the reins
Of royalty within your noble realm,
So hold them while the Gods, for our avails,
Shall stretch the thread of your prolongèd days.

And the Chorus:

And this great King that doth divide the land,
And yields the reign into his children's hand,
A mirror shall become, &c.

If Edgar sits in judgement on his father (v. iii. 170–3) we can hardly blame him.

[3] I. i. 40–2.

[4] I. iv. 73 f.

myself'.[1] His 'folly' in this, however, is infinitesimal compared with his injustice to Cordelia. He is an autocratic, masterful old man, accustomed to follow his own will, good or evil, and indulged because he suffers from the 'mother', which finally carried him off. And while he has gone his own way, his daughters have grown up outside his life, and are good or evil as they please or displease him. He is outrageously annoyed by Cordelia's little blunt speeches. Her sisters are right in saying, 'he hath ever but slenderly known himself, the best and soundest of his time hath been but rash'.[2] Self-knowledge, and the patience which is opposite to wilful rashness, both he and Gloucester acquire before death.

There is no trace of repentance in Sidney's 'Paphalgonian King'. On the contrary, he blames the 'base woman', his concubine.[3] Nor is there any conscious connexion between his adultery and the putting-out of his eyes. Exception has been taken to the 'cutting-out' of Gloucester's eyes in Shakespeare; but Puritan feeling favoured extreme punishment—death as in the Mosaic law,[4] or blinding in accordance with the doctrine, 'Whosoever looketh on a woman to lust after her, hath committed adultery with her already in his heart; wherefore if thy right eye cause thee to offend, pluck it out and cast it from thee'.[5] The Reformers quoted with approval the punishment by death; but blinding, as among the Locrensians,[6] was thought more Christian. When Isabella says of Angelo, 'O, I will to him and pluck out his eyes!',[7] she does not meditate revenge, but Puritan chastisement of the kind meted out to Claudio and Juliet. The injunction of the Sermon on the Mount (Matthew v. 29), which is headed in the Geneva Version, 'The plucking out of the eyes', suggests the reproach of Lear,

Old fond eyes,
Beweep this cause again I'll pluck ye out,
And cast you with the waters that you lose,
To temper clay.[8]

[1] I. iv. 120 f.
[2] I. i. 296–9.
[3] *Arcadia*, II. x. 3.
[4] Leviticus xx. 10: 'The adulterer and the adulteress shall die.'
[5] Matthew v. 28 f.
[6] Becon, *Homily against Adultery* (*Parker Soc.* ii. 649); Wilson, *Rhetoric*, ed. Mair, p. 28. See also *Willobie His Avisa*, xviii.
[7] *Meas. for M.* IV. iii. 124.
[8] *K. Lear*, I. iv. 323–6.

This is literal. Gloucester speaks in metaphor, driven to answer Regan,

> Because I would not see thy cruel nails
> Pluck out his poor old eyes.[1]

Cornwall replies to him with brutal realism,

> See it, shalt thou never. Fellows, hold the chair;
> Upon these eyes of thine I'll set my foot.[2]

Not only does he cut them out with his dagger, but he throws them on the ground and treads upon them:

> Out, vile jelly!
> Where is thy lustre now?[3]

No sooner is Gloucester blind than (a dramatic turn worthy of Dante) *he begins to see*:

> O my follies! then Edgar was abused:
> Kind gods, forgive me that and prosper him![4]

He wanders forth with 'bleeding rings' upon the heath:

> *I stumbled when I saw:* full oft 'tis seen
> Our means secure us—

in that security of carelessness (*sine cura*) which Hecate says is 'man's chiefest enemy',[5]

> and our mere defects
> Prove our commodities. Ah, dear son Edgar,
> Might I but live to see thee in my touch
> I'd say I had eyes again![6]

The Heavens have treated him cruelly—he is only beginning to see—

> As flies to wanton boys are we to the gods;
> They kill us for their sport.[7]

Yet he would that men might feel their stern hand, and learn to pity their fellows:

> Here, take this purse, thou who, the Heavens' plagues
> Have stumbled to all strokes: *that I am wretched*

[1] III. vii. 55 f.

[2] *Ib.* 67 f.

[3] 83 f. 'The blinding of Gloster is a complete reversion to the horrors of Titus Andronicus', 'What is the legitimate deduction to be drawn about the mentality of the audience that had provided for it the plucking-out of Gloster's eyes?' C. M. Haines and M. St. Clare Byrne in *The Shakespeare Association Papers*, 1927, pp. 57 and 199. They miss the point—as 'grave' and 'judicious' spectators of 1606 could not do.

[4] 91 f.

[5] *Macb.* III. v. 32 f.

[6] IV. i. 21–6.

[7] *Ib.* 38 f.

Makes thee the happier. Heavens, deal so still!
Let the superfluous and lust-dieted man
That slaves your ordinance, feel your power quickly,
So distribution should undo excess
And each man have enough.[1]

Weary, longing for death, he kneels on the edge of the cliff (as he believes) to the 'Opposeless Wills':

This world I do renounce, and in your sights
Shake patiently my great affliction off.[2]

But the world is not renounced, nor is great affliction patiently shaken off, by *suicide*. That is the work of the Devil—a Satan worthy of Albrecht Dürer:

methought his eyes
Were two full moons; he had a thousand noses,
Horns whelked and waved like the enridged sea.[3]

Miraculously preserved ('things impossible with men are possible with God')[4] he will 'bear affliction till it do cry out itself, 'Enough!'[5]

Lear enters; and the two fathers, one learning in his blindness to see, the other learning in his craziness to be sane, meet. The mad king's words probe deep:

I pardon that man's life. What was the cause?
Adultery?
Thou shalt not die: die for adultery? No,
Let copulation thrive: for Gloucester's bastard son
Was kinder to his father than my daughters.[6]

At the approach of the battle Gloucester is resigned:

Let not my worser spirit tempt me again.[7]

But when the battle is lost and Cordelia a prisoner, he despairs. Edgar reassures him:

What, in ill thoughts again? Men must endure
Their going hence, even as their coming hither:
Ripeness is all.[8]

This is better than Hamlet's 'the readiness is all'.[9]

[1] IV. i. 67–74. [2] IV. vi. 34.

[3] *Ib.* 69–71. Melville gives us a grotesque Devil from Scotland, which preached in a black gown to witches in the kirk of North Berwick, *Memoirs*, p. 194 f.

[4] Mark x. 26 f. ('The Gods make them honours of men's impossibilities': *K. Lear*, IV. vi. 73 f.). [5] IV. vi. 75 ff. [6] *Ib.* 111 ff.

[7] *Ib.* 222. [8] V. ii. 9–11. [9] *Haml.* V. ii. 234.

Edgar, finally, moralizes to the dying Bastard (Edgar's defeat of Edmund in the tournament is the one thing in that perverse world that went right),[1]

> The Gods are just, and of our pleasant vices
> Make instruments to plague us:
> The dark and vicious place where thee he got
> Cost him his eyes.

To which Edmund answers, with profound pathos, and significance:

> Thou hast spoken right, 'tis true
> The wheel is come full circle. *I am here.*[2]

And of his father, Edgar tells us,

> I asked his blessing, and from first to last
> Told him my pilgrimage; but his flawed heart
> Alack, too weak the conflict to support,
> Twixt two extremes of passion, joy and grief,
> *Burst smilingly.*[3]

There is the same only a greater sanctification in Lear. He is a titanic figure, vast in his presence and authority, in his explosions of wrath and terrific vehemence of speech ('wolfish visage', 'degenerate bastard', 'detested kite', 'blasts and fogs', 'rumble thy bellyful', 'darkness and devils', 'thwart disnatured torment'), his overwhelming grief and desperate yearnings, and, at last, his utter humility and sweetness. He is on a scale with the tempest which he defies, and with the Super-natural Powers which cast him down, and then raise him to a new majesty.

Fourscore and upwards, when our 'strength is labour and sorrow', he goes out into the hard world, to feel what 'wretches' feel, to learn to be just, and to become again as a little child. He loves his Fool—'Art cold? I am cold myself'.[4] He takes pity on the beggar. The storm, privation, his rage and sorrow, and mortification, the Fool's thoughtless gibes and Edgar's Bedlam-talk 'unsettle' his wits—another case of mental disorder which

[1] The tournament is the weak spot of the play, and its result is not determined by moral considerations. Edmund might just as well have won, and then ——? The strange thing is that Shakespeare, in his dark view of the world, did not make Edmund the winner.

[2] v. iii. 170–4. The occasion of Gloucester's loss of his eyes was not vice but virtue, an heroic defence of the poor old King. Yet the cause was the Bastard's treachery, and behind the treachery was the bastardy.

[3] v. iii. 195–9.

[4] III. ii. 68 f.

suggests 'observation' with Dr. Hall.[1] He is put to sleep, but is roused immediately and hurried off to Dover:

> This rest might yet have balm'd thy broken sinews,[2]
> Which, if convenience will not allow,
> Stand in hard cure.[3]

Cordelia cures him—provides the needed rest, and brings him to, after healing slumber, with soft music (always associated in Shakespeare with love and sanity).[4] He opens his eyes, and slowly recognizes his child bending over him like an angel in Heaven:

> CORDELIA. Sir, do you know me?
> LEAR. *You are a spirit.*[5]

Nothing matters now but Love. The battle is lost, and they must to prison; so be it, where love is, there is liberty—

> We two alone, will sing like birds in the cage;
> When thou dost ask me blessing, I'll kneel down
> And ask of thee forgiveness; so will live,
> And pray, and sing; and tell old tales; and laugh
> At gilded butterflies, and hear poor rogues
> Talk of Court news, and we'll talk with them too,
> Who loses and who wins, who's in, who's out;
> *And take upon us the mystery of things,*
> *As if we were God's spies.*[6]

'Thou art about my path and about my bed,' said the Psalmist, 'and *spiest* out all my ways.'[7] In the spirit of love, father and daughter will look above the glory of Court, to the knowledge that is 'too wonderful' for man, he 'cannot attain unto it'.[8] Here Shakespeare forgets the Act of Parliament, and writes out of his heart, *God*.

Gloucester and Lear die in their old age, and if their lives are somewhat shortened it is to gain what their previous many years have not given them. Nine others die, if we include Kent, who is left in a dying condition; and these, save Kent, do not live out half their days. They die young—Edmund, Goneril, Regan, Cornwall, Oswald, for their sins; the servant of Cornwall, the

[1] p. 652. [2] *nervos*. [3] III. vi. 105–7.
[4] And playing on his *nervos* (strings), as Apollo and Orpheus do in Ovid: *Met*. i. 518, x. 40.
[5] IV. vii. 48 f. [6] V. iii. 9–17.
[7] cxxxix. 3. [8] *Ib*. 6.

Fool, Cordelia, for the sins of others. Shakespeare is oppressed with the sense of human corruption. He was, as all thinking men then were, Calvinistic. He believed in the Fall, and in man's inability to rise without divine Grace. The villain of the play, like Iago, is a 'free-willer' such as the Protestant theologians regarded with horror. The Bastard scoffs at Divine Influence:

'This is the excellent foppery of the world, that when we are sick in fortune, often the surfeit of our own behaviour, we make guilty of our disasters the sun, the moon and the stars: as if we were villains by necessity, fools by Heavenly compulsion, knaves, thieves and treachers by spherical predominance, drunkards, liars and adulterers by an enforced obedience of planetary influence, and all that we are evil in by *a divine thrusting on*: an admirable evasion of Whoremaster Man to lay his goatish disposition to the charge of a star.'[1]

Such a parody of the doctrine of Necessity and Grace, under the guise of astrology, would sound blasphemous in 1606, and is hostile to the whole tenour of the drama, according to which good and evil, springing out of the depths of human nature rather than from circumstance, are overruled and guided to unseen ends by the Powers above. 'It is the Stars,' cried Kent, 'the Stars above us, govern our conditions.'[2] A glimmer of Grace in Edmund is his discovery of this fact: 'The Wheel (of Destiny) is come full circle: I am here.'

Kent is a character after Shakespeare's heart—fearless, plain-spoken, tender and true, religious: dear to him as Adam, Corin, and other faithful servants. He stands up for Cordelia, denounces Lear for his injustice, is unmoved when Lear lays hand on his sword, takes his banishment like a man. But he cannot leave his old master—he returns disguised and re-enters his service, with timely and welcome handling, in spite of his years (he is nearer seventy than 'forty-eight'), of the detestable Oswald. Shakespeare loathed a flunkey.[3] Few scenes are so satisfying as that of Kent's chastisement of the Steward, and request that he may treat him as Jehu dealt with the house of Baal.[4] Left by his mean persecutors in the stocks, he thinks of

[1] I. ii. 128–39.

[2] IV. iii. 34 f.

[3] Cf. Austria in *King John*; Le Beau in *As You Like It*; Osric in *Hamlet*.

[4] II. ii. 1–132. See 2 Kings x. 27: 'They threw down the house of Baal and made a jakes [a draught-house: Bishops' Bible] of it.' Says Kent, 'I will tread this unbolted villain into mortar, and daub the walls of a jakes with him . . . None of these rogues and cowards but Ajax is their fool.'

Lear, and comforts himself with a letter from Cordelia, which he reads at dawn:

> Approach, thou Beacon to this under-globe,
> That by thy comfortable beams I may
> Peruse this letter. *Nothing almost sees miracles*
> *But misery.*[1]

He cleaves to the King, goes through the storm, wanders to Dover, takes part in the battle. But the defeat of Cordelia breaks him up. He totters in to bid Lear 'good-night', and instead sees *him* die. He would not keep him, not stay himself, in this tough world—'O let him pass!'[2] To die is to *pass*. He will follow, 'My master *calls me*'.[3]

As faithful as Kent is the Fool—the most touching and, notwithstanding his sarcasm, most lovable, as he is also the most subtle in thought, of Shakespeare's Court-clowns.[4] He enlists our sympathy for Lear when our sense of his harshness and folly is yet lively, his youth contrasting with the King's grey hairs, and his delicacy of health matching the physical weakness of his master, pointing continually with his jests the moral and pathos of the situation. And then he disappears, as such dear creatures do, in the hurly-burly of the world. We do not know what becomes of him, and we have not time till all is over, to inquire. His place by the old King's side is taken by Cordelia.

This gracious heroine, whose eyes drop 'holy water' (a touch of the Old Faith amid the New),[5] is the presiding genius of the drama. She is little seen and less heard, but her effect is everywhere. She speaks altogether about one hundred lines—some forty at the beginning, sixty-odd at the end; but in absence she is present. 'I did her wrong'[6] is the thought her Father carries with him into the storm, and through it, and until they meet again, when he says,

> If you have poison for me, I will drink it.[7]

And the World might say this, whose innocent victim she is and redeemer. Like Desdemona, she is likened to Christ. Says one to Lear,

> Thou hast one daughter
> Who redeems nature from the general curse
> Which twain have brought her to.[8]

[1] II. ii. 170–3. [2] V. iii. 313. [3] *Ib.* 322.
[4] 'Tenderest of jesters' (Hales). [5] IV. iii. 31–5. See p. 724.
[6] I. v. 25. [7] IV. vii. 72. [8] IV. vi. 209–11.

As Christ redeemed the race from the reproach which Adam and Eve brought upon it, so Cordelia makes atonement for the disgrace inflicted by Goneril and Regan. And having manifested that spirit, there is no more that she can do. She died in its manifestation. 'The Gods defend her!'[1] is the prayer of Albany, well-meaning, orthodox. It is not answered, such prayers rarely are. Lear enters with her 'dead in his arms', his child and the victim of his headstrong past. 'What 's done is done' and 'what 's done cannot be undone . . . God forgive us all!'[2] We are left looking after them into the Unseen, feeling with Shakespeare the moral insufficiency and insipience of life, and its injustice and meaninglessness without life to come, convinced that goodness reveals not only human nature but the Divine:

Upon such sacrifices
The Gods themselves throw incense.[3]

Such are the lives they honour and love.

1606–8

§ 122. MARRIAGE OF SUSANNA SHAKESPEARE

SHAKESPEARE was probably in London on 18 October 1606 with his fellows, newly arrived from Dover, when Heminge received £30 for performances before King Christian in the summer.[4] This month he lost his friend, his hostess in Silver Street, Madame Montjoy. She was buried on the 30th. To take care of Monsieur and his 'sojourner', the Poet, the Bellots returned from George Wilkins's house to Silver Street; and presumably, Shakespeare continued to reside with Montjoy until the Bellots again left him in May 1607.

Shakespeare and his company performed *King Lear* at Whitehall on 26 December 1606,[5] and doubtless during the winter elsewhere, Burbage taking the part of 'Lear' and adding to the reputation he had acquired by his 'Richard', 'Hamlet', and

[1] v. iii. 256. [2] p. 649.
[3] v. iii. 20 f. [4] Chambers, iv. 173.
[5] See the entry of the play in the *Stationers' Register*, 26 Nov. 1607, 'as it was played before the King's Majesty at Whitehall upon St. Stephen's night at Christmas last, by his Majesty's Servants playing usually at the Globe on the Bankside' (Arber, iii. 366).

'Othello'. The impression left by his impersonation is suggested by the striking term of his elegist, '*kind* Lear'.[1] Did Shakespeare play 'Gloucester', Heminge 'Kent', Armin the 'Fool', Cowley 'Oswald'? At Whitehall the company also played on 29 December, 4, 6, and 8 January 1607, and 2, 5, 15 (Shrove Sunday), and 27 February.[2] On 30 March they received £90 by the hand of Heminge.[3] By the end of May or beginning of June, Shakespeare, we may believe, was in Stratford for his elder daughter's wedding. Master Greene was at home on 29 May, when he attended a meeting of the borough council and, we may assume, the Perrott sermon in the Chapel, followed by a banquet at Mistress Quyney's in the High Street.[4] She had lost, we will note, her revered old father-in-law, in the spring. His burial is thus entered in the register—

Mar. 7 Awdrianus Quinie, unus Aldermanus.[5]

Greene probably returned to London for Trinity Term, which began on 5 June. This day, which was Friday, Susanna Shakespeare was married at Stratford to Doctor John Hall. So we read in the register—

Junij 5 John Hall gentleman & Susanna Shaxspere.[6]

Susanna had just passed her twenty-fourth birthday, having been baptized on 26 May 1583. Her husband was seven years older, being sixty at the time of his death, 25 November 1635,[7] and only fourteen when he matriculated with his elder brother Dive at Cambridge from Queen's College in Michaelmas Term 1589.[8] Both are described as 'of Bedfordshire', and were the sons of William Hall, whom we find settled in Acton, Middlesex, at the time of his death in 1607. William Hall made his will at Acton on 12 December of that year,[9] six months after the marriage of John Hall, and was, as we gather from that document, also a medical practitioner.

He bequeathed 'all my books of physick unto my said son John'. He was, furthermore, an astronomer and astrologist, as his son had not made up his mind to be, and an alchemist, as

[1] *Elegy on the Death of Richard Burbage.*

[2] Chambers, iv. 121 f.

[3] *Ib.* 173.

[4] *Council Book B*, 147, and *Chamb. Acct.*, 8 Jan. 1608.

[5] p. 73.

[6] p. 22.

[7] See p. 891.

[8] *Alumni Cantabrigienses.*

[9] *P.C.C. 92 Huddleston* (Marcham, *William Shakespeare and his family*, p. 21).

Walter Scott, Bradford

'HALL'S CROFT', STRATFORD-UPON-AVON

definitely John had apparently decided *not* to be. Thus we conclude from the interesting bequests:

'I give and bequeath unto my man Matthew Morris all my books of astronomy and astrology whatsoever, conditionally that if my son John do intend and purpose to labour study and endeavour in the said Art, that the said Matthew should instruct him in consideration of his master's benevolence and free gift.

'Further I give and bequeath all my books of Alchemy unto my foresaid servant Matthew Morris and to be paid and given presently after my decease unto him.'

To Matthew Morris, of whom we shall hear again, and a good deal in Stratford-upon-Avon, William Hall also bequeathed four pounds. John's elder brother, Dive, had received his portion 'long ago', and had evidently caused his father trouble, especially since the mother's death, William Hall being a widower. There were daughters, Elizabeth married to Edmund Sutton, Damaris (?) to Michael Welles, Sara to William Sheapparde, doctor of physic of Oxford, and Martha to Benjamin Barlowe. Residuary legatee and executor is the younger son John; but the testator is uncertain whether he can act and makes provision accordingly. John, however, did act, and was present at the probate on 20 December following, in London, when there would be time for the journey from Stratford. Finally, the relationship of the two men is confirmed by the ultra-Protestant character of the preamble to the will.

John Hall had been admitted to his B.A. at Cambridge in 1593–4, and to his M.A. in 1597.[1] From Cambridge he went to the Continent, as many medical students did, and obtained a degree, probably in France.[2] In Stratford he enjoyed a large and fashionable practice, extending into and beyond the neighbouring shires.[3] Catholics were among his patients, notwithstanding his Puritan views,[4] in which, apparently, he had the full sympathy of his wife. We have noted his probable influence on Shakespeare—in *Hamlet*, *All's Well that Ends Well*, *Macbeth*, and *King Lear*—and shall note it again. Tradition connects him with the house in Old Town called 'Hall's Croft'. Already it may have been the Poet's intention that his daughter and son-

[1] I. Gray, *Shakespeare's son-in-law*. (*Genealogist*, Sept. 1936.)

[2] *Select Observations*, 1657.

[3] *Ib.*

[4] *Ib.* Preface by Doctor John Bird. See p. 833.

in-law should reside in *New Place*, for in the autumn of this year, on 7 November, Thomas Greene and his wife, Letitia, purchased from the Crown, in socage at a rent of eighteen shillings *per annum*, St. Mary's House adjoining the Churchyard. There was difficulty, however, in possession. The property in part was let to a recusant, George Browne, one of the Brownes of Ryon Clifford, and a 'papist'.[1] George Browne had married in 1594 Mistress Frances Barnes, a relative of Sir Henry Rainsford, and at length, by reference of the matter to Sir Henry, Greene at Michaelmas 1610 was able to leave *New Place* for his own abode.[2] The baptism of the Greenes' first child, Anne, has been noted.[3] Their second, a son, died in infancy and was buried on Sunday, 3 August 1606,[4] when Shakespeare was in attendance on King Christian. The third child, a son, was baptized in the parish church on Sunday 17 January 1608 and named William, no doubt after the Poet:

'1607 January 17 William, son unto Thomas Grene *generoso*.'[5]

Shakespeare was then in London, performing *twice* that day before the King.

In the early summer of 1607 Warwickshire was disturbed by 'tumultuous assemblies' against the enclosure of commons and 'depopulations'. Landlord aggression was worse than under Elizabeth, and the commoners, despairing of redress from James's weak and corrupt government, took the law into their own hands.[6] Cecil wrote to Winwood in Holland to reassure him against exaggerated rumours of riot, that the 'rabble' had done no 'harm to any person living but in pulling down hedges and ditches', and the Lieutenants of the shires had been 'directed to suppress them by fair *or foul* means'.[7] There was alarm in Stratford. Sir Edward Greville, as lord of the manor, was again to the fore. The gaol was put in order, and extra accommodation for prisoners, if needed, was provided at the Gild Hall, the

[1] He was presented as such in 1613.

[2] *Misc. Doc.* xi. 1. See below, p. 762.

[3] p. 620.

[4] *Register*, p. 73: 'Aug. 3 Infant son to Master Thomas Grene.'

[5] *Register*, p. 75.

[6] Stowe-Howes, *The Diggers of Warwickshire to all other Diggers*, New Shakspere Soc. 'Wit and Wisdom.'

[7] Winwood, ii. 315. See also 326 f. Such was 'capitalism' in 1607.

THE PAINTED ROOM IN CORNMARKET STREET, OXFORD

(by permission of E. W. Attwood, Esq.)

town-chest being removed from the armoury. The stocks, too, were mended.[1]

In London the plague increased, theatres were closed, and Shakespeare's company went on tour. They performed at Marlborough, Barnstaple, Oxford, and Cambridge.[2] They were at Oxford on 7 September.[3] Here Shakespeare would find himself among friends, chief of whom were the Davenants.

John Davenant, born in 1565, son of a London merchant-tailor, was educated at the Merchant Tailors' School, and admitted to the freedom of the Company in 1589. He may have known Shakespeare in London before his marriage some ten years later to his second wife, Jane Shepherd, the daughter, apparently, of Widow Tattleton, hostess of the *Salutation* Tavern[4] in Oxford.

Master and Mistress Davenant succeeded to the tavern, which was in the Corn Market (now no. 3 on the east side), a few yards from Carfax. They were a devoted couple, with a reputation for godliness, he 'grave and discreet', a reader and lover of books, she merry and handsome.[5] They had seven children, three girls and four boys, born in the years 1600–*c.* 1609. Robert, baptized in April 1603, became a doctor of divinity. He told Aubrey that 'Master Shakespeare had given him a hundred kisses'.[6] Master Davenant, though Puritan, loved plays, and was an enthusiastic admirer of the Poet, who frequently stayed at his house on his journeys between Stratford and London.[7] Shakespeare may have occupied the second-floor bedchamber, still in existence, overlooking the Corn Market, with a great fire-place in the east wall. In Widow Tattleton's time, at any rate, he would have read a black-letter admonitory stanza like that in the Priest's Chamber at Clopton, but running round the wall in a frieze:

[First of thi rysinge]
And last of thi rest
be thou god's servante
for that hold i best.

[1] *Chamberlain's Account*, 8 Jan. 1608.
[2] J. T. Murray, i. 151.
[3] *Ib.* 184.
[4] Afterwards *The Crown.*
[5] Wood, ii. 292.
[6] Clark, i. 204.
[7] Wood, ii. 292.

In the mornynge earlye
Serve god Devoutlye
Feare God above all thynge
[Honour all men] and the Kynge.[1]

Over the fire-place was (and is) an older monogram, 'I H S'. This writing was hidden by wainscoting subsequently erected by the Davenants.

The second son, William, baptized on Monday, 3 March 1606, had Shakespeare for a godfather and followed him in becoming a poet, but proved himself less worthy than his brother of Shakespeare's 'kisses'. When the 'Blatant Beast' defamed his mother with insinuations of a nearer relationship between him and Shakespeare, he was mean enough 'in his cups' to let it pass.

1607–8

§ 123. SHAKESPEARE'S PLAYS ON BOARD SHIP

NOT only at the Universities but among sailors on the far seas Shakespeare had his admirers. From journals[2] kept on the *Hector*, *Dragon*, and *Consent*, three of the East India Fleet, under command of William Keeling, captain of the *Dragon*, we learn of their departure on 4 March 1606/7 from Erith and arrival on 18 August at Sierra Leone. Keeling sent one John Rogers ashore to the native chief, Borea. Rogers returned on the 20th reporting his friendly reception by Borea and his interpreter, a negro, Lucas Fernandez, who spoke Portuguese very well. On the 27th Captain Hawkins of the *Hector* himself visited Borea, and supped with him and Fernandez, and found the latter very sensible. Next day the English were excited by the advent in the bay of a ship which tried to avoid them, and proved, on Keeling's inquiry, to be a Portingale from St. Iago under Bartholomew Andrea. On 4 September Fernandez came aboard the *Dragon* with a letter to Keeling from Andrea offering 'all kindly services'. Keeling, who thought Fernandez 'a man of marvellous ready wit', entertained him, and three negro companions, for the night, and sent him next morning, 'according to his desire', aboard the *Hector* for breakfast. 'And after', adds Keeling, all too

[1] The first and last line (cf. 1 Peter ii. 17) are conjecturally restored.
[2] F. S. Boas, *Contemporary Review*, July 1918.

briefly, in his log-book, 'he came aboard me, where we gave the Tragedy of Hamlet.' What a picture the entry calls up!—the little English *Dragon* anchored with her sister-ships in the bay of Sierra Leone, in summer, not ten degrees north of the equator,[1] and her crew, encouraged by the captain, entertain the chief's able interpreter and his fellow darkies with a performance in Elizabethan costume of 'The Prince of Denmark'. This was a means of promoting trade and friendship hardly within the calculation of modern advertisement, but entirely in the spirit of the Romantic Queen, now, alas! departed from the throne though not from her people, the secret of whose success was her gallant appeal to Imagination.

It is worth noting that this performance of *Hamlet*, two or three thousand miles away from home, took place on the Saturday before the exhibition of their 'quality' by Shakespeare and his fellows at Oxford on Monday 7 September, when the Mayor gave them 20*s*. out of the civic purse.

But this is not all we gather from these priceless journals. Keeling records, under date 30 September, 'Captain Hawkins dined with me, where my companions acted *King Richard the Second*'. And again, six months later, when the little fleet is becalmed in Indian waters and fresh food is a godsend, one Anthony Marlowe, a merchant on the *Hector*, is sent by Captain Hawkins to invite Commander Keeling 'to eat of dolphins taken of the mercy of God in sending fish to refresh us long sea-beaten travellers'. Next day, which was 31 March 1608, Keeling enters in his log-book, 'I invited Captain Hawkins to a fish dinner, and had *Hamlet* acted aboard me: which I permit to keep my people from idleness and unlawful games or sleep.'

1607

§ 124. *ANTONY AND CLEOPATRA*

FROM Oxford or Cambridge, we may believe Shakespeare returned to Stratford—to write *Antony and Cleopatra*, and to attend at least two domestic functions. On Wednesday, 14 October 1607, was baptized the son of his old friend, Richard Tyler.

[1] Hamlet might well be excused his perspiration and lack of breath.

The child was named William, the second to be so named. The first, christened in 1598, had died. The probability is that the Poet stood godfather to both infants. William the second lived to be an old gentleman and the honoured founder of a Charity in Stratford. The second function, again in the Parish Church, was the marriage on Sunday, 18 October 1607, of the Poet's nephew, Richard Hathaway. Born probably at Tysoe in 1582, the eldest son of Bartholomew Hathaway and his wife Isabella Hancocks of Tredington, Richard was 25 years of age, and one year older than his cousin, Susanna Shakespeare, now, since 5 June, wife to Doctor Hall. From what we know of these celebrations, there must have been a large gathering of the clans, Hathaways, Shakespeares, Halls, and kindreds, and 'a merry meeting', probably at *New Place*, after the not too solemn assemblage in the old Church porch. The bride, Mistress Priscilla Kyrdall, and her people, some of them it seems from Henley-in-Arden, would be welcomed into a leading Stratford circle as *cousins*.

Richard Hathaway was a baker, in Fore Bridge Street, near, perhaps next door to, the *Crown Inn*, of which in later life he became the host.

Antony and Cleopatra and *Pericles* were registered for publication on 20 May 1608.

Antony and Cleopatra is the sequel, after a lapse of years, to *Julius Caesar*, and must be regarded in the light of that drama. Brutus and Portia are an ideal man and wife. Their union is more intellectual than that of Coriolanus and Virgilia, graver, more ethical than that of Hotspur and Lady Percy. They are knit together, not by children, but by mental affinities and by years of companionship in happiness and suffering. Nothing disturbs their relationship but his mistaken sense of public duty, and her anxiety, which becomes despair, as to his safety.

According to Plutarch, Portia was a widow with a young son when Brutus married her. Shakespeare says nothing of this, he drops no hint of a former alliance. Portia, in his pages, is Cato's daughter, with enough of her father in her to inflict a wound in her side to test her power of keeping a state secret, and from first to last wife to 'Lord Brutus'[1] (who might be a Tudor noble), the gentle, clinging Lady of the great patriot, living and dying in

[1] *Jul. Caes.* II. i. 293, IV. iii. 238. Cf. II. i. 6, 233, 255, &c.

him. We see her twice, have but a glimpse of her in two brief scenes. They are sufficient, they reveal the sanctity of her wedded love. In the first the curtain is lifted for a moment on an interview so private that we seem like intruders and are almost glad when it drops again. She says to Brutus,

You have some sick offence within your mind,
Which, by the right and virtue of my place,
I ought to know of; and, upon my knees,
I charm you, by my once commended beauty,
By all your vows of love, and that great vow
Which did incorporate and make us one,
That you unfold to me yourself, your half,
Why you are heavy, and what men to-night
Have had resort to you; for here have been
Some six or seven who did hide their faces
Even from darkness.
BRUTUS. Kneel not, gentle Portia.
PORTIA. I should not need if you were gentle Brutus.
Within the bond of marriage, tell me, Brutus,
Is it excepted I should know no secrets
That appertain to you? Am I yourself
But, as it were, in sort or limitation,
To keep with you at meals, comfort your bed,
And talk to you sometimes? Dwell I but in the suburbs
Of your good pleasure? If it be no more,
Portia is Brutus' harlot, not his wife.
BRUTUS. You are my true and honourable wife,
As dear to me as are the ruddy drops
That visit my sad heart.[1]

The difference between the 'true and honourable wife' and the 'harlot' is the difference in character and colouring between *Julius Caesar* and *Antony and Cleopatra*. From the bracing atmosphere of the Seven Hills we enter a dazzling region of voluptuousness and superstition, where the scene shifts incessantly[2] and the ground reels under our feet.[3] We find ourselves in a golden

[1] II. i. 268–90. Montaigne knows nothing of such love: see p. 598.

[2] John Bailey (*Shakespeare*, p. 186) says well: 'We are not only constantly moving backwards and forwards between Alexandria and Rome, but we find ourselves also at Messina, at Misenum, on Pompey's galley at sea, on a plain in Syria, at Athens, and at Actium.' But he adds, erroneously, 'the continual changes of *Antony and Cleopatra* are its capital defect'. On the contrary, artistically they are absolutely right.

[3] There are thirteen scenes in the 3rd Act, fifteen in the 4th.

haze of splendour, in a languid intoxicating climate of wine and perfume, among slaves and eunuchs, fortune-tellers and the worshippers of Isis. And in place of the Stoic and his devoted helpmate, we have the lawless Epicurean and his gipsy quean.

What Shakespeare will present is told at once in a few words—

> The triple pillar of the world transformed
> Into a strumpet's fool: behold and see.[1]

Cleopatra enters with her victim and *mocks at his wife*.[2] Ambassadors have arrived with news from Rome, but he puts them off—

> Let Rome in Tiber melt, and the wide arch
> Of the ranged Empire fall! Here is my space.
> [*Embracing Cleopatra.*
> Kingdoms are clay: our dungy earth alike
> Feeds beast and man.[3]

Others have found kingdoms clay, and the earth food for man and beast, but Antony sacrifices these things for 'the strange woman' whose 'house inclineth unto death and her paths unto the dead'.[4]

What follows is the working-out of this theme, a subject which in lesser hands might merely repel, but as treated by Shakespeare is full of pathos. Antony is not like Dryden's hero, in his adaptation of the play, *All for Love*, a weak profligate, but the most attractive and, after Brutus, the greatest man of his time. Nor is Cleopatra a common wanton. Were she that, she would have no power over Antony. She is a brilliant and splendid creature, with mental as well as physical gifts, and as tragic in her fate as her lover in his.

Historically Cleopatra was a Greek. Shakespeare represents her as an Egyptian with 'tawny front', black in the sense that Othello was black and the heroine of Solomon's Song[5]—dark-featured as the gipsies, who attracted much attention in the Poet's lifetime. Plutarch is not enthusiastic about her beauty, says it

[1] I. i. 12 f.
[2] 20, 28, 31 f., 41.
[3] 33–6.
[4] Proverbs ii. 16 f.
[5] i. 5 ('I am black but comely').

was not beyond comparison with other women's. In the one passage in his *Life of Antony* where his imagination takes fire he describes glowingly the arts and accessories of her person, but he is silent about her features, tawny or otherwise. Shakespeare seized upon it and turned it into more glowing verse, adding a touch as to herself which is significant. Here is Plutarch in North's translation:

> 'When she was sent unto by divers letters, both from Antonius himself and also from his friends, she made so light of it and mocked Antonius so much that she disdained to set forward otherwise but to take her barge in the river of Cydnus. The poop whereof was of gold, the sails of purple and the oars of silver, which kept stroke in rowing after the sound of the music of flutes, haut-boys, citherns, viols and such other instruments as they played upon the barge. And now for the person of herself; she was laid under a pavilion of cloth of gold of tissue, apparelled and attired like the goddess Venus commonly drawn in picture; and hard by her, on either hand of her, pretty fair boys apparelled as painters do set forth god Cupid, with little fans in their hands, with the which they fanned wind upon her. Her ladies and gentlewomen also, the fairest of them, were apparelled like the nymphs Nereides, which are the mermaids of the waters, and like the Graces, some steering the helm, others tending the tackle and ropes of the barge; out of the which there came a wonderful passing sweet savour of perfumes, that perfumed the wharf's side.'

And here is Shakespeare's paraphrase, masterly in its soft, sensuous melody:

> The barge she sat in, like a burnished throne,
> Burned on the water; the poop was beaten gold,
> Purple the sails, and so perfumed that
> The winds were love-sick with them; the oars were silver,
> Which to the tune of flutes kept stroke, and made
> The water which they beat to follow faster
> As amorous of their strokes. For her own person,
> *It beggar'd all description*. She did lie
> In her pavilion, cloth of gold of tissue,
> O'er-picturing that Venus where we see
> The fancy outwork nature; on each side her
> Stood pretty dimpled boys, like smiling Cupids
> With divers-colour'd fans, whose wind did seem
> To glow the *delicate cheeks* which they did cool
> And what they undid did.
> Her gentlewomen, like the Nereides,
> So many mermaids, tended her i' the eyes
> And made their bends adornings; at the helm
> A seeming mermaid steers; the silken tackle

Swell with the touches of those flower-soft hands
That yarely frame the office. From the barge
A strange invisible perfume hits the sense
Of the adjacent wharfs.[1]

'Delicate cheeks', however, and 'a tawny front' with 'Phoebus' amorous pinches black', is all the Poet gives us of this 'thronèd Sensuality'. 'She beggar'd all description': so he dismisses her physical appearance, omitting the picture Marlowe would have painted with Renaissance appetite—of her hair and brows, her lips, her neck and arms, and 'naked glory', her 'white limbs', breasts, 'rising ivory' with 'azure circling lines empaled', 'by which Love sails to regions full of bliss'.

Leaving the flesh, with a fine phrase, Shakespeare gives us the mind in speech and action. She is Egyptian in character, as he has read of Egypt in the Bible since a child—as 'the house of bondage', the stronghold of oppression, the scene of 'fleshpots' and 'pomp' and faithlessness, the home of magic and enchantment, 'plagues', 'diseases', 'whoredoms', 'fornication', and other 'abominations':[2] from which 'the Lord delivered His people',[3] and from which 'by faith, Moses fled, refusing to be called the son of Pharaoh's daughter, choosing rather to suffer adversity with the people of God than to enjoy the pleasures of sins for a season, esteeming the rebuke of Christ greater riches than the treasures of Egypt'.[4]

Antony cries,
These strong Egyptian fetters I must break,
Or lose myself in dotage;[5]

again,

I must from this enchanting queen break off;
Ten thousand harms more than the ills I know
My idleness doth hatch.[6]

Twice there is an allusion to the prophet's warning that Egypt is a reed to lean upon, a broken staff that pierces the hand of him that trusts it.[7] More significant are references to the 'serpent' or 'crocodile' of Nilus, 'which hath said, *The River is mine, and I*

[1] II. ii. 196–218.

[2] Exodus xx. 2, i–xii, xvi. 3; Ezekiel xxxii. 12, xxiii. 2, 19, xvi. 26; Deuteronomy vii. 15, xxviii. 60; Ezra ix. 1, &c.

[3] Exodus xviii. 8–10, &c.

[4] Hebrews xi. 24–6.

[5] I. ii. 120 f.

[6] I. ii. 132–4.

[7] II. vii. 13–15, III. xiii. 68 f. Cf. 2 Kings xviii. 21.

have made it for myself. But I will put hooks in thy jaws and draw thee out of the midst of thy rivers'. This passage in Ezekiel[1] was in the Poet's thought when he wrote,

> We'll to the *River*; there
> My music playing far off, I will betray
> Tawny-finned fishes; my bended *hook* shall pierce
> Their slimy *jaws*, and as I *draw* them up
> I'll think them every one an Antony.[2]

Cleopatra is 'the strange serpent', born, as Ovid says, of the mud of the Nile, 'heated by the Sun's rays' (*aetherio exarsit sidere limus*).[3] 'In the midst of the feast', says Plutarch, Pompey's guests 'fell to be merry with Antonius' love unto Cleopatra'. Shakespeare develops Scripture, Ovid and Plutarch into a dialogue between Lepidus and Antony. The former, rather tipsy and facetious, chaffs Cleopatra's lover, who is more than a bit nettled:

LEPIDUS. You've strange serpents there?
ANTONY. Ay, Lepidus.
LEPIDUS. Your serpent of Egypt is bred now of your mud by the operation of your sun: so is your crocodile.
ANTONY. They are so.
LEPIDUS. What manner o' thing is your crocodile?
ANTONY. It is shaped, sir, like itself, and it is as broad as it has breadth; it is just as high as it is, and moves with its own organs; it lives by that which nourisheth it; and the elements once out of it, it transmigrates.
LEPIDUS. What colour is it of?
ANTONY. Of its own colour too.
LEPIDUS. 'Tis a strange serpent.[4]

This 'strange serpent' of the Nile is drawn on the lines of the 'strange woman' of Proverbs:

'She flattereth with her words; her lips drop as an honeycomb, and her mouth is more soft than oil; she forsaketh the husband and guide of her youth, and forgetteth the covenant of God; she weigheth not the way of life but her paths are movable and unsteadfast, they cannot be known; she is subtle in heart and decketh her bed with the ornaments of Egypt, with myrrh and aloes and cinnamon, but her end is bitter as wormwood and sharp as a two-edged sword, her feet go down to death and her steps pierce through into Hell.'[5]

Cleopatra has sweetness of the mouth and lips ('a kiss repays

[1] xxix. 3 f. (Bishops' Bible).
[2] II. v. 10–14.
[3] *Metamorphoses*, i. 416–47 (423 f.).
[4] II. vii. 27–32, 46–54.
[5] II. 16–18, V. 3–5, VII. 6–27.

all that was lost'),[1] flattery, unsteadfastness ('infinite variety'[2] of charm and principle), forsakes her husband and children, lies, deserts her lover on the instant, brings him to shame and suicide. Hence her 'grave-charm':

> Betrayed I am,
> O this false soul of Egypt! this grave-charm.[3]

She has the witchery that brings a man to the grave.[4] Her maid, Charmian, is licentious like herself. She is guilty of a speech more audacious than she knows. To the Egyptian soothsayer she says:

> 'Good now, some excellent fortune! Let me be married to three kings in a forenoon and widow them all. Let me have a child at fifty to whom Herod of Jewry may do homage. Find me to marry with Octavius Caesar and companion me with my mistress.'[5]

The 'kings' are the Wise Men of Matthew ii, the Three Kings of the mystery plays, who brought 'gold, frankincense, and myrrh' to the cradle of Christ, and to whom Herod professed his intention also to worship the Child. Cleopatra died in the year 30 B.C. If Charmian were then 20 years of age she would be 'fifty' at the Nativity. Her ambition is to rival her mistress in her loves. In the ears of her audience[6] she blasphemes. She would be mistress at once of the Three Kings, be the mother of Christ, be the wife of the Emperor, Caesar Augustus.

In such libertine company Antony is doomed. He has the qualities which expose him to ruin. In *Julius Caesar* he was Caesar's friend, the foil of Brutus, a 'shrewd contriver', victor with Octavius at Philippi, athlete and soldier, of a 'quick spirit', 'gamesome', a lover of plays and music, wine and revelry.[7] The ethical Brutus despised him, under-estimated, as the moralist often does, the power and influence of the artist. Brutus addressed the people from a height, in abstract terms, bade them be patient and *judge*. Antony was *of* them, among them, began with a beseeching note, and gradually, by use of concrete images and

[1] III. xi. 71.

[2] II. ii. 241.

[3] IV. xii. 24 f. Cf. Proverbs vii. 27: 'Her house is the way unto the *grave* (Geneva Version).

[4] The expression, so obvious in its meaning, to those who know their Bible, and so powerful, has been ludicrously misunderstood by commentators.

[5] I. ii. 25–30.

[6] In 1607: hardly at the present day, when the point of her audacity would probably be unrecognized.

[7] *Jul. Caes.* I. ii. 28 f., 203 f., II. ii. 116.

objects and the magic of verse, he captured their sympathy and sent them at last to wreak their fury on the conspirators.

On the death of Brutus and Cassius, he forms with Octavius and Lepidus the triumvirate. Pompey says his 'soldiership is twice the other twain'. When he is absent in Egypt all goes wrong with the State—the Parthians gain ground in Asia, pirates scour the Mediterranean, there is revolt in Rome. When he bestirs himself, Pompey's hopes vanish and Octavius is driven from Alexandria. Cleopatra calls him, justly, her 'Herculean Roman' and 'greatest soldier of the world'. His men love him, notwithstanding his faults. Scarus halts after him bleeding, with a wound enlarged from a T to an H. Enobarbus deserts him and takes his own life. Eros, rather than kill Antony with his sword, falls on it himself.

Most eloquent of greatness in his nature is the change his love works in Cleopatra. They meet in the prime of life. He is tall and handsome, his hair just touched with grey. She envies his inches, admires him walking, is proud of him on horseback, plays with his strong arms affectionately. She is in her ripe womanhood. Her 'salad days' of 'green judgment' are past; she has been mistress of Pompey and Julius Caesar, she has children growing up; but she is still 'fine Egyptian cookery', an 'Egyptian dish' (an appeal to *appetite*), a 'wonderful piece of work', her lover's 'great fairy'. And when they stand up together they are 'a peerless' pair.[1]

A worldly idealism, a brave recklessness, a spirit of *cameraderie* unites them as well as passion, and makes them indispensable to each other. They are never dull, as 'good' people often are. Their fellowship knows nothing of the unenterprising apathy which is often the curse of respectability.

Nevertheless, there is no meeting of souls. With all their fondling and kissing they are spiritually apart. They do not touch in the highest things. She is never quite sure of him, he can never quite trust her. 'She is cunning past man's thought.'[2] And both are subject to mad fits of jealousy. Two scenes in the play recall the words in Solomon's Song, 'Jealousy is cruel as the grave; the coals thereof are fiery coals and a vehement flame.'[3]

[1] *Ant. & Cleo.* II. vi. 64, I. ii. 159 f., IV. viii. 12, I. i. 40.

[2] I. ii. 150.

[3] viii. 6.

In the first (II. 5) Cleopatra is in her palace in Alexandria. Antony is away. She reclines on her couch, idle, restless, petulant:

CLEOPATRA. Give me some music—music, moody food
Of us that trade in love.
ATTENDANT. The music, ho! [*Enter Mardian.*

She changes her mind:

CLEOPATRA. Let it alone; let's to billiards: come, Charmian.

The transition from music to billiards is suggestive. Charmian is tired of billiards:

CHARMIAN. My arm is sore; best play with Mardian.

But she'll none. She will to the river and fish. A post arrives from Rome. She leaps to her feet to know the news. In her impatience she scarce allows the messenger time to speak, and overwhelms him, as his words come forth, with lavish promise and brutal threat. When he announces that Antony is married, and to the sister of Octavius, she strikes him, again and again, haling him up and down—

I'll unhair thy head,
Thou shalt be whipt with wire, and stew'd in brine.

She draws a knife, and he runs from the chamber.

Calmer, she sends for him, to know the looks of her rival—her stature, her age, the colour of her hair, how tall she is. And when she learns that Octavia is shorter than herself, has a round face and low forehead, is dull of tongue and is a widow, she bursts into laughter. These are not the attractions to hold her Antony.

Equally savage and gratuitous is Antony's wrath on coming upon Thyreus, Caesar's messenger, kissing Cleopatra's hand (III. xiii. 93–113):

Take hence this Jack and whip him. Moon and stars,
Whip him,
Till like a boy you see him cringe his face
And whine aloud for mercy.

Then he turns on Cleopatra,

You were half-blasted ere I knew you: ha!
CLEOPATRA. Good my lord—

ANTONY. You have been a boggler ever:
But when we in our viciousness grow hard,
O misery on't! the wise Gods seel our eyes,[1]
In our own filth drop our clear judgments.

Antony is too great for his fate. He repents, struggles, resolves to abandon the sorceress. But he leaves her to return. His ancestor, Hercules, gives him up, withdraws his warrior spirit from him. He commits blunder after blunder, strains the fidelity of his followers to breaking-point, throws away his chances, and, deserted in his last battle by his 'triple-turned whore', he is worsted by the 'boy', Octavius.[2] He cries to Hercules,

The shirt of Nessus is upon me: teach me,
Alcides, thou mine ancestor, thy rage:
Let me lodge Lichas on the horns o' the moon,
And with those hands that grasp'd the heaviest club
Subdue my worthiest self. The Witch shall die.[3]

He will murder Cleopatra, and take his own life. She escapes to the monument, and gives out that she is dead. He falls upon his sword. She says to him dying,

Shall I abide
In this dull world, which in thy absence is
No better than a sty?[4]

And when he is dead, she cries:

There is nothing left remarkable,
Beneath the visiting moon.[5]

What manner of woman is this, capable of such a desolation, and expression of it? She dies in her own way, *painlessly*,[6] by the poison of the asp (another 'serpent of old Nile'),[7] arrayed in robe and crown, with an eye to effect, so that Charmian can say,

Now boast thee, Death, in thy possession lies
A lass unparallel'd . . . Your crown's awry,
I'll mend it.[8]

[1] A term from falconry.

[2] IV. xii. 9–49.

[3] 43–7. 'Worthiest self' is counterpart to 'heaviest club', in the case of Antony as of Hercules, namely his life. For the 'Witch shall die', see Exodus xxii. 18: 'Thou shalt not suffer a witch to live.'

[4] IV. xv. 60–2.

[5] 67 f.

[6] A coward as regards pain, she has studied infinite forms of painless suicide and 'easy ways to die': V. ii. 357–9.

[7] V. ii. 243 ('the pretty worm of Nilus'). This Clown-scene, like the Porter-scene in *Macbeth*) is a grim comment on the play.

[8] *Ib.* 318–22.

And Octavius,

She looks like Sleep,
As she would catch another Antony,
In her strong coil of grace.[1]

She is the old Cleopatra. Yet she is a new, a greater creature. Her last words have the note of true womanhood:

Husband, I come!
Now *to that name* my courage prove my title.[2]
I am fire and air; my other elements
I give to baser life.[3]

She has outgrown the harlot, and *alta petit*. A sense of motherhood nestles in her bosom:

Peace, peace!
Dost thou not see my Baby at my breast
That sucks the Nurse asleep?[4]

We must note in the play the versification in certain passages of deep emotion. In Antony's great speech beginning,

Unarm, Eros, the long day's task is done,
And we must sleep—

we have these lines:

I will o'ertáke | thee, Cleopát|ra, and
Weep for my pár|don. So it múst | be, for now
All length is tór|ture; since the torch is out,
Lie down and stray no fár|ther: now all lá|bour
Mars what it does: yea, very force entáng|les
Itself with strength; séal | then, and all is done.[5]

And Cleopatra laments:

He was as rattling thún|der; for his bóun|ty,
There was no winter ín | it: an autumn 'twas

[1] v. ii. 349–51.

[2] Even this lawless character can talk law.

[3] v. ii. 290–4. See Ovid, *Metamorphoses*, xv. 239–43:

Quattuor aeternus genitalia corpora mundus
Continet; ex illis duo sunt onerosa suoque
Pondere in inferius, tellus atque unda, feruntur;
Et totidem gravitate carent nulloque premente
Alta petunt, aër atque aëre purior ignis.

'Four elementary substances doth the Eternal World comprise. Two of these, earth and water, have weight and by their heaviness are borne downward. And two, air and fire (which is lighter than air) are without weight and unobstructed seek the heights.' Without reference to Ovid, Cleopatra's noble aspiration is missed.

[4] v. ii. 311–13. A dull jest in Peele (*Edward I*, Dyce, *Old Dramatists*, p. 406) and Nashe (McKerrow, ii. 140) is here supreme poetry.

[5] IV. xiv. 44–9.

That grew the more by réap|ing; his delights
Were dolphin-like: they show'd his back above
The element they lívcd | in; in his livery
Walked crowns and crówn|ets; realms and ís|lands were
As plates dropp'd from his pó|cket.[1]

Here are the run-on lines, with weak or light ending, extra syllable and central pause with penultimate stress, which mark the Poet's emancipated and mature verse, especially in the utterance of grief. It is broken music for a broken heart, and draws us to the speaker.

1607–8

§ 125. *PERICLES*

SHAKESPEARE'S association with the Bellots, and their connexion with George Wilkins, doubtless had to do with the origin of *Pericles*. Wilkins ventured on novels and probably had encouragement from Shakespeare. He wrote a play, *The Miseries of Inforst Marige*, which was performed by Shakespeare's company in 1607. He was author of a novel, *The Painfull adventures of Pericles, prince of Tyre*, which was published in 1608.[2] This novel is based on the old story of Apollonius of Tyre, told by John Gower in his *Confessio Amantis* and, in Elizabeth's reign, by Laurence Twine in his *Patterne of painfull aduentures*. A new issue in 1607 of Twine's book (which first appeared in 1576) prompted Wilkins to write his *Painfull adventures*, with change of the hero's name to Pericles (the Pyrocles probably of Sidney's *Arcadia*) and those of his wife and daughter to Thaisa and Marina, and other alterations. A drama in verse of the *Painfull adventures*, by an unknown author, was brought to Shakespeare for performance by his company. He saw its possibilities and revised it, touching up the first two acts and re-writing the last three. The master-hand reveals itself unmistakably at the opening of the third act:

Thou God of this great vast, rebuke these surges,
Which wash both heaven and hell; and Thou, that hast

[1] v. ii. 86–92. Cf. 12–18.

[2] Wilkins, in the dedication of his novel to Master Henry Fermor, calls it the 'poor infant' of his 'brain'. He makes no claim to the *play* of Pericles, but only to the 'true history' on which it was based Had he been part-author of the play, he would almost certainly have said so.

Upon the winds command, bind them in brass,
Having called them from the deep! O still Thy deafening
Dreadful thunders, gently quench Thy nimble
Sulphurous flashes! O Lychorida,
How does my queen?

Great metre, Ovid, law, religion, the Bible, righteous handling (as the transformation of Lysimachus from a frequenter of the brothel to a governor inspector of its horrors) are Shakespeare's throughout Acts iii to v. They betray him here and there in Acts i and ii. The Gower-chorus may or may not be entirely his, but certainly it is largely his, from the beginning, with such lines as

Assuming man's infirmities,

and

So buxom, blithe, and full of face,
As Heaven had lent her all His grace,

which gave us Milton's

So buxom, blithe and debonair.[1]

It was not quite his first attempt at the dainty pseudo-archaic English of Spenser, and he is neither happy nor consistent in it He breaks away with:

the grisled North
Disgorges such a tempest forth.[2]

Shakespeare was familiar with Gower's monument in St. Saviour's. The old poet lies in effigy on his tomb, in cap and gown, his hands raised in prayer. His head rests for a pillow on his three volumes, in Latin, French, and English—*Vox Clamantis*, *Speculum Meditantis*, and *Confessio Amantis*. There was particular reason for Shakespeare's attachment at this time to St. Saviour's and to some spot a few yards from Gower's tomb. His youngest brother, Edmund, was buried here on New Year's Eve, 1607, in the forenoon of Thursday, 31 December, with 'a knell of the great bell', for which, and the interment within the church, the Poet doubtless paid the fees, amounting to 20*s*.[3]—about £15 in our post-War money. Edmund must have been a care to his brother, whom he followed to London to become a player. He

[1] *L'Allegro*, 24.

[2] iii. 47 f.

[3] The fee for burial in the churchyard was 2*s*., but 'the Churchwardens have for the ground for every man or woman that shall be buried in the church, with an afternoon's knell or without it, 20*s*.' ('Duties belonging to the Church', 1613).

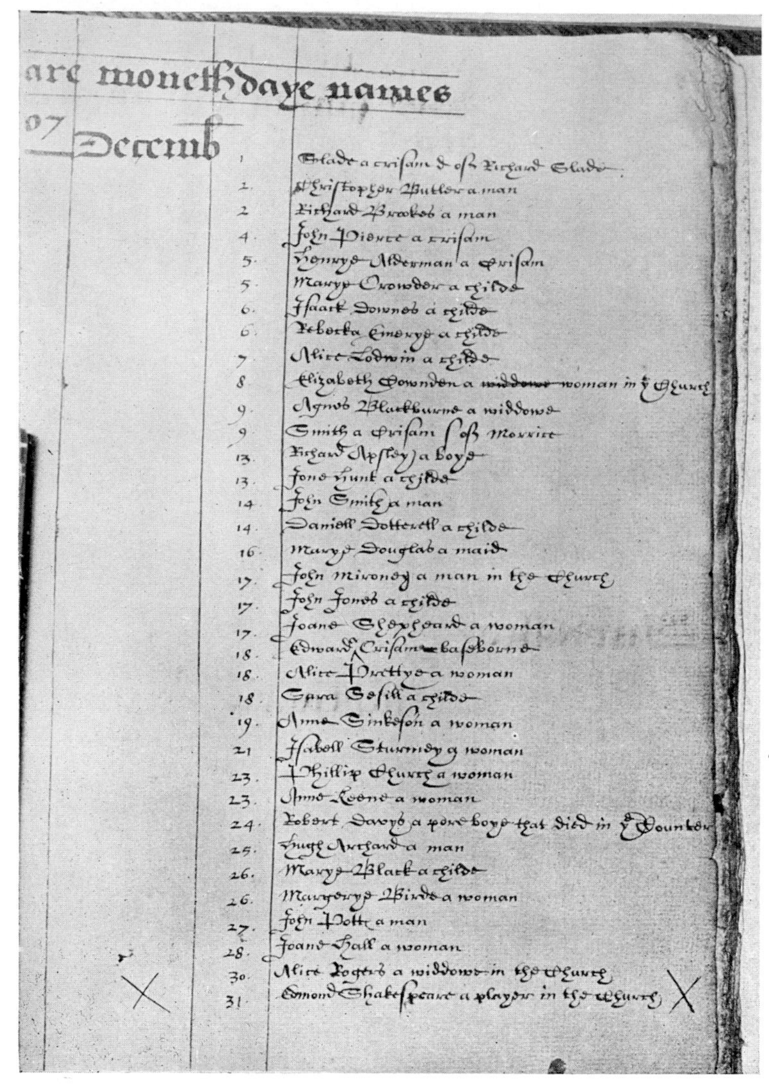

ENTRY OF BURIAL OF SHAKESPEARE'S BROTHER EDMUND,
ST. SAVIOUR'S, SOUTHWARK, 31 DEC. 1607

(by permission of the Rev. Canon J. B. Haldane)

was 27 years of age at the time of his death, and father of an illegitimate child who had died before him and been buried at St. Giles, Cripplegate, on 12 August of this year: 'Edward, son of Edward Shackspeere, player, base-born.'[1] Edmund and Edward, as said before, are interchangeable names in the registers.

The entry in the burial-register of St. Saviour's runs,

> '1607 December 31 Edmond Shakespeare, a player, in the Church';

and that in the sexton's account,

> '1607 December 31 Edmund Shakespeare, a player, buried in the church with a forenoon knell of the great bell, 20*s*.'

The spelling of 'Shakespeare' is the Poet's own in his published writings, *Venus and Adonis* and *Lucrèce*. Probably he is responsible for this form in the entries. The funeral was in the morning—Shakespeare and his fellows were on duty in the afternoon at the *Globe*.

It was bitterly cold weather. 'About the week before Christmas' the Thames just above the Bridge was frozen over. Ice-floes piled against the piers afforded a path, at first some five yards broad, for daring boys and youths from Cold Harbour to Bankside. This widened until at length it stretched to Westminster, providing a safe sheet of ice on which multitudes walked and sported. The unwonted spectacle presented itself for weeks of men shooting at pricks with bows and arrows, wrestling, running races, playing football, 'nine-holes', and 'pigeon-holes', as well as 'sliding'. There were refreshments. 'Would you drink a cup of sack, thirst you for beer, ale, usquebaugh (whisky), or for victuals, there you may buy it. If you want fruit after you have dined, there stand costermongers to serve you at your call.' Two barbers' shops 'in the fashion of booths with signs' were well patronized. The famous waterway became a highway. 'Of all ages, of both sexes, of *all professions*,' writes our informant, an eyewitness, here apparently quoting the Porter in *Macbeth*,[2] 'this is the common path'. Not exactly *the way to the Everlasting Bonfire*; yet were there fires on the ice, 'pans of coals' whereat 'to warm your fingers'.[3]

'Alas, poor watermen!' he says; 'the western barges might

[1] *Register*.
[2] II. iii. 21.
[3] *The Great Frost; cold doings in London, except it be at the Lottery* (Jan. 1608).

now wrap up their smoky sails.' Alas, too, poor players! The audience must have shivered at the *Globe* with its open roof, even if 'pans of coal' were provided. Sports on the river were more attractive than plays. But if the takings at the *Globe* suffered, and hastened Shakespeare and his company in their determination to have a covered winter-theatre in Blackfriars, the reward at Court was munificent. On 8 February they were paid £130 for performances at Whitehall—on 26 December, 27 December (Sunday), 28 December, 2 January, 6 January (two plays), 7 January, 9 January, 17 January (two plays), 26 January, 2 February (Candlemas), and 7 February (Shrove Sunday).[1]

In the early months of 1608, we may believe, Shakespeare reshaped *Pericles*. From St. Saviour's he brings the 'ancient Gower', with a staff in one hand and a bunch of bays in the other,[2] and from the Southwark-end of the Bridge the traitors' heads on poles, with their 'grim looks', 'dead cheeks', 'speechless tongues', 'and semblance pale', and no 'covering save yon field of Stars'—as the Poet had seen them on a winter's night. From the Bankside he introduces once more, in ghastly hideousness, the hateful 'Stews'. From Stratford, on the other hand, comes the familiar beadle who whips the beggars, the good physician Cerimon, and the fair Puritan girl among the flowers.

Pericles is a voyager over life's sea, who beholds the works of the Lord and His wonders in the deep; whose soul melteth because of trouble; who reels to and fro, and staggers like a drunken man; and is at his wits' end; who cries unto the Lord in his trouble, and is delivered from his distress; and then is glad because he is at rest, in the haven where he would be.[3]

His cry in pain is intenser than the storm, is heard above it, in appeal to pitiless deities. His wife dies, is thrown overboard by the superstitious mariners, as Jonah (whose story leaves more than one impress on the play) is cast from the ship,[4] and washed on shore at Ephesus. His child, Marina, daughter of the sea, is landed at Tarsus, and entrusted by him in flight to the governor Cleon and his wife, Dionyza.

Fourteen years go by, she is of Juliet's age. Her gifts and beauty

[1] Chambers, iv. 174. [2] Halliwell-Phillipps, *Outlines*, ii. 336.

[3] Psalm cvii. 23–30.

[4] III. i. 47–72. Cf. Jonah i. 5–15. With II. i. 29–47, cf. Jonah i. 17, II. i. 10.

excite in Dionyza, who has a daughter, jealousy. Like Imogen, she can use her needle, among other accomplishments:

> She sings like one immortal, and she dances
> As goddess-like to her admired lays;
> Deep clerks she dumbs; and with her needle cómposes
> Nature's own shape of bud, bird, branch, or berry,
> That even her art sisters the natural roses;
> Her inkle,[1] silk, twin with the rubied cherry.[2]

Like Perdita, she loves flowers:

> No, I will rob Tellus of her weed[3]
> To strew thy green with flowers: the yellows, blues,
> The purple violets and marigolds,
> Shall as a carpet hang upon thy grave
> While summer days do last.[4]

And like Cordelia and Imogen, she is religious. Her 'quirks' and 'reasons', 'prayers', and 'knees' would make 'a Puritan of the devil' and 'priests' of 'swearers'.[5]

Sent to death by Dionyza, she is captured by pirates and sold into a brothel—from flowers to filth. Here are the surroundings of Isabella, but a helpless girl, not a woman of station, confronts the pollution. She springs to womanhood—

> *An honest woman, or not a woman.*[6]

As in *Measure for Measure*, also, the Governor, Lysimachus, makes personal inspection of this haunt of wickedness, in the role not of a friar but of a patron of the stews. He makes trial of Marina, and is more than satisfied of her innocence:

> I did not think
> Thou could'st have spoke so well, ne'er dreamed thou could'st.
> Had I brought hither a corrupted mind,
> Thy speech had altered it. Hold, here's gold for thee:
> Persever in that clear way thou goest,
> And the Gods strengthen thee! . . .
> Fare thee well. Thou art a piece of virtue, and
> I doubt not but thy training hath been noble.
> Hold, here's more gold for thee.
> A curse upon him, die he like a thief,
> That robs thee of thy goodness! If thou dost
> Hear from me, it shall be for thy good.[7]

[1] A kind of narrow fillet or tape.
[2] Prol. v. 3–8. Cf. IV. vi. 194.
[3] Ovid, *Metam.* vii. 196.
[4] IV. i. 14–18.
[5] IV. vi. 8–13.
[6] IV. ii. 90.
[7] IV. vi. 109–14, 118–23.

With his gold she buys her freedom; and from him we hear,

> She is all happy, as the fairest of all,
> And with her fellow maids is now upon
> The leafy shelter that abuts against
> The Island's side.[1]

Like Cordelia, she brings her father back to life and love, and, unlike her hapless prototype, to years as full of blessing as the years he had known were full of adversity. Things happen 'too good to be true' after events beyond credit for their painfulness. He cries,

> O Helicanus, strike me, honoured sir;
> Give me a gash, put me to present pain;
> Lest this great sea of joys rushing upon me
> O'erbear the shores of my mortality
> And drown me with their sweetness . . .
> Down on thy knees, thank the holy Gods as loud
> As thunder threatens us; *this is Marina* . . .
> Give me my robes. I am wild in my beholding.
> O Heaven bless my girl! But hark, what Music?
> HELICANUS. My lord, I hear none.
> PERICLES. None?
> *The Music of the Spheres.*[2]

This happy conclusion,[3] the thought that 'in Pericles' was 'seen',

> Although assailed with fortune fierce and keen,
> Virtue preserved from fell destruction's blast,
> *Led on by Heaven and crowned with joy at last*—[4]

makes the play the first of a group of dramas which have been well described, in contrast with the terrible tragedies preceding, as Dramatic Romances. But for the present, 1608, such a play was an episode. Other work of a painful kind had to be done before Shakespeare could yield altogether to the new impulse. *Timon of Athens* and *Coriolanus* part *Pericles* from its sister-dramas, *Cymbeline*, *The Winter's Tale*, and *The Tempest*.

[1] v. i. 49–52.

[2] v. i. 192–6, 200 f., 224 f., 230 f.

[3] Such an ending, with other features, made *Pericles* popular, and encouraged Wilkins to publish his novel; which bore the title, *The painfull adventures of Pericles, prince of Tyre; being the true history of the play of Pericles, as it was lately presented by the worthy and ancient poet, John Gower* (1608). In the 'Argument' he asks his reader 'to receive this History in the same manner as it was under the habit of ancient Gower, the famous English Poet, by the King's Majesty's Players excellently presented'.

[4] v. iii. 87–90.

§ 126. SHAKESPEARE'S MEDICINE

CERIMON and Marina were not far from *New Place*. The former recalls the 'good doctor' in *Macbeth*, skilful and religious, but is a fuller portrait, and tells us something of contemporary treatment of sickness. He might be Doctor Hall, more keen about his cures than his fees and, if like his wife, the Poet's daughter, open-handed. Gentlemen roused from their beds by the storm find Cerimon up and about at dawn, ready for patients that the tempest might bring, dispatching his man to the apothecary. He says, in reply to their astonishment:

'Tis known I ever
Have studied physic, through which secret art,
By turning o'er authorities, I have
Together with my practice, made familiar
To me and to my aid the blest infusions
That dwell in vegetives, in metals, stones;
And I can speak of the disturbances
That Nature works, and of her cures; which doth give me
A more content in course of true delight
Than to be thirsty after tottering honour,
Or tie my treasure up in silken bags
To please the fool and Death.[1]

The lines that follow might be a prophecy of Hall's coming reputation:

Your honour has through Ephesus poured forth
Your charity, and hundreds call themselves
Your creatures who by you have been restored:
And not your knowledge, your personal pain,[2] but even
Your purse still open, hath built Lord Cerimon
Such strong renown as Time shall never end.[3]

Two of Cerimon's remedies must be noted, in one line:

The *music* there! I pray you, give her *air*.[4]

Sick mind and body could hardly have anything better—with warmth, 'make a fire within'.[5]

Shakespeare had been brought up on old medical knowledge

[1] III. ii. 31–42. For Doctor Hall's refusal of a knighthood see p. 884.

[2] Painstaking.

[3] III. ii. 43–8.

[4] 91.

[5] Gower's 'Maister Cerimon, a worthy leech, clerk and surgeon and eke a great physician' is responsible for the 'fire and cloths' ('a sheet warmed oft'), Shakespeare's Cerimon for the music and fresh air.

and superstition. He heard about 'elements'[1] and 'humours',[2] bleeding and the proper month for it,[3] water-casting,[4] lunar[5] and planetary influence.[6] He was perhaps bled himself before manhood, and warned to keep the air from a cut finger,[7] and not to sleep in the light of the moon. Homely Stratford remedies occur in his earlier writings—pills,[8] poultice,[9] plaster,[10] licking of a poisoned wound,[11] salves,[12] purgation,[13] 'potions and motions'.[14] He speaks there of plantain[15] and camomile,[16] aloes,[17] balsam,[18] syrup,[19] wormwood,[20] and ratsbane.[21] Occasionally also he ventures on a more technical term, like parmaceti,[22] aconitum,[23] *pia mater*, and 'ventricle of memory'.[24] There is nothing to suggest that he had been an apothecary's assistant or a medical student. On the other hand, from the time of his acquaintance with Doctor Hall (who was only eleven years his junior), and his proximity in Silver Street to the Barber-Surgeons' headquarters, he develops a wider and more curious interest in complaints and cures, introduces, as we have seen, doctors in his dramas, and delivers himself of lay convictions derived, no doubt, from his own experience. He talks not only of senna[25] and rhubarb[26] and purgative,[27] but of cataplasm,[28] clyster,[29] mandragora,[30] poppy,[31] rue[32] and fumiter,[33] colo-

1 *Sonnets*, 44 f.
2 *2 Hen. VI*, I. i. 247, I. ii. 97; *Sonnets*, 91; *Love's L. L.* II. i. 53, V. i. 10.
3 *Rich. II*, I. i. 157.
4 *2 Hen. IV*, I. ii. 1–6.
5 *Oth.* V. ii. 109; *Ant. & Cleo.* IV. ix. 12.
6 *1 Hen. VI*, I. i. 23, 54; *2 Hen. VI*, IV. iv. 16; *K. Lear*, I. ii. 135.
7 *3 Hen. VI*, II. vi. 27.
8 *Two Gent.* II. iv. 149.
9 *Rom. & Jul.* II. v. 65.
10 *Temp.* II. i. 139; *K. John*, V. ii. 13.
11 *Ven. & Ad.* 916 ('licking 'gainst venom'd sores the only sovereign plaster').
12 *Ven. & Ad.* 28; *Lucr.* 1116; *Sonnets*, 34, 7.
13 *Love's L. L.* III. i. 128.
14 *Sonnets*, 111, 119; *Merry W.* III. i. 105.
15 *Love's L. L.* III. i. 74; *Rom. & Jul.* I. ii. 52. Cf. Drayton, *Poly-Olbion*, xiii. 204.
16 *1 Hen. IV*, II. iv. 441.
17 *Lover's C.* 273.
18 *Com. of E.* IV. i. 89.
19 *Ib.* V. i. 104.
20 *Lucr.* 893; *Love's L. L.* V. ii. 857; *Rom. & Jul.* I. iii. 26, 30.
21 *1 Hen. VI*, V. iv. 29; *2 Hen. IV*, I. ii. 48.
22 *1 Hen. IV*, I. iii. 58.
23 *2 Hen. IV*, IV. iv. 48.
24 *Love's L. L.* IV. ii. 70 f.
25 *Macb.* V. iii. 55.
26 *Ib.*
27 *Ib.*
28 *Haml.* IV. vii. 144.
29 *Oth.* II. i. 178.
30 *Ib.* III. iii. 330; *Ant. & Cleo.* I. v. 4.
31 *Oth.* III. iii. 330.
32 *Haml.* IV. v. 181.
33 *K. Lear*, IV. iv. 3.

quintida,[1] infusions,[2] hemlock,[3] mallow,[4] hebenon.[5] He may have tried 'drowsy syrups',[6] otherwise sleeping draughts, for insomnia. He puts a horrible list of maladies, gathered from some source or other, in the mouth of Thersites, in gruesome language befitting the speaker, with intrusion of a term which betrays the author's familiarity with law rather than with medicine:

'Now, the rotten diseases of the South, the guts-griping, ruptures, catarrhs, loads o' gravel i' the back, lethargies, cold palsies, raw eyes, dirt-rotten livers, wheezing lungs, bladders full of imposthume, sciaticas, limekilns i' the palm, incurable bone-ache, and *the rivelled fee-simple of the tetter*, take and take again such preposterous discoveries!'[7]

Shakespeare also deals with specific cases, as *hysterica passio*[8] and *tremor cordis*,[9] and, not to mention mental sickness, the *fistula* pronounced incurable by the 'congregated College' (of Physicians) but healed by means of Gerard de Narbon's secret prescription.[10] We hear of Galen[11] and Paracelsus,[12] Hippocrates[13] and Ovid's Aesculapius.[14] Very striking and characteristic are the Poet's own views of health and sickness. We have noted his silence about tobacco,[15] his contempt for cosmetics, and his unmistakable verdict on the mischievous and criminal effects of alcohol. He believes in 'honest water, which ne'er left man i' the mire',[16] in fresh air[17] and sunlight,[18] in the free

[1] *Oth.* I. iii. 355.

[2] *Per.* III. ii. 35; *Wint. T.* IV. iv. 816.

[3] *Macb.* IV. i. 25; *K. Lear,* IV. iv. 4.

[4] *Temp.* II. i. 144.

[5] *Haml.* I. v. 62.

[6] *Oth.* III. iii. 331.

[7] *Tro. & Cres.* V. i. 20–8 (in modern terms: venereal diseases, colic, hernias, catarrhs, stone in the kidneys, apoplexies, paralysis, inflamed eyelids, liver troubles, asthma, cystitis, sciatica, palmar psoriasis, incurable scrofula or other skin disease). Thersites might have hung about a hospital. He speaks, in this scene, of a 'surgeon's box', the 'patient's wound' ('tented' or probed with lint) and the 'green sarcenet flap for a sore eye'. 'Preposterous discoveries' means 'forebackward indecencies' ('uncoverings'): a scholar and moralist's damning expression.

[8] *K. Lear,* II. iv. 57. See p. 663.

[9] *Wint. T.* I. ii. 110.

[10] *All's W.* I. i. 39.

[11] *2 Hen. IV.* I. ii. 133; *Merry W.* II. iii. 29, III. i. 67; *All's W.* II. iii. 12; *Cor.* II. i. 128.

[12] *All's W.* II. iii. 12.

[13] *Merry W.* III. i. 66.

[14] *Merry W.* II. iii. 29; *Per.* III. ii. 111.

[15] p. 238.

[16] pp. 237–8; *Tim. of A.* I. ii. 59 f.

[17] *2 Hen. IV,* IV. iv. 116; *Meas. for M.* II. iv. 24–6; *Love's L. L.* I. i. 236 ('The most wholesome physic of thy health-giving air': a line which might serve, as Sir St. Clair Thomson has suggested, for a Sanatorium).

[18] *Tam. Sh.* IV. v. 17 f. ('the blessed Sun'); *1 Hen. IV,* I. ii. 10, II. iv. 449.

movement of heart and lungs,[1] in keeping the teeth clean,[2] in washing and bathing,[3] in rest[4] and sleep,[5] cheerfulness at meals and in company[6] (for which a glass of good wine is commended),[7] and, last but not least, in physical exercise,[8] and change of scene[9] and condition,[10] as indispensable for mental and moral sanity. Such faith was part of his independence of observation and judgement, and magnificent common sense.

1607–8

§ 127. *TIMON OF ATHENS*

KING JAMES's lavish expenditure on plays was part of his prodigality. Of his wild extravagance in the summer of 1606 we have read in the Harington correspondence. By the end of the year officers and servants of the royal household were clamorous for their wages, and the Lord Treasurer, Buckhurst (King James's 'Flavius'), was stopped in his coach by a crowd demanding payment. In his speech to Parliament on 31 March 1607 the King replied to complaints of wasteful expense and favouritism, and promised amendment. But in July began his infatuation for Robert Carr, a handsome young Scot injured in the Tilting Yard, and brought prominently before the royal notice, on Coronation Day. Lord Thomas Howard wrote to Harington in the autumn:

'Carr hath all the favours. The King teacheth him Latin every morning; and

[1] *Rich. III*, IV. i. 34 f.; *Ant. & Cleo.* I. iii. 71; *Wint. T.* III. ii. 174 f.

[2] *Cor.* II. iii. 67.

[3] *Ib.* 66.

[4] *3 Hen. VI*, II. iii. 1–5; *Com. of E.* V. i. 83 ('life-preserving rest'); *Tro. & Cres.* V. viii. 3 f.; *Cymb.* IV. ii. 43; *Temp.* III. iii. 1–6.

[5] See pp. 758–9.

[6] *Com. of E.* V. i. 73–5, 83 f.

[7] *Hen. VIII*, I. iv. 5–7:

> He would have all as merry
> As first good company, good wine, good welcome
> Can make good people.

This is Shakespeare's one good word for alcohol.

[8] *Love's L. L.* I. i. 233–7 (Armado besieged with melancholy betakes himself to walk); *Cymb.* I. i. 110 ('were you but riding forth to air yourself'); *Wint. T.* IV. iv. 790 (The King goes aboard a new ship to purge melancholy and air himself).

[9] *Rom. & Jul.* I. i. 231–4, I. ii. 46–57, 90–2, 99–104.

[10] *K. Lear*, II. iv. 106–113. A remarkable passage, as pointed out by Sir St. C. Thomson (Lecture at Stratford, 23 April 1923).

I think some one should teach him English too, for as he is a Scottish lad he hath much need of better language. The King doth much covet his presence; the ladies, too, are not behind hand in their admiration. Where it endeth I cannot guess, but honours are talked of speedily.'

On 6 December he was appointed Groom of the Bedchamber with a salary of £600 a year, and on Christmas Eve was knighted. There were plays all the Christmas holidays, state dinners and masks and a great show of jewels—one lady wore £100,000 worth and Arabella Stuart even more. On 10 January a warrant was issued for the payment of £3,200 for jewels 'for New Year's tide' for the use of the Queen and her children, Elizabeth and Charles. The poor suffered from the intense cold, which continued into March. 'Ploughmen's children sit crying and blowing their nails, hunger pinches their cheeks,' wrote the author, already quoted, of *The Great Frost*, 'we grieve to behold the misery of our cattle, the ground is bare and not worth a handful of grass. Rich men had never more money, and covetousness had never less pity. Farmers are slaves to racking young landlords, those landlords are more servile slaves to their own riots and luxury.'[1] On 4 March the Earl of Nottingham was concerned for the deer at Hampton Court. 'The King', he wrote to Sir Thomas Lake, 'must be sparing of his gifts, this year being no year for tailors and shoemakers to eat venison.' On 22 March £300 was paid for presents from the King to 'Sir Robert Carr'. A month later the sorely tried old Lord Treasurer died at the Privy Council-table at Whitehall. He was succeeded by (a younger 'Flavius') Robert Cecil, Earl of Salisbury. Cecil, while he flattered Carr, and himself acquired an estate at the royal hands, did his best to restrain the King's lavishness towards the worthless young favourite. Carr amassed in a few years £200,000 in money, plate, and jewels, besides £19,000 per annum.[2] Roger Coke, our informant, tells us further that

'King James having given Sir Robert Carr a boon of £20,000, my Lord Treasurer Salisbury, that he might make the King sensible of what he had done, invited the King to an entertainment, and so ordered it that before the King should come at it, he should pass through a room wherein he had placed four tables, and upon each table lay £5,000 in silver. When the King came into the passage, he started and was amazed at the sight, having never before seen such a sum. He asked the Treasurer the meaning of it, who told

[1] Arber, *Garner*, i. 88 f.

[2] *Detection*, i. 80 f.

the King it was the boon he had given Sir Robert Carr. '*Swounds, man* (the oath he usually swore), *but five thousand should serve his turn.* And so for that time the Treasurer saved the King the other fifteen thousand pounds.'[1]

Players were more outspoken than statesmen. The French ambassador complained of a scene in George Chapman's *Duke of Biron*, wherein the Queen of France addressed a court lady with hard words and gave her a box on the ear. This was in March 1608 at the Blackfriars. Three of the actors were committed to prison, but the author escaped.

'A day or two before', says the ambassador, 'they had introduced their own King, his Scottish mien and all his favourites, on the stage in a very strange fashion. They made him curse and swear for the theft of a bird, and beat a gentleman for calling off the hounds, and represented him as drunk at least once a day.'

For this offence, we learn, the King forbade plays in London and dissolved the company of the 'Children' at Blackfriars.[2] For permission to play, four companies offered 100,000 francs; which, on 5 April, in the ambassador's opinion, they were likely to obtain, on the condition that they no more presented modern history or spoke of passing events on the penalty of losing their lives ('*à condition qu'ils ne représenteront plus aucune histoire moderne ni ne parleront des choses du temps à peine de la vie*').

In his more excellent way of Art, without fear of incurring any such penalty for himself or his fellows, Shakespeare, in a play of classical history, spoke clearly enough, and to the Court itself, of contemporary folly and danger. In the mouth of the Poet he disclaims personalities and 'malice':

> I have in this rough work shaped out a man
> Whom this beneath-world doth embrace and hug
> With amplest entertainment; my free drift
> Halts not particularly but moves itself
> In a wide sea of wax; no levell'd malice
> Infects one comma . . .
> I have upon a high and pleasant hill
> Feigned Fortune to be throned; the base o' the mount
> Is rank'd with all deserts, all kinds of natures,
> That labour on the bosom of this sphere
> To propagate their states; amongst them all,
> Whose eyes are on this Sovereign Lady fix'd,
> One do I personate of Lord Timon's frame,

[1] *Detection*, i. 53 f.

[2] Lake to Cecil, 11 March.

Whom Fortune with her ivory hand wafts to her . . .
All those which were his fellows but of late,
Some better than his value, on the moment
Follow his strides, his lobbies fill with tendance,
Rain sacrificial whisperings in his ear,
Make sacred even his stirrup . . .
When Fortune in her shift and change of mood
Spurns down her late beloved, all his dependants
Which laboured after him to the mountain's top,
Even on their knees and hands, let him slip down,
Not one accompanying his declining foot.[1]

Courteously, with the modesty of a subject, Shakespeare warns his Royal Patron of flatterers, and possible change of fortune, and even ventures, in the reference to the stirrup, to allude to a matter talked of at Court. Howard, in the letter to Harington above quoted,[2] says:

'The other day'—in the autumn of 1607—'a noble did come in suit of a place, and saw the King mounting the roan'—his favourite jennet—'delivered his petition, which was heeded and read, but no answer given. The noble departed and came to Court the next day, and got no answer again. The Lord Treasurer was then pressed to move the King's pleasure touching the petition. When the King was asked for answer thereto, he said in some wrath, *Shall a king give heed to a dirty paper when a beggar noteth not his gilt stirrups?* Now it fell out that the King had new furniture when the noble saw him in the Court yard, but he was over-charged with confusion and passed-by admiring the horse.'

Small is the resemblance between Timon and King James. Timon is a giant, like Hamlet, Macbeth, Lear, and Antony.[3] He is the titanic patron and feaster of men, who, on his patronage and feasting yielding its barren fruit, turns on them with Olympian scorn. There was nothing titanic about King James. We cannot imagine him hurling dishes at the heads of his Privy Council. Would that we could! His rage, which was frequent, took petty forms. He had not the strength of temper to be a passionate and eloquent misanthrope cursing the unrighteous. But Timon and James were Fortune's favourites and her dupes. They were easily flattered Lord Bountifuls, slaves of

[1] I. i. 43–8, 63–70, 78–82, 84–8.

[2] p. 694.

[3] Shakespeare read of him in Plutarch (*Life of Marcus Antonius*), Paynter (*Palace of Pleasure*), and Lucian (either in the Greek or a version).

the chase,[1] given to banquets[2] and noisy music,[3] believers in the friendship of presents and hospitalities. 'Lord Timon', indeed, is a lavish Stuart nobleman of the year 1608, reckless and irresponsible, up to the ears in debt, besieged by tradesman, jeweller, painter, poet, proffering their services and requesting payment. His table groans under the weight of meat and drink, and is crowded with guests. 'Our offices', says Flavius, Timon's faithful steward, 'have been oppressed'

> With riotous feeders, and our vaults have wept
> With drunken spilth of wine, and every room
> *Hath blazed with lights and bray'd with minstrelsy.*[4]

These 'feeders' are dismissed with gifts of money, plate, and jewels. Alcibiades is scarcely introduced when he is 'my Alcibiades' and a bosom friend. There is sentimental talk of 'friendship'. Timon addresses those gathered at his feast (I. ii. 91–112):

'O no doubt, my good friends, but the Gods themselves have provided that I shall have much help from you; how had you been my friends else? why have you that charitable title from thousands, did not you chiefly belong to my heart? I have told more of you to myself than you can with modesty speak in your own behalf; and thus far I confirm you. O you Gods, think I, what need we have any friends if we should ne'er have need of them? they were the most needless creatures living should we ne'er have use for them, and would most resemble sweet instruments hung up in cases that keep their sounds to themselves. Why, I have often wished myself poorer, that I might come nearer to you. We are born to do benefits, and what better or properer can we call our own than the riches of our friends? O what a precious comfort 'tis, to have so many like brothers commanding one another's fortunes! O joy, e'en made away ere't can be born! Mine eyes cannot hold out water, methinks: to forget their faults, I drink to you.'

It is the friendship, not of ideas and common causes and fellow suffering for goodness, but of the Five Senses, symbolized by the mask of Cupid and the Amazons:

> Hail to thee, worthy Timon! and to all
> That of his bounties taste! The five best senses
> Acknowledge thee their patron, and come freely
> To gratulate thy plenteous bosom: the ear,

[1] I. ii. 189, 194 f., 216 f., II. i. 5–10, II. ii. 8, 16, 197 f.

[2] Drinkings, I. ii. 1, 160, III. i. 32.

[3] 'Trumpets' (I. i. 94), 'loud music' (I. ii). 'Bray'd with minstrelsy' (II. ii. 170). 'Feast your ears with the music . . . if they will fare so harshly o' the trumpets sound' (III. vi. 36 f.).

[4] II. ii. 168–70.

Taste, touch, and smell pleased from thy table rise;
They only now come but to feast thine eyes.[1]

And as Apemantus says, in his churlish fashion, it is 'Friendship full of Dregs'.[2]

Such was King James's conception.

'The King', says Weldon, who knew him, 'never loved any man heartily until he had bound him unto him by *giving* him some suit, which he thought bound the other's love to him again. But that argued a poor disposition in him to believe that anything but a noble mind seasoned with virtue could make any firm love or union; for mercenary minds are carried away with a greater prize, but noble minds alienated with nothing but public disgraces.'[3]

'Feast-won' is 'fast-lost'.[4] Timon appeals in vain to his 'friends' for help. They turn from him, and he rounds upon them with fury for their ingratitude. His denunciation of Athens is the counterpart of his praise of 'Friendship', a superficial generalizing, great language and ineffectual, the fuming and foaming of Hamlet in another vein:

Timon will to the woods, where he shall find
The unkindest beast more kinder than mankind.
The Gods confound—hear me, you good Gods all!—
The Athenians, both within and without that wall!

Again the terrible *confound* of the Te Deum (it is continually in his mouth),[5]

And grant as Timon grows his hate may grow
To the whole race of mankind, high and lów!
Amen.[6]

Nothing comes of such a prayer. It is unjust, as the next scene shows. Timon's men are faithful. Their sorrow is real:

FLAVIUS. Good fellows all,
The latest of my wealth I'll share amóngst | you
Wherever we shall meet, for Timon's sake
Let's yet be fél|lows; let's shake our heads, and say,
As 'twere a knell unto our master's fór|tunes,
'We have seen better days'. Let each táke | some—
Nay, put out all your hands. Not one wórd | more:
Thus part we rich in sór|row, parting poor.
[*Servants embrace and part several ways.*[7]

[1] I. ii. 128–33.
[2] *Ib.* 240.
[3] *Court of King James*, p. 169 f.
[4] II. ii. 180. Cf. *Lucrece* 891.
[5] IV. i. 20, 21, 37, IV. iii. 74, 103, 127 f., 327, 339, 392, 452, V. i. 106.
[6] IV. i. 39–41.
[7] IV. ii. 22–9.

And here, and in what follows, Shakespeare gives us the verse we have heard before, and shall hear again, of fallen fortune, with its extra syllables, stress on the penultimate, run-on lines, weak or light endings, and frequent pause or 'breathing place', as Sidney says, 'in the midst of the verse':[1]

O the fierce wretchedness that glory bríngs | us! . . .
Who would be so mocked with glór|y, or to live
But in a dream of fríend|ship?
To have his pomp and all what state compounds
But only paint|ed, like his varnished friends?
Poor honest lord, brought low by his own heart,
Undone by góod|ness! Strange, unusual blood
When man's worst sín | is, he does too múch | good! . . .
My dearest lord, blest to be most accúrs|ed,
Rich only to be wrétch|ed, thy great fór|tunes
Are made thy chief afflíc|tions. Alas, kind lord!
He's flung in rage from this ingrateful seat
Of monstrous friends; nor has he with him *to*
Supply his life, or that which can commánd | *it*.[2]

Digging for roots Timon finds gold—

Gold! yellow, glittering, precious gold![3]

He is rich again, but will have no more to do with money. His hatred of it does not spring from poverty, but from its corrupting influence on man. He denounces it as the root of all evil:

You Gods, why this
Will lug your priests and servants from your sides . ..
Will knit and break religions, bless the accursed,
Make the hoar leprosy adored.[4]

But here he parts from the apostle. His pessimism, the consequence of his optimism, is Calvinism *without Grace*, a doctrine of human depravity without Redemption. He says:

All is oblique;
There's nothing level in *our cursed natures*
But direct villany.[5]
If thou wilt curse, thy father, that poor rag,
Must be thy subject, who in spite put stuff

[1] *Defence*, Feuillerat, iii. 44. The text of the play, which we have only in the Folio, is defective in many places, and here is not of the best.

[2] IV. ii. 30, 33–9, 42–7.

[3] IV. iii. 26. [4] 30 f., 34 f. [5] 18–20.

> To some she-beggar and compounded thee
> *Poor rogue hereditary.*[1]
> And nature, as it grows again toward *earth*,
> Is fashioned for the journey, *dull and heavy.*[2]

Flavius alone of those 'born of woman' escapes the general curse, Nature's and Timon's.[3]

All is futile raving. Alcibiades passes by, with drum and fife, bent on *action*. He is Timon's foil. He also has been wronged, he too has a fiery temper; but resentment with him does not take the form of mere mental writhing. He does not flee to the woods and pour out his heart to the Gods in ineffectual imprecation. In comparison with Timon he is a mean figure, the companion of harlots; but, like Fortinbras in relation to Hamlet, he has common sense and statesmanship. He knows, and does, the thing to be *done*. He takes the gold which Timon throws away and employs it against the unjust Senate. He brings his army to the gates of Athens, while Timon is engaged in a contest of words with the cynic Apemantus; and he is ready to enter the City, victorious, to punish offenders and spare the innocent ('using the olive with the sword'),[4] when news is brought of Timon's death, and burial apart from men on the verge of the sea, in proud isolation and impotence. Sentiment there may be in being covered daily by the waves, in their bitterness and purity, but not heroism.

It is the same Shakespeare. The world, whatever its evil, is good, and worth serving to our power. It has in it

> Piety and fear,
> Religion to the Gods, peace, justice, truth,
> Domestic awe, night rest, and neighbourhood,
> Instruction, manners, mysteries and trades,
> Degrees, observances, customs and laws.[5]

And we recognize the workmanship—the use of the Bible, the influence of *Metamorphoses*, familiarity with law, and the new feature, medical knowledge and terminology. Timon's wealth of vocabulary owes not a little, we may believe, to the Poet's intercourse with Doctor Hall.

New friendship and stimulus, however, will not hide from us, now or previously or to come, that of the old. Such neighbours,

[1] IV. iii. 271–4. [2] II. ii. 227 f. [3] IV. iii. 500–8.
[4] V. iv. 82. [5] IV. i. 15–19.

not to mention others, as Greene and Aspinall, were no mean asset in a country town. We must be just to the Schoolmaster. If Shakespeare did not love him, he must have found him an intellectual challenge. He had been elected, in 1606, Bailiff—the first and the last Schoolmaster to be so honoured in the borough. He declined, and was fined £10 for his persistent refusal. In the spring of 1608 there was dissatisfaction on the part of the assistant-master, a young graduate from Oxford named Richard Wright, with his chief. His criticism reached the ears of the Bailiff, who was Master Henry Walker, with the result that on 20 May 'Master Wright's allegations touching Master Aspinall's teaching, and the differences between them', were referred by the Council 'to the hearing of Master Rogers, the Ministers and Master Henry Sturley, and they to make report what they think concerning the same'. Rogers was the vicar; Henry Sturley, B.A., elder son of Abraham Sturley, had been assistant to Aspinall, and resident in 'Chapel' (succeeding Sir William Gilbert as tenant of the *camera juxta Aulam*), from 1598 to 1604, and was now vicar of Chipping Camden; and the 'Ministers' were the curates of Bishopton and Luddington. Their report is not forthcoming, but that it was of conciliatory nature we conclude from Wright's continuance in his post until he took his M.A. in 1611.

1608

§ 128. *CORIOLANUS*

CORIOLANUS is one more study of tragic failure. Plutarch's Marcius in Shakespeare's hands is a primitive, not to say barbaric, aristocrat, devoted to his home and family and class, brave and capable as a soldier, but unfit for statesmanship, contemptuous of the people, and as great a menace to his country in time of peace as indispensable in time of war. The Poet's judgement of him is that of Aufidius in one of his 'flashes'[1] of generous admiration:[2]

Whether 'twas pride,
Which out of daily fortune ever taints
The happy man; whether defect of judgment,

[1] Case, *Arden Shakespeare*, p. 181.
[2] It is short-lived. By the end of his speech he is resolved on revenge.

To fail in the disposing of those chances
Which he was lord of; or whether nature,
Not to be other than one thing, not moving
From the casque to the cushion, but commanding peace
Even with the same austerity and garb
As he controlled the war; but one of these—
As he hath spices of them all, not all,
For I dare so far free him—made him fear'd;
So, hated, and so, banished.[1]

We see the hero in his child—a lusty, pugnacious little fellow who chases the butterfly, and falling and losing his temper, pursues and 'mammocks' it (tears it, that is, to pieces with his teeth).[2] We see him also in his mother, the Lady Volumnia, a haughty masculine woman, who would rather have eleven sons 'die' nobly for their country than 'one voluptuously surfeit out of action'.[3] She says of him:

'When yet he was but tender-bodied and the only son of my womb, when youth with comeliness plucked all gaze his way; when, for a day of Kings' entreaties, a mother should not sell him an hour from her beholding; I, considering how honour would become such a person, that it was no better than picture-like to hang by the wall, if renown made it not stir, was pleased to let him seek danger where he was like to find fame. To a cruel war I sent him; from whence he returned, his brows bound with oak. I tell thee, daughter, I sprang not more in joy at first hearing he was a man-child than now in first seeing he had proved himself a man.'[4]

With such a mother, Coriolanus may be excused if his ideas of 'honour', 'renown', 'fame', and of 'a man' are those of a half-savage chieftain, triumphant in his hand-to-hand encounters with enemies like himself. He judges all from the point of view of caste and physical prowess. His inferiors in these respects, men of low birth or lacking animal courage, are 'rogues' or 'cowards'. He is the victim of what the Greeks called ὕβρις, an insolence of rank and strength, which thwarts the counsels of his friends, infuriates the 'populace', and exposes him to the designs of demagogues. He is 'whoop'd out of Rome',[5] not unjustly. Even his fellow nobles are relieved at his departure.

Such a Titan (he is the last of Shakespeare's 'giants'), without humour, culture, thought, or self-knowledge, devoid of the intellectual charm which raises Brutus high above princes, would

[1] IV. vii. 37–48. [2] I. iii. 65–71. [3] 26–8.
[4] I. iii. 6–19. [5] IV. v. 84.

have little interest, still less tragic interest, were it not for his deep domestic affections. These are most admirable. His love of his mother, wife, and little son redeems him from monstrosity. He is as filial as Hamlet, pure as Orlando, true as Brutus, fatherly as Leontes. He thinks of his home, as his home thinks of him, in the battle with the Volscians. He is warmly attached to his old family-friend, Menenius, and to his comrade, Cominius. He can care for one of the 'multitude' when he has known him in the house—though not sufficiently to remember, in a moment of weariness, his name. Few scenes are more perfect than that of the warrior's welcome home from Corioli, when he walks hand in hand with Volumnia and Virgilia, crowned with an oaken garland, amid the applause of the citizens, to the Capitol.[1] It is a great piece of Shakespeare.

The predominance of this home feeling, so marked at the beginning of the play, is questioned later by the 'deadly sin' of pride. The clash of these inconsistent passions is the psychological feature of the drama. One, then the other, gets the upper hand, and the higher weakens with the growing strength of the lower. Scorn, choler, recklessness increase, and revenge takes the place of 'noble carelessness'.[2] With greater difficulty rage is restrained by the presence and pleading of private friendship. Banished from Rome, Coriolanus says:

> Come, my sweet Wife, my dearest Mother, and
> My Friends of noble touch . . . I pray you, come.
> While I remain above the ground, you shall
> Hear from me still; and never of me aught
> But what is like me formerly.[3]

But in absence he broods over his wrongs, cherishes his hate, fails to write (and therefore, what he once despised, 'a promise-breaker'),[4] and turns up at last, embittered, disreputable, out-at-heel, at the house of the enemy, Aufidius. The great scene follows of the struggle for supremacy between the new revenge, 'the spleen of all the Underfiends',[5] and the old noble affection. Coriolanus believes in his own 'constancy'. Rome is at his feet. Cominius pleads in vain on her behalf, Menenius is sent back 'with a crack'd heart'. But the approach of his mother, wife,

[1] II. i. 179–220.
[2] II. ii. 16.
[3] IV. i. 48 f., 50–3.
[4] I. viii. 2.
[5] IV. v. 97 f.

and boy shakes him. He is swayed to and fro by contending tempests:

I will not—
My Wife comes foremost; then the honour'd Mould
Wherein this trunk was framed, and in her hand
The Grandchild to her blood.—*But out affection!*
All bond and privilege of nature, break!
Let it be virtuous to be obstinate.
What is that curtsy worth? or those doves' eyes
Which can make gods forsworn? I melt, and am not
Of stronger earth than others. My mother bows,
As if Olympus to a molehill should
In supplication nod: and my young boy
Hath an aspect of intercession, which
Great Nature cries, Deny not.—*Let the Volsces*
Plough Rome, and harrow Italy! I'll never
Be such a gosling to obey instinct, but stand
As if a man were author of himself
And knew no other kin. . . . O, a kiss
Long as my exile, sweet as my revenge!
Now, by the jealous queen of heaven, that kiss
I carried from thee, dear, and my true lip
Hath virgin'd it e'er since. You Gods! I prate,
And the most noble mother of the world
Leave unsaluted: sink, my knee, i' the earth. [*Kneels.*][1]

Love wins, and he returns to Antium to die. A final ungovernable outburst hastens his death. The taunt of 'Boy' inflames him:

'Boy!' False hound,
If you have writ your annals true, 'tis there
That like an eagle in a dove-cote I
Fluttered your Volscians in Corioli:
Alone I did it. 'Boy!'[2]

But from first to last Coriolanus was a 'Boy'. No term could better describe his mentality, or that of the young English aristocrat of 1608 onwards to the Civil War. We will note the 'broken-metre' of the hero's broken pride:

My name is Caius Márc|ius, who hath done
To thee particularly, and to all the Vóls|ces,
Great hurt and mís|chief; thereto witness may
My surname, Coriolán|us. The painful sér|vice,
The extreme dán|gers, and the drops of blood
Shed for my thankless cóun|try, are requí|ted

[1] v. iii. 21–50.

[2] v. vi. 113–17.

But with that súr|name; a good memory
And witness of the malice and displeás|ure
Which thou shouldst beár | me: only that name remains;
The cruelty and envy of the peó|ple,
Permitted by our dastard nó|bles, who
Have all forsoók | me, hath devoured the rest.[1]

1608

§ 129. THE MULTITUDE

FEUDAL bonds were loosening; nobles and retainers were on less congenial terms; the gentry, it was said, lived in London and left their estates to bailiffs; tumultuous assemblies in protest against enclosures in 1607 were followed by a dearth of corn in 1608 and further rioting. William Combe wrote to Cecil from Warwick on 2 June:

> I am overtold to acquaint your lordship with such grievances as the common people of this country (whereof for this year I have the custody under his Majesty)[2] are troubled with: *videlicet*, with the dearth of corn, the prices rising to some height, caused partly by some that are well stored, by refraining to bring the same to the market out of a covetous conceit that corn will be dearer, and by engrossing of barley by maltsters, of the chief townsmen in every corporation,[3] amongst whom the Justices of the country[4] have no intermeddling. These matters make the people arrogantly and seditiously to speak of the not reforming of conversion of arable land into pasture by enclosing.[5]

Through laws which they had no voice in making, and Courtly influence beyond their control, the people were ever the losers. Shakespeare blamed the authorities. The idea of political wisdom and righteousness springing from the workers and reaching to the privileged classes, was foreign to him, as to his age. The masses, in his opinion, were unfit for statesmanship, and easily misled into riot and chaos. He accepted the ancient classical and pagan dogma, expressed by Horace, *Populus . . . bellua multorum es(t) capitum*,[6] 'the people is a beast of many heads'. He puts it into the mouth of Rumour in *The Second Part of Henry the Fourth*:

the blunt monster with uncounted heads
The still-discordant, wavering multitude.[7]

[1] IV. v. 71–82.
[2] As High Sheriff.
[3] For example, Stratford.
[4] county.
[5] *S.P. Dom. James I*, xxxiv. 4.
[6] Epistles, i. 76.
[7] Induction, 18.

Coriolanus repeats it again and again—'the many-headed multitude',[1] 'Hydra the monster',[2] 'the beast with many heads',[3] with offensive variation, 'the mutable rank-scented many'.[4] But to Shakespeare's knowledge the 'multitude' had sterling qualities, including loyalty to fair-minded masters and unfailing native kindliness, which Coriolanus had not the upbringing or opportunity to recognize. When we think of Launce and Speed, the Dromios, Nick Bottom and his friends, the Gobbos, Francis Seacole, Old Adam and Corin, the Gardener in *Richard the Second*, and the Grave Digger in *Hamlet*, the Englishmen King Henry V talked with in camp before Agincourt, our gorge rises at the ignorant and insolent abuse of the young 'Roman' despot:

> What would you have, you curs,
> That like nor peace nor war? the one affrights you,
> The other makes you proud. He that trusts to you,
> Where he should find you lions, finds you hares,
> Where foxes, geese. You are no surer, no,
> Than is the coal of fire upon the ice,
> Or hailstone in the sun. Your virtue is
> To make him worthy whose offence subdues him,
> And curse that justice did it. Who deserves greatness
> Deserves your hate; and your affections are
> A sick man's appetite, who desires most that
> Which would increase his evil.[5]

Popular stupidity and aristocratic ineptitude are brought into fatal antagonism in the play. The people are starving and mutinous, in need of wise and sympathetic government. And three forms of political influence are exercised upon them—first, that of Menenius the old patrician, of which Shakespeare, in the main approves, the régime of the friendly and responsible Tudor nobility, in 1608 receding rapidly into the past;[6] second, that of the Tribunes, of which the Poet is more than suspicious, sectional, envious, and threatening the peace of the state; and third, more evil than the last, that of the arrogant and high-handed young cavalier, unequal to 'the interpretation of the time', unto himself

[1] II. iii. 18.
[2] III. i. 93, 95.
[3] IV. i. 1 f.
[4] III. i. 66.
[5] I. i. 172–83. The Tribunes are courtesy itself compared with Menenius, the best of the aristocrats, in II. i.
[6] Not a few Englishmen, in the year of Milton's birth, would question the claim of the aristocracy to be the serviceable 'belly' of the State.

'most commendable', who makes his 'tomb' most 'evident' in the 'chair' wherein he 'extols what he hath done'.[1]

Shakespeare censures the prince rather than the subject, the rich more than the poor. His Henry VI, Richard II, Timon, Coriolanus are the guilty.

In September 1608 the Poet lost his mother. She was buried on the 9th, no doubt beside the old Alderman, within the church or in 'the holy churchyard',[2] at Stratford:

Mayry Shaxspere, wydowe.[3]

From Henley Street, a fortnight later, was brought to the church and christened the Poet's nephew, Michael, son of his sister Joan—

Sept. 23 Mychaell sonne to Willyam Hart.[4]

On 16 October, which was Sunday, Shakespeare attended the christening of his friend Henry Walker's child and acted as sponsor, the boy being named after him, William—

William sonne to Henry Walker unus aldermannus.[5]

There was as little likeness, probably, between Mary Arden and Volumnia as between their sons. Had the Poet's mother in the least resembled the masterful Roman matron she would not have been so completely overshadowed by her husband. The 'gracious silence' of Virgilia better expresses her, else there were tempests (which have left no trace) in the Henley Street household. Nevertheless, her affection and the Poet's devotion are as unmistakable in *Coriolanus* as the memory of John Shakespeare in *Hamlet*. 'Mother', 'my mother', 'good mother', are the keynote of the play.

The beautiful scene, the very picture of peace and strength,[6] of the hero's mother and wife at their 'stitchery', is pure Stratford. They 'set them down on two low stools and sew'—such 'low stools' as those on which 'goodwives' sat in Shakespeare's native town, in 'the Hall' or the best chamber, with their 'cover' and cushion, more comfortable than the 'high stools' used at meals.[7] This simple 'interior', not surpassed in any painting,

[1] IV. vii. 49–53. The whole of this speech is Shakespeare rather than Aufidius.

[2] III. iii. 51.

[3] *Register*, p. 76.

[4] *Ib.*

[5] *Ib.* See further, p. 823.

[6] I. iii.

[7] See the Stratford inventories: 'In the Hall—two chairs, two low stools, a

was as dear and potent to the artist in London as to his rugged Roman at the wars.

Much may be from Stratford—the harvestman tasked to mow 'or all or lose his hire',[1] the proclamation in the market-place, in presence of 'all the officers of the town',[2] the 'prater in the stocks',[3] the greyhound in the leash,[4] 'halloaing a hare',[5] the rascal deer,[6] the 'quarry' (heap of deer's entrails) for the dogs,[7] 'conies outing of the burrows after rain',[8] the ripe mulberry that will not hold the handling[9] (perhaps in *New Place* garden), the channel dug for the overflow of the River in flood,[10] bowls on a subtle ground,[11] and

> Our tradesmen singing in their shops and going
> About their functions friendly.[12]

Something is from London—the coal of fire upon the ice,[13] the 'city mills' near London Bridge,[14] the London fog,[15] the tide rushing through the Bridge,[16] the pikemen trailing their weapons at a state funeral.[17]

Bible, Ovid, Law, Medicine are in evidence. The hero's vituperation, like Timon's, is nauseating in medical particulars—'rubbing the itch', 'scabs', 'a sick man's appetite' for what 'would increase his evil', 'the contagion of the South' (syphilis), 'boils and plagues', 'plastered over', 'infected', 'agued', 'dropping blood', 'wounds', 'decayed lungs', 'measles', 'tetter', 'dangerous physic for a body sure of death without it'. Menenius, too, has 'conversed' with Doctor Hall. In more senses than one he has studied his 'belly'—which is no mere recipient of food, 'still cupboarding the viand', but 'sends it through the rivers of the

table-frame, a form and two high joined stools' (Mary Mills, Nov. 1624): 'In her Bedchamber—four high joined stools, three low joined stools with coverings' (Rose Palmer, Aug. 1631).

[1] I. iii. 39 f.
[2] I. v. 27 f.
[3] V. iii. 159 f.
[4] I. vi. 38 f.
[5] I. viii. 7.
[6] I. i. 163, I. vi. 45, IV, v. 182.
[7] I. i. 202.
[8] IV. v. 225 f.
[9] III. ii. 79 f. There was much planting of the mulberry early in 1608 in the hope of cultivating the silkworm.
[10] III. i. 96 f. The Avon at Stratford was treated in this way.
[11] V. ii. 20.
[12] IV. vi. 8 f.
[13] I. i. 177.
[14] I. x. 31.
[15] II. iii. 32–4.
[16] V. iv. 50.
[17] V. vi. 152.

blood' to the 'heart and brain', through 'cranks and offices to the strongest nerves' (sinews) 'and small inferior veins':[1]

> The veins unfill'd, our blood is cold, and then
> We pout upon the morning, are unapt
> To give or forgive; but when we have stuff'd
> These pipes and these conveyances of our blood
> With wine and feeding, we have suppler souls
> Than in our priest-like fasts.[2]

A gangrened foot, a diseased limb that must be cut away, a man 'empoisoned', a 'palsied and decayed dotant', 'apoplexy', 'lethargy', 'sores', 'cicatrices', 'red pestilence', 'hoarded plague', 'murrain', rank sweat and stinking breath, are specified in the play; and Menenius is responsible for the following bit of medical humour, wherein again Shakespeare betrays himself lawyer rather than physician: 'A letter for me! it gives me *an estate of seven years'*[3] health . . . the most sovereign prescription in Galen is but empiricutic,[4] and, to this preservative, of no better report than a horse-drench.'[5]

This summer Shakespeare sued a neighbour, John Addenbroke, 'gentleman', for debt. He obtained a writ against him from the Court of Record on 17 August, which was served by the Serjeant, Gilbert Charnock. Addenbroke secured Thomas Hornby, the blacksmith of Henley Street, as his surety and promised payment. At any rate, Shakespeare took no further proceedings before his departure for London. But on 21 December, in his absence, a precept was granted for the summoning of a jury. Verdict was given for Shakespeare on 15 February 1609. On 15 March Thomas Greene obtained a precept for Addenbrooke's arrest or payment of the £6 due and 24*s*. awarded by the Court for costs and damages. The Serjeant, Francis Boyce, reported that he was not to be found within the borough. Nearly three months went by, and on 7 June a precept was issued for the appearance of Addenbroke's surety, Thomas Hornby.[6]

[1] I. i. 103, 139–42.
[2] V. i. 51–6.
[3] As of a lease. Cf. pp. 138–45.
[4] quackish.
[5] horse physic, II. i. 125–30.
[6] Lee's insinuations (*Life*, 321–3) as to Shakespeare's 'rigour' in business, with Rogers and Addenbroke and others, his 'triumph' over Addenbroke, and 'vengeance' on Hornby, his old 'playmate', and his 'scant regard for social ties', are wholly unwarranted.

1608–9

§ 130. SHAKESPEARE AND HIS FELLOWS

On 29 October 1608 Shakespeare's company performed at Coventry,[1] and later probably at Marlborough *en route* for London.[2] Two of his 'fellows' had died in the summer in London. William Sly made his nuncupative will on 4 August, and was buried from Holywell in St. Leonard's, Shoreditch, on the 16th.[3] Lawrence Fletcher was buried in St. Saviour's, Southwark, on 12 September, 'a man, in the Church, with an afternoon's knell of the great bell'.[4] Sly was one of the few unsatisfactory members of the company. We must associate him with Edmund Shakespeare as the father of a base-born child. He was unmarried—so we gather from his will, which was attested by several illiterate women. He left his hat and sword to Cuthbert Burbage, £40 to his brother-player, James Sands, and the residue of his property, including an interest in the *Globe*, to Robert and Cecily Browne and their daughter, Jane. Browne may have been the actor, Edward Alleyn's friend, who lived in 1612 in Clerkenwell.[5]

Shakespeare's 'fellows' figure prominently, and honourably, in Thomas Heywood's defence of his profession, *An Apology for Actors*, published in 1612 but written about 1608.[6] Heywood was a player (a member of the Earl of Worcester's and Queen Anne's company) and voluminous playwright. 'So bewitching a thing', he writes, 'is lively and well-spirited action, that it hath power to new-mould the hearts of the spectators and fashion them to the shape of any noble and notable attempt.' He instances 'a true portraiture' of 'King Edward the Third' (no doubt *The Reign of King Edward the Third*, published in 1596, with touches in it, as some suppose, of Shakespeare's workmanship) and 'of Henry the Fift' (assuredly Shakespeare's play). He praises by report actors he has not seen—'Knell, Bentley, Miles,

[1] Murray, ii. 244.
[2] *Ib.* 333.
[3] Collier, *Memoirs*, p. 156 ('William Slye gent.'); Chambers, ii. 340.
[4] *Ib.* ii. 318.
[5] *Ib.* 304. See Browne's letter to Alleyn on behalf of one Master Rose, 'amongst the Prince's Men', 'an old servant of mine always honest, trusty and true' (*Henslowe Papers*, 63).
[6] Chambers, iv. 250–4.

Cross, Laneham'—of whom one, Samuel Cross, was a performer, with Shakespeare in his earliest productions. And he says of those he has known—

I must needs remember Tarleton, in his time gracious with the Queen his sovereign, and in the people's general applause; whom succeeded Will Kemp, as well in the favour of her Majesty as in the opinion and good thoughts of the general audience. Gabriel [Spenser, whom Ben Jonson slew in a duel], Singer [a clown in Alleyn's company], Pope, Phillips, Sly—all the right I can do them is but this, that though they be dead, their deserts yet live in the remembrance of many. Among so many dead, let me not forget one yet alive, in his time the most worthy, famous Master Edward Alleyn [who had retired from the stage]. I could wish that such as are condemned for their licentiousness, might by a general consent be quite excluded our society; for as we are men that stand in the broad eye of the world, so should our manners, gestures and behaviours savour of such government and modesty, to deserve the good thoughts and reports of all men, and to abide the sharpest censures even of those that are the greatest opposites to the quality. Many amongst us I know to be of substance, of government, of sober lives and temperate carriages, house-keepers, and contributory to all duties enjoined them, equally with them that are ranked with the most bountiful; and if amongst so many of sort, there be any few degenerate from the rest in that good demeanour which is both requisite and expected at their hands, let me entreat you not to censure hardly of all for the misdeeds of some.

Contributors of commendatory verses to the author include Christopher Beeston and Robert Pallant, whom we saw performing with Shakespeare in *The Seven Deadly Sins* in 1592. Both were now 'fellows' of Heywood in the Worcester-Queen Anne company.

Between the making of his will and his death in August 1608, Sly was allotted a seventh share in the *Blackfriars Theatre* by the Burbages. Other sharers in this important venture were Shakespeare, Condell, Heminge, and Thomas Evans, probably a kinsman and representative of the previous lessee, late manager for the 'Children' of the Chapel, Henry Evans.[1] The 'Children' continued at the *Blackfriars* one more season,[2] rehearsing there (public performances were forbidden until December on account of the plague) with the King's men: who afterwards had sole possession, and took into their service at least three of

[1] Chambers, ii. 510.

[2] They played at Court on 1 and 4 Jan. 1609 as 'the Children of Blackfriars' (Chambers, iv. 123).

SHAKE-SPEARES

SONNETS

Neuer before Imprinted.

AT LONDON
By *G. Eld* for *T. T.* and are
to be solde by *william Aspley.*
1609.

THORPE'S EDITION OF 1609
Copy in Bodleian Library, Oxford

the abler 'Children'—William Ostler, John Underwood, and Nathan Field.

Twelve times Shakespeare and his company performed at Court at Christmas and Shrovetide 1608–9, before the King, the Queen, Prince Henry, and Prince Charles, and on 5 April they received for their services £120.[1] Three weeks later, the plague being severe and the theatres closed, they were paid £40 more 'by way of his Majesty's reward for their private practice in the time of infection, that thereby they might be enabled to perform their service before his Majesty in Christmas holidays 1609'.[2] They then went on tour—were at Ipswich on 9 May, Hythe on the 16th, New Romney on the 17th[3]—until, apparently, fear of infection in all parts of England made it impossible for them to get permission to act.[4] Shakespeare may have been at Stratford in June when further proceedings in his suit against Addenbroke were stayed.[5]

1609

§ 131. PUBLICATION OF SHAKESPEARE'S SONNETS

On 20 May, while Shakespeare was in Kent or Sussex, a collection of his sonnets was entered at Stationers' Hall to Thomas Thorpe as 'a book called Shakespeares Sonnettes'.[6] It had fallen into the hands of this piratical publisher and notorious procurer of manuscript,[7] possibly on the break-up of the Countess of Oxford's establishment at King's Place in the village of Hackney. The mansion passed this year, 1609, into the possession of Sir Fulke Greville.[8] The conjunction of names is suggestive. The late Earl of Oxford (he died in 1604) possessed, we may assume, a copy at least of Sonnets i–xxvi, wherein young Southampton was urged to accept the hand of his daughter, Elizabeth de Vere, and as a poet and patron of poets and players, he would value anything from Shakespeare's pen. The Countess, his second wife, Elizabeth Trentham, may have let the manuscript go, consisting of 154 sonnets and *A Lover's Complaint*, ignorant

[1] Chambers, iv. 123, 174.
[2] *Ib.* 175.
[3] J. T. Murray, i. 184.
[4] *Ib.* 152.
[5] p. 710.
[6] Arber, iii. 410.
[7] Lee, pp. 672–85.
[8] B. R. Ward, *National Review*, September 1922.

of its nature and literary worth. On the other hand, it may have escaped from the papers of the incoming occupant, the *litterateur* and sonnetter, Sir Fulke Greville. It has been suggested, also, that 'Master W. H.', the confidant to whom in audacious terms Thorpe expresses his gratitude for the copy, was one William Hall, married in Hackney Church on 4 August 1608,[1] who may have been William Hall the printer. This individual, the son of a Shropshire clergyman, served his apprenticeship with John Allde and was admitted to the freedom of the Stationers' Company in 1584. His first work was entered to him in 1598. He has been identified with the 'W. H.' who supplied George Eld in 1606 with the copy of Southwell's *Fourfold Meditation*.[2] Of the pieces comprising the *Meditation* 'W. H.' wrote, as probably he might have written, with less truth, of *Shakespeare's Sonnets* and *A Lover's Complaint*, 'Long have they lien hidden in obscurity, and haply had never seen the light had not a mere accident conveyed them to my hands'.[3] On 28 November 1608 Hall was entrusted with an edition of Justin in Latin 'to the use of the Company', paying *6d.* in the pound 'to the use of the poor for paper and printing';[4] and by 3 April 1609 he and his partner, Thomas Haviland, had acquired the business of Richard Braddock, with the printing of indentures concerning the licence of wines, recognizances for alehouses, sheriffs' warrants and bonds, and auditors' bills.[5] With such solid work in hand he might well dispose of a dainty literary 'find' to a younger man. Thorpe, the son of an innkeeper at Barnet, had taken out his freedom ten years later than Hall, but had published already important editions of poems and plays. More significant was his acquisition in 1600,[6] before he had set up for himself, of the unpublished 'Lucan' of Marlowe and issue of the same (by Peter Short and

[1] Ward (note 3).

[2] Charles Edmonds, in a letter to the *Athenaeum*, 1 Nov. 1873.

[3] Gray reminds us (*A Chapter, &c.*, p. 100, note) of the complaint of the publisher (Daye) of the authorized edition of *Ferrex and Porrex*, 1571, that the tragedy was 'never intended by the authors thereof to be published; yet one, W. G. [William Griffith], getting a copy thereof at some young man's hand, that lacked a little money and much discretion, about five years past [1565] put it forth much corrupted, neither of the authors being made privy'. Thorpe and Eld's text, however, is remarkably free of corruptions.

[4] Arber, iii. 396.

[5] *Ib.* 404.

[6] From Flasket, apparently, who had it from Linley on 26 June 1600.

Walter Burre) with a pert dedication to his 'kind and true friend, Edward Blunt' the publisher, once possessor of the manuscript:[1]

I purpose to be blunt with you, and out of my dulness to encounter you with a dedication in the memory of that pure elemental wit, Chr. Marlowe, whose ghost or genius is to be seen walk the Churchyard.[2] ... This spirit was sometime a familiar of your own ... But stay now, Edward, ... you are to accommodate yourself with some few instructions touching the property of a patron ... First, you must be proud ... then when I bring you the book, take physic and keep state, assign me a time by your man to come again ... censure scornfully ... commend nothing lest you discredit your judgment. These things if you can mould yourself to them, Ned, I make no question but they will not become you. One special virtue in our Patrons of these days I have promised myself you shall fit excellently—which is, to give nothing.[3]

This prepares us for his dedication of *Shakespeare's Sonnets* in 1609. The book appeared in June (in which month Alleyn bought a copy for 5*d.*)[4]—'*Shake-speares Sonnets. Neuer before Imprinted.* At London. By G. Eld for T. T. and are to be solde by Iohn Wright, dwelling at Christ Church gate. 1609.'[5] Appended to the Sonnets was '*A Louers Complaint. By William Shake-speare*'. Prefixed was the dedication, 'To the onlie begetter of these insving Sonnets, M(aste)r W. H. all happinesse and that eternitie promised by ovr ever-living Poet, wisheth the well-wishing Adventurer in setting forth, T. T.' 'The only begetter' is the writer's fantastic style (with an execrable pun on John i. 14, 'the only begotten'), and no doubt means the 'getter' or 'procurer' of the manuscript.[6] 'M(aste)r W. H.all', &c., probably ill disguises, intentionally, the dedicatee.[7] The 'adventurer T. T.' is a happy designation for Thorpe himself, who does not lack literary ability. His 'ever-living poet' recalls 'that pure elemental wit'. The printing of the *Sonnets* has been carefully supervised.

[1] He sold it to Linley in 1598.

[2] St. Paul's Churchyard, on the bookstalls.

[3] Tucker Brooke, *The Works of Christopher Marlowe*, p. 647.

[4] *Dulwich MSS.*, Warner, p. 92. 5*d.* is written on the title-page of the copy in Rylands Library, Manchester.

[5] Some copies read 'and are to be solde by William Aspley, 1609'.

[6] Cf. *Haml.* III. ii. 8.

[7] Cf. 'Blunt' and 'blunt' in the dedication of *Lucan* above. The idea of Thorpe addressing a lordly patron such as Lord William Herbert (the Earl of Pembroke), or an aristocratic scholar like Sir William Harvey, in these saucy terms is quite out of the question.

Sixteen years or more had passed since these closet-trifles saw the dim light of private perusal and appreciation, but the interval did not justify their being torn from their context and flung without a word of apology or explanation—rather with impudent effrontery—before the public eye. Shakespeare may or may not have cursed the insolent 'mercenaries', guilty of unpardonable trespass on his own and his friends' personal feelings; but, so far as we are aware, he made no public protest. His reputation, in the first place, was responsible for the publication. His circle of readers had grown greatly since 1597. Anything from his pen was marketable in 1609. His lightest effusions would find purchasers, and even the 'Will' sonnets would not be suffered to die. And with regard to such compositions, *Qui s'excuse s'accuse*, 'Sportive blood' must take the consequences. The Poet was content to leave his credit to his contemporaries. It stood high in 1609 among 'grand censors' 'most displeased with plays'. So we learn from the remarkable preface to an edition this year of *Troilus and Cressida*.[1] The writer, under the impression that the play was a new one and had not yet been acted,[2] delivers himself of the following:

A Never Writer to an Ever Reader,

News!

Eternal reader, you have here a new play, never staled with the stage, never clapper-clawed with the palms of the vulgar, and yet passing full of the palm comical; for it is a birth of that[3] brain *that never undertook anything comical vainly*. And were but the vain names of comedies changed for the titles of commodities or of plays for pleas, you should see all those grand censors[4] that now style them such vanities, *flock to them for the main grace of their gravities; especially this Author's comedies, that are so framed to the life that they serve for the most common commentaries of all the actions of our lives, showing such a dexterity and power of wit,*[5] *that the most displeased with plays are pleased with his comedies.* And all such dull and heavy-witted worldlings as were never capable of the wit of a comedy, coming by report of them to his representations, have found that wit there that they never found in themselves, and have parted better witted then they came, feeling an edge of wit

[1] G. Eld was the printer, as of *Shakespeare's Sonnets.*

[2] The title-page was altered and this preface omitted on the discovery that the play had been acted at the *Globe.*

[3] The text has 'your'—'yt' mistaken for 'y^r^'.

[4] Puritans as distinguished from 'worldlings'.

[5] Intelligence.

set upon them more then ever they dreamed they had brain to grind it on. So much and such savoured salt of wit is in his comedies, that *they seem (for their height of pleasure) to be born in that sea that brought forth Venus.* Amongst all there is none more witty[1] then this; and had I time I would comment upon it, though I know it needs not for so much as will make you think your testern[2] well bestowed; but for so much worth as even poor I know to be stuffed in it, it deserves such a labour as well as the best comedy in Terence or Plautus. And believe this, that *when he is gone* and his comedies out of sale, you will scramble for them and set up a new, English Inquisition. Take this for a warning, and at the peril of your pleasure's loss, and judgment's, refuse not, nor like this the less for not being sullied with the smoky breath of the multitude; but thank Fortune for the scape it hath made amongst you: since by the grand possessors' wills[3] I believe you should have prayed for them rather than been prayed. And so I leave all such to be prayed-for (for the states of their wits' healths) that will not praise it. *Vale.*

Here again is piracy; but with it is a priceless tribute. The thief is conscious of very much more than the money-value of Shakespeare's productions. He tells us of 'grave' men and 'censorious' at the *Globe*, as well as 'heavy witted worldlings'—in Hamlet's language, of 'the judicious' whose 'censure o'erweighs a whole theatre of the unskilful'.[4] He speaks also of the 'salt' in the Author which loses not its 'savour'.[5] The whimsical style must not disguise a fine appreciation. The birth of Shakespeare Comedy like the Goddess of Beauty from the Sea, and its 'height of pleasure', are splendid praise.

1609

§ 132. *CYMBELINE*

SHAKESPEARE'S work of 1609 merited all that could be said of it. He wrote his great and lovely *Cymbeline*. Imogen sprang of the sea-foam, and fancy attained the purest altitude of pleasure. The 'grandest censor' could not but admire the 'grace' and the 'gravity'.

Cymbeline, like *Pericles*, is a tragedy with happy ending. Like that play also, it has a Puritan heroine. No girl could suffer more—from 'hourly shot of angry eyes',[6] 'a father cruel and a

[1] Intellectual.
[2] Sixpence.
[3] The 'grand possessors' are the King's Men, the owners of the manuscript.
[4] *Haml.* III. ii. 28–31.
[5] Matthew v. 13.
[6] I. i. 89 f.

step-dame false', 'a foolish suitor' and a 'husband banished';[1] still further, from her husband's folly and want of faith, and an arch-villain's treachery. But she comes through all, unembittered, the same loving, winsome, Christ-like spirit. Not that she is a Griselda, tame and patient. On the contrary, she is full of fire, blazes out against iniquity, says things in the heat she afterwards regrets. 'Art thou mad?' asks her father, and she replies, 'Almost, sir; Heaven restore me!'[2] She apologizes to Cloten, after an outburst, 'I am much sorry, sir; you put me to forget a lady's manners'.[3] She is maddened by detraction of Posthumus, as her love of him (the 'touch more rare') 'subdues all pangs, all fears'.[4] Physically timid, she has great mental courage, and is fortified by her religion. The Gods are ever on her lips, though we might not notice it, so natural and unobtrusive is the utterance—when she parts from Posthumus (whom she would have charged

> At the sixth hour of morn, at noon, at midnight,
> To encounter me with orisons, for then
> I am in Heaven for him);[5]

when she sleeps; when she receives a letter from Posthumus; when she parts from Pisanio; when she enters the cave; when she eats;[6] when she is welcomed by Guiderius and Arviragus; when she sees the body, as she thinks, of Posthumus;[7] when she tells, guiltily, her little white lie to Lucius;[8] when she will bury her 'master',[9] on whose grave she will say 'a century of prayers' twice over.[10] Her faith is sorely tried—

> if there be
> Yet left in Heaven *as small a drop of pity*
> *As a wren's eye*, feared Gods, a part of it![11]—

but it holds, and brings her to the 'gracious season'.[12] She is of the clinging kind that Shakespeare loved, cultivated, a reader (far into the night) and a musician,[13] skilful with her needle (worker, probably, of the tapestry of 'silk and silver' in her handsome Elizabethan bed-chamber:

> the story,
> Proud Cleopatra when she met her Roman
> And Cydnus swell'd above the banks or for

[1] I. vi. 1–3. [2] I. i. 147 f. [3] II. iii. 109 f.
[4] I. i. 135 f. [5] I. iii. 31–3. [6] III. vi. 53.
[7] IV. ii. 295, 305. [8] *Ib.* 375–7. [9] *Ib.* 387.
[10] *Ib.* 391 f. [11] IV. ii. 303–5. [12] V. v. 401.
[13] III. iv. 177 f., IV. ii. 48.

The press of boats or pride: a piece of work
So bravely done, so rich, that it did strive
In workmanship and value),[1]

domestic, an early-riser,[2] neat at 'cookery',[3] diligent, 'feat' and 'nurse-like'.[4] She is 'Fidele', in household duties as in her virtue.

An 'Italian fiend', Iachimo, is one of her tormentors. He lays a wager with her husband in Rome that he will find her 'assailable'. He makes the venture and is spurned, 'disdained' as 'the devil'.[5] He only saves himself by cunning—by swift, lawyer-like craft, and praise of Posthumus. Nor is this all. In her bed she suggests to *him* what is innocent and beautiful. Nothing better illustrates the immense development of Shakespeare's genius since his long-winded *Lucrece* than Iachimo's brief and breathless soliloquy in her chamber:

The crickets sing, and man's o'er-labour'd sense
Repairs itself by rest. Our Tarquin thus
Did softly press the rushes, ere he waken'd
The chastity he wounded. Cytheréa,
How bravely thou becom'st thy bed! fresh lily!
And whiter than the sheets! That I might touch,
But kiss, one kiss! Rubies unparagon'd,
How dearly they do it! 'Tis her breathing that
Perfumes the chamber thus: the flame o' the taper
Bows toward her, and would under-peep her lids
To see the enclosed lights, now canopied
Under these windows, white and azure, laced
With blue of Heaven's own tinct. But my design,
To note the chamber: I will write all down:
Such and such pictures; there the window; such
The adornment of her bed; the arras, figures,
Why, such and such, and the contents o' the story.
Ah, but some natural notes about her body,
Above ten thousand meaner moveables,[6]
Would testify to enrich mine inventory.[6]
O Sleep, thou ape of Death, lie dull upon her!
And be her sense but as a monument
Thus in a chapel lying! Come off, come off!
[*Taking off her bracelet.*
As slippery as the Gordian knot was hard,
'Tis mine; and this will witness[6] outwardly,
As strongly as the conscience does within,

[1] II. iv. 69–74. For her needle see I. i. 168, I. iii. 19.
[2] II. ii. 6.
[3] IV. ii. 48.
[4] V. v. 86–8.
[5] I. vi. 147 f.
[6] Country-law terms.

To the madding of her lord. On her left breast
A mole cinque-spotted, like the crimson drops
I' the bottom of a cowslip: here's a voucher[1]
Stronger than ever Law could make: this secret
Will force him think I have pick'd the lock and ta'en
The treasure of her honour. No more: to what end?
Why should I write this down that's riveted,
Screw'd to my memory? She hath been reading late,
The tale of Tereus: here the leaf's turned down,
Where Philomel gave up. I have enough:
To the trunk again, and shut the spring of it.
Swift, swift, you dragons of the night, that dawning
May bare the raven's eye! I lodge in fear:
Though this a heavenly Angel, hell is here. [*Clock strikes.*
One, two, three: time, time!
[*Goes into the trunk. The scene closes.*[2]

What sort of a 'fiend' is this? The experience has done him good, has 'taught' him the 'difference 'twixt amorous and villanous'.[3] He is full of a wholesome dread. His repentance at the end of the play is not absurd. However audacious, he is not a depraved scoundrel like Iago, devoid of *Grace*. Nor is he a bragging lout like Cloten. Imogen cannot influence that boastful clod. Yet, be it noticed, by his means, she draws to her window musicians, with the loveliest of morning-songs—

Hark, hark! the lark at Heaven's gate sings,
And Phoebus 'gins arise,
His steeds to water at those springs
On chaliced flowers that lies;
And winking Mary-buds begin
To ope their golden eyes;
With everything that pretty is,
My lady sweet, arise,
Arise, arise![4]

'Loveliest', and one of the holiest, an exquisite blending of Ovid's and Shakespeare's purest fancies, with Christian symbolism. Ovid's Sun-god pastures the steeds of his chariot in the West—

Axe sub Hesperio sunt pascua Solis equorum,
Ambrosiam pro gramine habent![5]

Shakespeare waters them in the East on dew—

On chaliced flowers that lies—

[1] Country-law term. [2] II. ii. 11–51. [3] V. v. 193–5.
[4] II. iii. 21–30. [5] *Met.* iv. 214 f.

when the lark is in the sky, and the Marygold (which takes its name from the Virgin) wakens to the dawn:[1] a symbol of the soul, *ainsi mon âme*, opening her eyes to God.

Four times 'chalice' is used in Shakespeare—by Falstaff profanely,[2] by Claudius blasphemously,[3] by Macbeth religiously,[4] and with sweetest reverence in the matin to Imogen. The Poet, whatever his Protestantism, in 1609 preferred the holy vessel of the Old Faith to that of the New. The churchwardens of Rowington in 1567–8 sold their 'chalice' (for 51*s.* 4*d.*) and bought in Puritan Coventry a 'communion cup' (for 43*s.* 6*d.*).[5]

An Old London Sign of the Marygold, c. 1670 (Larwood and Hotten, p. 192).

More interesting and significant is the influence of Imogen on Posthumus. He is a headstrong young fool, caught by Iachimo as Othello was caught by Iago ('credulous fool' is the fitting description of both).[6] He boasts of his wife in the club or mess-room, when the wine is flowing, and he quarrels. He accepts Iachimo's challenge, and his circumstantial falsehoods.[7] In a fit of jealousy, as insane as Othello's, he would have Imogen put to death. He raves against her and all women.[8] On receipt, however, of the 'bloody cloth', the token from Pisanio that she was dead, he is filled with deep contrition—

Gods! if you
Should have ta'en vengeance on my faults, I never
Had lived to put on this: so had you saved
The noble Imogen to repent, and struck
Me, wretch, more worth your vengeance.[9]

[1] 'Their fair leaves spread as the Marygold at the Sun's eye' (Sonnet xxv).
'The Marygold that goes to bed with the Sun
And with him rises, weeping' (*Wint. T.* IV. iv. 105 f.).

[2] 'Take away these chalices—brew me a pottle of sack' (*Merry W.* III. v. 29 f.).

[3] 'I'll have prepared him a chalice for the nonce' (*Haml.* IV. vii. 160 f.).

[4] 'Even-handed justice commends the ingredients of our poison'd chalice to our own lips' (*Macb.* I. vii. 10–12).

[5] Ryland, *Records*, ii. 51.

[6] *Oth.* IV. i. 47; *Cymb.* V. v. 210.

[7] II. iv. 61–139.

[8] II. v.

[9] V. i. 7–11.

He seeks to die, leaves the Roman army to fight as a British peasant, and, when the Britons are victorious, joins again the Romans, to find himself the prisoner of Cymbeline, condemned to be hanged. He is glad:

> Most welcome, bondage! for thou art a way,
> I think, to liberty . . .
>   My conscience, thou art fettered
> More than my shanks and wrists: you good gods, give me
> The penitent instrument to pick that bolt,
> Then, free for ever . . .
> For Imogen's dear life take mine; and though
> 'Tis not so dear, yet 'tis a life; you coined it . . .
> If you will take this audit, take this life
> And cancel these cold bonds. O Imogen![1]

He sleeps in his chains; and in his dream, his father and mother and brothers come to him. They pray to Jupiter on his behalf; and Jupiter answers—in sententious rhyme, powerful in its simplicity and absence of rhetoric:

> Whom best I love I cross, to make my gift
> The more delayed, delighted. Be content;
> Your low-laid son our Godhead will uplift:
> His comforts thrive, his trials well are spent.[2]

Providence overrules and disentangles the many threads of the story, 'Grace' is stronger than 'contempt';[3] 'a true election' saves while it 'damns';[4] 'let ordinance come as the gods foresay it';[5] 'all was lost but that the Heavens fought';[6] 'the fingers of the Powers above do tune the harmony of this peace';[7] these are articles of the Poet's Creed.

His Bible, *Metamorphoses*, old Law and new Medicine, are easily recognized in the drama. The Queen has studied drugs

[1] v. iv. 3–11, 22 f., 27 f.

[2] v. iv. 101–4. To characterize this solemn dream-mask as 'silly' (*The New Shakespeare*, *Tam. Shrew*, p. ix) throws light on the critic rather than on the Author. Ben Jonson complained of the old-fashioned pageantry, the 'creaking throne' that 'comes down the boys to please' (*Works*, 1616, prologue to *Every Man in his Humour*), but not of the poetry.

[3] IV. ii. 27.

[4] I. ii. 29 f. (I fail utterly to see that the lords 'make merry' over these theological terms: Lee, *Life*, p. 424). Cf. I. i. 53 and v. v. 464 f.

[5] IV. ii. 145 f.

[6] v. iii. 3 f.

[7] v. v. 466 f. Cf. IV. iii. 41, 46 ('The Heavens still must work . . . Fortune brings in some boats that are not steer'd').

under Cornelius—perfumes, distillations, preservatives, 'confections',[1] 'cordials' which 'redeem from death',[2] 'poisonous compounds', 'the movers of a languishing death',[3] 'mortal minerals' which 'feed on life and lingering by inches waste you';[4] and, a potent factor in the story, 'a certain stuff',[5] which she mistakes for poison, able to 'stupefy and dull the sense awhile,' 'locking up the spirits, to be more fresh reviving'.[6] She experiments on cats and dogs and 'creatures not worth the hanging'.[7] Once more we may note the obtrusion of Shakespeare's Law in a passage on sickness:

> Yet am I better
> Than one that's sick o' the gout; since he had rather
> Groan so *in perpetuity* than be cured
> By the sure physician, Death.[8]

We are on familiar and loved ground—in *New Place* garden,[9] on the bowling-green 'in Chapel',[10] in Clopton Park,[11] in the Forest, among flowers (violets, cowslips, primroses, 'the azured harebell' and eglantine, 'fresh lily', 'winking marybuds'), trees (the pine and cedar, oak, elder, vine), 'wild-wood leaves', 'furred moss', and 'daisied plot'; birds (the wren and ruddock, lark, jay, crow, raven, puttock, owl), animals (the fox and deer, hare, weasel, goat), and fiercer creatures of the imagination (the eagle, wolf, and lion). 'Lud's town', with its gates and 'temple of great Jupiter' (St. Paul's) and 'South fog',[12] is in the distance. There, too, is the Court, whose affectations and hypocrisies are satirized. We hear of Courtiers who 'wear their faces to the bent of the King's looks',[13] and 'seem as does the King',[14] and of 'good *remainders*' (a legal tag) 'of the Court'[15] rarely loved or praised;[16] of the insolence of Lordship towards inferiors,[17] the liberty of Gentlemen to swagger, swear, and gamble,[18] of patriotic 'strutting',[19] of 'effects as good as promise, unlike our Courtiers',[20] of a Lord among the 'fliers', who asked of him who bravely 'stood', *What news?*[21] and of the 'slipperiness' of

[1] I. v. 10–15.
[2] *Ib.* 60–4.
[3] *Ib.* 8 f.
[4] V. v. 50–2.
[5] *Ib.* 255.
[6] I. v. 37, 41 f.
[7] *Ib.* 19 f., 38.
[8] V. iv. 4–7.
[9] Act I, sc. i.
[10] II. i. 1–3.
[11] II. iii. 73–5, III. iv. 111 f.
[12] V. v. 482, IV. ii. 99, II. iii. 136.
[13] I. i. 12–15.
[14] *Ib.* 2 f.
[15] *Ib.* 129.
[16] *Ib.* 46 f.
[17] II. i. 31 f.
[18] *Ib.* 11 f.
[19] III. i. 33.
[20] V. iv. 134–7.
[21] V. iii. 1 f., 64 f.

the Court, where 'fear is as bad as falling'.[1] Says Imogen of country men,

> These are kind creatures. Gods, what lies I've heard!
> Our courtiers say all's savage but at court:
> Experience, O, thou disprovest report![2]

But these cave-dwellers are of noble and princely blood, and Shakespeare believes in it. Imogen has it in her veins, and her brothers are as 'gentle'

> As zephyrs blowing below the violet,
> Not wagging his sweet head; and yet as rough,
> Their royal blood enchafed, as the rudest wind
> That by the top doth take the mountain pine
> And make him stoop to the vale. 'Tis wonder
> That an invisible instinct should frame them
> To royalty unlearn'd, honour untaught,
> Civility not seen from other, valour
> That wildly grows in them, but yields a crop
> As if it had been sow'd.[3]

Even Cloten is 'a Queen's son', and must, like Jezebel, be buried 'as a prince':[4] though 'mean and mighty', rotting

> Together, have one dust, yet reverence,
> That angel of the world, doth make distinction
> Of place 'tween high and low.[5]

Shakespeare in 1609, whatever his condemnation of 'courtiers', would have fought for the Crown against the Commons.

Again in this puritan drama we meet with a fine relic of Catholicism. It would be difficult to say which is the more beautiful, the 'chaliced flowers',[6] holding in their cups the morning dew, 'consecrate'[7] like the wine of the Eucharist, or the old King's tears, falling (like Cordelia's) as 'holy water' on his recovered child.[8]

Cymbeline's agitated speech at the close is in 'broken' metre:

> This fierce abrídge|ment
> Hath to it circumstantial brán|ches, which
> Distinction should be rích | in. Where? how líved | you?

[1] III. iii. 46–9. Cf. v. iv. 127–31.

[2] IV. ii. 32–4.

[3] *Ib.* 171–81. Cf. IV. iv. 53 f.

[4] 2 Kings ix. 34: 'And Jehu said, Visit now yonder cursed woman, and bury her; for she is a king's daughter.'

[5] IV. ii. 244–9.

[6] II. iii. 24.

[7] *Mid. N. D.* v. i. 422.

[8] v. v. 268 f. See p. 666.

And when came you to serve our Roman cáp|tive?
How parted with your bróth|ers? how first mét | them?
Why fled you from the Court? and whí|ther? These,
And your three motives, to the bát|tle, with
I know not how much more, should be demánd|ed.[1]

1609

§ 133. SHAKESPEARE'S PORTRAIT

THOMAS GREENE had difficulty, as we have seen,[2] in getting possession of his house adjoining the Stratford Churchyard. He was still living at *New Place*, with his wife and young children (Anne and William),[3] on 9 September 1609, when he submitted his case against the occupying tenant to Sir Henry Rainsford of Clifford Chambers for arbitration. In his memoranda he notes his willingness that Master George Browne should stay on for a time, provided he really intended to do, and sow the garden. Greene had cut down walnut-trees there, in Lent this year, and had sown peas; but there was difficulty in the carriage of the timber he wanted for the repair of the dwelling. He writes, '(Browne) doubted whether he might sow his garden, until about my going to the Term'—Easter Term began 3 May; 'seeing I could get no carriages to help me here with timber, I was content to permit it, without contradiction; and that rather, because I perceived I might stay another year at New Place.'

He continues, 'I desire I may have the possession at Our Lady Day next' (25 March 1610), 'that then I may begin to make it ready against Michaelmas next', i.e. following, 29 September 1610.

Shakespeare contemplated retirement. He wanted to have New Place to himself and his family not later than Michaelmas 1610. He probably had sole possession there in the spring of 1611.[4]

The Droeshout portrait of Shakespeare may have originated in his determination to retire from the stage. Much discussed and

[1] v. v. 382–9. [2] p. 670. [3] *Ib.*

[4] Greene said, in May 1617, he had spent £400 on St. Mary's House 'within this six years'. See p. 834, note 3.

criticized, this famous picture has triumphed over all attacks upon its authenticity. Richmond's judgement stands: 'The portrait is so alive in expression, so intelligent and passionate, that I feel convinced it was painted by a by no means incompetent artist, though not one of first-rate attainments, from life.' It has the inscription in the top left-hand corner, 'Willm Shakespeare 1609', and was doubtless the work in that year of Martin Droeshout, one of a group of Flemish artists in London. The lack of Gothic script in the lettering (e.g. S is written instead of the usual English and Shakespearean 𝔖) confirms the foreign nationality of the artist. Fellow-actors may have had the portrait painted in anticipation of the Poet's departure, though, as we shall see,[1] he did not succeed in complete retirement to Stratford until some years afterwards. Droeshout, who described himself as 'painter of Brabant', took out his naturalization on 25 January 1608. He had a nephew of the same name, baptized at the Dutch Church on 26 April 1601 (son of Michael Droeshout and his wife Susannaken van der Ersbek). Young Martin Droeshout perpetrated the engraving of Shakespeare in the Folio of 1623. The engraving, we cannot doubt, is made from the portrait. It is obviously the attempt of a novice, and so ill-drawn that it rises not much above the level of a caricature. Repeated efforts, as we shall note, to bring it into closer likeness with the painting have not improved it.[2]

'O sweet Master Shakespeare! I'll have his picture in my study' (at the Court), says Gullio in *Parnassus* (iii. 1), a students' play at Cambridge (1599); but there is no extant portrait of Shakespeare earlier than the Droeshout, 1609.[3] This, if crude, is not unworthy of the subject. The painter had sufficient skill to give us something of his stately sitter. The body of the Poet, which is cut-off by a starched ruff from the head, he entrusted, according to custom (when only a face was asked for), to an

[1] p. 817.

[2] The likeness gets worse instead of better. This fact is fatal to the theory that the portrait is a forgery, based on the latest form of the engraving. Spielmann's elaborate and interesting arguments for the priority of the engraving are convincing to me of the contrary.

[3] The 'Ely House' portrait is precisely what certain critics declare the Droeshout to be, namely, an idealization of the engraving in a late stage. It bears the forged date 'Aet. 39 1603'.

THE DROESHOUT PORTRAIT, 1609

Shakespeare Memorial Gallery, Stratford-upon-Avon

apprentice. The tunic is out of perspective,[1] and too narrow for a man of the proportions of the bust in Stratford Church. But the face, within the setting of the well-drawn ruff, is striking, and resembles the bust in almost every feature. In both are the tall domed forehead, the arching brows, the strong nose, the long upper lip (like Sir Walter Scott's), the auburn hair falling over the ears, the hazel eyes, and the sensitive mouth. In the portrait the eyes are clear and penetrating and the mouth with full under-lip is ready to smile; in the bust, which was evidently made from a death mask, the eyes are dull, the nose is shortened, perhaps by accident in the taking of the mask, and the upper lip correspondingly lengthened, the lips are drawn, and the hair is thinner on the crown and thicker below the chin than in the portrait. Evidently the Poet had grown his beard and lost hair at the top of his head between 1609 and his death in 1616.[2]

The face grows upon us and holds us. The gaze is searching and magisterial. Everything is observed, and little said. Iachimo shall be exposed, and Imogen shall come into her own. Mercy seasons Justice. From the picture, as in the book of the dramas, speaks the Lord Chief Justice of poets and all writers whatsoever. Subsequent 'portraits' are fanciful and feeble in comparison.

In December 1609 the theatres were reopened, and the King's men played at the Blackfriars.[3] They performed also at Court thirteen times, 'before Christmas and in the time of the holidays, and afterwards'. They were paid £130 on 2 March.[4] The *Globe* was open in April. Simon Forman witnessed *Macbeth* there on the 20th,[5] and Prince Lewis Frederick of Württemberg *Othello* on

[1] For example, the left arm (of the sitter) is far too much in profile compared with the right arm.

[2] On the elm panel has been laid a white gesso ground (whitening or slaked plaster and size), several coats. Over this, when dry, has been scumbled a thin warm red glaze, probably Indian red and a little umber in oil, after the practice of Flemish painters of the period. It is possible that this warm ground, which has been scumbled rather unevenly, suggested to some critics a portrait beneath. It shows through more in certain places than in others. Upon it has been painted the portrait in oil or oil varnish. In drying under the influence of time it has become very horny and cracked, separating at the slightest provocation from the gesso ground. The head has been prepared in a thick underpainting, probably in monochrome, and finished with glazes and thin paint.

[3] The Children of the Chapel, to make way for them, played at a theatre in the Whitefriars. Chambers, ii. 55, iv. 123.

[4] *Ib.* iv. 175.

[5] Ashm. MS. 208, f. 207.

the 30th.[1] Shortly before 20 April of this year, or shortly after 15 May 1611, Forman saw *Cymbeline* at the *Globe*. He was impressed, as he might well be, by the scene in Imogen's chamber.

Remember [he writes] how the Italian, that came from her love, conveyed himself into a chest, and said it was a chest of plate, sent from her love and others, to be presented to the King. And in the deepest of the night, she being asleep, he opened the chest and came forth of it, and viewed her in her bed and the marks of her body, and took away her bracelet.[2]

Cymbeline was immediately popular. It provided features for Beaumont and Fletcher's *Philaster, or Love Lies a Bleeding*, which was on the stage this summer, and the subject of commendation in John Davies of Hereford's *Scourge of Folly*. In *Philaster* are a king (who resembles King James) and his daughter, her worthless suitor (a Spanish prince) and her tempestuous lover, who, in a fit of insane suspicion, curses womankind. There is a girl, also, who wanders in boy's disguise through the wild. Imagery and phrase are borrowed, and the 'broken metre', which became a trick, repeated *ad nauseam* on any and every occasion, in Beaumont and Fletcher:

Oh, worthy sir, forgíve | me! Do not make
Your miseries and my faults meet togéth|er,
To bring a greater dán|ger. Be yourself,
Still sound amongst diséas|es. I have wróng'd | you,
And though I find it last, and beaten to it,
Let first your goodness knów | it. Calm the peó|ple,
And be what you were bórn | to.[3]

Philaster is a feeble production, in thought, ethics, verse, and characterization, and evidence of the impassable gulf which divided Shakespeare from his imitators.

In July the theatres were closed on account of plague,[4] and the King's men travelled. They performed at Dover[5] (where Shakespeare once more saw the sea, the shingle, and his cliff),[6] at Oxford[7] (where he would meet again, among others, the Davenants),[8] at Stafford,[9] and at Shrewsbury.[10]

[1] 'Lundi, 30. Son Excellence alla au *Globe*, lieu ordinaire où l'on joue les Commédies, y fut representé l'histoire du More de Venise.' Add. MS. 20001, f. 9b.

[2] Ashm. MS. 208, f. 206.

[3] *Philaster*, v. iii. 181–7.

[4] J. T. Murray, i. 155.

[5] *Ib.* i. 155, ii. 264 ('Bet. July 6 and Aug. 4').

[6] See p. 655.

[7] J. T. Murray, i. 155, ii. 379 ('August').

[8] See p. 671.

[9] Chambers, ii. 216.

[10] J. T. Murray, i. 155, ii. 392.

1610

§ 134. *THE SCOURGE OF FOLLY*

On 8 October was entered at Stationers' Hall a little volume of epigrams by a West countryman, John Davies of Hereford, the fashionable writing-master and poet (in Oxford), entitled *The Scourge of Folly*.[1] Three of the poems are addressed to Shakespeare and his fellows, Armin and Ostler. That addressed 'To our English Terence, Master William Shakespeare' is as follows:

Some say, good Will—which I in sport do sing—
Had'st thou not played some Kingly parts in sport,
Thou had'st been a companion for a King,
And been a King among the meaner sort.
Some others rail; but, rail as they think fit,
Thou hast no railing but a reigning wit;
  And *honesty thou sow'st*, which they do reap,
  So to increase their stock which they do keep.

Players were accustomed to the familiar terms of their admirers, but this is the first and last time Master Shakespeare was addressed in such free and easy fashion in print.[2] On that account the testimony to his aristocratic bearing and integrity is the more striking.

The epigram to Armin—

To honest, gamesome Robin Armin,
That tickles the spleen like an harmless vermin—

is more within the writer's ken, and altogether admirable:

Armin, what shall I say of thee but this,
Thou art a fool and knave? both? Fie, I miss
And wrong thee much, sith thou indeed art neither,
Although in show thou playest both together.
We all (that's Kings and all) but players are
Upon this earthly stage; and should have care
To play our parts so properly that we

[1] *The Scourge of Folly. Consisting of satyricall Epigramms, and others in honour of many noble and worthy Persons of our Land.* For Davies see p. 591.

[2] Heywood (*The Hierarchie of the Blessed Angells*, 1635) complains of the familiarity with which the audience *spoke* of their favourite actors, including even Shakespeare:

Mellifluous *Shake-speare*, whose inchanting Quill
Commanded Mirth or Passion, was but *Will*.

May at the end gain an applaudite;
But most men over-act, mis-act, or miss
The action which to them peculiar is,
And the more high the part is which they play
The more they miss in what they do or say;
So that when off the stage, by Death, they wend,
Men rather hiss at them than them commend.
But, honest Robin, thou with harmless mirth
Dost please the World,[1] and so amongst the earth,
That others but possess with care that stings,
So makst thy life more happy far than Kings;
And so much more our love should thee embrace,
Sith still thou livst with some that die to Grace,
And yet art honest, in despite of lets,
Which earns more praise than forced goodness gets:
So play thy part, be honest still with mirth;
Then, when thou'rt in the tiring-house of earth,
Thou, being His servant whom all Kings do serve,
Mayst for thy part well-played like praise deserve;
For in that tiring-house when either be,
You're One Man's men, and equal in degree.
So thou in sport the happiest men dost school,
To do as thou dost—*Wisely play the Fool.*

It is a fine poem, worthy of a fine actor, able to do some justice to Feste, Touchstone, and the Fool in *Lear*; worthy also of a wise man and religious, not over-blessed, though a 'goldsmith', with this world's goods,[2] nor, we suspect, with good health. From the epigram to Ostler, 'To the Roscius of these times, Master W(illiam) Ostler', we gather that not long since he had been almost killed in an assault, and recently had gained high reputation in the part of a slain monarch. He had lately joined Shakespeare's company, and probably shared his 'kingly parts'.

We must notice a fourth epigram in *The Scourge*, the subject of which is Sir Thomas Lucy of Charlecote, aged 24. He had been at the French Court with that dare-devil Welshman, three years older than himself, Sir Edward Herbert, huntsman, duellist, dancer, lutenist, linguist, philosopher—afterwards Lord Herbert of Cherbury and author of *De Veritate*. They were wrecked on the voyage from Dieppe, the ship in a storm driving against Dover pier.

[1] With play on the word *Globe* ('Mundus'): see pp. 521, 782.

[2] His 'boldness of a Beggar' (*armin*) in his dedication of *Phantasma* (1609) may be more than a play on his name.

SIR THOMAS LUCY, KT. (1585–1640)

Copied by G. P. HARDING, *c.* 1820, *from the miniature by* ISAAC OLIVER *at Charlecote*

They at Dover [says Herbert] adventured in a shallop of six oars to relieve us, which being come with great danger to the side of our ship, I got into it first with my sword in my hand and called for Sir Thomas Lucy, saying if any man offered to get in before him I should resist him; whereupon a faithful servant of his, taking Sir Thomas Lucy out of the cabin (who was half-dead of sea-sickness), put him into my arms; whom after I had received, I bid the shallop make-away for shore . . . from whence we sent more shallops and so made means to save both men and horses that were in the ship . . . In pity to the master, Sir Thomas Lucy and myself gave thirty pounds towards his loss.

This was in February 1609. One of the horses saved was a favourite French jennet of Herbert's. 'Sir Thomas Lucy', he says, 'would have given me £200 for this horse, which I would not accept.' Rapiers and horses played a prominent part in the lives of these Jacobean young bloods. Davies addresses Lucy—

Bright spark of wit and courage, yet enow
To set a world of hearts in love on fire . . .
Thou all-belov'd and highly prizèd gem
That in the Court's brows like a diamond,
Or Hesperus in Heaven, dost lighten them
For men to see their way on glory's ground.

He was apparently a little man, of spirit. Already he was keen about deer. In July 1610 he petitioned in the Star Chamber against gentlemen-poachers in his grandmother's park, now his, at Sutton.

We must glance at certain family and kindred happenings this year, 1610, in Shakespeare's life. On Sunday 14 January his wife's niece (and god-daughter), Anne Hathaway, daughter of Bartholomew Hathaway, was married in Stratford Church, in the face presumably of a large congregation, to Richard, son of Avery Richards, yeoman, of Drayton.[1] It was the 26th anniversary of the bride's christening in the same Church. On Sunday 4 March was christened here Mary, daughter of Master John Greene, the brother of the Town Clerk, Thomas Greene of *New Place*.[2] John Greene, a lawyer like his brother, had married, on 29 March 1609, Margaret Lane,[3] daughter of John and granddaughter of the late Nicholas Lane, and lived with or near the Lanes in Bridge Town. His child was buried in a week, on Sunday 11 March.[4] The same month an infant daughter was

[1] *Register*, p. 24.
[2] *Ib.*, p. 79.
[3] *Ib.*, p. 24.
[4] *Ib.*, p. 79.

born to Thomas Greene of *New Place* and buried.[1] On 1 April Bartholomew Hathaway purchased his farm at Shottery, his and his sister's old home, for £200 (subject to the old chief rent of 33*s.* 4*d.*)[2] Did Shakespeare help his brother-in-law to acquire this considerable estate? Was it the purchase he himself had contemplated in 1598 alluded to by Adrian Quyney?[3] His lawyer, Francis Collins of Warwick and Stratford, drew up the conveyance. Then, on 13 April, unless the statement in the *Finalis Concordia* is fictitious, Shakespeare bought of young William Combe and his brother, John Combe, twenty acres of pasture in Old Stratford for £100. Later in the year, at Michaelmas, when we may believe Shakespeare was at home, his wife's nephew, John Hathaway, second son to Bartholomew and future heir of the recently purchased Hewlands, married Elizabeth, daughter to Avery Edwards of Drayton.[4] Their families became thus doubly connected. On 29 December, when Shakespeare was in London, a newly-born daughter of John Greene, baptized Anne, to whom Mistress Shakespeare may have stood sponsor, was buried.[5]

1610

§ 135. DEATH OF WILLIAM COMBE OF WARWICK

THIS autumn died William Combe the lawyer, of the Middle Temple and Warwick. Resident in Warwick, where he was greatly respected ('an honest gentleman their neighbour well-known to them all', as the Bailiff described him in 1605[6]), he retained a close connexion with Stratford. He was Counsel for the Borough from 1597 until his death. In 1597 he represented the County in Parliament. Shakespeare bought land of him in 1602.[7] Early in 1606 he lost his wife,[8] Alice, by whom he had no children. This was the lady who thought poor Freeman's cheerfulness at his execution un-Christlike.[9] The same year Combe married Lady Jane Puckering,[10] widow of his neighbour

[1] *Register*, p. 79. 'Mar. 29, An Infant dawghter Mr. Thomas Grene.'

[2] Birthplace Museum (*Cat.* 59). [3] p. 496. [4] *Register*, p. 24.

[5] *Ib.*, p. 80. [6] *Black Book of Warwick*, p. 405. [7] p. 575.

[8] She was buried at St. Nicholas, Warwick, on 21 Jan. [9] p. 411.

[10] They were presented with wine by the Stratford Corporation on their visit to the College before Michaelmas (*Chamb. Acct.*, 9 Jan. 1607).

at Warwick, the late Lord Keeper of the Great Seal, Sir John Puckering, who had died in 1596. He went to live with her at her late husband's house, The Priory. It was the fine residence built on the site and out of the ruins of the dismantled priory by Thomas Fisher, John Dudley's 'man' and favourite, in 1565. Here Fisher entertained the Earl of Leicester at Michaelmas 1571, and his fellow-visitor, the old Earl of Northampton (William, brother of Queen Katharine Parr), who was taken ill, and died on 28 October, and hence was carried to his burial (at Queen Elizabeth's expense) on 5 December in St. Mary's Church.[1] At the Priory next year Fisher entertained the Earl and Countess of Warwick, who had vacated the Castle for the reception of the Queen. On the evening of Saturday 16 August her Majesty paid them a surprise visit on her return through the woods from Kenilworth, as described by their host's brother, John Fisher:

> And because she would see what cheer my Lady of Warwick made, she suddenly went unto Master Thomas Fisher's house, where my Lord of Warwick kept his house; and there finding them at supper, sat down awhile; and after a little repast, rose again, leaving the rest at supper, and went to visit the goodman of the house, Thomas Fisher, who at that time was grievously vexed with the gout. Who being brought out into the gallery-end would have kneel'd or rather fallen down, but her Majesty would not suffer it but with most gracious words comforted him.[2]

Fisher died in January 1577; and the Priory, after brief possession by his spendthrift son, was sold by him in 1581 to Sir John Puckering. For fifteen years the Priory was the residence of the Lord Keeper, and afterwards the home of his widow and her second husband, Master Combe. The north front faced the park, the south the garden. From the one to the other ran the gallery, with a chamber at each end, from one of which probably old Fisher was carried in a chair to receive the Queen's greetings. That facing the park was furnished in scarlet, red, and yellow with Dornix hangings, that facing the garden in purple and green. A chamber 'over the Hall-screen' was furnished in purple and tawny, with 'seven pieces of tapestry-hangings and four old window and chimney pieces of tapestry-work'. Two more bedrooms, called the 'Dornix chamber' and the 'Wainscot chamber', took their names from Dornix hangings and wains-

[1] *Black Book of Warwick*, pp. 51–6. [2] *Ib.*, p. 95.

coting. The former was furnished in yellow and purple and green, the latter in black and the 'changeable coloured taffeta'—recommended by the Clown to the unstable young Duke in *Twelfth Night.*[1] A sixth bed-chamber, named after the Earl of Warwick, was more elaborate, furnished in purple and yellow, and yellow splashed 'with drops of blood', with 'five pieces of tapestry', and 'a Turkey carpet for the cupboard there' (a side-board cloth). The 'Great Chamber over the Parlour' was a bed-room, furnished in crimson and hung with tapestries of the stories of Jacob and Esau (six pieces) and Abraham (one piece). Here were handsome andirons of brass or Northumberland metal (and not merely of wrought iron as in forementioned chambers) and a Turkey carpet for the cupboard. An oak stair-case led into the large 'Hall', with tall windows, on the ground-floor, where also was the 'Parlour' or dining-room. In the last were 'five pieces of tapestry of the story of Jacob and Esau, one long Turkey carpet, two cupboard cloths of Turkey work, a pair of andirons of brass or Northumberland metal, one dozen-and-a-half of Turkey work stools, one long table of walnut' (at which her Majesty may have sat for however brief a repast) 'and a dozen of stools of walnut-tree fitting the same table'. An heir-loom bequeathed by Lady Puckering to her son was 'two long cushions of purple velvet, embroidered with the crest of arms of Sir John Puckering late Lord Keeper'.[2]

For four years William Combe was master of the Priory, and not unworthy of his predecessor. His will, drawn up on Sunday 1 April 1610, opens with religious reflection and prayer:

> *Omnis gloria Dei et omnis salus hominum in Christi morte constituta sunt. Audi, Fili, verba oris mei eaque in corde tuo quasi fundamentum repone! Nescit homo diem suam: dies nostra quasi umbra super terram et nulla mora.*[3]

Such utterances were not formalities. The testator had studied theology as well as law, if only as a puritan layman. He continues:

> I bequeath my soul, a created substance invisible, incorporal and immortal, resembling the image of her Creator, unto the most holy and sacred hands

[1] II. iv. 76 f.

[2] *P.C.C. 52 Wood.*

[3] 'All the glory of God and all the salvation of men are established in the Death of Christ. Hearken, O Son, to the words of my mouth, and lay them in Thine heart as my foundation! Man knoweth not his day: our day is as a shadow upon the earth nor is there any delay.'

of the Maker and to God the Redeemer and Saviour thereof, to God the Holy Ghost the Comforter, one God in Trinity and Trinity in Unity, to whom be all honour, glory and power now and for ever and ever. Amen. I do confess and profess in all humility that I do very confidently believe that the promise of God's grace in the mercy of Christ belongeth unto me, and that I shall be saved by the only death and passion of that Jesus Christ who hath thereby satisfied his Father's wrath and just indignation for my most grievous sins and offences:

Disciplina pacis nostrae irruit per eum, et livore suo vulnera nostra sanata sunt.

He left a large estate, including Alvechurch Place and Park which he had acquired from the Sheldons, and interesting property in Warwick, such as The Vineyard House (probably his residence before he married Lady Puckering), three watermills called The Castle Mills (in the tenure once of Richard Brooke), the Castle Meadow, the Earl's Meadow, and a parcel of ground called 'The Gates'. To the poor of Warwick he bequeathed £20, of Alvechurch £10, of Stratford £10, of Broadway £10. His heirs, on his widow's decease, were his nephew John Combe, and his great-nephew William Combe, both of Stratford. Of Stratford also was the witness and no doubt *scriptor* of the will, Michael Olney, 'Master Lucas's man' and a lawyer, who about this time married Anne Parsons, daughter of Alderman Parsons of Wood Street, and god-daughter, there is some reason to think, of Mistress Anne Shakespeare. Master Combe died six months after making his will, and was buried at Warwick, in St. Nicholas Church and, in his right as leaseholder of the parish tithe, within the chancel, on Friday 5 October. There must have been a large gathering at the funeral, and we shall not be far out in the assumption that Shakespeare was present to do honour to his neighbour, not to use a stronger term. The demolition of the Priory in 1925 was a needless act of vandalism.

1610

§ 136. *THE WINTER'S TALE*

THE complex 'story' of *Cymbeline*, which Forman was able to follow at the *Globe*, has been traced to many sources—Holinshed, Spenser, Sidney, Boccaccio, and others. *The Winter's Tale*, which occupied Shakespeare in the summer of 1610, owes much to Robert Greene's novel, *Pandosto, the Triumph of Time*, something to Sidney's *Arcadia*, to Ovid's story of Pygmalion, and to the *Alcestis* of Euripides. So varied was the Poet's reading. But far more than books, Stratford, in both plays, stirred his imagination—the scenery, the quiet, the simplicity, the humour, the godliness of his native place. The fresh air of his loved Warwickshire blows through his work, scattering the clouds and the poison, and bringing health to diseased or sophisticated minds.

The Winter's Tale is the 'history' of a king seized, as were Othello and Posthumus, but for a cause different from theirs, by a mad fit of jealousy. They were victims of passion and circumstance; Leontes suffers from *physical* malady. A muscle or blood-vessel breaks and he is no longer himself. Love turns to hate—

> I have *tremor cordis* on me: my heart dances,
> But not for joy, not joy.[1]

Lear had similar attacks, the third of which killed him; but Leontes recovers from the first by the shock of the second, and again has his senses. This is medical, a matter which doubtless the Poet discussed with his son-in-law, Doctor Hall.

Under his first attack Leontes, on the question of his wife, is crazy. He believes that she is false and nothing will persuade him to the contrary. To argue or remonstrate only infuriates him and brings down his wrath on other innocent persons. For one in his shattered home he retains his affection—his little son. He loves the child the more in his desolateness. Mamilius is his own, if the baby daughter be a bastard, and on him he dotes while he sends the girl to her death. Then, from this object of his love comes his return to sanity. Confidently he has appealed to Apollo; the oracle arrives, and pronounces the Queen chaste and himself a tyrant; he blasphemes, declares it a 'falsehood'; the word is scarcely out of his mouth when a clap of thunder shakes the palace and a servant rushes in to say that Mamilius is dead. Hermione faints; Leontes, without realizing it, is restored:

> Apollo's angry, and the Heavens themselves
> Do strike at my injustice.[2]

His next thought is for his wife:

> Beseech you, tenderly apply to her
> Some remedies for life.[3]

[1] I. i. 110 f. [2] III. ii. 147 f. [3] 153 f.

He hears that she is dead, and bears Paulina's torrent of righteous indignation with relief. He welcomes it, embraces it, as an utterance of his own rage against himself:

O thou tyrant,
Do not repent these things, for they are heavier
Than all thy woes can stir: therefore betake thee
To nothing but despair. *A thousand knees,*
Ten thousand years together, naked, fasting
Upon a barren mountain, and still winter
In storm perpetual, could not move the Gods
To look that way thou wert.[1]

Here again is Dante in Shakespeare, the sense of the incommensurable in Sin. The scene closes with remorseful vows:

Bring me
To the dead bodies of my queen and son:
One grave shall be for both; upon them shall
The causes of their death appear, unto
Our shame perpetual.[2]

Hermione, outraged in every fibre of her noble nature, knowing nothing of the physical trouble in her husband, secludes herself. She can do no other. 'Time' alone may heal her wounds and sorrows. For sixteen years Leontes lives a solitary and, as he believes, a wifeless, childless man.

And strange things happen for his good.

In the first place, the baby daughter, cast on a wild shore, is preserved. A shepherd finds her and brings her to his cottage. She is reared, for her blessing, a country girl, the foster-child of rustic parents and sister to a yokel 'brother'. Then we see her aged 16, Perdita ('the Lost One'), at a shepherds' feast, the central figure in the longest scene but one in all Shakespeare.[3] The Poet delights in it, lingers over it, is loath to bring it to a close. Absolutely it is after his heart. Perdita in the stead of her 'mother', now dead, receives her 'father's' guests, as shy and sensitive as her buxom predecessor had been ready and hearty. 'Fie, daughter,' says he,

when my old wife lived, upon
This day she was both pantler, butler, cook,
Both dame and servant; welcomed all, served all;

[1] III. ii. 208–15.

[2] III. ii. 235–9.

[3] It contains 874 lines; *Love's L. L.* V. ii, with duplicate passages, has 942 lines.

Would sing her song and dance her turn; now here,
At upper end o' the table, now i' the middle;
On his shoulder, and his; her face o' fire
With labour, and the thing she took to quench it,
She would to each one sup.[1]

Perdita has no taste for familiarities and ale. She distributes flowers to old and young, according to their fanciful signification:

Reverend sirs,[2]
For you there's rosemary and rue;[3] these keep
Seeming and savour all the winter long:
Grace and remembrance be to you both,
And welcome to our shearing!
. . . Here's flowers for you;
Hot lavender, mints, savory, marjoram;
The Marygold, that goes to bed wi' the sun
And with him rises weeping:[4] these are flowers
Of middle summer, and I think they are given
To men of middle age. You're very welcome!
. . . Now, my fairest friend,
I would I had some flowers o' the spring that might
Become your time of day; and yours, and yours,
That wear upon your virgin branches yet
Your maidenhoods growing: O Proserpina,

(and Shakespeare here opened, in thought, his loved *Metamorphoses*)

For the flowers now that frighted thou let'st fall
From Dis's waggon! daffodils,
That come before the swallow dares, and take
The winds of March with beauty; violets dim,
But sweeter than the lids of Juno's eyes[4]
Or Cytheréa's breath; pale primroses,
That die unmarried, ere they can behold
Bright Phoebus in his strength, a malady
Most incident to maids; bold oxlips and
The crown imperial; lilies of all kinds,
The flower-de-luce being one![5]

She is wooed by Florizel, the prince of Bohemia in the guise of a shepherd. His father follows him to the sheep-shearing, and breaks in upon his betrothal with threat to bar him from suc-

[1] IV. iv. 55–62.
[2] Polixenes and Camillo, elderly gentlemen, in disguise.
[3] Rosemary for 'remembrance' and rue for 'grace': see next line but one.
[4] See p. 465.
[5] IV. iv. 73–7, 103–8, 112–27.

cession. But love knows not distinction of rank or occupation. It knits man and maid in deathless union. Nor is Perdita ashamed to be a shepherd's daughter—

> The selfsame Sun that shines upon [the] Court
> Hides not his visage from our cottage, but
> Looks on alike.[1]

As in *Cymbeline*, the Poet is emphatic about princely blood. He says of Perdita (IV. iv. 157–9),

> Nothing she does or seems
> But smacks of something greater than herself,
> Too noble for this place.[2]

But he satirizes, as in *Cymbeline*, with pitiless humour, the assumption of 'Greatness'. Autolycus masquerades as an aristocrat. Borrowed garments, and a superior tone of voice, give him the air of authority. He has been at Court and worn 'three-pile' velvet (mark of the pox),[3] was whipp'd out of the Prince's service, became ape-bearer, process-server, bum-bailiff, and having run a puppet-show of the Prodigal Son, married a tinker's wife, and 'settled' down to street-singing, peddling, and 'prigging'. Many a 'man of worship' in 1610 possessed fewer qualifications. Shakespeare cared for Autolycus infinitely more than for the corrupt official, and the costly, parasitic, often syphilitic young blood, who gathered from many parts about the King at Whitehall. What did courtiers think of the following?—

SHEPHERD. Are you a Courtier, an 't like you, sir?

AUTOLYCUS. Whether it like me or no, I am a Courtier. Seest thou not the air of the Court in these enfoldings? hath not my gait in it the measure of the Court? receives not thy nose Court-odour from me? reflect I not on thy baseness Court-contempt? Thinkest thou, for that I insinuate or toaze[4] from thee thy business, I am therefore no Courtier? I am Courtier *cap-a-pe*; and one that will either push-on or pluck-back thy business there: whereupon I command thee to open thy affair.

SHEPHERD. My business, sir, is to the King.

AUTOLYCUS. What advocate hast thou to him?

[1] 455–7. Cf. Matthew v. 45: 'That ye may be the children of your Father . . . He maketh His sun to arise on the evil and the good.'

[2] IV. iv. 157–9. 'Smacks of Something Greater than herself': a transcendent saying, of One with more Divinity than kingly blood in her. It might have been said of Christ.

[3] *Meas. for M.* I. ii. 31–6; *All's W.* IV. v. 100–3.

[4] pull or pluck, like the wool from a sheep's back.

SHEPHERD. I know not, an 't like you?

CLOWN (*aside to* SHEPHERD). Advocate's the Court-word for a pheasant: say you have none.

SHEPHERD. None, sir; I have no pheasant, cock, nor hen.

AUTOLYCUS (*breaking into poetry and morality*):

How blest are we that are not simple men!
Yet Nature might have made me as these are,
Therefore I'll not disdain.

CLOWN (*aside to* SHEPHERD). This cannot be but a great Courtier.

SHEPHERD (*aside to* CLOWN). His garments are rich but he wears them not handsomely.

CLOWN (*aside to* SHEPHERD). He seems to be the more noble in being fantastical. A great man, I'll warrant: I know by the picking on 's teeth.[1]

Autolycus, unlike Courtiers, renders real service to his fellows. He entertains them with ballads (and roguery), and sells genuine wares (with sham ones) from his pack. Shakespeare was acquainted with pedlars in Stratford, and may have known a female Autolycus, one Avice Clarke, the inventory of whose belongings on her death in the summer of 1624 was taken by Master John Sadler and Robert Wilson of the *Crown* in Bridge Street. She may or may not have sung ballads and picked pockets in the Market Place, but the goods she sold bear a striking resemblance to those of Shakespeare's delightful vagabond. They consisted of quoifs,[2] black and tawney, plain and drawn-work; handkerchiefs, crest-cloths, bands and garters, cross-gartering (such as Malvolio fancied), laces, points, white inkle,[3] loom-work, thread, band-strings, hand-carved (?) buttons, pins, boxes, brooches, thimbles, bound graces, bone-lace, loom-work lace, shreds of lace, calico.[4]

Autolycus, moreover, is the means whereby Perdita is recognized and 'Found'.

Leontes' trial ends. He recovers his daughter, he recovers also his wife. By Paulina he and Hermione are brought together when the time is ripe. The Statue becomes to husband and child warm and breathing life—as his 'ivory maid' to the hero of Paphos,

dedit oscula: visa tepere est;
Admovet os iterum, manibus quoque pectora temptat.[5]

[1] IV. iv. 753–80. [2] caps, hoods. [3] tape.

[4] *Misc. Doc.* i. 83; *Wills and Inventories*, 19. She made her will on 18 June and was buried on 5 July (*Register*, p. 106). The Inventory was made on 14 July.

[5] *Metamorphoses*, x. 281 f. Cf. *Wint. T.* V. iii. 109 ('O, she's warm'), 111 f.

Without a word she embraces him; and then she prays for blessing on Perdita:

> You gods, look down,
> And from your sacred vials pour your graces
> Upon my daughter's head![1]

Shakespeare's audience would recognize the allusion. In Heaven are four-and-twenty worshippers, having harps and golden vials full of odours, which are the prayers of the saints.[2]

We are in the puritan atmosphere of *Cymbeline* and *The Tempest.* There are references to Judas Iscariot ('that did betray the Best'),[3] Jacob and Esau,[4] the Lord's Prayer

> (You have paid down
> More penitence than done *trespass*: at the last,
> Do as the Heavens have done, forget your *evil*,
> With them *forgive* yourself),[5]

'amendment of life',[6] and probably to Elijah

> (Some Powerful Spirit instruct the kites and ravens
> To be thy nurses!)[7]

and Christ before Pilate

> (The silence often of pure innocence
> Persuades when speaking fails).[8]

Biblical language and thought are frequent—'hold my peace',[9]

('She embraces him, she hangs about his neck'). The Pygmalion of Shakespeare's Sicilia is 'that rare Italian master, Julio Romano, who had he himself eternity, and could put breath into his work would beguile Nature of her custom'. He had read the artist's epitaph (at San Barbara, Mantua) in Vasari (1550), or heard of it from Droeshout or some traveller:

> Videbat Jupiter corpora *sculpta* pictaque
> Spirare, aedes mortalium aequarier coelo
> Julii virtute Romani; tunc iratus,
> Concilio divorum omnium vocato,
> Illum aeternis sustulit; quod pati nequiret
> Vinci aut aequari ab homine terrigena.

[1] v. iii. 121–3. [2] Revelation v. 8. [3] I. ii. 419.

[4] IV. iv. 744. [5] v. i. 3–6. Cf. III. iii. 5–7.

[6] v. ii. 166. Cf. Matthew iii. 1, Geneva Version: 'Repent' ('amend your lives', Prayer Book); 8, Bring 'forth fruits worthy amendment of life' ('meet for repentence', Bishops' Bible); 11, 'I baptise you with water to amendment of life' ('unto repentence', B.B.; 'unto penance', Rheims); iv. 17, 'Amend your lives' ('repent', B.B.).

[7] II. iii. 186 f.; cf. 1 Kings xvii. 6.

[8] II. ii. 41 f.; cf. Matthew xxvii. 12.

[9] I. ii. 28 (some fifty times in the Bible).

'verily' (repeated again and again),[1] 'false as water',[2] sin to strike an anointed king,[3] slander 'sharper' than a 'sword',[4] Jove's better 'guiding spirit' for a 'babe',[5] 'commit adultery',[6] 'one jot',[7] 'harden the heart',[8] 'first-fruits of the body',[9] the 'sins of youth' forgiven,[10] 'grow in grace',[11] 'the life to come',[12] 'pace softly',[13] 'bring thee on thy way',[14] 'name put in the Book of Virtue',[15] 'a merry heart',[16] 'lift up your countenance',[17] 'flesh and blood',[18] stoned to death,[19] the Queen 'well' in death,[20] 'Heaven's spies',[21] a world ransomed or destroyed.[22] Dorcas is a Biblical name. Once or twice there is concession to Catholicism ('priest-like, thou hast cleansed my bosom',[23] and 'do not say 'tis superstition to kneel' to the image of Hermione);[24] and the Clown, after the manner of the foolish, gibes at the Puritan who 'sings psalms to hornpipes'.[25] But the leading characters

[1] I. ii. 46–55; John iii. 5, &c.

[2] I. ii. 131 f. (*Oth.* v. ii. 133), Genesis xlix. 4, 'Thou wast light ['unstable', B.B.] as water because thou wentest up to thy father's bed.'

[3] I. ii. 357–9; 1 Samuel xxiv. 6 f., xxvi. 9 f.; 2 Samuel i. 14. Cf. *Rich. III*, IV. iv. 150, v. iii. 124 f.; *Rich. II*, I. ii. 37–41; *1 Hen. IV*, IV. iii. 38–40; *2 Hen. IV*, Ind. 28–32; *Macb.* II. iii. 72 f.; *K. Lear*, III. vii. 56–8.

[4] II. iii. 85 f., Psalm lvii. 4 (margin: 'He meaneth calumnies and false reports').

[5] II. iii. 126 f., Matthew xviii. 10 ('little ones' whose 'angels behold the face of the Father').

[6] III. ii. 14 f.; Exodus xx. 14.

[7] III. ii. 51; Matthew v. 18.

[8] III. ii. 53; Exodus vii. 13.

[9] III. ii. 98; Micah vi. 7.

[10] III. iii. 124 f.; Psalm xxv. 7.

[11] IV. i. 24; 2 Peter iii. 18 (*Ant. & Cleop.* IV. ii. 38).

[12] IV. iii. 30; 1 Timothy iv. 8 (*Macb.* I. vii. 7).

[13] IV. iii. 121 f.; Genesis xxxiii. 14 (the wily Jacob says to Esau, 'I will drive softly according to the pace of the cattle').

[14] IV. iii. 122; Genesis xviii. 16; Acts xv. 3.

[15] IV. iii. 131; Revelation iii. 5 ('put his name out of the Book of Life').

[16] IV. iii. 134; Proverbs xv. 13, 15 (B.B.).

[17] IV. iv. 49; Numbers vi. 26; Psalm iv. 6 (reverential words to Perdita).

[18] IV. iv. 704–12 (kindred); Isaiah, xlix. 26 (*Tit. Andr.* IV. ii. 84; *Mer. of Ven.* III. i. 37–44; *K. Lear*, II. iv. 224–6, III. iv. 150 f.; *Temp.* v. i. 74 f.).

[19] IV. iv. 807; Exodus xix. 13, &c.

[20] v. i. 30; 2 Kings iv. 26 (B.B.) (*Rom. & Jul.* IV. v. 75 f., v. i. 14–19; *All's W.* II. iv. 1–13; *Macb.* IV. iii. 176–9; *Ant. & Cleop.* II. v. 31–46).

[21] v. i. 203; Psalm cxxxix. 3 (B.B.).

[22] v. ii. 16; 1 Timothy ii. 6, &c.

[23] I. ii. 237 f.

[24] v. iii. 43 f.

[25] IV. iii. 46–8: the Clown, like Aguecheek and Lavache, is a Prelatist.

converse, however freely (and Shakespeare is never a dogmatist), of doctrine they would not question:

POLIXENES. We were as twinn'd lambs that did frisk i' the sun,
And bleat the one at the other: what we changed
Was innocence for innocence; we knew not
The doctrine of ill-doing, nor dreamed
That any did. Had we pursued that life,
And our weak spirits ne'er been higher reared[1]
With stronger blood, we should have answered Heaven
Boldly, 'Not Guilty': the imposition cleared[2]
Hereditary ours.

HERMIONE. By this we gather
You have tripp'd since.

POLIXENES. O my most sacred lady!
Temptations have since then been born to 's: for
In those unfledged days was my wife a girl;
Your precious self had then not cross'd the eyes
Of my young play-fellow.

HERMIONE. Grace to boot![3]
Of this make no conclusion, lest you say
Your queen and I are devils: yet go on;
The offences we have made you do we'll answer,
If you first sinned with us, and that with us
You did continue fault, and that you slipped not
With any but with us.[4]

The best, and only contemporary, commentary on this passage is Romans v. 12 and 14, in the Geneva Version of 1587, with its marginalia:

'Wherefore as by one man sin entered into the world, and death by sin, and so death went over all men (*From Adam, in whom all have sinned, both guiltiness and death came upon all*), in whom all men have sinned (*By Sin is meant that disease which is ours by inheritance, and men commonly call it Original Sin*). Death reigned even over them also that sinned not (*The very infants, which neither could ever know nor transgress that natural law, are notwithstanding, dead as well as Adam*).'

The last note replaces in the older editions: '*He meaneth young babes, which neither had the knowledge of the Law, of Nature, nor any motion of concupiscence.*'

And Perdita is a puritan maiden, though she dances and sings at the shepherds' feast as if she were Flora, in 'unusual weeds', at her lover's wish and against her own, 'most goddess-like prank'd

[1] raised, roused by passion.
[2] the *imputed* sin paid and cancelled.
[3] Grace to my help!
[4] I. ii. 67–86.

up'.[1] She 'prized not' the 'trifles' of the pedlar's pack,[2] and will have 'no scurrilous words in his tunes'.[3] A 'bastard flower' offends her taste, like a 'painted' face.[4] The 'gifts' she looks for from Florizel are 'in his heart';[5] and the grace he admires in her blends with spiritual charm—

> What you do
> Still betters what is done. When you speak, sweet,
> I'ld have you do it ever: when you sing,
> I'ld have you buy and sell so, so *give alms*,
> *Pray* so.[6]

Alms, prayer, divine grace—

> This is a creature,
> Would she begin a sect, might quench the zeal
> Of all professors else; make proselytes
> Of who she but bid *follow*—[7]

are elements of her beauty and make her, as princess, 'the most peerless piece of earth that e'er the Sun shone bright on'.[8] She apologizes for kneeling to Hermione's 'statue', as to an image, seeking a mother's blessing, which subsequently she receives.[9]

The language of mythology ('Apollo', 'Jove', 'Gods', 'Fortune', 'Heavens') or what not ('Higher Powers', 'Great Creating Nature'),[10] as required by Act of Parliament, will not disguise for us the Poet's belief in God. 'Blessed be the great Apollo! praised!'[11] His Will, as in *Pericles* and *Cymbeline*, over-rules, 'strikes at injustice',[12] fulfils 'secret purposes',[13] and the lost (*perdita*) is found.[14]

Paulina once might utter the sentiments of the Poet's old recusant father:

> It is an heretic that makes the fire,
> Not (he) which burns in it.[15]

[1] IV. iv. 1–3, 10–12, 23 ('my borrow'd flaunts'), 133–5. [2] 368.
[3] 215 f. [4] 99–103. [5] 369–71. [6] 136–40.
[7] V. i. 107–10. Cf. Matthew iv. 19 f.: 'Follow me! . . . and they straightway followed him.' [8] V. i. 94 f.
[9] V. iii. 42–4:

> and give me leave,
> And do not say 'tis superstition, that
> I kneel and then implore her blessing.

And 119 f.
[10] IV. iv. 88. [11] III. ii. 138. [12] 147–50.
[13] V. i. 37. [14] V. iii. 120.
[15] II. iii. 115 f. A phrase in use among religious 'Brethren' occurs in I. i. 35: 'The Heavens continue their loves.' Sturley writes to Quyney, 'The Lord increase our loves' (Fripp, *Master Richard Quyny*, p. 148).

Hermione's defence in the Court of Justice should be noted for its religious faith, and for its versification—the 'broken metre' of a troubled speaker—

It shall scarce bóot | *me*
To say 'not guíl|ty': mine integrity,
Being counted fálse|hood, shall, as I expréss | *it*,
Be so receív|ed. But thus, if *Powers Divine*
Behold our human ác|tions, as They do,
I doubt not then but innocence shall make
False accusation blush, and tyranny
Tremble at pá|tience. You, my lord, best know,
Who least will seem to dó | so, my past life
Hath been as continent, as chaste, as true
As I am now unháp|py; which is more
Than history can pát|tern, though devís|ed
And play'd to take spectá|tors. For behóld | *me*,
A fellow of the royal bed, which owe
A moiety of the throne, a great King's dáugh|ter,
The mother to a hopeful prince, here stánd|ing
To prate and talk for life and honour fore
Who please to come and hear. For life, I príze | *it*
As I weigh grief, which I would spare: for hó|nour,
'Tis a derivative from me to mine,
And only that I stánd | for. I appeal
To your own cón|science.

This prepares us for the greater speech of a distressed queen, on her trial like Hermione in a foreign court, Queen Katharine in *Henry the Eighth*.

Medicine is to the fore,[1] with also the inevitable Law[2] and Ovid.[3] A feature of the drama is the shipwreck (the first since

[1] We may note, beside the malady of Leontes, 'sleepy drinks', 'the pin and web' (cataract), 'infected liver', 'cordial draught', 'rash potion', 'lingering dram', 'poison' and 'poisoner', 'distemper' and 'disease', 'a sickness caught', 'blood turn to an infected jelly', 'infection', 'venom', 'abhorr'd ingredient' which 'look'd upon' makes a man 'crack his gorge and sides with violent hefts', 'cold as a dead man's nose', 'purge', 'medicinal', 'physician', 'one infectious', 'cut my lace lest my heart break', a woman after childbirth longs 'to eat adders' heads and toads carbonadoed', 'stuffed with rheums' and 'bedrid', 'medicine' (physician), 'lethargy', '*aqua vitae* or other hot infusion', 'infirmity which waits upon worn times', 'the blessed Gods purge infection from the air', 'sweet cordial'.

[2] Conspicuous in II. ii. 58–63, II. iii. 200–5, III. ii. 1–142.

[3] IV. iv. 25–35, 116–27 and III. iii. 16–41 (the dream of Antigonus before his shipwreck: cf. the dream of Halcyone of the wreck and drowning of Ceyx in *Metamorphoses*, xi. 650–709).

The Comedy of Errors), off the coast (as Greene,[1] and Shakespeare after him, has it) of Bohemia. There is remarkable interest in the Sea. A dozen words—'unpath'd waters, undream'd shores', and 'all the profound seas hide in unknown fathoms'[2]—utter the fascination of the Deep for Elizabethan explorers, Gilbert, Frobisher, Drake, Raleigh, in their 'saucy' barks, liable to be engulfed like Gilbert's *Squirrel* with all on board. In *Othello* is a description of a storm at sea beheld from the 'foaming shore':

> The chidden billow seems to pelt the clouds;
> The wind-shaked surge, with high and monstrous mane,
> Seems to cast water on the burning Bear,
> And quench the guards of the ever-fixéd Pole.[3]

Finer is that by the Clown (notwithstanding its anticlimax):

> I have seen such sights by sea, . . . but I am not to say it is a sea, for it is now the sky; betwixt the firmament and it you cannot thrust a bodkin's point . . . I would you did but see how it chafes, how it rages, how it takes up the shore . . . the ship boring the moon with her mainmast and anon swallowed with yest and froth, as you'ld thrust a cork into a hogshead.[4]

It reminds us of Turner's picture of the sinking steamer off shore in a tempest,[5] of which Ruskin has written:

> 'Few people, comparatively, have ever seen the effect on the sea of a powerful gale continued without intermission for three or four days and nights; and to those who have not, I believe it must be unimaginable, not from the mere force or size of surge, *but from the complete annihilation of the limit between sea and air*. The water from its prolonged agitation is beaten, not into mere creaming foam, but into masses of accumulated *yeast*.'[6]

Something of the Bible (Genesis i. 6: the storm undoes the work of Creation), more of Ovid (*Metamorphoses*, xi. 497 f.:

> *Fluctibus erigitur caelumque aequare videtur*
> *Pontus et inductas aspergine tangere nubes*),[7]

but most of all, personal experience, are in Shakespeare's seascape.

[1] *Pandosto: The Triumph of Time*, a prose romance published in 1588, and republished as *Dorastus and Fawnia* in 1607.

[2] IV. iv. 500–2, 578.

[3] II. i. 12–15.

[4] *Wint. T.* III. iii. 84–7, 93–5. Cf. *Macb.* IV. i. 53 f.:

> Though the yesty waves
> Confound and swallow navigation up.

[5] National Gallery.

[6] *Modern Painters*, i. 402 f. For a Turner Sunrise, see p. 395.

[7] In waves the Sea is lifted, and seems to reach the Heaven and touch with spray the lowered clouds.

PRINCE HENRY

By WILLIAM HOLE

From Drayton's Poly-Olbion, 1613

Almost as remarkable is the observation in Florizel's speech to Perdita—

I wish you
A wave of the sea, that you might ever do
Nothing but that, move still, still so.[1]

Shakespeare was a landsman, and had small seamanship; but he met great seamen at Court, and read of their voyaging; met also sea-captains, sailors, and fishermen in London, below and above[2] the Bridge. He had looked, too, on the ocean, at various points from Dover Cliff to Plymouth Sound, in storm and calm; had felt the fury of it, and had watched, when it was at rest, the waves rise and break as in graceful play upon the shore.

1610–11

§ 137. PLAYS AT COURT, AND AT THE *GLOBE*

IN one respect the Jacobean Court compared pleasantly with the Elizabethan. It had children about it and young people. King James indeed 'would not endure his Queen and children in his lodgings',[3] but they were in evidence nevertheless at Whitehall. Prince Henry was nine years old at the accession, Princess Elizabeth in her seventh year, Prince Charles in his third. Charles was a delicate child, scarcely able to speak until his fifth year or walk until his seventh, but he then rapidly improved in health and grew into something of an athlete as well as a scholar. Henry shone in contrast with his father, was vigorous in body and mind, wilful as the King, but manly in his interests as the King was effeminate. 'He studies two hours in the day', says a writer in 1606, 'and employs the rest of his time in tossing the pike, or leaping, or shooting with the bow, or throwing the bar, or vaulting, or some other exercise of that kind, and he is never idle.'[4] To gallop on horseback pleased him better than hunting. He had his separate household and a large one, which drew into

[1] IV. iv. 140–2.

[2] The drawbridge was still occasionally used, as we may see in Visscher's view of 1616. Pl. XCI.

[3] Weldon, 125. Towards the end of his reign, under Buckingham's domination, he submitted to petticoat invasion until 'children did run up and down his lodgings like little rabbit starters about their burrows' (*ib.*).

[4] La Boderie.

it the best of the Court and a considerable faction. Raleigh was his friend, a prisoner in the Tower. 'No king but my father', said the prince, 'would keep such a bird in a cage.' Happily he had been brought up much away from his parents, and he imbibed his religious principles from an upright and able tutor, Sir Thomas Chaloner. He was the hope of the Puritan party. On 4 June 1610, in his seventeenth year, he was created Prince of Wales, with a dinner at Whitehall 'in such estate as greater could not have been done unto the King' and 'all kinds of most exquisite music'. Next day there was a mask in his honour, thus described by Fynnet:

Came first in, the little Duke of York [Prince Charles, aged nine years and a half] between two great sea-slaves, the chiefest of Neptune's servants, attended upon by twelve little ladies, all of them the daughters of earls or barons. By one of these men a speech was made unto the King and Prince, expressing the conceit of the mask; by the other a sword, worth 20,000 crowns at the least, was put into the Duke of York's hands, who presented the same unto the Prince his brother. This done, the Duke returned into his former place in the midst of the stage; and the little ladies performed their dance, to the amazement of all beholders, considering the tenderness of their years and the many intricate changes of the dance: which was so disposed that which way soever the changes went the little Duke was still found to be in the midst of these little dancers. These little skirmishers having done their *devoir*, in came the princesses—first the Queen, next the Lady Elizabeth's grace [she was fourteen in August following], then the Lady Arabella [Stuart].[1]

Shakespeare and his company played before Prince Henry repeatedly; and without doubt he had the prince and his sister in mind in his dramatic romances. Imogen and her royal brothers, Florizel and Perdita, Ferdinand and Miranda, cannot be dissociated from Henry and Elizabeth and their much-talked-of marriages. Fifteen times the King's men performed at Court in the Christmas of 1610–11, before their Majesties and the Prince; and they were paid £150 on 12 February 1611.[2] On 10 March they received £30 more, 'being restrained from public playing' —before Christmas—'within the City of London, in the time of infection, during the space of six weeks, in which time they practised privately for his Majesty's service'.[3] That month, or the next, proposals of marriage reached the King from the Duke

[1] Winwood, *Memorials*, iii. 179 f.

[2] Chambers, iv. 124, 176.

[3] *Ib.* 176.

of Savoy, between his eldest daughter and Prince Henry, and his son and Princess Elizabeth. Henry asked Raleigh for his opinion, who wrote two *Discourses* in disapprobation: 'Savoy from Spain is inseparable, Spain to England is irreconcilable . . . While the Prince is unmarried all the eyes of Christendom are upon him . . . I would advise the Prince to keep his own ground for a while, and no way to engage or entangle himself.'[1]

In April and May, Shakespeare and his company played at the *Globe*. Simon Forman witnessed their performance there, on Saturday 20 April,[2] of *Macbeth* and described it. He was impressed by the supernatural:

> There was to be observed first how Macbeth and Banquo, riding thorough a wood, there stood before them three women—fairies or nymphs, and saluted Macbeth saying three times unto him,
>
> '*Hail, Macbeth, thane*[3] *of Cawdor! for thou shalt be a King, but beget no kings!*' Then said Banquo, '*What, all to Macbeth and nothing to me?*' '*Yes,*' said the nymphs, '*hail to thee, Banquo; thou shalt beget kings yet be no king*' . . . And Macbeth contrived[4] to kill Duncan, and thorough the persuasion of his wife did murder the King, in his own castle being his guest. And there were many prodigies seen that night and the day before. And when Macbeth had murdered the King, the blood on his hands could not be washed off by any means, nor from his wife's hands which handled the bloody daggers in hiding them: by which means they became both much amazed and affronted.[5] He contrived[4] the death of Banquo, and caused him to be murdered on the way as he rode. The next night, being at supper with his noblemen, whom he had bid to a feast, to the which also Banquo should have come, he began to speak of noble Banquo and to wish that he were there. And as he thus did, standing up to drink a carouse to him, the ghost of Banquo came and sat down in his chair behind him. And he turning about to sit down again,[6] saw the ghost of Banquo which fronted him, so that he fell into a great passion of fear and fury, uttering many words about his murder, by which, when they heard that Banquo was murdered, they suspected Macbeth . . . Observe also how Macbeth's queen did rise in the night in her sleep and walk, and talked and confessed all, and the Doctor noted her words.[7]

[1] *Discourse touching a marriage between Prince Henry of England and a daughter of Savoy*, and *Discourse touching a match propounded by the Savoyan between the Lady Elizabeth and the Prince of Piedmont*.

[2] He gives the date as '1610, the 20 of April, Saturday', which is wrong. The new year has recently begun, and he writes 1610 instead of 1611.

[3] By a slip Forman has written 'king'.

[4] plotted.

[5] confronted, staggered.

[6] A bit of stage-business worth noting.

[7] *The Booke of Plaies and Notes there of performans for Common Pollicie*. Ashmolean MS. 208, f. 207.

On Tuesday 30 April he saw a play of *King Richard the Second* which was not Shakespeare's. One of his comments is worth quoting:

'Remember how the Duke of Lancaster asked a wise-man whether himself should ever be King; and he told him No, but his son should be King. And when he had told him, he hanged him up for his labour, because he should not bruit it abroad or speak thereof to others. This was a policy in the commonwealth's opinion, but I say it was a villain's part and a Judas-kiss to hang the man for telling him the truth. Beware, by this example, of noblemen, and of their fair words, and say little to them lest they do the like by thee for thy goodwill.'[1]

Forman, being a 'wise-man' or fortune-teller, spoke feelingly.

On Wednesday 15 May he was at a performance of *The Winter's Tale*. He says of Autolycus:

'Remember the rogue, that came in all tattered like Cole Pikcy,[2] and how he feigned him sick, and to have been robbed of all that he had, and how he cozened the poor man of all his money; and after came to the Sheep-shearing, with a pedlar's pack, and there cozened them again of all their money; and he changed apparel with the King of Bohemia's son, and then how he turned Courtier. Beware of trusting feigned beggars or fawning fellows.'[2]

A leading player, not in Shakespeare's company, Master Philip Rosseter, the lessee of the Whitefriars theatre and one of the royal lutenists, probably a Catholic, a friend of Thomas Campion (with whom he published *A Booke of Ayres* in 1601), was in trouble at Christmas 1610–11 with the Bishop of London for speaking against sermons, and affirming 'that a man might learn more good at one of their plays or interludes than at twenty of our roguish sermons'. He was let off, however, on 14 January, on the plea that these 'most vile, spiteful speeches' were old utterances, before 9 November 1609, and not since.[3] Doctor Simon Forman evidently expected to 'learn good' at the *Globe*, and was not altogether disappointed.

[1] *The Booke of Plaies and Notes there of performans for Common Pollicie.* Ashmolean MS. 208, f. 201.

[2] *Ib.* f. 201 f. Cole Pixy was a stage character, probably referred to by Thomas Becon in his *Displaying of the Mass*, *c.* Feb. 1555 (Parker Soc. iii. 260): 'Ye [priests] have not all your tools; therefore can ye not play *Cole under Candlestick* cleanly, nor whip Master Wynchard above the board as ye should do.' Becon likens the Mass to a play, and refers to *Hickscorner* and 'game-players' garments'.

[3] *Book of Detections*, f. 262. Rosseter was living in the parish of St. Dunstan's in the West. He was summoned on 19 December 1610 (*decimo quarto* should probably be *decimo nono*) and appeared in person next day.

On 26 May, 1st Sunday after Trinity, at St. Mary's Aldermanbury was baptized Master Henry Condell's child, William. Master Condell was a leading parishioner and office-holder in the church. This was his eighth child and third son baptized there. The three boys but only one daughter were living on 26 May 1611.

The first boy, Richard, baptized on Sunday 18 April 1602, may have had Burbage for godfather; the second, Henry, baptized on Sunday 6 May 1610, bore the father's name; the third may have had Shakespeare for sponsor—as yet a fourth son and last child, Edward, baptized on Monday 22 August 1614 (probably in some haste, for he died next day), may have had Edward Alleyn for godfather.[1] The fellowship of these men was not merely of the club and tavern but of the *Home.*

1611–12

§ 138. *THE TEMPEST*

THIS summer Shakespeare wrote *The Tempest.* He had been impressed, as were the British Court and public, by the disaster to the Virginia fleet in July 1609. Nine ships, with 500 colonists under Sir Thomas Gates and Sir George Somers, were on their way to the new settlement when the *Sea Adventurer,* with both Gates and Somers on board, ran ashore on the Bermudas. All got safe to land; Gates and Somers built vessels of cedar-wood, and setting sail for Virginia in May 1610 they arrived securely. Accounts of the adventure reached England in the autumn, and were published. Shakespeare read at least three of them, and made use of them in his drama. One, written by William Strachey and dated 15 July, was addressed to a lady of worship, who may have been the Countess of Southampton. The Earl was treasurer to the Virginia Company; after him was named the Southampton River. Another account, published in October, was by Silvester Jourdan, *A Discovery of the Barmudas, otherwise called The Ile of Divels.* A third appeared about December, *A True Declaration of the Estate of the Colonie in Virginia.* There was also a ballad on the subject.[2]

[1] See for the dates Chambers, ii. 311.

[2] For these sources of the play see the excellent introduction to the Arden *Tempest* by Morton Luce.

Shakespeare had written in *Twelfth Night*,

> Tempests are kind and salt waves fresh in love.[1]

He may have contemplated a drama on this theme while engaged on *The Winter's Tale*. A Latin sentence in *A True Declaration* might serve as the motto to *The Tempest*—

> *Quae videtur Poena est Medicina.*[2]

From Prospero to Caliban the characters suffer chastisement that is salutary. Prospero lost his dukedom, as Hamlet his kingdom, by 'bookishness'.[3] He gave to his prized 'volumes' attention due to the state, and allowed a brother, with help of an enemy, to dispossess him. King James had to be dragged to business from his studies in theological controversy. This summer, 1611, he was absorbed in the *Tractatus* and *Exegesis* of Vorstius. Prospero with his books and child, three years old, is sent adrift in a rotten boat, but carried by Providence to a desert island, where he lives twelve years. At the end of this period, when Miranda is fifteen, a storm throws the ship containing his false brother, Antonio, his ally, Alonzo King of Naples, and the latter's brother and son, Sebastian and Ferdinand, into Prospero's power. Any hatred he may have cherished is past. He wants his fellow men, welcomes enemies, and will change them by his magic into friends. They, like himself, shall 'suffer a sea-change'.

A tempest is no respecter of persons. The Boatswain has not time to consider worldly dignities. King and noble must get out of the way. Face to face with Nature and the fierce elements, men are men, and all men brothers. That is the first fact Alonzo, Antonio, and the rest are made to realize when tumbled below by the sailors. Next, Alonzo learns grief. His son, he believes, is drowned. Then he is betrayed by his confederates; and he and they are dragged up and down the island until footsore and ready to drop with weariness. A feast is held before them which, as they put out their hands to take it, disappears. Supernatural Voices speak in their ears and consciences. The 'Deity in the bosom'[4] is awakened:

> You are three men of sin,[5] whom Destiny,
> That hath to instrument this lower world

[1] III. iv. 419.

[2] 'What seems Punishment is Healing.'

[3] 'I, thus neglecting worldly ends, all dedicated to closeness, and bettering of my mind' (I. ii. 89 f.).

[4] II. i. 278.

[5] For 'man of sin' see 2 Thessalonians ii. 3.

And what is in it, the never-surfeited sea
Hath caused to belch up you . . .
The Powers, delaying not forgetting, have
Incensed the seas and shores, yea, all the creatures,
Against your peace; whose wraths to guard you from,
Which here in this most desolate isle else falls
Upon your heads, is nothing but heart-sorrow
And a clear life ensuing.[1]

Guilt, 'like poison given to work a great time after', 'bites their spirits' and makes them 'desperate'. Prospero's righteous anger dies at the first sign of repentance:

they being penitent,
The sole drift of my purpose doth extend
Not a frown further.[2]

The drunken butler and jester, and their 'savage and deformed slave' are also brought to their senses, after being led through briars and thorns into the mire, drenched to the skin, chased like beasts, and wrecked by cramps. Says Caliban,

I'll be wise hereafter,
And seek for *grace*.[3]

This is his 'sea-change' into 'something rare and strange'.

Blended with this central theme is the thought of Liberty. Ariel pants after freedom. He is from the Bible,[4] in Shakespeare's conception 'an airy spirit', whose being is in the Sunshine. Unlike Puck, who 'follows the darkness round the world' and loves men's homes and hearths, he lives in the light and fire, and shuns humanity. He flies 'after summer merrily'. His happiness is to float in the warm wind or on the crest of a wave, ride on a bat's back at the close of day, and couch, when owls do cry, in a cow-slip's bell or under the blossom on a bough. Prospero punishes him for his good after the manner of Isaiah.[5] In contrast is Caliban's notion of liberty. He is of the earth—earthly, sensual, devilish.[6] He hates work, plucks berries, gathers filberts, digs pig-nuts with his long nails, seeks the jay's nest,

[1] III. iii. 53–6, 73–5, 79–82.

[2] V. i. 28–30.

[3] *Ib.* 294.

[4] Ezra viii. 16 and Isaiah xxix.

[5] xxix. 4, 6, 10, 'So shalt thou be humbled, and shalt speak out of the ground, like him that hath a spirit of divination. Thou shalt be visited with thunder and shaking and a great noise, a whirlwind and a tempest, and a flame of a devouring fire . . . with a spirit of slumber.'

[6] James iii. 15.

snares the nimble marmoset, catches fish, gets young 'seamels'[1] from the rocks, drinks from the springs and freshes, and, with disastrous effects, from Stephano's bottle. 'Celestial liquor' makes him an anarchist. He sings,

> 'Ban, 'Ban, Cacaliban
> Has a new master—get a new man![2]

And again, with his comrades, in a catch,

> Flout 'em and scout 'em,
> And scout 'em and flout 'em;
> Thought is free![3]

In 'freedom of thought' he is ready to brain Prospero in his sleep, batter his skull with a log, paunch him with a stake, cut his weasand with a knife, or otherwise dispose of him in Caliban fashion.

Again, in contrast to these conceptions, neither of which is human, is the liberty of love in Ferdinand and Miranda. Ariel knows no sin, and cannot love nor pray. Caliban knows good and evil when at the end he is touched with Grace. Miranda is all grace, full of pity and reverence. She finds unbearable her father's recital of his wrongs. Ferdinand she loves with innocent passion. As Juliet and Romeo are 'saint' and 'pilgrim' to each other, Miranda and Ferdinand are like 'things divine'. When Prospero brings the son of his enemy to shore, and welcomes him in Ariel's song with sounds of the watchdog and the cock (the ancient symbols of Home), and Ferdinand, following the mysterious voices, looks up in wonder, and says, 'This is no mortal business'; Miranda, seeing him, a beautiful youth with worship in his countenance, asks, 'Is it a Spirit?'[4] And Ferdinand, seeing her, says, 'It is a Goddess!' Their love is tried and strengthened by adversity. Ferdinand is put in bonds, and made to fetch and stack the wood at Prospero's Cave. He does Caliban's work, and does it cheerfully. For love the King's son does that which the slave disdains—

> The mistress which I serve quickens what's dead
> And makes my labours pleasures.[5]

[1] seamews.
[2] II. ii. 188 f.
[3] III. ii. 130–2. 'Thought is free' was a proverbial saying: Heywood's *Proverbs*, p. 98. Cf. *Tw. N.* I. iii. 73; *Meas. for M.* V. i. 458.
[4] 'You are a Spirit' (Lear to Cordelia, IV. vii. 49): see p. 664.
[5] III. i. 6 f.

Might I but through my prison once a day
Behold this maid, all corners else o' the earth
Let liberty make use of, space enough
Have I.[1]

His freedom is that of the Collect for Peace—'Thy Service is perfect Freedom'.[2]

Lastly, there is the Freedom of Prospero. Give him an island to himself, make him monarch of all he surveys; yet he is not free. Let him have magical knowledge and power, and control of the elements; yet he has not freedom. He must return to Milan—to his fellow men, to duties and responsibilities, to faithful human service. For this he puts away his magic robe, breaks his staff, and drowns his book.[3]

Such is the Poet's farewell to his great and triumphant work as the master-mind of the King's Players. He himself, without doubt, played the part of Prospero and spoke the epilogue,

Now my charms are all o'erthrown,

with its conclusion—

Let your indulgence set me free.

He had, indeed, a right to the name *Prospero*—'I make you happy with my work!' Old and loved volumes, as well as recent publications, were employed by Shakespeare in his farewell play. He remembered, or read again, lines of *Hero and Leander*:

Far from the town, where all is *whist* and still,
Save from the *sea*, playing on *yellow sand*,
Sends forth a rattling murmur to the land,
My turret stands, and there God knows I play—
Come thither![4]

And,

The *waves* about him wound
And pulled him to the bottom, where the ground
Was strewed with *pearl*, and in low *coral* groves
Sweet singing mermaids sported.[5]

Thought and speech from his old Master's verse of twenty years since, he reshaped into nobler loveliness in Ariel's songs:

Come unto these *yellow sands*,
And then take hands,

[1] I. ii. 490–3. [2] *Book of Common Prayer*. [3] V. i. 50–6.
[4] I. 346–8, 351, 357. [5] II. 159–62.

Curtsied when you have and kist,
  The wild *waves whist*:[1]
Foot it featly here and there,
And, *sweet sprites*, the burthen bear:
  Hark, hark! (Bow-wow).
The watch dogs bark! (Bow-wow).
Hark, hark! I hear
The strain of strutting chanticleer
Cry, (Cock a diddle dow).

Full fathom five thy father lies;
  Of his bones are *coral* made;
Those are *pearls*, that were his eyes:
  Nothing of him that doth fade,
But doth suffer a *sea*-change
Into something rich and strange.
Sea nymphs, hourly ring his knell:
    (Ding dong)
Hark, now I hear them, (Ding dong bell).[2]

Shakespeare ventures on nautical terms in Act I, Scene i, and uses them accurately. They are such as would befit a vessel battling with a sou'wester on the South Coast, and driven ashore for want of 'room'.[3] The scene owes a good deal, as already said, to the shipwreck in *Metamorphoses*, XI.[4] Ovid is conspicuous also in IV. i and V. i, and is at least visible in I. ii and II. i.[5]

Medical matter,[6] for once, takes precedence of legal.[7] Bible language and imagery are everywhere.[8] For a comedy the play

[1] The wild waves being 'whist and still'. [2] I. ii. 376–88, 396–404.

[3] Unable to weather a point. [4] p. 109.

[5] pp. 102–14. Fripp, *Shakespeare Studies*, 101, 122 and n. 6.

[6] Infect, fever of the mind, entrails, blister, cramps, side-stitches, red plague, aches, rotten lungs, veins, rub a sore, plaster, chirurgeonly, kibe, infections that the sun sucks up make him by inch-meal a disease, ague, sinews, skull, paunch, belch, poison, fire in the blood, nerves, ardour of the liver, be more abstemious, grind the joints with dry convulsions, shorten up the sinews, brains boiled within the skull, the pulse beats, past cure—infirmity.

[7] Prerogative, surety, advocate, contract, succession, bound of land, kiss the book and swear, attach, estate on, release from bands.

[8] Ariel, Isaiah xxix. 4, 6, 10; 'The Wills above be done', Matthew vi. 10; 'safe . . . not a hair perished', Acts xxvii. 34 (and margin, 1587); 'the bigger light and the less, by day and night', Genesis i. 16; 'temple, spirit, dwell' (I. ii. 457–9), 1 Corinthians iii. 16; Alonso 'comforted' for the loss of his son by the 'visitor' (II. i. 10 f.), James i. 27 ('visit the fatherless'); 'Nature produce without sweat; pike, knife, gun would I not have; bring forth of its own kind in abundance' (II. i. 159–63), Genesis iii. 19, i. 25, i. 20 f.; 'almost persuaded' (another bit of

is remarkably grave and religious.[1] Miranda is 'a cherubin' to her father;[2] she smiles on him 'inspired with a fortitude from Heaven';[3] they 'come ashore by Providence divine';[4] 'bountiful Fortune' brings Prospero's enemies within his power;[5] his 'zenith' depends on 'a most auspicious star'.[6] To Gonzalo's prayer he would say, with Alonso, 'Amen':

> Look down, you gods,
> And on this couple drop a blessed crown!
> For it is you that have chalked forth the way
> Which brought us hither.[7]

After the nuptial he will retire to Milan, where

> *Every third thought shall be my grave.*[8]

'Third thought' literally is 'numbering', as in the Psalm, with its note in the Geneva version, xc. 12: 'Teach us so to number our days that we may apply our hearts unto wisdom (*which is by considering the shortness of our life, and by meditating the Heavenly Joys*).'[9]

Men, says Prospero, are 'spirits' which vanish; and the world, and all that is in it, will vanish before the Judgement:

> These our actors,
> As I foretold you, were all spirits, and

Antonio's mockery), Acts xxvi. 28; 'sea-swallowed, cast again' (II. i. 251), Jonah i. 17, ii. 10; 'supplant your brother', Genesis xxv. 26; 'cloven tongues', Acts ii. 3; 'men of Jude' (II. ii. 61) and 'more spotted than pard or cat o' mountain' (IV. i. 261 f.), Jeremiah xiii. 23 ('May a man of Jude change his skin, and the cat of the mountain [leopard: G.V.] his spots?', B.B.); 'knock a nail into his head', Judges iv. 21; 'one fiend at a time I'll fight their legions' (III. iii. 102 f.), Mark v. 15 ('him that was vexed with the fiend and had the legion', B.B.); 'Paradise' (IV. i. 124), Genesis ii. 8, 2 Corinthians xii. 4 (margin, 1587); 'flesh and blood' (V. i. 74, kindred), Isaiah xlix. 26; 'flesh and blood' (V. i. 114, physical, not spiritual), Matthew xvi. 17, &c.

[1] Shakespeare's sympathy with Puritanism in 1611 appears unmistakably from the mockery of it by Antonio and Sebastian, the two villains of *The Tempest* (in II. i. 43 f., 223–74) and their contempt for the little godly Gonzalo in his attempts to console Alonzo (in II. i. 1–90, 286: 'this ancient morsel, this Sir Prudence': as if he were a woman). In *The Tempest* he is ten times more akin to Milton than to Ben Jonson.

[2] I. ii. 152. [3] 153 f. [4] 158 f.

[5] 178–80. [6] 181 f.

[7] V. i. 201–4. Cf. Proverbs xvi. 9. [8] 311.

[9] We think of Sir Thomas More: 'He, therefore, irk and weary of worldly business, giving up his promotions, obtained at last the thing which from a child, in a manner, always he desired, that he might have some years of his life *free*, in which he might *continually remember* the immortality of the life to come' (Epitaph, 1532).

Are melted into air, into thin air:
And, like the baseless fabric of this vision,
The cloud-capp'd towers, the gorgeous palaces,
The solemn temples, the great globe itself—

as distinguished from the little *Globe* on the Bankside, with its imaginary men and women and children—

Yea, all which it inherit, shall *dissolve*,
And, like this insubstantial pageant faded,
Leave not a rack behind.[1]

As saith the Scripture:

'The Day of the Lord will come, in the which the earth with the works that are therein shall be burnt up; seeing, therefore, that all these things must be *dissolved*, what manner of persons ought ye to be in holy conversation and godliness?'[2]

He continues:

We are such stuff
As dreams are made on, and our little life
Is rounded with a sleep.[3]

Hamlet had said much the same thing.

To die, to sleep;
No more; and by a sleep to say we end
The heartache, and the thousand natural shocks
That flesh is heir to, 'tis a consummation
Devoutly to be wish'd. To die, to sleep;
To sleep: perchance to dream: ay, there's the rub;
For in that sleep of death what dreams may come,
When we have shuffled off this mortal coil . . .[4]

In contemporary theology Death was a sleep, a long refreshing sleep in preparation for the great Awaking. 'Them which are asleep will God bring with Him', we read in the Geneva Version (1 Thessalonians iv. 13 f.), with the comment, 'Death is but a sleep of the body until the Lord cometh, who will call their bodies out of their graves and join their souls to them again.' Stratford's great Bishop said,

'Death is a sleep to all that be faithful and fear God, from which they shall rise to Everlasting Life. Children weep when they shall go to bed because

[1] IV. i. 148–56.

[2] 2 Peter iii. 10 f. (Geneva Version. The Bishops' Bible has 'perish' for 'dissolve').

[3] IV. i. 156–8.

[4] *Haml.* III. i. 60–7. Hamlet's 'consummation' is that of the Burial Service.

they know not the commodities that be in sleep; they know not that the sleep refresheth a man's body and maketh him to forget all the labours which he hath had before. Death in very deed is the best physician.'[1]

Shakespeare had suffered from sleeplessness. He speaks of its tortures. Were he a martyr to it we should not be surprised. It would help to explain such a wonderful outburst as this—

I heard a voice cry, *Sleep no more!*
. . . the innocent sleep,
Sleep that knits up the ravell'd sleave of care,
The death of each day's life, sore labour's bath,
Balm of hurt minds, great Nature's second course,
Chief nourisher in life's feast.[2]

It would give personal significance to Prospero's further speech, which belongs as much to the thought of death and sleep as to Caliban's conspiracy:

Sir, I am vexed;
Bear with my weakness; *my old brain is troubled:*
Be not disturbed with my infirmity;
. . . *a turn or two I'll walk,*
To still my beating mind.[3]

Insomnia may have determined the Poet's retirement in the plenitude of his genius; and his inability, as we shall see, to leave the stage at this moment of desperately needed rest, may account for the funeral which all too speedily followed.

Shakespeare had entered into his own. He had created a demand for himself and his work, among high and low. At Court, at the Blackfriars theatre, at the *Globe*, his supremacy was assured. Never had he such a season as this last. Twenty-two times he and his company played at Court; and of their takings at the Blackfriars it was rumoured that they received 'more in one winter' (including, probably, this winter) 'by a thousand pound than they were used to get on the Bankside'.[4] Their performances before royalty were as follows: on 31 October 1611 (Hallowmas Eve) at Whitehall before the King; 1 November (Hallowmas Night) at Whitehall before the King, *The Tempest* being given; 5 November (anniversary of Gunpowder Plot) at Whitehall before the King, *The Winter's Tale* being the play;

[1] Hugh Latimer. See *Parker Soc.* i. 548 f.
[2] *Macb.* II. ii. 35–40.
[3] IV. i. 158–60, 162 f.
[4] Chambers, iv. 125 f., 177 f.

9 November (Prince Charles's birthday) before Prince Henry and Prince Charles; 19 November before Prince Henry and Prince Charles; 16 December before Prince Henry and Prince Charles; 26 December at Whitehall before the King, a play by Beaumont and Fletcher, *A King and No King*, being presented; New Year's Eve, before Prince Henry and Prince Charles; New Year's Day at night (a play by Richard Nicholls, *The Twins' Tragedy*, was given); Sunday 5 January 1612, Twelfth Night, at Whitehall before the King; 7 January before Prince Henry and Prince Charles; 15 January at Greenwich before Prince Henry and Prince Charles; on another date at Greenwich before the same; on Sunday 9 February before Princess Elizabeth, Prince Henry, and Prince Charles; 19 February (Prince Henry's birthday) and the following day before Prince Henry and Prince Charles, and again this latter day before Prince Henry; Sunday before Lent, 23 February, at Whitehall before the King; 28 February before Prince Henry and Prince Charles; 28 March before the Princess Elizabeth; 3 April before Prince Henry and Prince Charles; 16 April before Prince Henry and Prince Charles; and Sunday 26 April before Princess Elizabeth, Prince Henry, and Prince Charles. To such high favour, particularly that of the discerning Prince Henry, it was not easy, we may believe, for the Poet to say good-bye.

1612

§ 139. REST?

SHAKESPEARE may or may not have accompanied the King's men on a brief tour, between their performances at Court on 16 and 26 April, in Kent. They played at New Romney on the 21st.[1] On Monday 11 May the Poet was in London, and gave evidence in the Court of Requests at Westminster on behalf of Stephen Bellott against his unsatisfactory father-in-law, Christopher Montjoy, who had not paid his daughter, Mary, her marriage-portion nor given her the promised household goods.[2] His depositions show his friendly interest in the young couple with whom he had lived, before their marriage, in Silver Street.

[1] J. T. Murray, i. 184, ii. 335.

[2] pp. 629, 632, 667.

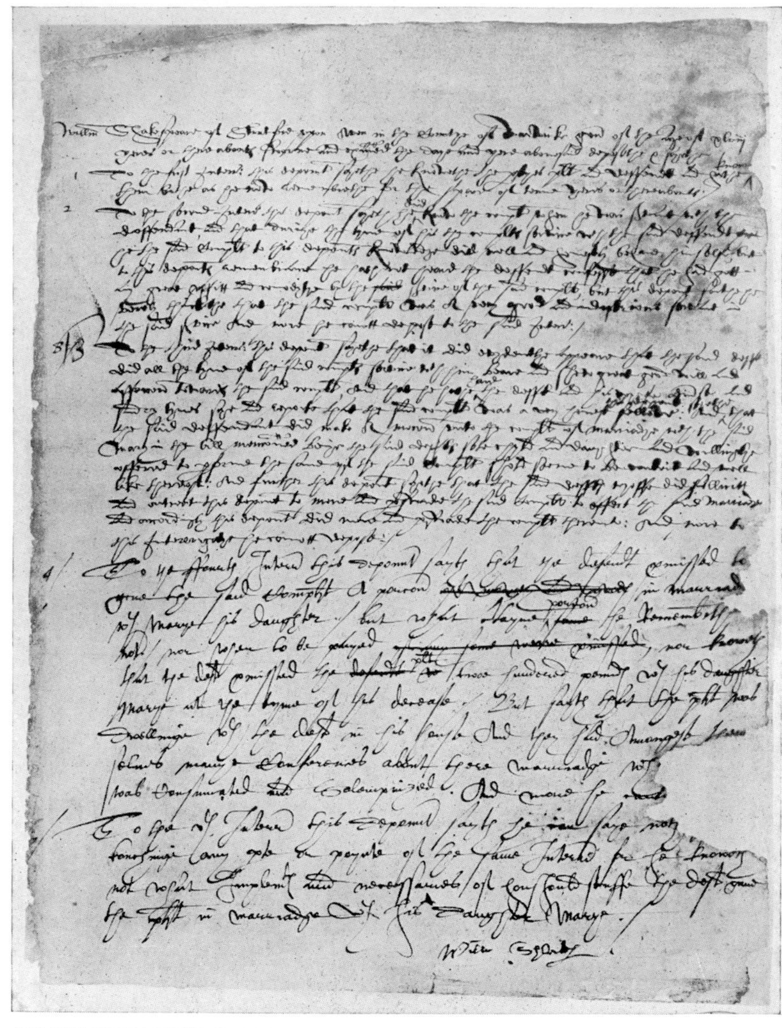

SHAKESPEARE'S DEPOSITIONS IN THE SUIT OF BELLOTT *versus* MOUNTJOY

He is described as *William Shakespeare of Stratford-upon-Avon gentleman*, of the age of 48 years. The report runs:

He knoweth the parties, plaintiff and defendant, and hath known them both for the space of 10 years or thereabouts. He did know the complainant when he was servant with the defendant, and during the time of his service he did well and honestly behave himself. The defendant did all the time of the complainant's service bear and show great goodwill and affection towards the complainant, and make a motion unto the complainant of marriage with the said Mary, the defendant's sole child and daughter; and the defendant's wife did solicit and entreat this deponent to move and persuade the complainant to effect the said marriage, and accordingly this deponent did move and persuade the complainant thereunto. The defendant promised to give a portion in marriage with his daughter, but what certain portion he remembereth not, nor when to be paid, nor knoweth that the defendant promised £200 at the time of his decease. The plaintiff was dwelling with the defendant in his house, and they had amongst themselves many conferences about the marriage, which was consummated and solemnized.[1] He knoweth not what implements and necessaries of household stuff the defendant gave the plaintiff.[2]

Shakespeare was more than familiar with such proceedings. He gave his evidence, and signed his name with a lawyer's abbreviation and a busy man's impatience, writing in his haste, with a bad pen on rough paper and a consequent blot in the *k*, '*Wittm Shakꝭe*' or '*Shakꝑe*', omitting either the *p* or the *s* in his surnãme.[3] The case was not concluded on 19 June, when he was expected to give further evidence for Bellott but made excuse which was accepted. Probably he had departed for Stratford, with his well-earned share of the £166 13*s*. 4*d*. paid to his company on 1 June for their performances at Court since 31 October.[4] With a glad sense of relief he may have ridden over Clopton Bridge, recently repaired and repaved at a cost of £27 19*s*. 5*d*., as if for his reception.[5] On 9 March his neighbours in Bridge Street, Master Robert Wilson of the *Crown* and Master John Samuel, had been appointed 'surveyors' of the work. Since he left Stratford he had lost his brother, Gilbert, who died in February

[1] p. 575. [2] Wallace, *University Studies*, Nebraska, 1910.

[3] Either *Shaks(er)e* or *Shakp(er)e*. The *Sh* are those of the signature to the conveyance of 10 March 1613 (p. 768), and the *a* is of the same tall type as that there, but roughly written. The *W* of the Christian name, with a dot in it, is a plain form of that in the Montaigne and Will chief signature (pp. 827–8). Again the *W* and *S* are detached letters.

[4] Chambers, iv. 177 f. [5] *Chamberlains' Account*, 8 Jan. 1612/3.

1612. We know little of Gilbert Shakespeare. He was two and a half years younger than the Poet, wrote a scholar's hand (so we may judge from his signature as witness to the lease of a piece of ground in Bridge Street on 5 March 1610),[1] and sufficiently commanded his brother's confidence to act on his behalf in the purchase of land from the Combes in 1602.[2] He seems to have lived quietly in the old home in Henley Street (where he may have succeeded his father as a glover) and died, unmarried, in the care of his sister, Joan Hart. His burial is thus recorded in the *Register*:

Feb. 3 Gilbert Shakspeare, adolescens.[3]

The old curate was buried the previous day, which was Sunday. The entry of his burial runs,

Feb. 2 Willmus Gilbert *alias* Higges, minister.

The vicar, John Rogers, or perhaps the new curate, Edward Wolmer, was therefore responsible for the term 'adolescens' applied to Gilbert Shakespeare, who was forty-five years old. It may have been roughly used for 'bachelor', as 'adolescentula' for 'spinster'.[4]

Shakespeare had now living his sister, Joan, aged forty-three, and his brother, Richard, aged thirty-eight. Richard may have resided, unmarried, with Joan in Henley Street.

Thomas Greene had left *New Place* for St. Mary's House. He had been active on behalf of the new charter for the Town, under which he was reappointed Steward and Town Clerk in July 1610, with George Carew, Baron of Clopton, as Chief Steward, and Sir Fulke Greville as Recorder.[5] By the terms of this document Old Stratford, with the Church and Church Way, was included in the Borough limits; and the Church Way, which led by the wall of St. Mary's House and was an old resort of 'beggars, vagabonds, and other persons loosely and depravedly living', came under the jurisdiction of the Borough officers. The Corporation, moreover, undertook in June 1611 'to repair the churchyard-wall at Master Greene's dwelling-house, and to keep it sufficiently repaired for the length of two hundred, ninety and

[1] Birthplace Museum, *Catalogue*, 58.
[2] *Ib. Cat.* 31.
[3] p. 81.
[4] i.e. three times on p. 81.
[5] New Charter, dated at Westminster 23 July 1610.

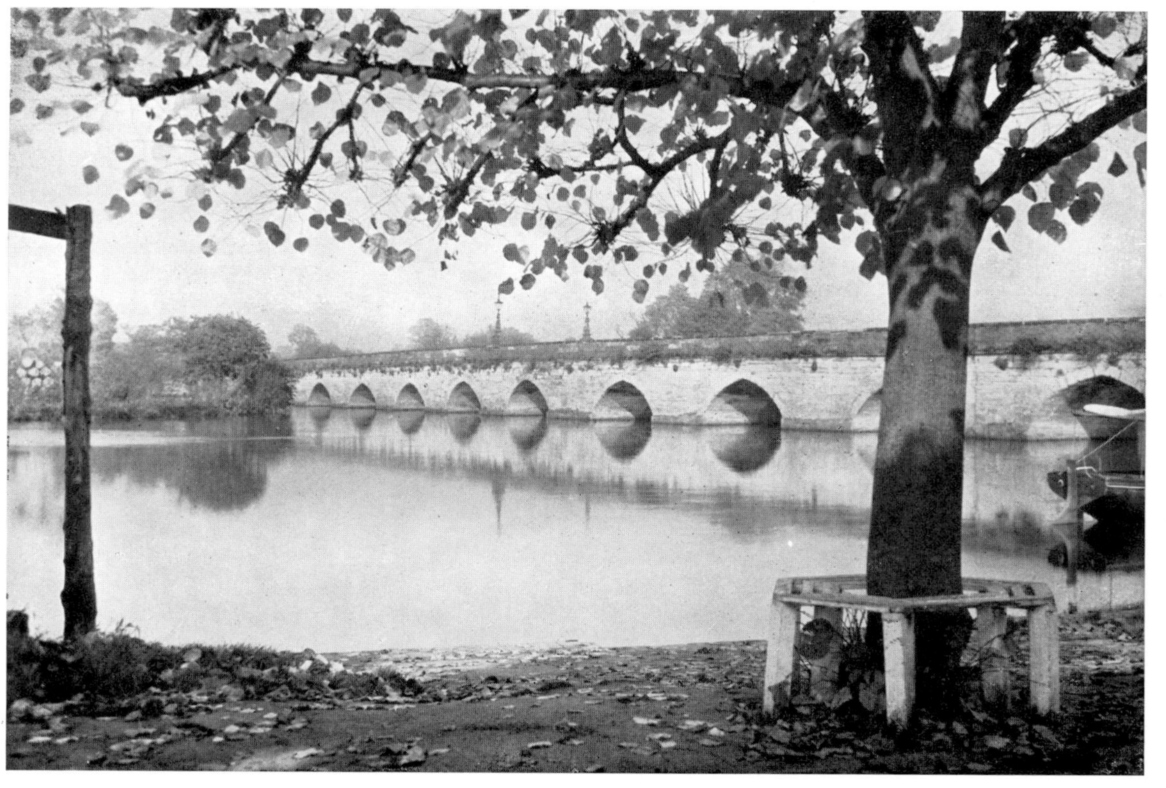

CLOPTON BRIDGE, STRATFORD-UPON-AVON

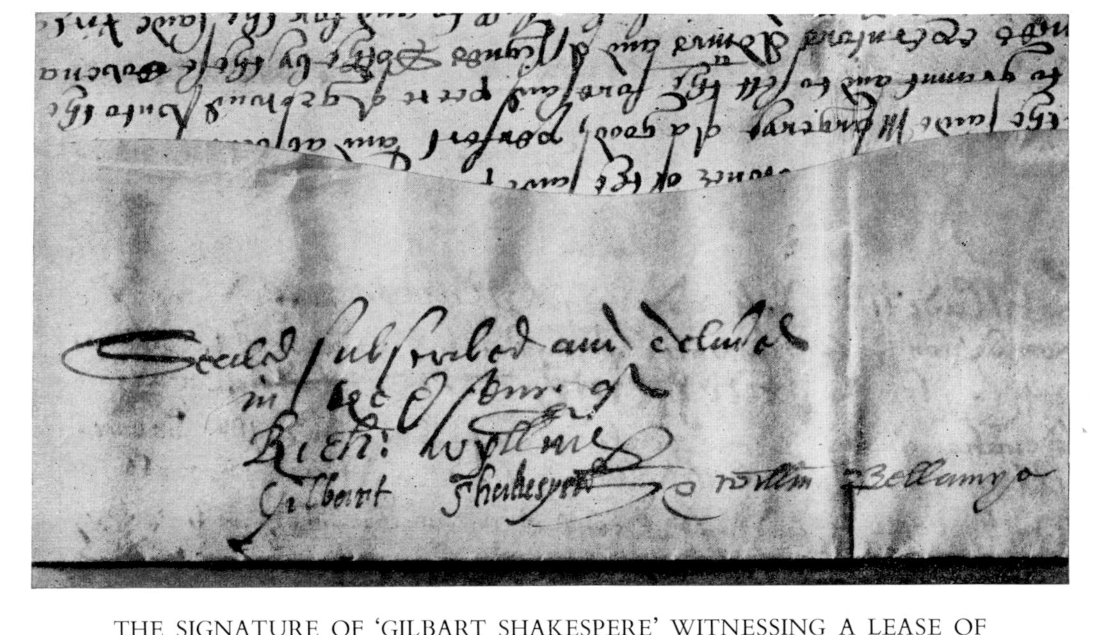

THE SIGNATURE OF 'GILBART SHAKESPERE' WITNESSING A LEASE OF 5 MARCH $16\frac{09}{10}$

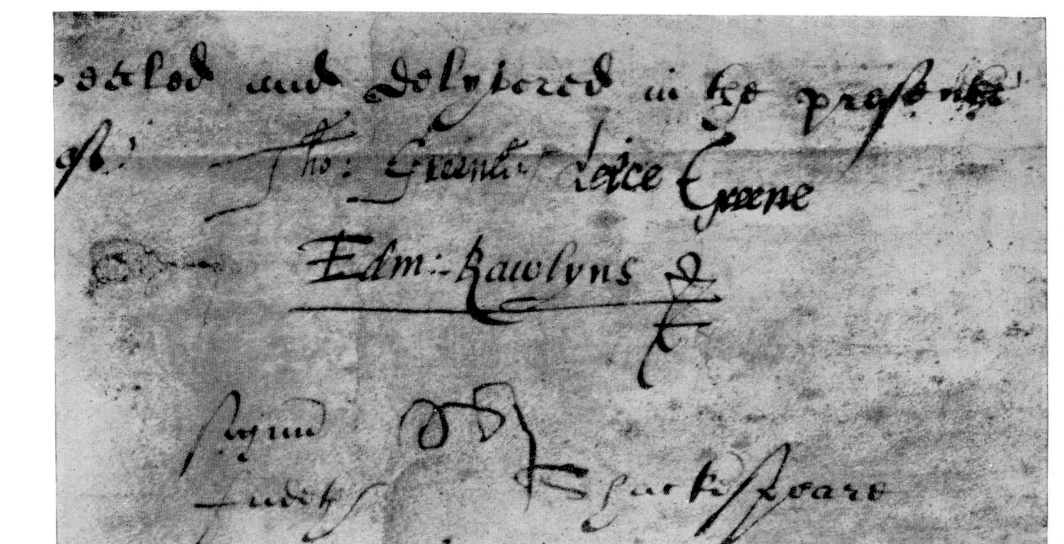

sealed and delyvered in the presence
of: Tho: Greene Lettice Greene
Edm: Rawlyns
Signum Judith Shakespeare

THE MARK OF SHAKESPEARE'S YOUNGER DAUGHTER, JUDITH, 4 DEC. 1611

seven foot'.[1] Greene paid his 2*s.* 6*d.* in September 1611 for St. Mary's House, as did Shakespeare for *New Place*, towards the charge of prosecuting a bill in Parliament for the repair of the Highways.[2] A deed of sale of 4 December by Mistress Quyney and her son, Adrian, of a house in Wood Street was witnessed among others by Thomas Greene, his wife Lettice, and their kinswoman and late fellow resident at *New Place*, Judith Shakespeare, younger daughter of the Poet. Judith Shakespeare, who was later to marry Mistress Quyney's son, Thomas, was now a young lady twenty-six years and ten months old.

Her future husband, four years her junior, was a vintner, who took a lease this Christmas of the old Atwood tavern, on the west side of High Street.[3] The sale of the house in Wood Street, which Judith witnessed, probably had to do with the setting up of her prospective bridegroom by his mother in High Street, and the young people (who were not so young) may already have been betrothed.

Some time before 10 July 1612, Shakespeare and Greene and Richard Lane put in a bill of complaint in Chancery to obtain 'a ratable and proportionable' payment by the various parties, and they were many, interested in the Stratford tithes, of the annual rent thereof of £27 13*s.* 4*d.* to the Corporation. As they were jointly and severally responsible, it fell too often to the good-natured complainants to pay what was owing by delinquents, 'against all equity and good conscience, for preservation of their estates'. It is interesting to observe that in this bill Master Greene stood socially higher than Master Shakespeare, being designated 'of Stratford, esquire', and not merely, like Shakespeare, 'of Stratford, gentleman'.[4]

On 28 June Master Greene's daughter, Elizabeth, was christened in the Parish Church.[5] It was Sunday. The Poet was probably present at the ceremony, and the babe may have received the name of his granddaughter, Elizabeth Hall, now four years and four months old.[6] In this case, Doctor Hall and Mistress Susanna Hall would attend as sponsors.

[1] *Misc. Doc.* i. 4.
[2] Birthplace Museum, *Catalogue*, 60.
[3] No. 36: Fripp, *Shakespeare Studies*, pp. 1–4.
[4] *Outlines*, ii. 25 ff.
[5] *Register*, p. 83.
[6] *Ib.* p. 75.

On 3 September 'Thomas Greene of Stratford, esquire' gave written notice to one Humfrey Collis of Bicknell that, according to a proviso made 1 March 1609, he would pay him £300 on 25 March 1613 'in the north porch of the parish-church' of Stratford.[1] Two days after this quaint announcement he attended as Clerk a meeting of the Council, at which his brother, John Greene 'gentleman', was elected a burgess.[2] Master John Greene for about a year[3] had been an attorney of the Stratford court. In October he was made the Borough solicitor for causes at London or elsewhere.[4] Later he was appointed deputy Clerk to his brother. Thomas Greene's connexion as a barrister was growing at the Middle Temple and in the Western Circuit. But he was attached to Stratford, and not the least attraction for him there was the residence at *New Place* of his cousin Shakespeare.

This year, 1612, Shakespeare's kinsman, Master Robert Fulwood of Little Alne,[5] was High Constable of Warwickshire;[6] and his old friend, Richard Tyler, a widower by the death of his wife (Susanna Woodward)[7] in May 1611, is referred to in a Corporation document[8] as a 'gentleman of honest conversation, and quiet and peaceable carriage amongst his neighbours and towards all people'.

1612–13

§ 140. THE MARRIAGE OF PRINCESS ELIZABETH

THE Poet's hope of retirement, however urgent on the ground of health, was disappointed. 'Clear as founts in July when we see each grain of gravel'[9] is the only hint of mental relaxation. As a King's man he was under command, and even had he resigned his groomship and royal livery he could hardly resist the call of friends and fellows to participate in the entertainment of the distinguished young Count who this winter wooed and

[1] *Misc. Doc.* xii. 99.

[2] *Council Book B*, 230. The same day Edmund Rawlins, a Stratford lawyer, was approved as deputy to Thomas Greene as Steward of the Court for 9 Sept.

[3] He was elected 11 Sept. 1611.

[4] *Council Book B*, 236 d.

[5] p. 530.

[6] See his warrant to the Constables of Stratford, 4 Feb. 1612 (*Misc. Doc.* vii. 74).

[7] p. 796.

[8] *Misc. Doc.* vii. 66 (16 June 1612).

[9] *Hen. VIII*, I. i. 154 f.

wedded the Princess Elizabeth. This was Frederick, the Elector Palatine, and future King of Bohemia.

Princess Elizabeth was sixteen on 19 August 1612, her boy suitor was seven days her junior. He was not cordially approved by the Queen, but for his Protestant opinions and on other grounds was greatly favoured by Prince Henry. The Earl of Southampton was one of the noblemen appointed with Prince Charles to receive him at the Whitehall stairs on 16 October, and conduct him into the royal presence in Inigo Jones's new Banquetting House. We are told:

'His approach, gesture and countenance were seasoned with a well-becoming confidence; and bending himself with a due reverence before the King, he told him among other compliments that in his sight and presence he enjoyed a great part (reserving it should seem the greatest to his mistress) of the end and happiness of his journey. After turning to the Queen, she entertained him with a fixed countenance, and though her posture might have seemed, as was judged, to promise him the honour of a kiss for his welcome, his humility carried him no higher than her hand. From which, after some few words of compliment, he made to the Prince [Henry], and exchanging with him, after a more familiar strain, certain passages of courtesy, he ended, where his desires could not but begin, with the Princess (who was noted till then not to turn so much as a corner of an eye towards him), and stooping low to take up the lowest part of her garment to kiss it, she most gracefully courtesying lower than accustomed, and with her hand staying him from that humblest reverence, gave him at his rising a fair advantage, which he took, of kissing her.'[1]

This charming greeting (so charmingly told) is not unworthy of that between Ferdinand and Miranda. From the same pen we learn:

'He hath most happily deceived good men's doubts and ill men's expectations. He is straight and well shaped for his growing years. His complexion is brown, with a countenance pleasing, and promising both wit, courage and judgment. He becomes himself well, and is very well liked of all. He is well followed—eight counts besides Count Henry of Nassau, some thirty-six gentlemen, and the rest do make up about one hundred and fifty.'[2]

There was love at sight, and immediate 'conjecture' of the marriage and its date, 'about Easter':

'In the meantime we talk of masks, tilts and barriers; but they are yet under invention, not in resolution.'[3]

[1] Fynnet to Trumbull, 23 Oct. 1612 (Winwood, iii. 403).
[2] *Ib.*
[3] *Ib.*

Festivities, however, were postponed by the illness of Prince Henry. He was 'seized with a fever' on 25 October, and was unable to accompany the Count to the Lord Mayor's Feast on the 29th. On 1 November he was 'let blood'; in the afternoon was 'very sick', so that the King and Queen, and Princess Elizabeth, 'went severally to visit him'. 'Revelling and plays appointed for that night [All Hallows'] were put off.'[1] Five days later the Prince died.

The shock and the grief were unspeakable.

'How shall I now answer', wrote Beaulieu from Paris to Trumbull in Brussels on 12 November, 'your kind letter of the 30th of the last month, but by pouring out my heart into the bosom of my dearest friend the torrent of grief wherewith it is ready to burst out, for that woeful and unexpected news which we had yesterday night of the untimely death of that brave Prince of Wales, the flower of his house, the glory of his country, and the admiration of all strangers; which in all places had imprinted a great hope in the minds of the well-affected, as it had already stricken terror into the hearts of his enemies . . . That vigorous young Prince, whose extraordinary great parts and virtues made many men hope and believe that God had reserved and destined him as a chosen instrument to be the standard-bearer of His quarrel[2] in these miserable times, to work the restoration of His Church and the destruction of the Romish idolatry. But the Lord's ways are not our ways, and His judgments are far above ours.'[3]

Henry had won admiration as his father gained contempt—

'a prince', says Roger Coke, 'adorned with wisdom and piety above his years, strength and ability of body equal to any man, of a noble and heroic disposition, and an hater of flatteries and flatterers—and therefore flat at odds with Rochester, not once giving him any countenance or vouchsafing him his company.'[4]

Rochester's hopes now rose high, as Raleigh's fell to the ground.[5] The contemptible favourite and his 'faction', says Weldon, now 'bare all down before them, disposing of all officers'. 'Of an open heart', he tells us, 'hating all baseness', the Prince 'would often say, of these Howards, "*If ever he were King he would not leave one of that family . . . to piss against a wall*" '.[6]

He was buried on 7 December in Westminster Abbey. Few would feel his death more keenly than Shakespeare.

[1] Chamberlain to Winwood, 3 Nov.

[2] 'God's quarrel' is an old Puritan expression. See *Rich. II*, I. ii. 37.

[3] Winwood, iii. 410.

[4] *Detection*, i. 60.

[5] Chamberlain to Carleton, 12 Nov.

[6] Weldon, 79. The contemptuous expression is Biblical (1 Samuel xxv. 22, 34).

On Sunday 27 December Princess Elizabeth and the Count Palatine were solemnly betrothed in the presence of the Archbishop of Canterbury.[1] There were plays at Court by the King's men from this date until the departure of the Princess and her husband on 10 April. Six times they performed before the King, fourteen times before Elizabeth, Frederick, and Prince Charles. The plays before His Majesty included *Hotspur* (*1 Henry IV*) and *Benedick and Beatrice* (*Much Ado about Nothing*); those before the young people included *Much Ado about Nothing, The Tempest, The Winter's Tale, Sir John Falstaff* (*2 Henry IV* or *The Merry Wives of Windsor*), *The Moor of Venice* (*Othello*), and *Caesar's Tragedy* (*Julius Caesar*).[2] The appropriateness of *The Tempest* is striking—with its undernote of sorrow, double betrothal (in private III. i and in public IV. i) and game of chess (V. i). It probably underwent revision for the pleasure of the Princess and the Count. Their wedding took place on Shrove Sunday, which was 14 February, St. Valentine's Day, 1613.

It is noticeable that Shakespeare's *Henry the Eighth* is not among the plays officially paid for at Court this season. That it was some time presented before His Majesty is clear from the allusion to King James in Act V, sc. V, ll. 40–55: a passage which seriously impairs Cranmer's speech, and was doubtless interpolated for a Court performance by the Poet himself.

Henry the Eighth was probably produced at the Blackfriars (where one of its chief scenes is laid),[3] not long after the performance at the Whitefriars on 31 January or 7 February 1613 of a piece called *The Hog hath Lost his Pearl*, of which we hear in a letter from Sir Henry Wotton, in King Street, Westminster, to his nephew Edmund Bacon, at Eton:

'On Sunday last some sixteen apprentices (of what sort you shall guess by the rest of the story), having secretly learned a new play, without book, intituled *The Hog hath Lost his Pearl*, took up the White friars for their theatre; and having invited thither, as it should seem, rather their mistresses than their masters, who were all to enter *per buletini* for a note of distinction from ordinary comedians. Towards the end of the play the Sheriffs (who by chance had heard of it) came in, as they say, and carried some six or seven of them to perform the last act at Bridewell. The rest are fled. Now, it is

[1] Chamberlain to Winwood, 9 Jan. 1613. 'The Queen was absent, not from distaste but a fit of the gout': Wake to Carleton, 31 Dec. 1612.

[2] Chambers, iv. 127 f., 180.

[3] II. iv.

strange to hear *how sharp-witted the City is*, for they will needs have Sir John Swinerton, the Lord Mayor, be meant by the *Hog*, and the late Lord Treasurer by the *Pearl*.'[1]

The late Lord Treasurer was Robert Cecil, Earl of Salisbury, who died at Marlborough on his return from fruitless treatment at Bath on 24 May 1612. The Sunday referred to by Wotton seems to have been a week or a fortnight before the Princess Elizabeth's wedding. To the performance of the apprentices' satire (suggested by 'the casting of pearls before swine', Matthew vii. 6) there is obvious allusion in the humorous epilogue to *Henry VIII*:

> 'Tis ten to one this play can never please
> All that are here: some come to take their ease,
> And sleep an act or two; but those, we fear,
> We have frighted with our trumpets, so 'tis clear
> They'll say 'tis naught: others *to hear the City*
> *Abused extremely, and to cry 'That's witty!'*
> Which we have not done neither.

Hence the 'gentle hearers' of the prologue,

> The first and happiest hearers of the Town,

are the audience at the Blackfriars. That at the *Globe* was more plebeian and, from what we know of the 'groundlings', or frequenters of the pit, there, less likely to 'take their ease and sleep'.

Shakespeare purchased a house near the Blackfriars theatre in March 1613. He paid £140 for it to the vendor, one Henry Walker, a minstrel of London, receiving from him again £60 on mortgage. He immediately leased the house to a friend, John Robinson. We wish we knew more of Robinson. He was one of the inhabitants in the Blackfriars who petitioned the Privy Council against the opening of a public theatre in their precincts in 1596. Richard Field, it will be remembered, was another. The interesting fact about John Robinson is that he was at *New Place* with Shakespeare in March 1616.[2] To the conveyance and mortgage-deed of the Blackfriars house are attached the Poet's signatures under date 10 and 11 March. The seal-tag in each case is parchment, which at the time of writing was rather greasy: whence the blot in the first and the 'printing' of the letters

[1] *Reliquiae Wottonianae*, p. 402 f.

[2] p. 828.

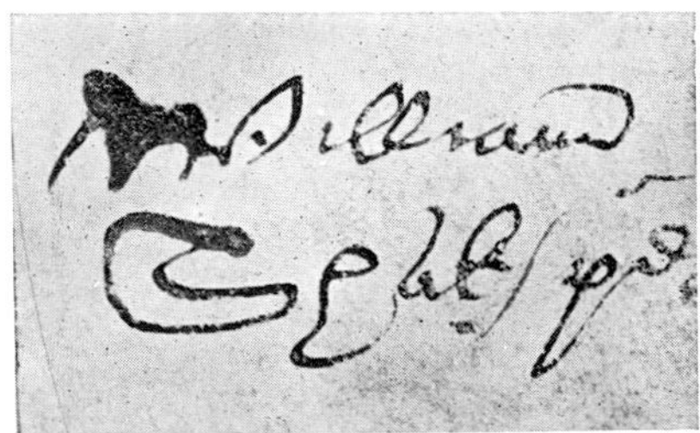

SHAKESPEARE'S AUTOGRAPH SIGNATURE TO THE DEED OF PURCHASE OF A HOUSE IN BLACKFRIARS, 10 MARCH 1613

(Guildhall Library, London)

(separately) in the second. Differences in the *W*'s, *h*'s, *a*'s, and *p*'s prove that Shakespeare did not write a rigid hand.[1] He had the artist's antipathy to uniformity.

This month he and Burbage executed an *impresa* for the Earl of Rutland in the tournament at Whitehall. Shakespeare designed, Burbage painted it. Would that Sir Henry Wotton, who was present at the tournament on 24 March, and mentions the Earl among the tilters, had sufficiently admired his device to describe it.

'The two best to my fancy', he wrote to Sir Edmund Bacon, 'were those of the two Earls brothers'—Pembroke and Montgomery—'the first a small, exceeding white pearl, and the word *Solo Candore Valeo*;[2] the other a sun casting a glance on the side of a pillar, and the beams reflecting, with this motto *Splendente Refulget*;[3] in which devices there seems an agreement, the elder brother to allude to his own nature and the younger to his fortune.'[4]

On 31 March Shakespeare was paid 44*s*. for his part in the *impresa* and Burbage the same for his, 'in gold', that is in 'Jacobuses', the new coins worth 22*s*. apiece.[5] On 29 April Wotton wrote to Sir Edmund Bacon: 'My lady Elizabeth and the Count Palatine, having lain long in our poor province of Kent, languishing for a wind, which she sees, though it be but a vapour, Princes cannot command, at length on Sunday last [25th] towards evening did put to sea.'[6] The Princess and Wotton might have remembered what the Boatswain said in *The Tempest*, 'What cares these roarers for the name of King? If you can command these elements to silence, we will not hand a rope more.'[7]

On 20 May 1613 Shakespeare received his share of £60 for performances before the King, and of £93 6*s*. 8*d*. for performances before the Princess and Count Palatine.[8] The following month, on St. Peter's day, Tuesday 29 June, the *Globe* theatre was burnt down during a performance of *Henry the Eighth*.

[1] The signature of 10 March recalls the one of the deposition of 11 May 1612 (see p. 761), that of 11 March the abbreviated signature in the Ovid (p. 113).

[2] 'By candour alone am I strong.'

[3] 'He flashes back the brilliant.'

[4] *Reliquiae Wottonianae*, p. 406.

[5] *Hist. MSS. Com.* iv. 494.

[6] *Reliq. Wott.*, p. 412.

[7] I. i. 18 f., 23–5.

[8] Chambers, iv. 180.

1612–13

§ 141. *KING HENRY THE EIGHTH*

'THE right happy and copious industry of Master Shakespeare', held up in praise this year,[1] was not yet ended. The series of Civil War plays was incomplete without *Henry the Eighth*. The story which Shakespeare in two sequences of dramas, the later first, had presented on the stage needed its conclusion. And to the crude *Richard the Third* he added, not as an afterthought but the fulfilment of old design, the ripe last work, *Henry the Eighth*, linking up grandly his youth and maturity.

This great play, for combination of noble character with splendid pageantry his greatest, Shakespeare brought with him, finished or unfinished, when summoned to London in the autumn of 1612 for the entertainment of the Court. That it was not presented at Court will hardly surprise us. It was unsuited for wedding festivities, especially, as it proved, with their background of sudden death. The 'happy ending' only partially relieves the tragic events preceding, which are such that if a man 'can be merry' at the sight of them he 'may weep upon his wedding-day'.[2]

We are warned at the outset—

> Be sad as we would make ye: think, ye see
> The very persons of our noble story
> As they were living; think, you see them great,
> And followed with the general throng and sweat
> Of thousand friends: then, in a moment, see
> How soon this mightiness meets misery.[3]

The pageantry, then, so far from being superfluous, as some critics would have us believe,[4] a concession to 'popularity', is an essential feature of the drama.[5] Amid scenes of worldly magnificence great personages, severally fit to be the central figure of the story, are presented and cast down—Buckingham, Wolsey,

[1] By Webster, in the preface to his *White Devil*, 1612.

[2] Prologue, 31 f.

[3] Prologue.

[4] Even Morton Luce ('A series of gorgeous pageants rather than a genuine drama', *Handbook*, p. 364). Such comment would be more appropriate for Alleyn's *Cardinal Wolsey* at the *Rose* in 1601.

[5] As Irving recognized in his great production at the *Lyceum* in 1892.

Queen Katharine. They occupy the first four acts, and hold us with moving interest. And we wonder, as these heroic souls depart, what sequel, what 'blessing' from time to time foreshadowed in their calamities—'a blessing to this land which shall in it be memorized',[1] 'a gem to lighten all this Isle'[2]—can compensate, still more justify, their loss. In the fifth act, however, is the promised and, for Shakespeare in 1612, all-sufficient, providential end.[3] In an atmosphere, still charged with emotion but no longer of lament and retrospect, of bustling energy and homely humour, we witness a great denouement. A little child is brought from her christening in Westminster Abbey, 'richly habited' beneath a canopy, preceded by the Archbishop of Canterbury and followed by her father, the King, in the presence of a surging multitude of citizens. Her name is ELIZABETH. Cranmer, his voice (and the verse richly responding) nearer tears of gladness than mere jubilation,[4] prophesies the glory of her reign—peace, prosperity, the settlement of the Reformation, triumph over Spain, poetry and song, chivalry, colonization, empire. He says:

> This royal in|fant,—Heaven still move abóut | her!
> Though in her crád|le, yet now promises
> Upon this land a thousand, thousand blés|sings,
> Which time shall bring to rípe|ness. She shall be—
> But few now living can behold that góod|ness—
> A pattern to all princes living wíth | her
> And all that shall succeed: Saba was név|er
> More covetous of wisdom and fair vír|tue[5]
> Than this pure soul shall be: all princely grá|ces
> That mould up such a mighty piece as thís | is,
> With all the virtues that attend the good,|
> Shall still be doubled on her.[6]

Was ever a babe so called? 'A Mighty Piece!' And here is a

[1] III. ii. 51 f.

[2] II. iii. 78 f.

[3] Cf. Sidney: 'God Almighty by a wonderful providence is ruling the Christian world in our time' (June 1574, Feuillerat, iii. 97 f., Latin). 'As it is the will of the Almighty that our safety should depend on so frail a thread as the Queen's health, she is commended to Him in the earnest prayers of the people' (June 1575, *Ib.* 103, Latin). And Naunton: 'God in His omnipotent providence had decreed the protection of the Mistress, and added His abundant blessing upon all and whatever she undertook' (*Fragmenta Regalia*, Arber, p. 60).

[4] See further, pp. 772–3.

[5] 1 Kings x. 1–3.

[6] V. v. 18–29.

hall-mark Shakespeare term, of endearment and excellence, again and again in his last plays—'this *piece* of your dead queen, a little daughter', for Marina;[1] 'a *piece* of tender air', for Imogen;[2] 'a *piece* of beauty rare', 'fresh *piece* of excellent witchcraft', 'the most peerless *piece* of earth that ere the Sun shone bright on', for Perdita; 'royal *piece*', for Hermione;[3] and 'a *piece* of virtue', for the mother of Miranda.[4]

Cranmer continues, in the same deep note:

Truth shall núrse | her;
Holy and heavenly thoughts still counsel her;
She shall be loved and feared: her own shall bléss | her;
Her foes shake like a field of beaten corn,|
And hang their heads with sór|row: good grows wíth | her:
In her days every man shall eat in sáfe|ty,
Under his own vine, what he plants; and sing|
The merry songs of peace to all his neígh|bours.[5]
God shall be truly known; and those abóut | her
From her shall read the perfect ways of hón|our,
And by those claim their gréat|ness, not by blood.|[6]

So speaks the true democrat. What follows has been interpolated and injured for the Court performance in compliment to the King, but can easily be restored:

Wherever the bright sun of Heaven shall shine |
(Her)[7] honour and the greatness of (her)[7] name |
Shall be, and make new ná|tions: (s)he[7] shall flóur|ish
And like a mountain cedar,[8] reach (her)[7] bránch|es
To all the plains abóut | (her).[7] Our children's | children
Shall see this and bless Heaven.
KING HENRY. Thou speakest wón|ders.
CRANMER. She[7] shall be, to the happiness of Éng|land,
An aged Prín|cess; many days shall sée | her,[7]
And yet no day without a deed to crówn | it,
'Would I had known no more! but she[7] must die— |
She[7] must, the Saints must háve | her;[7] yet a Vír|gin,
A most unspotted lily shall she[7] pass |
To the ground, and all the world shall móurn | her.

[1] *Per.* III. i. 17 f., 21.
[2] *Cymb.* V. v. 446.
[3] *Wint. T.* IV. iv. 32, 433 f., V. i. 94 f., iii. 38.
[4] *Temp.* I. ii. 56.
[5] 1 Kings iv. 20–5.
[6] V. v. 31–9.
[7] ll. 40–50 are an insertion, they anticipate ll. 60–3. 'She' and 'her' in 57–63 more than suggest the original readings in ll. 52–5.
[8] Psalm xcii. 12, 14.

KING HENRY. O lord Archbishop,
Thou hast made me now a man: never, before
This happy child, did I get anything.
This oracle of comfort hath so pléas'd | me
That when I am in Heaven I shall desire
To see what this child does, and praise my Mák|er.[1]

Henry VIII, as we know him, looking down from Heaven is an anti-climax; but as conceived by the Elizabethan puritan he was the giver of the Bible and the Truth to England, and her deliverer from the Pope and the mass. Shakespeare represents him as not unworthy of his illustrious daughter. He shows us Katharine's love for him,[2] and his love for Katharine,[3] whatever his passion for Anne Boleyn and desire for male issue; Buckingham's allegiance—'my vows and prayers yet are the King's';[4] Wolsey's devotion to the last—'I know his noble nature';[5] and whatever the monarch's failings as a man, his 'sacred person'.[6]

The play ends in rejoicing—

This little one shall make it holiday.[7]

It could only end so, whatever critics may say of a second hand giving a conclusion other than Shakespeare intended. Politically it is a great finale.

Here is the Poet's tribute—and there is none finer, though some regarded it as belated—to Queen Elizabeth. It would delight the hearts of Raleigh and the old Earl of Nottingham, and thousands who remembered their late Sovereign with adoration, and contrasted her virile and adventurous personality with the mean effeminacy of King James.

But if *Henry VIII* by its 'happy ending' has affinity with the Dramatic Romances—*Pericles*, *Cymbeline*, *The Winter's Tale*, *The Tempest*—it has in it not a little of the great tragedies. It reminds us of *Lear*, and the problem that drama raises, the outstanding problem of Shakespearean tragedy, of personal suffering, and spiritual attainment. Buckingham, Wolsey, and Katharine rise to magnitude in misfortune which is beyond them, and even foreign to them, in worldly greatness, and which

[1] v. v. 18–39, 51–69.
[2] III. i. 180, 'he has my heart yet'.
[3] II. iv. 133–41, 'Go thy ways, Kate', &c.
[4] II. i. 86 ff.
[5] III. ii. 419.
[6] II. iv. 41, III. ii. 173.
[7] v. v. 77.

we may doubt whether 'children's children' will achieve in the palmy days of Elizabethan 'Peace' and 'Truth'.

Shakespeare had been reading, among other authorities (Holinshed, Hall, Foxe), the *Life of Wolsey*, in manuscript, by Cavendish, one of the few choice classics of Mary's reign, wherein the author sought to replace the 'light tales' and 'innumerable lies' with the 'truth' (whence *All is True* as the second title to *Henry VIII*), and to convey the lesson, as he regarded it, of the Cardinal's fate:

'I would wish all men in authority and dignity to know and fear God, considering in all their doings that authorities be not permanent but may slide and vanish as Prince's pleasures.[1] . . . Let all men to whom Fortune extendeth her grace not trust too much to her fickle favour; for when she seeth her servant in most highest authority, and that he assureth himself most assuredly in her favour, then turneth she her visage unto a frowning cheer and utterly forsaketh him.[2]

'Mark this history, good reader, and note every circumstance, and thou shalt espy the wonderful work of God against such persons as forgetteth God and His great benefits.[3] . . . What thing so-ever a man purposeth, yet God disposeth all things at His will and pleasure.[4] . . . This Lord Cardinal was the haughtiest man that then lived, having more respect to the worldly honour of his person than to his spiritual profession, wherein should be all meekness, humility and charity.[5] He hath felt both of the sweet and the sour in each degree, as fleeting from honours, losing of riches, deposed from dignities, forsaken of friends and the inconstantness of Princes' favour. Wherefore the prophet said full well, *Thesaurizat et ignorat cui congregabit ea*.'[6]

He quotes Psalm xxxix. 7, thus rendered in the Prayer Book: 'Man walketh in a vain shadow and disquieteth himself in vain; *he heapeth up riches, and cannot tell who shall gather them*.'

In Shakespeare's hands King Henry is the god Fortune.[7] He smiles, men rise; he frowns, they fall—Buckingham, Wolsey, Katharine. And echoes of Cavendish's moral may be heard again and again in the play.[8] But while the biographer can see no 'end in all', Shakespeare both contemplates Elizabeth's reign as the providential purpose and *transforms the sacrificed lives into ends in themselves, noble and worthy of immortality*. The 'meekness, humility and charity' which Cavendish regretted Wolsey had not, the Poet gives him at last in overflowing measure. Such is

[1] Morley, p. 15 f. [2] 25. [3] 54.
[4] 64. [5] 254. [6] 262.
[7] Morley, *English Writers*, xi. [8] III. ii. 356–8, 366 f.

his treatment also of Buckingham and Katharine. Not only is there national blessing from their sufferings by the Will of God ('the Will of Heaven be done, in this and all things!',[1] 'Heaven has an end in all',[2] 'Heaven is above all yet',[3] 'It's Heaven's Will'),[4] but personal faith, strong and convinced through a changed heart, in the life to come. Buckingham on his way to execution calls to his friends,

> Go with me, like good angels, to my end;
> And as the long divorce of steel falls on me,
> Make of your prayers one sweet sacrifice
> And lift my soul to heaven.[5]

Wolsey cries, in his majestic grief,

> Farewell
> The hopes of court! my hopes in heaven do dwell.[6]

Katharine, dying, dreams of Heaven (her vision is the loveliest of all masques, without a word spoken) and, 'as it were by inspiration', make signs to angels:

> Spirits of Peace, where are ye?[7]

Here is peace deeper than that of the Elizabethan era.

The portrait of Katharine is beautiful at the beginning and only more beautiful at the close. Not a fault is left in her—save a pardonable touch of the old Spanish pride—

> Garlands I am not worthy yet to wear—*I shall, assuredly*.[8]

We are drawn to Henry for what she says of him:

> In death I bless'd him;[9]

and to Wolsey by her forgiveness:

> So may he rest; his faults lie gently on him![10]

We love the words that fall from her, so simply:

'Alas, poor man!'[11] (of Wolsey, unable to sit his mule);
'And something over to remember me by'[12] (wage to her faithful poor);

[1] I. i. 209 f., 215. [2] II. i. 124. [3] III. i. 100.

[4] III. ii. 128. Contrast Norfolk, 'Some spirit put this paper in the packet' (129), with Wolsey, 'What cross devil made me put this in the packet?' (214 f.). The 'cross devil' in Shakespeare's philosophy was the overruling Providence.

[5] II. i. 75–8. [6] III. ii. 458 f.

[7] IV. ii. 83. [8] *Ib.* 91 f. [9] *Ib.* 163.

[10] *Ib.* 31. [11] IV. ii. 16. [12] *Ib.* 151.

'On that celestial harmony I go to';[1] and (wonderful touch, from Cavendish,[2] given by Shakespeare also to Laertes and Antony)[3] '*I can no more*'.[4]

The Spaniard's will at last gave out.

She is one of Shakespeare's perfect women, and (what artists have so rarely drawn or had the power to draw) the perfect Wife.[5]

Buckingham's development is finely sketched, from a haughty, headstrong, young aristocrat to the model of Christian patience:

> he fell to *himself* again, and sweetly
> In all the rest showed a most noble patience.[6]

Wolsey learns to 'know *himself*'. The picture of his transformation is one of the very greatest of the Poet's achievements.

Nothing can excel the speeches, in soliloquy and in confidence to Cromwell, wherein he lays bare his soul after his fall. It has been the ambition of nearly every great actor to pronounce them. In sensitiveness of feeling, in thought so true and deep, in metrical expression so subtle in its changes, and moving in cadence, they are unsurpassed:

> Farewéll! a lóng farewéll to áll my gréat|ness!
> Thís is the státe of mán: to-dáy he púts | forth
> The ténder léaves of hópe; to-mórrow blós|soms,
> And béars his blúshing hónours thíck upón | him;
> The thírd day cómes a fróst, a kílling frost, |
> And whén he thínks, good éasy mán, full súre|ly
> His gréatness is a-rípe|ning, | níps his róot, |
> And thén he fálls, as Í | do. Í have vén|tured,
> Like líttle wánton bóys that swím on blád|ders,
> This mány súmmers in a séa of glór|y
> But fár beyónd my dépth: my hígh-blown príde |
> At léngth broke únder me, and nów has léft | me,
> Wéary and óld with sér|vice, to the mér|cy
> Of a rúde stréam that múst for éver híde | me.
> Vain pómp and glóry of this wórld, I háte | ye:
> I féel my héart new ó|pen'd. Ó how wrétch|ed
> Is thát poor mán that hángs on prínces' fá|vours!
> There ís, betwíxt that smíle we wóuld aspíre | to,

[1] IV. ii. 80. [2] Morley, p. 253 (but spoken by Wolsey).
[3] *Haml.* V. ii. 331; *Ant. & Cleop.* IV. xv. 59. [4] IV. ii. 173.
[5] The critic who denies Katharine to Shakespeare is the victim of some theory.
[6] II. i. 36.

That swéet aspéct of prín|ces, and their rú|in,
More pángs and féars than wárs or wómen have: |
And when he fálls he fálls like Lŭcifer,[1] |
Néver to hópe agaín.[2]

Here, in perfection, is the 'broken metre' we have noted from time to time in the later plays. It occurs in a few lines in *Antony and Cleopatra*,[3] throughout a scene in *Timon of Athens*,[4] in a passage in *Coriolanus*,[5] a passage in *Cymbeline*,[6] and a great speech in *The Winter's Tale*.[7] It occurs also in *The Tempest* in Ferdinand's speech in Act III, Scene i,[8] and the dialogue of Prospero and Miranda in Act I, Scene ii.[9] In *Henry the Eighth* it appears frequently, is so conspicuous, indeed, that it calls for explanation. This may be found in the peculiar sentiment of the drama,

Those that can pity, here
May, if they think it well, let fall a tear;
The subject will deserve it.[10]

For such a theme as fallen greatness and noble grief no metre could be more appropriate; and if Shakespeare needed suggestion

[1] A more terrible fall than that of Phaethon: *Rich. II*, III. iii. 178 f.; *Metamorphoses*, ii. 319–21.

[2] III. ii. 351–72. I have given the stress as I think Shakespeare would have laid it; but as to the Master's fine music who will dogmatize? Some profess not to hear it. Even Morton Luce complains of 'jingle'. He is hard to please. George Brandes wrote, 'Fletcher has spoilt the character by the introduction of the badly-written monologues uttered by Wolsey after his fall. We recognise the voice of the clergyman's son in their feeble pastoral strain' (*William Shakespeare*, ii. 319). This is light, not on Shakespeare, but on Brandes.

[3] IV. xiv. 44–9, V. ii. 12–18, 86–92. See p. 684.

[4] IV. ii. See p. 699.

[5] IV. v. 71–82. See p. 705.

[6] V. v. 382–92. See p. 724.

[7] III. ii. 26–47. See p. 745.

[8] 1–15, e.g.:

This my mean task
Would be as heavy to me as ó|dious, *but*
The Mistress which I serve quickens what's dead,
And makes my labours pléa|sures: O, she *is*
Ten times more gentle than her father's cráb|bed,
And he's composed of hársh|ness. I must ré|move
Some thousands of these logs, and pile them up
Upon a sore injúnc|tion: my sweet Mís|tress
Weeps.

[9] 1–21, 55–9, 74–83, 140–3, 151–3. For example,

O, I have suffer'd
With those that I saw súf|fer! a brave vés|sel
Who had, no doubt, some noble creature ín | her,
Dash'd all to píe|ces.

[10] Prologue.

of its suitability, he might receive it from Cavendish. Queen Katharine's speech at the Blackfriars, as reported by him in the fine prose of his *Life of Wolsey*, has in it not a little of the moving cadence of Shakespeare's verse. Here is the opening of it, in verse-formation for the sake of comparison:

Sir, I beséech | you,
for all the loves that hath been betwéen | us,
and for the love of God,
let me have justice and right.[1]
Take of me some pí|ty and compás|sion,
for I am a poor wó|man and a strán|ger,
born out of your domí|nion.
I have here no assúred | friend,
and much less indifferent cóun|sel.
I flee to you as to the head of jús|tice,
within this realm. Alás, | Sir,
wherein have I offended you?
or what occasion of displéa|sure
have I designed against your will and pléa|sure,
intending, as I perceive, to put me fróm | you?
I take God and all the world to wít|ness,
that I have been to you a true, humble and obedient wife,
ever conformable to your will and pléa|sure.[1]

And here is Shakespeare's verse:

Sir, I desire you, do me right and jús|tice,[2]
And to bestow your pity ón | me; for
I am a most poor wó|man, and a strán|ger,
Born out of your domí|nions; having here
No judge indíffer|ent, nor no more assúr|ance
Of equal friendship and procéed|ing. Alás, | sir,
In what have I offénded you? what cause
Hath my behaviour given to your displéa|sure?
That thus you should proceed to put me off,
And take your good grace fróm | me? Heaven wít|ness,
I have been to you a true and humble wife,
At all times to your will conformable.[3]

Verbally Shakespeare has followed Holinshed rather than Cavendish. Here is Holinshed, in verse-order:

Sir, I desire you to do me justice and right
and take some pity upón | me, for

[1] Morley, p. 116.
[2] Note the Poet's skilful change of 'justice and right' to 'right and jus|tice'.
[3] II. iv. 13–24.

I am a poor wó|man | and a strân|ger,
born out of your domí|nion, | having here
no indifferent cóun|sel, and less
assurance of fríend|ship. | Alás, | sir, |
what have I offended you, or what occá|sion
of displéa|sure | have I shówed | you,
intending thus to put me fróm | you |
after this sort? I take God to my judge,
I have been to you a true and humble wife,
ever conformable to your will and pléa|sure.[1]

'Desire', 'do', 'on me' (after 'pity'), 'having' (for 'have'), 'assurance of friendship' (for 'assured friend'), and 'ever' are Holinshed's verbal changes from Cavendish, and are taken by Shakespeare from Holinshed; from Cavendish, Shakespeare takes the original 'from (you)' and 'witness'.[2] Holinshed has reproduced something of the rhythm of Cavendish, Shakespeare has added to it.

Shakespeare, moreover, has intensified the effect of this rhythm by the skilful interspersal of lines which contain none of its features and throw them into relief by contrast. There is no penultimate stress, or extra, overhanging syllable, in the direct, challenging declaration,

I have been to you a true and humble wife.

It has no sob in it or at the end of it; and it is from Holinshed. Of the same character are the lines in Wolsey's soliloquy:

The third day comes a frost, a killing frost : . .
But far beyond my depth: my high blown pride . . .
And when he falls, he falls like Lucifer.

And if there is a penultimate stress within, a sharp emphasis suitable to the thought, like a knife, concludes the line:

His greatness is a-rípe|ning, *nips his root.* |[3]

[1] *Chronicles*, p. 908.

[2] In the rest of the speech in Shakespeare 'reckoned', 'deemed', 'of every (realm)' are from Holinshed, 'Ferdinand' (for 'Ferdinando') and 'be advised' are from Cavendish.

[3] Spedding led the critics a wild-goose chase when he detected, as he thought, a double hand in *Henry VIII*, and attributed the metrical peculiarities of the play to Fletcher. There is no inconsistency, as he imagined, between Acts I–IV and Act V; nor is there sound reason for assigning the *metrik* to another hand than Shakespeare's. Not only is *Henry VIII* one of the best attested, as to its authorship, of the Poet's dramas, but the suggested participation of Fletcher is singularly unhappy. It was a new play so late as 1613; was this year performed at the

In *The Tempest* Shakespeare observed scrupulously the 'dramatic unities'. The scene shifts but a few yards, and the time of the story is that of the performance at the *Globe*—from a little after two o'clock until shortly before six.[1] Doubtless he had heard of his breaches as a playwright of the laws of Classical Drama. For once he worked within its restrictions, and demonstrated to the critics his capacity to do so as triumphantly as the Ancients. But he had small respect for such rules and limits. Life was too large and incalculable; and having made his obeisance to the idol of classical correctness, he cast it down and trampled it to pieces. In *Henry VIII* he revelled in the freedom of Gothic art, of medieval sculpture and building and painting. While the spirit of history, for once almost contemporary, is preserved, its mere chronology is thrown to the winds, and the events of twenty-four years are gathered up into as many or fewer days. *Men*, not happenings, and what is written on the faces and the hands of them, the marks of the *Soul* or the lack of it, are the Poet's concern.

The Ovid in the play has been noted.[2] Medicine is once more in evidence,[3] but altogether secondary to Law. And Law, in its turn, has to yield the first place to Shakespeare's earliest and latest literary companion, the Bible. The storm at sea, of *Othello*,[4]

Globe by Shakespeare and his fellows, among them John Heminge and Henry Condell; and was included by the editors, Heminge and Condell, in the Folio of 1623, without a word of protest from Fletcher or any other claimant. And nowhere does Fletcher reveal the mentality capable of the speeches of Buckingham, Wolsey, Katharine, Griffith, and Cranmer. He has not the thought, still less the ethics and religion, for these things. His verse, too, is slipshod and indiscriminate, devoid of the subtle and telling variations of Shakespeare's. He could indeed write 'sob-verse' (with penultimate stress, eleventh syllable, weak and double ending, or what not), anywhere and everywhere, loose and languid *ad libitum*, but was entirely unequal to the *metrik*, as to the sentiment, of Wolsey's 'Farewell'. Wolsey and Katharine have had the moral experience of fifty Fletchers.

[1] I. ii. 239 f., 241, V. i. 3–5, 136 f., 186, 223.

[2] p. 109.

[3] Ague, disease, flow of gall, infect, not wholesome, pestilent, sick, sickness, give physic, catching diseases, good digestion, cure, 'a sufferance panging as soul and body's severing', 'he brings his physic after his patient's death', 'brain and function', poison to the stomach, cured me, sick to death, fell sick suddenly, 'altered on the sudden, her face is drawn, pale, earthy cold, mark her eyes', gentle physic, embalm, Butts the King's physician, contagious sickness, farewell all physic, general taint.

[4] p. 628.

Pericles,[1] *The Winter's Tale,*[2] and *The Tempest*[3] has not quite subsided. We hear it in the 'noise' such

> As the shrouds make at sea in a stiff tempest,
> As loud and to as many tunes.[4]

This summer, 1613, during a performance of *Henry the Eighth*, the *Globe* theatre was burnt to the ground.

1613

§ 142. THE BURNING OF THE *GLOBE*

SIR HENRY WOTTON writes to Sir Edmund Bacon on Friday 2 July:

'Now, to let matters of State sleep, I will entertain you at the present with what hath happened this week at the Bank's Side. The King's Players had a new play called *All is True*[5] representing some principal pieces of the reign of Henry VIII, which was set forth with many extraordinary circumstances of pomp and majesty, even to the matting of the stage, the Knights of the Order, with their Georges and Garter, the Guards with their embroidered coats, and the like: sufficient in truth within a while to make greatness very familiar, if not ridiculous. Now, King Henry making a mask at the Cardinal Wolsey's house,[6] and certain cannons being shot off at his entry,[7] some of the paper or other stuff wherewith one of them was stopped, did light on the thatch; where being thought at first but an idle smoke and their eyes more attentive to the show, it kindled inwardly and ran around like a train, consuming within less than an hour the whole house to the very ground.

This was the fatal period of that virtuous[8] fabric; wherein yet nothing did perish but wood and straw, and a few forsaken cloaks;[9] only one man

[1] p. 685. [2] p. 746. [3] p. 756. [4] IV. i. 71–3.

[5] The second title, no doubt, of Shakespeare's play. See Prologue: 'May here find truth' (9), 'our chosen truth' (18), 'that only true we now intend' (21), 'think ye see the very persons as they were living' (25 f.). Cf. Cavendish, *Life of Wolsey*, 'prologue': 'lies' with 'a visage of truth', 'nothing more untrue', 'until the truth be known', 'true intelligence', 'untrue imaginations', 'most untrue', 'according to truth', 'their untruth', 'malicious untruth', 'I commit the truth to Him who knoweth all things'.

[6] *Hen. VIII*, I. iv.

[7] At the entry, rather, of the maskers, including the King: at I. iv. 49, *Drum and trumpet: chambers discharged.*

[8] The *Globe* evidently had the character of ultra-respectability.

[9] This statement requires some qualification (see p. 782), but there is no reason to suppose, with Lee (p. 448), that 'the players' books' and 'Shakespeare's original manuscripts' perished. Such a catastrophe to the King's men, and to the Poet in particular, would almost certainly have been mentioned. When the *Fortune* was 'burnt down, in two hours' on Sunday night 9 Dec. 1621, the players, we are informed, were 'quite undone' by the loss of their 'apparel and playbooks'.

had his breeches set on fire, that would perhaps have broiled him if he had not by the benefit of a provident wit put it out with bottle-ale.'[1]

The old Knight writes facetiously, with some sensitiveness as to the display of Court orders and dignities on the public stage. If he was not present, his informant was; and his information is confirmed and augmented from various contemporary sources. The mishap took place 'on St. Peter's day',[2] Tuesday 29 June, 'Burbage's company were acting the play of *Henry the Eighth*',[3] 'the house' was 'filled with people',[4] who had 'enough to do to save themselves',[5] 'having but two narrow doors to get out'.[6] 'A dwelling-house adjoining'[7] was consumed, apparently an ale-house,[8] whence perhaps the 'bottle-ale' mercifully at hand for the man in burning breeches. Ben Jonson was a witness to this Vulcan's 'mad prank'

> Against the *Globe*, the glory of the Bank,
> Which though it were the fort of the whole Parish,
> Flank'd with a ditch and forc'd out of a marrish,
> I saw with two poor chambers taken in
> And razed ere thought could urge this might have been!
> See *the World's*[9] ruins! nothing but the piles
> Left.[10]

A few other details, and amusing references to Burbage, Condell, and Heminge, and probably Armin (as chief Fool in the company), are given in a ballad, entitled *A Sonnet upon the Pitiful Burning of the Globe playhouse in London*. It is an example of the use of the ballad, sung and printed, as a means for the spread of news.[11] It well deserves quoting:

> Now sit thee down, Melpomene,
> Wrapp'd in a sea-coal robe,
> And tell the doleful tragedy
> That late was played at *Globe*.

[1] *Reliquiae Wottonianae*, 425 f. [2] Chamberlain to Winwood, iii. 469.

[3] Thomas Lorkin to Sir Thomas Puckering at Venice, 30 June. *Harl. MS.* 7002, f. 268. [4] Stow-Howes, *Annals*.

[5] Lorkin. [6] Chamberlain. [7] *Ib.* [8] See p. 783.

[9] This recalls Kemp's allusion to the *Globe*, p. 521.

[10] 'Execration upon Vulcan' (*Underwoods*, lxi. 129–35).

[11] Two ballads on the subject were entered at Stationers' Hall on 30 June (Arber, iii. 528). The second, *A Doleful Ballad of the General Ouerthrowe of the famous theater on the Banksyde called the Globe*, by William Parrat, may be the 'Sonnet' quoted above.

For no man that can sing and say
Was scaréd on St. Peter's day.
  O sorrow, pitiful sorrow,
  And yet 'All this is True'.[1]

All you that please to understand,
Come listen to my story,
To see Death with his raking brand
'Mongst such an auditory,[2]
Regarding neither Cardinal's might,
Nor yet the face of Henry Eight:
  O sorrow, &c.

This fearful fire began above,
A wonder strange and true,
And to the stage-house did remove
As round as tailor's clue,
And burned down both beam and snag,
And did not spare the silken flag:
  O sorrow, &c.

Out run the Knights, out run the Lords,
And there was great ado;
Some lost their hats, and some their swords—
Then out ran Burbage too:
The reprobates, though drunk on Monday,[3]
Pray'd for the Fool and Henry Conday:
  O sorrow, &c.

The periwigs and drumheads fried,
Like to a butter firkin,
A woeful burning did betide
To many a good buff jerkin:
Then with swol'n eyes, like drunken Fleming's,
Distressed stood old stuttering Hemings:
  O sorrow, &c.

There are many more verses, in one of which is mention of the ale-house destroyed with the theatre. Armin ('the Fool', in the part of the Porter) and Condell seem to have been in some danger, salving, no doubt, properties and papers. The sketch, in a couple of lines, of 'old Hemings', with eyes inflamed by the smoke, standing and 'stuttering', is good. We welcome a glimpse of Burbage, running out of the building, energetic. Unfortunately there is no mention of Shakespeare. Did he take the role of Wolsey? Another not named is John Lowin,

[1] p. 781, and note 5.
[2] A distinguished audience.
[3] The previous day, 28 June.

who was instructed by Shakespeare, we are told, in the part of the King.[1]

Whatever Shakespeare's intentions of retirement at this time, Edward Alleyn left Southwark in October for Dulwich. He had probably given up acting since 1605 to devote himself to business, theatrical and other, of his own and his father-in-law, Henslowe. He made money by growing land-values, and purchased the manor of Dulwich, which he now made his home, after being a churchwarden of St. Saviour's in 1610. For many years Shakespeare and Alleyn had been neighbours under the shadow of the Cathedral.

§ 143. STRATFORD IN SHAKESPEARE'S LAST YEARS

BURNED out of the *Globe* the King's Men went on tour—into Kent, where we find them at Folkestone, and thence by Oxford to Shrewsbury.[2] Before or after this tour Shakespeare returned to Stratford.

His native town was much changed, in appearance and in personnel, since the Fires of 1594 and 1595. Handsome three-story houses replaced the old-fashioned dwellings. In 1613 the Poet would hardly recognize the Henley Street, Wood Street, Bridge Street, High Street, and Sheep Street of his youth. The outstanding features, however, were the same—the Avon and Bridge (with its 'causey'), Middle Row (little altered), the High Cross, Rother Market and the Mere, the Chapel and its group of buildings, the Church and its churchyard and College, St. Mary's House, and *New Place* (save that it was restored) wherein he might say—

I could be well content
To entertain the lag end of my life
With quiet hours.[3]

And if many old friends were gone, not a few remained, with their proud welcomes and congratulations; while his contemporaries occupied positions of affluence and trust.

[1] 'The part of the King was so right and justly done by Mr. Betterton, he being Instructed in it by Sir William [Davenant], who had it from Old Mr. Lowen, that had his Instructions from Mr. Shakespear himself' (Downes, *Roscius Anglicanus*, p. 24).

[2] J. T. Murray, i. 155.

[3] *1 Hen. IV*, v. i. 24.

His last brother, indeed, was dead. Richard Shakespeare was buried on 4 February 1613, not quite 39 years of age. We know even less of him than of his brother, Gilbert. Living in the old home in Henley Street was their sister, Joan, aged 44, with her husband, William Hart, the hat-maker, and their three sons, William, Thomas, and Michael, boys from twelve to four years old. In Henley Street resided the Poet's friend, William Shaw, glover, probably his father's old apprentice, now prosperous and on his way to be Master Shaw and 'gentleman'. He married (for his second wife) Alice Lane, on 22 April 1611, and had a child, christened William on 16 October 1613, to whom the Poet may have stood godfather. In Henley Street also, next the *Angel*, lived William Smith, a prosperous haberdasher, son to the Poet's godfather (as we have assumed) of the same name. Host of the *Angel* was Master Arthur Cawdrey. At the corner shop in Middle Row, facing the High Cross, dwelt Master Francis Smith, elder brother of William, a 'gentleman' of means and exceptional character, with his wife and daughter. He was Bailiff in 1603–4. He served a second time in 1614–15. He outlived Shakespeare.

Neighbour and friend of Francis Smith, and a kinsman of Shakespeare through Thomas Greene, was William Chandler. He seems to have come from Leicestershire,[1] with his infant son and a step-mother named Lettice, who married Thomas Greene. He set up as a mercer in the *Cage* in High Street, and on 8 November 1603,[2] being a widower, he married Elizabeth Quyney, the daughter of the late Richard Quyney, Shakespeare's friend, thus linking the Quyney and Shakespeare connexions. He was elected a Burgess in 1608, and when Chamberlain in 1611 was commissioned by the Council to 'assay to procure Master John Price of Harvington to be Underschoolmaster'. He was then *generosus*. In January 1614 he purchased an interest in the tithes of Old Stratford, Welcombe, and Bishopton, and in March he was made an Alderman in place of John Sadler the second. As an Alderman of the Corporation and an interested party in the tithes, and as a devoted follower of his step-father, the Town Clerk, he was conspicuous in opposition to the enclosure of the

[1] His son was born in Leicestershire in 1600: see p. 871.

[2] *Register*, p. 21.

commons by the Combes. He figures largely in Greene's 'diary'.[1] He lived to send a son to Oxford.[2]

In Wood Street were Abraham Sturley and William Parsons. Sturley never recovered, financially, after the Fire of 1594; but he stood high in the estimation of his fellow townsmen. He was Thomas Greene's deputy as Steward of the Court of Record, had been active with his 'brother' Daniel Baker in obtaining the Charter in 1611, was excused his second bailiwick in 1612 on the ground of 'unability', otherwise his lack of means, and was in failing health when Shakespeare entered on his period of retirement. His sons, Henry and Richard, on leaving Oxford took orders, and were clergymen in the neighbourhood of Stratford, Henry at Broadway, Richard at Alcester. After eleven successive absences from 'halls' (most unusual with him) Sturley, early in 1614, sold his interest in the Wood Street property to a farrier, John Ingram. His last recorded attendance at the Council was on 30 July, and he died the month following. We read in the burial register,

August 28 M[agiste]r Abrahamus Sturley, gener[osus].

He was probably interred in the Hill tomb in the Church. His widow, Anne Hill, survived him more than twenty years.

William Parsons had a struggle after the Fire of 1594. What became of his son, John, the student at Balliol, we are not informed. To help her housekeeping, Mistress Parsons took a boarder, Master Thomas Lucas, a lawyer and a member of Gray's Inn, a pronounced Puritan. When Parsons sued his tenant at Spernall, for non-fulfilment of contract, in 1607, and drew his lawyer-lodger into the case, the latter was offended and went to live with Master Sturley at the other end of Wood Street. On the departure, however, of Master Lucas a more welcome visitor succeeded. This was Michael Olney, his clerk, a kinsman probably of the Olneys of Tachebrook, who were gentlefolk. He lived with Mistress Parsons, and married her eldest daughter, Anne, whom we have supposed to be god-daughter to Mistress Shakespeare. They continued to reside in her parental home, and here their children were born in 1612 and 1614. Master Parsons served his second bailiwick in 1611–12. He had not

[1] p. 809. [2] p. 871.

changed since 1593. He opposed the Combes, as he had opposed Sir Edward Greville,[1] for encroachment on the Town rights. Thomas Greene records a conversation between him and William Combe, as reported by Parsons, on Sunday 2 April 1615:

> Master Combe questioned him why he was so against the enclosure at Welcombe; and he said, as Master Baker had said to him, they were all sworn men for the good of the Borough and to preserve their inheritances; and therefore they would not have it said in future time that they were the men which gave way to the undoing of the Town.[2]

Parsons was at that time High Alderman and a Magistrate. With the exception of old Thomas Barber, he was senior member of the Council. On Barber's death in August he became, for a few months, Father of the Corporation. By 1 January 1616 he made up his mind to retire to Spernall. He sold the lease of his house in Wood Street to Michael Olney for £70, and on 19 April, four days before Shakespeare's death, he attended for the last time in the Old Gild Hall, a few yards from *New Place*. On 26 June it was resolved that 'for so much as Master William Parsons is removed forth of this Borough to dwell at Spernall', he 'be amoved from the office of an alderman, and is discharged of any further attendance in this place'.

Below the *Cage* in Fore Bridge Street lived Shakespeare's nephew, Richard Hathaway, the baker. Had he been an apprentice of Thomas Allen, baker, whose Will he signed and wherein he was appointed an overseer, on 13 December 1612? The schoolmaster, Aspinall, signed the Will with him, and probably was the writer thereof. The document reveals the fact that the vicar, 'Master Rogers preacher', owed the testator 33*s.* 4*d.*, a very large amount if for bread; and that Master Richard Lane of Bridgetown owed him 'lent money' (money lent) '52*s.*, more in horse-breads 8*s.* 6*d.*, in bread for his own table 18*s.* 6*d.*', and money 'lent to his son, Edward', of late a student at Oxford, 10*s.* The largest debt, and it is to be feared a bad one, was from 'Master Bushell for bread, £6 17*s.* 0*d.*' This was 'Harry Bushell gentleman', who matriculated at Oxford in 1598 when he was sixteen, the son of a Gloucestershire gentleman, probably of Cleeve, and seems, like Edward Lane, to have

[1] p. 670. [2] Ingleby, *Shakespeare and the Welcombe Enclosures*, p. 9.

left the University without a degree. In 1610, aged 28, he married a cousin of Edward Lane—Mary, the seventeen-year-old daughter of Master John Lane of Bridge Street, sister of a young gentleman, John Lane, junior, who was shortly to bring himself into disgrace by defamation of Shakespeare's daughter, Mistress Hall. Harry Bushell ran up a very much larger account at the Quyneys' in High Street. He was a kinsman, perhaps brother, of Eleanor Bushell, whom Adrian Quyney (eldest son of Mistress Quyney and her late husband, Alderman Richard Quyney), aged 27, married in May 1613. Eleanor died in November 1616, and Adrian followed her to the grave eleven months later. Harry Bushell then owed him £40, which was inventoried as 'uncertaine to be gott'.[1] Then Bushell died in July 1618, when his age was 36, to be followed by his young wife in January 1625, aged 32. Drink had to do with this tragic mortality—how much we cannot say.

It is a pleasure to return to Richard Hathaway. Old Allen in his Will directed that 'Richard Hathaway shall see the building, which as yet is not finished on Sir Thomas Puckering's ground (which I am in possession of) according to the lease performed, out of that part of the corn which is amongst us, that is to say, Richard Hathaway, Francis Ainge, and myself'. Ainge was a baker, in Back Bridge Street, and the three men apparently had stores of grain in a common barn.

Hathaway's wife bore him a daughter, an only child, baptized on 18 October 1608 and named after his mother, Isabella. In September 1614 he was elected a Burgess, and the same month a Constable of his ward. Further evidence of his character and standing is his election as a Churchwarden at Easter 1616. He held this position on his illustrious uncle's burial in the Church in April 1616.

Below the *Cage* in High Street dwelt Sturley's 'brother', Daniel Baker. He was a forcible and influential person, leader of the ultra-puritan party in the borough, narrow-minded and pugnacious, and very different from the Puritan of a previous generation. He objected to plays and may-poles, and to old Master Barber, whom he would have had removed from the

[1] Worc. Prob. Reg. 1617, 174^{b}. Another debt 'uncertaine to be gott' was 'by Sir Edward Grivell, xxx^{li}', the late grasping, bankrupt lord of the manor.

Council on the ground of his wife's Romanism; was antagonistic to Vicar Rogers (who had his failings) and was instrumental in his deprivation, and strongly supported his successor, the hot-tongued preacher, Thomas Wilson, whereby in May 1619 he gained the title of 'ancient leading hypocrite'. He excited antipathy in individuals, as in Master John Smith, ironmonger, nephew of the late Bishop Watson, and in Robert Ingram, fisherman, tenant of the waters below the Mill, who could hardly be restrained from thrusting his dagger into him. He 'had no more conscience', it was said, 'than a dog'. Rather he lacked humanity. His want of humour appears in his early drafting of his Will and ostentatious delivery of the same (a document of eight folio pages) to the Stratford Corporation to be kept for safety in the Town Chest. He had a son, his namesake, at Oxford, demy of Magdalen College from 1605 until 1611, whence he took his B.A. in 1609.[1] A testimonial to this scholar's 'progress in learning, civility, behaviour and other passages', when supplicating for his M.A., was signed at Banbury on 18 February 1612 by a distinguished company of Puritan divines, namely John Dodd, Robert Cleaver, Robert Harris, William Whateley, Henry Scudder, and Thomas Lydiat[2]—the famous poor savant commemorated by Johnson in his *Vanity of Human Wishes*,

> If dreams yet flatter, once again attend,
> Hear Lydiat's life and Galileo's end.[3]

Harris and Whateley, at least, were well known in Stratford as 'lecturers', or preachers of courses of Sermons before the Bailiff and his Brethren, and duly rewarded by them. Harris, born at Broad Campden in Gloucestershire, was educated at Magdalen College, Oxford, matriculating in 1597, at the age of 16, and taking his B.A. in 1601. His Puritan theology was acceptable to Sir Anthony Cope of Hanwell, where he preached after the deprivation of John Dodd in 1605. He married a sister of William Whateley, and thus had kinsfolk in Stratford. Whateley belonged to the Henley-Stratford clan, so sharply divided in religion, and was probably connected with the Henley-Stratford family of Baker. He was born in 1583 in Banbury, where his

[1] *Register of the University*, ii. 2. 269, 3. 283. [2] *Ib.* ii. 1. 38.

[3] 163 f. Born in 1572. Fellow of New College, Rector of Okerton, near Banbury, ranked in his time with Bacon, and died unrewarded in 1646.

father (or grandfather) had settled from Henley. He went to Christ's College, Cambridge, graduated in 1601, was incorporated B.A. of Oxford in 1602, proceeded to M.A. of Oxford in 1604, was appointed lecturer at Banbury this year or the next, and vicar early in 1611.

Opposite Daniel Baker in High Street, Stratford, dwelt Mistress Quyney, widow of the late Richard Quyney. Old Adrian had died in 1607, and she kept on the business with the help of her son, Adrian, who on 7 May 1613 married Eleanor Bushell. Her younger son, Thomas Quyney, had the tavern next door (36).

Below Daniel Baker's house were the new and handsome premises of Willy Walford (17 and 18), Mistress Quyney's half-brother. Their mother, Margaret Dickson of the *Swan*, had married Thomas Phillips, and on his death, in 1557, Edward Walford of Evenlode. Willy inherited a house in Chapel Street, next door to *New Place*, but lived and prospered as a woollen draper in High Street. He may have served his apprenticeship with George Badger in Sheep Street, whose eldest daughter, Anne, he married in 1595, when she was only sixteen. We have letters from him to Richard Quyney in London dated 17 October and 16 November 1598. Three days before the former his first child was christened, a few days before the latter his young wife had followed this child to the grave. He does not mention either event. With stoical repression, worthy of Brutus in his 'insupportable and touching loss', he opens the second letter thus: 'Master Quyney, with my most hearty commendations to you, hoping you are in good health *as we are all in Stratford*'—and plunges into business. There was grit in those Puritan folk, worthy of the Poet and his drama.

Walford's second wife was also Anne, daughter of William Ainge of Bishopton, whom he married about Christmas-time 1600. He was elected a Burgess on 2 September 1601, when Richard Quyney was chosen for a second time Bailiff, and he was present at the memorable meeting of the Council summoned on the day of Quyney's funeral, 31 May 1602. He served as Chamberlain from 1605 to 1607. His 'accompt' shows the business man rather than the scholar. On 21 April 1609 he was elected an Alderman in succession to old Master Rogers. He almost rivalled Rogers as a builder. His fine three-gabled dwelling still faces the house of Rogers opposite. He was Bailiff (as well as Churchwarden) in 1610–11, and the Buck Feast was held in his handsome abode on New Year's Day 1611. In the rent-roll of 1614 the house is entered as in the possession of 'William Walford gentleman, a messuage by him of late newly builded'.

Walford took a leading part, as we shall see, in resistance to the Combes. He and Chandler, spade in hand, threw down the 'ditches' or mounds which their men were erecting, to the exclusion of 'commoners', at Welcombe, and suffered assault in December 1614. He was associated with Shakespeare's friend, Henry Walker, as Bridge Warden in 1616–17, was again Churchwarden in 1617–18, and a second time Bailiff in 1620–1. He died in May 1624, one of the richest men in Stratford.

Alderman Thomas Rogers had left his mark on the town as a wealthy butcher and maltster, the builder of at least one beautiful house, a devoted Borough Councillor, 'gentleman', and father of a very notable family. He had signed in 1604, with a shaky hand, the testimonial on behalf of the elementary Schoolmaster, Thomas Parker. His daughter, Katharine, married Robert Harvard at Stratford on 8 April 1605. Harvard lived in Southwark, near the *Globe* theatre, and in St. Mary Overy's was christened his son, John Harvard, on 29 November 1607—a month before the burial there of Shakespeare's brother Edmund. This child became famous as the founder of Harvard University. In August 1608 Rogers lost his wife Alice; and on 12 April 1609, after nearly a year's absence, he attended his last Council meeting, doubtless to request that he might resign. On the 21st it was agreed 'that Master Thomas Rogers, by reason of his great age and his grown unable through infirmity to bear the office of Alderman, be, *with great allowance of his good desert of this place*, amoved from this office'.

The old man's merits (and those of the delinquent) helped his son-in-law, John Wilmore's return to the Corporation. Wilmore's name, it will be remembered, was removed in 1603 from the list of Burgesses for a false declaration respecting his apprenticeship. From 1605 until 1609, however, he served as a Churchwarden, and in February 1610 he was re-elected a Burgess. He was Chamberlain in 1613–14. On 3 January 1611 Rogers's youngest daughter, Frances (who was barely seventeen), married William Harvard of Southwark, the brother of her sister's husband, Robert. On 20 February Thomas Rogers was buried at Stratford,[1] as 'one of the Aldermen', that is, with aldermanic honours within the Church. He was succeeded in his beautiful house by his son, Thomas Rogers the younger.

At the corner of High Street and Sheep Street lived the Poet's friend, Hamlet Sadler, in a new-built house which may have strained his resources. Glimpses of him and his wife, Judith, in the Sturley–Quyney correspondence do not suggest affluent circumstances. She died in March 1614, and he sold his business and the lease of his house in August following. Shakespeare left him 26*s.* 8*d.* for a memorial ring in 1616. He survived the Poet eight years, dying at the time of the Shottery epidemic in October 1624, within a few days of Fulke Sandells and Bartholomew Hathaway. His son William, probably Shakespeare's godson, we shall note later.[2]

In High Street was the shop of Philip Rogers the apothecary.[3] He sold confections and concoctions of many kinds, including some powerful purgatives. Men's lives were sometimes saved by evacuation, if they survived it. He sold also 'tobecka' and pipes and ale. A patient feeling sore after a dose of 'diagredium' or 'corrosive sublimate' might purchase consolation on the premises. His pipe and a modicum of the soothing weed would cost him threepence—some three shillings in our money. We are not told that Rogers went in 'tattered weeds' or had 'overwhelming brows', but he was frequently in financial difficulty, notwithstanding his lease from Master Richard Lane of five cottages, which he sublet to poor inhabitants.[4] We have noticed his indebtedness to Master Shakespeare.[5] He owed Master Daniel Baker £8. It was a pity, some might think, he did not administer to Master Baker a compound like that poor Romeo swallowed. He had to do with doctors, was something of a doctor himself, owned a copy of Gale's *Chirurgerie* which he lent to one Valentine Palmes and had to recover at law, was once

[1] His Will was proved in London, 27 April, by his son Thomas, executor, but unfortunately it was not registered and the original is lost (*P.C.C.*, *P.A.*, April 1611).

[2] p. 897.

[3] Fripp, *Shakespeare's Stratford*, p. 36 f.

[4] 12 Jan. 1613/4.

[5] p. 620.

himself in the doctor's hands for an ulcer *in virga ipsius.* Master George Agar the surgeon undertook to cure him. He both cured him and sold him a cerecloth, and then sued him for payment. The cerecloth was for his daughter, Margaret, who died in 1609. Rogers had three other children, Thomas, Francis, and Rose. Thomas, born in 1598, probably studied under Aspinall and learned pharmacy in his father's shop before going to Oxford, where he described himself as *filius generosi conditionalis*, son of a gentleman bound in certain services. After seven years *in studio et praxi chirurgiae duas anatomias et tres curationes*, he obtained the testimonials of three resident doctors in the University, and on 12 December 1635 was licensed *ad practicandum per universam Angliam.*[1]

In High Street also resided the Poet's friend, Henry Walker, with his little son, William, the Poet's godson, aged 5 in 1613. And round the corner from High Street, at the rebuilt *Shrieve's House* in Sheep Street, lived Henry Walker's sister, Elizabeth Rogers, widow of William Rogers, Serjeant-at-the-Mace. This edifice was not altogether destroyed by the Fire of 1595: 'the greater part of a tenement in Sheep Street in his possession having been destroyed by fire' are the terms of the new lease to Rogers in October 1595. A year later he had reconstructed and enlarged it. Then he died, in January 1597. The widow kept the house as a tavern and prospered, bringing up a son and four daughters. Her daughter, Elizabeth, baptized 15 April 1582, interests us. On 13 October 1613 she married a friend of the Halls, Master Matthew Morris. After Shakespeare's death, his house in the Blackfriars, London, was transferred on 10 February 1618, in accordance with the terms of his Will, to trustees, who were John Greene, of Clement's Inn and Bridge Town, and Matthew Morris of Stratford 'gentleman'. If the Poet was in Stratford in October 1613, we can hardly doubt that he attended the wedding. The names of the children born of the union confirm the friendship between the two families. Susanna was baptized on Sunday, 21 August 1614, a second Susanna on All Hallows' 1616, Elizabeth on 9 September 1618, John on 6 December 1620, Matthew on 23 July 1623. Elizabeth and Matthew are the names of the parents; Susanna and John, the names which

[1] *Register*, II. i. 125.

have the priority, are those of Shakespeare's daughter and her husband, Mistress Susanna and Doctor John Hall. When Widow Rogers died, in that fatal year 1624, she made Matthew Morris executor, and her 'well-beloved brother' Henry Walker and 'loving cousin' John Greene the lawyer, overseers of her Will. She bequeathed the house and residue of her property to the Morrises and their children, who no doubt were living with her.

The *Shrieve's House*, then, has an attraction for us beyond its venerable and picturesque structure. It was rebuilt, in the days of Shakespeare's 'reparation' of *New Place*, by his friend's sister and her husband, and inhabited in his last years by trusted friends of his daughter and son-in-law. He must have known it within and without—have knocked at the 'entry' and sat in the 'hall', or making his way through the yard, have climbed the staircase, looked through the glass 'going up', approved of the lifting of the floors and ceilings, and on one occasion at least, joined in 'a good man's feast'.

George Badger and Nicholas Barnhurst, the old rivals in Sheep Street in woollen drapery and religion, had parted. Both had suffered from the Fires, and from ill-temper. Badger was Chamberlain in June 1596 when Barnhurst called him 'knave' and 'rascal'. Nothing could be more offensive to the officer responsible for the Borough finances, and only Barnhurst's apology saved him from expulsion from the Council. After presenting his 'accompt' as Chamberlain in January 1597, Badger absented himself. He refused to return. In July he was fined £5 for absence. He still refused. In September he was fined £10 for declining the Bailiwick. Catholics could be as 'obstinate' as Puritans. In January 1598 it was resolved that he should 'no longer be one of the aldermen, for that he will not be ordered by the statutes'. It was a short-lived triumph, however, for Barnhurst. His turn followed. In 1599 he was 'removed' out of the Corporation 'for his great abuse' of the same. He went to live in Warwick. And here in 1606 the greatest of his troubles befell him. His second wife, Millicent, 'was shamefully murdered in her own house by one Richard Elliot'. So we read in the register of St. Nicholas Church, which records her burial on Sunday, 7 September. What became of Alderman Shakespeare's old comrade in recusancy after this tragic event, we have no sure

THE SHRIEVE'S HOUSE
SHEEP STREET, STRATFORD-UPON-AVON

evidence. He paid his rent for the Sheep Street houses for the last time in 1609. He may have retired to his native place, and been the 'Nicholas Bannister de Henley' who was buried at Wootton Wawen on 5 March 1616.

No longer a member of the Stratford Council, Badger left fewer traces of his stormy career. What we have, however, are characteristic. He was said (as was William Parsons) to be 'outlawed', and one debtor at least refused him payment as a consequence of the rumour. More convincing was the discovery that a 'cloak-bag' of 'massing relics' had been sent to him in Stratford from Northbrooke, by way of Clopton House, at the time of Gunpowder Plot (November 1605). Eight years later he was in prison in Warwick, whence he wrote a remarkable letter to his 'good friend', the Town Clerk of Stratford, Shakespeare's kinsman, Thomas Greene:

Worshipful Sir,

I humbly commend me unto you, with desire of your good health.

May it please you, of late one William Slater, as I take it as yet of Stratford, came unto the place where I am, to release William Reynolds of Stratford, and brought with him into the place a very large skin of parchment. One of his acquaintance demanded of him what use he would put that skin unto. His secret speeches were, unto the party, that it was to set down many interrogatives of *great abuses that were committed* in Stratford by Master Baily, Master Alderman, and the rest of his Brethren, with other great abuses suffered in the town of Stratford by *the idle life and conversation of the Company*.

Now, if it may please you, though I am not of the place yet I love the place; and I thought it good to acquaint your worship with the speeches. And you, if it please you to acquaint Master Baily and Master Alderman, with the rest of the Brethren, with the speeches, I would entreat of you not to signify unto all the Company who it is that hath made known so much unto you; for it may be that I shall know more hereafter of the party that did tell me of these speeches.

So leaving myself unto your good considerations, I humbly take my leave of you.

From my uncomfortable being, Warwick, the second of October anno 1613. Your worship's to command to my poor power,

George Badger.

Of William Reynolds, a friend of Shakespeare, we shall see something shortly. He was a Catholic, and in Warwick jail with Badger for recusancy. William Slater (Slaughter), who came to offer security for his release, was an old Catholic recusant of 1592, a wheelwright in Rother Market, ever ready with his hammer for the Puritan Corporation of Stratford. The Bailiff and Head Alderman at the time of this effort to obtain evidence, undoubtedly slanderous, of their 'idle life and conversation', were Daniel Baker and good John Gibbs, Slater's well-to-do neighbour in Rother Market. Badger had small faith in Slater, and was not willing that the Council should be libelled, to which, though no longer a member, he was warmly attached. His information probably exposed the detractor to the searching scrutiny of the Town Clerk. In the minutes of the 'hall' held 5 December 1616 we read, in Greene's handwriting:

It is agreed that articles and a petition be provided against William Slater, since he is a common troubler and breaker of good order.'

In 1613 Richard Tyler still resided in Sheep Street. Had he continued a member of the Corporation we might have followed step by step his advancement in prosperity and social status. He was allowed to resign in 1594, and from this date until his death in 1635 we have but tantalizing glimpses of this interesting friend of the Poet. His children who lived were Richard, Susanna, Frances, Elizabeth, Esther, and William. The last, who was baptized 14 October 1607, and a previous William,[1] probably had Shakespeare for godfather. On 12 May 1607 Tyler came to blows with the contentious Thomas Lucas.[2] On 11 May 1611 he buried his wife, who had braved so much for his love.[3] He did not marry again. Shakespeare calls him 'Master Richard Tyler the elder' in his Will, January 1616.[4] Richard the younger was then in his twenty-fourth year.

Before we leave Sheep Street, we will look in on the old shoemaker, John Jordan.[5] It was said of him by a Romanist critic, 'F.S.', who may have been Master Francis Smith of Shottery Manor, that he was a 'cobbler turned divine'.

The Catholics, if few, included influential parishioners, among them Master and Mistress Reynolds and their son, Shakespeare's friend, William. Early in 1604, after the death of Queen Elizabeth, when Romanist hopes for a moment revived to lapse into desperation, a priest found refuge with the Reynoldses from

[1] Baptized 9 July 1598, *Register*, p. 60.
[2] *Misc. Doc.* xii. 93.
[3] *Register*, p. 81.
[4] See p. 823.
[5] Buried 23 Jan. 1620. *Ib.*, p. 98.

savage pursuers. Report of the runaway reached the Town Clerk, Thomas Greene, then resident at *New Place*, who immediately, on 14 January, held an inquiry. The Jesuit father was disguised in unbecoming attire—green round hose, white stockings, and high-heel'd shoes—and moreover had fallen in the mud, and ran down the street in great haste, threatening to overthrow a boy in his path. He stopped at Master Reynolds's door, laying his hand on the 'cheek-post'—whether in Corn Street or Old Stratford is not stated.

John Combe in his Will of January 1613 made bequests to Master and Mistress Reynolds and their six children. Reynolds, however, died before Combe, being buried in the chancel of the Parish Church on 8 September 1613. Combe was buried in the same place on 12 July 1614. Shakespeare probably attended both funerals. Widow Reynolds was on friendly terms, notwithstanding religious differences, with Master Thomas Greene and his wife, Lettice. Their dwellings in Old Stratford were within a few yards of each other in the Church Way: now a well-paved thoroughfare but still beset by noisy crowds at Fair-time. Greene refers to Mistress Reynolds in his diary under dates 28 and 29 March, and 3 and 19 April 1615 in connexion with the Combe enclosures to which she was opposed. She was in his house on 29 March, with Shakespeare's attorney, Francis Collins. On 3 May she was in her grave, within the chancel of the Church, by the side of her well-beloved husband. Her Will, of 2 May, was witnessed by Shakespeare's son-in-law, Doctor Hall, no doubt her medical attendant; by Shakespeare's cousin, John Greene, probably her lawyer; by William Barnes of Clifford Chambers, esquire, step-father to Michael Drayton's friend, Sir Henry Rainsford; and last but not least, old Master Barber of the *Bear*. She appointed Hall and Greene overseers, and her son, William, executor. Three months after her funeral in Stratford, William, in his fortieth year, married. His wife was Mistress Frances de Bois. The wedding, which took place at Clifford Chambers, on 3 August, was probably attended by the Poet. In his Will of March 1616 Shakespeare left to William Reynolds, gentleman, 26*s.* 8*d.* to buy him a ring.

In Corn Street, opposite to *New Place*, lived Master William Court the lawyer. His office, the old gatehouse, had been 'burned to the ground' in the Fire (which spared *New Place*) of 1594; but it was reported 'newly re-edified and tiled' in April 1599. He occupied it until his death in 1634. Few inhabitants can have been more familiar to Shakespeare than Master Court. He had a son, William Court junior.

Above *New Place* the Poet had old neighbours—George Perry, Widow Tomlins, Julyne Shaw, and Henry Norman. Perry, a glover, we have seen before. Widow Tomlins was the relict of John Tomlins, a tailor, who succeeded Master Walter Roche as tenant in 1596. Tomlins interests us for his suit against the Poet's uncle, Henry Shakespeare of Ingon, in the autumn of 1596. Julyne Shaw interests us as a signatory of the Poet's Will, and a leading fellow-townsman worthy of his friendship.

From Henley Street, Julyne Shawe, wooldriver and maltster, followed Shakespeare to Corn Street, taking a lease in 1597 of the house recently occupied by Robert Gibbs, the Serjeant-at-the-Mace, two doors from *New Place*. It was reported in 1599 to be of 'two bays on the street tiled, on the back side a barn, a deep lean-to thatched, a cross back-house of two bays thatched and a garden as long as Tomlins' '—that is, it stretched to the boundary of the Poet's 'great garden'. The premises in the rear were considerable, housing the wool and the malt; but the dwelling was of very modest dimensions, consisting of a hall, a parlour bed-chamber, a little chamber, a kitchen, a cellar, and, over the hall, a 'great chamber'. The furniture is known to us very much as Shakespeare saw it. In the hall were two tables, a cupboard, eight stools, two chairs, two 'low-stools' (such as Volumnia and Virgilia sat on in *Coriolanus*), a halbert (carried by Master Shaw when he did duty as Headborough), a pair of bellows, a lantern, and pot-hooks. The kitchen, among other things, held a great brass kettle, brass pots, a brass basting ladle, a brass mortar and pestle; an old warming pan, a flagon, candlesticks and a basin of pewter; platters, a pie-plate, porringers, salad dishes, a double and single salt, trencher-plates, spits, a flesh fork, an *aqua vitae* bottle; the 'little chamber' had a bedstead and a truckle-bed (such as Mercutio slept on—

I'll to my truckle-bed:
This field-bed is too cold for me),

which was on wheels, to be pushed under the bedstead (or

standing bed), with their bedding, a mat and cover, curtain and coffer. The 'chamber over the hall' was a dining-room as well as the principal sleeping-chamber. Here was the 'best joined-bedstead' (with a truckle-bed) which Mistress Shaw inherited from her first husband, Arthur Boyce, with a down-bed (worth 50*s.*). Here were five green curtains, a green carpet, a green rug, another curtain of green, a wainscot chair, a handsome wainscot chest (another inheritance of Mistress Shaw as Widow Boyce), a court cupboard, a long dining-table (worth 46*s.* 8*d.*), twelve joined-stools, and six Turkey-cushions. Here also, or in the parlour, were linen (valued at £5 10*s.* 0*d.*), silver (a bowl, another bowl gilt, and ten spoons, valued together at £7), a basin and ewer of pewter, a close-stool, a looking-glass, a trunk, a box, and a 'pin-chest', with apparel, including Mistress Shaw's riding-cloak and 'safe-guard', worn when she mounted her husband's gelding behind him.

In and from this comfortable little abode Julyne Shaw (without children) fulfilled the functions of a rising member of the Borough Council. He was elected a Burgess in 1603, in place of John Wilmore, when the latter was 'put out' for false declaration of his apprenticeship. His 'Accompt' as Chamberlain, presented in 1611, might satisfy Alexander Aspinall. It is a full document, the chief items are dated, the writing is excellent, the spelling is consistent and marks an approach to Biblical standard. The author will not be regarded as uneducated because he drops the letter *e* at the end of *George* and adds it at the end of *buck*. Shakespeare would not find fault with Shaw's orthography. In 1613 he was made an Alderman. The terms of his appointment in Master Greene's minute of 4 January are an extraordinary testimony to his character:

> The Aldermen, much approvyng his well-deservynges in this place, have, for his honesty, fidelity and good opinion of him, chosen Julins Shawe to be an Alderman.[1]

He was elected in place of that esteemed member, just deceased, Master John Smith, ironmonger, nephew of the late Bishop of Winchester. Then followed his Bailiwick. From 6 October 1615 (when he was sworn, and after presided at the Buck Feast, the buck being presented by Sir Philip Sidney's old

[1] *Council Book B*, 239.

friend, Sir Fulke Greville, the recorder, now of Warwick Castle) until Friday 4 October 1616 he was chief magistrate of the borough. He was present at many 'halls', had arduous duties, and was diligently supported by his Head Alderman, Daniel Baker, and by the Town Clerk, Thomas Greene. The Council were engaged in collecting for the victims of a serious fire in 1614 which devastated a part of Sheep Street, and resisting the right of Master William Combe, this year High Sheriff, to enclose the commons at Welcombe. They lost an experienced supporter in William Parsons, and were not helped by the advice or manners of their hot-headed counsel, Thomas Lucas. Of Lucas it was said that he had 'no religion in him', but Baker probably found him a man after his heart.

Next to *New Place*, in the last eight years of the Poet's life, resided Henry Norman, with his wife, Joan (daughter of William Ainge of Bishopton), and four children. Norman leased the house from Willy Walford and occupied it until his death in 1635. His relations with Doctor John Hall were close, not to say intimate.

The Chapel Quad, a few yards from *New Place*, was still occupied, though no longer dominated by Master Alexander Aspinall. Not that he had ceased to be a dominating person. In 1611 the names of seventy-two leading inhabitants, including Shakespeare, were presented as having paid their contribution to the charge of prosecuting a Bill in Parliament for the better repair of the Highways. The list, apparently, was drawn up by the Town Clerk's brother, Master John Greene, who mischievously enters the Schoolmaster (it can only be he) as 'Great Philip Macedon'. He may have acquired this nickname as in constant need of the reminder, 'Thou art a man mortal'. Of the Prince of Macedonia the Latin-English dictionary in Stratford School (Eliot-Cooper) said he was 'so excellent' in 'language and utterance as neither readiness of tongue wanted fine ornaments of eloquence, neither flowing speech sharp invention of witty matter'. This recalls Holofernes.

'Great Philip' was capable, and whatever Richard Wright[1] thought of his teaching, he prepared a lengthy succession of youths for the University. But in 1611 he terminated his lease

[1] Aspinall's assistant, 1608–12. His allegations about Aspinall's teaching were referred by the Council to the Vicar, 20 May 1608.

of the 'Priests' House' and his undivided sway in the Chapel precinct. The dwelling was converted into a vicarage for Master Rogers. Side by side lived Vicar and Schoolmaster in the quiet court; and opposite in the old *camera* and rooms above the Council Chamber lived their assistants, the curate and the usher. These in 1613 were young men fresh from Oxford, Edward Wilmore *alias* Brocke of Oriel and All Souls, and Richard Watts of Jesus.

In 1614 Aspinall succeeded Sturley as Deputy Town Clerk to Thomas Greene, and was 'amoved' from his aldermanship in flattering terms:[1]

> Master Aspinall, with most worthy commendations of his continual and faithful service, secrecy, fidelity and diligence, with exceeding and hearty thanks by this Company to him for his very many and great pains taken in the affairs and for the good of this borough, is, at his earnest request, discharged from the office of an alderman; and he is now by a common consent of courtesy (in regard he is an ancient Master of Art, and a man learned, and Schoolmaster of the King's Free School) placed in the first place amongst the Chief Burgesses.

We have this resolution in his own handwriting, and no doubt it was drawn up by himself. He was still 'Holofernes', as when twenty-eight years previously he framed the following receipt for his salary, a model of fussy long-windedness:

> *Sexto die Novembris anno Domini 1585 et Regni Regine Elizabethe vicesimo septimo.* Witnesseth that I, Alexander Aspinall, Schoolmaster of the Free School in Stratford-upon-Avon, have received of George Bardell, Chamberlain of the same town, at four several payments, that is to wit, every quarter Five Pounds, the whole and full sum of Twenty Pounds: due to be paid to the foresaid Alexander as Schoolmaster by the said George as Chamberlain, from the feast of Saint Michael the Archangel in the year of the Lord 1584 until the said feast of Saint Michael next after in the year of our Lord 1585, being the first year of his Chamberlainship: which said sum of £20 I acknowledge myself to have received, and for that year do acquit the said Chamberlain by these presents. In witness whereof I, the said Alexander Aspinall, to this mine acquittance have put to my hand the day and year above written. By me, Alexander Aspinall.

In such terms, and similar, should money be receipted, and 'continual and faithful service, secrecy, fidelity and diligence' be acknowledged.

Vicar Rogers was not flattered by the Corporation. He

[1] *Council Book B*, 259.

succeeded, as he preceded, a remarkable man, and was himself very noteworthy, but he was not favoured latterly by the 'chiefs' of the Council or of his congregation.

Richard Byfield, who followed Bromhall in 1597, and preceded Rogers, was the father of scholars and preachers. His eldest son, Nicholas, studied at Exeter College, Oxford, and became assistant to Aspinall in 1604. He took orders, and preaching in St. Peter's, Chester, on his way to Ireland about 1608, was invited to be 'preacher' there and consented. He was Vicar of Isleworth from 1615 until his untimely death at the age of 44 in 1622. His half-brother, Richard, was born in Stratford in September 1598. He went to Queen's College, Oxford, matriculating thence on 26 April 1616—the day after Shakespeare's funeral. Ejected from his rectory of Long Ditton by the Act of Uniformity, he died at Mortlake in 1664.

John Rogers was an old protégé of the Earls of Leicester and Warwick and disciple of Thomas Cartwright. From Byfield in Warwickshire he was presented to St. Nicholas, Warwick, in 1599. Thence he was instituted in Stratford in June 1605, where he was Vicar until after Shakespeare's death. No doubt he officiated at the Poet's funeral.

There were presbyterians *and* presbyterians, and Master Rogers seems to have been of the liberal wing. He had 'faults and failings' which exposed him to censure.

We must look at John Sadler—John Sadler the Second—before we pass to the Combes. We saw him last in 1594, father of four children. From the Corn Inquiry of 1595 we learn that besides his mills he had malt and barley, and was in household ten persons. He was then living in Rother Street, next door to Alderman Gibbs. He was elected an Alderman in 1598, and served as Bailiff in 1599–1600. He was Head Alderman to Richard Quyney in the latter's tragic term of office in 1601–2. His brother, Thomas, inheritor of the *Bear*, went to the wars in Ireland, and did not return. John took care of his children, and the widow was admitted to the Almshouse in 1601. In 1609 he lost his highly respected mother, Mistress Dickson of the *Swan*, and inheriting his father's house in Church Street, he occupied it—within a few yards of *New Place*. His second Bailiwick, which (as he professed, but his colleagues would not believe) his 'decayed estate' hardly permitted, fell in the year 1612–13. In February 1614 he was allowed to retire from the Corporation. He must have been happy in his children, who married into good families of the town and neighbourhood, as we shall see,[1] one of them linking the Sadler, Quyney, and Shakespeare connexions.

Of Master Thomas Combe of the College[2] we read in the Corn Inquiry of 1595 that he possessed '17 quarter of wheat and rye, 52 of barley and 7 of malt', and was 'of household fourteen'. He purchased the College in 1596, and bequeathed it, in his Will of 22 December 1608, to his wife, Mary, for thirty years 'if she shall so long live sole', and then to his elder son, William. Thomas Combe was buried 11 January 1609.

John Combe the bachelor, co-heir of Lawyer Combe of Warwick, made his Will 28 January 1613 and died July 1614. The Will was evidently drawn up by Collins. It begins:

> In the name of God, Amen. I, John Combe, of Old Stratford, gentleman, being both in perfect health and memory, God be thanked, do make my last Will and testament in manner and form following:
>
> First, I commend my soul to God my Maker, hoping and steadfastly believing that thorough the only merits of Jesus Christ, my alone Saviour and Redeemer, I shall, after this life ended, be partaker of the life everlasting; and my body to be buried in the parish church near to the place where my mother was buried.
>
> [He directs that] a convenient tomb of the value of three score pounds shall be within one year after my decease set over me.

The bulk of his estate he leaves to his nephew, Thomas Combe, the younger brother of William. Among his lands in Hampton Lucy are Ingon Grove and Parsons's Close *alias* Shakespeare's Close. The Poet's uncle, as we have seen, probably gave his name to the latter. Bequests include 'to Master William Shakespeare £5', 'unto Francis Collins the elder of Warwick £10', 'to Master Henry Walker 20*s*.', to Mistress Reynolds 'grounds called Salmon Tail' for her life and after to William Reynolds her son, 'unto Sir Francis Smith £5 to buy him a hawk, and to the Lady Anne his wife £40 to buy her a bason and ewer', 'to my god-daughter Gardiner £20', 'to every one of my god-children before not named 5*s*.', 'to a learned preacher 20*s*. to make a sermon twice a year at Stratford Church', to poor people 'ten black gowns every one worth 13*s*. 4*d*.', 'to the poor of Stratford

[1] p. 870.

[2] pp. 811, 823.

£20', and £100 to be lent 'unto 15 poor or young tradesmen', '20 nobles apiece for 3 years, paying 3*s.* 4*d.*' at Michaelmas and Lady Day.

Prominent in the Will is his half-brother, John, son of his father's second wife, Mistress Rose Clopton. He was thirty-five years of age and married, with children.

> I give and bequeath [we read] to my brother, John Combe, all that messuage or tenement wherein William Cawdrey *alias* Cooke now dwelleth situate in Warwick near and adjoining to the Gable there, [and] to the children of my brother, John Combe, £300 to be set forth to the best use, and the profit paid yearly to my said brother during his life to his own use and the bringing up of his children.

The Cawdreys of Warwick were kinsmen of the Cawdreys of Stratford and, like them, Catholics. William had been a recusant in 1592. His house was in the High Pavement. Shortly before his half-brother's death, John Combe the younger settled in Warwick, in the parish of St. Nicholas, where his daughter Mary was born in September 1613.

Bachelor John Combe's release in his Will of one shilling in the pound to his 'good and just debtors' did not save the old usurer from satire. On his tomb were 'fastened', some time before 1618, lines printed in that year as follows:

> Ten-in-the-Hundred must lie in his grave;
> But a hundred to ten whether God will him have.
> Who then must be interr'd within this tomb?
> 'Oh! oh!' quoth the Devil, 'my John-a-Combe'.[1]

The tomb, with recumbent effigy in a gown, by the Dutch sculptor, Gerard Johnson of Southwark,[2] stands in the north-east corner of the Chancel. At the foot of the inscription enumerating his charitable bequests, is the Latin *Virtus post funera vivit.*[3]

[1] Richard Brathwaite, *Remains*, 1618. Aubrey and Rowe give variant versions. Fane (Commonplace Book, p. 177) merely has the couplet:

> 'Hay, hay,' saith Tom Foule, 'who is in this tome?'
> 'Ho, ho,' quoth the Deuill, ' 'tis my John a Come.'

[2] *Dugdale's Diary* (Hamper, p. 99): 'Shakespeare's and John Combe's monuments were made by one Gerard Johnson.'

[3] Master William Knight of Banbury, who died in 1631, aged 73, had the following on his monument in St. Mary's:

> Virtus funera post vivit aeternum,
> Deteriora cadunt sed meliora vigent.

The doggerel verses above were ascribed in course of time to Shakespeare[1] (and Shakespeare could write doggerel as well as any when it suited his purpose). Others were attributed to the same source—as the impromptu epitaph for Combe's 'brother', apparently John the younger.[2] 'Offended' at the lines on the Stratford monument, he 'wished to know what Shakespeare would say upon him when he was gone; whereupon' the Poet 'said *extempore*',

Thin in beard but thick in purse;
Never a man beloved worse;
He went to his grave with many a curse;
And the Devil and he had both one nurse.[3]

1614–15

§ 144. THE CORPORATION FIGHT AGAIN FOR THEIR COMMONS

William Combe lost his head on his sudden accession of fortune. His uncle was scarcely in his grave when there was report of his intention to enclose the common fields of Welcombe. It proved true, and Thomas Greene as Town Clerk, on 5 September 1614, drew up as a precaution a list of the freeholders. At the head stands:

Master Shakespeare, four yardland, no common, nor ground beyond Gospel Bush, nor ground in Sandfield, nor none in Sloe Hill Field beyond Bishopton, nor none in the enclosure beyond Bishopton.

Next is the preparatory Schoolmaster:

Thomas Parker, in right of his wife, half a yardland, no land in Sandfield nor ground beyond Gospel Bush nor in Sloe Hill Field, but hath common over all the Fields.

Others are Master Lane, Sir Francis Smith, Macey, Arthur Cawdrey, and Master Richard Wright now curate of Bishopton.[4]

Farmers of the tithes—Shakespeare, Greene, Henry Smith, and many more—and leaseholders at Welcombe (such as old Alder-

[1] By a visitor to Stratford in 1634 (*Lansdowne MS.* 213, f. 332).

[2] The brother George lived at Alvechurch, and was apparently less affluent.

[3] *B.M. Add. MS.* 29, 264 f. (Collection by T. Ward for Continuation to 1830 of Dugdale's *Warwickshire*.)

[4] *Misc. Doc.* i. 94.

man Barber) were also interested. On 23 September, when Greene expressed his fears to the Council, they unanimously voted not to agree to any enclosure. Combe's intentions came out, but, save by Greene, were not taken very seriously. It must have seemed incredible that a young man, not yet eight-and-twenty, and merely *armiger*, could hope to succeed where Sir Edward Greville, the late lord of the manor, had failed. He proceeded, nevertheless, to square, as he thought, the chief parties concerned. On 28 October, by his agent, William Replingham of Great Harborough, he covenanted with Shakespeare to compensate him for any loss to his tithes. Greene's name was added in the agreement on the suggestion of Thomas Lucas, one of the witnesses. Shakespeare evidently regarded the matter lightly, though one evening at St. Mary's House he advised his kinsman to 'hold out for his tithes', in which he had just invested £300. Greene was in London and knew nothing of the agreement with himself and the Poet until some time later. On 12 November, when Aspinall deputed for him as Clerk, the Stratford Council agreed unanimously (save for Cawdrey) 'that all lawful means shall be used to prevent the enclosing that is pretended'. The resolution was communicated to Greene at the Middle Temple, who received it on the 16th in the afternoon. The previous day, he says, 'Against Whitehall Wall I met with Master Replingham; who promised to come to me at afternoon, saying I should be satisfied; and I asking him how the Town should be satisfied; he said he cared not for their consents.'[1]

Bringer of the Council's letter to Greene on the 16th was Alderman William Wyatt. In his presence Greene's clerk reported, after inquiry, that William Combe was not in London.[2] That day Shakespeare arrived in London from Stratford. Next morning Greene wrote:

My cousin Shakespeare coming yesterday to town, I went to see him how he did. He told me that they assured him they meant to enclose no further than to Gospel Bush, and so up straight, leaving out part of the Dingles to the Field, to the gate in Clopton Hedge and take in Salisbury's piece; and that they mean in April to survey the land, and then to give satisfaction and not before. And he and Master Hall say they think there will be nothing done at all.

Master Wyatt after noon told me that Master Combe had told Master

[1] *Diary*, f. 1.

[2] *Ib.*

Wright[1] that the enclosure would not be, and that it was at an end. I said I was the more suspicious, for those might be words used to make us careless. I willed him to learn what he[2] could, and I told him so would I.[3]

On 22 November Alderman Henry Smith from Stratford was in London. He, says Greene, 'told me that Master Wright told him that my Lord Carew would not agree to further any enclosure at Stratford but would rather hinder it if he could'.[4]

On 24 November Wyatt told Greene that Master Mannering —Arthur Mannering or Mainwaring, steward to Lord Chancellor Ellesmere—whom Combe had partly won over to cooperate with him, had said, 'that if he might not do it well &c, he cared not for enclosing, and cared not how little he did meddle therein'.

Greene had returned to Stratford by 3 December. With the Bailiff (Francis Smith, of the *Corner House* in Middle Row), High Alderman (William Parsons of Wood Street), Daniel Baker (of High Street), Julyne Shawe (Chapel Street), and William Chandler (of the *Cage*, High Street), he waited on Combe at the *College* on 9 December, to 'present the loves of the Company' and 'their hearty desires that he would be pleased to forbear further proceedings touching the enclosure, and to desire his love towards the Town as they shall study to deserve it'. To this courteous and friendly deputation, the young bully replied offensively—that it was Master Mannering's undertaking rather than his own, and he would not move him to stay it; that the Council would do well to pray for the continuance of the frost, for as soon as it broke Mannering would begin 'to hedge-in the enclosure'; and that the Council, by their stirring in the business, had made 'almost the greatest men of England' their enemies. Next day Replingham was in Stratford, and called at the *Bear* for Alderman Barber, and at *New Place* for Shakespeare. Greene followed him to these houses, and came upon him 'on the narrow side' (wherever that was), but 'he was not to be spoken with'. Shakespeare was still in London, where he

[1] Greene writes in haste and almost illegibly, for his private reading only, and makes mistakes. He has written 'Master Wright had told Master Combe', which is assuredly wrong.

[2] Greene's 'he' here might be read 'I'. He has a way of writing, in his haste, 'I' and 'he' indistinguishably.

[3] *Diary*, f. 1.

[4] *Ib.*

spent Christmas. On 15 December Greene urged 'that some course might be taken for staying the enclosure', and advised Aspinall and Baker 'what a commoner might do as touching throwing down of ditches', i.e. the hedge-mounds and their trenches. Bailiff Smith told him that day, in his shop at the top of Middle Row (where he was busy, it being Thursday, market-day), that he and Arthur Cawdrey (of the *Angel*) had taken a view of the land affected and found that 516 plots were under the plough. On 19th the frost had broken, and labourers under Combe's directions began 'a great ditch and bank', which by 10 January was 'at the least fifty perches in length' (275 yards). The Corporation immediately took action, communicating with local gentlemen—Master Thomas Spencer of Claverdon, whom Greene personally visited, *Custos Brevium* of the Court of Common Pleas, and father of Lady Lucy; Master Archer, Justice of the Peace; Master John Randall (that he might acquaint Sir Francis Smith of Wootton Wawen, lord of the manor of Shottery); Sir Henry Rainsford and Master Shakespeare. At their meeting on 23 December they 'almost all' (there were twenty-one aldermen and burgesses present) put their hands to a letter to the Poet. 'I also', says Greene, in his diary, 'writ of myself to my Cousin Shakespeare the copies of all our oaths made then, also a note of the inconveniences would grow by the enclosure.' They wanted his influential declaration and action against Combe. Unfortunately neither their letter nor his answer is extant. The rough draft of a letter the same day, similarly signed by the Company, to Mannering is preserved. They have heard that he would endeavour an enclosure at Welcombe, and entreat him in his 'Christian meditation' to bethink him of 'the great disabling' such enclosure would tend to, and the ruin of the Borough, 'wherein live about seven hundred poor which receive alms; whose curses and clamours will be daily poured out to God against the enterprisers of such a thing'.[1]

Incidentally we hear of Greene and Bailiff Smith, and others, being engaged one day (9 December) 'some four or five hours with the Overseers of the Poor'.[2]

The year 1614 closed with hard work and some anxiety,

[1] *Wheler MS*. i. 66.

[2] Greene's *Diary*, p. 3.

public and private, for the faithful Town Clerk. He wrote in his diary:

Heu! vivunt homines tanquam mors nulla sequetur,
Et velut informis fabula vana fide.
Mors certa est; incerta dies, hora agnita nulli;
Extremam quare quamlibet esse puta.
Fleres si scires unum tibi tempora mensem;
Rides cum non sit forsitan una dies.
Qui modo sanus erat nunc lecto egrotus adheret,
Estque cinis subito qui modo civis erat.[1]

His wife was near confinement. On 30 December her child, a boy, was baptized in the Church (a few yards from the house) and named after his father, Thomas.[2] On 1 January 1615, which was Sunday, Greene, 'after evening prayer', received in his study at St. Mary's House, the Bailiff, Head Alderman, Master Barber, and other members of the Council, to consider the legal opinion of one Master Gilbert respecting the enclosure.[3]

The digging went forward and Combe defied interference. When it was told him 'that some of the better sort would go to throw down the ditch, said he, O *would they durst!* in a threatening manner, with very great passion and anger'. He abused the Corporation, called them 'factious knaves', 'Puritan knaves', 'underlings in their colour', and declared he would do them 'all the mischief he could'. On 9 January Walford and Chandler, being 'commoners', went to throw down the 'ditch'. Calling first at St. Mary's House, Chandler informed his step-father of their purpose. 'Privately' they 'had sent on their spades before'. 'I advised', notes Greene, 'that they would go in such private manner as that none might see them go, lest others might perhaps follow in companies and so make a riot or a mutiny.' There was nothing on which the authorities were so sensitive

[1] 'Alas! men live as though no death will follow, and as if it were a hideous fable void of credit. Death is certain; uncertain is the day, the hour known to none; wherefore think any to be the last. Thou would'st weep if thou knewest thy time to be but a month; thou smilest when perchance it may not be a day. He that late was well now keeps his bed sick, and he of late a citizen is straightway a cinder.' *Mors certa est* is Englished by Shallow (*2 Hen. IV*, III. ii. 40–2). The lines *Fleres* . . . *Rides* . . . occur in St. Sebald's, Nuremburg, in an inscription in a side-chapel. Two lines follow:

Heu! quam nulla fides est et constantia rebus;
Nosse Deum vita est: cetera cuncta nihil.

[2] *Register*, p. 87.

[3] *Diary.*

(as Greene and Shakespeare knew) as 'a riot', and it was important that the 'assault' should be from Combe's side. The Aldermen, therefore, 'in the gentlest manner they could, endeavoured to hinder the malefactors from their unlawful digging', and were 'diversely assaulted' and 'wrongfully by force put from their lawful and rightful common' with 'riotous disorder'. The diggers, encouraged by Combe, who sat on his horse and laughed, closed with them and threw them to the ground.

But this collision with Justices of the Peace brought Combe, when he had time to reflect on it, to St. Mary's House. Greene notes:

About three of the clock after noon he came to me; willed me to propound a peace; promised me £10 to buy a gelding to do it; liked not amiss of a friendly suit to end it; willed me to move Sir Henry Rainsford; . . . threatened that within this twelvemonth all the Fields should be laid down greensward if they did not agree; . . . confessed that there was now about 600 lands to be laid down from arable to pasture, and that Sir Thomas Lucy promised he would help him to a lease of the tithes of ground adjoining for the falling of his lambs in yearning-times; . . . and after many promises and protestations that I should be well dealt withal, departed, and I brought him to the door.[1]

That evening a petition was drawn up by Walford, Henry Smith, and Chandler for presentation next day at the Warwick Assizes. There, however, it was agreed by the representatives of Combe and the Corporation, 'for the preventing of tumults and avoiding of meeting of the people', that 'ditching' on the one hand and ploughing on the other should be stayed until 25 March, and that the ditch set up should stand until then, save where it interfered with 'ways'.[2] In the meantime women and children gathered in force from Stratford and Bishopton, and throwing down the mounds, filled up the trenches. So easy was it to excite the exasperated working people against their oppressors.

On 11 January, Greene notes:

At night Master Replingham supped with me, and Master William Barnes was [there] to bear him company; where he assured me, before Master Barnes, that I should be well dealt withal, confessing former promises by himself—Master Mannering and his agreement for me with my Cousin Shakespeare.[3]

[1] *Diary.* [2] *Misc. Doc.* v. 18; *Diary.* [3] *Diary.*

This, apparently, was the first he heard of the agreement of 28 October: such little importance had Shakespeare attached to it. Proceedings were to be taken by both parties against the poor 'women-diggers' (of whom Replingham furnished names) to 'bind them to their good behaviour'—in spite of Greene's advice that the law should not be executed upon them. He knew the odium that would be visited upon the Corporation and upon himself, as Town Clerk, in particular.

Greene went to London for Lent Term (23 January–13 February), and was followed thither by Master Richard Tyler with a letter from Chandler, requesting subpoenas out of the Star Chamber against Master Combe and Master Anthony Nash and their principal diggers, John Terry of Welcombe, Stephen Sly of Stratford, and two more. Chandler concludes his letter:

> I purpose, by God's help, to be with you the next Tuesday at night myself [31 January]. I would entreat you, if you have not the note of remembrance that you took concerning Master Combe and other business [that is, his so-called *Diary*] at London already, then, I would entreat you, to write to my mother Greene [Mistress Lettice Greene at St. Mary's] that she may send you the note up to you by the next return of the carrier. Thus, being in haste, I humbly take my leave. Your son, in all duty, William Chandler, Stratford the xxvjth of January 1614. To my loving father, Thomas Greene esquire, at his chamber in the Middle Temple give these with all speed.[1]

Greene had returned to Stratford before 24 February when the Corporation, on his advice, decided to petition the Lord Chief Justice, Edward Coke, against the enclosure at the coming Assizes at Coventry. Thither he rode with it, and on 25 March presented it in Court; but Coke put it off until his sitting at Warwick. Here on the 28th his lordship ordered that no enclosure should be made, for that it was against the laws of the realm, by Master Combe or any other until he showed cause at open Assizes.

Combe took his defeat badly, avenging himself on poor commoners (impounding their sheep and pigs and railing on them at the plough), and on individual members of the Corporation like old Alderman Barber. His brother, Thomas Combe, who lived at Welcombe, and was his abettor in this enclosure business, actually beat and kicked Barber's shepherd on Meon.

[1] *Misc. Doc.* v. 151.

Barber's death this summer elicited from Shakespeare his disapprobation of the enclosure. The old man buried his wife, the Catholic Joan, on 10 August 1615. He died four days later, as we learn from the entry in Greene's note-book, '14 *Augusti* Master Barber died'. He was buried on the 15th.[1] At the next meeting of the Council, on 1 September, it was recorded, in Greene's handwriting,

At this Hall, for that it hath pleased Almighty God lately to take to his mercy Master Thomas Barber, an ancient alderman of this borough, Robert Butler, one of the Chief Burgesses, is chosen in his stead.[2]

A day or two afterwards follows the entry in Greene's note-book:

Septembris. M[3][aster] Shakespeare's telling J[ohn] Greene that he[4] was not able to bear the enclosing of Welcombe.

Then this:

5 *Septembris*. His[5] sending James for the executors of Master Barber to agree, as is said, with them for Master Barber's interest.[6]

Barber, it will be remembered, was a leaseholder of land in Welcombe.[7]

Greene would be grateful for the declared, as for the moral, support of his influential kinsman, in the renewed conflict, which he saw was inevitable, with the arrogant and wealthy young Squire of the College, who this year was elected High Sheriff of the County.

1613–16

§ 145. SHAKESPEARE'S LAST YEARS

SHAKESPEARE, who did not find Stratford sleepy, avoided its controversies and personalities. The latter, which sometimes grew out of the former, touched him once rather nearly. His elder daughter was slandered in a speech which may have owed

[1] *Register*, p. 88. [2] *Council Book B*, 290. [3] or W[illiam].

[4] *Diary*. Easily misread 'I'. It is Shakespeare's sentiment that is recorded. Why should Shakespeare tell John Greene, Thomas Greene's brother, what John Greene had long known and Shakespeare perfectly well knew was known to him? And why should Thomas Greene, in his confidential note-book, enter such an inane memorandum?

[5] Shakespeare's sending James (whoever he was).

[6] *Diary*. [7] pp. 807–11.

something to drink, something to anti-Puritan rancour. In June 1613 John Lane junior[1] 'reported' that Mistress Hall 'had the running of the reins' and 'had been naught with Rafe Smith at John Palmer's'. Rafe Smith, aged 35 (Susanna Hall was 30), son of the late Alderman John Smith, vintner and nephew of Hamlet Sadler, was a haberdasher (like his well-to-do uncles, Francis, William, Roger, and Henry Smith) and had a wife. Master Marshall had married him in Bishopton Chapel to Anne Court in 1604. We have noted his Bible among Marshall's books in 1607.[2] John Palmer was a gentleman of Compton, grandson of the late Alderman William Smith, Bishop Watson's brother-in-law. Lane, aged 23, was the son of Master John Lane, the Romanist with a taste for fine clothes, and nephew of Master Richard Lane of Bridgetown. His sister Margaret, aged 25, was the wife of Master John Greene, the Town Clerk's brother and Shakespeare's cousin. The 'defamation' was uttered in the hearing of Robert Whatcott, a friend of the Shakespeares (he was afterwards a signatory of the Poet's Will),[3] who duly related it, to the wrath and grief, we may believe, among others of the culprit's uncle, Master Richard Lane.

At this moment Richard Lane had reason for gratitude to the Shakespeare connexion. In ill-health (he died eight weeks later) he settled property on his son and daughter, appointing on 9 July Thomas Greene[4] and Doctor Hall their trustees.[5] The son, Edward, who matriculated at Oxford from Exeter College in 1605, *filius generosi aet. 16.*[6] (he was baptized at Alveston 5 February 1589), contemplated matrimony. Friendship prompted Doctor Hall to act in such capacity for the cousin of the young man who so grossly libelled his wife. Shakespeare would probably have treated the matter with contempt. Not so his son-in-law, who prosecuted John Lane and obtained his excommunication at Worcester on 27 July.[7]

[1] In 1619 John Lane was a ringleader in the amazing attack on the Puritan Vicar, Wilson (see p. 839), and was presented by the Churchwardens as a 'drunkard'.

[2] p. 123.

[3] p. 828.

[4] Thomas Greene kept the minutes of the Council meeting that day.

[5] *Inquis. p.m.* Richard Lane, Series II, vol. 334 (74).

[6] *Register*, II. ii. 281.

[7] *Ecclesiastical Causes in Gloucester and Worcester, 1609–1613, Act Book*, No. 9, Worcester Diocesan Registry. More fortunate than his daughter, in his lifetime

Richard Lane died 'esquire' on 6 September 1613. His widow (Joan, sister of Henry Whitney 'esquire') died on the 29th of the same month. On Saturday 11 December their son, Edward, in the presence doubtless of Thomas Greene[1] and the Halls, married, in the Parish Church, Mistress Mary Combe, daughter of the late Thomas Combe of the College, sister of William and Thomas, aged 21, thus linking these prominent Stratford families.

Shakespeare may have gone to London for the Court season 1613–14, which began on 1 November and ended on Shrove Tuesday, 8 March. If so, he took no play with him, and acted, presumably, in old parts. His company, at any rate, performed three times before the King and twice before Prince Charles in November; four times before the King at Christmas and Candlemas; five times before Prince Charles in January and February, and twice before the King at Shrovetide.[2] That they played no less than seven times before the young Prince suggests the presence of Shakespeare, whom he greatly admired and of whose dramas, in the Folio of 1623, he was a diligent reader.

On 25 February a junior but honoured member of their fellowship was buried in St. Saviour's, Southwark—'Alexander Cooke, a man, in the Church'. This was Heminge's old apprentice, 'Saunder', who played 'Videna' and 'Progne', when his master impersonated 'Lydgate', and Shakespeare 'King Henry VI', in *Four Plays in One* in 1592.[3] He probably took female parts in Shakespeare's early dramas.[4] He was one of the 'King's Men' of 1603, and doubtless the 'Master Cooke' whose commendations with those of his recently married wife 'in the kindest sort' Mistress Alleyn sent to her husband at Bexhill in October 1603.[5] His four children (of whom Rebecca probably had Mistress Heminge for godmother) were baptized, one posthumous, in St. Saviour's, and were entrusted in his Will (dated 3 January 1614) to the care of Heminge and Condell. These veterans, and Shakespeare, and others of the company, probably attended his funeral.

A few yards from St. Saviour's, and Master Cooke's house,

Shakespeare escaped all but the merest bespattering of the Blatant Beast, but less fortunate after he and his friends were dead and there was none to take the traducer into court, he suffered considerable 'defamation'.

[1] He was in Stratford. [2] Chambers, iv. 128 f., 181 f.

[3] p. 292. [4] p. 293. [5] p. 588.

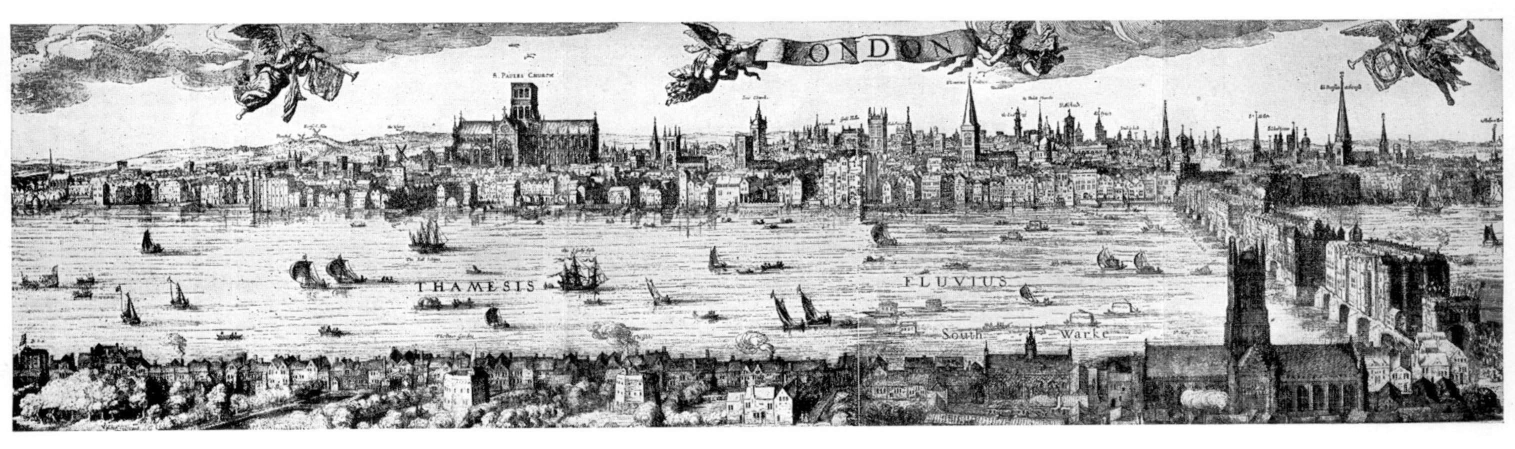

VISSCHER'S VIEW OF LONDON, 1616

the Poet saw the rebuilding of the *Globe*, of which he was a shareholder, in preparation for the open-air season. It was again of timber, but octagonal instead of circular, with tile in place of thatch. It was finished and opened before midsummer. John Chamberlain wrote from London on 30 June to Lady Carleton at Venice:

> I have not seen your sister Williams since I came to town though I have been there twice. The first time she was at a neighbour's house at cards, and the next she was gone to the new *Globe* to a play. Indeed, I hear much speech of this new playhouse, which is said to be the fairest that ever was in England, so that if I live but seven years longer I may chance to take a journey to see it.[1]

John Taylor the 'water-poet' set the 'new *Globe*' high above the old:

> As gold is better that 's in fire tried,
> So is the Bank-side *Globe* that late was burn'd;
> For where before it had a thatchéd hide,
> Now to a stately theatre 'tis turn'd.

We see it in Visscher's view of London of 1616, with its three turrets and flagstaff, pleasantly situated in the fields, among trees, at the back of the houses on the Bank-side. To the west is the Bear Garden, and beyond this the *Swan*; to the east is St. Saviour's, and then the approach to the Bridge. What a glorious old bridge! and what a City it leads to! both beautiful almost beyond our dreams. What Visscher *delineavit* Shakespeare loved. It had sunk into the Poet's heart, as we may realize in *Henry the Eighth*. Though his home was in Stratford, as it had always been, he had no intention in 1614 of breaking his association with London.

He may or may not have been in Stratford on Saturday 9 July, when the town suffered for a third time in his life from a calamitous fire. 'Within the space of less than two hours' it burned fifty-four dwelling-houses, besides barns and stables, with great store of corn, hay, and timber, to the value of £8,000: 'the force of which fire was so great, the wind sitting full upon the town, that the whole town was in very great danger to have been utterly consumed.'[2] John Combe died the next day, and it is not unreasonable to connect his decease with the excitement and the peril of the disaster. *New Place* escaped, and after the fire,

[1] Birch, *James I*, i. 329.

[2] *Wheler MS*. i. 65.

if not before it, the Shakespeares entertained a visiting Preacher: to whom, in his capacity of Bailiff, Daniel Baker sent a gift of sack and claret-wine costing 20*d.*[1] On 26 August was buried at Snitterfield from his grandfather's old home, the Poet's aunt, Margaret Cornwall, formerly Webbe *née* Arden, his mother's last surviving sister. In the autumn he rode as usual to London, on probably his last visit. He arrived, as we have seen, on Wednesday, 16 November, and Greene called upon him next day 'to see him how he did'. Was he in ill-health? The fact that the King's Men played only eight times this season,[2] and that Prince Charles had his own company of players (who performed six times in his presence),[3] points to the conclusion that Shakespeare's participation in the Court festivities, if indeed he did participate, was confined to a few favourite roles. Hence the complaint voiced by Chamberlain to Carleton 5 January 1615:

> They have plays at Court every night, both holidays and working-days, wherein they show great patience, being for the most part such poor stuff that instead of delight they send the auditory away with discontent. Indeed, our poets' brains and inventions are grown very dry, in so much that of five new plays there is not one pleases; and therefore they are driven to publish over their old, which stand them in best stead and bring them most profit.[4]

The Court no longer inspired 'poetry' and 'invention'. It fed on the nullity divorce of Lady Essex and her marriage with Rochester, now Earl of Somerset, and on rumours, which were shortly to become nauseating facts, of youthful lust and crime.

Just before Christmas, 1614, the King's Men lost another junior member, William Ostler. He was an old Royal Chapel boy, who was 'taken to strengthen the King's service' from the *Blackfriars* in 1608 or 1609.[5] He had talent, and swiftly acquired a reputation in some 'kingly part'. Davies,[6] it will be remembered, praised him in 1610 as 'the Roscius of these times', reproving him at the same time for taking instead of inflicting a broken head in a brawl:

> Ostler, thou took'st a knock thou would'st have given,
> Near sent thee to thy latest home: but, O,
> Where was thine *action* when thy crown was riven,
> Sole King of actors? Then wast idle? No,

[1] 'Item for one quart of sack, and one quart of claret wine, given to a Preacher at the New Place, 20*d*.' (*Chamberlains' Account*, 13 Jan. 1615).

[2] Chambers, iv. 130, 182.

[3] *Ib.*

[4] Nichols, iii. 26.

[5] Chambers, ii. 59.

[6] *Scourge of Folly.*

Thou had'st it for thou would'st be *doing*. Thus
Good *actors' deeds* are oft most dangerous.
But if thou play'st thy dying part as well
As thy stage parts, thou hast no part in Hell.[1]

Such praise was more calculated to swell the young man's head than heal it. He married John Heminge's daughter, Thomasine, a girl of sixteen, in 1611, and their child, Beaumont (godson possibly of Francis Beaumont the dramatist), was baptized on 18 May 1612 in St. Mary Aldermanbury.[2] He obtained shares, probably as a marriage-gift from Heminge in the *Blackfriars* (on 20 May 1611) and the *Globe* (20 Feb. 1612), which after his death became a subject of litigation between his young widow and her father. She claimed that they were worth £600. On 31 March 1615 (the Friday before Good Friday) Heminge and Burbage appeared before the Privy Council to answer for playing by the King's Men in Lent. Other companies, represented by Christopher Beeston and Robert Lee (Queen Anne's), William Rowley and John Newton (Prince Charles's), Thomas Downton and Humphrey Jeffes (Prince Palatine's), and players not named, were summoned for the same offence.[3] Immediately afterwards the King's Men travelled, and were in Nottingham in April.[4]

Shakespeare was possibly in London until 26 April 1615, when a bill of complaint by himself and six others was addressed in Chancery against Matthew Bacon of Gray's Inn for withholding deeds of their properties in Blackfriars—Bacon being the vendor of the house he purchased from Henry Walker in 1613.[5] Short or long, his sojourn in the capital this season, whatever his hopes or intentions, seems to have been his last.

Coincident, as it happened, with his departure from the scene of his triumphs was the publication of a remarkable tribute to his genius. The writer, as we might expect, was a lawyer and a dramatist. He was a Gloucester man, John Stephens of Lincoln's Inn, author of a play, *Cinthia's Revenge*, published in 1613. His *Satyrical Essayes, Characters and Others* came out in 1615, and again the same year with the new title, *Essayes and Characters, Ironicall and Instructive*. Both editions contain the sketch of a

[1] Chambers, ii. 331.
[2] *Ib.*
[3] Collier, *Memoirs*, 43 f.
[4] J. T. Murray, ii. 376.
[5] C. W. Wallace, *The Standard*, 18 Oct. 1905.

'Worthy Poet', which is unquestionably a word-portrait of Shakespeare. This conclusion is confirmed by additions in the second impression which complete the picture.[1] Here is the enlarged essay (Bk. i. 6):

A Worthy Poet[2] is the purest essence of a worthy man.[3] He is confident of Nature in nothing but the form and an ingenious fitness to conceive the matter; so he approves Nature as the motive not the foundation or structure of his worthiness.[4] His works do every way pronounce both nourishment, delight and admiration to the reader's soul: which makes him neither rough, effeminate nor windy; for by a sweet contemperature[5] of tune and ditty he entices others to goodness, and shows himself perfect in the lesson.[6] He never writes upon a full stomach and an empty head, or a full head and an empty stomach.[7] For he cannot make so divine a receptacle[8] stoop to the sordid folly of gall or envy without strength, or strength of brain stoop and debase itself with hunting out the body's succour.[9] He is not so impartial[10] as to condemn every new fashion or tax idle circumstance, nor so easy as to allow vices and account them generous humours. So he neither seeks to enlarge his credit of bitterness by a snarling severity, nor to commend his substance by insinuating courtship. He hath more debtors in knowledge among the present writers than creditors among the ancient poets.[11] He is possessed with an innocent liberty,[12] which excludes him from the slavish labour and means of setting a gloss upon frail commodities. Whatsoever,

[1] See further, p. 889.

[2] A worthy ποιητής or Maker.

[3] Cf. Milton: 'He who would not be frustrate of his hope to write well hereafter in laudable things ought himself to be a true poem.' (*Apol. to Smectymnuus.*)

[4] A worthy 'maker' trusts in 'Nature' for the form and substance of his structure, and in God his 'Maker' for the foundation and edifice. For Nature in this lower sense see the speech of the atheist Edmund, 'Thou, Nature, art my goddess' (*K. Lear*, I. ii. 1).

[5] 'Contemperament' in first impression. Concord, keeping time together.

[6] Cf. Sidney on the Poet: 'He doth not only show the way, but giveth so sweet a prospect into the way as will entice any man to enter into it. He cometh to you with words set in delightful proportion, and with a tale which holdeth children from play and old men from the chimney-corner, and pretending no more, doth intend the winning of the mind from wickedness to virtue.' (*Defence*, Feuillerat, iii. 19 f.)

[7] He is neither an ascetic nor a gourmand.

[8] The stomach is one of the members which 'God hath set in the body' (1 Cor. xii. 18).

[9] He does not fill his belly with the sordid bitterness and feeble envy of some writers, nor debase his thought with the pleasures of the table.

[10] Strict.

[11] Shakespeare's chief 'creditor' among the ancient poets, as we have seen, was Ovid. His 'debtors' were a swarm of imitators—Beaumont, Fletcher, Massinger, and the rest.

[12] Cf. Shakespeare's own phrase for himself in Sonnets cxxi. 6: 'sportive blood'; and that for his Friend in xli. 1: 'pretty wrongs that liberty commits'.

therefore, proceeds from him, proceeds without a meaning to supply the worth when the work is ended by the addition of preparative verses at the beginning, or the disperst hire of acquaintance to extol things indifferent. Neither does he passionately affect high patronage, or any further than he may give freely and so receive back honest thanks.[1] The dangerous name and the contempt of poets[2] sprung from their multitude of corruptions[3] proves no disadvantage or terror to him, for such be his antidotes that he can walk untouched even through the worst infection. And indeed that mountebank's preparing oil which kept his hands unscalded, was a toy of nothing to this Poet's rarity of discretion, which so prepares his mind that he can bathe it in the strains[4] of burning lust, fury, malice or despite, and yet be never scalded or endangered by them. He only among men is nearest infinite; for in the scenical composures[5] of a tragedy or comedy he shows the best resemblance of his High Creator, turning his quick passions and witty humours to replenish and overcome[6] into matter and form as infinite as God's pleasure to diversify mankind.[7] He is no miserable self-lover, nor no unbounded prodigal; for he can communicate himself wisely to avoid dull reservedness, but not make every thought common to maintain his market.[8] It must be imputed to his perfect eyesight that he can see error and avoid it without the hazard of a new one: as in poems so in projects, by an easy conjecture. He cannot flatter nor be flattered. If he gives desert he gives no more, and leaves hyperbole in such a matter of importance. As for himself, he is so well known unto himself that neither public fame[9] nor yet his own conceit can make him overvalued in himself. He is an enemy to Atheists, for he is no Fatist nor Naturalist. He therefore excludes luck and rime from the acceptance of his poems, scorning to acknowledge the one as an efficient,[10] the other as an essence of his Muses' favour. He pays back all his imitation with interest;[11] whilst his authors (if revived) would confess their chief credit was to be such a pattern:[12] otherwise (for the most part) he proves himself the pattern and the project in hand.[13] Silver only and sound metal comprehend[14] his nature; rubbing, motion, and customary usage makes the brightness of both more eminent. No marvel though[15] he be immortal, seeing he converts poison into nourishment, even the worst objects and societies to a

[1] Shakespeare's one patron was the Earl of Southampton.

[2] Especially among Puritans.

[3] Cf. Gosson in *School of Abuse* in 1579. Later, Shakespeare's younger contemporaries quickly brought poets into contempt.

[4] Dregs.

[5] Compositions.

[6] Come-over, flow-over.

[7] Make varied human nature.

[8] Does not make himself cheap, unbosom to everybody.

[9] Evidence, if it were needed, of Shakespeare's great reputation.

[10] A first cause.

[11] Shakespeare enriched everything he borrowed from his predecessors, turning their alloy into gold.

[12] The chief interest of these predecessors is that Shakespeare honoured them by making use of them—Greene, Kyd, Lodge, and others.

[13] He himself is the originator of what he undertakes.

[14] Comprise.

[15] that

worthy use. When he is lastly silent[1] (for he cannot die), he finds a monument prepared at other's cost and remembrance, while his former actions[2] be a living epitaph.[3]

Nothing finer has been written of Shakespeare. Every sentence is weighty and discriminating; and if the writer strains after epigram, his phrases are often most happy. What could be better than 'every way pronounce nourishment, delight and admiration to the soul', 'entices others to goodness and shows himself perfect in the lesson', 'not so impartial as to condemn every new fashion or tax idle circumstance, nor so easy as to allow vices and account them generous humours', 'possessed with an innocent liberty', 'walk untouched through the worst infection', 'this Poet's rarity of discretion', 'bathe in the streams of burning lust' (we think of Anthony and Cleopatra), 'fury' (Othello, Lear), 'malice' (Iago, Edmund), 'or despite' (Timon), 'and yet be never scalded', 'he only among men nearest infinite', 'in tragedy or comedy the best resemblance of his High Creator' (the makers' Maker), 'his quick passions and witty humours', 'so well known unto himself that neither public fame nor his own conceit can make him over-valued in himself', 'an enemy to Atheists, no Fatist nor Naturalist', 'silver only and sound metal: rubbing, motion and customary usage make the brightness of both more eminent', 'immortal[4] seeing he converts poison into nourishment' (we recall the brothel-scenes in *Pericles*), 'silent he cannot die', 'a monument at others' cost and remembrance'? Of one, and only one, poet could this possibly be said in 1615, and of him it was absolute truth—the great dramatist on whose beautiful work Stephens had feasted, and whose friendship assuredly he could claim. The crowning praise seems the fruit of personal acquaintance. 'It must be imputed to his perfect eyesight that he can see error and avoid it without the hazard of a new one'—a new error and a worse, namely, of thinking himself better than others. It is this supreme virtue that has ever exposed Shakespeare to the misinterpretation of mean judgements.

[1] There was a brief silence before, as a long silence after, the Poet's death

[2] Literary and histrionic performances.

[3] Cf. Milton in 1630:

> What needs my Shakespeare for his honoured bones
> The labour of an age in piled stones?

[4] Exempt from death, poison not killing him.

The eulogist, on the other hand, is very conscious of 'poets' less modest—of one, at least, who is 'rough' and guilty of 'a snarling severity', ready to 'condemn new fashion' and 'tax idle circumstance'—the censorious, if 'rare', Ben Jonson; and of poets less honest—'effeminate and windy, engaged in the slavish labour' of 'setting a gloss on frail commodities' and even 'allowing vices and accounting them generous humours'—the decadent and popular playwrights, Francis Beaumont and John Fletcher, and others who brought the drama to so low a level in 1630 that Jonson in disgust penned his fierce ode,

> Come, leave the loathed stage
> And the more loathsome age,
> Where pride and impudence, in faction knit,
> Usurp the chair of wit!

1616

§ 146. SHAKESPEARE'S WILL AND DEATH

OF Shakespeare, from 5 September 1615, when he sent for Master Barber's executors to *New Place*,[1] until the drawing up of his Will in January 1616, when he was 'in perfect health and memory', there is no record. He lost his fellow and friend, Robin Armin, chief clown in his plays since 1599, a refined and cultivated actor, probably of a delicate constitution, in November 1615. The burial is recorded at St. Botolph, Aldgate, on the 30th of this month, 'free of the Goldsmiths' and a Player'.

Apparently Shakespeare spent Christmas in Stratford, where preparations were in hand for his daughter Judith's wedding. In anticipation of her marriage-portion, Thomas Quyney negotiated with his brother-in-law, William Chandler, for the exchange of his little house in High Street, 'Atwood's',[2] for the more commodious and prominent *Cage* at the corner of High Street and Bridge Street.[3] Banns were put up in the Parish

[1] p. 812. [2] p. 763.

[3] On 15 Dec. 1615 Quyney's elder brother, Adrian, undertook to produce the deeds of 'Atwood's House' (now 36) to the Council at their meeting on 12 Jan. 1616 (*Council Book B*, 298). On this latter date a new lease of the *Cage* was granted to Chandler, for thirty-one years from 21 Dec. 1615 at the rent of 40*s*. It was sealed on 1 March 1616. The exchange of the premises and leases was formally sanctioned on 19 July 1616 (*Council Book B*, 312 f.).

Church,[1] possibly on the 7th, 14th, and 21st of January in view of a wedding at the end of the month, and Shakespeare made a Will to be signed and sealed after the ceremony.[2]

The main portion of this Will is embodied in a second draft, drawn up in haste and signed, as we shall see, two months later, and the Poet's intentions in January are clear.[3] He divided his estate, save for a few bequests, between his daughters, with their husbands. Judith and Thomas Quyney were to have £150 or 10 per cent interest on the same from the date of the Will, *provided that Quyney assured his wife and prospective children in lands to the value of £100.* Judith was also to receive £150 or 10 per cent interest thereon from the date of the Poet's decease—£100 in discharge of her marriage-portion, and £50 in lieu of claim to the cottage in Chapel Lane.[4] *New Place* and this cottage, the houses in Henley Street (described as '*two* messuages'), the

[1] Otherwise the irregularity would be mentioned in the excommunication of 12 March: see p. 824.

[2] This first draft was certainly drawn up for signature in January, and *Vicesimo Quinto Die* may just possibly have been reproduced from it (correctly) as *Januarij* (wrongly). See p. 828.

[3] Shakespeare's Will, fortunately the original document as well as the official copy, is at Somerset House. Its two stages can only be understood when studied in the original, or a photographic reproduction. It is in the hand of Francis Collins, on three sheets of paper. The second begins with *a cancelled paragraph*, which demands our close attention:

'to be set out for her within one year after my decease by my executors, with the advice and directions of my overseers, for her best profit until her marriage, and then the same with the increase thereof to be paid unto her'.

This undoubtedly refers to £100 which was to go to Elizabeth Hall (Shakespeare's grand-daughter) as a marriage-portion in the event of her aunt Judith's death. The item which follows, *uncancelled*, refers also to the grand-daughter:

'Item, I give and bequeath unto her all my plate that I now have at the date of this my Will.'

Above the cancelled paragraph is inserted an item respecting the Poet's nephews, the Harts, which is carried on from the first sheet. Nor is there anything at the end of, or elsewhere in the first sheet, hingeing-on to the cancelled paragraph in the second sheet. Moreover, to connect the item about the Harts with the item about the plate (following the cancelled paragraph), Collins has had to amend the latter, crossing out *her* and writing over it *the said Elizabeth Hall.* The inference is obvious. The second sheet is a *revised* draft, the first sheet is a *re-written* one. The third sheet continues the second, and is of the same character: it has been revised, not re-written. We have to do, then, with a document which consists of three sheets of writing, the second and third being an *amended* portion of a former Will, the first a *new* draft of the opening portion of that Will. Further evidence entirely confirms this conclusion: see pp. 824, 826–8.

[4] p. 578.

house in Blackfriars, London,[1] and all landed property, including 'hereditaments' in the tithes of Stratford, were to go, at the testator's death, to Susanna; and to Susanna and her husband, Doctor John Hall, was demised the residue—'all goods, chattels, leases, plate, jewels, and household stuff whatsoever', less plate in the Poet's possession on the date of his Will,[2] bequeathed to his grand-daughter ('my niece'),[3] Elizabeth, child of Susanna and John Hall, and a 'broad silver and gilt bowl' left to Judith. 'Leases' would include the Poet's shares in the *Globe* and *Blackfriars* theatres, and the 'household stuff whatsoever', his library and manuscripts. Doctor Hall, then, himself a writer and a scholar, was to be his chief literary executor. Susanna Hall was more interested in her 'works of mercy' than in her father's or her husband's writings.[4] The minor bequests are noteworthy—£10 to the poor of Stratford; 'my sword' (worn as a King's Man on State-occasions) to Master Thomas Combe; £5 to Thomas Russell esquire; £13 6*s.* 8*d.* to Francis Collins of Warwick (writer of the Will, the Poet's trusted attorney);[5] 26*s.* 8*d.* for a memorial ring to Master Richard Tyler the elder (of the romantic marriage),[6] Anthony Nash gentleman (of Welcombe) and his brother Master John Nash; and 20*s.* in 'gold' (a memorial coin) 'to my godson William Walker' (now seven years old and not yet confirmed). Conspicuous by his absence from the Will is Master William Combe, the blustering young *dominus* of the College and High Sheriff. It has been plausibly suggested that the gift of the sword to his pugnacious younger brother had a touch of irony in it—'for all that take the sword shall perish with the sword'.[7] Tom Combe readily took to his fists, not to say his

[1] p. 768.

[2] The expectation of further plate, implied by this wording, is another indication that the Poet did not contemplate death in Jan. 1616. See p. 829.

[3] Cf. 'my niece, Plantagenet' (*Rich. III*, IV. i. 1), Lat. *neptis*, grand-daughter: as 'nephew' originally 'grandson', from Lat. *nepos*.

[4] pp. 901–4.

[5] Collins's script is familiar to us in the Stratford records as Deputy Town Clerk from 1602 to 1608 and Town Clerk in the last months of his life, April–Sept. 1617. The will of Thomas Combe, the elder, of Old Stratford, 22 November 1608, is also in his writing.

[6] p. 796.

[7] Matthew xxvi. 52. Shakespeare knew the text: King Henry VI says of Cade's followers,

God forbid so many simple souls
Should perish by the sword. (*2 Hen. VI*, IV. iv. 10 f.)

feet: we remember his beating and kicking the shepherd.[1] About 8 September 1616 he fought Valentine Taunt, a member of the Stratford Corporation, at the Dingles. In November, as a consequence or not of this assault, Taunt died.

Shakespeare's Will was ready for signature and sealing in January, but for some reason the wedding was postponed. His illness might or might not be the occasion. The 28th of January was Septuagesima, the first day of the inhibited season for marriages, which lasted until 6 April. Between these dates, inclusive, a costly special licence was necessary. Neither Thomas Quyney nor Judith Shakespeare took steps to obtain such a licence; nevertheless, they were married, with Puritan obstinacy, on Saturday, 10 February; the broad-minded Vicar, John Rogers, or his assistant, Richard Watts, 'minister', officiating. They did not escape episcopal detection and punishment. An apparitor of the Consistory Court, William Nixon, lived in Bridge Town, who reported the irregularity. He was no exception to his class, took bribes for non-presentment, himself made false presentments, and even forged (it was alleged) the signature of the registrar of the Consistory Court, William Warmstrey.[2] The Quyneys were not people to bribe him, and the date of their marriage was manifest in the parish register. Twice they were cited to Worcester, and failing to appear they were fined seven shillings (plus the licence-fee) and excommunicated, on 12 March (or April):[3] *quod nupti fuerunt absque licencia bis citati per Nixon non comparuerunt in Consistorio: 12 (die) non comparuerunt, excommunicati.*[4]

Shakespeare would hardly approve of this behaviour. He did not sign his Will after the wedding on 10 February. Quyney had further transgressed. *He had failed to settle the £100 in land on his wife and prospective children.* Time passed, and Shakespeare proved, or became, the victim of a malady, probably typhoid fever, which killed him.

The scrap of truth in the otherwise worthless legend for which the Vicar, John Ward (1662–81) is responsible, that 'Shakespeare, Drayton and Ben Jonson had a merry meeting

[1] p. 811. [2] Star Chamber Proceedings, James I, 26/10 m. 2.
[3] The date falls between 10 Feb. and 11 May (next entry).
[4] Visitation Book, Kington Deanery, Worc. Dioc. Reg.

and, it seems, drank too hard, for Shakespeare died of a fever there contracted', is the association of the Poet's illness with 'a merry meeting'.[1] The festivity was doubtless that of his daughter's wedding. That Drayton was present is not unlikely—he was often at Clifford Chambers[2] as the guest of his 'Idea', Lady Henry Rainsford; but Jonson's presence is highly improbable.[3] To hard drinking Shakespeare was as little given as Drayton,[4] though Ward may be pardoned for accepting the Restorationist view of players and playwriters. To his credit, he says, 'it seems'. He knew even less of Shakespeare's work than some of his contemporaries. 'Remember', he adds to the above unedifying gossip, 'to peruse Shakespeare's plays and be versed in them, that I may not be ignorant in that matter.'[5]

[1] See his Commonplace Book in MS. late in the library of the Medical Society of London: begun, as Ward tells us, on 14 Feb. 1661/2 and finished 2 April 1663 at the house of Master Brookes in Stratford. Festivity, fever, and funeral are the three stages of the story. The Bidford legend has also a grain of truth in it. There was a hedge at Bidford called 'Shakespeare Hedge'. 'Why Shakespeare Hedge?' asked somebody. 'Because Shakespeare slept under it,' volunteers somebody. 'Why did he sleep under it?' continues the questioner. 'Because he was drunk, I suppose,' replies the informant. Joseph Greene, the Stratford schoolmaster, traced this foolery to its source. 'The story of Shakespear's tippling with the men of Bidford, and giving name to a hedge near that village, is rather too mean to appear in print. Sir Hugh Clopton has often told me that story, and seemed to think it true; but I am inclined to believe it is no more than a fiction of some wag who, for want of a better, thought that some reason however ludicrous must be assigned why the Hedge went by his name: as it still continues' (Letter to James West, London, from Stratford 8 Nov. 1758; discovered at Alscot by Mr. F. C. Wellstood in 1927).

Hedge, sleep, drunk, is the order; not, drunk, hedge, sleep.

For further developments of the tale see Halliwell-Phillipps, *Outlines*, ii. 325–7.

[2] 'Dear Clifford's seat, the place of health and sport,
Which many a time hath been the Muse's quiet port.' (*Poly-olbion*, xiv. 161 f.)

Later in life his visits seem to have been in the summer. He writes from Clifford on 14 July 1631 to Drummond of Hawthornden: 'from a Knight's house in Gloucestershire; to which place I yearly use to come in the summertime to recreate myself and to spend two or three months in the country.'

[3] There is nothing to connect Jonson with Stratford, save his 'Sweet Swan of Avon': see p. 866.

[4] The Rev. Francis Meres says in *Palladis Tamia*, 1598, 'Michael Drayton, *quem toties honoris et amoris causa nomino*, among scholars, soldiers, poets, and all sorts of people, is held for a man of virtuous disposition, honest conversation, and well governed carriage' (Arber, *Garner*, ii. 97). Shakespeare did not need this laudation, still less did he call for it.

[5] Ward also says, 'I have heard that Master Shakespeare was a natural wit without any art at all' (which we will take with a very large dose of salt); 'he

In March Shakespeare's illness took a serious turn, and he sent for Collins to revise his Will. The document of (25) January consisted of three sheets. Under the Poet's instruction the first sheet was cancelled and the second and third amended. It was his object to ensure his daughter Judith an immediate income and future prospects without admitting her husband (who still failed of the £100 in land) to more than conditional benefit. Thomas Quyney, indeed, is not mentioned in the new draft, and the only hint that Judith already has a husband is a slip of the pen, of which there are several, in the hasty revision of the document. It occurs in the first item of the re-written first sheet. Collins wrote, following the old draft, 'I give and bequeath unto my son-in-L', and then scoring through 'son-in-L', substituted 'daughter Judith'.

The Poet made other changes. He omitted the 'setting-out' for his grand-daughter, Elizabeth Hall, of the reversionary £100. He added Hamlet Sadler, William Reynolds gentleman, and 'my Fellows, John Hemynges, Richard Burbage and Henry Cundell', to the recipients of *26s. 8d.* for a ring.[1] On the other hand, he omitted the name of Master Richard Tyler, to whom, no doubt, he made during his illness some personal gift. God-children were probably so remembered—such as William Greene (now eight years old), by the hand of his father, the Poet's kinsman. Nor, we may be certain, would this devoted kinsman, his late fellow resident at *New Place*, be overlooked. Wills rarely contained all such souvenirs. Bequests to the Harts are reproduced in the second draft—to the mother, Joan Hart, Shakespeare's sister, of her house in Henley Street (the tenement on the west) for life, at the nominal rent of *12d. per annum*, with a reversion of the second £50 bequeathed to Judith Quyney; and £5 apiece to her sons, William, [Thomas] and Michael. Last, in the third sheet, is the afterthought, interlined, 'Item, I give unto my wife my second-best bed with the furniture'. The four-poster bedstead, with its furnishing, is prominent in Tudor and

frequented the plays all his younger time' (whatever this may mean), 'but in his elder days lived at Stratford and supplied the stage with two plays every year' (good confirmatory evidence of what we have noted in the Poet's career from 1592 onwards), 'and for that had an allowance so large that he spent at the rate of a £1000 a year, as I have heard' (which is a ridiculous exaggeration). Halliwell-Phillipps, *Outlines*, ii. 70.

[1] p. 823.

Sheet One (his second signature in order of time)

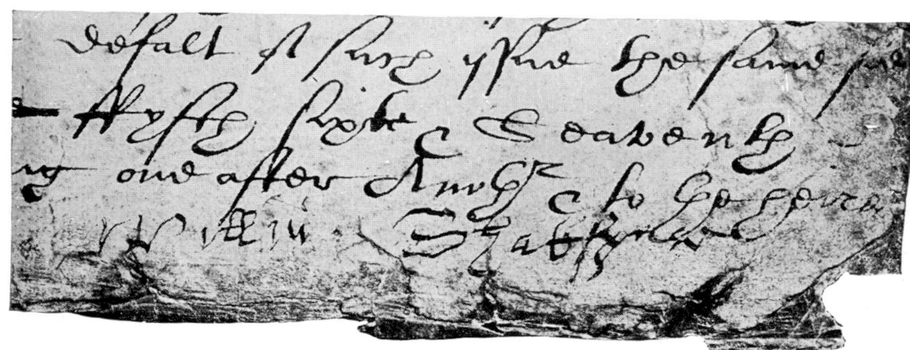

Sheet Two (the third and last in order of time: hence the shakiness. The S is *not* written in one stroke, as in the Bellott depositions, but in two, the lower part first, then the upper part, as in the Ovid initials)

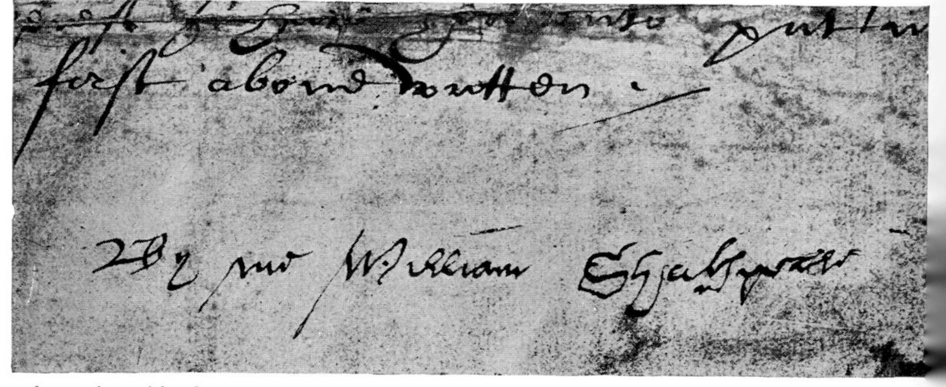

Sheet Three (the first in order of time. The S is written in one stroke, from the top. Note the dot in the W, as in the Ovid initials)

WILLIAM SHAKESPEARE'S SIGNATURES TO THE THREE SHEETS OF HIS WILL

Stuart legacies, and not unfrequently we meet with a 'best' and a 'second'. Thomas Greene of Warwick, in his Will of 22 July 1590, left to his daughter, Margaret, his 'best bedstead with the furniture', and to his son, Thomas, later Town Clerk of Stratford, Shakespeare's 'cousin', his 'second feather bed furnished'. More apposite is the bequest in the Will of William Bracey of Snitterfield, 14 January 1557: 'My wife Margery shall have to her use all my household stuff except one bed, the second best, the which I give and bequeath to John my son with three pair of sheets.'[1] At *New Place* the 'best bed' was, doubtless, in the guest-chamber, to be occupied by such a visitor as the 'preacher' to whom the Bailiff in 1614 sent a gift of wine. The 'second best' was the less sumptuous bed the Poet had shared with his wife, in which he lay dying, and which he desired her to have after he was dead. It was a 'standard' or fixture, and would ensure her occupation of the old bed-chamber in the changes that were imminent on the coming of the Halls into the house, or at least their inheritance of the same. There was no need to leave her property. She was entitled to the Widow's Dower, was sixty years of age, and probably infirm, and would be well looked after by her daughter and the Doctor, her son-in-law. Shakespeare, moreover, had been generous, we may believe, to her people.

The Poet signed but did not seal the Will, writing his name firmly in the third sheet, less firmly at the bottom of the first, then shakily, as if exhausted by his efforts, at the bottom of the second. The first signature bears a striking resemblance to that in his copy of Montaigne, bold and free and full of character. It is preceded by the words *By me*, in legal fashion, in undoubtedly the Poet's hand. The *W* is that of the *Ovid* but contains a dot; the *S* is that of the *Ovid* but untouched, with the angular base-line characteristic of the *S* also in the third signature to the Will. The last letters of the surname, which is *Shakspeare*, are tremulous, and prepare us for the second signature. This has largely disappeared, and should be studied in an early facsimile, such as that by Steevens in 1776. The *W* and *S* differ from those of the first signature, and the *W* contains no dot. The *a*, too, in

[1] 'Among the Shakespeare Archives' (*Notes and Queries*, 1920–21) and *Shakespeare's Haunts*, p. 23 f. and n. 1. See also the Will of John Combe, p. 803.

the surname, which is spelt *Shakspere*, is peculiar. The third signature, of which the surname is *Shakspere*, again differs from the other two, in the *W*, which is without the dot, the *S*, which is in two strokes instead of one, and the curiously twisted *p*.

From these, as from the five previous examples of his penmanship, we conclude that the Poet could write beautifully when he wished (and was well), as in his books and Will; carelessly when impatient (or unwell); tended to lift the line as he wrote, as one who pressed somewhat heavily on the table; did not link his capitals with letters following (note the detachment of the *B* from the *y*); like a lawyer never dotted his *i*'s; and abhorred a dull uniformity as Nature abhors a vacuum.

Witnesses to the Will are 'Fra: Collynes,[1] Julyns[2] Shawe, John Robinson, Hamnet Sadler, Robert whattcott'.

Oversights in the re-writing of the first sheet prove Collins's trepidation on finding Shakespeare dangerously sick. He began with the date at the top, *Vicesimo Quinto Die Januarij Anno Regni Domini nostri Jacobi nunc Regis Anglie &c decimo quarto & Scotie xlix° annoque Domini 1616*—that is, 'On the twenty-fifth day of January in the 14th year of the reign of our lord James now King, of England &c and of Scotland the 49th, and the year of our Lord 1616'. He reproduced, unconsciously, the *Januarij* of the first draft, which was before him, and the rest of the paragraph until he came to the end, when realizing his error, he wrote '1616' instead of '1615', which must have been the reading of the first draft: the '(25) January 1616' was (25) January 1617. Further, he erased *Januarij*, and wrote over it '*m̄tii*', i.e. *Martii*, possibly leaving the day (which presumably was correct) unaltered.

The religious preamble must not be dismissed as a formality. Whatever convention may be in it, it is not altogether conventional. No devout Catholic, for example, would be content with the statement. Protestant formulae were of great variety, and the one adopted, no doubt, had Shakespeare's approval. It is as follows (much like John Combe's):[3]

I commend my soul into the hands of God my Creator, hoping and

[1] The signature of Francis Collins is in a Latin hand, not the Gothic script of the Will. He used it also for marginal notes in the Corporation Minute Book.

[2] Not Julyus; but Julyns, apparently, has been revised into Julyne.

[3] p. 803.

I

II

III

SHAKESPEARE'S SIGNATURES

I. Depositions in the Bellott–Mountjoy suit, 11 May 1612 (*Public Record Office*).

II. Purchase deed of a house in Blackfriars, 10 March $161\frac{2}{3}$ (*Guildhall Library*).

III. Deed of mortgage of a house in Blackfriars, 11 March $161\frac{2}{3}$ (*British Museum*).

assuredly believing through the only merits of Jesus Christ my Saviour, to be made partaker of life everlasting; and my body to the earth whereof it is made.

It is curious that the Poet did not specify the place of his burial —within the Parish Church of Stratford and, according to his right as a lessee of the tithes, within the chancel. He was not sure, perhaps, early in January 1616, 'in perfect health and memory, God be praised' (this, as well as the religious preamble, is taken over from the first draft) that he might not die in London, and be buried with his brother, and so many of his fellows, in St. Mary Overy's, Southwark. But the progress of his sickness determined the spot; and, his end approaching, he wrote or spoke the lines for his grave in Stratford Church,[1] near the 'bone-house',[2] in warning to the sexton in days to come:

Good Frend, for Iesvs' sake forbeare,
To digg the dvst encloased heare:[3]
Bleste be ye man yt spares thes stones,
And cvrst be he yt moves my bones.

GOOD FREND FOR IESVS SAKE FORBEARE,
TO DIGG THE DVST ENCLOASED HEARE:
BLESE BE YE MAN YT SPARES THES STONES,
AND CVRST BE HE YT MOVES MY BONES.

Inscription on the Poet's grave.

His brother-in-law, William Hart, died in Henley Street a few days before, and was buried on 17 April.[4] Shakespeare outlived

[1] 'Made by himself a little before his death' (Dowdall to Edward Southwell, 1693: Halliwell-Phillipps, *Outlines*, ii. 71).

[2] 'There is in this church a place which they call the Bone House, a repository for all the bones they dig up: which are so many that they would load a great number of waggons. The Poet being willing to preserve his bones unmoved, lays a curse on him that moves them. . . . They have laid him full seventeen foot deep, deep enough to secure him' (William Hall to his friend, Edward Thwaites, 1694: *Ib.* ii. 72).

[3] Is there an echo here of his loved *Hero and Leander*? (i. 343 f.)

Gentle youth, forbear
To touch the sacred garments which I wear.

[4] *Register*, p. 90.

the 22nd,[1] thus entering his fifty-third year, and passed away on the 23rd, which was Tuesday, St. George's day. Thomas Mills would toll the passing-bell at the Chapel. On 25th, Thursday and market-day, his body was borne to its resting-place[2]—to await that 'Last Day', when

> Particularities and petty sounds
> (Do) cease.[3]

Julyne Shaw, as Bailiff, and, no doubt, his Brethren of the Corporation, attended the funeral, to do honour to a King's servant and their illustrious fellow townsman.

This year a talented young player, Nathan Field, son of the preacher, John Field, one of the young men taken over by Shakespeare and his company from the old *Blackfriars* theatre, wrote in 'defence of his profession' against the restrictions of a preacher at St. Saviour's, Master Thomas Sutton, in the following terms:

> You have so laboured to banish me from mine own parish-church that my conscience cannot be quiet within me. . . . Pardon me, sir, if in patience and humbleness of spirit I expostulate a little with you.
>
> You waded very low with hatred against us when you ransacked Hell to find the register wherein our souls are written *damned*; and I make no question that *if you had with charity cast your eyes to Heaven, you might more easily have found our names written in the Book of Life.*
>
> And herein is my faith the stronger, because in God's whole Volume, which I have studied as my best part,[4] I find not any trade of life except conjurers, sorcerers and witches *ipso facto* damned, nay, not expressly, spoken against, but only the abuses and bad uses of them. And in that point I defend not ours; nor should have disagreed with you, if you had only struck at the corrupt branches, and not laid your axe to the root of the tree.[5]

'My fellow-labourers', wrote the apostle, 'whose names are in the Book of Life.'[6] The King's Men and the whole theatrical profession were lamenting the death of their 'fellow-labourer' at Stratford.

[1] His birthday? See p. 38. Had he died on his birthday there would almost certainly have been mention of the fact in the inscription on his monument.

[2] *Register*, p. 90.

[3] A great line in an early play, *2 Hen. VI*, v. ii. 44.

[4] This letter is full of Biblical expressions.

[5] *State Papers Dom. Jac. I*, lxxxix. 105.

[6] Philippians iv. 3.

NATHANIEL FIELD

From the painting in Dulwich Gallery

RICHARD BURBAGE

From the painting in Dulwich Gallery
(probably painted by himself)

1615–17

§ 147. RICHARD BURBAGE

NONE would feel the master's loss more keenly than the chief disciple, Burbage. What did Shakespeare owe to this gifted interpreter, or the interpreter owe to his teacher? He is sketched in one of the characters added to *Sir Thomas Overburie his Wife* in 1615, entitled 'An Excellent Actor', a reply to 'A Common Player', 'a friend's satire' admitted by John Stephens in his *Satyrical Essayes, Characters, and Others* of this year.[1] Force, and a fine restraint of strength and passion,[2] charm of movement, grace and music of speech, memory and imagination, enriched by skill in painting, deep thought and gravity, a lovable presence, and perfect command of his audience, are the qualities commended here, and elsewhere, in the great tragedian:

Whatsoever is commendable in the grave orator is most exquisitely perfect in him; for by a full and significant action of body he charms our attention. Sit in a full theatre, and you will think you see so many lines drawn from the circumference of so many ears while the actor is the centre. He doth not strive to make nature monstrous—she is often seen in the same *scaena* with him, but neither on stilts nor crutches; and for his voice, 'tis not lower than the prompter nor louder than the foil and target. By his action he fortifies moral precepts with example, for what we see him personate we think truly done before us. A man of a deep thought might apprehend the ghost of our ancient heroes walked again, and take him at several times for many of them. He is much affected to painting; and 'tis a question whether that make him an excellent player, or his playing an exquisite painter. He adds grace to the Poet's labours; for what in the Poet is but ditty, in him is both ditty and music. He entertains us in the best leisure of our life, that is, between meals, the most unfit time either for study or bodily exercise.[3]

The flight of hawks and chace of wild beasts are delights noble, but some think this sport of men the worthier, despite all calumny . . . I observe of all men living a worthy actor in one kind is the strongest motive of affection that can be, for when he dies we cannot be persuaded any man can do his parts like him . . . I value a worthy actor by the corruption of some few of the quality, as I would do gold in the ore—I should not mind the dross but the purity of the metal.

[1] The 'Excellent Actor' has been attributed to John Webster, the 'Common Player' to J. Cock. See Chambers, iv. 255–8.

[2] Not always characteristic of him off the stage—at least in his youth.

[3] Plays were in the afternoon, between 2 and 6 o'clock.

This vivid sketch of the actor may be supplemented by a description of his audience, no doubt, from the season (December in 1617) and the character of the assemblage, at the *Blackfriars*, and presumably in a play by the King's Men for so distinguished a visitor, namely Orazio Busino, chaplain to the Venetian ambassador. He writes:

> The other day they resolved to take me to one of the many theatres here in London, where comedies are recited; and there we saw the performance of a tragedy, which affected me very little, chiefly because I cannot understand a single word of English. One could get some pleasure only by gazing at the magnificent dresses of the reciters, and observing their gestures, and the various interludes of music, dancing, singing, and such like things. The best entertainment was to see and contemplate so many noblemen, so finely arrayed that they looked like so many princes, and listening with such silence and respect (*con tanto silenzio e modestia*). And many honourable and fair ladies come there with perfect freedom, and take their seats amongst the men without hesitation.[1]

Burbage married late, perhaps more than once, and lost five, if not all, of his six children born to him in 1603–14, before the baptism of a son in St. Leonard's, Shoreditch, on 6 November 1616. This was his second son; the first, Richard, named after himself, died in 1607. Shakespeare was not living to be the godfather of the second boy, but we can hardly doubt that his loved name was given to him. William Burbage was alive in 1635.

1616–22

§ 148. AFTER SHAKESPEARE'S DEATH

QUYNEY and Chandler exchanged leases, and the Poet's younger daughter left *New Place* for the *Cage*.[2] Judith, like her mother, was considerably older (by four years) than her husband. Like her mother, also, she had but three children. The first, a boy, was born in November 1616 and christened, on the 23rd, Shakespeare. This child, Shakespeare Quyney, united in his name the two families so long connected by friendship, and now 'consanguineous'. Unfortunately, this first grandson of the Poet lived less than six months, and was buried on 8 May 1617.

[1] Smart, *Shakespeare Truth and Tradition*, p. 156.
[2] *Council Book B*, 315 f., 318 f.

The other children were also boys—Richard, baptized 9 February 1618, and Thomas, baptized 23 January 1620.

Quyney, who was 'Master Thomas' and 'gentleman', was elected a Burgess on 28 August 1617 and a Constable in September. He served as a Chamberlain from 1621 to 1623, and presented his Accompt on 9 January 1624. In his absence it was voted 'imperfect'; but on the 29th, with some explanation from him, it was passed.[1] The document exists in his own handwriting, with flourishing signatures and a motto in French:

> Bien heureux est celui qui pour devenir sage
> Qui par[2] le mal d'autrui fait son apprentissage.

The original lines by Saint Gelais, run:

> Heureux celui qui pour devenir sage
> Du mal d'autrui fait son apprentissage—

'Happy is he who, to become wise, serves his apprenticeship from other men's troubles.'

Doctor Hall, with his wife and daughter (eight years old), if not already in residence there, came to live at *New Place*. He proved Shakespeare's Will in London on 22 June 1616, and exhibited the inventory of the Poet's goods, which unfortunately is lost. The Stratford Corporation, eager to have him as a member, elected him a Burgess on 14 March 1617. He pleaded his professional duties, and was excused. A letter from him to the Corporation respecting the dissolution of the College is alluded to in their minutes of 6 November 1618,[3] but is not extant. He was an active Churchman and Puritan, and a devoted admirer of the eloquent, headstrong Vicar, instituted in 1619, Thomas Wilson. We find him at the parish meeting for the election of Churchwardens on 3 April 1621. Again he was elected a Burgess, in 1622, and excused.

There is a regrettable gap in Thomas Greene's 'diary' from 10 April to 4 September 1616, the period of Shakespeare's last days, death, and burial, and his own determination probably to leave Stratford. Combe troubled him to the end of his Stewardship; but it was the loss of his great kinsman, evidently, that

[1] *Council Book B*, 444.

[2] By a slip Quyney has repeated *pour* from the previous line.

[3] *Council Book B*, 364.

decided him to sell his house and interest in the tithes and remove to Bristol. A defiant letter from Combe was received by Chandler 'at Master Greene's gate' on Trinity Sunday, 26 May 1616. The diary of 4 September informs us of his abuse of his powers as High Sheriff to distrain on the cattle of the commoners. The entry of 5 September is:

> Master Hall told me of G. Bonner's saying what he would do to Lucas; and that Master Sheriff said Lucas could not be an honest man, for he had no religion in him;

and of 7 September:

> The Sheriff's lying in the ditches a-field to keep other men's sheep forth of Welcombe Meadow.

Sir Edward Coke's dismissal from the Lord Chief Justiceship in November encouraged Combe still further. His diggers continued, in spite of protest, their mound and trench. A *latitat*[1] against him in the King's Bench was, on Greene's advice, sent for. The last entries in the diary are of 19 February 1617. One reports:

> Combe to the diggers, *Masters, go on with your business; I will bear you out, though it costeth me £500.*

Greene had intimated about Christmas his intention to resign, and gave in his notice on 24 March: by which date Combe's 'ditch' had extended to 402 perches (or 2,211 yards), 350 perches (or 2,025 yards) being 'upon the continual common greensward'; whereon '400 or 500 of his sheep all summer ate up the grass'. On 8 April the Council elected Francis Collins to succeed Greene, provided he left Warwick and resided in Stratford.[2] Sir George Carew wanted John Greene to succeed his brother, but his recommendation (on 28 May, from the Savoy) was too late. Thomas Greene was in London for the Easter term (7 May–2 June) and wrote from his chambers at the Middle Temple on 22 May to the Bailiff and Alderman (the half-brothers, Henry and Francis Smith) relative to the purchase by the Council of his house[3] and interest in the tithes.

[1] 'He lies hid.' A writ whereby all persons were originally summoned to answer in personal actions in the King's Bench; so called because it is supposed by the writ that the defendant lurks and lies hid or has gone into some other county, to the sheriff of which this writ was directed to apprehend him there.

[2] *Council Book B*, 326.

[3] 'A pretty, neat, gentlemanlike house, with a pretty garden, and a little young

In the friendliest manner he declines their offer:

I have received your letters of the 15 of this May; and do see, if we agree I must lose a hundred marks on the true value of my things I sell, to the place which has more reason, if I may speak it without offence, to give me recompence to a greater value for my golden days and spirits spent in Stratford's service.[1]

He writes again on 27 May, accepting their revised terms:

Yet with this, I will deal with *you*, and not with a corporation . . . as you amongst yourselves shall think meet, for the safety of yourselves and the good of that Borough to which I shall ever wish happiness and prosperity.

It will be Whitsun Eve[2] before I come home; and on Trinity Monday[3] I must needs take my journey for Thornbury without return before the term.[4] Wherefore if it please you to provide on your parts . . . I offer to you whether you shall not think it fit, to have this term a *dedimus potestatem*[5] of my wife and me, and to think in whose names you will take it . . .

Haste makes me break off—yet I shall not be hasty to leave to love you: but shall ever rest your very loving friend.[6]

Greene received £240 for St. Mary's and £360 for his tithes in two payments of £340 on 23 June 1617 and £260 on 3 February 1618. The money was raised by loans from members of the Council, Henry Smith advancing £80, Francis Smith £80, John Gibbs £20, Henry Wilson £40, Daniel Baker £80, William Walford £50, Julyne Shaw £50, William Chandler £50, John Wilmore £20, Alexander Aspinall £5, Francis Ainge £50, Thomas Rutter £10, Thomas Greene of Henley Street £20, Richard Robins £20, Richard Hathaway £20, and William Mountford £5.[7] Of the money promised on 3 February 1618 the bulk of it was to be paid at *New Place* (as neutral ground), either to Master Hall, Francis Collins, or, as Greene writes, 'to me there'.[8]

This was a large and popular investment by the Corporation, and there was rejoicing at the taking possession of St. Mary's

orchard standing very sweet and quiet: the place and building within this six years' (see p. 670) 'cost above £400' (*Misc. Doc.* vii. 125).

[1] *Misc. Doc.* i. 1. [2] 7 June. [3] 16 June.

[4] Trinity Term: 20 June–9 July.

[5] *We have given the power.* A writ or commission to one or more private persons for the speeding of some act, granted most commonly upon a suggestion that the party who is to do something before a judge, or in a Court, is so weak tha the cannot travel.

[6] *Misc. Doc.* i. 2. [7] *Ib.* xi *Council Book B*, 329.

[8] *Misc. Doc.* xiii. 42.

House at Michaelmas 1617, 'two dozen silk points' being given to 'the boys', Master Aspinall's pupils, wherewith to deck themselves.[1] The rejoicing, however, had other ground than the purchase of the ancient School-house, which was speedily sold for £200 to the late Bailiff, Master Henry Smith, on his undertaking to pay £90 a year for seven years for Master Greene's late moiety of the tithes. The Corporation probably congratulated themselves that Greene's estate in Stratford had not fallen into the grasping hands of the Combes. Mistress Henry Smith, daughter of Mistress Aspinall and sister of Julyne Shaw, therefore succeeded Mistress Greene at St. Mary's House; and, by a vote of the Corporation on 8 October 1617, 'the seat where Mistress Greene did sit' at Church was allocated to 'Mistress Bailiff and Mistress Alderwoman'.[2]

One of Greene's last services for the town was to draw up a petition in 1619 to the Privy Council requesting their aid against Combe. He knew the whole story of the enclosure, and he tells it ably and briefly.[3] We learn that Combe had 'bought three farms at Welcombe, pulled down one of them and taken the land from another', both 'ancient houses of husbandry', and that 'the village of Welcombe, except his own house', was 'wholly depopulated'. Baker and Chandler rode to London to see Lord Coke—as he now was, though no longer Lord Chief Justice—and prosecute the suit, sending the Town Charter by carriage in 'a fardel'.[4] They might say with the Shepherd in *The Winter's Tale*: 'Let us to the King: there is that in this fardel will make him scratch his beard.'[5] They spent £15 7*s*. 6*d*. and, by Coke's help, obtained a stern reprimand from the Council, signed by the Archbishop of Canterbury, the Lord Chamberlain, and five others, on 12 March, confirming the orders of Assize, and requiring Combe on his 'peril' to 'lay open' the enclosed fields 'as formerly they were', 'convert the pasture into arable again', and 'restore the meres and banks'. In gratitude, the Corporation sent a present of ten cheeses, weighing 55 lb., to the Lord Coke, carriage paid.[6]

[1] *Chamberlains' Account*, 7 Jan. 1618. An indication of the number of the boys in the School.

[2] *Council Book B*, 336.

[3] *Misc. Doc.* vii. 3.

[4] *Council Book B*, 367, 369. *Chamberlains' Account*, 7 Jan. 1620.

[5] IV. iv. 727 f.

[6] *Misc. Doc.* vii. 6 (2).

On 15 June 1621 Greene was appointed Autumn Reader (*Lector pro tempore autumnali*) at the Middle Temple, with two other masters to assist him, John Hopkins and Thomas Trist.[1] On 8 August his son, William (Shakespeare's godson, we may believe), was admitted to the Middle Temple, aged 13½ years. Francis Collins did not long survive his succession to Greene as Town Clerk of Stratford. He signed his Will on 26 September 1617 and was buried next day in the Church. On 18 October Anthony Langston of Evesham was elected in his stead, with Alexander Aspinall for deputy.

Widow Hart, Shakespeare's sister, continued to live in Henley Street. Her youngest son, Michael, was buried 1 November 1618, and she was left with the two sons, William and Thomas, aged respectively 18 and 13. Bartholomew Hathaway, the Poet's brother-in-law, lived at Shottery, owner of the old home, Hewlands Farm. He lost his wife, Isabella, in February 1617. He made his Will on 16 September 1621, 'in good and prosperous health', and lived four years afterwards. The occasion of the Will may have been the betrothal of his third and youngest son, Edmund, and Margaret Cotterell of Shottery, who were married on 17 July 1622. The eldest son, Richard Hathaway, and the daughter, Annes, wife to Avery Edwards of Drayton, had received their portions. John, the second son, who was married and had children, was to inherit Hewlands, Edmund £120 in instalments. One of two bedsteads in the 'Over Chamber', probably the four-poster still at Hewlands, was bequeathed to John, the other (with 'my best featherbed, my best healing, two pair of sheets, one pair of my best blankets, my best bolster, and one of my best pillows') to Edmund. The handsome legacies to John and Edmund, as doubtless the portions to Richard and Annes, more than suggest the Poet's liberality to his wife's brother.

Richard Hathaway, who had a daughter, Isabella, was a Churchwarden when his uncle Shakespeare was buried in the Church in April 1616, and still when his mother was interred in the Church in February 1617. He was Chamberlain from 1617 to 1618, and presented his account on 8 January 1619. The document exists, and is worthy in its penmanship, consistent spelling,

[1] *Bench Book*.

Latinity (what there is of it—*anno Domini, imprimis, videlicet, vidua, summa totalis, item, per*), and business-like order, of a pupil of Master Aspinall. Friends of Shakespeare appear in the items—Master Shaw, Master Henry Smith, Master Richard Tyler (rent behind for 'the burned ground' in Sheep Street since the Fire of 1614), Master Greene ('use' or interest of money lent to the Chamber for the purchase of his property), and Master Hall (receipt of his £17, the rent of his moiety of the tithes).

Two items concern the Vicar:

Paid Master Baker for Master Rogers's gown, £3 12*s.* 0*d.*

Paid for facing Master Rogers's gown, and other things to Master Chandler, £1 2*s.* 6*d.*

It had been 'agreed' in the Council on 30 January 1618 'that there shall be a fit gown of good broad cloth given to Master John Rogers, our vicar, in hope that he will well deserve the same hereafter and amend his former faults and failings';[1] and on 8 May, 'that the Chamberlains shall pay for the furring of Master Rogers's gown, and for the outside and lining'.[2]

But this handsome present, if it improved the Vicar's appearance in the pulpit, did not make either his ways or his preaching more acceptable. The Corporation wanted an orator, like the well-known Puritan minister, Robert Harris of Hanwell, whose sermons at Stratford in October 1617 excited enthusiasm.[3] The opportunity for a change occurred in the spring of 1619, when Rogers inadvertently became a 'pluralist'. He 'got another benefice' and thus suffered 'a lapse', which, on the advice of lawyer Lucas, was promptly seized upon for the presentation of a successor.[4] This was obtained on 16 March, from no less a person than Francis Bacon, now Lord Verulam, Lord Chancellor, and as representative of the Crown, lord of the manor, for a gifted young preacher at Evesham, Thomas Wilson, a native of Kent and Master of Arts of Oxford.[5] Rogers and his friends protested; but the Council on 5 May, by a majority of eighteen to seven, resolved to petition for a confirmation of the appointment.[6] Wilson's eloquence and opinions had taken the Puritan

[1] *Council Book B*, 349.
[2] *Ib.* 354.
[3] *Chamberlains' Account*, 7 Jan. 1618.
[4] *Misc. Doc.* xi. 3.
[5] Not improbably grandson of his namesake the late Dean of Worcester.
[6] *Council Book B*, 372.

leaders by storm—including Shakespeare's son-in-law, Doctor Hall. On the other hand, 'libels' by supporters of Rogers, in verse and prose, were scattered in the town and parish denouncing fiercely the prime-movers—the 'Chief Rulers', as one rhymster called them, 'in the Synagogue of Stratford'.

A 'confederacy' against the Corporation and Churchwardenship, headed by Master John Nashe and, as was alleged, Master William Reynolds, enlisting the secret services of the disreputable apparitor to the Consistory Court, William Nixon, had been in existence for some time (at least since November 1617), and was ready for violence, however drunken, on the (practical) dismissal of the easy-going, faultful old Vicar. When Wilson attended evening service in the church on Sunday 30 May 1619, previous to his induction the next day, he was met by an infuriated crowd, armed with swords, daggers, bills, pikes, and stones, who shouted: 'Hang him, kill him, pull out his throat, cut off his pockie and burnt members, let us hale him out of the church!' Wilson, for safety, was hurried into the chancel (where Shakespeare was buried), and the church doors were closed. Certain of the crowd broke in, others battered on the walls and threw stones through the windows, terrifying the congregation.

The induction, nevertheless, took place on the 31st; and the Sunday following, 6 June, Wilson read himself in, before a congregation which included the Bailiff and his Deputy (John Wilmore of High Street and Henry Smith of St. Mary's House); Lucas the Town Clerk; Aldermen Gibbs, Henry Wilson, Daniel Baker, William Wyatt, Shakespeare's friend Henry Walker, his neighbour Julyne Shaw, his kinsman (through Master Thomas Greene) William Chandler; the Schoolmaster, Aspinall; Mistress Shakespeare's nephew, Richard Hathaway; the Churchwardens Richard Baker (son and partner of Daniel Baker) and William Smith (son-in-law and partner of Mistress Quyney, widow of Shakespeare's old friend, Richard Quyney), and others who signed as witnesses.

Connected with this riot was a fierce brawl about a May-pole. King James for once had been in the neighbourhood of Stratford. On 2 September 1617, on his return from Scotland, he was received at Coventry, where Philemon Holland, schoolmaster and translator, addressed His Majesty 'in a suit of black satin'; on the

4th he was entertained at supper by Sir Fulke Greville ('friend of Sir Philip Sidney', lord of Warwick Castle, but not yet Lord Brooke) in the ancient burger-hall (Leicester Hospital) at Warwick (the Castle probably undergoing reparation); and on the 5th he proceeded on his way to Woodstock. It was the royal practice to lecture the Puritans where, as at Coventry, it gave most offence. The following Whitsuntide, 1618, appeared the *Declaration concerning Lawful Sports to be Used*, commonly known as the King's 'Book of Sports', though it had as much to do with Recusancy as with Games on Sunday. The royal 'pleasure' here expressed (intended and in many quarters accepted as 'law') was, that Papists and Puritans, if they were dissatisfied and would not conform, should leave the country; that people should be suffered, if they wished, after divine service, to enjoy themselves with dancing, archery, leaping, vaulting, and 'such harmless recreations', and that May-poles, May-games, Whitsun-ales, morris-dancing, and rush-bearing should be permitted. On the other hand, it disapproved of bear-baiting, bull-baiting, and plays on the Sabbath, and of bowls at all times 'by the meaner sort', being a game only for bishops and gentlemen.

On the strength of this manifesto a May-pole was erected in 1619 at the entrance to the Church Way in Stratford, and here it stood as a rallying-point for the anti-puritanical in the Rogers-Wilson conflict. The Churchwardens complained on 9 June of the bad state of the Way by Master Reynolds's house. In the summer the 'road surveyors' repaired it, making a 'very fair pavement for the parishioners to and from the Church', and the Borough authorities resolved to remove the pole at the autumn fair. On 11 July, at a meeting of the Churchwardens and parishioners, a levy of £24 was agreed upon for the repair of the Church, £12 in the Borough, and £12 in the rest of the parish. The Bailiff and his Deputy subscribed their names to the resolution, and others including Doctor Hall, Bartholomew and Richard Hathaway, Henry Walker, William Chandler, Daniel and Richard Baker, Francis Smith (of the 'Corner House', Middle Row), William Walford (of High Street), William Richardson and Stephen Burman of Shottery, and, of course, the much-tried Churchwarden, William Smith, who was also acting-Chamberlain of the Borough, busy on the repair of the

Gild and School premises and the Vicar's house there, as well as of the Church. *On 16 July the Corporation resolved to contribute 'towards the keeping dry the Chancel'* (*Shakespeare's resting-place*). On 29 July five women and a man were presented at the Vicarial Court (presided over by the curate, John Owen) for rioting in Church (sterner steps were in contemplation for the ring-leaders); and Master Lucas, on the other part, was presented for losing his temper with a minister, Master John Bursye (a friend, presumably, of Master Rogers), 'striking and using him un-reverently, calling him *scurvy, rascal Knave*'. Such conduct and speeches were not tolerable even from the Town Clerk on behalf of an innocent young new Vicar. In the meantime, taking alarm, Nixon turned round upon the 'confederates', and without warrant summoned John Pink, the author of a slanderous libel against 'the ancient leading hypocrite' (John Gibbs was Senior Alderman) and a tailor's wife, to acknowledge his fault before the Churchwardens and six of the parishioners, forging for the purpose the signature of the registrar of the Consistory Court, William Warmstrey, Esquire. This was in August.

The Fair came (it was held on 13–15 September), and the Bailiff and his Deputy (John Wilmore and Henry Smith) on the opening day had the May-pole ('Summer-pole' it was called) removed—'not', as they professed, 'for any dislike unto the pole', but because it was an obstruction to 'carts and carriages' and diverted them on to the new pavement. In expectation of this action, 'forty' persons at least, the former rioters in the Church, gathered armed in the Church Way, and with shouts of triumph proceeded to set the pole up again, rearing it, though assured by the Bailiff that they were at liberty to re-erect it in a spot 'six yards distant', half-way up on the 'very self same place', to 'the great danger of raising a mutiny' amongst the 'great number of people which then resorted thither'.

The result of these two outrages was a bill in Chancery, drawn up with much local information by Lucas and committed to the Attorney-General, Sir Henry Yelverton, against 'one John Nashe, William Reynolds, Thomas Rutter, Richard Wyatt, John Lane, gentlemen; John Rogers, John Pincke, William Nixon, William Hathaway, yeomen; Thomas Milles, weaver; Thomas Courte, blacksmith; William Smith, maltster; Raphe

Smith, haberdasher; Joan Askewe, wife of Richard Askewe, and divers other persons, for malicious, libellous and riotous behaviour'.

Here are friends of Shakespeare, and a half-brother of his wife, in company with men he would hardly approve, charged with offences, whatever their motive, 'irreverent', 'murderous', 'slanderous', and 'outrageous', in the judgement of leading townsmen and magistrates who were his friends and relatives, and one of them his son-in-law. Master John Nashe, to whom he bequeathed 26*s.* 8*d.* for a memorial ring, was uncle to young Thomas Nashe, who in 1626 married Doctor Hall's only daughter and child, Elizabeth; and Master William Reynolds, recipient of a like gift, was the Catholic living in the Church Way. Master Thomas Rutter was less reputable, a Burgess in the Corporation, who gave trouble by neglect of his duties and an abusive tongue, and was pronounced in 1611 'unfit to continue a burgess'. Younger men were Master Richard Wyatt, son of the law-abiding Alderman William Wyatt, and Master John Lane, the defamer of Shakespeare's daughter, and 'drunkard'; Wyatt was aged 27, Lane 29. These five, 'gentlemen', were the ringleaders.

Of their supporters, William Hathaway was the youngest son of Mistress Shakespeare's father, Richard Hathaway, by his second wife, born in 1578 at Shottery, and being now a parishioner, not to be confused with his kinsman, William Hathaway of Weston-upon-Avon. His participation in these disreputable tumults probably throws light on the non-appearance of himself and his brother, John, in the records and Wills of the Hall-Nashe connexion, and the prominence there of his cousins, Thomas and William of Weston. Nixon, now or a little later, was 'excommunicate'. His relationship with Pinke recalls that of Master John Lane with Rafe Smithe in 1613. Such breaches and alliances give us little faith in the 'confederacy' of 1617–19. Of William Smith, maltster (son of Daniel Smith, maltster), Thomas Milles, weaver, Thomas Courte, blacksmith, and the women, Joan Askewe and the rest, we know very little, and will credit them with being 'persuaded, abetted and procured' by their betters.

A few quotations will indicate the quality of the 'libels' scattered, in song, recitation, or writing, up and down the parish 'in or about the month of May and at divers other times before and sithence'. One is *A Satire to the Chief Rulers in the Synagogue of Stratford*, the Bailiff Wilmore, and his Brethren the leading Aldermen:

Stratford's a town that doth make a great shew,
But yet it is governed but by a few:
O Jesus Christ of Heaven,
I think they are but seven;
Puritants without doubt,
For you may know them, they are so stout . . .

. . . .

A heavy curse, O Lord, upon them send,
Because they've bereft us of our best Friend,
And in his stead here have they placed
A fellow that hath neither shame nor grace,
Yet these men are True Religious without quirks,
For one of the chiefest hath read far in Perkins' Works . . .

. . . .

But soft, my satire, be not too free,
For thou wilt make them spurn at thee;
For rub a horse where scabbe be thick
And thou wilt make him wince and kick.

Lucas comes in for special attention:

Be sure their lawyer is of God accurst,
For he begun this mischief first,
And with his malice and his spite
Was first that brought this 'lapse' to light.

Another, in prose, is livelier. It begins:

Sirra ho! the greatest news since Pentecost. Where there is report that all the old biting, and young sucking, Puritants of Stratford are joined with their two Justasses a piece maliciously to displace and utterly undo their Minister, and to bring in his place as arrant a k—— as themselves, of purpose to assist them in their hypocrisy; and now seeing they have set all the Town together by the ears, which is the true office of a Puritant, and finding their plot hath not their wished effect it is thought that divers of them will run horn-mad: therefore I would have thee to make haste up hither.

The writer 'skibs' at one 'too busy', another who 'shows like a monster with four elbows', a third who is 'a cobbler turned divine'; but 'some death-unconscionable knaves will hearken to nothing but to fulfil their greedy desires. Therefore, farewell from Romany, this merry month of May: thy honest friend (if thou do not turn Puritant), F.S.'

A third piece, in rhyme, is signed Joh(n) P(incke). It is headed, *Stratford to the Magistrates*, and begins:

The Puritants are now found out, their walking late and early,
Beshrew their hearts, they spoil men's grass, and do not spare the barley.
The ancient leading Hypocrite, that is of all that sort,
(Some say) a sermon lately lost to wait afield for sport;
But now 'tis meant in better sort (as some of them do say):
The cause why he neglected church was but to save his hay.
But take heed how you do him charge with doing any harm;
He'll drive the countery of him that tells him of the Farm.

whereby is 'intended', we are told, 'one Margery Gunne, wife of John Gunne; and that one had carnal knowledge of her in a barley-close called The Farm'.

A fourth and last effort is a 'Sonnett' with a 'burden', otherwise a lamentation with a chorus. Apparently it is put (with sonnet-like disguise) into the mouth of the late defeated Vicar:

Who will relieve my woe? my heart doth burn
To see man's state, wane as the wind doth turn:
He wars and wins, and winning's lost by strife;
War is another death, a sure uncertain life.
Try and then trust, give credit by delay;
The feigned friend with feigned looks betray;
Baker had never lived to vanquish me,
Had it not been for Lucas treachery,
Shall I of Chandler and busy William speak?
That bade to make a tale and it to break?
Hence I conclude, what all the world doth see—
There is no peace where is no unity.
  Though I on earth for thee receive disgrace,
  Live I in Heaven, see Jesus face to face.

From this height, however, of sympathy, the singer drops to earth, and into the mire, with his 'burden' to please the clown and yokel at the Fair:

June, July, August and September,
Although he come he shall not mortify one member:
A very Rogue he is—
He cannot draw his pintle for to piss.

Here tragic and comic are mixed without dramatic effect! On 15 October, under the new Bailiff, William Wyatt *generosus* (William Chandler *generosus* being his chief Alderman), the Corporation passed a resolution (the old Vicar not having vacated the vicarage in the Chapel Quad) 'that Master Rogers shall have £3 more to that £2 which is lent him by Master Wilmore: for which sum he is to give his bond, and to give security for his avoiding out of his house within a week, and to deliver up peacably possession to the Chamberlain'.[1] Three days later Churchwardens Smith and Baker presented women for 'reviling and miscalling Master Wilson our vicar, giving him the title of *a knave*'. Rogers had vacated his dwelling before 10 December when the Corporation agreed to repair it for Wilson—'the hall floor shall be boarded', the 'clay of the floor in the great chamber shall be taken away' and boarding substituted, and the rest 'of the house set in sufficient repair'.[2]

We have Reynolds's answer to the Attorney-General—that he is 'persuaded his name is inserted upon some causeless malice and he is not guilty of the misdemeanours as set forth'. But the result of the proceedings is unknown.

§ 149. DRAMA

WHATEVER the King might say of bowling 'by the meaner sort', the Stratford fathers, including Daniel Baker, were careful of their 'alley' in the Chapel Garden. In Richard Hathaway's 'accompt' of January 1619 are items for 'remaking' it, 'picking stones' there, and 'sanding'.

Other items call for notice:

Delivered Master Bailiff, which was given to a company that came with a Show to the town, 3*s*. 4*d*.

Delivered *per* Master Bailiff's appointment to a Company of Players, 5*s*.

Paid for a pottle of wine sent to Master Grant the preacher, 1*s*. 4*d*.

These entries recall Shakespeare's youth, when Sermons and Plays equally had the patronage of the Corporation. In Daniel Baker's first Bailiwick, on 17 December 1602, a stern resolution had been carried that,

there shall be no plays or interludes played in the Chamber, the Gild Hall, *nor in any part of the House or Court* from hence forward: upon pain that whosoever of the Bailiff, Aldermen and Burgesses shall give leave or licence thereunto, shall be forfeit for every offence, 10*s*.

[1] *Council Book B*, 380.
[2] *Ib*. 382 f., and *Chamberlains' Account*, 7 Jan. 1620.

Were Baker not Bailiff we might assume from the sweeping terms of this resolution (which cover the Council Chamber, Schoolroom and Quad as well as the Hall) that the ground of objection was damage to the building and its precincts. School plays are forbidden, as well as interludes by travelling players, and we might suppose, for example, that there was dread of fire. But a resolution of 7 February 1612, when William Parsons was Bailiff, was even more drastic and definitely specified other grounds than 'inconvenience':

> The inconvenience of Plays being very seriously considered-of, *with the unlawfulness*, and how contrary the sufferance of them is against the orders heretofore made, *and against the examples of other well-governed cities and boroughs*: the Company here are contented, and they conclude, that the penalty of 10*s*. imposed in Master Baker's year for breaking the order shall from henceforth be £10 upon the breakers of that order. And this to hold until the next Common Council and from thenceforth for ever, excepted that it be then finally revoked and made void.[1]

The 'inconveniences', which were many—rowdy assemblies, breaking of forms and windows, drink, bad company, bad air, contagion—were largely due to the decline in the character of the players' productions, and the withdrawal of the old grave type of spectator. But feeling was widespread against the drama as such—as a playing at life, as a game, a dressing-up, an array, a scenical display of things too solemn and serious for actors on a stage. Such feeling had been strong among the 'lollards' against the miracle plays, and it was again strong among the Puritans as civil war drew on and the triumph of Cromwell. A sense of the 'unlawfulness' of their calling added sharpness to the mandate of corporations which bade players 'be gone', or 'rid them' (with a fee if they had an influential patron) 'out of the town'. Still, not all their 'commodities' were 'frail', and some were irresistible; and 'Master Bailiff' of Stratford in 1618, who was William Chandler (the step-son of Shakespeare's cousin, Master Greene), incurred no penalty for directing Richard Hathaway to pay 5*s*. to a 'company of players' and 3*s*. 4*d*. to the exhibitors of a puppet-show.

The fall of the Drama after Shakespeare's death was itself a tragedy. On Shrove Tuesday, 4 March 1617, a Puritan mob destroyed a new playhouse in Drury Lane. Shakespeare's old

[1] *Council Book B*, 220.

fellowship began to break up. Richard Cowley made his Will on 13 January 1619. He had acted with Shakespeare and Richard Burbage in 1592, and lived since 1596 (if not earlier) in St. Leonard's parish, Shoreditch, in Holywell (save for a short period), where Cuthbert and Richard Burbage resided. The brothers were probably godfathers to his sons, Cuthbert and Richard, baptized in St. Leonard's in 1597 and 1598. His name stands tenth on the list of 'principal actors' in Shakespeare's plays given in the Folio. He saved money and became a 'gentleman', with coat-armour before 1605 (to the vexation of Ralph Brooke). He lost his wife in 1616, and appointed his young married daughter, Elizabeth Birch, aged seventeen, his executrix in 1619. Cuthbert Burbage witnessed his Will, as did John Heminge, John Shanks the player (who had joined the King's Men from the Prince Palatine's, and lived in St. Giles's parish, Cripplegate), and Thomas Ravenscroft, who may have been the madrigalist. Cowley was buried in St. Leonard's on Friday, 12 March 1619. Richard Burbage that day had a seizure, and made a nuncupative Will, drawn up by his brother Cuthbert and witnessed by his devoted old apprentice, Nicholas Tooley. He died next day. The death of his old friend and neighbour may have deeply affected him and hastened his end. On the 16th he was buried in St. Leonard's. A friend who admired him both as an actor and a painter wrote a Funeral Elegy. 'He's gone', he laments, 'that could the best both limn and act my grief'; and continues, with valuable testimony to his genius as a player,

> He's gone, and with him what a world is dead!
> Which he revived, to be revivéd so
> No more! Young Hamlet, old Hieronimo,
> Kind Lear, the grieved Moor, and more beside
> That lived in him have now for ever died.
> Oft have I seen him leap into the grave,
> Suiting the person, that he seem'd to have
> Of a sad lover, with so true an eye
> That then I would have sworn he meant to die—
> Oft have I seen him play this part in jest
> So lively that spectators, and the rest
> Of his sad crew, whilst he but seem'd to bleed,
> Amazed thought even that he died indeed.

Henry Condell gave up acting, though still a member of the

King's company, after Burbage's death. His name appears (third in the list of twelve) in the royal patent of 27 March 1619, licensing them to play at the *Globe* and at their 'private House in Blackfriars', as also in any 'City, University, Town or Borough whatsoever within our said Realms and Dominions'; and again (second in the list of twelve) in the Livery Allowance of 19 May 1619; but this summer we find him in Shakespeare's country, and probably at Stratford in connexion with the Poet's monument and the Folio edition of his plays. He had invested, for some reason, in the moiety of an estate at Brockhampton near Broadway in May 1617, and he sold the same in the summer of 1619, personally attending at Brockhampton (or at Broadway) on 18 August[1] and attaching his signature to the conveyance in the presence of seven local witnesses, including William Sheldon of Broadway, John Hales of Coventry, and Anthony Langston, Town Clerk of Stratford. News of the destruction to the Church at Stratford on 30 May may have reached him, and his visit possibly accelerated the reparation of the Chancel.

1619–23

§ 150. THE STRATFORD MONUMENT

ATTENTION was drawn after Shakespeare's burial to the condition of the Church. A levy was made for reparation at a parish meeting on 22 April 1617; another on 13 October, in which month (on the 24th) the Churchwardens were cited to the Episcopal Court at Worcester. Expenditure to the amount of £27 16*s.* 10*d.* was reported on 7 April 1618, and among the receipts 8*s.* from Master Hall and 4*s.* from Richard Hathaway. William Chandler 'of his own free goodwill' gave 'the wainscot canopy that is over the pulpit'. The Chancel was pronounced 'ruinous and out of repair', and the lessees of the Tithes, including Master Hall, were called upon to restore it. On 4 December it was resolved that all fees for burials in the Chancel should be devoted to its reparation.[2] On 9 June 1619 Master Hall, Lord Carew, William Combe, Henry Smith, and others, were presented 'for not repairing the Chancel'. This was a few days after

[1] Barnard, *New Links with Shakespeare*, 4.

[2] *Council Book B*, 365.

Walter Scott, Bradford

SHAKESPEARE'S MONUMENT

WILLIAM SHAKESPEARE

Profile from a cast of the monumental effigy in the Parish Church, Stratford-upon-Avon

the new Vicar, Thomas Wilson, had been locked in there for his personal safety. A further levy for the Church (as distinct from the Chancel) was imposed on 11 July 1619; and on 16 July the Corporation resolved 'to bestow some charges' on keeping the 'Chancel dry'. The advent of George Quyney as the assistant minister at Michaelmas 1620 probably hastened matters. The uncollected levy of 1619 was raised and expended; and on 30 April 1621 Quyney and the Churchwardens (of whom Master Richard Tyler was one and the chief) presented Lord Carew, Master Combe, Doctor Hall, and *the Bailiff and Burgesses*[1] for the Chancel's decay.

The new Curate was the youngest son of Shakespeare's friend, Master Richard Quyney, a graduate of Oxford, fresh from Balliol, aged 21 in April 1621, a delicate enthusiast, usher in the School to Master Aspinall, as well as assistant to the Vicar, Wilson. As nothing is said of the old grievance in presentments of 25 February and 6 March 1622, nor in the minute of the parish meeting on 23 April, when yet another levy was agreed to for the repair of the Church, we may believe that the restoration of the Chancel was in hand. Bailiff and Burgesses did their part, as we learn from the Chamberlains' 'Accompt' presented 10 January 1623. The items are worth quoting:

> Paid the painters for painting the Chancel 20*s*., Samuel Scriven for glazing the Chancel 20*s*., to the same glazier 6*s*. 8*d*., George Burgess for mending the Chancel-walls 3*s*. 4*d*., the same for digging two load of stone 8*d*., to Hemmings for 7 strike of lime 4*s*. 8*d*., Nicholas Tybbotts for 9 strike of hairs 3*s*.

The entry following these items is to the effect that a preacher on 7 July, which was Sunday, received 6*s*. 8*d*.

We cannot disassociate these long-needed reparations from the erection of the mural monument to the Poet. This was the work of Gerard Johnson, the sculptor of John Combe's tomb. It occupied him in his workshop at Southwark near the *Globe*, where the Poet's old friends could drop in to criticize it, and eventually was brought down to Stratford and put up in the restored Chancel for the admiration of his relatives and neighbours—and, if our conjecture is right, of the King's Men on tour that summer in Warwickshire.

[1] As owners of the Tithe it was their duty to see that the lessees fulfilled their contract.

The Poet, bare-headed, looks up from his writing, his hands resting on a green cushion (crimson underneath) with gilt edges and tassels. In his right hand is a pen, beneath the left is a sheet of paper. The head was evidently carved accurately from a death-mask. The face is heavy and puffy as with fever, the eyes stare, the nose is sharpened, and the upper lip elongated by the shrinkage of the muscles and nostrils. Over a scarlet doublet, with white turned-back cuffs and turned-down collar, the Poet wears a sleeveless black gown. The tall domed head is bald, but the hair falls thickly over the ears. Eyes are light hazel, hair, moustache, and short-pointed beard (which has grown since the portrait of 1609–10) are auburn.[1] The likeness to the Droeshout portrait is unmistakable.[2] Above are the familiar arms and crest,[3] flanked by nude boy-figures, with spade and inverted torch, representing Labour and Rest.[4] Below is the inscription in Latin and English:

Iudicio Pylium, genio Socratem, arte Maronem,
  Terra tegit, populus maeret, Olympus habet.[5]
Stay Passenger, why goest thou by so fast?
Read, if thou canst, whom envious Death hath plast
Within this monument: Shakspeare! with whome
Quick Nature dide; whose name doth deck this Tombe
Far more than cost; Sith[6] all that He hath writt
Leaves living Art but page to serve his witt.
    Obiit anno Domini 1616
    Aetatis 53 die 23 Aprilis.

The praise, whoever the writer,[7] is enthusiastic. It tells of public grief, whatever the Court taste and contempt for 'Populus', and of a servile drama, only fit to wait at the table of the Master. We remember what the Poet himself wrote to his Friend in 1592:

The earth can yield me but a common grave
When you entombéd in men's eyes shall lie.[8]

[1] 'Your chestnut was ever the only colour' (Orlando's hair, *As You L. It*, III. iv. 12).

[2] See p. 725. [3] See p. 520. [4] *Art Journal*, 1903, p. 335 f.

[5] 'In judgment a Nestor, in genius a Socrates, in art a Virgil: the earth covers him, the people mourn him, Olympus has him.' For Pylium see Ovid, *Amores*, III. vii. 41, and Horace, *Carmina*, I. xv. 22.

[6] Sieh: the usual confusion between e and t.

[7] Probably a Londoner, who intended his inscription for a tomb ('placed within this monument') not for a mural tablet, and could speak with some knowledge of contemporary dramatic Art. We must notice his eye-rime.

[8] Sonnet 81.

There had been talk of the removal of Shakespeare's body to Westminster Abbey, to the spot (afterwards known as the Poets' Corner) where Chaucer, Spenser, and Beaumont were buried. This ceased on the erection of the Stratford monument. So we gather from a sonnet by William Basse:

> Renowned Spencer, lye a thought more nye
> To learned Chaucer, and rare Beaumont lye
> A little neerer Spenser, to make roome
> For Shakespeare in your threefold, fowerfold Tombe.
> To lodge all fowre in one bed make a shift
> Vntill Doomesdaye, for hardly will a fift
> Betwixt this day and that by Fate be slayne
> For whom your Curtaines may be drawn againe.
> If your precedency in death doth barre[1]
> A fourth place in your sacred sepulcher,
> Vnder this carued marble of thine owne,
> Sleepe, rare Tragœdian, Shakespeare, sleep alone:
> Thy vnmolested peace, vnshared Caue
> Possesse as Lord, not Tenant, of thy Graue,
> That vnto us and others it may bee
> Honor hereafter to be layde by thee.[2]

Condell, then, did not take part, as sometimes alleged, in *Sir John van Olden Barnaveldt* at the *Globe* in August 1619. Nor, so far as we are aware, did he participate in any of the Beaumont-Fletcher plays by his Company after this date. Heminge had not acted in a non-Shakespearean play since *Cataline* in 1611, and now Condell followed suit, leaving to half a dozen juniors of the old fellowship, headed by Lowin and Joseph Taylor, the production of the new, degenerate drama, such as *Custom of Country*, *Laws of Candy*, *False One*, *Island Princess*, *Women Pleased*, *Little French Lawyer*, *Pilgrim*, *Wild Goose Chase*, all produced in 1619–21, and *Double Marriage* and *Sea Voyage*, produced in the spring or early summer of 1622. Of eleven performances at Court by the King's Men in the winter 1621–2, only one was of a play by Shakespeare—*Twelfth Night*, under the significant title, *Malvolio*. A satire on a Puritan with Ass's Ears, saying, 'Is it now a time to

[1] Basse was a lawyer.

[2] *Lansdowne MS.* 777, f. 67 b. If, as some think, Basse's lines were written as early as 1620 (*Works*, Warwick Bond, pp. 113 ff.), we may suppose that they were inspired by a visit to Johnson's workshop rather than to Stratford Church and its dilapidated Chancel.

give gifts and to make merry?' was more in favour than *Timon of Athens*.

The King's Men toured in the Midlands in the summer of 1622 and visited for the first and only time Stratford-upon-Avon. They were in Leicester on 8 June and in Coventry on 9 August before returning to London to play *The Spanish Curate* on 24 October. They received 10*s.* at Leicester, and at Stratford were paid 6*s.* for *not* performing (as was their right) in the Gild Hall.

What brought them for once and now to Shakespeare's native town and home and burial-place? Heminge, Condell, and the rest of the old fellowship—Lowin, Underwood, Tooley, Eccleston, Taylor, Benfield, Gough, Robinson, Shank, Rice, if they were all there—but to pay homage to the man and his monument, and to receive 'papers', without a blot on them, from his Widow and Daughter and Son-in-law at *New Place*?

Nicholas Tooley died before the Folio appeared. His Will, made 3 June 1623, throws light on one of Shakespeare's oldest pupils and associates, and his relations with his fellows. We read:

I do give unto Mistress Burbage, the wife of my good friend, Master Cuthbert Burbage, in whose house I do now lodge, as a remembrance of my love in respect of her motherly care over me, the sum of £10, over and besides such sums of money as I shall owe unto her at my decease.

I do give unto her daughter, Elizabeth Burbage *alias* Maxey, the sum of £10.

I do give to Alice Walker, the sister of my late Master Burbage deceased, the sum of £10, to buy her such things as she shall think most meet to wear, in remembrance of me.

I give unto Mistress Condell, the wife of my good friend, Master Henry Condell, as a remembrance of my love, £5.

I give unto Elizabeth Condell,[1] the daughter of the said Henry Condell, £10.

Residuary legatees were Cuthbert Burbage and Henry Condell; and beneficiaries, by forgiveness of their debts, were three other King's Men—Joseph Taylor, John Underwood, and William Eccleston. The debt of yet another, Richard Robinson, he did *not* forgive, but directed that it should be paid to Sarah Burbage,[2] the daughter of his old master; nor did he leave anything to her mother, Richard Burbage's widow,[3] whom Robinson had married.

[1] Baptized 26 Oct. 1606. [2] Baptized 5 Aug. 1619. [3] Winifred.

Other bequests prove his piety:

I give unto my good friend, Master Thomas Adams, preacher of God's Word, whom I do entreat to preach my funeral sermon, £10.

I do give for the perpetual relief of the poor of Saint Leonard in Shoreditch four score pounds . . . every Sunday morning after morning prayer out of the increase shall be distributed thirty-and-two penny wheaten loaves.

I do give for the perpetual relief of the poor of Saint Giles without Cripplegate twenty pounds: . . . every Sunday morning . . . eight penny wheaten loaves.'

He commended his soul to God the Father, trusting by the merits of Christ to 'obtain full and free pardon of all my sins, and enjoy everlasting life amongst the elect children of God'. He was buried in St. Giles, on 5 June, 'gentleman'.

He is the 'Nick' who as a boy played with Burbage and Shakespeare in *The Seven Deadly Sins, part 2*, in 1592.

Nor did Shakespeare's widow see the Folio edition of his plays. This year, on 8 August, she was buried[1] by his side, next the

HEERE LYETH INTERRED THE BODY OF ANNE WIFE
OF WILLIAM SHAKESPEARE WHO DEPTED THIS LIFE THE
6TH DAY OF AVGV: 1623 BEING OF THE AGE OF 67 YEARES
Vbera, tu mater, tu lac, vitamq dedisti.
Væ mihi: pro tanto munere saxa dabo?
Quam mallem, amoueat lapidem, bonus angl? ore
Exeat, christi corpus, imago tua
Sed nil vota valent. venias cito Christe; resurget
Clausa licet tumulo mater et astra petet

Inscription on the grave of the Poet's widow

Chancel wall. She 'did earnestly desire', says Dowdall's[2] informant (the old sexton, Castle, who was nine years of age when Mistress Shakespeare died), 'to be laid in the same grave with him', but 'not one, for fear of the curse abovesaid, dare touch his gravestone'. A brass on her grave has this inscription:

Heere lyeth interred the body of Anne, wife of William Shakespeare,

[1] *Register*, p. 104.

[2] To Southwell, 1693: Halliwell-Phillipps, *Outlines*, ii. 72.

who departed this life the 6th day of August 1623, being of the Age of 67 yeares.

Vbera, tu mater, tu lac vitamque dedisti:
  Vae mihi: pro tanto munere saxa dabo?
Quam mallem amoueat lapidem bonus Angelus orem!
  Exeat, ut Christi corpus, imago tua.
Sed nil vota valent; venias cito, Christe! resurget
  Clausa licet tumulo mater et astra petet.[1]

The grief is Susanna's, the Latin, probably, Doctor Hall's.

1623

§ 151. THE FOLIO

HEMINGE and Condell at this time were busy on an edition of Shakespeare's plays. Behind the Poet's bequests to them of memorial rings[2] there may have been an understanding respecting his dramas. Shakespeare knew, as every great artist knows and alone knows, the value of his work; and that he was indifferent to its fate, as some allege, is unthinkable. It was his intention to revise and publish it. This is clearly implied in what Heminge and Condell say in their interesting (if also disappointing) Epistle to the Readers in the Folio:

> It had been a thing, we confess, worthy to have been wished *that the Author himself had lived to have set forth and overseen his own writings*; but since it hath been ordained otherwise, and he by death departed from that right, we pray you do not envy his friends the office of their care and pain to have collected and published them.

The task of revision, then, was interrupted by the Poet's death; and the fact that the editors had to 'collect' the dramas is evidence that the work had not proceeded far. Internal testimony confirms both conclusions.

Even if Shakespeare, as he probably did, kept a copy of every one of his plays, yet the original work underwent change in

[1] 'Breasts, O Mother, milk and life thou didst give: Woe is me! for so great a boon shall I give stones? How rather would I pray that the good Angel should move the stone, that, like Christ's body, thine image might come forth! But nought avail my prayers. Come speedily, O Christ! that my Mother, though shut within this tomb, may rise again and seek the stars.' The allusion is to Matthew xxviii. 2, Mark xvi. 3 in the *Vulgate: Angelus . . . revolvit lapidem ab ostio monumenti.*

[2] p. 826.

rehearsal and successive production, and the copyright of the playbooks passed out of his hands to the company (in almost every case his own) to whom he sold the drama. Moreover, certain of the playbooks were stolen and disposed of to printers, who thus secured an interest in them. Quarto editions of no less than nineteen of the thirty-seven plays appeared before the publication of the Folio, some excellent, obviously from the author's manuscript, others very imperfect, made up of a few good parts and the garbled results of stenography (sound and unsound version side by side). 'You were abused', say the editors of the Folio to their readers, 'with divers stolen and surreptitious copies, maimed and deformed by the frauds and stealths of injurious imposters that *exposed* them'—i.e. printed and offered them for sale. Such language would apply to the quartos of *2 Henry VI* (1594), *3 Henry VI* (1595), *Romeo and Juliet* (1597), *Henry V* (1600), *The Merry Wives of Windsor* (1602), and *Hamlet* (1603); and of these plays in the Folio Heminge and Condell might justly say, 'they are now offered to your view cured and perfect of their limbs'. On the other hand, the quartos of *Richard II* (1597), *Love's Labour 's Lost* (1598), and *A Midsummer Night's Dream* (1600, Fisher) are so good, and in some respects so superior to the Folio that we may suspect that Heminge and Condell were either not acquainted with them or failed to obtain permission to use them. Great pains were taken by Shakespeare's company, as his fame grew, to prevent this piracy, and of the following plays there are no quartos, unfortunately, for our collation and correction of the Folio text: *Julius Caesar*, *As You Like It*, *Twelfth Night*, *All 's Well that Ends Well*, *Measure for Measure*, *Macbeth*, *Antony and Cleopatra*, *Coriolanus*, *Timon of Athens*, *Cymbeline*, *The Winter's Tale*, *The Tempest*, and *Henry VIII*. Efforts of publishers to get a copy of these pieces seem to have been frustrated. Some early dramas, also, to our loss, escaped their hands—*1 Henry VI*, *The Two Gentlemen of Verona*, *The Comedy of Errors*, *The Taming of the Shrew*, and *King John*. These eighteen plays were first published in the Folio. Lastly, inferior to the Folio, but not to be described as 'maimed and deformed', are quartos of *Titus Andronicus* (1594), *Richard III* (1597), *1 Henry IV* (1598), *The Merchant of Venice* (1600), *2 Henry IV* (1600), *Much Ado about Nothing* (1600), *King Lear*

(1608), *Troilus and Cressida* (1609), and *Othello* (1622). They include some of the most popular of Shakespeare's productions, and we can understand the difficulty of keeping them from the press. In one case, *Troilus and Cressida*, unpopularity left it a prey to the pirates.

From one source or another, including Shakespeare's manuscripts, Heminge and Condell had collected versions of thirty-six plays by the summer of 1623; and without waiting for *Pericles*, a play of dual authorship, pirated in 1609, and still popular, in demand on the stage and the bookstall, they brought out in the autumn the famous volume, *Master William Shakespeare's Comedies, Histories and Tragedies, Published according to the True Original Copies, 1623*. An advance copy presented by Jaggard to Augustine Vincent, the Herald, bears the inscription, 'Ex dono Wil(elm)i Jaggard Typographi a(nn)o 1623'.[1] Jaggard died on the completion of the work, his Will being proved on 17 November, nine days after the entry of the book at Stationers' Hall.

Among these 'original copies', as already said, were drafts from the Poet's own hand, first or later versions. The editors claim to give the reader not only the plays 'deformed by imposters' cured and perfect, but 'all the rest absolute in their numbers' as the Author 'conceived them'. And they add this most valuable piece of information:

> As he was a happy imitator of Nature, so was he a most gentle expresser of it. His mind and hand went together, and what he thought he uttered with that easiness that *we have scarce received from him a blot in his papers*. But it is not our province, who only gather his works and give them you, to praise him.

Reiterated is their protest to be merely collectors. They can have been little more. The Folio contains a host of misprints, omissions, and other errors of compositors, which no educated and careful editor would have permitted. We lament, indeed, with Heminge and Condell, that 'the Author himself', as they repeat in their dedication, had 'not the fate to be executor to his own writings', and we cannot forgive them for their negligence at least in the correction of the proofs. 'We have done an office to the dead', they declare, 'without ambition either of self-profit

[1] Lee, *Life*, p. 566 f.

or fame, only to keep the memory of *so worthy a Friend and Fellow alive*.' They might have been a little more jealous of their 'fame', and done higher service to their 'Friend and Fellow' by engaging, if they were unequal to the task, some competent scholar, even at expense to themselves, to 'oversee' the work of the printers. The cost, we know, was great (the Folio has more than 900 pages) and was borne by a group of stationers. It was 'printed by Isaac Jaggard and Ed(ward) Blount',[1] at the charges of W(illiam) Jaggard, Edward Blount, J(ohn) Smithweeke and W(illiam) Aspley'.[2] Whatever we owe to these men, editors, printers, and publishers, for their splendid enterprise (and our debt is incalculable)[3] we cannot acquit them of remissness in the supreme matter of the purity of the text. Where was Richard Field? why was he not in the undertaking? He was high in his profession—Master of the Stationers' Company in 1619 and in 1622. What did he think of the Folio? His supervision would have added greatly to its merits. He died in the autumn of 1624. By his Will,[4] which was proved 14 December of that year, he left a third of his estate to his widow, his house *The Splayed Eagle* to his son Richard, and property in Wood Street to his son, Samuel. He remembered his step-sons, Manasses and James Vautrollier, and his sister, whom we saw at Stratford, Margaret Young. He desired to be buried in his Parish Church of St. Michael: 'a proper thing', as Stow describes it, 'and lately well repaired'.[5]

Comparison of the Folio with the Quartos, notwithstanding errors in both, reveals certain lines of the Poet's revision. He follows more or less strictly the Act about the Use of the Divine

[1] Title-page. [2] Colophon.

[3] The praise of a contemporary is not too high: 'To my good friends, Master John Heminges and Henry Condell—

To you that jointly with undaunted pains
Vouchsafed to chant to us these noble strains,
How much you merit by it is not said;
But you have pleased the living, loved the dead;
Raised from the womb of earth a richer mine
Than Cortez could with all his Castiline
Associates: they did but dig for gold,
But you for treasure much more manifold.

Discovered by Sir Israel Gollancz among the papers of the Salusbury family (*Times Lit. Sup.* 26 Jan. 1922).

[4] *P.C.C.* 107, *Byrde*. [5] *Survey*, p. 286.

Name, and abandons oaths like 'Sblood' and 'Zounds'. He tends to drop old-fashioned expletives, such as 'Tush!', 'Pish!', 'Go to, go to!' He substitutes, to our regret, for homely Stratford words terms of London and Court culture—for trow, know; buss, kiss; dearn, stern; and or an, if; forfend, forbid; unpossible, impossible; perfit, perfect; thorough, through; sprite, spirit; pelting, petty; murther, murder; till, to; vilde, vile; aby, abide; a, he; afeard, afraid; faith, sooth, or troth; bepray, pray; Don, Dan; doth, does; maister, master; pleated, plighted; powther, powder; pottage, porridge; justicers, justices; presageth, presages; spake, spoke; further, farther; voice, noise; compt, count; sneak, steal. He corrects double negatives and comparatives, and turns old singulars into plurals—as in *Lear*, 'keep thy foot out of brothel, thy hand out of placket, thy pen from lender's book, and defy the foul fiend' (III. iv. 99–101). Such alteration was not improvement, and we are glad that it did not proceed further. But more subtle change has the touch of the master-hand, as in *Lear*, one of the plays undoubtedly loved and elaborated by Shakespeare: I. i. 41, 'confirming on younger years' to 'conferring on younger strengths'; 54, 'merit doth most challenge it' to 'Nature doth with merit challenge'; 163, 'recreant' to 'miscreant' ('recreant' recurring in 169); 177, 'diseases' to 'disasters' ('disease' has occurred in 167); 184, 'friendship' to 'freedom' as antithesis to 'banishment'); 185, 'protection' to 'dear shelter'; 231, 'unclean' to 'unchaste'; 242, 'respects' to 'regards' ('respects' occurs again in 251), and others in the same scene.

More striking is the cutting-down of the longer dramas. To restrain the flow of his thought and diction, in the interest of the dramatic situation, was ever the task of the Poet. He had 'an excellent phantasy', said Jonson, 'brave notions and gentle expressions, wherein he flowed with that facility that it was necessary he should be stopped'. Shakespeare omitted much at the last. A dozen passages in the *Lear* quarto, more than 200 lines, are excised in the Folio. As readers we should miss them; but the Poet wrote, and revised, for players and their audience. If he himself had edited the Folio, it would have been as a magnified 'playbook' for the green-room, rather than a volume in the Bodleian.

On the other hand, the Folio preserves much that is not in the Quartos. In *Richard III*, for example, it gives upwards of 200 lines not found in the earlier editions; in *Titus Andronicus* a scene (III. iii) not published before; in *Othello* some 150 lines not in the fine Quarto of 1622; in *King Lear* 50 new lines, notwithstanding the shortening; in *Hamlet*, and the rest of the plays, it republishes many independent lines or readings. Without the Folio, indeed, in these republished dramas, we should be at as great a loss as without the Quartos. Without the Folio, *Henry V* would be a ghost of itself, lacking the magnificent Chorus, the Epilogue, and some 500 lines more.

Again, if of less value than the Quartos in the restoration of Shakespeare's spelling and pronunciation, the Folio is indispensable. The printers have taken even greater liberties with his script—economizing their type and paper, bringing the verse-line into its space, dropping provincialisms and old-fashioned forms, conforming to new usage as well as convenience; but much of the original is retained both in plays long since staged and in recent productions. In *The Two Gentlemen*, for instance, we find *apparant* and *trewant* (pronounced *apparaunt* and *trewaunt*) *vertue*, *emperour*, *coulour*, *counsaile*, *travaile* and *travailer*, *soveraigne*, *Millaine*, *raigne*, *deigne*, *convaye*, *sodaine*, *glaunce*, *guift*, *queint*, *ghesse*, *howre*, *powre*, *towre*, *dowre*, *scowre*, *atchieve*; *imploye*, *injoyne*, *injoye*, *inrage*, *extreame*, *compleat*, *seaven*, *sommer*, *aboord*, *bloud*, *shepheard*, *moneth*, *tyger*, *fryer*, *neyther*, *ayme* and *ayre* (pronounced thus, for *aim* and *air*), *loyter*, *rejoyce*, *cloyster*, *starre* (the *r* rolled), *farre*, *jarre*, *warre*, *chidde* (not merely *chid*), *shedde*, *kisse*, *mistresse*, *worthlesse*, &c., *sonne* and *sunne*, *wrack*, *yong*, *musique*, *embarque*, *cloase*, *betroath*, *rime*, *yeelde*, *neere*, *heere*, *deere*, *beleeve*, *theefe*, *peece*, *pillorie*, *solitarie*, *legacie*, *perjurie*, *beeing*, *comming*, *doe*, *goe*, *mee*, *bee*, *shee*, *hee*, *noe*, *ore*, and survivals of the old preterites, *beautif(y)de*, *d(y)de*, *dynd(e)*, *falne*, *stolne*, &c. Scattered up and down the text are bits of pure Shakespeare, or almost such: e.g. 'My Mother weeping(e), my Father wayling(e), my Sister crying(e), our(e) Ma(y)d(e) howling(e), our(e) Catte wringing(e) her hand(e)s, and all(e) our(e) ho(w)se in a great perplexitie; yet did(de) not this cruell-hearted Curre shedde one teare: he(e) is a stone, a ver(ie) pibble stone, and has no(e) more pitt(ie) in him then a dogge: a Jew(e) wold have wepte to have seen(e) our(e) parting(e): why(e) my Grandam(e) having(e) no(e) eyes, looke you, wept her selfe blinde at my parting(e): nay(e), Ile shew(e) you the manner of it. This shooe [pronounced *shewe*] is my (F)ather, no(e), this left shooe is my (F)ather, no(e), no(e), this left shooe is my (M)other, nay(e) that cannot bee so(e) neyther' (II. iii. 7–18).

On the other hand, Shakespeare's words are attenuated in such lines as,

> VAL. Now, tell me, how do al from whence you came?
> PRO. Your frends are wel, & have them much commended (II. iv. 122 f.);

and

> And then I offerd her mine owne, who is a dog as big as ten of yours & therefore the guift the greater (IV. iv. 61 f.).

He probably wrote, 'Nowe telle mee, howe doe alle', 'are welle and', 'offerde', and 'a dogge as bigge as tenne of yours and therefore'.

Similar results are forthcoming from *The Tempest*. Here are the familiar *daunce*, *graunt*, *Millaine*, *barraine*, *sodaine*, *vertue*, *aboord*, *credulous*, *theame*, *ouglie*, *boudge* (budge), *porredge*, *sommer*, *fadom*, *burthen*, *murther*, *bloud*, *fowre* (four), *flowre*, *showre*, *powre*, *towre*, *sowre*, *warre*, *farre*, *marre*, *stirre*, *logge*, *dogge*, *digge*, *dragge*, *madde*, *witte*, *chinne*, *finne*, *shippe*, *toppe*, *guift*, *queint*, *wracke*, *twincke*, *stunck*, *suncke*, *trunck*, *kybe*, *lyon*, *clymate*, *pyne*, *pyde Ninnie*, *byde* (bide), *ayde*, *ynch*, *ayre* and *ayrie*, *hayre* (hair), *fayre*, *wayte*, *nayle*, *toyle*, *coyle*, *oyle*, *hoyst*, *sayle*, *poyson*, *foyzon*, *urchyn*, *rejoyce*, *joyne*, *noyse*, *demy*, *heere*, *deere*, *yeere*, *neere*, *cheere*, *peece*, *shreek*, &c., *blew* (blue), *fewell* (fuel), *swolne*, *stolne*, *falne*, *confinde*, *propheside*, *bedymnd*(e), *moap*, *stroake*, *snoare*; and new forms, *philbirt*, *scarph*, *turph*, *mushrump*. We are not far from Warwickshire. Shakespeare old as young writes, and talks—

> Fowre legges and two(e) voyces,—a most delicate Monster! . . . If thou beest Trinculo, come [pronounced *coome*] foorth; Ile pull(e) thee by the lesser legges, if an(ie) be(e) Trinculo's legges (II. ii. 93 f., 107–9).

Frequently we hear him in the Folio, as often we just miss him. Here he is, unmistakably:

(*a*) Yong Orlando that tript up(pe) the wrastler's heeles and your hart both in an instant (*As You L. It*, III. ii. 224 f.).

(*b*) What ere the Ocean pales or Skie inclippes
Is thine, if thou wilt ha't (*Ant. & Cleop.* II. vii. 74 f.).

(*c*) MENENIUS. You are ambitious for poore knaves cappes and legges: you weare out a good wholesome Forenoone in hearing(e) a cause betweene an Orendge w(y)fe and a Forset-seller, and then rejourne the Controversie of three-pence to a second day of Audience. When you are hearing(e) a matter between part(ie) and part(ie), if you chaunce to bee pinchd(e) with the Colli(que), you make faces like Mummers, set(te) up(pe) the blo(u)die Flagge against all Patience, and in roaring(e) for a Chamber [pronounced *chaumber*] pot(te), dismisse the Controversie bleeding(e), the more intangled by your hearing(e): all the peace you make in their Cause is calling(e) both the parties Knaves. You are a payre of stra(u)nge ones. BRUTUS. Come, come [pronounced *coome, coome*], you are well(e) understood to bee a perfecter gyber for the Table then a necessar(ie) bencher in the Capitoll (*Cor.* II. i. 76–92).

One more sketch of a country Law Court, though Menenius is a London magistrate.

(*d*) There was a Habberdashers W(y)fe of small(e) wit(te) neere him, that ra(y)ld(e) up(p)on me(e), till her pinckd(e) porrenger fell(e) off her head for kindling(e) such a combustion in the State. I mis(sde) the Meteor once, and hit(te) that Woman; who cryde out, Clubbes! When I might see from farre some fowrt(ie) Truncheoners draw(e) to her succour, which were the hope o' th' Strond, where she was quarterd(e); they fell(e) on, I made good my place; at length they came to th' broome-staffe to me(e); I defyde 'em stil(le), when sodain(elie) a f(y)le of boyes behind(e) 'em, loose shot(te), deliverde such a showre of pibbles, that I was faine to draw(e) mine honour in(ne) and let 'em win(ne) the Woorke (*Hen. VIII.* v. iv. 48–62).

(*e*) Yon (ribaudred) Nagge of Egypt—
Whom Leprosie oretake!—ith mid(de)s oth fight,
Wh(a)n vantage l(y)ke a payre of Twinnes appeard(e),
Both as the same, or rather our(e)s the elder,
(The Breeze up(p)on her l(y)ke a Cow(e) in June),
Ho(y)st(e)s Sa(y)les and flyes (*Ant. & Cleop.* III. IX. 10–15).

(*f*) Come, thou monarch of the V(y)ne,
Plumpie Bacchus with pincke eyne;
In thy Fattes our(e) Cares be(e) drownd(e),
With thy Grapes our(e) Ha(y)res be(e) crownd(e).
Cup(pe) us till the Wo(o)rld(e) go(e) round(e),
Cup(pe) us till the Wo(o)rld(e) go(e) round(e).
(*Ant. & Cleop.* II. vii. 120–5.)

(*g*) So(e) Bees with smoake, and Doves with noysome stench,
Are from their Hyves and Houses driven away(e).
They calld(e) us, for our(e) fiercenesse, English Dogges;
Now(e), l(y)ke to Whelpes, wee crying(e) runne away(e).
Hearke, Countreymen! eyther renew(e) the fight,

Or teare the Lyons out of Englands Coat(e);
Renounce your Soyle, give Sheepe in Lyons stead.
(*1 Hen. VI*, I. v. 23–9.)

(*h*) You Shames of Rome, you heard of—Byles and Plaigues
Plaister you ore, that you maye bee abhorrd(e)!
(*Cor.* I. iv. 30 f.)

And in such phrases as these, which lose force in modern speech: 'combynate husband',[1] 'verie Midsommer madnesse',[2] '*monstruousnesse*'[3] (cf. '*monstruositie*'),[4] 'measurelesse Lyar!'[5] (outburst of Coriolanus against Aufidius: as inexpressible in modern spelling as Juliet's '*auncient damnation!*'). *Murther*, not *murder*, is the Warwickshire word that runs through *Macbeth*.

The above is from plays only published in the Folio. Occasionally there is more of Shakespeare in the Folio than in the Quartos, even the best of them. By its means we obtain such results as in Brabantio's denunciation of Othello:

O thou fowle Theefe! where hast thou stowde my Daughter?
Damnde as thou art, thou hast inchaunted her;
For Ile referre mee to alle thinges of sence
(If shee in chaines of Magique were not bound),
Whether a Mayde, soe tender, fayre and happie,
So opposite to marriage that shee shunnde
The wealthie, curled dearlinges of our Nation,
Wold ever have (t' incurre a general mocke)
Runne from her guardage to the sootie boosome
Of such a Thinge as thou![6]

and in Othello's lamentation:

I found not Cassio's kisses on her lippes:
He that is robbde, not wanting what is stolne,
Let him not know't, and hee's not robbde at alle![7]

and in Emilia's 'swan-song':

What did thy Songe boade, Ladie?
Hearke, canst thou heare mee? I wille playe the Swanne,
And dye in Musique: *Willough*, *Willough*, *Willough*,
Moore, shee was chaste; shee lovde thee, cruell Moore;
Soe come my soule to blisse as I speake true;
Soe speakinge as I thinke, alas, I dye.[8]

[1] *Meas. for M.* III. i. 231.
[2] *Tw. N.* III. iv. 61.
[3] *Tim. of Athens*, III. ii. 79.
[4] *Tro. & Cres.* III. ii. 87.
[5] *Cor.* V. vi. 103.
[6] *Oth.* I. ii. 62–71.
[7] *Ib.* III. iii. 341–3.
[8] *Ib.* V. ii. 246–51.

The same assistance gives us the lofty strain of Shallow's friend, Silence, moved to utterance in the orchard:

Doe nothinge but eate and make good cheere,
And prayse God for the merrie yeere,
When flesh is cheape and females deere,
And lustie laddes rome heere and theere,
Soe merrilie,
And ever amonge soe merrilie![1]

Falstaff is delighted at the inspiration.

More worth having at first hand is Hamlet's ridicule of Rosencrantz:

H. Besides, to be demaunded of a Spundge, what replycation[2] shold be made by the Sonne of a Kinge.

R. Take you mee for a Spundge, my Lord?

H. I, sir; that soakes uppe the Kinges Countenaunce, his Rewardes, his Auctorities; but such Officers doe the Kinge best service in the ende: hee keepes them lyke an Ape in the corner of his jawe, first mouthde to be last swallowde, when hee needes what you have gleande: it is but squeezinge you; and, Spundge, you shalbe drye againe.[3]

and 'Spundge's' flattery of the King:

The cease of Maiestie
Dyes not alone, but lyke a Gulfe doth drawe
What's neere it with it. It is a massie Wheele,
Fixde on the somnet of the highest Mount,
To whose hudge Spoakes tenne thousand lesser thinges
Are mortizde and adjoynde: which, when it falles,
Each smalle annexment, pettie consequence,
Attendes the boystrouse Ruyne: never alone
Didde the Kinge sighe, but with a general grone.[4]

and again, Hamlet's ridicule of Polonius:

Slaunders, sir: for the Satyricall rogue sayes heere, that olde menne have graye Beardes, that their faces are wrinckled, their eyes purginge thicke Aumber and Plumtree gumme; and that they have a plentifulle lacke of Witte, togither with most weake Hammes.[5]

Sometimes an ending of a word puts all right, as in the Prologue to Hamlet's play:

For us, and for our Tragedie,
Heere stoupinge to your Clemencie,
Wee begge your hearinge Patientlie.[6]

[1] *2 Hen. IV*, v. iii. 18–23.
[2] A touch, for the thousandth time, of the Poet-lawyer.
[3] *Haml.* IV. ii. 12–23.
[4] *Ib.* III. iii. 15–23.
[5] *Ib.* II. ii. 198–202.
[6] *Ib.* III. ii. 159–61.

A passage in *King Lear* is almost letter for letter as it dropped from the Poet's pen, at *New Place*, in the autumn of 1606, Harsnet's book by his side, nearly within sight of his loved Cotswolds:

FOOLE. Prythee, Nunckle, be contented; 'tis a naughtie night to swimme in. Nowe a litle Fyre in a wilde Fielde were lyke an olde Letcher's hart; a small sparke, alle the rest ons bodie colde. Looke! heere comes a walkinge Fyre.

EDGAR. This is the foule fiende Flibbertigibbet; hee beginnes at Curphewe, and walkes to first Cocke. Hee gives the Webbe and the Pinne, Squeintes the eye, and makes the Hare-lippe; Mildewes the white Wheate, and hurtes the poore Creature of earth.

Swithold footed thryce the Olde:
Hee mette the Night-Mare, and her Nynefolde;
Bidde her alight, and her troth plight,
And 'Aroynt thee, Witch, Aroynt thee![1]

1623

§ 152. PREFATORY MATTER

THE title-page of the Folio contains a copper-plate engraving of the Poet inscribed 'Martin Droeshout sculpsit London'. On the fly-leaf facing it are lines by 'B.I':

To the Reader.

This Figure, that thou here seest put,
  It was for gentle Shakespeare cut;
Wherein the Grauer had a strife
  with Nature, to out-doo the life:[2]
O, could he but haue drawne his wit
  As well in brasse, as he hath hit
His face; the Print would then surpasse
  All, that was euer writ in brasse.
But, since he cannot, Reader, looke
  Not on his Picture, but his Booke.

'B.I', who was Ben Jonson, is more complimentary to the engraver than the engraver to Shakespeare. 'Martin Droeshout junior' was a young man of two-and-twenty years of age in 1623, a novice and unequal to his task. That the work should have been

[1] III. iv. 115–29. Cf. p. 886.

[2] This is Shakespeare's own image in *Ven. & Ad.* 11 f., 'Nature that made thee with herself at strife, Saith that the world hath ending with thy life'; and 289, 291, 'Look, when a painter would surpass the life, His art with nature's workmanship at strife'.

ENGRAVED PORTRAIT OF SHAKESPEARE

By MARTIN DROESHOUT

From the First Folio, 1623 (first state)

MR. WILLIAM
SHAKESPEARES
COMEDIES,
HISTORIES, &
TRAGEDIES.

Publiſhed according to the True Originall Copies.

LONDON
Printed by Iſaac Iaggard, and Ed. Blount. *1623.*

ENGRAVED PORTRAIT OF SHAKESPEARE (re-touched)
from the First Folio (reduced)

To the great Variety of Readers.

FRom the most able, to him that can but spell: There you are number'd. We had rather you were weighd. Especially, when the fate of all Bookes depends vpon your capacities: and not of your heads alone, but of your purses. Well! It is now publique, & you wil stand for your priuiledges wee know: to read, and censure. Do so, but buy it first. That doth best commend a Booke, the Stationer saies. Then, how odde soeuer your braines be, or your wisedomes, make your licence the same, and spare not. Iudge your sixe-pen'orth, your shillings worth, your fiue shillings worth at a time, or higher, so you rise to the iust rates, and welcome. But, what euer you do, Buy. Censure will not driue a Trade, or make the Iacke go. And though you be a Magistrate of wit, and sit on the Stage at *Black-Friers*, or the *Cock-pit*, to arraigne Playes dailie, know, these Playes haue had their triall alreadie, and stood out all Appeales; and do now come forth quitted rather by a Decree of Court, then any purchas'd Letters of commendation.

It had bene a thing, we confesse, worthie to haue bene wished, that the Author himselfe had liu'd to haue set forth, and ouerseen his owne writings; But since it hath bin ordain'd otherwise, and he by death departed from that right, we pray you do not envie his Friends, the office of their care, and paine, to haue collected & publish'd them; and so to haue publish'd them, as where (before) you were abus'd with diuerse stolne, and surreptitious copies, maimed, and deformed by the frauds and stealthes of iniurious impostors, that expos'd them: euen those, are now offer'd to your view cur'd, and perfect of their limbes; and all the rest, absolute in their numbers, as he conceiued thē. Who, as he was a happie imitator of Nature, was a most gentle expresser of it. His mind and hand went together: And what he thought, he vttered with that easinesse, that wee haue scarse receiued from him a blot in his papers. But it is not our prouince, who onely gather his works, and giue them you, to praise him. It is yours that reade him. And there we hope, to your diuers capacities, you will finde enough, both to draw, and hold you: for his wit can no more lie hid, then it could be lost. Reade him, therefore; and againe, and againe: And if then you doe not like him, surely you are in some manifest danger, not to vnderstand him. And so we leaue you to other of his Friends, whom if you need, can bee your guides: if you neede them not, you can leade your selues, and others. And such Readers we wish him.

A 3

Iohn Heminge.
Henrie Condell.

ADDRESS 'TO THE GREAT VARIETY OF READERS' FROM THE FIRST FOLIO

PHILIP HERBERT, EARL OF MONTGOMERY

From an etching after VAN DYCK

entrusted to one so incompetent is another mark of inefficiency in the promoters of the Folio. Young Droeshout's relationship to the painter of the portrait of 1609–10 is almost his sole qualification. He may have seen Shakespeare in his uncle's studio, but he has not drawn on recollections. He endeavours a parrot-like copy of the Portrait, and he fails. The nose is wrong, too broad at the top and snubbed at the end. The forehead is bulbous, as if the Poet died of water-on-the-brain. The eyes, the distinguishing feature of the Portrait, are not a pair, the left being lower and larger than the right. Of the ear, because little or nothing was visible in the Portrait and the youthful engraver falls back on knowledge, he makes a sorry mess. Subsequent efforts to improve the likeness of the Engraving to the Portrait, by enlargement of the moustache, addition of shadows on the ruff and deepening of them on the cheek and brow,[1] only emphasize, as already said,[2] the lack of resemblance and the apprentice-hand.

After the title-page follows the Dedication—'to the most noble and imcomparable pair of brethren', William and Philip Herbert, sons of Philip Sidney's sister, Mary Countess of Pembroke, who had recently died in London and been buried in Salisbury Cathedral, in October 1621. 'Since your Lordships have been pleased to think these trifles something heretofore, and have prosecuted both them and their Author with so much favour, we hope', said the Editors, 'you will use the like indulgence toward them you have done unto their Parent.'

Then comes the Epistle 'to the great variety of Readers' with a startling request to *purchase* (the Folio was offered at 20*s*.)—'Whatever you do, Buy! Censure will not drive a trade or make the Jack go.' Want of funds, we may believe, was answerable for the poor proof-reading and cheap engraving in the Folio. Commendatory verses are added by Leonard Digges, 'I. M.', Ben Jonson, and Hugh Holland. Jonson is at last enthusiastic, all carping done and envy gone:[3]

Soule of the Age!
The applause! delight! the wonder of our Stage!

[1] The darkening of the shadow at the roots of the hair intensifies the swollen forehead and gives the appearance of a wig. [2] p. 726.

[3] Almost: he must bring in his superiority in Classical Learning, for which we will forgive him.

II D d

My Shakespeare rise; I will not lodge thee by
Chaucer, or Spenser, or bid Beaumont lye
A little further, to make thee a roome:[1]
Thou art a Moniment, without a tombe,
And art aliue still, while thy Booke doth liue,
And we have wits to read, and praise to giue.
That I not mixe thee so, my braine excuses;
I meane, with great, but disproportion'd Muses;
For, if I thought my iudgment were of yeeres,
I should commit thee surely with thy peeres,
And tell, how farre thou didst our Lily out-shine,
Or sporting Kid, or Marlowe's mighty line;
And though thou hadst small Latine and lesse Greeke,
From thence to honour thee, I would not seeke
For names; but call forth thund'ring Æschilus,
Euripides, and Sophocles to vs,
Paccuuius, Accius, him of Cordoua dead,[2]
To life again, to heare thy Buskin tread,
And shake a Stage: Or, when thy Sockes were on,
Leaue thee alone, for the comparison
Of all that insolent Greece, or haughtie Rome
Sent forth, or since did from their ashes come.
Triumph, my Britaine, thou hast one to showe,
To whom all Scenes of Europe homage owe:
He was not of an age, but for all time!

. . . .

Sweet Swan of Auon, what a sight it were
To see thee in our waters yet appeare,
And make those flights upon the bankes of Thames,
That so did take Eliza, and our Iames!

Holland, 'I. M' (if he was James Mabbe), and Digges were University men, the first from Cambridge, the others from Oxford. 'His days are done', writes Holland in his laudatory sonnet,

that made the dainty plays
Which made the *Globe* of heaven and earth to ring.

Mabbe also refers to the *Globe*, under its common name 'The World':

Wee wondred (Shake-speare) that thou went'st so soone[3]
From the World's Stage, to the Graue's Tyring-roome.

[1] He had read Basse's elegy (see p. 851) and thought it altogether inadequate.

[2] Here Jonson spoils his praise with pedantry. Paccuvius and Accius are little more than names and, like Seneca's birth at Cordova, 'caviare to the general'.

[3] So young, 52 years old.

Wee thought thee dead, but this thy printed worth,
Tels thy Spectators, that thou went'st but forth
To [re-]enter with applause.

Leonard Digges, a Londoner, born in 1588, and B.A. of Oxford in 1607,[1] takes us, as nobody else has done, to the productions at the *Globe*, both before and since the Poet's death. His father, Thomas Digges, the mathematician, died a parishioner of St. Mary Aldermanbury, in 1595, 'esquire'.[2] The boy, who matriculated from University College when he was fifteen, knew Shakespeare, as well as his neighbours, Heminge and Condell. He tells of 'the glad rememberance I must love of never-dying Shakespeare'. He will not speak of his 'works' for the plays were written with such ease,

Art without Art unparaleld as yet.

Only Nature helped him:

All that he doth write
Is pure his owne—plot, language exquisite.

Pardonable exaggeration in a worshipper. He continues—

But oh! what praise more powerfull can we give
The dead then that by him the King's Men live? . . .
How could the *Globe* have prospered since? . . .
So have I seene when *Cesar*[3] would appeare,
And on the stage at halfe-sword parley were
Brutus and Cassius,[4] oh how the audience
Were ravish'd! with what wonder they went thence;
When some new day they would not brooke a line
Of tedious (though well-laboured) *Catiline*;[5]
Sejanus[6] too was irkesome, they prizde more
'Honest Iago' or the jealous Moore,
And though *The Fox*[6] and subtill *Alchimist*,[6]
Long intermitted, could not quite be mist
Though these have sham'd all the ancients, and might raise
Their authours merit with a crowne of bayes—
Yet these sometimes, even at a friend's desire
Acted, have scarce defrai'd the sea-coale fire

[1] *Register*, II. ii. 267, iii. 265.

[2] Barnard, *New Links*, p. 93.

[3] *Julius Caesar.*

[4] In the great quarrel-scene, IV. iii.

[5] Jonson's *Catiline*. Cf. 'Shakespeare puts them all down, aye, and Ben Jonson too. Shakespeare hath given him a purge that made him bewray his credit' (*Return from Parnassus*).

[6] Plays by Jonson.

And doore keepers; when, let but Falstaffe come,
Hall, Poines, the rest, you scarce shall have a roome,
All is so pester'd; let but Beatrice
And Benedicke be seene, loe, in a trice
The cock-pit, galleries, boxes, all are full,
To hear Malvoglio, that crosse-garter'd gull,
Briefe, there is nothing in his wit-fraught booke
Whose sound we would not heare, on whose worth looke
Like old coynd gold, whose lines in every page
Shall passe true currant to succeeding age.

This entry evidently was written for the Folio, but declined by the Editors as severe on Jonson and somewhat slighting to the King's men.[1] Digges therefore wrote another and shorter, which was accepted. In it he refers to 'the Stratford monument', to the quarrel-scene in *Julius Caesar*, and to 'our bankrout Stage'. He applies to the Folio Ovid's prophecy of the *Metamorphoses*, which Shakespeare had applied to his Sonnets:

Nor Fire nor cankring Age, as Naso said
Of his, thy wit-fraught Booke shall once invade.

A list of the 'Principal Actors in all these Plays' and a 'Catalogue' of the dramas (from which *Troilus and Cressida* is absent, the Editors not knowing how to classify it) conclude the prefatory matter. The names of Shakespeare's twenty-five fellows must here be given in full:

Richard Burbage, John Heminge, Augustine Phillips, William Kemp, Thomas Pope, George Bryan, Henry Condell, William Sly, Richard Cowley, John Lowin, Samuel Cross, Alexander Cooke, Samuel Gilborne, Robert Armin, William Ostler, Nathan Field, John Underwood, Nicholas Tooley, William Eccleston, Joseph Taylor, Robert Benfield, Robert Gough, Richard Robinson, John Shank, and John Rice.

Most of these were dead before the publication of the Folio, and Gough and Underwood died just after it, in February and October 1624. Gough was Pope's old apprentice, and as a youth played Aspasia in *The Seven Deadly Sins, Pt. 2*, 1592. Pope left him apparel and arms. He married a sister of Augustine Phillips, and witnessed his Will in 1605. He lived near the *Globe*, and was

[1] It was published, after the author's death in 1635, as a prefix to *Poems written by Wil. Shakespeare, gent.* 1640. See Halliwell-Phillipps, *Outlines*, ii. 88 f.

JOHN LOWIN IN 1640

(By permission of the Visitors of the Ashmolean Museum, Oxford)

buried in St. Saviour's, the resting-place of so many of his fellows. Underwood, like Ostler, was 'taken' by the King's men from the Chapel children at Blackfriars in 1609. From his Will (made 4 October 1624) we learn that he lived in Smithfield, in the parish of St. Bartholomew the Less, had shares in the *Blackfriars*, *Globe*, and *Curtain* theatres, was a 'gentleman', and the father of five children. He appointed Henry Condell an executor, and John Heminge and John Lowin overseers.

1622–1628

§ 153. LATE FRIENDS AND NEIGHBOURS OF SHAKESPEARE

THE Shakespeare circle was fast diminishing. Mistress Davenant died at Oxford in April 1622, and her husband, who was mayor of the city, followed her to the grave eighteen days afterwards.[1] His desire was to be buried 'as near my wife as the place will give leave where she lieth'. A local eulogist wrote—

If to be great or good deserve the bays,
What merits he whom great and good doth praise?
What merits he? why, a contented life,
A happy issue of a virtuous wife,
The choice of friends, a quiet honour'd grave.
All these he had; what more could Davenant have?
Reader, go home, and, with a weeping eye
For thy sins past, learn thus to live and die.

His sons, Robert and William (Shakespeare's godson), were nineteen and sixteen years of age. Robert was at St. John's College, about to take his degree.

Another couple, old neighbours of Shakespeare, passed away together in the winter of the publication of the Folio, Mistress Aspinall in November 1623, and her husband, the venerable Schoolmaster, in February 1624. His late assistant, the curate George Quyney, died a few weeks later. Doctor Hall attended him in 1623 for a 'grievous cough', which proved consumptive. *Multa frustra tentata*, he records in his visiting-book, *placide cum Domino dormit. Fuit boni indolis et linguarum expertus et pro juveni*

[1] She was buried on the 5th, he on the 23rd.

omnifariam doctus—'many remedies were tried in vain; peacefully he slept with the Lord. He was of a good wit, expert in tongues and, for a young man, learned in every way.' Such praise would have given pleasure to his father, Shakespeare's old friend, Richard Quyney. He was buried on Sunday 11 April, aged just four-and-twenty. His sister-in-law, we remember, was Shakespeare's daughter, Judith Quyney.

Hamlet Sadler was a widower for the last ten years of his life, and died, as we have noted,[1] in October 1624. John Sadler survived him less than a year. His son, John, prospered as a grocer in London; and his daughter, Eleanor, married his son's partner there, who was Richard Quyney (of the schoolboy Latin letter of 1598). Another daughter, Margaret, married Leonard Kempson, gentleman, of Arden's Grafton, and brought her husband, who was a skilled musician, to live in the parental home in Church Street. Music and the Bible were features of that home, as well as painted cloths, wainscot, simple oak furniture, four-post bedsteads, a handsome cupboard, and a fine display of pewter.[2] Master Sadler died, if not so well off as his father in worldly goods, 'gentleman', and was buried 1 July 1625. Overseer of his Will, besides Leonard Kempson (to whom he bequeathed his municipal gown 'furred with foins'), was William Smythe, the 'busy puritant' of High Street, son-in-law of old Mistress Quyney, and her right hand in the business, certainly since and probably before the death of her son Adrian in 1617 at the early age of 31.

Master Francis Smythe of the Corner House, uncle (or certainly kinsman) of this William, served as Bailiff for a third time in 1623–4. In his Will[3] of 15 April 1623 he left £20 a year 'to the use and bringing up at School' (the University) of his nephew and probably godson, Francis, son of his half-brother William of Henley Street, otherwise for his maintenance until the age of 21, and then the sum of £200. Other nephews and nieces received legacies. To sons of neighbours in High Street, Master Smythe bequeathed £10 apiece—'to William Chandler now in Oxford, son of William Chandler, and to Richard Castle, son of Richard Castle'. He was buried in the Church 20 April 1625, Chandler,

[1] p. 792.
[2] Fripp, *Shakespeare Studies*, pp. 62–6.
[3] *P.C.C.* 52 *Clarke*.

Castle, John Eston, and a fourth friend, Baldwin Brookes, bearing his corpse to the grave.[1] A brass records,

> Hereunder lieth buried the body of Francis Smith the Elder, mercer, who was born and bred in this town, and bore the chief office of the same three several times. He died the 17 day of April 1625, being 66 years of age.
>
> If honesty be honour, let him have
> All honour that lies buried in this grave:
> Here born, here bred, a constant friend
> Of God[2] and goodness to his end.

Richard Castle, mercer, was William Chandler's tenant (of no. 36) in the High Street. He was one of the 'Chief Rulers in the Synagogue of Stratford', 'a monster with four elbows' ('because he useth in his gait or going, as some observe, to shake his elbows'). His son, Richard, legatee of Master Smythe's £10, was a child, baptized 7 May 1620.

Young Chandler matriculated at Oxford from Lincoln College on 9 May 1617 (born in Leicestershire, son of a 'gentleman', aged 17), and he took his B.A. in 1622.[3] The father had lost his wife, Elizabeth Quyney, in 1615, who left him a son, Richard, seven years of age, and a baby daughter, Elizabeth. By a third wife, whom he married that year, he had eight children, bearing, save one, Biblical names. He exchanged his house *The Cage* for that of Thomas Quyney in the High Street (no. 36) in 1616.[4] We have his letter to his 'father', Master Thomas Greene, of 26 January 1615,[5] and a letter to him from the young squire Combe offering him one hundred angels 'on Midsummer Day 1616 or sooner', if he would help him in his enclosure. Combe was High Sheriff and exultant. His letter was written on Trinity Sunday, and pious as well as tempting and threatening:

> If I may lay down my land from tillage by law, and without your consents [*i.e.* of the Corporation] then methinks you, being surety for the good of your town, do hazard the breach of your oaths in refusing this my offer; which may turn you to much prejudice but accepting of it much benefit and peace; which the prophet David saith we ought to seek and follow after it.[6]

[1] So, at least, he desired in his Will.

[2] 'Abraham . . . was called the friend of God' (James ii. 23).

[3] *Register*, II. ii. 361, iii. 404.

[4] p. 832. See p. 821.

[5] *Misc. Doc.* i. 108.

[6] 'seek peace and follow after it.' The Bishops' Bible and the Prayer Book have 'seek peace and ensue it'. The Authorized (1611) has 'seek peace and pursue it'.

But he mistook his man. Chandler was not to be beguiled by 'angels', nor by Psalm xxxiv. 14, even in the Geneva Version. He served as Bailiff in 1617–18. Julyne Shawe was his deputy, whose wife stood godmother at the christening of his child, Samuel, on the first Sunday of the new year 1618 (4 January), in the face, no doubt, of a large congregation, including his 'brethren' and their wives of the Corporation. In April following it was placed on record, in the Churchwardens' minutes, that

> This year last past Master William Chandler, now Bailiff, did, of his own free goodwill, give the wainscot canopy that is over the pulpit.

In May, when Master Combe erected a 'ditch' to enclose the Butt Close by the Bridge, the Bailiff paid 2*s*. 4*d*. unto workmen for throwing it down, and 10*s*. unto Master Lucas for his advice—Lucas being Thomas Lucas of Gray's Inn and Stratford, and counsel to the Corporation.

As Thomas Greene had missed Shakespeare in Stratford, so Chandler must have regretted his step-father's departure. He would enjoy a visit to him, we may think, at the Middle Temple. We find him in London again and again on Borough or Parish Church business—in Hilary Term 1619 with Daniel Baker, in Lent Term with the same, and in the Easter Term unaccompanied; in February 1623 with the Town Clerk, Anthony Langston, 'attending the Right Honourable the Lord Treasurer with our charter, at Chelsea'; in January 1625, lodging in Chelsea, and 'going twice to London by water with Master Catchmay', ecclesiastical counsel (at a cost for both of 6*s*.), and in February following when he spent 'a fortnight and upwards' in Town, and in May of this year to 'inform the Earl of Middlesex'—the corrupt Lord Treasurer—'of the state of the Vicar's peculiar jurisdiction and what belongs to it'.

Shakespeare's friend, Richard Tyler, yeoman and gentleman, and his son of the same name, lawyer, are not easily at times distinguished. The latter, no doubt, in his 26th year, drew up the deed of the transference of the Poet's house in the Blackfriars to trustees (in accordance with the terms of the Will) in February 1618.[1] On Sunday 10 January 1619, in Stratford Church, he married Anne, the surviving child and heir of the late Thomas

[1] Halliwell-Phillipps, *Outlines*, ii. 365–41.

Mills (Miles) of Rother Market,[1] and in her right inherited the lease of his house (once occupied by Rafe Downes and John Sadler the second[2]). Master Tyler senior followed his son to this home from Sheep Street, and ended his days there. In her Will of 2 September 1620 Mistress Woodward[3] made over to her grandson two houses in Rother Market in affectionate terms. She was the mother (Frances Perrott) of the young Susanna Woodward who gave her heart, notwithstanding the displeasure of her people, to Richard Tyler of Sheep Street, and became the mother of Richard Tyler junior. These houses seem to have been the King's House tavern by Mereside and the dwelling beyond it at the corner of Henley Lane.

On 3 April 1621 Master Tyler senior, ever reluctant to take office, consented to be a Churchwarden, with Vicar Wilson and the young 'reading minister', George Quyney. His colleagues were, for the borough Richard Castle (of the 'four elbows'), for the 'country' (i.e. the parish outside the borough limits) Stephen Burman of Shottery and William Court, son of the old lawyer of Corn Street. Subscribers to his election, besides Doctor Hall, were Daniel Baker, Francis Smythe, July (for Julyne) Shawe, William Chandler, Bartholomew Hathaway, William Smythe, and Daniel Baker's son, Richard.[4] It is an interesting group of Shakespeare's nearest kinsmen and neighbours. And noteworthy are the presentations by Tyler and his colleagues: of 'George Badger and Alice his wife and Alice their daughter for not receiving sacrament at Easter' (1 April), and with them 'John Lane gentleman' (the slanderer of Mistress Hall and leader in the riot against Vicar Wilson), Rafe Smith, and Thomas Combes esquire; of 'Thomas Clarke, taborer, for playing in time of divine service being Ascension Day' (10 May)—he was presented at Bishopton 'for playing with his tabor and pipe' the previous Sabbath, 6 May, 'in evening prayer-time';[5] of 'four who came not to Catechism, one as a common drunkard, a man

[1] *Register*, p. 29.

[2] Fripp, *Shakespeare Studies*, pp. 64 f.

[3] She was buried 30 Sept. within the Church, probably in the Chancel, the fee being the large sum of 20*s*. (*Vestry Minute Book*, p. 18).

[4] *Vestry Minute Book*, p. 18.

[5] The chirpy piping and tum-tum of this form of music, suitable for Kemp on his dance to Norwich (p. 519) or Ariel's charm to drunkards, would be trying to people at worship. See p. 753.

and woman for incontinency, two for opening their shops to sell meat on Sundays, a man and his wife for defaming a woman' (all presentments of 30 July); of two couples for incontinency, a case of adultery, and another of concealment of birth, and of 'Master Holder, curate of Bishopton, for baptizing the child concealed secretly', and of 'a shoemaker as a common departer out of the Church before the sermon be ended' (presentments of 25 February 1622); of 'Thomas Cowper and others for playing at cards in prayer-time on the Sabbath-day' (March). A confession of sin by one Eleanor Fletcher, extracted by Quyney, Tyler, and Court, may be given as an example of their Puritan discipline. Drawn up by Court in legal form, it is signed by Quyney and Tyler.

The 23[ty] daie of Marche Anno dom[in]i 1621 m[emoran]d[um] that I, Elionor ffletcher the daie and yeare aboue wrytten doe acknowledge my ffaultes & offences heretofore Comytted, Trustinge in god to become a newe Wooman, Confessinge them before Will[ia]m Courte and Richard Tyler, Churchwardens, & George Quyney, Minister of the p[ar]ishe Churche of Olde Stratford.

Tyler's term of office ended on 23 April 1622, when he and his late efficient colleagues were elected sidesmen. He was not responsible, therefore, for the presentment of five men 'for dancing the Morris in evening prayer-time on the Feast day of Philip and Jacob', otherwise May Day; nor of a couple in July for 'incontinency before marriage and their offence in being married without banns or licence', whose child Quyney had christened on 28 April on their promise to live henceforth 'as Christians ought to do'. But as sidesman it was his duty to take round the wine at Communion on the first Sunday in August (the 4th) when eight quarts and a half were distributed at the cost of 5*s.* 6*d.*, and on the first Sundays of September (the 1st), November (the 3rd), December (the 1st), February (the 2nd), and March (the 1st), when similar quantities were consumed.

But the outstanding act with which Master Tyler was associated as an officer of the Parish Church was the bold resolution of 30 April 1621 (at the first meeting of the Churchwardens after his election), calling upon the owners of the tithe, including the Corporation, to repair the Chancel. None would be more interested in the resting-place of his life-long friend. Richard Tyler junior began his career in the Corporation, of which he became a faithful and honoured member, by his election on 12 April 1623 as a Burgess. He was present at two meetings on 18 March 1625 when, under the bailiwick of Shakespeare's old friend, Henry Walker, 'the Company granted Master Wilson their certificate for his conformity to the Church ceremonies'. Vexed by the episcopal citations from Worcester, he knelt at the sacrament, wore the surplice, baptized with the cross, and married with the ring, and a petition for his relief and assistance was sent in the name of the Company to the Lord Treasurer. The same month Tyler was appointed, with William Smythe and another, to receive a church offering and 'sell the tythe pigges' (the latter duty, which recalls Mercutio's 'tithe-pig's tail', he probably delegated to his yeoman father). And on 19 April he was chosen a Churchwarden. He attended a meeting of the Corporation on 7 September, when a member was expelled for adultery and refusal to be censured by the Vicar's court; a meeting on 14 October, when he was elected 'Headborough' of his ward (Wood Street ward, which included Rother Market); and a meeting on 21 October, when a petition was drawn up, on the much-tried-and-trying Vicar's behalf, to Lord Brooke, and two were appointed to 'go over with it to my lord' at Warwick Castle, in company with the Vicar. The cordial feeling of the old Warwickshire magnate, better known to us as Fulke Greville (Sir Philip Sidney's Fulke Greville), for Stratford (of which he was Recorder) is evidenced by a letter from him, dated 'from the Court at Whitehall this 12th of May 1625', on behalf of Richard Townsend of Warwick for the post of steward (Town Clerk) on the death of Thomas Lucas.

He is a man [he writes] passinge well knowne to manie of yow, a neere neighboure of yours, and beside by his profession everie waie qualified. . . . If therefore yow shall thinke fitt to doe him curtesie in this for my sake, I shalbe readie to acknowledge it to yow all with thankfullnes And remayne your lovinge freind, F. Broke.[1]

Whatever their opinion of Master Townsend, they preferred, and with characteristic independence elected, 'Master Job Dighton of Middle Temple esquire', a fellow-bencher, and perhaps the commended, of Shakespeare's Cousin Greene.

On 3 December 1625 Tyler and his co-Churchwarden for the

[1] *Misc. Doc.* xiii. 69.

borough obtained the following apology from a Londoner who had been misbehaving himself in Stratford:

I, Richard Hill, Cittizen and habberdasher of London, doe hereby freely Acknowledge my ffalts Comitted at Stratford uppon Avon in unlawfull frequenting and haunting of Alehouses, and playeinge at unlawful games within the said Towne, and in giveinge evell words to the officers and Constables there: for all which I ame hartily sorry, and promise Amendment for the tyme to Come.

Witness my hand hereunto the day and yeire aboveseid

Richard Hills

Wm. Smith }
Rich: Tyler } Churchwardens[1]

This William Smythe was a kinsman, if not a grandson, of our old acquaintance of the same name of Henley Street, Shakespeare's godfather (as there is good reason to believe). He, too, was a haberdasher, and a chip of the same block, independent, masterful, puritan. He married the second daughter of the late Richard Quyney, Anne (baptized 5 January 1592), on 2 May 1614; was elected a Burgess 2 June 1615 ('William Smith junior', Thomas Greene denominates him, to distinguish him from his elder relative, probably his uncle now in Henley Street); was appointed executor to the Will of his wife's brother, Adrian Quyney, 28 June 1617; was elected Chamberlain in 1617 with Richard Hathaway, Headborough for the High Street ward in 1618 with William Chandler, and Churchwarden in 1619 with Richard Baker (son of the Puritan Alderman Daniel Baker) immediately prior to the troubles on the appointment of Thomas Wilson to the vicarage. Swiftly he had taken his place in family, borough, and parish, and not inappropriately was nicknamed by Wilson's opponents the 'busy'. He warmly supported the new Vicar, rode to Worcester, Hartlebury, and London on his behalf, and spent money (advancing it out of his own pocket) on the Vicar's house (in the Chapel Quad) as well as on the Chancel (the meeting-place of wardens and parishioners, and burial-place among others of William Shakespeare) on keeping it dry: all in 1619. Again and again he served as Churchwarden, and more than once he got into trouble for his officiousness, as when he sold trees in the churchyard for the cost of church repairs without permission of the Corporation. On 5 June 1623 the follow-

[1] *Misc. Doc.* vii. 76.

ing formal and severe resolution, in Aspinall's Holofernian manner, was passed (in spite of his supporters):

> At this Hall it is considered by the Company that William Smith, being one of the Capital Burgesses of this Borough and sworn of the Company, for divers of his misdemeanours against the Company and the Principal Officers of the Borough, and other his contempts against the government of the town, as is conceived: be, from his attendance and service of the affairs of the town and of his place of Capital Burgess, clearly discharged, and another be elected in his place.[1]

He retaliated with a writ for illegal removal, and proceedings seemed imminent; but by the good offices of the lawyer Lucas, on his submission and signature he was restored to his place and its privileges. He was a beneficiary by Lucas's Will, which he witnessed on 30 April 1625. On 17 May he was deputed by the Corporation to go to London with William Chandler, and on 1 June he was made an Alderman in succession to his kinsman, Master Francis Smythe. He helped to make the inventory of John Sadler's goods on 25 July, after witnessing his Will on 12 May 1625. He was Churchwarden again this year, and again Headborough of his ward. On Easter Sunday, 9 April 1626, was buried his kinsman (his uncle?) and namesake of the familiar dwelling in Henley Street, the lease of which now passed to his cousin, Thomas, a young man of twenty-one years of age, a glover. Henley Street was still a centre of the glove industry. On 2 May 1626 William Smythe made his account as Churchwarden with Richard Tyler, and was paid something of what he had advanced. He was paid more next year—10*s.* in money and 28*s.* 4*d.* in the metal of an old bell. The account is subscribed by the curate, Simon Trapp, and five leading parishioners, including William Smythe, Richard Hathaway, Henry Walker, and Richard Tyler. Hathaway was Bailiff, Walker Chief Alderman.

In September Alderman Smythe was in London. In November, after Hathaway had laid down his office, Smythe was charged with having 'caused' him, whilst Bailiff, 'to seal a letter of licence, assigning over a lease, under his private seal' instead of the Borough Seal. Smythe denied it, declaring that if he had done so, he was not fit to remain of the Company. Mistress Shakespeare's nephew, apparently, had the character of com-

[1] *Council Book B*, 433.

pliance, as Smythe that of domination. In due course Smythe was nominated for the Bailiwick, as on 3 September 1628 when Henry Smythe was elected, with Richard Hathaway as his Chief Alderman. Two days before, Lord Brooke had been stabbed mortally in his house in Holborn by an exasperated servant, an old attendant who was disappointed at not being mentioned in his Will. His lordship died on 30 September; and on 6 October the Stratford Corporation appointed Sir Thomas Lucy their Recorder in his stead. The funeral took place at Warwick in St. Mary's Church on 27 October. Round the tomb which the deceased had erected for himself (in, and practically occupying, the ancient chapter-house) is the inscription, more impressive than the tomb:

> Fulke Grevill, servant to Queene Elizabeth, Conceller to King Iames, and frend to Sir Philip Sidney.

1626

§ 154. DEATH OF EDWARD ALLEYN

More than two years younger than Shakespeare, Alleyn enjoyed his retirement more than ten years longer. He gave himself to the planning, building, and endowment of a school and hospital on his estate to be called 'the College of God's Gift at Dulwich'. He inherited wealth by the death of his father-in-law, Henslowe, in 1616, and was able to inaugurate his venture, on which he bestowed £10,000, in 1619, publicly reading the deed of Foundation in the College Chapel ('Christ's Chapel' he named it) on 13 September, in the presence of a distinguished company, including the guest of honour, Francis Bacon Lord Verulam, Lord Chancellor. His last years were spent in sociability and hospitality, to rich and poor, actors, literary friends, courtiers, and members of his College. In 1623 he lost his wife, Joan, the beloved 'mouse' of his youth. She left him no children. The same year he married the young daughter of the Dean of Paul's, Constance Donne. Gossips 'doubted the match would diminish his charity and devotion', but their fears were groundless. He died in 1626—the same year as Lord Bacon—desiring to be buried 'without any vain funeral pomp or show, in the quire of that Chapel which God of his goodness hath

EDWARD ALLEYN

From the painting at Dulwich College

From the *Resuscitatio*, 1657

caused me to erect and dedicate to the honour of my Saviour'. He was universally respected. The legend that the actual appearance of the Devil to him while playing Faustus, caused him to forsake the stage, is of the kind told of actors. Very different is the testimony from the theatre itself, even in 1662:

> What scurrility [asks Baker in reply to contemporary critics] was ever heard to come from the best actors . . . Alleyn and Burbage? yet what plays were ever so pleasing as where their parts had the greatest part? . . . Have we not seen Edward Allen a player, famous as well for his honesty as for his acting? who hath left behind him a worthy testimony of his Christian charity to all posterity?

His portrait, at his College, confirms what we are told of his physique and fitness for a 'majestic part', and especially what Marlowe wrote of his hero in *Tamburlaine*—'of stature tall' (though the painter has somewhat cut down the long, black-gowned figure), 'large of limbs', 'joints strongly knit' (though now he is old), 'breadth of shoulders', 'piercing' eyes (if now mild with years), 'lofty brows', 'amber hair in curls', 'arms and fingers long and sinewy', 'betokening' (in younger days) 'valour and excess of strength'.

1625–30

§ 155. EXEUNT CONDELL AND HEMINGE

'OLD Heminge' and 'Harry Condell' were the Fathers of the King's Company, rich in worldly goods, richer in memories—of the Drama and the Court, of players and theatres, of the efforts and triumphs, laughter, changes, and tears of probably the most distinguished brotherhood in the Annals of Art. Had they recorded them, could they have done justice to them, few books would have been more precious. And without doubt, they would have attempted it, however imperfectly, could they have realized the evil days that were coming, with their oblivion and their gossip.

Condell lived until 1627, an honoured parishioner of St. Mary Aldermanbury, with a 'country house' at Fulham. With Heminge he marched at the head of the Players in the funeral procession of King James to Westminster on 7 May 1625, and their names lead the list of King Charles's Men in the patent of

24 June. In the plague that followed that summer he entertained at Fulham certain players who had fled from London, and incurred the reproach of Thomas Dekker. To a pamphlet by Dekker, entitled *A Rod for Runaways*, they replied with *The Runaways' Answer*, which they dedicated 'to our much respected and very worthy friend, Master H. Condell', thanking him for his 'free and noble farewell' on setting forth on their 'peregrination' in the provinces. 'You are nearer to London than we', they wrote, 'by many miles, and therefore entreat you to publish this.' They dated their communication from 'Oxford and elsewhere, September 10 1625'.[1]

At Fulham, Condell made his Will,[2] on 13 December 1627, leaving much property, including shares in the *Globe* and *Blackfriars*, to his wife, two youthful sons, and a young married daughter. To his elder son, Henry, aged 17, he bequeathed £30 a year 'for his maintenance either at the University or elsewhere'; to William, Shakespeare's godson (?),[3] apprentice to a grocer, he left £300: a legacy which proved (as we gather from his mother's Will) baneful rather than a benefit. To an old servant, Elizabeth Wheaton, he demised, among other things, 'that place or privilege which she now exerciseth and enjoyeth' at the *Blackfriars Theatre* and at the *Globe* 'for the term of her natural life'.[4] As overseers he appointed Cuthbert Burbage and John Heminge. He was buried in St. Mary Aldermanbury on 29 December.

Heminge was now left, also wealthy, but with a large grown-up family. His son, William, who may have been a godson of Shakespeare, was at Oxford, after being at Westminster School. He took his B.A. from Christchurch in 1625, his M.A. in 1628. He became a dramatist of small reputation, but might have won fame and the gratitude of posterity with a volume of recollections from his father's lips.

Old Heminge may have died of the plague which kept the theatres closed in the summer and autumn of 1630. He had ceased to reside in St. Mary Aldermanbury, perhaps on account of the frequent and long-continued infection. On 20 September

[1] Collier, *Memoirs*, 141–3.

[2] *Ib.* 144–9.

[3] p. 751.

[4] Widow Condell, in her Will of 1 Sept. 1635, left her a similar post, 'the gathering Place at the *Globe* during my lease'. She would collect the payments due from those who had taken seats in the galleries.

a royal warrant was issued to pay the King's Players £100 'in regard of their great hindrance' through the pestilence.

We have given order [runs the document] that our servant John Heminge and the rest of our players shall attend upon us and our dearest Consort the Queen at our next coming to Hampton Court; and for as much as we are graciously pleased in regard of their great hindrance of late received, whereby they are disabled to attend this service, to bestow upon them the sum of one hundred pounds, we do hereby will and command you to pay unto the said John Heminge, for himself and the rest of our said servants, the said sum as of our free gift and bounty.

To Heminge, then, fell the distribution of the money, probably in and around the plague-stricken city. He was taken ill, made his Will on 9 October, which was Saturday, died that day or the next, and was buried in his old church of St. Mary Aldermanbury, a 'stranger' (non-parishioner), on Tuesday the 12th, 'near unto his loving wife and under the same stone' as conveniently might be. She had been interred there on 2 September 1629. He left bequests of 'ten shillings unto every' of his fellows and sharers, his Majesty's Servants, 'to make them rings' (we recall Shakespeare's legacy to him of 26*s.* 8*d.* for a ring: which presumably his son William inherited), and 'twenty shillings unto John Rice clerk of St. Saviour's in Southwark for a remembrance of his love to him' (John Rice being his former apprentice who had of late taken orders). He appointed his 'loving friends, Master Burbage and Master Rice' overseers, his son, William, executor.[1] Master Burbage was Cuthbert Burbage, who survived Heminge nearly six years, being buried in St. Leonard's, Shoreditch, on 17 September 1636.[2]

§ 156. DOCTOR JOHN HALL, M.A.

FROM Shakespeare's fellows, friends, and neighbours, let us come at last to his distinguished son-in-law.

Doctor Hall had an extensive and fashionable practice. He rode, with his 'surgeon's box'[3] behind him, so far afield as Northampton, Worcester, and Ludlow. His patients included the Earl of Warwick, the Earl and Countess of Northampton, Lady Beaufoy ('godly, honest, being of a noble extract, healthful

[1] Chambers, ii. 322. [2] *Ib.* 306. [3] *Tro. & Cress.* v. i. 12.

till the age of 28, which was 1617 July 1'), Lady Rouse, Mistress Mary Talbot ('a Catholic, fair': 'such as hated him for his religion often made use of him'), Lady Puckering, Lady Browne of Radford, Lady Smith ('Roman Catholic, cruelly afflicted with wind'), Lady Dickenson ('fair, pious, chaste, vexed with pain of the head'), Lady Underhill and others of her family, Sheldons, Throgmortons, Rainsfords, Barneses, and 'Master Drayton' ('an excellent poet, labouring of a tertian'), Combes, Nashes, Lanes, Pearses of Alveston, Kempsons, Mistress Chandler (sister of George Quyney and sister-in-law to Judith Quyney),[1] Mistress Smith (sister to Julyne Shawe), one Browne ('a Romish priest, labouring of an ungarick fever in danger of death'), Mistress Grace Court ('wife to my apothecary'), John Nason, barber, and many more. We will note his 'observations' on Master Leonard Kempson and his wife, resident in her father, John Sadler's house in Church Street, within a few yards of *New Place*. 'Master Kempson: oppressed with melancholy; a fever with extraordinary heat; very sleepy so that he had no sense of his sickness' (*Obs.* 31). 'Mistress Kempson, being for many days and nights cruelly tormented with a hollow tooth and had used many medicines, as also *charms*'—anything to avoid the dread 'tooth-drawer', with a brooch in his cap,[2] and on it the design of the Rose and the Crown,[3] and a string of old tusks in his shop for the victim's edification[4]—'and yet not profited, came running to me'—she had not far to run—'and I prescribed to her' (*Obs.* 82). Leonard Kempson suffered from the prevalent *melancholia*, notwithstanding his music,[5] and died a few weeks after his father-in-law, being buried 26 August 1625. Margaret, his wife, found relief from bereavement (and toothache) in marriage on 20 April following with one John Norbury.

More interesting are the Doctor's notes on his wife and daughter. He writes of the former (in Latin): 'Mistress Hall of Stratford, my wife, being miserably tormented with the colic . . .';[6] and again, 'was troubled with the scurvy, accompanied with pain of the loins, melancholy &c. . . . I freed her

[1] p. 785.
[2] *Love's L. L.* v. ii. 622–4.
[3] Taylor, *Wit and Mirth*, 1630 (Hindley, p. 62).
[4] If his shop was like that of the German *Zaubrecher* in Jost Amman.
[5] p. 130.
[6] *Obs.* xix.

from pain Feb. 9, 1630/1'.[1] Of their daughter, Shakespeare's grand-daughter, he records:

Elizabeth Hall, my only daughter, was vexed with *tortura oris* or the convulsion of the mouth, and was happily cured as followeth . . . 5 January 1624/5.[2] In the beginning of April she went to London and returning homewards the 22nd of the said month she took cold and fell into the said distemper on the contrary side of the face, and although grievously afflicted with it, yet, by the blessing of God, she was cured in sixteen days as followeth: . . . her neck was fomented with *aqua vitae*, in which was infused nutmegs, cinnamon, cloves, pepper; she ate nutmegs often. In the same year, May the 24th, she was afflicted with an erratic fever: sometimes she was hot, by and bye sweating, again cold, all in the space of half an hour, and thus she was vexed oft in a day . . . Thus was she delivered from death and deadly disease, and was well for many years, to God be praise!

His efforts to cure a consumptive girl were heroic—

Mary Wilson aged 22 afflicted with a hectic cough. There were appointed meats boiled, as veal, hens, capons (fed either with barley or crammed with paste made of barley-meal), frogs, snails, and river-crabs. By these she got flesh. Our restorative was a caudle made of the yokes of eggs, wine, and sugar. She also used the following panatella: ℞ crumbs of bread moistened with milk, and after mixed with almond milk, rose-water and sugar; a ptisan or cream of barley was thus prepared: ℞ barley oz. ii, purslane, borage, each Mſs, boil them in 10 lb. of water till a fourth part be wasted, after strain it and drink of it. She frequently used sugar of roses. For a clyster this was used: ℞ chicken broth oz. x, in which was boiled seeds of poppies, flowers of water-lilies, violets, mallows, each Mſs; being strained there was added oil of violets oz. i ſs, white sugar oz. ii, honey of violets oz. i ſs, lemon salt oz. i ſs, the yoke of one egg; mix them. She sucked woman-milk, nourished with cooling and moistening diet, as lettuce.

He thought he had arrested the disease, but confesses, 'a year after this she died'. Convalescent patients he sent to Bath and to the Hotwells at Bristol.

All that he tells us in his 'no less than a thousand observations' we would willingly exchange for a few words about the last illness, or any illness, of his great father-in-law. Did his attendance and prescription retard or accelerate his decease? We should have been grateful also for information about the deadly epidemic in Shottery in the autumn of 1624 and following winter. From 22 August to 9 March there were at least seventeen funerals in the little hamlet, including those of Bartholomew Hathaway, Fulke Sandells (the Poet's old surety for his marriage-

[1] *Obs.* xxxiii. [2] *Ib.* xxxvi.

bond), and William Richardson (son to the other surety for that bond, John Richardson). Other friends of Shakespeare who died in the autumn of 1624 were Hamlet Sadler (as stated above) and the Earl of Southampton. The latter, with his son, fell victim to a fever in November at Bergen-op-Zoom in Holland, whence their bodies were brought to Titchfield and, on 28 December, interred within the Church.

The journey of Shakespeare's grand-daughter to London early in April 1625 may have been to participate, with her father, in functions consequent on the death of King James on 24 March and the accession of Charles I. She was at home, but ill, on Sunday 1 May when her mother, as we have surmised, stood sponsor at the baptism of Master Henry Walker's child, Susanna. Doctor Hall was offered a knighthood on the Coronation in February 1626, but declined it. William Combe and the Poet's kinsman, Thomas Fulwood of Little Alne, also declined the honour. The Crown was in need of money, and those who would not receive a title had to compound for their refusal. Doctor Hall paid £10, Combe £15, Fulwood, who was evidently wealthy, £16. George Carew, Baron of Clopton, accepted a peerage as Earl of Totnes.

On Saturday 22 April 1626 in the Parish Church, within a few yards of her grandfather's grave and monument, young Mistress Hall was married to Master Thomas Nash of Lincoln's Inn, son of Anthony Nash of Welcombe, to whom her grandfather left a memorial ring. She was just over seventeen, he just under thirty-three years of age. The wedding is thus entered in the register:

Apr. 22 M(aste)r Thomas Nash to M(ist)r(i)s Elizabeth Hall.

No doubt the Vicar, Thomas Wilson, to whom Doctor Hall was warmly attached, officiated.

Wilson's popularity was great while it lasted. Francis Smith of the Corner House in Middle Row, by his Will of 15 April 1623, as we have seen, left £5 a year for a weekly sermon on a week-day so long as Wilson was Vicar. The Corporation supported him loyally, spending freely on his house in the Chapel precinct and augmenting his salary. When he was excommunicated in 1625, for some nonconformity, by Bishop Thornborough, they were active on his behalf and sent a deputation to old Fulke Greville, now Lord Brooke and Chancellor of the Exchequer, their Recorder, to plead for him. On 12 January 1627 they voted him £20 a year for his 'learned sermons' and 'great pains' in the late sickness and pestilence in the parish. Possibly the confidence turned his head. He exceeded his right to the timber in the Churchyard, a point on which the Corporation were always jealous, and refusing to yield he gave offence to old supporters. It was a small matter on which to quarrel, and it led to a serious breach. On 14 December 1627, within a twelvemonth of their signal mark of favour, by an overwhelming majority they voted the withdrawal of the grant of half the profits of the Churchyard. Feeling grew strong against the Vicar. In July 1629 the Corporation rescinded their grant of £20 a year to his 'wages' and invited their old favourite, Robert Harris of Hanwell, to deliver a weekly sermon. In October 1630 they restored the £20 to the Vicar on the condition that he secured Harris for another year as their lecturer. Seventeen months later there was an open breach, and the Corporation called in Sir Thomas Lucy (Recorder since Lord Brooke's death in 1628) and Sir Greville Verney to arbitrate between them and Wilson 'to hear his grief and complaints' and 'wherein they have wronged or abused him'.

Doctor Hall was his champion. He consented to be his Churchwarden, busy man as he was, in 1628–9. With his colleagues, Anthony Smith, and George Barton of Welcombe, he fulfilled his duties energetically, presenting parishioners for 'loitering forth of church at sermon-time', 'sleeping in the belfry with a hat on upon the Sabbath', 'keeping drinking in a house' on the Sabbath and in 'the company of an excommunicated person', keeping 'naughty company', 'wearing a hat in Church' and being 'a common romler', 'being abroad seen by the Constable at sermon time', 'for late coming to Church' and having 'no employment but laziness'; 'using beastly behaviour' and putting hand under plackets, calling a woman 'whore' and 'witch', being 'a common swearer and blasphemer' or 'drunkard'. Most interesting, for the light it throws on an execration in *Macbeth* and *King Lear*, is the account by the wardens of a brawl between two Stratford women:

Item the wife of Adrian Holder saith Goody Bromley is *an ill-book woman*[1] and *I would overlook her and hern as I overlook others* and bid me *Arent thee, witch!* and saith *I was a whore and my bastards maintained me*, and bid me *get me home*, how 'a *would brush the motes forth of my dirty gown*.[2]

The *oratio* is somewhat mixed (as sometimes in Master Greene's note-book), but the sense is clear enough. The speaker is Holder's wife, who addresses the Churchwarden with quotation of scraps of Goody Bromley's abuse of her. 'Arent thee witch!' means 'Get thee back to Hell!' *aroint*,[3] whatever its origin (*averruncate?*), signifying 'Avoid!' and 'Avaunt!'

Shakespeare had listened to such spirited dialogue.

Doctor Hall had scarcely laid down his Churchwardenship, on 7 April 1629, before George Carew Earl of Totnes (who died in the Savoy on 27 March) was buried on 2 May[4] in Stratford Church among his wife's people, the Cloptons. Sir Greville Verney succeeded him as High Steward of the borough. Another funeral to be noted was that of Julyne Shawe on 24 June.[5]

In her Will of 5 January 1630 Mistress Shawe bequeathed to Alderman William Smythe her 'best joined bedstead in the chamber over the Hall' (in her house next door but one to *New Place*) 'and the truckle-bed to it', and to his wife (Anne Quyney) her green rug, her malt-mill, and her close-stool. She further made Smythe a residuary legatee and executor. But Mistress Smythe did not long possess her bequests. Mistress Shawe was buried on 25 October this year, and Mistress Smythe four weeks later, on 22 November.

But to return to Doctor Hall. Like William Smythe he was more devoted to the Parish Church and Vicar than to the Corporation, of which against his will he was elected a Burgess in May 1632. Twice he had successfully made excuse, but now he had to yield: partly to answer for his determined countenance of Wilson and participation with him in suits against them. His membership lasted sixteen months, and his presence when he attended was disturbing. In the minutes of 30 June his name is entered on the list of Burgesses thus:

Jo[*hannes*] *Hall*, *generosus*, *in Artibus Magister*, *a*[*bsens*],

[1] 'Black-book woman.'
[2] *Misc. Doc.* i. 160.
[3] Cf. *K. Lear*, III. iv. 129.
[4] *Register*, p. 115.
[5] *Ib.*

and a note is added:

Master Hall, at the last hall elected a chief-burgess of this Borough, hath neglected to come to take his oath, being thereunto warned by both the Chamberlains and Serjeants.

He was 'warned' again for 6 July, but in response to a pleading and indignant letter from a patient, Sidney Davenport of Bushwood, demanding his attendance,[1] he again, as it is recorded, 'made default'. He was sworn, however, on 11 July. At the end of August he 'fell into a most cruel torture' of his teeth, and struggled against it, visiting his patients, until driven to his bed with 'a burning fever which then raged killing almost all that it did infect . . . I was not only much maciated but weakened so that I could not move myself . . . My wife sent for two physicians . . . my friends . . . and I became perfectly well, praised be God'—about 29 September. We have the prayer he wrote on his recovery:

Thou, O Lord, which hast the power of life and death, and drawest from the gates of death: I confess without any art or counsel of man, but only from Thy goodness and clemency, Thou hast saved me from the bitter and deadly symptons of a deadly fever beyond the expectations of all about me, restoring me as it were from the very jaws of death to former health: for which I praise Thy name, O most merciful God and Father of our Lord Jesus Christ, praying Thee to give me a most thankful heart for this great favour for which I have cause to admire Thee.[2]

Mistress Quyney died in October, the long surviving widow of Shakespeare's friend, Richard Quyney (writer to him of the letter in London of 25 October 1598). Doctor Hall had trouble with her son, his brother-in-law, Thomas Quyney of the *Cage* tavern. Notwithstanding his French, and his sound philosophy in that language, 'Blessed is the man who learns wisdom from others' follies', the vintner, like his older kinsman, Bardolf, fell a victim to the temptations of his calling. He was fined for absence from halls, for swearing, for suffering tippling in his house, and was not promoted to aldermanic rank. On 13 March Doctor Hall and Master Thomas Nash, together with Richard Watts, Vicar of Harbury (who had married Mary Quyney, sister of Thomas), took over the lease of the *Cage* in trust for his wife and boys.

[1] *Wheler MS*. i. 94.

[2] *Obs*. lx.

On 11 January 1633 Doctor Hall was called upon to answer and submit himself for 'abusive speeches' against the Bailiff, who was Master Richard Castle ('Shake-elbows'). Influence with Master Wilson and the Bishop had enabled the doctor to change his pew in the Church from one near the pulpit on the south of the nave (that hitherto allotted to *New Place* and no doubt occupied by Shakespeare and his family[1]) to another on the north side of the nave, at the upper end, 'enjoyed time out of mind' by the Aldermen and their wives. Bailiff and Brethren not unnaturally resented this exchange. They objected also to Doctor Hall's denunciation of them for breach of contract with Wilson. There were unseemly doings on both sides. In September, Alderman William Smythe was in danger of losing his *nomination* for the Bailiwick. Daniel Baker, Henry Walker, Henry Smythe, and Thomas Quyney opposed his right, against fifteen who upheld it, including Richard Hathaway, Richard Tyler, Richard Castle the Bailiff, and Doctor Hall. William Shawe, brother of Julyne, had the *election*.

This was one of Hall's last attendances and doubtless a stormy one. On 9 October, when Castle laid down his office, a resolution was carried that he should have 'precedency of place of Master William Smythe, in respect he hath borne the office of Bailiff; and so every person hereafter to be elected and shall undergo the said office, shall have place of all which shall not undergo the office before him'.[2] Hall was furious, and used such language that by nineteen votes to three he was expelled from the Council—for 'wilful breach of orders, sundry other misdemeanours, and continual disturbances'.[3] This was Wednesday. On Sunday following (or a Sunday shortly after) Castle endeavoured, on his return to the aldermanic pew in Church, to take his seat above Master Smythe, but found this gentleman in possession. The result (then or later) was a scuffle, in

[1] The award of June 1635 (see p. 833) was, 'That the said Master Hall and his Wife' (Susanna Shakespeare) 'and Master Nash and his Wife' (Elizabeth Hall) 'and Mistress Woodward and Mistress Lane should have the seat now in question, to and for them to sit and kneel in, if the same seat were large enough for them.'

[2] *Council Book C*, 82.

[3] *Ib.* The minority consisted of Alderman Richard Tyler and Burgesses Francis Walford and John Eston. Burgess Henry Norman was unavoidably absent. Henry Walker and Richard Hathaway voted in the majority.

which the vintner of (36) High Street (with his 'four elbows') did his best to dislodge the mercer, his next-door neighbour of the same street, from his seat in this pew, without success. Such proceedings by the town-fathers called for inquiry; and on Thursday, 19 December, the Vicar held a special court, at nine o'clock in *New Place* (instead of the usual Chancel, it probably being cold), in the presence of a public 'notary', John Stephens.

Being then and there demanded why he disturbed the congregation, and wherein and in what particular he did the same, Alderman Smythe answered, that for his part he never gave occasion of any disturbance there; but if any such thing were done, it was occasioned by the intrusion of Master Richard Castle of the said town, who went about lately upon the Sabbath Day, in the morning, but before divine prayers, by violence to thrust out the said Smythe out of his usual sitting-place. And the said William Smythe doth further allege that for so much as he is *ancient* to the said Richard Castle, as well in bearing offices of Churchwarden, and Alderman of the foresaid Borough, and hath always held his place among Aldermen in the said parish-church next unto one Master Thomas Greene; and for that the said Master William Smythe is above the said Castle in all taxations and payments, and hath always had precedency in the said parish-church before the said Castle as his ancient, and lastly for so much as the said parish-church is out of the limits of the Corporation of the foresaid borough; he desireth that he may not be reputed, by keeping of his accustomed place in the said church, to be a disturber, but that he may be settled in the quiet and peaceable possession of his said usual and accustomed sitting-place.

Who is this John Stephens, 'notary', attending 'the vicarial court' at Stratford, at Christmas time, in Shakespeare's old home, in the presence of his son-in-law? Is it the Gloucestershire man, the bencher of Lincoln's Inn, who wrote, himself a dramatist, the incomparable essay in 1615 on *A Worthy Poet*, with knowledge of Shakespeare only derivable from friendship? He was probably living in 1631 when a further edition of his *Essayes* appeared.

The breach between Vicar and Corporation widened. Wilson and Hall filed a petition in Chancery for the increase of the stipends of both Vicar and Schoolmaster, 'according to the intent of the Charters'. Notwithstanding the Doctor's sale to the Corporation of his lease of tithes 'for less money than the same was worth by a hundred pounds at the least', to maintain the Vicar's salary to £60, they had reduced it; and also, for about the space of ten years last past, they have 'utterly suppressed, omitted and neglected the payment of £20 per annum to the Schoolmaster'.[1] The meagre stipend, apparently, had not tempted a successor to Aspinall, and the condition of Shakespeare's old school, for ten years under an usher or the curate, was a source of concern to his able son-in-law and the Oxford B.D. They charged the Corporation, moreover, with 'feasting and private use of the revenues'. On the exhibition of this bill the Corporation, in April, gave answer upon oath that it was 'false and scandalous' (William Smythe, Henry Norman, Richard Walford, Francis Walford, and John Eston alone dissenting) and put their defence in the hands of the lawyers. In May they deprived Wilson of his 'key of the Chancel-door in the Chapel to have passage there through to his house'. He had ill-used the Chancel (as a superstitious sanctuary), allowing his children to play ball there and other games, to the breaking of the windows and 'defacing of the pictures', permitting washing to be hung, fowls to roost, and pigs to lie there.[2] More serious complaints were forthcoming—he annoyed his congregation by walking in the Church during service ('meditating his sermon') and he 'grossly particularized' in his preaching. Matters came to a head on Tuesday 12 May 1635, at the funeral of Mistress Henry Smythe (sister of the late Julyne Shawe). The Vicar, not invited to preach the sermon, sat on the pulpit stairs to prevent the curate, Simon Trappe, from delivering it. On 5 June Doctor Nathaniel Brent, the Vicar-General of the diocese, opened his inquiry in Stratford. He awarded Doctor Hall his new pew ('on the north side of the nave at the upper end'), if he decided within a month to take it. Among the witnesses examined respecting the Vicar and the Corporation, were John Eston (mercer, aged 36), Anthony Smith (gentleman, aged 52), William Chandler (gentleman, now of Milcote, aged 58), John Greene (gentleman, aged 60, the lawyer, brother of Master Thomas Greene of the Middle Temple, Shakespeare's cousin), and Richard Tyler (senior, 'three score and eight years of age', gentleman, Shakespeare's old friend). Wilson pleaded guilty, and was suspended, on 16 July, for three months, promising amendment, as one recognized 'to be a very good scholar, and the son of a very grave, conformable

[1] *Misc. Doc.* viii. 303.

[2] *Wheler MS.* i. 124.

Doctor of Divinity'.[1] On 31 July Master William Smythe was deprived of his Alderman's gown.[2]

That Doctor Hall approved of all Wilson's proceedings we may more than doubt; but he felt that the Vicar had been meanly treated (with six young children—one named Grindal after the old Puritan Primate)[3] and he admired his learning. He did not long survive his friend's suspension. He died suddenly this autumn, on 25 November, within a few days of his neighbours, also stout supporters of the Vicar, Henry Norman and Richard Walford (Richard Hathaway's son-in-law). They may have been carried off by the same malady[4]—for which perhaps he attended his fellow victims, with fatal consequence. On his grave, next but one to Shakespeare's, were inscribed the lines, perhaps of Wilson's authorship:

> Hallius hic situs est, medica celeberrimus arte,
> Expectans regni gaudia laeta Dei;
> Dignus erat meritis qui Nestora vinceret annis,
> In terris omnes sed rapit aequa dies.[5]

He had dictated a nuncupative will to his son-in-law, Thomas Nash, witnessed and, no doubt, written by the Curate (from the Chapel Quad). It is as follows:

> The last Will and Testament nuncupative of John Hall of Stratford upon Avon in the County of Warwick, gentleman, made and declared the five and twentieth of November 1635.
>
> *Imprimis* I give unto my wife my house in London. *Item* I give unto my daughter Nash my house in Acton. *Item* I give unto my daughter Nash my Meadow. *Item* I give my goods and moneys unto my wife and my daughter Nash to be equally divided betwixt them. *Item* concerning my study of Books, I leave them (said he) to you, my son Nash, to dispose of them as you see good. As for my manuscripts, I would have given them to Master Boles if he had been here; but forasmuch as he is not here present, you may (son Nash) burn them or else do with them what you please.
>
> Witnesses hereunto Thomas Nashe, Simon Trappe.[6]

The 'Meadow' was his moiety of 'three closes in Stratford, called Square Meadow, Washie Meadow, and a little meadow adjoin-

[1] *State Papers, Domestic, Chas. I.* [2] *Council Book C*, 117.

[3] *Baptism Register*, p. 115.

[4] Norman was buried 11 Nov., Walford the 21st, Hall the 26th.

[5] 'Hall is laid here, very renowned for his medical skill, looking for the joys of the Kingdom of God. Worthy was he, for his merits, to outdo Nestor in years, but on earth a like Day lays hands on all.'

[6] *P.C.C.* 115 *Pile.*

ing', purchased jointly by himself and Nash about the time of the latter's marriage (22 April 1626).[1] We should like to know more of that 'study of Books', otherwise the library, at *New Place*, and what became of it. It doubtless included volumes inherited from Shakespeare. Master Bowles presumably was the Doctor's assistant, from home, perhaps, in a case: Magister Josephus Bowles, who was settled in Stratford in 1640, in a house exactly opposite to *New Place* (now the Falcon Inn), married, and father of a child, Josephus (baptized 25 March 1639, but buried 16 April 1641). Hall would entrust his 'manuscripts' to him, including his case-books and other confidential papers, as one professional man to another. Some of these have survived and await publication in their original Latin. There is an allusion, most interesting and tantalizing, to the 'study' and 'books' at *New Place* eighteen months after Doctor Hall's death. A member of the Corporation, of whom from time to time we have had a glimpse, Baldwin Brookes, a prosperous mercer, acting-Chamberlain of the Borough in 1635–6, then or later 'gentleman', had a claim on the estate of the deceased Doctor, to some extent at least disputed and resisted by his widow and son-in-law. Brookes obtained a judgement for £77 (probably, it being a large sum, at the Warwick Assizes), and as payment was still refused, he filed a bill in Chancery. Widow Hall, on the direction of Anthonie Smith (her late husband's old colleague in the Churchwardenship) and the lawyer, Edmund (Edward) Rawlins, signed her answer at Stratford on 5 May 1637, which was delivered to Robert Riche, a master in Chancery in London, on the 10th. Two days later she filed a bill in Chancery against Brookes, thus staying his further prosecution. From her answer we learn that she was seized of two messuages in Stratford and other property by the Will of her father, 'William Shackspeare, gentleman', and continued to reside, with her daughter and son-in-law, at *New Place*, 'the messuage wherein John Hall lived and died'; that her late husband's goods and chattels were worth a thousand pounds; and that Brookes had sent bailiffs to the house, who 'did then and there break open the doors and study, and rashly seize upon and take divers books, boxes', and other things. The seizure of the books as security for the debt is evidence of the value set upon them.

[1] Barnard, *New Links with Shakespeare*, p. 118 f.

JOYCE CLOPTON, COUNTESS OF TOTNES, †1637

(from her effigy at Stratford-upon-Avon)

1635–36

§ 157. THE MARKET HOUSE

OTHER burials of 1635 were those of the old Catholic recusant, George Badger, on 1 May, and of Mistress Sturley on 7 November. Richard Hathaway died in 1636. He made his Will on 1 September, leaving considerable property (four tenements, five lands in the Common Fields of Old Stratford, and the lease of the *Crown*) to his wife for life, and was buried in the Church on 8 October. Shakespeare's friend, Richard Tyler, died in December 1636, a little over seventy years of age; and Joyce Clopton, Countess of Totnes, died on 14 January 1637. Her ladyship was buried by the side of her husband in the Church. Their altar-tomb is the finest monument in it. They lie in effigy in coronets and robes of scarlet. Arthur Cawdrey of the *Angel* died in July 1637, in his seventy-fifth year; and in October 1638, after prolonged negotiations with the Council for peace, passed away the unhappy Vicar. On 7 November the Council resolved that 'all the best means be used to gain Master Harris of Hanwell to be our Vicar, in the place of Master Wilson deceased'. For more than a year they tried to get him in vain. He would probably have united the Corporation. William Smythe favoured him, and entertained him at his house in High Street (the old Quyney shop and residence) on behalf of the Corporation on his visits to lecture in Stratford. A letter from him to the Bailiff, dated 23 March 1635/6, is worth quotation for its reference to Harris, and allusions to the building of *The Market House*, at the corner of Sheep Street and Chapel Street, destined to be blown up within a very short period by the Cavaliers.

In April 1634 the Corporation resolved to build a market house on the site referred to (purchased in 1626 of Thomas Walker), and contracted with a mason, John Page of Chipping Campden, for its erection by Michaelmas following. But plans were altered, promises were unfulfilled (so it was alleged) on both sides, and more than two years passed before the building was completed, and then an outside staircase (itself an afterthought) did not give satisfaction. The result was litigation, and the acceptance at length of £20 by Page in settlement of his claim, early in 1640.

The edifice interests us, though Shakespeare never saw it, because among its chief promoters were his friends—William Shawe of Henley Street, Henry Walker of High Street, and Richard Tyler (junior) of Rother Market.

Smythe's letter, moreover, abovesaid, is so admirable in its restraint and courtesy that it will serve as our reluctant farewell to a public-spirited younger contemporary of the Poet, his fellow-native of Stratford, and the close ally of his son-in-law. Here, then, it is in full:

To the Worshipful Master Bailiff and his Brethren of Stratford these.

Gentlemen, I understand by my cousin, Thomas Smythe, your late Chamberlain, that you would not accept of his Accompt unless he would accompt for, and make payment of, the rent of the tenement wherein John Hunt and Widow Hinshue inhabiteth, which I hold of you. What he hath done I know not, only I hope you are not ignorant of the damage which I have and do still sustain ever since the Market House hath been in building—that is, about two years. For John Hunt, you pulled down his pig-sty and house-of-office; and the place to lay his soil in you took away, as also it is his backside. You know he is a poor man and hath little need of such hindrances. I have and must abate his rent in some measure answerable thereunto. For the widow Hinshew, the house that she lived in was much defaced in the pulling down of the old house which joined to it, insomuch it cost me above x^{s} to repair it, and now since is by your workmen so broken down and ruinated that she could not live in it. And for these two years I could get little or no rent of her. She paid willingly before xx^{s} per annum, and for this time I have not had x^{s} of her, and now the house stands void.

I hope you do not desire that I should bear this loss by you and yet pay you the rent. I desire you to [make] my case yours, and do as you would be done by. Your heretofore request is of the house and backside to enlarge your passage about the Market House, and [you] promised reasonable satisfaction for the same. I was not, neither yet am, unwilling thereunto. You may have what you please, only I desire you would consider what you would have and let it be done; or if you will not have it, then I desire that everything be made in as good state as it was and satisfaction for such losses as I have and do sustain, and I shall not be unwilling to pay the rent.

There is also money due to me for Master Harris' diet and entertainment for the last quarter. I hope you do not expect I should bear it. Master Alderman and Master Baker promised, as Master Harris informed me, and no longer ago than the last week but one at his being here doth affirm it, that I should have satisfaction; which I desire to have in love.

You have much prejudiced me in my name and credit undeservedly, as I hope it will appear; and still you go on, as I am informed, to do me further harms. I must be content if you take away my name and ruin my estate, yet I hope my trust in God shall not fail. I desire of God you may use your

GEORGE CAREW, EARL OF TOTNES, †1629

From his effigy at Stratford-upon-Avon

Ben Jonson,
after Gerard Honthorst.

power to better purpose, and however you deal with me yet my prayers may not be wanting for the good and prosperity of this place wherein I was born and for which I owe my best endeavours. Wherein I have damaged the Corporation, if I may know it I shall and will, if I be able, make satisfaction; if not I willingly desire pardon.

Thus praying for your true prosperity, craving pardon for my boldness, desiring your answer by whom you shall appoint, and ever resting at your service. Wm Smythe

23 of March 1635[/6].

c. 1623–37

§ 158. *TIMBER*

BEN JONSON died 6 August 1637. After his death was published a collection of his notes, in carefully written prose, made in his riper years, on men and things, as a result of his daily reading or observation of the time, entitled *Timber or Discoveries.* It is a precious little book, a bit of sound ὕλη, which brings us near to the honest heart of the writer, and admirer, if always critical and sometimes scornful, of literature and men of letters. He has an exalted conception of Poetry and a poor opinion of his late contemporary poets:

'We do not require in the Poet', he says (in words absolutely befitting Shakespeare), 'mere elocution or an excellent faculty in verse; but the exact knowledge of all virtues and their contraries, with ability to render the one loved, the other hated, by his proper embattling them.'[1]

And he laments

The time was when men would learn and study good things, not envy those that had them. Then men were had in price for learning, now letters only make men vile: *jam literae sordent.* He is upbraidingly called *a poet,* as if it were a contemptible nickname. But the professors, indeed, have made the learning cheap-railing, and tinkling rimers, whose writings the vulgar more greedily read, as being taken with the scurrility and petulancy of such wits. He shall not have a reader now unless he jeer and lie.[2]

And again, of poets

a kind of tuning and riming fall in what they write: it runs and slides and only makes a sound. *Women's poets* they are called, as you have women's tailors—

> They write a verse as smooth, as soft as cream,
> In which there is no torrent nor scarce stream.

You may sound these wits and find the depth of them with your middle finger.[3]

[1] Gollancz, p. 53. [2] *Ib.* 18. [3] *Ib.* p. 38.

Once more, of a contrary type, 'hobbling' rimers, whose 'poems run like a brewer's cart upon the stones'.[1]

Rare Ben preferred Machiavelli to Montaigne, *The Prince* to *The Essayes*; had his 'beadroll of English writers', including Sir Thomas More, Sir Philip Sidney, and Master Hooker ('great masters', these two, 'of wit and language, in whom all vigour of invention and strength of judgment met'); and praised immeasurably *Dominus Verulamius*, whose 'hearers could not cough or look aside from him without loss', and 'within whose view and about whose times were all the wits born that could honour a language or help study'; and in whose 'adversity I ever prayed that God would give him strength, for greatness he could not want'.[2] But the gem of the volume is the 'observation' *De Shakespeare Nostrati*, 'of our Shakespeare'. We can only connect it with the praise expressed by Heminge and Condell in their preface to the Folio (1623), that what Shakespeare 'thought, he uttered with that easiness that we have scarce received from him a blot in his papers'. Jonson says,

> 'I remember the players have often mentioned it as an honour to Shakespeare, that in his writing (whatsoever he penned) he never blotted out a line. My answer hath been, *Would he had blotted a thousand!* which they thought a malevolent speech. I had not told posterity this but for their ignorance who chose that circumstance to commend their friend by wherein he most faulted; and to justify mine own candour, for *I loved the man, and do honour his memory on this side idolatry as much as any. He was, indeed, honest, and of an open and free nature*; had an excellent phantasy, brave notions, and gentle expressions, wherein he flowed with that facility that sometimes it was necessary he should be stopped. *Sufflaminandus erat*, as Augustus said of Haterius.'[3]

Jonson was buried, two days after his death, in Westminster Abbey. A projected monument on account of civil troubles came to nothing. In the meantime an admirer gave eighteenpence to a mason to cut the words which still mark his gravestone, 'O Rare Ben Jonson!'

[1] Gollancz, p. 134. [2] *Ib.* 46 f.

[3] *Timber*, p. 35 f. For Haterius see Seneca, *Exc. Controv.* iv, pref. § 7.

1639–41

§ 159. DEATH OF SHAKESPEARE'S GRANDSONS, AND HIS COUSINS GREENE

UNTIL 1639 Shakespeare had two grandsons living, Thomas and Richard Quyney, at the *Cage*. Early this year they both died. Thomas, who had just reached nineteen, was buried on 28 January, Richard, a few days over twenty-one, on 26 February.[1] Judith Shakespeare's cup of sorrow was full. These young men, their cousin Mistress Thomas Nash having no son (nor child), were heirs to the Shakespeare estate. Upon their death Mistress Hall settled her property on her daughter and Thomas Nash with a remainder to him and his heirs—on 27 May 1639.[2] We get glimpses of the Poet's daughters. Thomas Hathaway had settled in Stratford from Weston-upon-Avon as a carpenter and builder in 1636, paying his 50*s.* for his 'freedom' as a 'stranger'. He lived four doors above *New Place*, and had the confidence of his kinswomen, Mistress Hall, Mistress Nash, and Mistress Quyney.[3] Doubtless the last stood sponsor to his child, Judith, at her christening on Sunday, 25 February 1638; as with equal certainty we may believe that Mistress Hall on Sunday, 8 December 1639, acted as godmother at the baptism of Susanna Sadler, grand-daughter of the Poet's old friend, Hamlet Sadler, and daughter of William Sadler, who was probably the Poet's godson.

Another bereavement must be noted. On 29 March 1639, William Hart of the 'Birthplace' was buried,[4] a month after young Richard Quyney. He was Shakespeare's nephew, eldest son of his sister Joan, and probably his godson. He was in his thirty-ninth year. Master John Greene died in August 1640 at Stratford, whither he had returned from Bidford about the time of his brother's departure to Bristol. Lord Carew, as we have seen, wanted him to succeed his brother as Steward and Town Clerk of Stratford. He did not obtain the appointment, but he served the Corporation in various legal capacities while keeping his chambers near Clement's Inn. He was about sixty-five years

[1] *Register*, p. 33 f.

[2] *Birthplace Catalogue*, no. 68.

[3] Fripp, *Shakespeare's Haunts*, pp. 26–7.

[4] *Register*, p. 35.

of age at the time of his death. His brother resided at Bristol while a distinguished member of the Middle Temple. We have his will made on 5 November 1640 in London.[1] The religious exordium is no formality but very sincere indeed, typical of the 'Puritan knave' of 1615:

I do bequeath my soul, so dearly redeemed by my Lord Saviour Jesus Christ unto the hands of my Lord God which gave it me, confidently relying upon the mercy of my most gracious God, through the merits and mediation of my Lord and Saviour of mankind, Jesus Christ; and my body to the earth to be buried in Christian burial, where it shall seem best to my executrix, with as little charge as may be.

After bequests to the Cathedral Church of Bristol (which he probably attended) and 'the Hospital of St. John's Churchyard', to his son William (40*s*. for a ring), his daughter (? Anne) and her husband Gifford (30*s*. and 25*s*. for rings), his daughter (? Elizabeth) Holloway (£5) and her children Thomas and Humfrey (66*s*. 8*d*. apiece), his daughter Margaret (born since he left Stratford, £10), his two clerks and maidservant, he left the residue of his estate 'unto Lettice, my most dear and loving wife, being sorry that I have no more to leave to so good a woman'.

He made her his sole executrix, without overseers 'because I know her very justly minded'.

She proved the will in London on 1 July 1641—the day after the burial in Stratford Church of the indomitable old Puritan, Daniel Baker.

1639–41

§ 160. ANOTHER OLD 'PURITAN KNAVE'

BAKER died a devout Churchman, dating his Will 'according to the Accompt of the Church of England', and bequeathing his body to be interred in the south aisle of the Parish Church 'near unto my wives deceased', his first and second, Joan and Eleanor. He bequeathed also 'to the same church, there to remaine for ever, my book of M[aste]r Greenham's Works for the use and benefit of such as shall be so well disposed to read the same, and the same Book to be made fast with a Chain in some convenient place in the same church for the more better and

[1] *P.C.C.* 88 *Evelyn.*

WILLIAM WHATELEY, VICAR OF BANBURY, ÆT. 56

safe keeping thereof'. Master Greenham was the 'practical divine', R. Greenham, praised by Bradford, and author of *Comfort for an Afflicted Conscience*, to which one 'H.C.' prefixed three stanzas of praise, the first as follows:

> The thirsty soul, that fainteth in the way,
> Or hunger-bit for heavenly food doth long;
> The wearied heart that panteth all the day,
> Oppressed with fears and homebred griefs among;
> The blinded eye that hunts the shining ray,
> Or mind enthralled through Satan's wily wrong;
> Let hither fare for comfort in their need,
> For smothered flames a greater fire will breed.[1]

To his native town of Henley-in-Arden he left 26*s*. 8*d*. yearly, to make gowns of 'strong cloth or frieze' for 'two poor widows' who 'are or have been during their abilities diligent frequenters of the Church'. At his funeral feast in his house in High Street meat and home-brewed beer were consumed by mourners. He left property, besides his thriving woollen-draper's business, in lands and tithes, tenements and cottages, two 'Sault Phattes in Droyght' (otherwise salt-pits in Droitwich), corn, malt, furniture, bedding, linens, jewels, rings, silver, pewter, and a limbeck and a still for the home-making of strong waters. His sons, Daniel (the Oxford scholar), Richard, and Abraham, were dead; and to their children, five girls and a youth, Samuel, aged 19, he made handsome legacies, especially to Samuel ('whom God graunt longe to live!'), including 'during his minority, a larger sum than his sisters, to his study in the University or elsewhere'. To his widow, Katharine, in addition to £400 settled upon her (at their marriage ?) on 1 December 1619, he bequeathed 20 nobles (£6 13*s*. 4*d*.) per annum and household possessions. Cousins, godchildren, servants, and the poor benefited from his generosity, and friends, among them Richard Castle of 'the elbows' and Squire Thomas Combe of Welcombe, forgiven, apparently, for his youthful misbehaviour to the Borough.

Baker's friend, William Whateley, the Vicar of Banbury, predeceased him. He died on 10 May 1639, at the comparatively early age of 56. His portrait at the time of his death gives us the

[1] *Select Poetry*, Parker Society, ii. 470.

bearded Puritan preacher, in tight-fitting scull-cap (as opposed to the square cap) and voluminous black gown. His critics called him 'Roaring Willy'. Robert Harris remained with the Copes at Hanwell, and Wilson's successor at Stratford, instituted in May 1640, was a Cambridge scholar, Henry Twitchett, M.A. Harris preached the funeral sermon of Sir Thomas Lucy the Third, the mild-eyed Lucy with the spade beard, at Charlecote on 20 January 1641. More significant was his sermon before Parliament on 25 May 1642, on the eve of the Civil War.

1642–74

§ 161. THE CIVIL WAR AND AFTER

Civil War was drawing on. Warwickshire refused to pay 'Ship-money'.[1] Coventry had been assessed for £266, Warwick for £100, Birmingham for £100, Stratford for £50, without result. Fulke Greville's successor at Warwick Castle, Robert Greville Lord Brooke (who followed Sir Thomas Lucy the third as recorder of Stratford on 11 December 1640), was a leader on the Parliamentary side. In July 1642, aged 34, he garrisoned the Castle, and on 3 August he defeated the Earl of Northampton at Kineton. The Earl then laid siege to Warwick Castle, which was held by Sir Edward Peyto until Lord Brooke relieved it on 23 August. In Stratford, Thomas Nash was a Parliamentarian. He made his will on 25 August (leaving *New Place*, on the assumption of his survival of his wife and Mistress Hall, to Edward Nash, his cousin, the son of Master George Nash), and sent £100 in money and plate to the Parliamentary collector at Warwick. That he joined the Parliamentary army we are not informed, but his prospective heir fought as a captain under Cromwell.

Warwickshire was the scene of the first hostilities. The Earl of Essex (Robert Devereux), general of the Parliament forces, intercepted the King on his march to London on Edge Hill, near Kineton, on Sunday 23 October. The result was indecisive, the

[1] 'In Gloucestershire, they say, the Sheriff refuseth to execute the commission. Nothing at all is collected in Warwickshire' (a correspondent to a resident at Lyme, Cheshire, 8 Nov. 1635. *House of Lyme*, p. 140.

King diverging to Oxford and Essex falling back on Warwick. Soldiers wounded on the Parliament side were brought to Stratford to be cared for. The Corporation voted money to be 'disbursed and given unto the Parliament-soldiers which were wounded and died in the Town after Kineton battle'.[1] In February 1643 Cavalier horsemen seized, and for a moment held, Stratford Bridge, as a point of vantage counter to Warwick Bridge. Lord Brooke, who was at Coventry, immediately dispatched 'dragooners' to Stratford, and followed with artillery, arriving at Warwick on the night of 23 February. Next morning he drove the Cavaliers (300 of them) out of Stratford, and narrowly escaped being blown up, with his captains, in the new Market House, 'a very fair' edifice (at the corner, as we have seen,[2] of Chapel Street and Sheep Street), where a mine was laid for him and exploded. 'The Lord Brooke taking time to send away his prisoners to Warwick, and to settle the town in quiet (as to cause by strict order that none should pillage), heard a noise as if some house had fallen down, and saw the Town Hall' (so it is called) 'torn in pieces, and a great smoke: which caused a most lamentable and pitiful cry in the town.'[3] One Captain Hunt was wounded but none slain. Thomas Hathaway lost a valuable table in the building, for which he received 20*s*. compensation.

Spared at Stratford, Lord Brooke was shot dead six days later (2 March 1643) while directing the siege of the Cathedral close at Lichfield. He was one of the ablest and bitterest opponents of Episcopacy. Milton praised him as 'right noble and pious' and a staunch friend of toleration.

In the summer (July) Stratford was again in the hands of the Cavaliers. Under the escort of Prince Rupert and 3,000 men, Queen Henrietta herself arrived in the town, in her coach with drivers, footmen, and porters, amid the ringing of the church bells. For three days she was quartered at *New Place*. 'She preferred it', we are told, 'to the *College*, which was in the possession of the Combe family, who did not so strongly favour the King's party'[4] as Mistress Hall. William Combe professed to be a

[1] Chamberlains' Accompt: 12 Jan. 1643/4. [2] p. 893.

[3] *The Last Week's Proceeding of the Lord Brooke*, 1 March 1642/3 and *A True Relation of the Death of Lord Brooke*.

[4] Theobald, Preface to *Works of Shakespeare*, 1733, p. xiv.

royalist, but it was complained that he 'sat at home'.[1] The Corporation supplied her Majesty and servants with quails, poultry, meat, cakes, bread and cheese, and beer, together with 'fees' (or wages), and fodder for the horses, at a cost of £15 4*s*. o*d*. The Borough Chamberlain (Thomas Horne of the *Swan*) had to pay for these things. He also paid, we must note, on behalf of the Corporation, £3 for the fortifications at Warwick, against the royalists. Sympathy of the Corporation with the Parliament is indicated by the change of the name of their inn in Bridge Street, *The Crown*, in the tenure of Widow Hathaway, to *The Woolsack*.[2]

Next year the Parliamentarians were in possession. A surgeon of Warwick, James Cooke, medical attendant on the late Lord Brooke, and 'a Congregational member meeting at Warwick Castle',[3] was in attendance on the regiments which held the Stratford Bridge. He was a friend of the late Doctor Hall, and with him was a relative of the doctor's, who invited him 'to the house of Mistress Hall to see the books left by Master Hall'. He continues:

After a view of them, she told me she had some books left, by one that professed physic, with her husband for some money. I told her if I liked them, I would give her the money again. She brought them forth, amongst which there was this [*Observations*, in Latin], with another of the author's [Doctor Hall's], both intended for the press. I, being acquainted with Master Hall's hand, told her that one or two of them were her husband's and shewed them her. She denied, I affirmed, till I perceived she began to be offended. At last I returned her the money.

The Latin *Observations*, with their many and difficult contractions, may well have perplexed the good lady, over sixty years of age and more given to 'works' than to letters. It was well, perhaps, that Master Cooke purchased them. Would that he had acquired some of Shakespeare's papers!

Several times we see Mistress Hall in her old age, and once more her signature—with that of her daughter, Elizabeth Nash. We think of the mother and daughter together in *New Place*. If, as we may believe, Mistress Hall stood sponsor at the baptism of William Sadler's child, Susanna, in the Parish Church on Sunday 8 December 1639, we shall not be far wrong in thinking that

[1] *Symonds' Diary* (Camden Society, p. 191 f.). [2] *Misc. Doc.* xiv. 34.

[3] This Sunday meeting at the Castle was the parent of the Dissenting Congregation in High Street.

Unus ex Libris Edm: Pytt

Select Observations

ON

ENGLISH

BODIES:

OR,

Cures both Empericall and Historicall, performed upon very eminent Persons in desperate Diseases.

First, written in Latine by Mr. *John Hall* Physician, living at *Stratford* upon *Avon* in *Warwick-shire*, where he was very famous, as also in the Counties adjacent, as appeares by these Observations drawn out of severall hundreds of his, as choysest.

Now put into English for common benefit by *James Cooke* Practitioner in *Physick* and *Chirurgery*.

London, Printed for *John Sherley*, at the *Golden Pelican*, in *Little-Britain*. 1657

Hall's *Select Observations*, 1657

Mistress Nash filled this office for his child, Elizabeth, in the same place on Sunday 26 June 1642, both infants being Hamlet Sadler's grand-daughters. William Sadler, a cordwainer, had married a wife, Elizabeth, and owned a house, perhaps in her right, at Quinton. He owned also £100, which he lent to Thomas Kingerley (Kinserley), husband of his sister, Mary. He died in the plague of 1645, making a nuncupative will on 20 September, leaving his house at Quinton to his wife, with £80 of the £100 on loan, and the remaining £20 to Kingerley's children. The lawyer, Michael Olney, who had lost his wife and a daughter in this plague, attended at his bedside to take his declaration. Olney, it may be remembered, 'Master Lucas' man', lived in William Parsons's house at the corner of Wood Street and Rother Street, having married Parsons's daughter, Anne, godchild probably of Mistress Shakespeare (Anne Hathaway, Mistress Hall's mother), Anne Parsons's mother being Margaret Sadler, daughter of old Alderman Sadler, and cousin therefore of Hamlet Sadler. Whence, we may assume, Olney's devotion in this perilous season to his late wife's kinsman. He had buried his wife on 26 August. How numerous and close are the domestic links in Stratford with Shakespeare!

On 4 April 1647 Mistress Hall lost her son-in-law, Thomas Nash. He died suddenly, adding a nuncupative codicil to his will of 1642, as follows:

> To his mother, Mistress Hall £50; to Elizabeth Hathaway £50; to Thomas Hathaway £50; to Judith Hathaway £10; to his uncle and aunt Nash each 20*s*. to buy them rings; to his cousin Sadler and his wife the same; to his cousin, Richard Quyney, and his wife the same; to his cousin, Thomas Quyney, and his wife the same.

Here are old and new relationships. Elizabeth Hathaway is Thomas Hathaway's youngest child, baptized on 10 January previous, with, doubtless, Elizabeth Nash as sponsor. Thomas Hathaway is the joiner in Chapel Street, Judith Hathaway is his eldest daughter, nine years old, god-daughter of Mistress Judith Quyney. Uncle and aunt Nash are Master George Nash and his wife Mary, daughter to Edward Cox of Southwark (one more of the many links between Stratford and Southwark). Cousin Sadler and his wife are John and Susanna Sadler of London; Cousin Richard Quyney and his wife are Richard and Ellen (*née*

Sadler) Quyney of London and Stratford; and cousin Thomas Quyney and his wife, of course, are Richard Quyney's brother, the vintner of the *Cage* (Stratford), and Judith (*née* Shakespeare), Mistress Hall's sister.

Thomas Nash was buried, on 5 April,[1] in the chancel of the Church, next to Shakespeare. On his grave were inscribed the verses—

> Fata manent omnes; hunc non virtute carentem
> Ut neque divitiis abstulit atra dies,
> Abstulit at referet lux ultima. Siste, viator;
> Si peritura paras, per mala parta peris.[2]

Immediately, on the strength of his inheritance from Master Nash, on 8 April, Thomas Hathaway purchased the house he occupied in Chapel Street, from Richard Lane—'all that messuage with the backside, between the dwelling-house of John Loach on the north side and the house of Henry Tomlins on the south, the land of [the late] Master Hall on the east and the said street on the west'. In view, too, of Master Nash's death, Mistress Hall and her daughter resettled the Shakespeare property on themselves for life, with remainder to the heirs of the daughter's body, and in default to the use of her right heirs for ever. The indenture, dated 2 June, is sealed and signed by them both. The daughter's handwriting is remarkably bold and good.[3]

By this deed they made Thomas Hathaway and his brother, William of Weston-upon-Avon, their trustees. Next year, on 11 June, Mistress Hall still further showed her confidence in Thomas Hathaway by acting, apparently, as sponsor to his new-born child, Susanna.[4]

On 15 August 1647, we may believe, the kindly mistress of *New Place*, ever loyal to her father's friends, stood godmother at the christening of Susanna Walker, first-born daughter of William Walker, 'gentleman', son of Henry Walker, and Shakespeare's godson, the boy to whom he bequeathed a 20*s*. gold piece in his will in 1616. William Walker had married a wife, Frances, who bore him two sons, Henry (in 1640) and

[1] *Register*, p. 144.

[2] 'Fate awaits all; this man, wanting in neither virtue nor wealth, the Black Day carried off—carried off, but the Light at last shall bring him again. Stay, passenger; if thou preparest perishable things, thou by evil offspring perishest.'

[3] *Birthplace Catalogue*, no. 69.

[4] *Register*, p. 148.

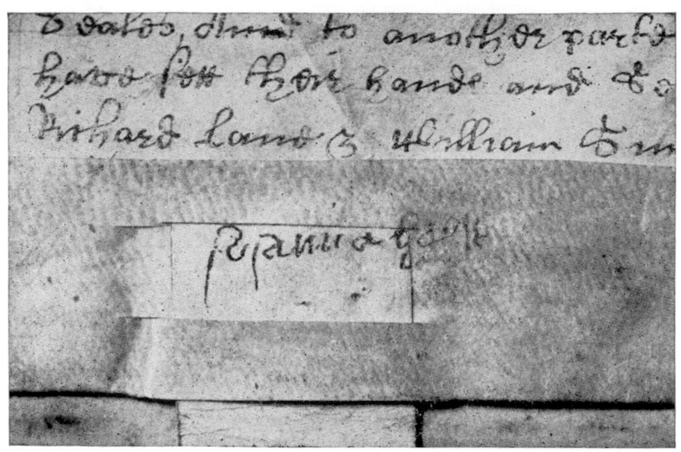

SIGNATURE OF SUSANNA HALL

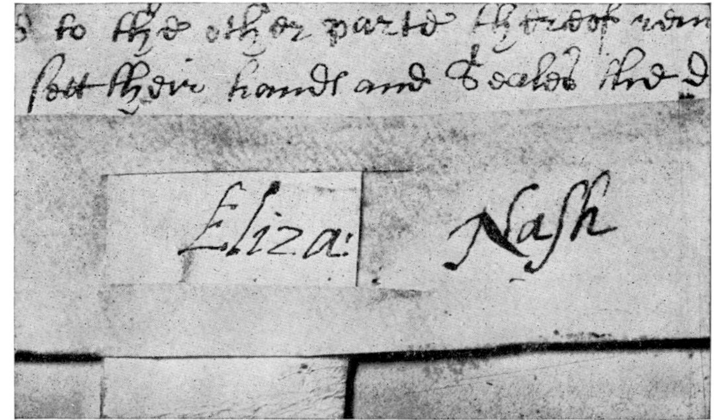

SIGNATURE OF ELIZABETH NASH

SIGNATURE OF ELIZABETH BARNARD

William (in 1642), and a third son, Samuel (in 1650). He was acting-Chamberlain in 1645–6, and served as Bailiff in 1649–50.

Changes also were taking place in Henley Street. Shakespeare's sister, Joan Hart, died in November 1646. She had outlived her eldest son, William, who was buried 29 March 1639. Her surviving son, Thomas, had married one Margaret about 1632, and had four children—Michael, Thomas, George, and Mary, aged respectively thirteen, twelve, ten, and five, in 1646. Thomas Hart, his wife, and four children, continued to reside in the western house of the Birthplace. The adjoining eastern house was an inn called the *Maidenhead*.

Widow Nash on 5 June 1649, when her age was forty-one, married at Billesley Master John Barnard, lord of the manor of Abington, near Northampton. He was a widower, two years her senior, with four sons and four daughters, the children of his first wife (who died in 1642), daughter to Sir Clement Edmonds of Preston near Abington. He was a reader, and patron of literature, and possessed a library. To him, no doubt, descended books of Shakespeare and Doctor Hall, and pictures.

Mistress Hall survived the wedding rather more than a month. She died on 11 July, and five days later was buried in her husband's or the adjoining grave. So we learn from the concluding lines on his tombstone (this addition, or the whole, was written after her decease):

> Ne tumulo quid desit, adest fidissima conjux,
> Et vitae comitem nunc quoque mortis habet.[1]

Her own epitaph is on the adjoining stone:

> Witty[2] above her sex; but that's not all—
> Wise to Salvation was good Mistress Hall:
> Something of Shakespeare was in that, but this
> Wholly of Him with whom she's now in bliss.
> Then, passenger, hast ne'er a tear
> To weep with her that wept with all
> That wept, yet set herself to cheer
> Them up with comforts cordial?[3]
> Her love shall live, her mercy spread,
> When thou hast ne'er a tear to shed.

[1] 'Lest aught should be wanting to his tomb, his very faithful wife is at hand, and the companion of his life he has now also in death.'

[2] Intelligent.

[3] Cf. *The Winter's Tale*, v. iii. 76 f.: 'For this affliction has a taste as sweet as any cordial comfort.'

The writer, who may have been the able minister appointed by Cromwell, Alexander Beane, had not heard of saving grace in Shakespeare, a player and author of plays; but his testimony to the pious and benevolent disposition of the Poet's daughter is first-hand and emphatic. Not less striking is his association of her with Scripture. 'Wise to salvation' is from 2 Timothy iii. 15: 'Thou hast known the Holy Scriptures of a child, which are able to make thee wise unto salvation, through the faith which is in Christ Jesus'; and 'Weep with her that wept with all that wept' is from Romans xii. 15: 'Weep with them that weep.'

After Mistress Hall's death the Barnards resided at *New Place* until 1653, when Mistress Barnard appointed Henry Smythe and Job Dighton trustees of her estate instead of William and Thomas Hathaway. William was probably dead, and Thomas had not long to live. The latter was buried 15 January 1655. Richard Quyney died in May 1656 at his residence in Shottery. He left a considerable estate, including property in Virginia, and a share in the ship *The Seven Sisters*, which may have been so named after his seven daughters. He left an annuity of £12 to his brother, Thomas Quyney, and £5 for his funeral expenses. Among those mentioned in his will (16 August 1655) as still living is his 'brother-in-law, William Smythe'.

The Barnards had returned to Abington before Christmas 1656, when the minister there, John Howes, preached a sermon, much criticized, on 'Christ God-Man'. He published this sermon in the spring of 1657, with a dedication to Master Barnard as his Mæcenas, *splendididissimo patrono suo semper colendo bonarum literarum.*

In 1657 appeared two 'centuries' of Doctor Hall's 'Observations', selected out of not 'less than a thousand', and translated by Cooke. He had sent the note-books to a practitioner in London, who pronounced the Latin too 'abbreviated or false' for reproduction. The manuscript had evidently puzzled this gentleman as it had perplexed Mistress Hall. Cooke had the volumes returned, and with assistance from the author's apothecary, Master Court of Stratford, he brought out the above *Select Observations on English Bodies, or Cures both Empirical and Historical, performed upon very eminent Persons in desperate Diseases.*

At the Restoration John Barnard was created a baronet, on 25 November 1661, and for the last eight or nine years of her life Shakespeare's grand-daughter was Lady Barnard. The Restoration vitally affected Stratford. The long succession of Puritan vicars came to an end. Beane resigned the living on the Act of Uniformity, and went out, one of the 'Two Thousand', on the memorable St. Bartholomew's Day, 1662 (24 August). Ten days later the Corporation voted him his salary to that date, with a gratuity of £5 13*s.* 4*d.* on the condition he left the vicarage-house 'peaceably'. Beane had a wife and seven children, and he left peaceably; but he took with him followers who became the founders of Nonconformity in the borough. His successor, who had no scruples about episcopacy and the Prayer Book, was John Ward, aged 33, a Master of Arts of Oxford. He was inducted on 10 December 1662, and lodged with one Master Brookes in Stratford until 25 April 1663, when presumably he took up his abode in the Chapel Quad.

It was Ward's intention (of which he makes a note in his diary) 'to see Mistress Quyney'. Unfortunately she died just too soon, in February 1662. She was seventy-seven years old. The entry of her burial is thus in the register:

1661[/2] February 9 Judith uxor Thomas Quiney gent.

Had Ward met her, he would have handed on something better than his feeble memoranda about the Poet. Nor, apparently, did he take the trouble to communicate with Lady Barnard. William Combe was still alive, from whom he may have had the report of the Poet's latter-day prosperity. Combe died in January 1667, over eighty years of age. He was spoken of as 'a miserable old churl'. His younger and more respected brother, Thomas, of Welcombe, deceased nearly ten years before him. From 1648 to his death in 1657 Thomas was Recorder of Stratford.

Lady Barnard died at Abington in 1670. In her will of 29 January she directed that, after her husband's decease, *New Place* and the land in Stratford, Welcombe, and Bishopton should be sold, and out of the proceeds £5 a year (or the sum of £40) should be paid to Judith Hathaway, the sum of £40 apiece to Rose, Elizabeth, and Susanna Hathaway, all daughters of the late Thomas Hathaway of Chapel Street, Stratford, and £50 to their married sister Joan Kent, with £30 to her son, Edward Kent, 'towards putting him out as an apprentice'. The houses in Henley Street she left to the Harts.

Thomas Hart, Shakespeare's nephew, died in 1661. His sons, Thomas and George, were living, men of thirty-five and thirty-three years of age, on Lady Barnard's death. Thomas had no children (he died without issue), but George (to whom 'the Birthplace' descended) had three young daughters, Elizabeth, Jane (Joan), and Susanna, and a son, Shakespeare, in 1670. As the names of his children prove, George Hart, who was a tailor, had a proud consciousness of his relationship to the Poet, Mistress Hall, and Lady Barnard. He was probably not the least of the 'neighbours' whom Aubrey consulted, sometime before 1680, respecting William Shakespeare.

Sir John Barnard died in 1674. We have the inventory of his goods and chattels. Among the items are:

In the Study: desks, chests, cabinets, trunks and boxes, £5 1*s.* 6*d.*; all the plate there, £29 10*s.* 0*d.*; in rings, jewels, and a watch, £30; *all the books*, £29 11*s.* 0*d.*

A rent at Stratford-upon-Avon, £4.

Old goods and lumber at Stratford-upon-Avon, £4.

In the Parlour: all the pictures there, £5 10*s.* 0*d.*

In the Best Chamber: pictures and andirons, £2.

In the Little Chamber: pictures, hangings, table and a carpet £6.

What became of these 'books' and 'pictures'? Little seems to have been left at *New Place* in 1674. Sir Edward Walker purchased the house next year.

An old man was alive in Stratford in 1680 (he died in March that year) who might have told Ward something worth recording, if he had cared to inquire, about Shakespeare. This was Master William Walker, son of Henry Walker and godson of the Poet, who left him, when seven-and-a-half years old, 20*s.* for a memorial ring. He was, perhaps, the last who had spoken to Shakespeare and received his 'kisses'.[1]

[1] p. 823.

1642–98

§ 162. SHAKESPEARE'S DRAMA ON EVIL DAYS

THE playhouse fell low after Ben Jonson's departure,[1] and Cromwell shut it up. We remember old Willis's lamentation in 1639, 'how far unlike the plays and harmless morals of former times are to those which have succeeded, many of which may be termed schoolmasters of vice and provocations to corruption'.[2] Plays were forbidden in 1642 during 'these times of humiliation' and altogether suppressed in 1647. The Civil War put Shakespeare out of men's heads and seriously broke the Shakespeare tradition. Otherwise the Protector's interdict did little harm. Thought on the stage had degenerated, and, with it, art and verse. And all three were debased on the reopening of the theatres under the licentious Charles II. Two playhouses instead of six met the diminished demand in spite of a larger population. The 'grave', who had appreciated Shakespeare, were conspicuous by their absence.

There were, of course, old Shakespeareans like John Milton, who knew what great verse was and noble drama, and therefore honoured Shakespeare. There were also *readers* of the Poet's works. Four impressions of the Folio (1623, 1632, 1663, 1685) had taken his plays from the dissolute theatre to quiet chambers and libraries before Nicholas Rowe ventured on his edition of 1709 in six octavo volumes. The second Folio (1632) contained Milton's lofty praise, his first published verse:

> Dear Son of Memory, great Heir of Fame.

About the same time Milton wrote in *L'Allegro*, after reading *A Midsummer Night's Dream*,

> sweetest Shakespeare, Fancy's Child,
> Warble his native wood-notes wild.

He lived, a devotee of the Poet and his disciple in verse, far into the reign of Charles, a Samson among the Philistines.

But the theatre-going public did not ask for thought, and they got neither art nor verse. No chapter in English Literature is more pitiful than that of the Restorationist Drama. The chief

[1] p. 895. [2] p. 66.

dramatist and poet of the period, Dryden, made an opera of *Paradise Lost* in rhyme, with dialogue between Adam and Eve; and turned *Antony and Cleopatra* into a play of lust, under the title *All for Love, or The World Well Lost*. Fletcher's moral tag to his *Maid's Tragedy*—

> On lustful kings
> Unlooked for sudden deaths from Heaven are sent—

gave offence to Charles II, and therefore was changed by Waller, with re-writing of the fifth act, to

> Long may he reign that is so far above
> All vice, all passion, but excess of love!

Davenant has the credit of suggesting to Dryden his adaptation of *The Tempest* by adding to the part of Miranda (a girl who had never seen a youth) that of a youth who had never seen a girl. A lordly writer of plays, one John Sheffield, who was Earl of Mulgrave and Duke of Buckingham, reconstructed *Julius Caesar* into a pair of correct pieces observant of the classical unities of place and time. It was vain for such authors to profess admiration for Shakespeare and perpetrate these atrocities.

The fashionable spectator's view is expressed by Pepys. He records in his diary on 29 September 1662, 'To the King's Theatre, where we saw *Midsummer Night's Dream*; which I had never seen before, nor shall ever again, for it is the most insipid, ridiculous play that ever I saw in my life'; and on 1 March 1662 of *Romeo and Juliet*, 'It is the worst that ever I heard'; on 15 August 1667 of *The Merry Wives of Windsor*, 'It did not please me at all, in no part of it'; on 7 March 1667 of *Richard III*, 'It was pretty good but nothing eminent in it'. Not that these judgements are altogether to the discredit of the diarist. What he saw was Shakespeare 'improved', adapted, that is, to the foolish taste. *Romeo and Juliet* was fitted with a happy ending—the lovers recover and live happy ever after. On 19 April 1667 Pepys witnessed *Macbeth*—'one of the best plays for a stage *and variety of dancing and music that ever I saw*'. On 18 February 1662 he enjoyed a version of *Measure for Measure* by Davenant, enlivened by the introduction of Benedick and Beatrice: 'a good play and well performed'. Pepys could sometimes appreciate good acting. He admired Betterton. Evelyn said, 26 November 1661,

'I saw *Hamlet*; but the old plays begin to disgust the refined age'. Pepys liked *Hamlet* on 28 May 1663 when Betterton took the part of the hero.

More than any Restorationist actor, Betterton kept alive the Shakespeare tradition. He was coached in Hamlet and King Henry VIII by Davenant, who had seen Shakespeare's fellows, Joseph Taylor and John Lowin, in these parts. From the same or another direct source he probably had the Poet's conception of Pericles, Sir Toby Belch, Brutus, and Othello. He did not rant, his voice moved with the metre, and his face was expressive. Born in 1635 he lived, and played, until 1710, receiving in his old age the enthusiastic admiration of Steele. To Betterton and Davenant, Rowe was indebted for much in his sketch of Shakespeare's life and work. Biographical detail has also come down from older players—William Beeston, who died in 1682, 'the chronicle of the stage', as Dryden called him, son of Christopher Beeston; and John Lacy the clown; who was committed to prison for blunt speech to the 'King' in the role of a country gentleman newly arrived at Court.

Without these actor-informants—Lacy, Beeston, and Betterton—Shakespeare's biography would have suffered even more than it has done from neglect and tattle. When interest in the Poet's life manifested itself in the latter end of the seventeenth century, the character of his calling was very much lower than in the former end, and it had become a matter of astonishment that a stage-player, or a writer of stage-plays, should be other than a profligate. Almost alone Betterton was guiltless of the condemnation launched like a thunderbolt in 1698 on the theatrical profession by Jeremy Collier's *Short View of the Immorality and Profaneness of the English Stage*. The *Short View* was an octavo of 300 pages and unanswerable. Vanbrugh and Congreve offered futile defence; Dryden, to his credit, recanted:

> I have pleaded guilty to all thoughts and expressions of mine which can be truly argued of obscenity, profaneness or immorality, and retract them. If he be my enemy, let him triumph; if he be my friend, he will be glad of my repentance.

No greater misfortune could have happened to Shakespeare than to be viewed through 'the fog and filthy air' at last disturbed by Jeremy Collier's honest outburst.

§ 163. SHAKESPEARE LEGENDS

FOURTEEN years after the Poet's death Stratford was spoken of as 'most remarkable for the birth of famous William Shakespeare';[1] but visitors to the town, clerical or other, in 1660–1708 would hardly bring with them or expect to find honourable report of the strangely belauded genius whose work had been degraded almost beyond recognition on the London stage, and whose 'harlotry' fellows had been banished from his native town for half a century. What would the Rev. John Ward (who apparently had not read a line of Shakespeare) be prepared or likely to hear in 1663? or John Aubrey shortly before 1680? or Master Dowdall in 1693? or William Hall in 1694? or the Rev. Richard Davies (whose acquaintance with the text of the Poet was little better, if any, than Ward's) sometime between 1688 and 1708? or even Betterton himself, who made a pilgrimage to Stratford some time probably before his illness in 1701, 'to gather up what remains he could of a name for which he had so great a value'? Betterton's 'unconsidered trifles' are less mixed and more consistent than Aubrey's but of a later date.

All legend has its value. Every story tells something either of the subject or *the narrator*, and it is worth while in Shakespeare's case to trace, if possible, the most extravagant to its source. Certain stories we have already examined; others, not the least important, call for notice.

a. THE POET BUTCHER-BOY

'How was it a Stratford youth found his way to London to become the monarch of the stage?' was a question that early excited inquiry and is still a matter of controversy. Aubrey heard that he was an inspired butcher-boy, that inclination drew him to town, and natural ability ensured him success. He says:

> His father was a butcher, and I have been told heretofore *by some of the neighbours*, that when he was a boy he exercised his father's trade; but when he killed a calf he would do it in a high style and make a speech. This William, being inclined naturally to poetry and acting, came to London—I guess about eighteen—and was an actor at one of the play-houses, and did act exceedingly well.

[1] *A Banquet of Jeasts*, 1630.

Such was the report, among the Harts and others, shortly before 1680, and notwithstanding its obvious (if intelligible) errors it is the most plausible that has come down to us. John Shakespeare was not a butcher, but as a whittawer and glover he had to do with skins; and *a portion of his late property had probably been let before 1680 as a butcher's shop*. Nor is there the least indication in Shakespeare's writings of the author having been in his youth a butcher (as there is evidence abundant of his service in an attorney's office); but his youthful muse had been guilty of a grandiloquence, not beyond the admiration of Shakespeare Hart, which may have suggested the story of the speechifying in 'high style':

> And as the butcher takes away the calf,
> And binds the wretch and beats it when it strays,
> Bearing it to the bloody slaughter-house—
> And as the dam runs loving up and down,
> Looking the way her harmless young one went,
> And can do naught but wail her darling's loss—
> Even so . . . (*2 Hen. VI*, III. i. 210 ff.).

b. THE RUNAWAY BUTCHER-BOY

That Shakespeare was a butcher-boy Master Dowdall heard in Stratford in April 1693. But he heard more, that *he ran away from his master to London*. His informant was not George Hart (who lived until 1702), but the old parish clerk or sexton, William Castle.

'The clerk', he says, 'that shewed me the Church' and the Poet's grave 'is above 80 years old; he says that this Shakespeare was formerly in this town bound apprentice to a butcher, but that he run from his master to London, and there was received into the playhouse as a servitor, and by this means had an opportunity to be what he afterwards proved. He was the best of his family, but the male line is extinguished.'

Castle, who was of a lower station than 'Master Richard Castle mercer', was baptized in the Church on 17 July 1614 and was not quite so old as he thought himself in April 1693. He relinquished his post on 11 March 1698, and was buried 19 November 1701. He correctly said that the male line was extinguished—Shakespeare's last grandson died in February 1639. The Poet's daughters and his grand-daughter were also dead. Only the Harts remained, and for them the old sexton, who showed the graves in the Chancel, had probably no great respect. The room over the butcher's shop in Henley Street was probably now shown as the Poet's birth-chamber.

c. THE RUNAWAY POACHER

The story of the deer-stealing and disreputable flight from Stratford makes its first appearance more than a hundred years after the supposed event, and not in Stratford. In 1693 gossip in Stratford, in the mouth of the sexton, was of a butcher's apprentice who ran away from his master. But Richard Davies, rector from 1695 to 1708 of Sapperton in Gloucestershire (about 40 miles south-west of Stratford[1]), was guilty of *memoranda* (not unworthy of a divine described by Anthony Wood in 1692 as 'looking red and jolly as if he had been at a fish-dinner at Corpus Christi College and afterwards drinking, as he had been') to the effect that Shakespeare 'was much given to all unluckiness in stealing venison and rabbits, particularly from Sir —— Lucy, who had him oft whipt and sometimes imprisoned, and at last made him fly his native country, to his great advancement; but his revenge was so great that he is his Justice Clodpate, and calls him a great man, and that in allusion to his name [he] bore three louses rampant for his arms'. For this surprising information, after so many days, wherein the informant betrays his ignorance of Lucy's Christian name and non-possession of a deer-park, and of the law respecting poachers (who could not be whipped nor imprisoned), and of the name of Justice Shallow, and wags an uncurbed tongue (as in '*much* given', '*all* unluckiness', 'stealing venison and rabbits *particularly* from Lucy', and therefore from others besides, '*oft* whipt', '*times* imprisoned', as in a further irresponsible statement that Shakespeare 'died a papist'), we need not go beyond the college dining-hall and Falstaff's abuse of Shallow (as Oldys recognized in 1773) in the first scene of *The Merry Wives of Windsor*. Davies probably was not the first (as certainly he has not been the last) to identify the mentality of Shakespeare with that of Falstaff.

The story, however, caught on. Rowe in 1709 tells, apologetically, of the young Shakespeare's 'extravagance' and 'mis-

[1] Between Cirencester and Stroud.

fortune', his family being 'of good figure and fashion' and 'mentioned as gentlemen', in falling into ill company, who engaged him with them more 'than once in robbing a park that belonged to Sir Thomas Lucy' (as it certainly did not). He speaks also of 'a ballad', since 'lost', 'the first essay of (Shakespeare's) poetry', 'so very bitter that it redoubled the prosecution against him to the degree that he was obliged to leave his business and family in Warwickshire for some time and shelter himself in London'. Evidently Rowe did not believe that he 'left his family' for a long time. In due course a 'ballad' turns up, a 'misfortune' indeed to a young poet of such good breeding that in after life, as Rowe reports, 'every one who had a true taste of merit and could distinguish men had generally a just value and esteem for him'. It is found in a manuscript of 1727–30 ('full of forgeries and falsehoods', Malone declares), as sung by an old woman in Stratford in the hearing of Joshua Barnes, a professor of Greek at Cambridge, 'about 40 years since'; to whom the professor, for the two stanzas she could remember, presented, 'such was his respect for Master Shakespeare's genius', a new gown. He must have had a poor opinion of the young Poet's abilities and good breeding if he thought him capable of the following:

Sir Thomas was too covetous
  To covet so much deer,
When horns upon his head
  Most plainly did appear.
Had not his worship one deer left?
  What then, he took a wife
Took pains enough to find him horns
  Should last him during life.

The abuse is as pointless as it is vulgar. Sir Thomas and Lady Lucy, as it happens, had a reputation for matrimonial happiness. Any visitor to their tomb at Charlecote might know that if young Shakespeare wrote these lines he singularly lacked intelligence as well as good manners.

Hence perhaps the disappearance of the 'ballad' a second time, and reappearance about 1750 in a new form, as 'remembered' by 'a very aged gentleman', Master Thomas Jones of Tardebigge[1]

[1] So Capell in 1780, who adds that he died in 1703 aged upwards of 90.

(about 18 miles from Stratford), who 'died fifty years since'. It now begins:

> A Parliament Member, a Justice of Peace,
> At home a poor scarecrow, at London an ass:
> If lousy is Lucy, as some volk miscall it,
> Then Lucy is lousy whatever befall it.

Lucy's contemporaries, acquainted with his services as a magistrate, a member of Parliament, a frequent commissioner to the Privy Council, and a recipient of the Council's special thanks for his services, would have treated such vilification with contempt. But he was forgotten, as was Shakespeare, before 1700, and the object of vituperation (he was a Puritan), as Shakespeare of dissolute suggestion, at the hands of clownish and townish wits. Fabricator Jordan eventually added to the Jones 'ballad' six stanzas, which he declared he discovered in 1790 'in a chest of drawers', said to have come from Shottery, and discovered again, apparently the same month, 'amidst some deeds given to a tailor' for 'measure strips'. This is not the end of the Poaching Legend. Later gossip has pointed out the lodge where Shakespeare, after beating the knight's men and killing his deer, *seduced* the 'keeper's daughter'. So the legend grows under our eyes. The only value of it is its testimony to the delight of the English public (as old as the story of Beowulf) in a hero who begins badly and ends well. Shakespeare himself played on this deeply rooted sentiment in *Henry IV* and *Henry V*.

d. POVERTY AT HOME AND WITHDRAWAL FROM SCHOOL

Ben Jonson started the idea that Shakespeare wanted learning. Justly proud of his own scholarship, he unjustly depreciated his great rival's. Fuller, who pecked up wit and epigram as pigeons peas, discovered 'little Latin and less Greek' (Jonson said 'small Latin and less Greek'), and interpreted it as, we may be sure, the author never intended. 'Plautus', he says, 'was an exact comedian yet never any scholar, as our Shakespeare, if alive, would confess himself. He was an eminent instance of the truth of that rule *poeta non fit sed nascitur*, one is not made but born a poet. Indeed his learning was very little . . . Nature was all the art used upon him.' He then draws a fanciful comparison of Jonson as a Spanish great galleon with Shakespeare as an English man-of-war: one of his many figures-of-speech more quaint than true. Ward follows suit about Shakespeare being 'a natural wit without any art at all'. Aubrey quotes Jonson's dictum, but questions it. Shakespeare, he says, 'understood Latin pretty well, for he had been in his younger years a schoolmaster in the country'. So, apparently, he heard at Stratford. The report is inconsistent with the butcher-boy story, and has this truth in it that it attributed to the Poet an intellectual occupation. William Hall is also sceptical of the current opinion. Quoting from memory, after a visit to the Church, the lines on the Poet's tombstone, he remarks,

> The little learning these verses contain would be a very strong argument of the want of it in the author did not they carry something in them which stands in need of a comment. Having to do with clerks and sextons, for the most part a very ignorant sort of people, he descends to the meanest of their capacities and disrobes himself of that art which none of his cotemporaries wore in greater perfection.

But Rowe is confirmed in the accepted belief by what he has derived from Stratford. 'Master Shakespeare', he says, 'was the son of *Master* John Shakespeare. His family, as appears by the register and public writings relating to (Stratford), were of good figure and fashion there, and are mentioned as *gentlemen*. His father was a considerable dealer in wool' (and therefore not a butcher), but he '*had so large a family, ten children in all, that though he was his eldest son he could give him no better education than his own employment*'—namely that of a wool-driver. He, however, qualifies this statement: 'He had bred him, 'tis true, for some time at a free school, where 'tis probable he acquired that *little Latin* he was master of; but *the narrowness of his circumstances and the want of his assistance at home forced his father to withdraw him from thence*, and unhappily prevented his further proficiency in that language.' He confesses, however, 'There is one play of his, indeed, *The Comedy of Errors*, in a great measure taken from the *Menaechmi* of Plautus. How that happened I cannot easily divine, since I do not take him to have been master of Latin enough to read it in the original, and I know of no translation of Plautus so old as his time.' Some one, perhaps Betterton, has taken the trouble to glance at the registers and town records, and he has discovered that the Poet's father had the status of 'gentleman', and that William was the eldest of 'ten' children born to a John Shakespeare. He might have found eleven, and that three of these were the children of a second and younger John Shakespeare. He might, also, have discovered that the Poet's father never had more than five children living at one time, and that in April 1579, when Shakespeare was fifteen years of age, he had only four. His conclusion, therefore, that John Shakespeare's 'large family' rendered his 'circumstances narrow', and 'forced him' to 'withdraw' his eldest son from the Free School and employ him in his own business as a wool-driver, is unwarranted. A casual survey of the minutes of the Corporation, if permitted to him, might have confirmed his opinion of John Shakespeare's lack of resources; but of this evidence, of which further study would give a very different estimate, he says nothing. He is wrong, too, in his conclusion that John Shakespeare was 'a dealer in wool'. The wool-driver's craft was emphatically distinct from that of the whittawer. We are grateful, however, for the statement that the Poet did go to the Free School and learn Latin, prior to entering on an employment which enabled him 'while yet very young' to 'marry the daughter of one Hathaway, a substantial yeoman in the neighbourhood' of Stratford. 'In this kind of settlement', he goes on to say, 'he continued for some time'—until the poaching escapade. It is worth noting that Rowe knows nothing of the modern legend that Shakespeare ran away from his wife. That calls for information of which there is no trace among contemporaries or successors.

e. HOLDING HORSES AT THE THEATRE DOOR

Old Castle told Dowdall that Shakespeare 'ran from his master to London, and was received into the playhouse as a servitor'. Rowe says he was 'obliged to leave his business and family in Warwickshire', and was received into 'the company then in being in a very mean rank'. A development of this humble admission, of a runaway and a scapegrace (of which Aubrey knows nothing), is in a story which Davenant told Betterton (who did not hear it in Stratford), but which Rowe refused to believe, that the penniless youth held horses at the theatre door; and held them so faithfully that he was in request; and with business energy (which the runaway butcher-boy and disgraced poacher stories scarcely reveal in him) he organized a band of waiters, who were known after a time as 'Shakespeare's Boys', and announced themselves as 'I am Shakespeare's boy, Sir'. Pope also declined this nonsense, which Doctor Johnson reported to Robert Shiels before 1753 and introduced into his own Life of Shakespeare in 1765. If the Poet ever organized (as he certainly did) a troup of 'boys', it was within the theatre, and not among the horses.

f. SHAKESPEARE DIED A PAPIST

He 'died a Papist', says Davies, the Vicar of Sapperton, and we are not altogether surprised at the report. Neither his father nor his son-in-law would have judged him sound in the Protestant faith. He was no zealot, and he has drawn none, Jesuit or Puritan. Shylock and Isabella are his nearest approaches to fanaticism; and the one he would have abjure his Judaism, the other leave the convent door and be a wife. He cared for man more than doctrine, and for God more than creed. The Bible was a book of men and women rather than of saving truth. Worship was dearer to him than sermons, and worship was not always at Church. Much as he loved the House of God, and in particular his noble Parish Church—

> If ever been where bells have knoll'd to church—
> And have with holy bell been knoll'd to church—

yet the field-dew was 'consecrate', and flowers were 'chalices', tears were 'holy water', and love was 'Divine'. No sect could claim him. He was too broad and deep for any *one*. He had the artist's sense of proportion which took now the form of kindly or devastating humour, at the expense of confession, rite, or Scripture; now that of spiritual discrimination and discernment worthy of Dante and St. Paul. He stands supreme among English laymen for his Reverent Liberalism. From his writings, and from his will, we conclude that he lived, and died, a member of our National Communion, a lover of his Church in days when, before the Act of Uniformity, it included in pulpit and pew a rich variety of thought, ancient and modern, and enjoyed, if sometimes painfully, a salutary clashing of brains.

INDEX